FUNDAMENTALS
OF CLINICAL SUPERVISION

FUNDAMENTALS OF CLINICAL SUPERVISION

FOURTH EDITION

JANINE M. BERNARD

Syracuse University

RODNEY K. GOODYEAR

University of Redlands

**This book is not for sale or
distribution in the U.S.A. or Canada**

Merrill
is an imprint of

PEARSON

Upper Saddle River, New Jersey
Columbus, Ohio

Library of Congress Cataloging in Publication Data

Bernard, Janine M.
  Fundamentals of clinical supervision / Janine M. Bernard, Rodney K. Goodyear.—4th ed.
    p. cm.
  Includes bibliographical references and indexes.
  ISBN-13: 978-0-205-59178-7
  ISBN-10: 0-205-59178-7
  1. Psychotherapists—Supervision of. 2. Counselors—Supervision of. 3. Clinical
psychologists—Supervision of. I. Goodyear, Rodney K. II. Title.
  [DNLM: 1. Health Personnel—organization & administration. 2. Mental Health
Services—organization & administration. 3. Clinical Competence. 4. Health Facility
Administrators—education. 5. Interprofessional Relations. 6. Models, Organizational.
7. Personnel Management—methods. WM 21 B519f 2009]
  RC480.5.B455 2009
  362.2'04250683—dc22   2008025784

Vice President and Executive Publisher: Jeffery W. Johnston
Publisher: Kevin M. Davis
Acquisitions Editor: Meredith D. Fossel
Editorial Assistant: Maren Vigilante
Senior Managing Editor: Pamela D. Bennett
Senior Project Manager: Linda Hillis Bayma
Production Coordination: Shylaja Gattupalli, TexTech International Pvt Ltd
Design Coordinator: Diane C. Lorenzo
Cover Designer: Candace Rowley
Cover image: PhotoDisc
Operations Specialist: Susan Hannahs
Director of Marketing: Quinn Perkson
Marketing Manager: Jared Brueckner
Marketing Coordinator: Brian Mounts

This book was set in Times Roman by TexTech International. It was printed and bound by Hamilton
Printing Company. The cover was printed by Phoenix Color Corp.

Pearson Education Ltd., London
Pearson Education Singapore, Pte., Ltd.
Pearson Education Canada, Inc.
Pearson Education–Japan
Pearson Education Australia PTY, Limited

Pearson Education North Asia, Ltd., Hong Kong
Pearson Educación de Mexico, S.A. de C.V.
Pearson Education Malaysia, Pte. Ltd.
Pearson Education Upper Saddle River, New Jersey

Merrill
is an imprint of

PEARSON

10 9 8 7 6 5 4 3 2 1

ISBN-13: 978-0-205-59178-7
ISBN-10:   0-205-59178-7

PREFACE

No book would warrant multiple editions if the field it covered were not evolving. There-fore, the publication of this fourth edition of *Fundamentals of Clinical Supervision* can be understood as one important indicator that clinical supervision remains a vital, dynamic area for mental health practitioners and researchers.

Certainly *Fundamentals of Clinical Supervision* has changed across its four editions and the 17 years they span. For example, the first edition had no chapter that focused specifically on supervisory relationships, but now two chapters explicitly address that relationship; this edition presents supervision models that have been published only recently. And, of course, the literature and the ideas it presents have been updated with each edition.

Regardless of specific content, we have remained true to the following goals across all four editions:

- The book is both *scholarly* (accomplished through a comprehensive review of the lit-erature) and *pragmatic* (accomplished through our choice of topics and manner of writing). We are heartened at the rapid growth in the supervision literature, including the publication of a number of new books devoted to the topic. Despite the prolifera-tion of books, though, we believe that this book has remained the one that best meets the twin goals of scholarship and pragmatism.
- The book provides a resource that will be useful to both the student of supervision as an overview of the field, and to the supervision practitioner as a professional resource.
- We draw broadly from the mental health professions to address an intervention that is common to them. Supervision literature has often existed in separate disciplinary silos, so that there has been a social work literature on supervision, a marital and fam-ily therapy literature, and so on. As a result, the same issues often have been addressed in a duplicative way and there have been limited opportunities for synergies that might otherwise occur.
- The book covers the essentials for professional training. The conceptual model of supervision presented in Figure 1.2 provides an overview of what we cover in the book. The figure and the content it describes are consistent with the content required in courses/training for the Approved Clinical Supervisor (ACS) credential, a credential available to all licensed or certified mental health practitioners (see http://www.cce-global.org/credentials-offered/acs), and it addresses the core supervision competencies articulated by the Association of Psychology Postdoctoral and Internship Centers (APPIC) supervision task group (Falender et al., 2004).

Fundamentals of Clinical Supervision underwent a major restructuring in its third edi-tion, along with our addition of a conceptual model to organize it. We find that the structure we imposed on the third edition continues to work well for us, and so we have continued it in this edition. We focused our quality improvement efforts in this edition primarily on identifying and incorporating the best of the new literature.

Of course, one challenge always has been how to add new material while holding the size of the book relatively constant from edition to edition. We have attempted to meet that challenge by deleting some of the more dated materials while also tightening some of our prose. This constraint forces us with each edition to reconsider what concepts and information are most essential.

This edition does have a more international tone than in previous editions. Clinical supervision is of interest in all countries with organized mental health systems and so we have worked to (1) better acknowledge supervision conventions and regulations other than those of the United States, and (2) draw more fully from supervision scholarship being published in other countries. As more scholars are included in professional conversations about supervision, our understandings of this important intervention can only become richer as a result.

As with the third edition, *Clinical Supervision: A Handbook for Practitioners,* by Marijane Fall and Jack Sutton, supplements this text. The *Handbook* is intended to be used in conjunction with the text and contains vignettes of supervision sessions, activities to help the student of supervision assimilate material, discussion questions, and suggestions for workshop activities. It is our hope that the addition of the *Handbook* will help us significantly in meeting our goal of offering our readers a resource for both academic and practitioner use.

As we complete this edition of *Fundamentals of Clinical Supervision,* we want to thank colleagues both at our institutions and elsewhere for the many discussions we have engaged in with them around this topic. We thank the reviewers—Clyde Beverly, Lehigh University; Mathew R. Buckley, Delta State University; Karla D. Carmichael, The University of Alabama; Cindy Juntunen, University of North Dakota; Anju Kaduvettoor, Lehigh University; Yoko Mori, Lehigh University; Tiffany O'Shaughnessy, Lehigh University; and Ryan Weatherford, Lehigh University—whose feedback informed the decisions we made in writing this edition. We want to extend our appreciation to present and former students as well. They allow the literature to come alive on a regular basis, many have been thoughtful critics, and some have been research collaborators.

Brief Contents

Contents

Note: Every effort has been made to provide accurate and current Internet information in this book. However, the Internet and information posted on it are constantly changing, and it is inevitable that some of the Internet addresses listed in this textbook will change.

CHAPTER 1

INTRODUCTION TO CLINICAL SUPERVISION

Many professions have a "signature pedagogy" (cf. Shulman, 2005), a particular instructional strategy that typifies the preparation of its practitioners. In medicine, for example, during clinical rounds a team of physicians and medical students visit a prescribed set of patients, discussing diagnostic and treatment issues related to each, along with what has happened since the team last discussed that patient. In law, students come to class prepared to be called upon at any moment to describe the essential arguments of a particular case or to summarize and respond to the arguments another student has just offered. During these interactions, their professor engages them in a type of Socratic dialogue.

Clinical supervision is the signature pedagogy of the mental health professions (Barnett, Cornish, Goodyear, & Lichtenberg, 2007; Goodyear, Bunch, & Claiborn, 2005). Like the signature pedagogy of other professions, it is characterized by (a) engagement, (b) uncertainty, and (c) formation (Shulman, 2005): *engagement* in that the learning occurs through instructor–learner dialogue; *uncertainty* because the specific focus and outcomes of the interactions typically are unclear to the participants as they begin a teaching episode; and *formation* in that the learner's thought processes are made clear to the instructor who helps shape them so that the learner beings to think "like a (physician, lawyer, psychologist, and so on)." In this book, we also are concerned with a higher level shift, which is to that of "thinking like a supervisor" (cf. Borders, 1992).

Shulman (2005) notes that these are:

> . . . *pedagogies of action, because exchanges typically [end] with someone saying, "That's all very interesting. Now what shall we do?"* (p. 14)

Clinical supervision qualifies as a signature pedagogy against all these criteria; criteria that underscore both supervision's importance to the mental health professions and its complexity. This book is intended to address that complexity by providing the technical and conceptual tools that are necessary to supervise.

We assert that every mental health professional should acquire supervision skills, for virtually all eventually will supervise. In fact, supervision is one of the more common activities in which mental health professionals engage. For example, Norcross, Hedges, and Castle (2002) summarized data from surveys of members of the American Psychological Association (APA)'s Division of Psychotherapy in 1981, 1991, and 2001. In each of the three surveys, supervision was the third most frequently endorsed professional activity (after psychotherapy and then diagnosis/assessment). Surveys of counseling psychologists (e.g., Goodyear et al., 2008; Watkins, Lopez, Campbell, & Himmell, 1986) have shown similar results.

This is true internationally as well. In a study of 2,380 psychotherapists from more than a dozen countries, Rønnestad, Orlinsky, Parks, and Davis (1997) confirmed the commonsense relationship between amount of professional experience and the likelihood of becoming a supervisor. In their study, the percentage of therapists who supervised increased from less than 1% in the first 6 months of practice to between 85% and 90% for those who have more than 15 years of practice.

In short, this book is for all mental health professionals. Its focus is on a training intervention that is not only essential to, but defining of those professions.

FOUNDATIONAL PREMISES

One challenge in writing this book has been our recognition that almost anyone who reads it will do so through a personal lens that reflects beliefs, attitudes, and expectations about supervision that they have formed through their own experiences as supervisees; perhaps also as supervisors. Such foreknowledge can make the reading more relevant and personally meaningful. But it also can invite critical responses to material that readers find dissonant with their beliefs. We hope readers who have that experience will find we have presented material in a manner that is sufficiently objective that they will be able to evaluate dispassionately any dissonance-producing content or ideas.

Two premises are foundational to what follows:

- *Clinical supervision is an intervention in its own right.* It is possible, therefore, to isolate and describe issues, theory, and technique that are unique to it. Moreover, as with any other psychological intervention, the practice of supervision demands that those who provide it have specific, appropriate preparation.
- *The mental health professions are more alike than different in their practice of supervision.* Most supervision skills and processes are common across these professions. There are, of course, profession-specific differences in emphasis, supervisory modality, and so on. These might be considered the unique flourishes each profession makes on our common signature pedagogy. But we assume there are core features that occur whether the supervision is offered by psychologists, counselors, social workers, family therapists, psychiatrists, or psychiatric nurses: "irrespective of professional and theoretical background, supervisors engage in very similar supervisory practices" (Spence, Wilson, Kavanagh, Strong, & Worrall, 2001, p. 138). Therefore, we have drawn from an interdisciplinary literature to address the breadth of issues and content that seems to characterize clinical supervision in mental health practice. We also draw from the growing

international literature on supervision, especially that from Britain.

This chapter is intended to lay the groundwork for those that follow. Therefore, we address the professional context for it, as well as its importance. We then consider definitions, both formal and more personal. We conclude by presenting the conceptual model that both informs our understanding about supervision and guides the organization of this book.

SUPERVISION'S CENTRALITY TO THE PROFESSIONS

Supervision's crucial role in the preparation of professionals has been recognized for thousands of years, as is suggested in the first few lines of the famous Hippocratic oath:

> *I SWEAR by Apollo the physician, and Aesculapius, and Health, and All-heal, and all the gods and goddesses, that, according to my ability and judgment, I will keep this Oath and this stipulation—to reckon him who taught me this Art equally dear to me as my parents, to share my substance with him, and relieve his necessities if required; to look upon his offspring in the same footing as my own brothers. . . .* (Hippocrates, ca. 400 BC; bold added for emphasis)

In this oath, the veneration being accorded a teacher or supervisor is clear. Moreover, the comparison of that teacher to one's parents suggests the power and influence the neophyte physician cedes to the teacher.

To appreciate that power and influence requires an understanding of the nature of the professions (see, for e.g., Goodyear & Guzzardo, 2000), especially of the ways in which they are distinct from other occupations. Those distinctions include that: (a) professionals work with substantially greater autonomy; (b) professionals need to make judgments under conditions of greater uncertainty (Sechrest et al., 1982), an attribute of the work that Schön (1983) vividly characterized as "working in the swampy lowlands" of practice (this is in contrast to technicians who work from a prescribed protocol on situations that typically are carefully constrained); and (c) professionals rely on a knowledge base that is sufficiently specialized that the average person would have difficulty grasping it and its implications.

Because of these qualities of professions, it is generally understood that lay people would not have the knowledge necessary to regulate them. Therefore, society permits the professions to self-regulate in return for the assurance that they will place the welfare of society and of their clients above their own self-interests (see e.g., Schein, 1973; Schön, 1983). This self-regulation includes controlling who is admitted to practice, setting standards for members' behavior, and disciplining incompetent or unethical members.

Within the mental health professions, three primary mechanisms of self-regulation are: (1) state regulatory boards, (2) professional credentialing groups, and (3) program accreditation. Supervision is central to the regulatory functions of each, for it provides a means to impart necessary skills, to socialize novices into the particular profession's values and ethics, to protect clients, and, finally, to monitor supervisees' readiness to be admitted to the profession. In short, "supervision plays a critical role in maintaining the standards of the profession" (Holloway & Neufeldt, 1995, p. 207).

State Regulatory Boards

State regulatory boards treat supervision as a regulated activity and therefore codify its practice. They stipulate: (a) the *qualifications* of those who supervise; (b) the *amounts* of supervised practice that licensure candidates are to accrue; and (c) the *conditions* under which this supervision is to occur (e.g., the ratio of supervision to hours of professional service; what proportion of the supervision can be in a group format; who can do the supervising). Some regulatory boards require a separate license in order to supervise within a particular profession. For example, Alabama licenses supervisors of counselors as a separate category.

Professional Credentialing Groups

Independent groups, such as the Academy of Certified Social Workers (ACSW), the American Board of Professional Psychology (ABPP), the National Board for Certified Counselors (NBCC), the American Association for Marriage and Family Therapy (AAMFT), and the British Association for Counselling and Psychotherapy (BACP) also credential mental health professionals. The credentials that these groups award usually are for advanced practitioners and certify competence above the minimal level necessary for public protection (the threshold level of competence for licensure is not actual competence, but rather the reasonable assurance that the person will do no harm). Like the regulatory boards, these credentialing groups typically stipulate amounts and conditions of supervision a candidate for one of their credentials is to have.

These groups mentioned above credential clinical practitioners. At least three of them (AAMFT, NBCC, and BACP) also have taken the additional step of credentialing clinical supervisors. In so doing, they have made clear their assumption that supervision is made up of a unique and important skill constellation.

Accrediting Bodies

Whereas licensure and credentialing affect the individual professional, accreditation affects the training programs that prepare them. Each of the mental health professions has its own accreditation body and their guidelines address supervision with varying degrees of specificity. For example, the American Psychological Association (APA, 2008) leaves it to the individual training program to establish that supervised training has been sufficient. But other groups are very specific about supervision requirements. For example, any graduate of an AAMFT-accredited program is to have received at least 100 hours of face-to-face supervision and this should have been in a ratio of at least 1 hour of supervision for every 5 hours of direct client contact (American

Association for Marriage and Family Therapy, 2006). The Council for Accreditation of Counseling and Related Educational Programs (CACREP, 2001) requires that a student receive a minimum of 1 hour per week of individual supervision and 1.5 hours of group supervision during practicum and internship; CACREP doctoral program standards also specify requirements for supervision-of-supervision.

CLINICAL SUPERVISION IN THE PREPARATION OF MENTAL HEALTH PROFESSIONALS

The foregoing speaks to the responsibilities supervisors have to the professions and to the broader society they serve. The next level of responsibility is to the supervisees with whom they work, to ensure that they develop the necessary competencies. The next section addresses the competencies supervisees are to develop and the role of supervision in that process.

Science–Practice Integration

The training of mental health practitioners can be thought of as having two major components: (1) the formal theories and research that typically are taught in a traditional didactic manner and (2) the practice-based knowledge of expert practitioners. These components, which can be thought of broadly as science and the art of practice should complement each other. In fact, this assumed complementarity is at the heart of the scientist–practitioner model in which most psychologists and many other mental health professionals are trained.

Yet these two domains of knowledge are differentially valued. Within universities the first too often is regarded as that of real knowledge, whereas the latter is either ignored or even regarded with some disdain. The reverse prejudice too often is true among practitioners. As a result, it is often difficult to reach an optimal balance between the two; it is even more difficult to integrate them.

These prejudices are one barrier to students being able to appropriately integrate the two knowledge domains. Another barrier is that students typically are exposed to these knowledge domains sequentially, learning formal theory and research first, in the classroom. They later gain the practitioner-driven knowledge when they begin to participate in the delivery of human services and to solicit the wisdom of other service providers.

Clinical supervisors are key to the integration of these two types of knowledge. Supervised practice provides the crucible in which supervisees can blend them and it is the supervisor who can help provide a bridge between campus and clinic (Williams, 1995), the bridge by which supervisees begin to span the "large theory–practice gulf" to which Rønnestad and Skovholt (1993, p. 396) have alluded.

Supervised Practice: Key to the Development of Competence

Supervised practice provides the opportunity for science–practice integration. In fact, it is absolutely essential as a means for supervisees to develop professional skills. This was Peterson's (2002) point when he told a joke about a New York City tourist who, lost, stopped a cabbie to ask, "How can I get to Carnegie Hall?" The cabbie's response was "practice, practice, practice." Peterson noted that this joke's punch line is significant in that the cabbie did not say "read, read, read."

But practice alone is an insufficient means by which to attain competence: Unless it is accompanied by the systematic feedback and guided reflection (the operative word being "guided") that supervision provides, supervisees may gain no more than the illusion that they are developing professional expertise. Dawes (1994) asserted:

> Two conditions are important for experiential learning: one, a clear understanding of what constitutes an incorrect response or error in judgment, and two, immediate, unambiguous and consistent feedback when such errors are made. In the mental health professions, neither of these conditions is satisfied. (p. 111)

Dawes's assertions about the two conditions necessary for experiential learning are compelling. But we believe his assertion that *neither* condition is met in the mental health professions is overstated. We predicated our writing of this book on the assumption that supervision can satisfy these and other necessary conditions for learning.

It is true a "supervisor" (by whatever name) may be unnecessary for attaining many motor and performance skills. In these domains, simply to perform the task may provide sufficient feedback for skill mastery. Learning to type is one example. Learning to drive an automobile is another (Dawes, 1994): When driving, the person who turns the steering wheel too abruptly receives immediate feedback from the vehicle; the same is true if he or she is too slow applying the brakes when approaching another vehicle. In these and other ways, experience behind the wheel gives the person an opportunity to obtain immediate and unambiguous feedback. Driving skills are therefore likely to develop and improve simply with the experience of driving.

But psychological practice skills are of a different type. In this domain, experience alone rarely provides either of the two conditions that Dawes stipulated as necessary for experiential learning to occur. The practitioner's skills cannot be shaped by simple experience in the same automatic manner that occurs with the development of driving skills. She or he must receive intentional, clear feedback such as is available in supervision. Research data confirm that unsupervised counseling experience does not accelerate the clinical progress of trainees (Hill, Charles, & Reed, 1981; Wiley & Ray, 1986), a conclusion complemented by that of educational psychologists who have examined the broader domain of instruction (see, esp. Kirschner, Sweller, & Clark, 2006).

In short, (a) practice is essential, but (b) insufficient or even counterproductive if not guided in the ways supervision can provide. As Brashears (1995) noted, "arguments have been made about how long supervision should last and how much supervision is needed, but not over its necessity" (p. 692).

NECESSARY PREPARATION TO SUPERVISE

The material immediately above focused on the role of supervision in helping supervisees to develop professional competence. But, whereas a great deal of attention has been given to supervision in the development of new professionals' competence, a great deal less attention has been given to the development of competence in the supervisors themselves. Milne and James (2002) commented that this is something of a paradox that the field needs to address.

Fortunately, there seems to be observable progress on that front. During the 17 years since the first edition of this book was published, we have observed mental health practitioners' attitudes about obtaining formal preparation as supervisors to change substantially. They are much less likely now to entertain either of two erroneous assumptions. The less frequent of these is that having been a supervisee is itself sufficient preparation to be a supervisor. This, though, is analogous to believing that one could be a therapist simply on the basis of having been a client.

The more frequent assumption is that to be an effective therapist is a sufficient prerequisite to being a good supervisor. Yet to assume that therapy skills translate automatically to supervisory skills is analogous to assuming that a good athlete inevitably will make either a good coach or perhaps a good sports announcer. We all can find an instance in which that has not been the case. In fact, the great players tend not to become the great coaches, and vice versa, although most coaches at least have "played the game." Carroll (1996) spoke to this problem when he asserted "It sounds a terrible choice, but given the option between a good counsellor who was a poor educator, or a poor counsellor who was a good educator, I would choose the latter as a supervisor" (p. 27).

Although many fewer mental health professionals now entertain these and related erroneous beliefs, those beliefs have been one barrier to the formal preparation of supervisors. Another has been circumstance. That is, many mental health professionals find themselves thrust into a supervisory role, regardless of training. In performing that role, they often come to believe they are doing a pretty good job. But self-assessments of competence and actual competence are often independent of one another (cf. Dunning, Johnson, Ehrlinger, & Kruger, 2003). Professionals who have assumed supervisory roles in this manner are more inclined to believe that, if they have learned it without formal preparation, their students and supervisees can as easily do so. These faculty and field supervisors serve as role models to supervisees, who then receive mixed messages about the actual importance of supervision training. In this way, then, they hinder more general acceptance that training in supervision is necessary.

Yet another barrier to obtaining preparation as a supervisor had been difficulty obtaining training (e.g., Hess & Hess, 1983; McColley & Baker, 1982). Fortunately, this is changing because accrediting bodies now are stipulating that students receive this preparation. Both CACREP- and AAMFT-accredited doctoral programs are required to offer a supervision course, and the accreditation guidelines for APA stipulate supervision as a competence area, bolstered by the report of the Association of Psychology Postdoctoral and Internship Centers (APPIC) task group on supervision competencies (Falender et al., 2004) which similarly declared supervision a core competence; the Association for Counselor Education and Supervision (ACES) has endorsed Standards for Counseling Supervisors (1990), a variant of which later was adopted by the Center for Credentialing and Education as the basis for its Approved Clinical Supervisor credential. As well, AAMFT has a supervisor membership category that requires specified training.

Although it does not stipulate specific training the Canadian psychology regulatory boards have declared supervision to be a core competence that requires specific skills (Mutual Recognition Agreement, 2001). In Britain, supervision training is readily available to qualified professionals through a number of freestanding training "courses" (i.e., programs).

Fortunately, attitudinal and structural barriers to supervision preparation have diminished

substantially and are continuing to do so. Supervision training now is much more frequently offered than in the past, although its availability is uneven across the various mental health professions and even between specialties within a profession. For example, whereas a supervision course is required for all CACREP accredited doctoral programs, Scott, Ingram, Vitanza, and Smith (2000) found psychology specialty and setting differences in the emphasis given to supervision training. For example, among counseling psychology programs, 85% had a didactic course in supervision and 79% had a supervision practicum; those percentages for clinical psychology programs were 34% and 43%, respectively. Among internship sites, university counseling centers were more likely than other sites to offer a supervision seminar (73% vs. 27%) or to offer the opportunity to supervise (89% vs. 44%).

The good news is that the availability of supervisor training seems steadily to be increasing. It helps, too, that state licensure boards also are beginning to require that mental health professionals who provide supervision receive at least some supervision training. For example, a 2003 regulation requires California-licensed psychologists who want to supervise to participate in one 6-hour supervision workshop during every 2-year licensure cycle. Sutton (2000) reported that 18% of counselor licensure boards required a course or its equivalent for persons providing supervision and another 12% required training in supervision, but do not specify the type or amount. Sutton reported that three of these boards had a specialty license for supervisors.

The cumulative effect of these changes is to ensure better and more systematic preparation for supervisors, especially for newer ones. But there still are many practitioners who were trained during an earlier era, and so it will take some time for the field to catch up entirely. Within the past decade, for example, Johnson and Stewart (2000) found that only a very few of the Canadian psychology supervisors they surveyed reported having received training in supervision while in graduate school. Yet two of their findings were encouraging: (1) those who had received supervision training reported themselves to feel more ready to supervise than those who had not, and (2) more than half (55.1%) reported that their initial supervision experience was itself supervised.

DEFINING SUPERVISION

We have been able to get this far into this chapter without defining supervision because we assume anyone reading this book has some understanding of what it is. But a deeper appreciation of supervision requires a more formal definition.

Before offering that definition, we want first to acknowledge the most simplistic way of looking at it, which is that it involves the supervisor's use of "super vision." In fact, it is possible for a supervisor to find that she or he has gained a clarity of perspective about counseling or therapy processes precisely because she or he is not one of the involved parties. The supervisor works from a vantage point that is not afforded the therapist who is actually involved in the process.

Levenson (1984) spoke to this when he observed that, in the ordinary course of his work as a therapist, he spends considerable time perplexed, confused, bored, and "at sea." But "when I supervise, all is clear to me!" (p. 153). He reported finding that theoretical and technical difficulties were surprisingly clear to him. Moreover, he maintained that people whom he supervised and who seemed confused most of the time that they were supervisees reported that they attained a similar clarity when they were supervising. He speculated that this is "an odd, seductive aspect of the phenomenology of the supervisory process itself" (p. 154) that occurs at a different level of abstraction than therapy. Perhaps this is the perspective of the Monday-morning quarterback.

Haley (1996) provided his own, sardonic take on how a supervisor might embrace the notion of having "super vision:"

> *Two vision mannerisms are helpful: (1) a faraway look that implies one is considering all aspects of the larger situation, and (2) a keen incisive look that*

> *shows the student that one is alert and quickly grasping the essentials. . . . The faraway look and thoughtful silence can, at times, cause the trainee to become impatient enough to come up with an idea of something to do. The supervisor can accept the trainee's idea, perhaps implying that he or she had that very thing in mind and merely wanted the trainee to think of it spontaneously. If a student already has a plan and is seeking approval for it, a sharp, knowing look by the supervisor is correct even if he or she doesn't understand the plan.* (p. 216)

The etymological definition of supervision is simply *to oversee* (Webster's, 1966). This is the function of supervisors in virtually any occupation or profession. Yet it is an insufficient definition for what occurs during the clinical supervision of trainees and practitioners in the mental health professions. It is important, therefore, to have a more precise and specific definition.

Definitions that various authors have offered differ considerably as a function of such factors as the author's discipline and training focus. Our intent in this book is to offer a definition that is specific enough to be helpful, but at the same time broad enough to encompass the multiple roles, disciplines, and settings associated with supervision. Before providing this definition, it is useful to consider two others that have been suggested.

We have offered, with only the slightest of changes, the following working definition of supervision since the first edition of this book (Bernard & Goodyear, 1992):

> *Supervision is an intervention provided by a more senior member of a profession to a more junior member or members of that same profession. This relationship*
>
> - *is evaluative and hierarchical,*
> - *extends over time, and*
> - *has the simultaneous purposes of enhancing the professional functioning of the more junior person(s); monitoring the quality of professional services offered to the clients that she, he, or they see; and serving as a gatekeeper for those who are to enter the particular profession.*

Milne (2007) has observed that this definition has been informally adopted as the standard in both the United States and the United Kingdom. He argued, though, that it is insufficiently specific. So he offered his own modification in which he broke the definition into the components of *form* (e.g., intensive, relationship based, case focused) and *function* (e.g., quality control, facilitating supervisee competence, helping supervisees work effectively).

Although Milne's comments are useful, we stand by our definition. It is succinct, though, and so merits further explication. To that end, it is useful to isolate each of its elements and then engage in a more extended consideration of each element. Prior to doing this, however, we wish to offer a brief discussion of other terms we will use in this book.

We will use *counseling, therapy,* and *psychotherapy* interchangeably, for distinctions among these terms are artificial and serve little function. We also will follow the convention first suggested by Rogers (1951) of referring to the recipient of therapeutic services as a client.

We also distinguish between supervision and training. Stone (1997) made the point that the definition of supervision "occasionally suffers from cycles of inflation and deflation" (p. 265), depending on whether authors are confusing supervision with training. Training differs from supervision, however, in its more limited scope, its following of prescribed protocols, and its focus on specific skills (e.g., how to offer restatements of client affect and content). Also, such training often takes place in laboratory courses, rather than with real clients.

Paralleling this training versus supervision distinction is the one that we make between *trainee* and *supervisee*. We believe that *supervisee* is the more inclusive term. *Trainee* connotes a supervisee who is still enrolled in a formal training program; it seems less appropriate for postgraduate professionals who seek supervision. Therefore, in most cases we will use *supervisee*.

We turn now to a more complete explication of our working definition of supervision. Each of the following sections will address a specific element of this definition.

Supervision Is a Distinct Intervention

Supervision is an intervention, as are teaching, psychotherapy, and mental health consultation. There are substantial ways in which supervision overlaps with these other interventions (see Table 1.1). In fact, in later chapters we will discuss how good supervisors will draw from each of these roles. But, despite these overlaps, supervision is a unique intervention.

Teaching versus Supervision.   One goal of supervision is to teach, and the supervisee does have the role of learner (cf. the title of the classic Ekstein and Wallerstein book, *The Teaching and Learning of Psychotherapy* [1972]). Moreover, teaching and supervision are alike in that each has an evaluative aspect. Relatedly, each ultimately serves a gatekeeping function, regulating who is legitimized to work in a particular area.

Teaching, however, typically relies on an explicit curriculum with goals that are imposed uniformly on everyone. But even though the focus of supervision at its broadest level might seem to speak to common goals (e.g., to prepare competent practitioners), the actual intervention is tailored to the needs of the individual supervisee and the supervisee's clients. Eshach and Bitterman's (2003) comments about the challenges in preparing physicians to address the needs of the individual—and therefore about the need for an educational context that is flexible and adaptive to the needs of the trainee and the person she or he is serving—apply just as well to the training of mental health practitioners.

> *The problems are often poorly defined. . . . The problems that patients present can be confusing and contradictory, characterized by imperfect, inconsistent, or even inaccurate information. . . . Not only is much irrelevant information present, but also relevant information about a case is often missing and does not become apparent until after problem solving has begun.* (p. 492)

As well, the focus of supervision typically is on some problem the supervisee has encountered

TABLE 1.1 Supervision versus Teaching, Counseling, and Consultation

	SIMILARITIES	DIFFERENCES
Teaching	• Both have the purpose of imparting new skills and knowledge • Both have evaluative and gatekeeping functions	• Whereas teaching is driven by a set curriculum or protocol, supervision is driven by the needs of the particular supervisee and his/her clients
Counseling or therapy	• Both can address recipients' problematic behaviors, thoughts, or feelings	• Any therapeutic work with a supervisee must be only to increase effectiveness in working with clients • Supervision is evaluative, whereas counseling is not • Counseling clients often have greater choice of therapists than supervisees have of supervisors
Consultation	• Both are concerned with helping the recipient work more effectively professionally. For more advanced trainees, the two functions may become indistinguishable.	• Consultation is a relationship between equals whereas supervision is hierarchical • Consultation can be a one-time event, whereas supervision occurs across time • Consultation is more usually freely sought by recipients than is supervision • Supervision is evaluative, whereas consultation is not

during his or her work. The idiosyncratic nature of these problems will not lend themselves to a pre-planned curriculum.

Counseling versus Supervision. There are elements, too, of counseling or therapy in supervision. That is, supervisors often help supervisees to examine aspects of their behavior, thoughts, or feelings that are stimulated by a client, particularly as these may act as barriers to their work with the client. As Frawley-O'Dea and Sarnat (2001) observe, to have "a rigidly impenetrable boundary between teaching and 'treating' in supervision is neither desirable nor truly achievable" (p. 137). Still, there should be boundaries. Therapeutic interventions with supervisees should be made only in the service of helping them become more effective with clients: To provide therapy that has broader goals is ethical misconduct (see, e.g.,

Ladany, Lehrman-Waterman, Molinaro, & Wolgast, 1999; Neufeldt & Nelson, 1999).

There are other differences, too. For example, clients generally are free to enter therapy or not; when they do, they usually have a voice in choosing their therapists. On the other hand, supervision is not a voluntary experience for supervisees. Moreover, they often have scant voice in who their supervisor is to be. Given this circumstance, it is salient to note that Webb and Wheeler (1998) found in their study that supervisees who had chosen their own supervisors reported being able to disclose to their supervisors more information of a sensitive nature about themselves, their clients, and the supervisory process than supervisees who had been assigned a supervisor.

Page and Woskett (2001) differentiated supervision from counseling according to their respective *aims* (in counseling, to enable a fuller, more satisfying life versus, in supervision, to develop counseling skills and the ability to conceptualize the counseling process); *presentation* (clients present material verbally whereas supervisees present in multiple ways including not only verbally, but via audio and videotape, live observation, and so on); *timing* (clients choose the pace whereas supervisees often need to have new understanding or skills in time for their next counseling session); and *relationship* (in counseling, regression may be tolerated or even encouraged whereas that is not so in supervision; although some challenging of boundaries is expected in counseling, there is not that expectation in supervision).

The single most important difference between therapy and supervision may reside in the evaluative responsibilities of the supervisor. Although few would maintain that counseling or therapy is or could be free of values, most therapists actively resist imposing their values on clients or otherwise making explicit evaluations of them. On the other hand, supervisees are evaluated against criteria that are imposed on them by others.

Consultation versus Supervision. Mental health consultation is yet another intervention that overlaps with supervision. In fact, for more senior professionals, supervision often evolves into consultation. That is, the experienced therapist might meet informally on an occasional basis with a colleague to get ideas about how to handle a particularly difficult client or to regain needed objectivity. We all encounter blind spots in ourselves, and it is to our benefit to obtain help in this manner.

Despite the similarities, there are distinctions between consultation and supervision. Consultation, for example, is more likely than supervision to be a one-time-only event and the parties in the consultation relationship often are not of the same professional discipline (Caplan, 1970; e.g., a social worker might consult with a teacher about a child's problem).

Two consultation–supervision distinctions echo distinctions already made between therapy

and supervision. One is that supervision is more likely imposed, whereas consultation typically is freely sought. More significantly, whereas evaluation is one of the defining attributes of supervision, Caplan and Caplan (2000) observed that consultation

> . . . *is non-hierarchical. Our consultants reject any power to coerce their consultees to accept their view of the case or to behave in ways the consultants may advocate. . . . consultants have no administrative power over the consultees or responsibility for case outcome.* (pp. 18–19)

In summary, then, specific aspects of such related interventions as teaching, therapy, and consultation are present as components of supervision. Supervision should be thought of as an intervention comprised of multiple skills, many of which are common to other forms of intervention. Yet their configuration is such as to make supervision unique among psychological interventions. Moreover, there is at least one phenomenon, that of parallel or reciprocal processes (e.g., Doehrman, 1976; Searles, 1955), that is unique to supervision and distinguishes it from other interventions (parallel processes are discussed in Chapter 6).

Member of Same Profession

The widely acknowledged purpose of supervision is to facilitate supervisees' development of therapeutic and case management skills. It is possible to accomplish this purpose when the supervisory dyad is comprised of members of two different disciplines (e.g., a marital and family therapist might supervise the work of a counselor). In fact, almost all supervisees will be supervised by someone outside their immediate profession. The limitation of this arrangement is that it overlooks the socialization function that supervision serves. Supervisees are developing a sense of professional identity, and this is best acquired through association with more senior members of the supervisees' own professional discipline.

Ekstein and Wallerstein (1972) spoke to this when they noted that it would be possible for a training program to prepare its supervisees with all the basic psychotherapeutic skills, but still fall short: "What would still be missing is a specific quality in the psychotherapist that makes him [or her] into a truly professional person, a quality we wish to refer to as his [or her] professional identity" (p. 65).

Most state laws that govern the licensure of mental health professions stipulate that the licensure applicant have a certain portion of his or her supervised clinical hours from supervisors of a like profession. It is instructive to note that Kavanagh et al. (2003) found that Australian public mental health workers perceived that the extent of supervision they received was related to its impact on them but only when the supervisor was of the same profession; not otherwise.

In a cautionary tale concerning the use of members of one profession to supervise neophyte members of another profession, Albee (1970) invoked the metaphor of the cuckoo: The cuckoo is a bird that lays its eggs in the nests of other birds, who then raise the offspring as their own. His case in point was clinical psychology, which had used the Veterans Administration system as a primary base of training in the decades following World War II. From Albee's perspective, this was unfortunate, for the clinical psychology fledglings were put in the care of psychiatrists, who then socialized them into their way of viewing the world. Albee asserted that a consequence of this pervasive practice was that clinical psychology lost some of what was unique to it as its members incorporated the perspectives of psychiatry.

Supervision Is Evaluative and Hierarchical

We have already mentioned several times that evaluation stands as one of supervision's hallmarks, distinguishing it from both counseling or therapy and consultation. Evaluation is implicit in the supervisors' mandate to safeguard clients, both those currently being seen by the supervisee and those who would be seen in the future by the supervisee if the he or she were to finish the professional program.

That supervisors have an evaluative function provides them with a tool, giving them an important source of interpersonal influence. For example, although most supervisees have a very high degree of intrinsic motivation to learn and to use feedback to self-correct, evaluation can provide supervisees with an additional, extrinsic motivation to use supervisory feedback.

But, despite its importance as a component of supervision, both supervisor and supervisee can experience evaluation with discomfort. Supervisors, for example, were trained first in the more nonevaluative role of counselor or therapist. Indeed, they may well have been attracted to the field because of this feature of counseling. The role of evaluator therefore can be not only new, but uncomfortable as well.

> The role of evaluator also affects the trainee's perception of the supervisor. Students are not only taught psychotherapy by their supervisors, they are also evaluated by them. The criteria for evaluating students' performances tend to be subjective and ambiguous, in large part because the skills being evaluated are highly complex, intensely personal, and difficult to measure. Students know that their psychological health, interpersonal skills, and therapeutic competence are being judged against unclear standards. . . . Supervisors are thus not only admired teachers but feared judges who have real power. (Doehrman, 1976, pp. 10–11)

That supervision is evaluative means that it is hierarchical. To the extent that hierarchy recapitulates issues related to ethnicity and gender, this can be problematic. Feminists, for example, have wrestled with the best means by which to balance their collaborative stance with the fact of hierarchy in supervision (see, e.g., Prouty, Thomas, Johnson, & Long, 2001). Some (e.g., Edwards & Chen, 1999; Porter & Vasquez, 1997), in fact, have suggested the term *covision* as an alternative to supervision, to signal a more collaborative relationship. Yet hierarchy and evaluation are so intertwined with supervision that to remove them makes the intervention something other than supervision.

Evaluation, then, is an important, integral component of supervision. But it is one that often is the source of problems for supervisors and supervisees alike. Therefore, we have devoted an entire chapter of this book to the topic of evaluation (see Chapter 2). Although there is no way in which evaluation could (or should) be removed from supervision, there are ways to enhance its usefulness and to minimize problems attendant to it.

Supervision Extends over Time

A final element of our definition of supervision is that it is an intervention that extends over time. This distinguishes supervision from training, which might be brief, for example, in a short workshop intended to impart a specific skill; it distinguishes supervision, too, from consultation, which might be very time limited as one professional seeks the help of another to gain or regain objectivity in his or her work with a client.

The fact that it is ongoing allows the supervisor–supervisee relationship to grow and develop. Indeed, many supervision theorists have focused particular attention on the developing nature of this relationship. In recognition of this, we devote three chapters of this book to the supervisory relationship, including the ways in which it evolves and changes across time (see Chapters 5, 6, and 7).

Purposes of Supervision

In our definition, we suggest that supervision has two central purposes:

1. *To foster the supervisee's professional development* (a supportive and educational function)
2. *To ensure client welfare* (the supervisor's gatekeeping function is a variant of the monitoring of client welfare)

Each is an essential purpose. It is possible, however, for a supervisor to more heavily emphasize one than the other. For example, a student working at a field placement might have both a university-based and an on-site supervisor. In this situation, it is possible for the university-based supervisor to give relatively greater emphasis to the teaching–learning goals of supervision and the on-site supervisor to give relatively greater emphasis to the client-monitoring aspects. Feiner (1994) alluded to this dichotomy of goals when he suggested that

> *Some supervisors assume that their most important ethical responsibility is to the student's patient. This would impel them to make the student a conduit for their own expertise. Others make the assumption that their ultimate responsibility is to the development of the student. . . . Their concern is the possible lowering of the student's self-esteem when confronted by the supervisor and his rising fantasy that he should become a shoe salesman.* (p. 171)

It is important to acknowledge other possible purposes for supervision. For example, Proctor (1986) asserted that supervision serves three purposes that she labeled *formative* (equivalent to our teaching–learning purpose), *normative* (generally equivalent to ensuring client welfare), and also *restorative*. This last purpose is to provide supervisees the opportunity to express and meet needs that will help them to avoid burnout.

Occasionally, too, supervision is mandated as a method to rehabilitate impaired professionals (see, e.g., Frick, McCartney, & Lazarus, 1995). This overlaps with both the training and client-protective purposes of supervision, but really should be considered an additional purpose. We will not specifically address this purpose of supervision in this book and refer interested readers to discussions of the topic by Cobia and Pipes (2002) and Walzer and Miltimore (1993).

Both the restorative and rehabilitative purposes of supervision are important in some supervision. But they are not common to *all* supervision, as are the two purposes that are part of our definition of supervision. We address each in turn in the sections that follow.

We would add one additional, ultimate goal, which is to prepare the supervisee to self-supervise. At the point of licensure, practitioners, at least in the United States, no longer are required to be supervised and so must be able to monitor their own work, knowing how to learn from it and also when to seek consultation. Supervisees work with a number of supervisors; a psychologist will have worked with about eight prior to obtaining a doctorate (M. V. Ellis, personal communication, August 31, 2006, from data obtained as part of an instrument validation study). In the process of that work, they should develop a sort of "internal supervisor" that incorporates what they have learned from each of their supervisors.

Enhancing Professional Functioning. We state the teaching–learning goal simply as "to enhance professional functioning." This is a pragmatic definition that meets our need to provide a succinct and generally applicable definition of supervision. It is silent about any performance criteria that supervisees are to meet or even about the content of learning (though in Chapter 2 we flesh this out with a discussion of performance criteria).

To enhance professional functioning, then, is a broad conceptual goal. In actual practice, supervision will have goals that vary both in specificity and time orientation. That is, the supervisor should have some very precise and concrete goals to accomplish with the supervisee during their work together; in the best of circumstances, the supervisee will share these goals. Typically, these derive from some combination of the supervisor's own theory or model, the supervisee's particular developmental needs, and the supervisee's expressed wishes.

In addition, the supervisor almost certainly would want the supervisee to be developing skills and competencies necessary for eventual licensure or certification. This is a utilitarian goal that has the virtue of specificity. That is, supervisors generally know what competencies the supervisee will have to demonstrate for licensure, at least in his or her own state. Moreover, this is a logical target in that to attain licensure is the point at which the supervisee makes the transition to an autonomously functioning professional who no longer has a legal mandate to be supervised.

The truth is that no one knows or tracks in any systematic way what transpires between therapist and client once the therapist escapes the onus of training and supervision, and unlike most medical procedures of significant consequence, there's generally no one present to observe other than the provider and the recipient—neither of whom is apt to be vested with an unbiased view or recollection. (Gist, 2007)

The assumption undergirding this right to practice without supervision is that the person has developed what Falender and Shafranske (2007) call "metacompetence," or "the ability to assess what one knows and what one doesn't know" (p. 232). Moreover, it is expected that the licensed professional will know to seek consultation when faced with an issue beyond his or her expertise.

Whereas it is the norm in the United States to permit licensed professionals to work without formal supervision, this is not true in other countries, which may be wise given Gist's observation above. In the United Kingdom, for example, many mental health professionals are expected to continue receiving supervision throughout their professional lives (West, 2003). This is codified in the British Association for Counselling and Psychotherapy's (BACP) ethical code, which stipulates that "There is an obligation to use regular and on-going supervision to enhance the quality of the services provided and to commit to updating practice by continuing professional development" (BACP, 2007, p. 3). BACP expectations are that practitioners will participate in supervision at least 1.5 hours per month. Such a convention recognizes that professional development is ongoing and extends even after a professional develops expertise; supervision in this context is understood to have more than a training function.

Fried (1991) offered the folk wisdom that it takes 10 years to become a really good psychotherapist. In fact, Hayes (1981) estimated that it requires about 10 years to become an expert in *any* skill domain; Ericcson and Lehmann (1996) referred to this as "the ten year rule of necessary preparation." Yet, for many professionals, time alone will be insufficient to attain expert status. The same is true of clinical wisdom. But even if expertise or even wisdom is attained, it still is useful to have supervision, if only for the support it provides.

In fact, many—perhaps most—postgraduate, credentialed practitioners *want* and do continue some level and type of supervision even if it is not mandated (see, e.g., Borders & Usher, 1992; McCarthy, Kulakowski, & Kenfield, 1994; Wiley, 1994). This is good for them, and it also is good for their clients. Slater (2003) stated:

> I remember a patient once asking me, "Who do you talk about me with?" He wasn't asking out of fear, but hope. What suffering person doesn't want many minds thinking about how to help?

Monitoring Client Care.   In addition to their responsibilities to the supervisees' professional development, supervisors must also ensure that supervisees are providing adequate client care. This professional responsibility is well understood by virtually all supervisors. It is a responsibility that also comes with some professional risk, for the supervisor can be held liable for any harm done by his or her supervisees, though the legal concept of vicarious liability (Chapter 3).

The original purpose of clinical supervision was to monitor client care. Supervision in the mental health disciplines almost certainly began with social work supervision, which "dates from the 19th-century Charity Organization Societies in which paid social work agents supervised the moral treatment of the poor by friendly visitors" (Harkness & Poertner, 1989, p. 115). The focus of this supervision was on the client.

Eisenberg (1956) noted that the first known call for supervision to focus on the professional, rather than exclusively on the client, was in 1901 by Zilphia Smith. This supervisory focus did not become more prominent until "the 1920s when Max Eitington, a psychoanalyst in Berlin, proposed that psychoanalysts in training conduct supervised psychoanalysis sessions" (Hutto, 2001).

But, despite its importance, the need to ensure quality of client care is one job demand with particular potential for causing dissonance in the supervisor. Most of the time, supervisors are able to perceive themselves as allies of their supervisees. Yet they also must be prepared, should they see harm being done to clients, to risk bruising the egos of their supervisees or, in extreme cases, even to steer the supervisee from the profession. From the perspective of supervisees, especially those with autonomy conflicts, this aspect of supervision can lead to the perception that supervisors are conducting "snooper vision" (Kadushin, 2002).

PERSON-SPECIFIC UNDERSTANDINGS OF SUPERVISION

A formal definition of supervision is important. But it is inevitable that supervisors and supervisees also will operate according to their own idiosyncratic, personally nuanced definitions. Because these more individualized, and usually implicit, definitions can affect supervision processes in important ways, they too should be acknowledged as complements to the more formal definition.

To consider these nuanced definitions, it is useful to invoke the concept of the schema (in the plural, schemata) that Bartlett (1932, 1958) introduced and which now is widely used among cognitive psychologists and mental health professionals. A schema helps us to interpret our world by providing a mental framework for understanding and remembering information. More formally stated, it is a knowledge representation based on our past experiences and inferences that we use to interpret a present experience. In short, people have a tendency to understand one domain of experience in terms of another; that is, to think metaphorically. Mental health professionals, in fact, base much of their work on the assumption that a person's previous life experiences can and often do function metaphorically for current ones (i.e., the very notion of transference is based on this assumption).

In other words, then, particular life experiences and patterns serve us as something of a template for understanding other situations in our lives: Our perceptions and responses to a new situation are organized and structured as they were in a previous similar situation. Because of their apparent similarities, we then respond to the new situation as if it were the earlier one. Moreover, the more ingrained the role, the more it is likely to intrude on later learned roles. The schema people

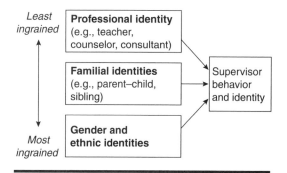

FIGURE 1.1 Life and Professional Roles That Affect Supervisory Role Behavior

develop for supervision is shaped in this manner. Figure 1.1 shows, for example, that gender and ethnicity roles are among the most ingrained and therefore permeate much of our behavior, including supervision (see Chapter 5 for a discussion of these roles in supervision).

Professional roles are learned later and therefore are less an ingrained part of ourselves. But, even so, earlier learned professional roles (such as that of counselor) are likely to affect later learned professional roles. For those taking on the later learned roles, it is natural, perhaps inevitable, to attempt to understand them in terms of things we do know: It is merely human to attempt to understand that which is the new in terms of that which is familiar.

It should be no surprise, then, that the roles of supervisor and supervisee are at least partially understood as metaphoric expressions of other life experiences. Proctor (1991), for example, invoked the concept of archetypes, which actually could be understood as schemata:

A number of my colleagues asked me what archetypes went into taking the trainer role; we immediately identified a number. There are the Guru, or Wise Woman, from whom wisdom is expected, and the Earth Mother—the all-provider, unconditional positive regarder. In contrast there is the Clown or Jester—enjoying performance, and cloaking his truth in riddles, without taking responsibility for how it is received. The Patriarch creates order and

unselfconsciously wields power. The Actor/Director allocates roles and tasks and holds the Drama; the Bureaucrat demands compliance to the letter of the law. The Whore gives services for money, which can be indistinguishable from love, and re-engages with group after group. There is even the Warrior— valiant for truth; and of course the Judge—upholding standards and impartially assessing. The Shepherd/ Sheep-dog gently and firmly rounds up and pens. (p. 65)

These are some possible metaphors for the supervisor. There also are metaphors that speak to the process or experience of supervision, independent of other life roles. Therefore, a supervisee (or supervisor) might understand supervision as akin to a lighthouse beacon that provides one with bearings in often foggy situations. Participants in workshops that our colleague, Michael Ellis, has run have described supervision as a shepherd and flock, as an oasis in the desert, and (more ominously) as going to the principal's office.

Page and Wosket (1994) employ the metaphor of bicycle riding to describe the supervisory process. They suggest that the domain of counseling or therapy might be

represented by bicycles. There are many different types of two-wheel cycles, some different because they are designed and made by different manufacturers who give priority to a particular quality in their product. . . . [W]e could liken counsellor supervision to the tandem—having two riders rather than the usual one . . . [and that they] offer a means whereby an experienced rider might coach an inexperienced one in the saddle. (pp. 3–4)

Milne and James (2005) developed the same metaphor of supervision as tandem bicycle riding, apparently independently of Page and Woskett. In fact, they have elaborated on that metaphor to present it as a supervision model.

We believe that these metaphors exist at various levels of awareness. But they often are present and affect participants' expectations and behaviors. The following discussions of more frequently occurring metaphors are therefore in the service of making them available for consideration.

Family Metaphors

Family metaphors (midprint Figure 1.1) seem especially common in supervision. The most basic of these is that of the parent–child relationship. Lower (1972), for example, employed this metaphor in alluding to the unconscious parent–child fantasies that he believed are stimulated by the supervisory situation itself. In fact, Itzhaky and Sztern (1999) cautioned supervisors against allowing themselves to behave without awareness of what they termed a "pseudo-parental role" (p. 247).

Many theorists have, of course, employed this metaphor of parent–child relationship as a way to think about therapy. As it may apply to supervision, the metaphor simultaneously is both less and more appropriate than for therapy. It is *less* apt in that personal growth is not a primary goal of the intervention, as it is in therapy, but rather is an instrumental goal that works in the service of making the supervisee a better therapist. It is *more* apt, on the other hand, in that supervision is an evaluative relationship just as parenting is—and therapy presumably is not.

Just knowing that they are being evaluated is often sufficient to trigger in supervisees an expectation of a guilt–punishment sequence that recapitulates early parent–child interactions. Supervisors can, through their actions, intensify such transference responses among supervisees, triggering perceptions of them as a good or bad parent. We have heard, for example, of instances in which supervisors posted publicly in the staff lounge the names of supervisees who had too many client "no-shows." The atmosphere created in situations such as this can easily establish supervisory staff as "feared parents."

Still another parallel between parent–child and supervisor–supervisee relationships is that status, knowledge, maturity, and power differences between the participants eventually will begin to disappear. The parties who today are supervisor and supervisee can expect that one day they might relate to one another as peers and colleagues.

The parent–child metaphor is suggested, too, in the frequent use of developmental metaphors to describe supervision. Hillerbrand (1989) suggested, for example, that supervisors consider the theorizing of Vygotsky (1978), who also recommended this. The following description of Vygotsky's thinking really derives at the most basic level from the manner in which parents teach life tasks to their children:

> [Vygotsky] *proposed that cognitive skills are acquired through social interaction. Unskilled persons learn cognitive skills by assuming more and more responsibility from experts during performance (what he called "expert scaffolding"). Novices first observe an expert's cognitive activity while the experts do most of the work. As novices begin to perform the skills, they receive feedback from the experts on their performance; as they learn to perform the skill correctly, they begin to assume more responsibility for the cognitive skill. Finally, novices assume the major responsibility for the cognitive skill, and experts become passive observers.* (Hillerbrand, 1989, p. 294)

A second family metaphor that can pertain to supervision is that of older and younger sibling. For many supervisory dyads, this probably is more apt than the parent–child metaphor. The supervisor is further along on the same path being traveled by the supervisee. As such, she or he is in a position to show the way in a nurturing, mentoring relationship. But, as with siblings, issues of competence can sometimes trigger competition over who is more skilled or more brilliant in understanding the client.

The older–younger sibling metaphor is structurally similar to the relationship between master craftspersons and their apprentices. Such relationships have existed for thousands of years and are perpetuated in supervision. In these relationships, master craftspersons serve as mentors to the people who aspire to enter the occupation, showing them the skills, procedures, and culture of the occupation. In this manner, too, master craftspersons help to perpetuate the craft. Eventually, after what is usually a stipulated period of apprenticeship, the apprentices become peers of the craftspersons.

These metaphors, particularly those of parenting or sibling, occur at fundamental and often primitive levels. Because they influence in an immediate and felt way, they have special and probably ongoing influence on the supervisory relationship. Moreover, such metaphors probably operate outside the awareness of the supervisor.

If it is true that supervision is a unique intervention, then one might reasonably infer that there is a unique role characteristic of supervisors in general. In a broad sense, this is true, and we can identify at least two major components of this generic supervisory role. The first of these is the perspective from which the supervisor views his or her work; the second pertains to the commonly endorsed expectation that the supervisor will give feedback to the supervisee.

This topic of supervisor roles is one to which we will give greater attention in Chapter 4, as we discuss social role models of supervision. There are, though, aspects of it that are important to cover at this point.

Liddle (1988) discussed the transition from therapist to supervisor as a role-development process that involves several evolutionary steps. An essential early step is for the emerging supervisor to make a shift in focus. That is, the supervisor eventually must realize that the purpose of supervision is neither to treat the client indirectly through the supervisee nor to provide psychotherapy to the supervisee.

Borders (1992) discussed this same step in the supervisor-to-be's professional evolution. She maintained that the supervisor-to-be must make a cognitive shift as he or she switches from the role of counselor or therapist. To illustrate how difficult this often is for new supervisors, she gave the example of a neophyte supervisor who persisted for some time in referring to his supervisee as "my client." Until he was able to correctly label the supervisee's role in relation to himself, his perceptual set remained that of a therapist.

This shift, then, requires the supervisor to give up doing what might be thought of as "therapy by proxy," "therapy by remote control," or what

Fiscalini (1985) called therapy "by ventriloquism." We would note, however, that the pull to doing this may always remain present, even if unexpressed in practice. In part, this is reinforced by the supervisor's mandate always to function as a monitor of client care, vigilant about how the client is functioning. Similarly, the longer the person has functioned as a therapist, the harder it may be for the supervisor to make the necessary shift in perspective. It is interesting to note, for example, that Carl Rogers talked about having occasionally experienced the strong impulse to take over the therapy of a supervisee, likening himself to an old fire horse heeding the call (Hackney & Goodyear, 1984).

Borders (1992), in fact, observed that untrained professionals do not necessarily make this shift on their own, simply as a result of experience as a supervisor. As a matter of fact, some "experienced" professionals seem to have more difficulty changing their thinking than do doctoral students and advanced master's students in supervision courses. This is consistent with what we depict in Figure 1.1: The more ingrained the role, the more pervasive and influential it is on current behavior.

A CONCEPTUAL MODEL OF SUPERVISION

The conceptual model depicted in Figure 1.2, an adaptation of the competencies cube developed by Rodolfa and colleagues (2005), is the framework that guides our thinking about supervision. It also has influenced our organization of this book. This is a three-dimensional model in which the three dimensions are what we have labeled *Supervisor Tasks, Parameters of Supervision,* and *Supervisee Developmental Level.*

Parameters of Supervision

These are the features of supervision that undergird *all* that occurs in supervision, regardless of the particular supervisory function or the level of the supervisee. For example, the supervisor's

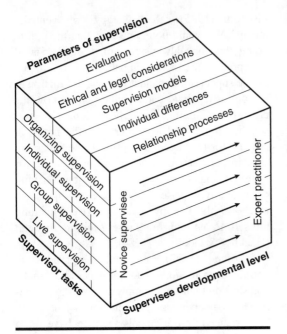

FIGURE 1.2   Conceptual Model of Supervision

model or theory is a factor at all times. So, too, is the supervisory relationship and each of the other of the parameters listed in the figure.

Supervisee Developmental Level

We assume that supervisees need different supervisory environments as they develop professionally. Although we discuss supervisee developmental levels specifically in only Chapters 5 and 6, concern with this issue pervades the entire book. The manner in which supervisors intervene differs according to supervisee level. As well, the expression of each parameter (e.g., relationship or evaluation) is affected by developmental level.

As we discuss later in the book, different supervision theorists each have suggested a different number of stages through which supervisees progress. We have drawn Figure 1.2, though, in a way to suggest that we do not take a stand on exactly how many of these stages there actually are. We believe it is sufficient here simply to make

clear that developmental processes affect all that we do as supervisors.

Supervisor Tasks

Supervisor tasks are the actual behaviors of the supervisors. In this book, we discuss the four depicted in Figure 1.2 (organizing supervision, individual supervision, group supervision, and live supervision). It is possible, of course, to think of more. But we believe these four are the most frequently employed.

Using the Model

We assume that the three dimensions interact with one another. To illustrate, consider the supervisor who is using individual supervision: He or she will do so within the context of a relationship and that work will be guided by the supervisor's particular theory or model, attention to supervisee's individual differences (e.g., ethnicity or gender), and ethical and legal factors; the fact of evaluation will affect it as well. The developmental level of the supervisee, then, moderates each of these things.

We should note that we are not attempting in this model to capture *all* that occurs in supervision. This is especially true with respect to our discussion of supervisor tasks. We recognize, for example, that individual, group, and live supervision are not the only modalities. Kell and Burow (1970), for example, discussed the use of conjoint treatment as a supervision modality. But, although this is not a modality included in Figure 1.2, it is easy enough to see how conjoint treatment might be fit into the conceptual model.

The next 10 chapters each address features of this model. We hope that with this conceptual framework the reader will more readily see how the particular topic being covered fits within the larger picture of supervision, as least as we envision that picture.

The book's final chapter does not speak specifically to the conceptual model. Instead, it addresses topics—the teaching of supervision and supervision research issues—that have the purpose of enhancing supervisory practice.

CONCLUSION

The purpose of this chapter was to lay the groundwork for the material that follows. We hope we have been effective in establishing the basis for and importance of supervision, by offering a formal definition of supervision and considering possible idiosyncratic definitions of supervision that occur at less manifest levels. We also hope our conceptual model will be useful in thinking about supervision and the ways its various aspects relate to one another.

We also addressed the historical context, importance, and prevalence of supervision. We then considered definitions, both formal and more personal. We concluded by presenting the conceptual model that both informs our understanding about supervision and guides the organization of this book.

We alluded early in the chapter to the two realms of knowledge (Schön, 1983) that are the basis of professional training: the theory and research that are the focus of university training and the knowledge derived from practitioners' experience. We asserted, too, that these actually are complementary knowledge domains (e.g., Holloway, 1995). Because of this conviction, material in this book is drawn from both realms of knowledge with the belief that each informs the other. That is, in the course of our work we draw both from theoretical and empirical literature and from literature that describes the insights and practices of supervisors themselves.

CHAPTER 2

EVALUATION

Evaluation could be viewed as the nucleus of clinical supervision. In fact, as we noted in Chapter 1, evaluation is a defining aspect of supervision. Supervisors direct and encourage, but also monitor, those who enter the helping professions. The ethical and legal issues surrounding supervision are primarily embedded in the evaluation function. Many of the more direct methods for conducting clinical supervision have developed, in part, as a response to a need for better data for the evaluation process.

As central as it is to proper functioning of clinical supervision, most supervisors are troubled by evaluation, at least occasionally. Some view it as a necessary evil; a few see it as antithetical to the helping professions (Cohen, 1987). Part of the problem is that clinical supervisors were first trained as counselors or therapists, and their values often lie within that domain. Therapists are taught to accept their clients' limitations and to respect their clients' goals. Like good parents, good therapists learn to respect the boundary between clients' ambitions for themselves and therapists' ambitions for them. The good therapist is a facilitator of another's change and is not a decision maker about what change is necessary.

Many of the working conditions within supervision reflect those for therapy or counseling. Yet there is an essential, paradigmatic difference: The supervisor might want to use the supervisee's progress as the critical criterion for evaluation, but responsibility to the profession and to the supervisee's future clients would preclude this (referred to as the gatekeeping function). The supervisor is charged to evaluate the supervisee based on some external set of criteria. These criteria must meet institutional standards, but also reflect national standards of practice (Robiner, Fuhrman, Ristvedt, Bobbitt, & Schirvar, 1994).

An essential assumption underlying evaluation is that the criteria chosen or derived from professional standards reflect competent practice. Herein lies the first major obstacle in conducting sound evaluation. Robiner, Fuhrman, and Ristvedt (1993) described clinical competence as a "moving target with an elusive criterion" (p. 5). Although the accrediting and state regulatory bodies of the helping professions prescribe knowledge and skill standards, the research continues to undermine the assumption that particular types of therapist knowledge, skill, or level of experience determine client outcome (Herman, 1993). Reviews of the outcome literature have produced mixed results (e.g., Pinsof & Wynne, 1995; Shaw & Dobson, 1988), and some continue to support the notion that nonspecific factors such as the counselor's personal characteristics might be the more predictive of successful outcome with clients (Herman, 1993; Orlinsky, Grawe, & Parks, 1994; Shaw & Dobson, 1988). Because of this, helping professionals have not yet determined definitively the educational experiences that yield competent practitioners, nor have they developed performance measures that reliably distinguish competent from incompetent practitioners (Robiner et al., 1993).

Of course, any stark conclusion that some or much of training may be irrelevant to producing a competent practitioner makes highly credentialed professionals defensive, including most clinical supervisors. Intuitively, most professionals believe, even in the absence of conclusive data, that training and experience matter and that there are specific knowledge and skills which professionals must possess. As a logical outgrowth of this belief, clinical supervisors assume that they are responsible for monitoring supervisees' development of knowledge and skills. The helping professions continue to seek better research to indicate which aspects of training are especially important (e.g., Binder, 2004); in the meantime, it is safe to assume that supervisors will continue to evaluate supervisees based on their own knowledge of what is understood in their professional community to constitute acceptable standards of practice.

Given the consistent finding that personal characteristics of therapists are highly predictive of success (Herman, 1993; Jennings, Goh, Skovholt, Hanson, & Banerjee-Stevens, 2003; Sakinofsky, 1979), it may be of some comfort to clinical supervisors that the personal characteristics of supervisees and supervisors alike have always been considered relevant to supervision, as is evidenced in this text by the amount of space given to the supervision relationship, individual and cultural differences, and ethics as personal morality. On the other hand, these same personal characteristics often lead to some of the most difficult evaluation moments, as we will review later in this chapter (Forrest, Elman, Gizara, & Vacha-Haase, 1999; McAdams, Foster, & Ward, 2007). Finally, this is a time when the call for more rigorous evaluations has increased due to legal accountability (e.g., McAdams et al., 2007). In summary, then, clinical supervisors must evaluate within professional guidelines (that may reflect the accumulated experience of the profession in the absence of clear outcome research), be sensitive to the importance of supervisees' personal characteristics (including cultural characteristics) that parallel training but are not necessarily affected by it, and remain cognizant of an increasingly litigious society. They often do this in the absence of any comprehensive understanding of what exactly contributed to their own competence, as either a counselor/practitioner or a supervisor.

These two factors, then, the possible incompatibility of evaluation with their professional identity as helping professionals and the inadequacy of relevant outcome studies to determine the salient ingredients of therapeutic competence, can combine to cause considerable dissonance when supervisors are required to evaluate. Supervisors have two choices for managing this dissonance: They can throw up their hands and minimize the function of evaluation in their supervision or they can work to counteract both dissonance-causing factors by thoughtful planning, structuring, intervening, and communicating. The rest of this chapter can be viewed as an outline of topics for consideration by those who will face evaluation responsibly and attend to its requirements to the best of their ability, even in light of imperfect or incomplete criteria, within a social context that exhibits greater demands for accountability.

The first step for the supervisor is to recognize a clear distinction between *formative* and *summative* evaluation. Robiner et al. (1993) described formative assessment as the process of facilitating skill acquisition and professional growth through direct feedback. As such, they contended that formative evaluation causes little discomfort for clinical supervisors. Formative evaluation indeed represents the bulk of the supervisor's work with the supervisee and does not necessarily feel like evaluation, because it stresses the process and progress of professional competence, rather than outcome. Nevertheless, it is important to remember that there is an evaluative message in all supervision. When supervisors tell supervisees that an intervention was successful, they are evaluating. When supervisors say nothing, supervisees may decide that their performance was exemplary or too awful to discuss. In other words, by virtue of the nature of the relationship, evaluation is a constant variable in supervision (Briggs & Miller, 2005). Some of the supervisor's evaluative comments are deliberately sent (encoded) by the supervisor to the supervisee; others are received (decoded) by the supervisee and may or may not be an accurate understanding of the supervisor's assessments, especially in light of individual and cultural differences. Because we are always communicating, an evaluative message can always be inferred.

Summative evaluation, on the other hand, is what many of us mean when we discuss evaluation, and it causes far more stress for both supervisors and supervisees. This is the moment of truth when the supervisor steps back, takes stock, and decides how the supervisee measures up. To do this, supervisors must be clear about the criteria against which they are measuring supervisees. Furthermore, the supervisee should possess the same yardstick.

In truth, summative evaluations are often stressful because they are disconnected from what has come before in the supervision relationship. Either because of lack of organization, lack of a clear set of standards, or lack of a positive working relationship, the supervisor may conduct summative evaluation in a vague or biased way. A supervisor who is helpful and articulate during the formative contacts can appear rushed and insecure at a summative conference. Robiner et al. (1993) asserted that, because of the trepidation or ambivalence caused by summative assessment, a generalized disdain for evaluation may result "despite its central importance in the supervisory process" (p. 4). Because summative evaluations are those that influence major educational, regulatory, and administrative decisions, such disdain is highly problematic. The chief antidote to summative disdain is the amount of time and care invested in the formative evaluation process. But before any evaluation begins, the difficult task of identifying criteria must be addressed.

CRITERIA FOR EVALUATION

Choosing criteria for evaluation is a less-than-perfect process when the research regarding what is essential for therapists-in-training to learn is generally wanting. Ironically, although the professions lack clear empirical direction about the necessary conditions for competence, the increasing fear of litigation has forced professionals to grapple with the issues of impairment or gross lack of competence. We will address these issues later in this chapter.

Overholser and Fine (1990) cited five areas of competence that should be established for any supervisee: factual knowledge, generic clinical skills, orientation-specific technical skills, clinical judgment, and interpersonal attributes. Each of the mental health professions tends to address similar areas of competence. For example, Perlesz, Stolk, and Firestone (1990) tracked criteria for competence in marriage and family therapy and used perceptual skills (ability to make pertinent and accurate observations), conceptual skills (the process of attributing meaning to observations), and executive–intervention skills (ability to respond within sessions in a deliberate manner), as well as demonstrated personal development, as the targeted criteria. With the growing sensitivity to cultural variables in therapy, multicultural competence is increasingly identified as essential as well (e.g., Hatcher & Lassiter, 2007; Vasquez, 1999).

Interpersonal and intrapersonal skills are also essential. Frame and Stevens-Smith (1995) made a concerted effort to operationalize and categorize those skills. Based on a review of the literature, Frame and Stevens-Smith (1995) identified nine supervisee functions that have been cited as necessary for success as professional counselors. They recommend that supervisees be: open, flexible, positive, and cooperative; willing to accept and use feedback; aware of one's impact on others; and able to deal with conflict, accept personal responsibility, and express feelings effectively and appropriately. Frame and Stevens-Smith suggested that these functions be published for student consumption and that students be evaluated on them on a regular basis.

Over several years and by virtue of multiple initiatives, psychology has focused on competencies for the training of doctoral-level psychologists (Kaslow, 2004; Kaslow et al., 2004; Rodolfa et al., 2005). Recently, an outline of competencies for the first doctoral practicum emerged (Hatcher & Lassiter, 2007) that draws from these previous initiatives. These competencies include baseline knowledge, skills, and attitudes, as well as those that are developed during the practicum. Baseline competencies include prerequisite knowledge and abilities such as basic helping skills, knowledge and awareness of cultural difference, and ethical and legal parameters. They also include personality characteristics and personal skills that largely echo the list developed by Frame and Stevens-Smith (1995). Additions to those presented by Frame and Stevens-Smith are interpersonal communication skills, including the ability to be empathic; intellectual curiosity and the ability to think critically; personal courage; and reflective skills. While those entering doctoral training may have acquired some of the prerequisite skills in a master's program, Hatcher and Lassiter (2007) made the salient point that "it is inappropriate to undertake formal clinical professional training with students who have not acquired or do not possess these critical skills at an acceptable level, because the work of subsequent clinical training is to shape and refine these baseline skills into professional skills" (p. 54). In addition to listing competencies, Hatcher and Lassiter have developed a rubric to assist supervisors in assessing each competence. This outline of descriptors lends itself to the task of identifying criteria for evaluation. For the complete list of Hatcher and Lassiter's competencies and their rubric, see the Supervisor's Toolbox.

Moving from the beginning of training to its culmination, Robiner et al. (1993) reported the result of APA's Joint Council on Professional Education in Psychology's (Stigall et al., 1990) attempt to delineate exit criteria for psychology doctoral internships. The eight areas of competence identified by the council are: effective interpersonal functioning; ability to make sound professional judgments; ability to extend and expand basic assessment and intervention techniques to meet the needs of different settings, problems, and populations; ability to apply ethical and legal principles to practice; ability to assess and intervene appropriately with clients manifesting diverse characteristics; development of a primary professional identity as a psychologist; awareness of personal strengths and limitations and the need for continued supervision, consultation, and education; and preparedness to enter residency training and to choose appropriate advanced training. In addition to these, the Joint Council recommended that personal characteristics such as psychological health and awareness of self be considered as entry-level criteria for admission to professional training programs. Although generic in nature, this list offers a place to begin in establishing criteria and can easily be generalized to other mental health professions.

The sentiment of attending to the psychological health of supervisees was echoed by Johnson and Campbell (2002), who chastised the profession of psychology for not establishing character and fitness criteria for entrance into professional programs. Noting that the remediation efforts of troubled or incompetent practitioners have not been particularly promising, they asserted that criteria for entrance and retention in programs must be more rigorous. As cited earlier, Frame and Stevens-Smith (1995) and Hatcher and Lassiter (2007) have provided some assistance here as well.

Although there are frequent messages in the professional literature about the importance of theoretical consistency, published information about the formation of criteria refers to this criterion only in the most general way (e.g., Overholser & Fine, 1990). For training programs that insist on theoretical consistency, criteria must be developed that are also theoretically consistent. Because professional standards tend to be theory neutral, it is up to training programs and clinical sites to translate standards into adequately specific criteria. For example, if a supervisor is working with a supervisee who has declared cognitive behavioral theory as the theory of choice, the supervisor needs to measure the supervisee's progress based on criteria that reflect a cognitive behavioral approach to working with clients. If the supervisor uses, for example, Bernard's (1979, 1997) Discrimination Model, the supervisor must develop criteria that describe the interventions used in cognitive behavioral therapy, the ways to conceptualize a problem that reflect a cognitive behavioral approach, and the therapist's appropriate use of self when conducting cognitive behavioral therapy. Developing such criteria would in and of itself be a highly worthwhile supervision activity and could become part of the supervision contract (see Chapter 8). And, of course, if the supervisor feels uncomfortable, inadequate, or simply unwilling to supervise according to a particular model of treatment, that too would be negotiated as an aspect of the contract.

The point is that models of delivering therapeutic services and models of supervision are not independent from the task of establishing criteria. If criteria do not directly reflect the models, the criteria will be less helpful to the supervisee. If they contradict the models, they become an obstruction to learning, rather than a guide.

Criteria can attend to global characteristics or more distinct skill sets. Focusing on the ability to conduct a diagnostic interview, Rudolph, Craig, Leifer, and Rubin (1998) identified the following necessary steps: structure the interview, forge a working alliance, facilitate interviewee participation and disclosure, collect data and pursue inquiry, and maintain professional conduct. Rudolph et al. asserted that supervisees welcome clear communication of expectations. Therefore, they argued that the faculty time spent in developing and agreeing on criteria for each major clinical function was worthwhile.

Accrediting bodies have become central in defining criteria, though they tend to avoid any reference to personal characteristics except in terms of admissions and termination policy. All the mental health professions have accrediting bodies that establish standards for the education of persons entering the profession. These standards include core areas of knowledge and often specialized curricular areas (e.g., school counseling or mental health counseling), as well as stipulations for clinical training. These standards, then, become the criteria for evaluation, at least for pre-degree candidates. Bradley and Fiorini (1999) found that CACREP programs' translation of standards for criteria demonstrating clinical competence are fairly uniform.

Accreditation standards also tend to increase in number over time, whether because of the increased complexity of mental health delivery (Hahn & Molnar, 1991) or because it is human nature to add rather than subtract when it comes to criteria (Mohl, Sadler, & Miller, 1994). For better or worse, professional standards are used by training institutions and state regulatory bodies to assess persons entering specific mental health professions and are therefore legitimate compilations of criteria for evaluation. It should be noted, however, that even when criteria are specified, expected competency *levels* often remain elusive to both supervisees and supervisors (Magnuson, 1995).

Job analyses, or an investigation of the knowledge and skills used by persons in targeted mental health positions, are also used as a method for arriving at criteria for evaluation (e.g., Fitzgerald & Osipow, 1986; National Board for Certified Counselors, 1993). The limitation of job analyses, however, is that they inform us of *what is* rather than what *should* or *could be*. While this process is legally defensible (e.g., to determine items for a licensure exam), it does not move a profession forward. Forward movement occurs in the interplay among market forces, training programs, and accrediting bodies (Goodyear et al., 2000).

In summary, establishing criteria for evaluation may be the most challenging and conceivably most labor-intensive aspect of the evaluation process. To meet this challenge, the supervisor should draw from many sources of criteria, including accrediting body standards, program values, research, and general advice of professionals found in the mental health literature and in practice. The difficulty of establishing criteria for evaluation and the equally difficult task of measuring them is a professional reality. We do not presume to offer a definitive list of criteria. Rather, we stress that, regardless of what criteria the supervisor identifies, the formative and summative evaluations should relate directly to these same criteria. It is not unheard of for supervisors to find themselves hunting for an evaluation form at the end of the supervisory relationship as if the summative evaluation had no relationship to the formative sessions that had preceded it. On the contrary, whatever is to be used at the end of supervision to summarize the supervisee's progress should be introduced early in supervision, should serve as teaching–learning objectives, and should be used throughout supervision as the basis for formative feedback (Ladany, 2004).

FAVORABLE CONDITIONS FOR EVALUATION

A major problem with evaluation in the helping professions is that it hits so close to home. Because counseling and therapy draw heavily on interpersonal and intuitive abilities, it can be difficult for supervisees to draw a boundary between their performance as helping professionals and their worth as a person. For this reason and because of the vulnerability accompanying any evaluation process, it is important that supervisors do all that is possible to create favorable conditions when evaluating. Favorable conditions not only make evaluation more palatable, but directly influence the overall outcome of supervision. As Ekstein and Wallerstein (1972) noted, when the context of supervision is favorable, the supervisee stops asking "How can I avoid criticism?" and starts asking "How can I make the most of this supervision time?"

Several authors have addressed the conditions that make evaluation a more positive experience. Several of these conditions also ensure that the evaluation process is conducted in an ethical manner (see Chapter 3). The following list of conditions draws on our own thoughts as well as the work of others (Borders et al., 1991; Briggs & Miller, 2005; Coffey, 2002; Ekstein & Wallerstein, 1972; Forrest et al., 1999; Fox, 1983; Fried, Tiegs, & Bellamy, 1992; Kadushin, 1992a; Ladany, 2004; Ladany, Hill, Corbett, & Nutt, 1996; Lopez, 1997; Mathews, 1986; Murphy & Wright, 2005; Olson & Stern, 1990; Ramos-Sanchez et al., 2002):

1. Supervisors must remember that supervision is an unequal relationship. No amount of empathy will erase the fact that supervisors' reactions to supervisees will have consequences for them, some of which may be negative. Being sensitive to the position of the supervisee will make supervisors more compassionate evaluators.

2. Clarity adds to a positive context. Supervisors need to state clearly their administrative as well as clinical roles. Who will be privy to the feedback that supervisors give supervisees? Will the supervisor be making decisions regarding the supervisee's continuation in a graduate program or job? If not, what is the supervisor's relationship to those persons who make these decisions? For example, most graduate programs conduct periodic student reviews. At these reviews the evaluation by the clinical supervisor is often weighed more heavily than other evaluations. Students should be aware, at the very least, that their performance in the clinical component of the program will be discussed by the total faculty at some point in the future.

3. Supervisees' defensiveness should be addressed openly (Coffey, 2002; Costa, 1994). Supervision makes supervisees feel naked, at least initially. It is natural, if not desirable, that they attempt to defend themselves. Supervisees differ in their coping styles, some exhibiting behaviors that are far more productive than others. Some will deal with their feeling of defensiveness by "digging in deeper" and doing all that they can to get on the same page as the supervisor; others will defend by trying to outguess the supervisor; still others will appear vulnerable and helpless. The truth is that all supervisees are vulnerable, and supervisors need to be sensitive to this fact and not hold their vulnerability against them.

Coffey (2002) suggested that supervisors take time at the outset of supervision to teach students how to receive corrective feedback. The source of defensive reactions and how they have served one in the past need to be understood by supervisees so that they can process these reactions in light of the present situation. Coffey proposed that the use of awareness-enhancing exercises is well worth the time spent so that supervisees can understand their defensive reactions and process them when they occur; this puts them in a better position to determine the usefulness of the supervisor's corrective feedback.

4. Along with defensiveness, individual differences should be addressed openly. Evaluation may well be affected by differences of cultural background, gender, race, and so forth, particularly if these differences are not understood to be relevant to supervision. Furthermore, competence in therapy includes the ability to communicate in ways that are culturally flexible. The first cultural context to be addressed, therefore, is the supervision context.

5. Evaluation should be a mutual process and a continuous process. The supervisee should be actively involved in determining what is to be learned (Briggs & Miller, 2005; Ladany, 2004; Lehrman-Waterman & Ladany, 2001). In a sense, the supervisor is there to serve the supervisee, and this contractual dimension should not get lost. Also, the formative aspect of evaluation should be the most active. Although both parties know that the supervisor will be taking stock down the road, the process and evaluation of the learning should not feel static.

6. Evaluation must occur within a strong administrative structure. Whether in an educational or work setting, supervisors must know that their evaluations will be taken seriously. Nothing is as frustrating and damaging as when a supervisor risks the consequences of a negative evaluation only to have this overturned by an administrator in the organization. When this happens, more often than not, one of two things has happened. Either due process was not followed, or the supervisor did not have a clear sense of administrative support beforehand. In other words, the supervisor assumed that he or she would be backed up without bothering to check. Or the supervisor did not have the political savvy to inform his or her superiors prior to the evaluation, both to warn them and to make sure that the process would be supported. Whether the supervisor is correct in the evaluation can be a moot issue if the supervisee's rights were not protected, or appeared not to be protected, during the evaluation process. It is important that the system be perceived as trustworthy by both supervisor and supervisee. If the history of the system is that evaluation is arbitrary or capricious, supervisees will risk less and will be more defensive overall in their interactions with supervisors.

Finally, it is as important that the supervisee be cognizant of a supportive structure as it is for the supervisor. Supervisees must know that there is a place to go if they think an evaluation is unfair or incomplete. On university campuses, the grievance committee is usually the administrative body of choice once the head of the department has been consulted; in employment settings, the supervisor's immediate superior would be the appropriate person. If there is no such protective body or person, it is up to the supervisor to establish some sort of safeguard for the supervisee (e.g., through a Professional Disclosure Statement that provides pertinent information in this regard). Supervision objectives will be greatly handicapped if anyone in the system feels trapped. (Chapter 8 addresses administrative practices that assist the evaluation process.)

7. Premature evaluations of supervisees should be avoided. Whether a supervisor is working with one supervisee or several, it is important to resist overreacting to the person who shows unusual potential or the person who seems to be faltering. We are not implying that one should withhold feedback or be dishonest. Rather, we believe that supervisors often react too quickly and, by evaluating too soon, can do serious disservice to talented supervisees, as well as to those who need more grounding to begin their better work. If supervision occurs in a group, morale is hurt when it becomes obvious that early distinctions have been made among supervisees. On the contrary, when the group is challenged to ensure that everyone achieve competence, the atmosphere is energetic, supportive, and competitive in the best sense.

Some supervisees will enter supervision expecting to be recognized and treated as stars. It is the supervisor, however, who makes such a designation happen (Murphy & Wright, 2005) by relying on initial impressions and forgetting that some counseling or therapy skills can only be assessed accurately over the long term. Whether a supervisee wears well will be terribly important to the supervisee's future colleagues, supervisors, and clients. This cannot be determined in a few weeks, regardless of the strength of the supervisee's entry behavior or the intuitive abilities of the supervisor.

8. Supervisees need to witness the professional development of their supervisors. As a supervisor, the best way to accomplish this goal is to invite feedback and use it. Supervisees feel empowered if they sense that they have something valuable to offer their supervisors. Additionally, a supervisor's involvement and sharing of continuing-education activities models the need for development across the life span of one's career. For supervisors to present new ideas that they have recently been exposed to gives a much more accurate picture of professional growth than for them to play the part of the all-knowing guru. Also, presenting some tentativeness in thinking will remind the supervisor to be tentative about the work of supervisees. Supervisors must constantly remind themselves that they do not deal in a profession of facts, but of concepts.

9. Supervisors must always keep an eye to the relationship, which influences all aspects of supervision (Barnett, 2007). Evaluation becomes especially difficult when the relationship has become too close or too distant. In fact, it is the reality of evaluation that behooves the supervisor to maintain both a positive and supportive relationship with the supervisee—yet one that is professional, not personal. If relationships are strained for whatever reason, supervisors must ask themselves if they can evaluate objectively enough. (No evaluation is totally objective; the goal is to keep objective standards in mind while considering subjective impressions.) This point was underscored by Ladany et al. (1996) who found that negative reactions to the supervisor, personal issues, clinical mistakes, and evaluation concerns were the top four categories of supervisee nondisclosures in supervision. A weak relationship between supervisor and supervisee, then, can cause the supervisee to withhold essential supervision information. Burkard et al. (2006) found that needed discussions about cultural differences did not take place when favorable conditions were not evident to the supervisee. In short, when supervisees are guarded because the supervision context feels unsafe, it is virtually impossible for the supervisor to get an accurate picture of the supervisee's strengths and areas for growth.

10. No one who does not enjoy supervising should supervise. For this final condition, we go back to the point we made at the beginning of this chapter: Evaluation is difficult, even for those supervisors who love the challenge of supervision. For the supervisor who is supervising for any lesser reason, evaluation may feel like too great a burden. When this is the case, the supervisor will shortchange the supervisee and give perfunctory evaluations or avoid the task, especially if the evaluation could carry negative consequences. Supervisors always have many other responsibilities to use as rationalizations for keeping a supervisee at arm's length. It is not difficult to find helping professionals who can attest to the frustration of being supervised with unclear expectations, getting little or no constructive feedback, or receiving mostly negative feedback (Magnuson, Wilcoxon, & Norem, 2000; Ramos-Sanchez et al., 2002). It is little wonder that the absence of favorable conditions for evaluation have been found to compromise the working alliance between supervisor and supervisee (Ramos-Sanchez et al., 2002). Whenever a supervisee is denied appropriate supervision and evaluation, the professional community is diminished.

THE PROCESS OF EVALUATION

We have discussed the important task of choosing criteria and have made brief reference to using some sort of evaluation instrument to communicate a final assessment regarding the supervisee's level of competence. These, respectively, comprise the beginning and the end of evaluation. *Process* defines how supervisors conduct their business between these two markers and how they incorporate the issue of evaluation from the beginning of supervision to its completion. In other words, the process of evaluation is not separate from the process of clinical supervision, but is embedded within it. The evaluation process also includes the means by which supervisors obtain the data that they use to make their assessments, a topic more completely addressed in Chapters 9, 10, and 11. For our discussion here, the process of evaluation will be considered as having six elements, most of which interact throughout the supervision experience: negotiating a supervision–evaluation contract, choosing evaluation methods and supervision interventions, choosing evaluation instrument(s), communicating formative feedback, encouraging self-assessment, and conducting formal summative evaluation sessions.

The Supervision–Evaluation Contract

When students register for a course, they receive a syllabus identifying requirements, course objectives, an outline of activities or topics to be discussed, and the instructor's plan for evaluation. Whether or not clinical experience is gained within a course structure, each supervisee should be provided with a plan that parallels a syllabus. Unlike most course syllabi, however, the supervision contract should include components that are individualized. Described as goal-directed supervision, Talen and Schindler (1993) asserted that supervisee-initiated goals set the stage for a collaborative relationship with the supervisor. Similarly, Lehrman-Waterman and Ladany (2001) found that goal setting with supervisees was highly correlated with a positive supervisory working alliance and to overall supervisee satisfaction with supervision. Mead (1990) suggested that ample time be given during this process to considering discrepancies between the supervisee's goals and those set for the supervisee by the supervisor. Mead advised that some goals identified by the supervisee may be a residue from past experiences in supervision and may need thorough discussion and modification. An initial focus on the supervision contract serves a purpose for new supervisees also in that it helps them to understand the difference between clinical supervision and other learning experiences. Although plans can vary, all supervision contracts should establish learning goals, describe criteria for evaluation, establish supervision methods that will be used, describe the length and frequency of supervision contacts, and establish how a summative evaluation will be achieved. The relationship of formative feedback to summative feedback should

also be explained to the supervisee. (A more thorough discussion of the makeup of a supervision contract is included in Chapter 8.)

To proceed in a manner that is consistent with goal-directed supervision, each supervisory conference can and perhaps should end with a plan of action for goal attainment and a time frame for completion of the plan. In the same way, each conference should begin with an update on progress toward the goals set at the beginning of the supervisory relationship (Briggs & Miller, 2005). Middleman and Rhodes (1985) suggested that formative evaluation occur often enough for changes to be suggested with time to implement them before the summative evaluation. In other words, evaluation should be dynamic and relevant throughout the supervision experience, not just at the beginning and end.

A final note about the supervision contract, and one that was confirmed by Talen and Schindler (1993), is the compatibility between this activity and the developmental needs of relatively inexperienced supervisees (Stoltenberg, McNeill, & Delworth, 1998). The structure offered through the process of establishing learning goals supplies the supervisee with a concrete anchor to help weather the onslaught of clinical sessions that include many unknowns.

Choosing Supervision Methods for Evaluation

Each method of supervision—process notes, self-report, audio- or videotapes of therapy sessions, or live supervision—influences evaluation differently. Some supervisors rely heavily on group supervision and may even encourage some form of peer evaluation among supervisees. This approach provides markedly different information than that gathered from, for example, self-report. When the ultimate responsibility to evaluate is paramount in the supervisor's awareness, however, the supervisor will seek supplemental data if they are needed to arrive at a balanced evaluation.

Supervisees can be at a disadvantage when the form of supervision changes from one setting to the next. For example, Collins and Bogo (1986) have observed that early training experiences (on campus) tend to use a good amount of technology, whereas field supervision is more likely to be based on self-report and case notes. Therefore, they found that supervision in the field was far more reflective in nature than that on campus, which focused more on skills and their development. Perhaps supervisors need not only to inform their students about the forms of supervision that they use, but also to educate them about the forms that they do not use.

Of paramount importance is that supervisors realize that supervision methods have both instructional and evaluation consequences. A supervisor may favor one form of gathering supervision material (e.g., audiotape), but the supervisor must realize that each method is a lens through which to view the work of the supervisee. Some lenses provide a sharper image of one aspect of the supervisee's work, but a wide angle may be desirable on occasion to allow the supervisor a different perspective from which to evaluate. Therefore, multiple methods are the surest way to get an accurate picture of the supervisee's strengths and weaknesses (Harris, 1994).

Choosing Evaluation Instruments

There are nearly as many evaluation instruments as there are training programs in the helping professions. Supervisors tend to develop and use Likert-type measures for summative purposes. Depending on how well a measure reflects criteria that already have been selected and communicated by the supervisor (or negotiated between supervisor and supervisee), the measure may help supervisees to appreciate their progress toward predetermined goals. When evaluation measures have not been integrated into the supervision experience, their use can be superficial or frustrating from the standpoint of the supervisee.

A scientist–practitioner model would call for evaluation measures that are more than communication tools. And yet, to date, most evaluation measures are homegrown and have not been validated. Gonsalvez and Freestone (2007) were

critical of the lack of efforts to remedy the situation: "It appears that psychology has applied its considerable expertise in measurement and evaluation more assiduously to a wide array of other domains and disciplines, while neglecting what is arguably the most important component of its professional training" (p. 24). Despite this critical call to action, most evaluation measures of clinical practice continue to be used primarily as a way to organize feedback for the supervisee and little more.

The most common evaluation instrument continues to be unvalidated, using a Likert scale, perhaps with some open-ended questions as well. Because of the subsequent quantification of evaluations, supervisees may need some assistance in translating the feedback received. For example, the supervisor must decide what is adequate (numerically speaking) for supervisees to be assured that they are receiving a positive evaluation. Additionally, it should be clear what level of performance is below standards and what level would be considered as meeting the highest standards. If a supervisee comes into supervision with superior ability in several areas, the Likert-scale ratings should reflect this. Some supervisors use scales differently, deciding that no supervisee should receive a score higher than a certain number (e.g., 5 out of a possible 7) until the supervisory experience is at least half complete. If this is the supervisor's policy, it is important that the supervisee know this. When the supervisor uses a scale in this way, however, the supervisor sidesteps the issue of competence level.

One positive trend in the development of more useful assessment instruments has been an increasing interest in the development of anchored rubrics (Hahn & Molnar, 1991; Hanna & Smith, 1998; Hatcher & Lassiter, 2007). Hahn and Molnar supported their 7-point scale with adequate descriptions at each level in the supervision process (see Table 2.1), especially for summative evaluation. Because rubrics describe behaviors expected at different levels of competence, Hanna and Smith argued that they give supervisees a more accurate picture of the level at which

TABLE 2.1   Intern Rating Scale

Rate intern using the following 7-point scale:

Level 1	Performs inadequately for an intern in this area. Requires frequent and close supervision and monitoring of basic and advanced tasks in this area.
Level 2	Requires supervision and monitoring in carrying out routine tasks in this area and requires significant supervision and close monitoring in carrying out advanced tasks in this area.
Level 3	Requires some supervision and monitoring in carrying out routine tasks in this area. Requires guidance, training, education, and ongoing supervision for developing advanced skills in this area.
Level 4	Displays mastery of routine tasks in this area. Requires ongoing supervision for performance of advanced skills in this area. The intern occasionally, spontaneously demonstrates advanced skills in this area.
Level 5	Displays mastery of routine tasks in this area. Requires periodic supervision for refinement of advanced skills in this area.
Level 6	Displays mastery of routine tasks in this area. Could continue to benefit from some supervision on advanced and/or nonroutine tasks in this area.
Level 7	Performs at the independent practice level in this area and is capable of teaching others in this area. Performs without the general need of supervision, but consults when appropriate.

Source: From "Intern Evaluation in University Counseling Centers," by K. Hahn and S. Molnar, 1991, *The Counseling Psychologist, 19,* pp. 414–430. Copyright 1991 by the Division of Counseling Psychology. Reprinted by permission of Sage Publications, Inc.

they are performing, thus communicating the essential message that clinical competence is a developmental process more than an outcome. They also acknowledged that developing rubrics for clinical assessment is a time-consuming process. It requires consensus building among all those responsible for the supervision and training of individual supervisees. To aid those serious about developing rubrics for assessment purposes, the authors suggested a 15-step process that begins and ends by seeking consultation from others and includes identifying standards to be evaluated, operationalizing goals, revising on a regular basis, including specific goals for individual supervisees, and encouraging self-evaluation for supervisees.

Supervisees also can be encouraged to use Likert-type formats to communicate with their supervisors. Marek, Sandifer, Beach, Coward, and Protinsky (1994) suggested asking supervisees to scale themselves from 1 to 10 on three different issues: satisfaction with therapy, level of confidence in achieving their goals, and level of

willingness to meet goals. By having supervisees make such judgments, communication between supervisor and supervisee is enhanced around these key aspects of supervisee development. In addition to challenging supervisees to reflect on their progress, Marek et al. suggested using scaling to encourage open communication about the supervision process itself.

> *The supervisor can also utilize these questions in connection to other issues brought forth by the supervisee and/or to assess how the supervisee's needs are being met in the present context. For example, "Where are you on the scale right now in terms of the case related issues you brought in to supervision today?" "What happened to allow you to move from a seven (7) to an eight (8)?" "What would it look like if you were at an eight and a half (8½)?" "What would you be doing differently?"* (p. 62)

Ranging from the simplest measure to a comprehensive rubric, most evaluation tools continue to be paper-and-pencil instruments that reflect a traditional view of assessment. However, some research activity in the development of different evaluation tools (e.g., Lambert & Meier, 1992) takes advantage of computer technology and may offer ways to standardize supervisee evaluation. Guth and Dandeneau (2007) described the use of the Landro system to track and categorize each supervisee intervention, thus providing rich data for feedback purposes (see Chapter 9). Still, modern advancement notwithstanding, the traditional evaluation tool continues to be almost universal.

Finally, and congruent with a scientist–practitioner posture, supervisors may seek client input or client outcome data for the sake of formative or summative evaluation of supervisees (Galassi & Brooks, 1992; Lichtenberg, 2007). The Session Evaluation Questionnaire developed by Stiles and Snow (1984), for example, is a brief evaluation tool that can be used after each therapy session to obtain impressions from both supervisees and clients regarding session depth (i.e., felt power and value) and smoothness (i.e., comfort and pleasantness) using pairs of bipolar adjective scales. These quantitative scales can be supplemented with open-ended sentence stems such as "I believe the *most* helpful things that happened in today's counseling session were . . . ," "I believe that the *least* helpful things that happened in today's counseling session were . . . ," and "In my next counseling session I would like. . . ." With the relatively high level of control available in many training programs, various types of data, including that derived from single-case designs, can become part of the evaluation strategy (Galassi & Brooks, 1992; White, Rosenthal, & Fleuridas, 1993).

As well, repeated measures of client outcome (i.e., data obtained at each session) can be plotted to provide important supervisee feedback. Lambert et al. (2001), for example, demonstrated that such feedback to therapists increases levels of eventual gains. To that end, a number of university counseling centers now use the Outcome Questionnaire-45 (Lambert et al., 1998) which includes items such as "I get along with others," "I work/study too much," and "I feel something is wrong with my mind."

The choices are expanding for clinical supervisors when selecting evaluation instruments. What each supervisor must determine is whether a particular instrument is consistent with the supervisor's criteria, when and how to introduce the instrument to the supervisee, and how to use the instrument as an evaluation *intervention,* rather than simply a completed form to be filed and forgotten. The Supervisor's Toolbox at the end of this text includes several supervision instruments, each with a different focus, that can be of assistance to the practicing supervisor.

Communicating Formative Feedback

When supervisees reflect on their supervision, what comes to mind most often is the quality and quantity of the feedback that they received. Giving feedback is a central activity of clinical supervision and the core of evaluation (Hahn & Molnar, 1991). Curiously, researchers have given little specific attention to feedback within supervision. The study of Friedlander, Siegel, and Brenock (1989) is a notable exception. It described feedback as a process in which the supervisor verbally shares thoughts and assessment of the supervisee's progress. The evaluation can be either explicit or implicit. For their study, they did not include questions or nonevaluative observations as feedback. Three raters were trained to high levels of agreement (median interjudge agreement rate of 0.92) about the presence or absence of feedback in a particular supervisor speaking turn. These raters then examined each speaking turn of one supervisor across nine supervision sessions (ranging from 45 to 60 min in length) with one supervisee. They identified only 14 speaking turns as containing feedback. Eight speaking turns occurred in the last two sessions; sessions 3, 4, and 6 had no feedback whatsoever.

The Friedlander et al. (1989) study was an intensive case study. Therefore, the results might be idiosyncratic to the particular dyad studied and may not apply to supervision in general. A more recent study, however, also found that giving feedback can be difficult for supervisors. Hoffman, Hill, Holmes, and Freitas (2005) interviewed 15 supervisors of predoctoral psychology interns and found varying levels of directness, especially if the feedback was perceived as difficult to deliver. There were also difficult situations in which supervisors admitted that they refrained from offering feedback. In general, it seemed that feedback delivered easily had to do with supervisees' work with their clients. More challenging feedback to deliver either addressed issues more personal to the supervisee or about the relationship between the supervisor and the supervisee. Not surprisingly, Hoffman and colleagues (2005) found that conditions such as supervisee openness, a strong positive relationship, a clear need for feedback, and the supervisor feeling competent to impart the feedback worked to facilitate the delivery of feedback. Supervisors reported that timing was also important to them in delivering feedback, as was outside support if difficult feedback was not received well. When asked if they would change anything if they could start the process over, none of the supervisors interviewed stated that they would give less feedback. Rather, some supervisors reported that they would operate as they had while others noted that they would give feedback sooner, more directly, and more often regarding supervisees' personal issues.

These studies serve as corollaries to other research in which supervisees reported receiving far too little feedback (Kadushin, 1992b) and that the lack of feedback negatively affects their feelings about the value of the supervision they received (cf. Ladany, 2004; Lehrman-Waterman & Ladany, 2001; Magnuson, Wilcoxon, & Norem, 2000). In fact, rather than perceiving the delivery of feedback as being detrimental to the supervisory relationship, Lehrman-Waterman and Ladany recommended that supervisors engage in increased goal setting and feedback if they feel they have a troubled relationship with a supervisee. Feedback, then, is viewed by these researchers as a corrective measure to put the supervisory relationship back on good footing. Sapyta, Riemer, and Bickman (2005) stressed that, in the long run, what is key is for feedback to be accurate, whether it is positive or critical.

The feedback described thus far relies primarily on a linear model, originating from the supervisor to the supervisee. Another view of feedback is what Claiborn and Lichtenberg (1989) referred to as *interactional*, which allows us to think of feedback as ongoing and constant between the supervisor and the supervisee. Two premises are basic to understanding the interactional or systemic perspective. The first is that you cannot *not* communicate. This premise was suggested as an axiom of communication by Watzlawick, Beavin, and Jackson (1967). It means, for example, that even the act of ignoring another person is feedback to that person, communicating a message such as "Leave me alone" or, perhaps, "You are not important enough for me to talk with."

The second premise essential to understanding the interactional perspective is that any communication to another person contains both a message about the relationship between the two parties and a message about some particular content (Watzlawick et al., 1967). For example, within the context of supervision, the content may be about a particular, difficult moment in the supervisee's session with a client; the message about the relationship, however, might be "I enjoy working with you" or "This relationship is very tenuous." If the feedback about the relationship is negative or more pronounced than the content, it will be more difficult for the supervisee to hear the content in the way that the supervisor would like. Similarly, the message back from the supervisee might be, "I find your feedback very useful," as well as "I am too intimidated by you to ever tell you otherwise" (the second message being unverbalized). If cultural differences are pronounced between supervisor and supervisee, dissonance within the relationship may complicate feedback even more. For these reasons, the relationship between supervisor and supervisees receives much attention in the professional literature (see Chapters 5, 6, and 7). Finally, it is imperative to remember that the supervisor is not only delivering both levels of feedback, but receiving (and reacting to) both levels. The idea of supervisor feedback, therefore, is deceptively simple when compared to the actual interactive process.

There are instances when supervisor and supervisee do not see eye to eye. Ratliff, Wampler, and Morris (2000) studied communication styles using a qualitative design when there was a lack of consensus between supervisor and supervisee. Their findings suggested that supervisors tend to be subtle more often than not in attempting to direct supervisees toward their own position. At the same time, Ratliff et al. found that supervisors engaged in a progression of supervision strategies, from low confrontation (e.g., asking leading questions) to high confrontation (e.g., giving explicit direction), when lack of consensus about the direction of therapy emerged. In their discussion, these authors raised the issue of increased autonomy (i.e., accurate self-evaluation) among supervisees as an important goal of supervision. They suggested that supervisors consider the negative consequences when consensus is the goal, especially if they rely on confrontational strategies to accomplish consensus, potentially leading to heightened supervisee dependency in the process.

Despite an acknowledgment that supervision includes give and take, convergence of thinking and occasional divergence, most supervisors conceptualize feedback per se as communicating to the supervisee an assessment of particular behaviors as either on target or off, as either progressing toward competence or diverging. The clarity of supervisors' communications for this purpose is of paramount importance. Each message will affirm, encourage, challenge, discourage, confuse, or anger a supervisee. If the metamessage is different from the stated message, the result will be an unclear communication. The most serious communication problem is when the message is dishonest, either intentionally or unintentionally. This typically occurs when the supervisor does not want to deal with the fact that the supervisee is not meeting expectations. As a result, the supervisor is not prepared to address the critical issues at hand (Hoffman et al., 2005; Magnuson, Wilcoxon, & Norem, 2000).

Several authors have offered suggestions for giving formative feedback, including feedback that is critical or corrective in nature (Abbott & Lyter, 1998; Borders, 2006; Borders & Brown, 2005; Chur-Hansen & McLean, 2006; Hawkins & Shohet, 1989; Heckman-Stone, 2003; Lehrman-Waterman & Ladany, 2001; Munson, 2002; Poertner, 1986; Sapyta et al., 2005). Drawing from these various sources as well as our own experience, we have compiled the following:

- Feedback should be based on learning goals (criteria) that have been negotiated between the supervisor and the supervisee;
- Feedback should be offered regularly and as much as possible should be based on direct samples of the supervisee's work;
- Feedback should be balanced between support/reinforcement and challenge/criticism as either extreme over time is eventually rejected by supervisees as disappointing supervision (Gross, 2005);
- Especially when feedback is corrective, it should be timely, specific, nonjudgmental, behaviorally based, and should offer the supervisee direction in how to improve;
- Feedback should address learning goals that are achievable for the supervisee;
- Because communication is, in part, culturally determined, supervisors should use listening skills to conclude if feedback was received as intended;
- Feedback should be owned by the supervisor as professional perception, not fact or truth. Supervisors need to model self-critique, flexibility, and brainstorming in conjunction with formative feedback;
- Supervisors must understand that supervisees want honest feedback yet are fearful of it;
- The acceptance of feedback is integrally related to the level of trust the supervisee has for the supervisor. Supervisees must trust that formative feedback has a different purpose than summative feedback;
- Feedback should be direct and clear, but never biased, hurtful, threatening, or humiliating.

To help supervisors remember some essential aspect of good formative feedback, Hawkins and Shohet (1989) have suggested the use of the mnemonic CORBS, which stands for Clear, Owned, Regular, Balanced, and Specific.

Example: Dana has been supervising Nicole for 2 months. Until now she has attempted to focus on Nicole's strengths while gently suggesting other strategies for Nicole to consider. Nicole has found supervision to be a very positive experience thus far. Unfortunately, in Dana's opinion, Nicole has not picked up on Dana's suggestions and therefore has not progressed at all in her counseling. Of particular concern is Nicole's work with one client, Shirley. During the sessions that Dana has observed, Shirley regularly brings up her difficulties with her husband. Shirley is upset with his relationship with his ex-wife; the husband thinks that she is overly jealous. Nicole seems to keep the entire issue at arm's length and usually finds another topic to focus on.

DANA: I wanted to spend some time talking about Shirley's issues with her husband. These seem to keep coming up. What do you think is going on there?

NICOLE: I think Shirley's self-esteem is low and so she is insecure about her husband and his ex-wife. She doesn't like it that he has to deal with her around his kids. His behavior certainly seems reasonable to me.

DANA: I don't think there's any question that Shirley's self-esteem is low. I agree with you. But she keeps bringing up her husband and I don't see you doing much with that in the session. Is there a reason you avoid addressing that issue?

NICOLE: I just didn't see it as the real problem. Besides, Dr. M said that we can't deal with a marital issue if only one spouse is in the room.

DANA: OK. So you've been avoiding it because of Dr. M's advice. Is there any way you can view the problem that would allow you to focus on Shirley and not the interaction between her and her husband?

NICOLE: And still deal with her jealousy about her husband?

DANA: Right.

NICOLE: I could ask her how she feels about her husband, but I already know that.

DANA: Yes, I think you do. What about her thought processes?

NICOLE: I'm not sure what you mean.

DANA: Well, I've noticed that you pretty much focus on the client's feelings in all of your counseling. I

think you're doing well there, but I don't think it's a complete enough approach. You need to figure out some way to address the client's thoughts if you're going to help Shirley any more than you have. And remember, addressing her thoughts will lead you to more of her internal life, including more of her feelings.

NICOLE: So, you don't think I'm helping Shirley?

DANA: I think you've gone about as far as you can go with the approach you've taken. But the issue is bigger than your work with Shirley. In order for you to become a better counselor, I think you need to start looking at how you address cognitive issues. I'd like to focus on that for a while.

NICOLE: OK.

From the perspective of formative evaluation, we might ask the following questions: How successful was this segment between Dana and Nicole? Was Dana's intent clear? Did she hear all of Nicole's messages? Did she react adequately to Nicole's feedback? What was the content of Dana's communication? The message about the relationship? What was the content of Nicole's communication? The message about the relationship? In the past, Nicole has not picked up on Dana's suggestions. Has Dana done anything to ensure that Nicole has heard her this time?

Finally, Talen and Schindler's (1993) study found that an attitude of trust and positive regard from the supervisor, validating supervisees' strengths and accepting them at their present skill level, were considered to be the most important supervision strategies from the perspective of supervisees. With this in mind, has this session compromised the supervision relationship between Dana and Nicole? How might the session have been conducted differently if a different approach is called for?

Encouraging Self-Assessment

Assisting supervisees to evaluate their own work has been identified as an important aspect of supervision (Bernstein & Lecomte, 1979; Borders et al., 1991; Borders & Brown, 2005; Falender et al., 2004; Munson, 2002; Perlesz et al., 1990). Relatedly, Rønnestad and Skovholt (2003) found that a commitment to ongoing self-reflection is a skill that characterized good therapists at all points across the professional life span. Kadushin (1992a) asserted the importance of supervisee self-assessment and noted that supervisory evaluation, in and of itself, makes learning conspicuous to the supervisee and helps to set a pattern of self-evaluation. Ekstein and Wallerstein (1972) were more cautious about the notion of self-evaluation, reminding the supervisor that asking supervisees to self-evaluate will stimulate all their past experiences of being selected, rejected, praised, and so on. We challenge the thoughts of Ekstein and Wallerstein in that self-evaluation, we believe, takes some of the parent-like authority away from the supervisor, rather than adding to it. If negative feelings are going to be experienced as a result of evaluation, these will be there regardless of whether the supervisee is given an opportunity to contribute to the assessment.

Although the idea of supervisee self-assessment is intuitively appealing and generally endorsed by the professional literature, research has produced mixed and sometimes contradictory results about the ability of the supervisee to productively engage in self-assessment. We will review key research on the topic and end this section with recommendations.

An early study by Dowling (1984) found evidence that graduate student supervisees were both accurate self-evaluators and good peer evaluators, a finding consistent with Hillerbrand's (1989) observation. More recently, Dennin and Ellis (2003) found mixed results when using self-supervision with four doctoral students to increase distinct skill sets. While self-supervision appeared to have some effect in increasing the students' use of metaphor in counseling, it did not significantly increase the use of empathy. Dennin and Ellis concluded that their research did not support some of the robust effects claimed in the literature regarding self-assessment and self-supervision. They suggested that current literature regarding self-supervision is overly simplistic because mediating variables such as supervisee developmental level and skill level are not typically

addressed. They concluded that, especially for neophyte supervisees, any use of self-assessment should be paired with feedback from a more advanced supervisor. Indeed, it seems that self-assessment is best perceived as a skill to be developed under supervision (Barnes, 2004) rather than some parallel evaluation activity.

Though the research to date is limited, we have some evidence that supervisors influence the development of their supervisees' self-assessment skills based on distinct factors. Steward, Breland, & Neil (2001) studied supervisee self-evaluation, including self-efficacy (which was defined as counselors knowing what to do and having judgments about their capabilities to effectively respond to upcoming counseling situations). In a study that initially appeared to be counterintuitive, Steward et al. found that accurate self-evaluation on the part of supervisees was negatively associated with supervisor attractiveness. In other words, the more friendly, flexible, supportive, open, positive, and warm the supervisor, the less accurate the novice supervisee's self-evaluation. These authors noted that, in general, supervisees tend to underestimate their abilities and supervisor attractiveness may reinforce this tendency. Finding one's supervisor as less attractive may stimulate the supervisee's own determination to approve of one's own work, thus resulting in making more accurate self-assessments. Steward et al. did not suggest that supervisors aspire to be unattractive to their supervisees. They did, however, state that their study may underscore the importance of supervisors engaging in both supportive and challenging interventions. Steward et al. speculated that consistently supportive supervisors might not expect their supervisees to move beyond their comfort zones. This may, in turn, have negative implications for training, resulting in supervisees whose self-confidence, self-efficacy, and sense of accomplishment are reduced.

In a seemingly contradictory study, Daniels and Larson (2001) found that performance feedback from the supervisor influenced supervisee self-efficacy and anxiety in the directions expected (i.e., positive feedback increased self-efficacy and lowered anxiety, while negative feedback had the opposite effect). Unlike the Steward et al. (2001) study, Daniels and Larson used bogus feedback to manipulate supervisee reactions. They cautioned that their negative feedback in particular may have been too extreme. At the same time, the authors noted that the degree of anxiety that a supervisee presents in supervision should modify a supervisor's behavior. In other words, the balance between support and challenge needs to be tailored for each supervisee to arrive at optimal results. (We discuss the ramifications of supervisee anxiety in Chapter 7.)

As yet another consideration regarding supervisee self-efficacy, Steward (1998) raised the issue of the relationship between supervisee self-efficacy and supervisor self-efficacy. He cautioned training programs in particular to consider the degree to which they have integrated and monitored field supervisors who may be unaware of program expectations and/or may be inadequately trained as supervisors. Prior to assessing counselor self-efficacy and competence, Steward advised that training programs seek to provide supervisees with uniform supervisory experiences.

Based on scant empirical work on the topic, paired with consistent calls for the practice of self-assessment, we offer the following guidelines:

1. Self-assessment is best viewed as a developmental issue for supervisees rather than a parallel process of evaluation. Supervisees have been known to either overestimate or underestimate their abilities (Barnes, 2004). Both can have negative consequences for supervisee development and for client care. Therefore, making self-assessment a goal of supervision rather than an activity for evaluation seems a reasonable approach.

There are several highly productive ways that the supervisee can be involved in self-assessment within the context of supervision. The most obvious is for the supervisor to communicate an expectation that the supervisee will do some sort of self-assessment prior to each supervision session. It has been our experience that unless the supervisor follows through on this expectation, however, most supervisees will falter in their intentions to self-assess.

A useful self-evaluating activity is to ask the supervisee to periodically review a segment of a counseling session in greater depth for response patterns (Collins & Bogo, 1986). If the supervisee can identify nonproductive patterns, this exercise can be instrumental in breaking bad habits.

2. To the extent possible, the supervisor might share how he/she arrives at assessments of the supervisee. This should be done regularly. It is one thing to say "You're not attending to the client's affect." It is another thing to say, "When I'm assessing a session, I listen for important affect and whether the counselor picks up on it. I thought your client expressed important feelings twice during the session. These were when he said he felt overwhelmed by life and when he said that he was disgusted with his son. While you have told me that you reacted to each of these statements internally, you didn't express to your client that you heard him. So, I would assess the skill of attending to client affect as needing to be improved." The supervisor should be equally explicit when a skill of the supervisee has been assessed positively.

3. Self-assessment should never be a "test." In other words, like other skills that are viewed developmentally, self-assessment should be monitored as a series of approximations toward a goal, not in a dichotomous right/wrong fashion. For this reason, it is perhaps unwise to ask supervisees to complete evaluation forms of their skills using Likert scales. Instead, a supervisor might ask the supervisee to choose items on a form to identify areas in which they are having difficulty self-assessing. This would move the discussion to the area for assessment and the issues making self-assessment difficult rather than setting up a tug-of-war between the supervisee and the supervisor regarding a particular skill.

4. At the time for summative evaluation, evaluate self-assessment as a skill set rather than asking the supervisee to prepare an alternative final self-evaluation. This method would complement the approach to self-assessment throughout the supervisory experience.

In summary, the rationale for emphasizing self-assessment within supervision is that it ultimately may have utility beyond the formal training context. In other words, part of the responsibility of clinical supervisors is to assist supervisees in establishing a habit of self-scrutiny that will follow them into their professional careers. Although supervision is always warranted in the early years of practice, it is not always forthcoming, at least not always at an optimal level. Even though our knowledge about self-assessment is modest, it makes intuitive sense to include self-assessment as part of clinical supervision.

Communicating Summative Evaluations

Although the word summative might imply a single final evaluation, summative evaluations usually occur at least twice during a typical supervisory relationship. In academic settings, there is usually a mid-semester and a final summative evaluation. For off-campus externships, internships, and work settings, the summative evaluations are given at the halfway mark and at the end or as annual reviews, respectively. If all has gone well within supervision, a final summative review should contain no surprises for the supervisee. In other words, the summative review should be the culmination of evaluation, not the beginning of it. The initial summative review is perhaps the more important because it is at this point that the supervisor will learn if the supervisee has understood the implications of formative assessments. If so, the summative evaluation will provide an opportunity to take stock and to plan a productive sequel to the supervision that has transpired to this point—a second supervision contract, so to speak. If formative assessment has been resisted by the supervisee, the first summative evaluation must be specific regarding the progress that is required for the supervisee to remain in good standing and must be conducted early enough for the supervisee to have a reasonable opportunity to achieve success. In all cases, summative evaluations should be conducted face to face and should also be put in writing (Belar et al., 1993).

Even when a correct process has been established for summative evaluations, their ultimate success depends in large part on the communication skill of the supervisor. Unfortunately, supervisor training often gives short shrift to the process of conducting summative evaluation sessions. What follows are two segments taken from actual summative evaluation conferences conducted by supervisors-in-training with counselors-in-training. Both supervisor and counselor are female in each case. In the first segment, the pair begins by reviewing the Evaluation of Counselor Behaviors—Revised form (Bernard, 1997) that the supervisor completed prior to the session. The person referred to as Dr. P. is the counselor's faculty instructor.

S: Uh, I would put this more here, I think, and more here . . . And I think, you know, again, I did this here. I may go back and circle . . . if you see anything that you don't agree with, just go ahead and question it. I think you know how I look at it. I see you just having started to work.

C: Oh, I . . .

S: You know, you may not like that. I just think since that one big leap, when you started to consciously try to do things differently . . .

C: I can't even visualize 10 years down the line having you say that everything is excellent. I don't know. To me, you're asking for close to perfection.

S: It would be hard for me to get there (*laughs*). I wouldn't want to be evaluated.

C: So much that comes to me comes through experience.

S: Yeah. I suppose, you know, maybe it's the teacher part of me . . . whenever I see the word "always" (*referring to the evaluation form*), I just can't . . . we're in trouble.

C: Yeah.

S: Even for me (*laughs*).

C: I understand. You know, as I look at this, it looks like a positive evaluation because of what you've said so far.

S: Um, well, you have a lot of 2's and 1's, but "good" to me is good. Letter grade wise, I don't know. I can't tell you. Part of me says, because of what has gone on the whole semester, you know, and part of me says, "Okay. What are you doing now?" So, you know, I don't assign grades. It won't be an A. I'm not too sure. I'd say probably a C+ to B– in that area.

C: But there are no pluses or minuses in the grading schedule.

S: That's right.

C: To me, a C is a failure and I'm assuming that you are not . . .

S: I don't think I look at it as a failure. I think that maybe, you know, when you do course work and things like that, maybe you could look at it that way. But I don't look at it as a failure because failure is an F.

C: Um hum.

S: If I were to have to assess a grade by skill level, it probably would be close to a C/D. But in looking from the beginning, you know, you've come a long way. But that isn't for me to assess. That's for Dr. P. to assess and I don't know how he will do it. I definitely think that there has been a lot of improvement.

C: And to me, it seems like it's been such a short time.

S: Yes, a very short time.

It is not difficult to see that there are several communication problems in this example. Actually, four things contribute to the ambiguity presented here: (1) the supervisor's personal style of communication is clouded. She does not finish many of her statements. She is not crisp. She would do well to practice the delivery of her feedback for clarity. (2) The process is ambiguous. Either Dr. P. has not been clear regarding procedures or neither supervisor nor counselor has attended to these details. The result is that the supervisor does not seem to know her role in the evaluation process. Another possibility is that, because of her discomfort, she is playing down her role and referring the counselor to Dr. P. for the difficult task of final evaluation. From the conversation as it stands, we cannot know which of these is the case. (3) Criteria for evaluation also seem to be ambiguous to the

supervisor. She vacillates from references to skill level and references to progress. It is obvious that she is not clear about how Dr. P. will weigh each of these two factors. (4) The supervisor seems to be uncomfortable with the responsibility of evaluation, especially in this case where the practicum seems to be ending on a down note. We do not know if the supervisor has not prepared adequately for this conference or whether any amount of preparation would have countered her personal discomfort. The result is a series of mixed messages:

1. "You're not a very good counselor."/"'C' isn't a bad grade."
2. "You've come a long way."/"You still aren't very good."
3. "I'm trying to be fair."/"I wouldn't want to be in your shoes."
4. "I'm recommending between a C+ and a B–."/"I don't assign grades."

In our second summative session, the supervisor and counselor have had a better working relationship and the results are more positive.

S: I came up with some agenda items, things I thought we needed to touch base on. You can add to this agenda if you'd like. The concern that you expressed previously about the deadlines, wrapping up, dealing with your clients, and then talking about termination–continuation issues. Kind of finishing up, so that it concludes not only your client situations, but practicum. Again, the other issue I have down is evaluation. I am not sure how he (Dr. P.) . . . did he mention that in class today? How he's going to handle that? Do you have a conference with him?

C: There will be the conference next Monday with the three of us and then it seems to me that the other was kind of nebulous as to if we had another conference with him about you. Is that what you mean?

S: No, no. I meant about you. See, I was not aware that we were meeting on Monday (*laughs*).

C: Yes, yes . . .

S: Well, that's nice to be aware of. Surprise!

C: So it will be the three of us for evaluation.

S: So I thought, depending on if you had any concern about that, that maybe we can discuss that ahead of time. I don't know if we need to here today or not or whatever, but that was something that I had as a possibility at least.

C: There are other things that are more urgent . . . (*Supervisor and counselor then talk about a particularly difficult case. The following occurs later in the same session.*)

C: You've been very supportive. I really appreciate your feedback that you give me. A lot of good supportive feedback. It's not all the positive. There's been good constructive criticism you give too. I appreciate that.

S: You perceive that there has been enough of a balance?

C: Um, you've been heavier on the positive, but maybe it's just because I've done such a good job (*laughs*).

S: (*Laughs*) I'm laughing because you're laughing.

C: You very nicely have couched the constructive criticism, preceding it with a lot of positive. "I like the way you did this, and then when you said this, it was very good, and then this was good and now you, probably if you had said this, perhaps you would have. . . ." You preceded criticism with about two or three positive things, which helps, helps the ego. I've appreciated that a lot. (*counselor continues*)

S: I've seen you do continually more intervening and trying different things, being aware of this and trying to do things about it. Do you feel like, as you go away from here, you'll be able to take away something so that you can do that when you get into situations like this again?

C: Yeah, I've really learned that, and I do feel that I am doing it more.

The most dramatic difference between this pair and the previous pair is the quality of the relationship. Apparently, this has been a positive experience for both supervisor and counselor. There may or may not be some lack of comfort for the supervisor with evaluation in that what might

have been a summative conference became a preconference by their mutual choice. But the important characteristic of their interaction, as it appears here, is that they seem to be current with each other. Evidently, there has been enough formative feedback along the way that each person appears to know where she stands. Notice, however, that the same administrative problem that appeared in the first example appears here, too. Again, we see that communication between the instructor and the supervisor has not occurred and this leaves the supervisor at a disadvantage in the conference. Because both of these sessions transpired in the same training program, we could come to the conclusion that the doctoral supervisors need more support from the faculty in the form of clearer guidelines about their role in the evaluation process and clearer communication down the administrative hierarchy.

Thus far we have discussed summative evaluations as they relate to the instructional needs of the supervisee. The process of arriving at the summative evaluation can also be a valuable learning experience for the supervisor. Too often this is an activity done alone. There is great value, however, in the use of additional evaluators to arrive at summative assessments. The following evaluation format was used in a counseling center where doctoral students served as the individual supervisors for master's-level counselors: One doctoral student was assigned to three master's-level students. Most semesters, there were 12 counselors and 4 supervisors. In addition to working closely with the supervisees, each doctoral student was required to observe (usually through a two-way mirror) three other counselors at least twice during the semester. The doctoral students did not have to share their observations with the counselors; their charge was simply to have some knowledge of the counselor's ability. Additionally, weekly supervision-of-supervision conferences were held, which included listening to taped supervision sessions between the doctoral supervisors and their three supervisees. When it was time to evaluate the counselors, the faculty instructors for both groups (supervisors and counselors), the center coordinator (who read all counselors' intake and termination reports), and the group of doctoral supervisors met together. Therefore, the work of each counselor was known by at least four people, and all were encouraged to voice their opinion.

These evaluation meetings provided both a learning experience for supervisors and the opportunity to arrive at consensus evaluations of the counselors. One of the most obvious dynamics in these meetings was the investment that each supervisor had in the three supervisees that they had mentored. At times the supervisor would get noticeably defensive if the supervisor's counselors were seen as weaker than some others. Such reactions were always processed, and awareness was increased that the supervisory relationship can be a powerful one and can cloud a supervisor's ability to be objective.

A secondary issue was whether the supervisor felt responsible for the counselor's level of performance. Sometimes it was thought that the supervisor might have been partially responsible for a counselor's modest improvement over the semester, but usually this was not the case. The most important lesson, however, was appreciating that different views could be held about the same supervisee, even when seemingly objective criteria were in place.

PROBLEMATIC STUDENTS, IMPAIRMENT, AND INCOMPETENCE

Virtually all training programs in the helping professions admit students with the intention of graduating and ultimately endorsing them. Similarly, mental health agencies hire professionals with optimistic expectations about their performance. The unpleasant idea of dismissal of students or employees is something most supervisors attempt to repress. And yet evaluation of mental health professionals must include the possibility that the person being evaluated may fail to meet minimal criteria. Though supervisors typically exhibit a high commitment to their supervisees, they must be ever cognizant that "duty to the public and the profession takes precedence" (Pearson & Piazza, 1997, p. 93).

Definitions

For the past 20 years or so, the mental health professions have leaned toward the word *impairment* to describe either a troublesome reversal in performance or an inability to meet the requirements of (usually) the clinical component of a training program (Lamb, Cochran, & Jackson, 1991; Lamb et al., 1987; Muratori, 2001; Oliver, Bernstein, Anderson, Blashfield, & Roberts, 2004; Vacha-Haase, Davenport, & Kerewsky, 2004). Impairment has also been described as affecting several areas of a supervisee's functioning, going beyond problems typically expected of supervisees, and impervious to feedback (Burgess, 1994). Reversals in performance have typically been hypothesized as a consequence of emotional and physical depletion or burnout. Manifestations of such impairment can include substance abuse, boundary violations, misuse of power, and diminished clinical judgment (Muratori, 2001). We speculate that the more typical problem, at least for training programs, is the supervisee who never attains adequate clinical competence. Often these students perform quite well in their academic courses; rather, it is when they embark on supervised clinical work that issues emerge that are serious enough to cause supervisors significant concern. Michaelson, Estrada-Hernández, and Wadsworth (2003) differentiated unprepared supervisees from unqualified supervisees, suggesting that the former might benefit from additional training while the latter are more likely to be dismissed from training programs. Therefore, these authors seem to equate unqualified supervisees with impaired supervisees.

Falender, Collins, and Shafranske (2005) asserted that the Americans with Disabilities Act (ADA) has "preempted" the word impairment and that supervisors are advised to refrain from use of the term lest they be accused of discrimination if they have not followed ADA guidelines. They recommended, instead, that the word "problematic" be used to describe students and that supervisors refrain from diagnosing students. Others have also discussed the ADA implications of the use of the word impairment (e.g., Oliver et al., 2004; Vacha-Haase et al., 2004) and some have suggested the modified term *professional* impairment (Oliver et al., 2004); however, the word impairment continues to appear in the mental health literature, including in the 2005 American Counseling Association Code of Ethics (i.e., sections C.2.g., F.8.b). For our purposes here, we will use the terms *problematic* and *professionally impaired* interchangeably.

Incidence

Problematic students and supervisees are endemic to the supervision process. There is an increasingly robust body of anecdotal and empirical literature attesting to the fact that a small percentage of supervisees are found to be unqualified to practice in the helping professions by their supervisors (e.g., Elman & Forrest, 2004; Forrest et al.,1999; Gaubatz & Vera, 2006; Gizara & Forrest, 2004; Lamb & Swerdlik, 2003; McAdams et al., 2007; Oliver et al., 2004; Rosenberg, Getzelman, Arcinue, & Oren, 2005; Russell & Peterson, 2003; Vacha-Haase et al., 2004). In their seminal review of the literature on this topic, Forrest and colleagues (1999) documented the consistent incidence of problematic supervisees and the numerous struggles of supervisors to determine appropriate responses to problematic behaviors. Research documenting the ongoing incidence of professional impairment continues to surface (e.g., Gizara & Forrest, 2004; Russell & Peterson, 2003). Not surprisingly, it appears that not only supervisors are aware of problematic supervisees. In an exploratory study in which researchers interviewed clinical psychology students about professional impairment among their peers (Oliver et al., 2004), students identified a host of observed behaviors including what they labeled as depression, anxiety disorders, personality disorders, eating disorders, alcohol abuse, and boundary

concerns. Another study surveying counseling and clinical psychology students (Rosenberg et al., 2005) reported a similar awareness among peers regarding problematic behaviors of others. Rosenberg et al.'s study participants identified lack of awareness of impact on others, emotional problems, clinical deficiency, and poor interpersonal skills as among the most common problematic behaviors. Less frequently reported behaviors included isolative behavior, eating disorders, substance abuse, and anger/aggression.

Gaubatz and Vera (2006) surveyed both students and faculty of counselor education programs and found that students reported a higher rate of peer deficiency than did the faculty. One of the interesting outcomes of all of the investigations seeking student perspectives was that students were not aware if or when their training directors or faculty became aware of the troublesome behavior they were observing. As a result, there was some frustration among these students directed at their supervisors and faculty. Student participants in the Gaubatz and Vera study thought that nearly 18% of deficient students received no faculty intervention, whereas faculty subjects in the same study estimated their rate of slippage to be under 3%. Additional results reported by Gaubatz and Vera included some insight into student posture toward the issue of professional impairment in relationship to themselves. In general, students reported that they would be open to remediation if they were identified as being deficient. However, 22% reported that they would pursue legal action if dismissed from a program, and 43% of student respondents noted that they would attempt to be admitted to another counseling program if dismissed from their present program. In short, it seems that at least some students take a consumer approach to their training and are not open to their supervisors' opinion if it is a negative assessment of their ability to be a successful mental health professional.

Students seem not to be aware of any policies or procedures regarding problematic peers (Oliver et al., 2004; Rosenberg et al., 2005). Rosenberg et al. reported that in the absence of policies, students reported that their most common response to problematic peers was to gossip with other peers or to seek consultation with peers. It seems then that there is a great need in educational and supervision contexts for clearer protocol so students know how to address the issue of problematic peers in a way that is both caring and professional. Engaging students in a discussion about the possibility of encountering a professionally impaired peer, and discussing appropriate due process with them, may have an additional benefit of encouraging reflection regarding their own coping styles.

Responses. Despite ongoing documentation of incidence, educators and supervisors continue to struggle in their attempts to respond appropriately to problematic supervisees (Vacha-Haase et al., 2004). Psychotherapy has been occasionally reported as a remediation of choice even though there is little support that such an intervention will remediate these supervisees adequately for competent practice (Elman & Forrest, 2004; Vacha-Haase et al., 2004). Furthermore, suggesting a need for therapy blends the supervisory role with a therapeutic one (Russell, DuPree, Beggs, Peterson, & Anderson, 2007) and may represent an ethical dilemma (see Chapter 3). Other reported responses from directors of marriage and family therapy programs were increased supervision, requiring a leave of absence, increased contact with one's academic advisor, and a requirement to repeat coursework (Russell et al., 2007).

In general, clinical supervisors report feeling unprepared to respond to professionally impaired supervisees (Gizara & Forrest, 2004). One issue that has affected preparedness is that training programs often view problematic behaviors as "nonacademic" traits that interfere significantly with trainee performance. Forrest et al. (1999) found that studies of supervisee professional impairment identified clinical deficiencies, interpersonal problems, problems in supervision, and personality disorders as the four most common forms of impairment. Because of the view that

these behaviors are nonacademic, some training program faculty and supervisors have considered them to be outside of their purview. University legal counsel has often reinforced this position. Lumadue and Duffey (1999) and Kerl, Garcia, McCullough, and Maxwell (2002) reviewed court cases that have addressed this issue. Their conclusion is that courts have consistently viewed personal attitudes or behaviors that are necessary for adequate performance within a profession as academic issues. Therefore, characteristics such as low impulse control, limited empathy for clients, debilitating anxiety, and pronounced cultural insensitivity could be defended as part of an academic dismissal. This is important because, legally, academic dismissals are the right and responsibility of the faculty, while disciplinary dismissals require additional documentation and a formal hearing. The due process obligation for the faculty when the issue is an academic one is met simply by notifying the supervisee prior to dismissal regarding his or her failure or impending failure to meet program standards (Kerl et al., 2002).

Related to the above is the importance of processes that assist supervisors and inform supervisees that parameters exist regarding their interpersonal functioning. While these may not be legally necessary for a dismissal of a supervisee, the parameters help build a training culture that is perceived as healthy (Gizara & Forrest, 2004) and capable of addressing the crisis of a professionally impaired supervisee.

Although Chapter 3 addresses informed consent and due process extensively, we include some discussion here as part of a description of processes to address problematic supervisees. Lamb et al. (1987) suggested that information given to new supervisees include agency and/or training program expectations; agency and/or program responsibilities in assisting supervisees to meet expectations; and evaluation procedures, including time frame, content of evaluations, use of verbal and written feedback, evaluation forms, and opportunities for supervisee feedback. Describing it as a "gatekeeping model," Lumadue and Duffey (1999) outlined the six informed consent goals that faculty of one counselor training program agreed on:

1. To identify the qualities and behaviors expected of students
2. To reach faculty consensus on the expectations for student fitness and performance
3. To devise a rating form listing these qualities and behavior
4. To standardize evaluation procedures within the department by using these forms
5. To communicate these expectations to all students in each class
6. To include these expectations in the admissions packets issued to interested students (p. 106)

The rating form developed by this training program was published later (Kerl et al., 2002) and included five areas of evaluation: counseling skills and abilities, professional responsibility, competence, maturity, and integrity. Students are assessed as meeting, meeting minimally, or not meeting each criterion. Similarly, after reflecting on a long (and unsuccessful) legal challenge from a dismissed student, McAdams et al. (2007) formulated a rubric that assists students to understand acceptable and unacceptable behaviors across 10 domains. This valuable evaluation tool is provided in the Toolbox.

In addition to informed consent that alerts supervisees about expectations and procedures, due process needs to be addressed when supervisors judge that a supervisee is incompetent or professionally impaired. Lamb et al. (1991) outlined four intensive due process steps for interns that ensure both supervisee protection and institutional credibility:

1. *Reconnaissance and identification.* This phase encompasses that period of time when the supervisee is seeing clients under supervision and the areas of strength or vulnerability are observed. Lamb et al. suggested that supervisors meet regularly to consult with each other as these evaluations are occurring. Gizara and Forrest (2004) also emphasized the importance of a supportive supervisor group when confronting problematic supervisees. Forrest

et al. (1999) recommended that behaviors that cause concern be matched to evaluation criteria, a recommendation that has been reiterated by others as well.

2. *Discussion and consultation.* Once an intern has been identified as displaying problematic behaviors, Lamb et al. suggested that extreme care be taken to protect both the intern and the staff through extensive discussion among all relevant personnel. Furthermore, all former impressions and interventions should be reviewed. Finally, supervisors need to make a judgement about the seriousness of the situation and review their documentation of the process up to this point.

3. *Implementation and review.* If more serious action is called for, this is the point at which it will occur. Probation or even termination may be the decision of the staff. (It is also possible that, after careful scrutiny of their own behavior and consultation, the staff will find a less dramatic intervention that is appropriate.) If probation is the avenue of choice, Lamb et al. suggested that a letter be sent to the intern that should include the following:
   a. Identify the specific behaviors or areas of professional functioning that are of concern.
   b. Directly relate these behaviors to the written evaluations (e.g., not showing up for counseling sessions as an example of inadequate professional functioning). Provide several specific ways that these deficiencies can be remediated (e.g., from additional training to personal therapy).
   c. Identify a specific probation period after which the performance of the intern will be reviewed (long enough for reasonable changes, but not so long that further action cannot be taken).
   d. Stipulate, if appropriate, how the intern's functioning in the agency will change during the probation period (e.g., additional time in supervision).
   e. Reiterate the due process procedures available to challenge the decision (Lamb et al., 1991, p. 293). McAdams et al. (2007)

emphasized the importance that any written notification provided to the student is documented with the student's signature as evidence of receipt and acceptance.

Lamb et al. advised that a probation period be an active time of ongoing feedback to the intern and frequent consultation and documentation among staff. Finally, Lamb et al. are equally compendious if the decision is to terminate, advising that all implications be reviewed before action is taken, that the intern receive a letter reiterating the probation conditions and the reasons for dismissal, and that the intern be provided with an opportunity to appeal. Only then should the dismissal occur.

4. *Anticipating and responding to organizational reaction.* Lamb et al. (1991) wisely concluded that removing a professionally impaired or incompetent intern is not only an action that will call for support of that intern, but a systemic intervention as well. All levels of the system should be considered, including clients of the intern, supervisors who were pivotal in the decision, administration, and other staff and interns. Although the intern's rights to privacy must be protected, all persons who are aware of the decision will have a reaction, and there should be some mechanism for their reactions to be addressed.

In summary, there is no more dreaded evaluation situation than the possible assessment of a supervisee as unable or unfit to practice in the profession that he or she has chosen. At the same time, this task is representative of the gatekeeping function required of all clinical supervisors. Historically, when supervisors avoided this responsibility, they have done so using the nebulousness of the professions as their argument. Stepping up to the challenge of addressing problematic supervisees has required more specificity about a range of behaviors, attitudes, and characteristics from acceptable to unacceptable. This specificity assists all supervisees—not only those who struggle, and sometimes fail—to meet professional standards.

ADDITIONAL EVALUATION ISSUES

At the beginning of this chapter, we mentioned that evaluation is a difficult task because of the personal nature of the skills being evaluated. Relatively clear criteria, good evaluation instruments, and a credible process go far to diminish the difficulty of evaluation. But the supervision process is not sterile and neither is the evaluation process. What is called for when supervisors evaluate is a judgment based on as much objective data as possible. But the judgment will still include a subjective element.

The Subjective Element

Clinical supervisors work hard to be fair and reasonable in their evaluations. Without some awareness of the pitfalls to objective evaluation, however, supervisors are at a disadvantage for attaining this goal. At the same time, supervisors must know that the subjective element of evaluations cannot and should not be totally eliminated. There is something intrinsically intuitive about counseling and psychotherapy, and this is equally true for clinical supervision. Evaluation is a delicate blend of subjective judgment and objective criteria. Yet sometimes our *personal subjectivity* contaminates our *professional subjectivity,* and evaluation becomes less intuitive and more biased (Gonsalvez & Freestone, 2007; Robiner, Saltzman, Hoberman, Semrud-Clikeman, & Schirvar, 1997). No clinical supervisor is above this dilemma. Being aware of the possibility, however, may help the supervisor to draft a checklist of personal vulnerabilities and potential blind spots to review when evaluating. Each clinical supervisor will have a separate list of subjective obstacles to navigate when facing the task of evaluation. Our list is only a partial one of some of the more common problems that we have experienced or that have received attention in the professional literature.

Similarity. An assumption that has spawned a good deal of empirical investigation is that attraction (which includes the concept of similarity) influences the therapeutic process and, likewise, the supervision process (Turban & Jones, 1988). Although Kaplan (1983) reported findings that were mixed, similarity with one's supervisor is probably more of an advantage than a disadvantage. Still, there are times when this is not so. If the supervisor is suffering from a poor self-image, this may spill over to a supervisee perceived as similar. From another vantage point, dissimilarity is an advantage for the supervisee if the lack of similarity gives the supervisee additional influence in the relationship. For example, if the supervisor is young and relatively inexperienced and the supervisee is older and has more life experience, such dissimilarity might translate to a better evaluation than if the supervisor were the same age as the supervisee, especially if the supervisee is male (Granello, 2003). There is evidence also that females rate males higher in competence; therefore, a female supervisor might rate a male supervisee higher than would a male supervisor (Goodyear, 1990). (Goodyear cited several such studies, but in his own study found no evidence of gender bias in supervisee evaluations.)

There is a situation-specific form of similarity that the supervisor should consider. When life has dealt two people the same hand, or at least some of the same cards, this tends to create a bond between them. Both supervisor and supervisee might have recently been through a divorce, have children of the same age, or have a parent who abuses alcohol. Depending on the amount of self-disclosure that has occurred in supervision, and each person's comfort level about these life situations, such similarity can be an advantage or a disadvantage. Regardless, how these similarities might influence evaluation must be considered.

Liking one's supervisee seems more important than similarity, though the two concepts are related. Turban, Jones, and Rozelle (1990) found that liked supervisees received more psychological support during supervision than disliked supervisees, supervisors extended more effort in working with liked supervisees, and supervisors evaluated liked supervisees more favorably than disliked supervisees. It is difficult to determine whether liking leads to inflated performance evaluation or if better-performing supervisees are more liked; perhaps both are true. The fact that liking affects the interactions between supervisor and supervisee long before summative evaluation, however, makes this a variable to which supervisors should be alerted.

Familiarity. "He's difficult to get to know, but he wears well." How many of us have had negative first impressions of people we now hold in high esteem? Not all of a person's qualities are apparent in the short run, and sometimes it takes a significant amount of time (in graduate-training terms) to arrive at what later would look like a balanced view of the trainee's strengths and weaknesses. In conjunction with this, when affection for someone has grown over time, it can become more and more difficult to evaluate objectively (Robiner et al., 1997).

Some empirical evidence supports the case that familiarity affects evaluation. Blodgett, Schmidt, and Scudder (1987) found that supervisors rated the same trainees differently depending on how long they knew the trainees. If a supervisor had had the trainee in a class prior to the supervision experience, the supervisor was more likely to evaluate the trainee more positively. Blodgett and colleagues noted that the trainees who had received their undergraduate and graduate training at the same institution had a distinct advantage in this particular study. The authors warned that it would be unwise, however, to assume that familiarity always works to the trainee's advantage. Our experience would support this admonition. Just as some trainees wear well, others do not.

A corollary to the issue of familiarity is the perseverance of first impressions (Sternitzke, Dixon, & Ponterotto, 1988). Although we have already stated that our first impressions are not always our last, it is important to mention that first impressions can be long lasting. If supervisors attribute dispositional characteristics to their trainees early in their relationship, it may require an inordinate amount of evidence for the trainee to reverse the supervisor's opinion. In this case, the trainee may be familiar to the supervisor, but the trainee might be far from known.

Priorities and Bias. Each supervisor has an individual set of priorities when judging the skill of a supervisee. Most often, supervisors are not cognizant that their priorities are partially subjective and that an equally qualified supervisor might have a somewhat different list of priorities. All perception is selective, and we process more quickly what is familiar to us (Atwood, 1986) or what we value more.

Bernard (1982) found that supervisors tended to rate supervisees lower on skills that the supervisors perceived as more important for a particular counseling session being reviewed. Although this makes sense intuitively, it is important to note that different supervisors watching the same videotaped session occasionally identified different skills as most essential and then rated the supervisee lower on these. In other words, it appears that supervisees were rated relative to the supervisor's bias and independent of a more objective set of criteria. Yet all supervisors thought that they were being objective and, in several cases, were not aware of having a bias in their assessments. These results are supported by attribution theory as explained by Sternitzke et al. (1988). Building on the work of Ross (1977), they identified egocentric bias as a common problem for supervisors when observing supervisee behavior and explained the nature of the bias as follows:

> One's estimate of deviance and normalcy are egocentrically biased in accord with one's own behavioral choices, because observers tend to think about what they would have done in a similar situation and then compare their hypothesized behavior with the actor's actual behavior. If the observers believe they would have acted differently, then there is an increased tendency for them to view the actor's [behavior] as deviant. If the observers believe they would have acted in a similar fashion, then their tendencies are to view the actor's behavior as normal. (p. 9)

Robiner et al. (1993) addressed idiosyncratic tendencies for individual supervisors to demonstrate

a leniency bias, a strictness bias, or a central-tendency bias. In a subsequent study of 62 supervisors, Robiner et al. (1997) found that an acknowledgment of evaluation bias was commonplace (59%), with only 10% of supervisors believing that their evaluations were free from bias and 31% being unsure. Of those supervisors who admitted bias, 40% felt that they leaned toward leniency in their ratings of supervisees; 45% felt that they leaned toward central tendency; and only 7% felt that they exhibited a strictness bias.

According to Robiner et al. (1993), a leniency bias—that is, the tendency to evaluate more favorably than objective data might warrant—may result from any of four sources: (1) measurement issues, such as a lack of clear criteria; (2) legal and administrative issues, such as a concern about a grievance procedure; (3) interpersonal issues, such as experiencing the anguish about damaging a supervisee's career; or (4) supervisor issues, such as having limited supervision experience. In all, Robiner et al. listed 23 potential bases for a lenient evaluation (see Table 2.2).

Strictness bias is the tendency to rate supervisees more severely than warranted. This kind of bias would seem to be the most difficult for the supervisee. Ward, Friedlander, Schoen, and Klein (1985) suggested that such ratings can lead to excessive defensiveness on the part of the supervisee or attempts to manipulate the supervisor to gain more positive ratings. Robiner et al. (1993) suggested that consistent critical ratings are likely to suggest problems within the supervisor (e.g., unrealistic standards or displaced personal frustration).

The central-tendency bias is the tendency to rate supervisees uniformly average. When this is the supervisor's bias, supervisees are denied feedback that would allow them to address deficits seriously or to appreciate that their performance was above average.

Gonsalvez and Freestone (2007) conducted an important follow-up to the Robiner et al. (1997) study. They collected data on 130 field supervisors over 12 years and found that these supervisors indeed reflected a leniency bias. (Their data did not support a central-tendency bias or a strictness bias.)

TABLE 2.2   Factors Contributing to Leniency or Inflation in Faculty Evaluations of Interns

---

Definition and Measurement Issues
  1. Lack of clear criteria and objective measures of competence or incompetence in psychology
  2. Lack of clear criteria and objective measures of impairment or distress in psychology
  3. Supervisor awareness of subjectivity inherent in evaluation
  4. Apprehension about defending evaluations due to lack of clear criteria and objective measures

Legal and Administrative Issues
  5. Concern that negative evaluations may result in administrative inquiry, audit, grievance, or litigation
  6. Lack of awareness of internship or institutional policies and procedures involved in negative evaluations
  7. Social and political dynamics: feared or perceived lack of support from institutions, directors of training, and colleagues for providing negative evaluations
  8. Concern that failing to "pass" an intern may result in loss of future training funds or training slots or the need to find additional funds to extend the intern's training
  9. Concern that failing to "pass" an intern may result in adverse publicity that could affect institutional reputation and the number of internship applicants

Interpersonal Issues
 10. Fear of diminishing rapport or provoking hostility from supervisees
 11. Fear of eliciting backlash from current or future trainees
 12. Anguish about damaging a supervisee's career or complicating or terminating his or her graduate training

Supervisor Issues
 13. Supervisors' wish to avoid scrutiny of their own behavior, competence, ethics, expectations, or judgment of their clinical and supervisory practices
 14. Limited supervisory experiences with impaired or incompetent trainees
 15. Inability to impart negative evaluations (e.g., deficit in assertive communication skills)
 16. Indifference to personal responsibility for upholding the standards of the profession
 17. Discomfort with gatekeeper role
 18. Identification with supervisee's problems
 19. Inadequate attention to supervisee's performance or problems
 20. Supervisors' presumption of supervisee competence (e.g., overreliance on selection procedures)
 21. Minimization of incompetence or impairment in supervisees
 22. Inappropriate optimism that problems will resolve without intervention
 23. Preference to avoid the substantial energy and time commitment necessary to address or remediate deficient trainees

---

Source: From "Evaluation Difficulties in Supervising Psychology Interns," by W. Robiner, M. Fuhrman, and S. Ristvedt, 1993, *The Clinical Psychologist, 46*(1), pp. 3–13. Copyright 1993 by the Division of Clinical Psychology, Division 12 of the American Psychological Association. Reprinted by permission.

Additionally, Gonsalvez and Freestone found that early field supervisor assessments of supervisees regarding particular competencies did not predict later assessments on the same competencies. As a reflection regarding the documented leniency bias, the authors stated: "It is possible that the supportive and nurturing role supervisors are called to play in their own therapy with clients, and the formative role they play in building up skills and confidence in an often anxious and sometimes vulnerable trainee, conspire against objective and critical supervisory judgments" (p. 28). The research of Bogo, Regehr, Power, and Regehr (2007) supported this conclusion. Bogo et al. found that social work field supervisors felt the task of evaluation collided with some highly valued professional values such as being nonjudgmental and sensitive to individual learning needs. Therefore, though acknowledging the importance of making evaluative judgments, these field supervisors acknowledged that the process of facilitating learning was far more appealing to them than being gatekeepers for the profession.

Regarding the low predictability of field supervisor ratings in the Gonsalvez and Freestone (2007) study, the authors speculated that assessments may need to be considered in more discreet circumstances. In other words, a supervisee's ability to intervene with clients who represent one clinical population may not generalize to intervention skills with a different population. Most presently used assessment tools, however, tend to refer to skills independent of clinical populations.

Their findings led Gonsalvez and Freestone (2007) to state a concern that a leniency bias might translate to a "halo" effect for supervisees, with negative consequences. In particular, these authors were concerned that supervisees might bypass additional supervision or professional development, thinking they are better than their peers. Referring to processes like the use of outside readers for dissertations, Gonsalvez and Freestone suggested that at least some aspects of supervisee performance should be assessed by persons other than the field supervisors.

We concur with Gonsalvez and Freestone's (2007) recommendation. Although several different types of subjective variables can influence evaluation, a single action may serve to counter their effect: consultation. Supervision will be less vulnerable to subjective confounding when others are brought into the process. Supervisors are more likely to involve other opinions when there is a supervision crisis, especially if the situation has ethical or legal implications. The wise supervisor, though, involves others in the evaluation process when things are seemingly at their smoothest. Not only is this good practice, it affords the supervisor ongoing professional development that will assist him or her in becoming a better evaluator.

Consequences of Evaluation

Like most activities of any importance, the process of evaluation contains some risks. There have been false positives and false negatives in the evaluation experience of most clinical supervisors. Possibly because supervisors all know that they have evaluated incorrectly in the past, the consequences of their evaluations can loom before them like an unforgiving superego. Supervisors know that a positive evaluation may mean that a supervisee will be competitive in the job market or an employee will be promoted, while a negative evaluation may result in a student's being dropped from a training program or an employee's being the first to be let go. Because of supervisors' awareness of the consequences of evaluation, they find themselves doing extra soul searching over the evaluations of the strongest and weakest supervisees.

But even for the average evaluation, there are consequences. Levy (1983) referred to the "costs" of evaluation as the inordinate time it requires of the supervisor, the anxiety it causes the supervisee, and the stress it puts on the supervisory relationship. Burke, Goodyear, & Guzzard (1998) found that evaluation interventions that resulted in breaches in the supervision working alliance left the supervision relationship vulnerable. Yet, Levy noted that program or agency integrity and the welfare of future clients placed the costs and benefits of evaluation in alignment.

In a highly pragmatic discussion, Kadushin (1992a) mentioned the administrative consequences for the supervisor when a negative evaluation is necessary. If in a work environment an employee is let go because of an evaluation, the supervisor will often be the person to feel the brunt of the extra workload until a replacement can be found. In a training program, a negative evaluation will typically mean more extensive documentation, the possibility of an appeal process or even a court case (McAdams et al., 2007), or, at the very least, lengthy interviews with the supervisee involved. Robiner et al. (1997) established that, indeed, legal and administrative issues played a role in supervisor leniency bias. It is understandable, although not acceptable, that some supervisors shy away from giving negative evaluations in order to avoid unattractive consequences. Such shortsightedness, however, does not acknowledge the much more significant consequences when evaluations are not done properly.

CONCLUSION

Evaluation poses a range of issues for the clinical supervisor. It is at the same time the most disconcerting responsibility, the most challenging, and the most important. There are, however, conceptual and structural aids to help supervisors in this process that can increase confidence and competence and contribute to a productive evaluation process experience for the supervisee.

CHAPTER 3

ETHICAL AND LEGAL CONSIDERATIONS

It is perhaps a sign of the times that ethics is an increasingly visible topic in the literature of the mental health professions. The passage of the first code of ethics specific to clinical supervision in the United States (Supervision Interest Network, 1993) advanced an awareness of the responsibilities and expectations of the supervisory role distinct from other professional roles. Practitioners in the mental health disciplines continue to search for answers to troubling ethical dilemmas and to identify the appropriate posture supervisors must take in a variety of situations. In more recent years, increased attention has been paid to precursors of unethical behavior. In this chapter, we will present the areas most critical and relevant to the ethical practice of clinical supervision.

In addition to their increased attention to ethics, the mental health professions have also become highly reactive to legal matters. This plight is not unique to the mental health professions, for litigiousness has become a characteristic of United States society. Furthermore, counseling and psychotherapy are sought by a wider range of consumers than in generations past, thus making it a more public enterprise. With increased exposure has come increased accountability. If the practice of psychotherapy was ever tranquil, it is no longer so. One result is that, although suits against mental health professionals are still relatively rare, the fear of litigation has been a factor affecting how much of practice now is operationalized.

Even if ethics and legal matters are often related, each has a distinct purpose. Ethical codes are conceptually broad in nature, limited in number, and occasionally open to interpretation. Although they are sometimes perceived as safe-guards to avoid legal liability, following ethical codes does not guarantee total safety. Rather, ethical standards are a statement from a particular profession to the general public regarding what they stand for.

The law is "defined as the body of rules governing the affairs of persons within a community, state or country" (Committee on Professional Practice, 2003, p. 596). Despite their separate purposes, professional ethics and legal tenets have a relationship to each other. For a professional to be considered liable, it is generally accepted that the professional must have acted outside the bounds of accepted professional practice (Ogloff & Olley, 1998; Remley & Herlihy, 2001). As Guest and Dooley (1999) pointed out, the emergence of standards and ethical codes for supervisors has made those persons working outside these parameters more vulnerable to being held liable. At the same time, the presence of these standards and codes protects those who follow them.

The reader could assume that, because ethical codes tend to be more stringent, avoiding litigation in one's supervision practice is simply a matter of behaving ethically. Unfortunately, it is not that simple. A moral act can at times subject one to retaliatory litigation. The opposite tendency, however, seems to be the more prevalent. That is, it is more common to see professionals more concerned about the law than their profession's ethical standards. As Pope and Vasquez (1991) admonished, this tendency "can discourage ethical awareness and sensitivity. It is crucial to realize that ethical behavior is more than simply avoiding violation of legal standards and that one's ethical and legal duties may, in certain instances, be in conflict" (p. 48). At the same time,

Meyer, Landis, and Hays (1988) advised that ethical standards can become legally binding for two reasons: (1) they may be used by the courts to determine professional duty, and (2) they are indirectly influential because they guide the thinking of others in the field who may be asked to testify.

It seems then that ethical standards and legal matters have a symbiotic rather than a perfectly symmetrical relationship. In this chapter, we will discuss first ethical issues and then legal ramifications. Because ethical situations typically are not black and white, we have offered some case examples throughout the ethics sections and have followed with questions to stimulate reflection.

MAJOR ETHICAL ISSUES FOR CLINICAL SUPERVISORS

The following are the major ethical themes of which clinical supervisors should be cognizant. We will present the implications of these themes for the practice of supervision based on our understanding and a review of the literature. We will limit our discussion to issues that have direct relevance for clinical supervisors and therefore will not discuss topics such as research. At the same time, several ethical issues have implications for both the supervisory relationship and the therapy relationship that the supervisor oversees. We will address each dimension separately.

Due Process

Due process is a legal term for a procedure that ensures that notice and hearing must be given before an important right can be removed (Disney & Stephens, 1994). As with other concepts that have legal precedents, due process has been adopted as an ethical mandate as well. In the human services, due process has surfaced as an issue mostly around the proper route to take if a client needs to be committed to a mental health hospital (Ponterotto, 1987; Schutz, 1982). Most hospitals are aware of their due process duties, and professionals who work with volatile populations also are aware of correct procedures.

The helping professions have taken the position that supervisees have due process rights as well. Forrest et al. (1999) described the distinction between substantive due process and procedural due process. Substantive due process means that "the criteria and procedures that govern a training program must be applied consistently and fairly" (p. 656). Procedural due process has to do with the rights of the individual to be notified. This is understood to mean that the supervisee–student should be apprised of the academic and performance requirements and program regulations, receive notice of any deficiencies, be evaluated regularly, and have an opportunity to be heard if their deficiencies have led to a change in status (e.g., put on probation). Most of the supervision literature that addresses due process focuses on procedural due process.

The ethical codes of the mental health professions and divisions within professions give some attention to supervision, but their primary purpose is still in detailing ethical behavior for the provider of counseling and therapy (cf. American Association for Marriage and Family Therapy [AAMFT], 2001; American Counseling Association [ACA], 2005; American Psychological Association [APA], 2002; National Association of Social Workers, 1999). It is not surprising, therefore, that ethical guidelines developed specifically for the practice of supervision (Center for Credentialing and Education, 2001; Supervision Interest Network, 1993) address the issue of due process concerning supervisees most directly (see Supervisor's Toolbox). For example, the Ethical Guidelines for Counseling Supervisors (Supervision Interest Network, 1993) states that:

> Supervisors should incorporate the principles of informed consent and participation; clarity of requirements, expectations, roles and rules; and due process and appeal into the establishment of policies and procedures of their institution, program, courses, and individual supervisory relationships. Mechanisms for due process appeal of individual supervisory actions should be established and made available to all supervisees. (section 2.14)

The most blatant violation of Guideline 2.14 occurs when a supervisee is given a negative final evaluation or dismissed from a training program or job without having had either prior warning that his or her performance was inadequate or a reasonable amount of time to improve (a procedural due process issue). Ladany et al. (1996) found that being denied adequate performance evaluation was the most frequently cited supervisor violation reported by supervisees in their study. This ethical dilemma seems to originate, at least in part, from an avoidance of evaluation by supervisors in training programs and clinical sites. Perhaps, as a consequence, they tend to take a reactive posture to the issues of supervisee inadequacy or professional impairment. They place their emphasis on screening for admission (Bradey & Post, 1991) with the unrealistic expectation that accepted students will uniformly complete training successfully. As a result, it seems that training programs and internship sites across mental health professions have not established adequate and public due process procedures (Boxley, Drew, & Rangel, 1986; Koerin & Miller, 1995; Oliver et al., 2004; Rosenberg et al., 2005). Koerin and Miller went so far as to say that the gatekeeping assumption of training programs is at odds with the absence of policies for termination of problematic students.

When a full due process procedure is followed (see Chapter 2 for the process suggested by Lamb et al., 1991), the supervisee in question is guaranteed a respectful review of the situation and the expert opinions of professionals, in addition to that of the person initiating the complaint. Following such a procedure also protects the institution from the accusation that its action was capricious or arbitrary, which is a due process violation.

Although most supervisees do not challenge violations of due process rights, several authors have documented those cases for which litigation followed such violations (cf. Disney & Stephens, 1994; Forrest et al., 1999; Knoff & Prout, 1985; Meyer, 1980). As we stated in Chapter 2, when due process procedures have been followed, the courts have shown great deference to faculty evaluations (Forrest et al., 1999; McAdams et al., 2007). Disney and Stephens (1994) advised that, strictly speaking, due process (legal) rights are only protected within public institutions. Therefore, private institutions of higher learning and/or mental health sites that do not receive significant public funding would not be held legally accountable regarding due process procedures unless they were stipulated in the institution's official published materials. Because of the legal variability of due process protections, the ethical mandate to employ due process is especially important for supervisors.

Forrest et al. (1999), Frame and Stevens-Smith (1995), and McAdams et al. (2007) proposed developing policy statements to guide the evaluation process and establishing descriptive criteria about personal characteristics that are determined to be essential for success as a mental health practitioner. These criteria must then be used for ongoing evaluation of students during their training program. In short, students' due process rights are protected by published policy statements and criteria, and by the availability of the regular evaluations. When students are found to be in jeopardy, Frame and Stevens-Smith utilized a procedure very similar to that described by Lamb et al. (1991).

Example: Hannah is in a master's program in mental health counseling. She has completed 10 courses in the program and is currently in practicum. Hannah has received a great deal of formative feedback throughout the practicum indicating that she has many areas that needed improvement. At the conclusion of the practicum, Hannah's instructor assigns Hannah a grade of F for the course. At this time, Hannah is informed that a failing grade in the practicum is grounds for dismissal from the program. Hannah is told that she may retake the practicum one time, but that the faculty are not optimistic that she will improve enough to receive a B or better, a condition for her continuing in the program. Although Hannah knew that she was not doing as well in the practicum as some others, she had no awareness that she was in danger of being terminated from the program until the final evaluation.

It is likely that Hannah will take the advice of the faculty and will discontinue the training program. However, have her due process rights been protected? How vulnerable is her practicum instructor and the program if she should decide to challenge their decision? Even if Hannah does not appeal, what are the potential systemic implications of such a process? While there is no ill will evident in the action of the faculty and no indication that their decision was capricious or arbitrary, did the process that they followed adequately protect the student and was it legally defensible?

Informed Consent

The concept of informed consent has been handed down to us from the medical profession. Within this context, informed consent requires physicians to inform patients about medical procedures that could be potentially harmful to them. Patients should also be apprised of any risks of a recommended treatment and of the alternative treatments available. The failure of physicians to inform their patients constitutes malpractice and leaves the physician vulnerable to liability should injuries occur as a result of treatment. The doctrine of informed consent has been extended to other health service providers, including those in the mental health fields (Disney & Stephens, 1994).

There is perhaps no ethical standard as far-reaching as that of informed consent for the practice of psychotherapy. This is underscored by Woody and Associates (1984), who asserted that informed consent is the best defense against a charge of malpractice for the practitioner. For the supervisor, there are really three levels of responsibility: (1) The supervisor must determine that clients have been informed by the supervisee regarding the parameters of therapy, (2) the supervisor must also be sure that clients are aware of the parameters of supervision that will affect them, and (3) the supervisor must provide the supervisee with the opportunity for informed consent. We will discuss each of these separately.

Informed Consent with Clients. It is essential that clients understand and agree to the procedures of therapy prior to its beginning. This is not

to imply that there will be no ambiguity in therapy or even that the therapist should be able to predict everything that will happen during the course of therapy. But it does imply that some assessment must occur that will be shared with clients, that goals will be determined, and that the general course of therapy will be outlined for the clients' approval. If it is determined later that a redirection of therapy would be beneficial, this process should be repeated.

Partly because of theoretical orientation, some therapists have resisted this process. But even less directive forms of therapy can and should be explained to clients prior to their commitment to the process. As Woody and Associates (1984) stated,

> [T]he professional should be the last person to object to a requirement of informed consent. If anything, the professional should reach to the maximum allowed by public policy to ensure that the service recipient does, in fact, understand and consent to the treatment. To do otherwise is to court a disciplinary action for unethical conduct and/or a legal suit for malpractice. (p. 376)

According to Haas (1991), there are seven categories of information that, if revealed, would constitute necessary and sufficient informed consent. The first four apply to the therapeutic relationship. Haas began with the information most directly related to the medical precedent, that of the risks and benefits of treatment. In both cases, only what is reasonable needs to be covered. The risks may be mild, such as embarrassment if others should learn that one is receiving counseling (Disney & Stephens, 1994), or they may be serious, such as the risk of terminating a marriage if one begins to address chronic relationship issues. Likewise, the potential benefits of therapy (Haas's second category) should be discussed.

Haas's (1991) third category encompassed the logistics of treatment, including the length of sessions, cost, opportunity for telephone consultations, and the like. Depending on insurance parameters, the limits of treatment in terms of number of sessions is a critical area that must be covered by the supervisee (Acuff et al., 1999; Haas & Cummings,

1991). Finally, if the supervisee is a student assigned to a site for a limited amount of time (say, one semester), this information is important to convey for purposes of informed consent.

The fourth category described by Haas (1991) includes information about the type of counseling or therapy that clients will be offered. If one is behaviorally oriented and will require homework, if the supervisee is in training as a marriage and family therapist and will require additional family members to be present, or if one's approach to working with particular issues includes the use of group work, such stipulations should be explained at the outset of therapy. Disney and Stephens (1994) suggested that preferred alternatives to the type of treatment being suggested, as well as the risks of receiving no treatment at all, should be explained at this time as well.

> *Example:* Julian is a supervisee in a mental health agency. He has been seeing Ellen for four months in individual counseling. It has become apparent that Ellen and her husband need marriage counseling. Julian has been trained in marriage and family therapy. He very much wants to follow this case to its conclusion. Without discussing alternatives, he suggests that Ellen bring her husband to the next session. Ellen says that she is relieved that he is willing to work with them. She was afraid that Julian would refer them to another therapist. Having Julian work with both her and her husband is exactly what she was hoping for.

In this example we must ask if Ellen has been given the opportunity of informed consent. Has her husband? Is there information about the therapy process that Julian should have offered to help both Ellen and her husband make the best decision for their present situation? At the very least, Julian has erred in not discussing alternatives. Julian's supervisor must now help Julian backtrack. If the supervisor had any inkling that marital therapy might be indicated, the supervisor was negligent for not coaching Julian regarding the client's informed consent rights, as well as her husband's.

Informed Consent Regarding Supervision. The client must not only be aware of therapeutic

procedures, but also of supervision procedures. Whether sessions will be taped or observed, who will be involved in supervision (one person or a team of persons), how intrusive will be the supervision—all these need to be communicated to the client.

Haas's (1991) final three categories regarding informed consent are related to supervision. The fifth area of information about which clients should be apprised is emergency procedures that are in place. Because the supervisor should always be involved in an emergency situation, we have placed this category here. Clients should know if direct access to the therapist is available in case of emergency. Will the supervisor be available to the client? This leads to the next category of confidentiality. Most supervisees are apprised of their obligation to inform clients when confidentiality will be breached for reasons other than supervision; for example, if there was an indication that the client might do harm to another. However, the issue of confidentiality is equally relevant to the supervisory relationship. According to Disney and Stephens (1994), "supervisees place themselves in a position to be sued for invasion of privacy and breach of confidentiality if they do not inform their clients that they will be discussing sessions with their supervisor" (p. 50). Most training programs use written forms to alert clients of the conditions of supervision. It may be wise for the supervisor to meet with clients personally before the outset of therapy for a number of reasons: (1) By meeting the supervisor directly, the client usually is more comfortable with the prospect of supervision, (2) it gives the supervisor an opportunity to model for trainees the kind of direct, open communication that is needed to ensure informed consent, and (3) by not going through the trainee to communicate with clients, it is one less way that the supervisor could be vicariously responsible should the trainee not be clear or thorough.

The last area of information to be given to clients has to do with the qualifications of the provider (Haas, 1991). As several authors have noted (e.g., Disney & Stephens, 1994; Harrar, VandeCreek, & Knapp, 1990; Knapp & VandeCreek, 1997; Pope & Vasquez, 1991; Worthington,

Tan, & Poulin, 2002), it is vitally important for ethical and legal reasons that clients understand when they are in therapy with a supervisee who is in training. Any attempt to obscure the status of a supervisee may expose both supervisee and supervisor to civil suits alleging fraud, misrepresentation, deceit, and lack of informed consent.

Even when clients are aware that their therapist is under supervision, informed consent can be compromised when trainees downplay the parameters of supervision. Situations occur when supervisees use ambiguous language like, "If it's all right with you, I'll be audiotaping our session," when what they mean is, "I am required to audiotape our sessions if I am to work with you." This leaves the trainee in the awkward position of setting an unwise precedent or of having to backpedal to explain the true conditions of therapy and supervision.

Example: Beth is a social worker who counsels women who have experienced domestic violence. She is well trained to do initial interviews with women in crisis, and her supervisor is confident in Beth's abilities to carry out these interviews without taping them. Additionally, there is the obvious concern that the use of audiotape would be insensitive to women who are frightened and vulnerable during the interview. The conditions of supervision, however, require Beth to audiotape all subsequent sessions.

Janell was one of Beth's interviewees. After the initial session, Janell decided that she was ready to receive counseling regarding her abusive marriage. She explained to Beth that she was afraid of her husband's reaction to counseling, so she made her first appointment for a day when she knew he would be out of town. When Janell arrived for counseling, Beth discussed the conditions of counseling, including the requirement that she audiotape sessions for supervision. Janell became quite upset and told Beth that she never would have agreed to counseling if she had known that the sessions would not be held in strictest confidence. Beth attempted to explain that would still be the case, but Janell left and did not return.

How do you react to Beth's method of handling this situation? Were Janell's informed consent rights violated? What alternatives did Beth have that would protect both her and her client?

Informed Consent with Supervisees. It is best practice that supervisees be as well informed as clients even though this is not a uniform requirement across mental health professions (Knapp & VandeCreek, 2006). In addition to being informed about the personal and interpersonal strengths required of them for retention in a training program (Forrest et al., 1999), supervisees should enter the supervisory experience knowing the conditions that dictate their success or advancement. In other words, the gatekeeping responsibility of supervisors should be clarified with supervisees and done so at the outset of supervision (Russell et al., 2007). It also should be clear to them what their responsibilities are and what the supervisor's are. Consider the following examples:

1. Ronald, a student in a professional counseling master's program, makes an appointment to see his academic advisor to discuss his internship now that he is near the end of his training program. He plans to do his internship in a local mental health agency. His advisor tells Ronald that the faculty recently evaluated students and that he was viewed as not having the capacity to be successful in clinical work. It was suggested that he pursue an internship in a "softer" area such as career counseling. Ronald states that he has no interest in career counseling. Ronald's advisor states that such an internship site is the only type that will be approved for him.

2. Ruth has been assigned to a local mental health hospital for her field placement to work with patients who are preparing to be discharged. It is her first day at the site and she is meeting with her site supervisor. He gives her a form to fill out, which asks for information regarding her student malpractice insurance. When Ruth tells her supervisor that she does not carry such insurance, he advises her that it is their policy not to accept any student who does not have insurance. The supervisor also expresses some surprise, because this has always been the hospital's policy and Ruth is not the first student to be assigned to them from her training program.

3. Latoya is in her predoctoral internship, working with very difficult clients. In supervision she shares that one client in particular has been "getting to her," most likely because some of the client's situation is so similar to Latoya's past. Latoya's supervisor immediately suggests that Latoya receive counseling regarding this issue. When Latoya says that she believes her past therapy was sufficient and that she would prefer to view the situation as a supervision one, her supervisor states that she will only continue to work with Latoya if she commits to counseling.

In each situation, how egregious is the violation of the supervisee's right to informed consent? To what extent can institutional materials cover issues of consent? How might each situation have been handled to better address the rights of the supervisee?

Whiston and Emerson (1989) addressed the informed consent violation if supervisors refer their trainees for therapy as a condition for continuing in a training program when their trainees were not aware of this possibility from the outset of training. In other words, if there is a possibility that personal counseling will be recommended for any trainees in a given program, all trainees should be cognizant of this practice upon entering the program (e.g., Standard 7.02 in APA's Ethical Principles of Psychologists and Code of Conduct, 2002, is very explicit about this).

While not directly related to informed consent, Russell et al. (2007) posed additional issues if trainees are referred to therapy, including the fact that the efficacy of therapy to remediate supervisee functioning has not been established. Furthermore, Russell et al. noted that referring students to therapy implies a diagnosis, thus blending the educational relationship between supervisor and trainee with one that is more clinical. As others have noted as well, Russell et al. stressed that a referral to therapy opens the door for the supervisee to claim discrimination based on a disability by virtue of the Americans with Disabilities Act. Russell et al., therefore, might challenge a recommendation of therapy for a supervisee, even if the informed consent parameters had been met. Instead, they suggested that training programs wishing to encourage outside personal therapy for trainees keep that separate from any action involving an individual trainee.

Their conclusion, therefore, was that "(p)sychotherapy as an integral part of training for supportive and preventive purposes is different from selecting out students for therapy as a part of remediation" (Russell et al., 2007, p. 238).

More routine matters that the supervisee should be apprised of as part of informed consent include supervision methods that will be used, the time that will be allotted for supervision, the expectations of the supervisor, the theoretical orientation of the supervisor, and the type of documentation required for supervision (Cohen, 1987; McCarthy et al., 1995; Pope & Vasquez, 1991). Simply put, the surprises in store for the supervisee should be due to the learning process itself and the complexity of human problems, not to oversights on the part of the supervisor.

Attending to informed consent with supervisees may seem rather straightforward yet it is fairly complex and requires that the supervisor balance what may appear to be disparate functions of supervision with skill and sensitivity. Thomas (2007) noted that informed consent is only partially applicable to supervision because once a person has entered a training program (thus entering a profession), that person's options become limited. Requirements for success (e.g., program completion, licensure) are largely predetermined. The supervisor's role from this angle would stress the function of the gatekeeper. Yet, Barnett (2007) emphasized a different supervisory task and focused on the importance of a productive relationship to effective supervision, including demonstrated empathy for the supervisee, investment in the supervisee's development, and sensitivity to the supervisee's cultural vantage point. Although measuring the supervisee's performance against standards is not necessarily in any opposition to forming a supportive relationship with a supervisee, these dual tasks require skill and open communication. They also may require ongoing supervision of supervision. This leads us to our final comment about informed consent and the work of Stout (1987) who advised that supervisors and supervisors-in-training also be forewarned about the parameters of supervision. "Supervisors, as such, should be allowed the prerogative of informed consent, that is, they need to be fully aware of the heavy responsibility, accountability, and even culpability involved in [providing] supervision" (p. 96).

Multiple Relationships

Just as the term "impaired" has gone out of favor to describe problematic students, the term "dual relationships" has been replaced by the term "multiple relationships." Ethical standards of all mental health disciplines strongly advise that multiple relationships, or engaging in relationships in addition to the professional relationship between therapists and clients be avoided. Probably the most flagrant type of multiple relationships are sexual relationships between therapists and clients, which are condemned (e.g., ACA, 2005; APA, 2002). In most states, sexual exploitation of a client is grounds for the automatic revocation of licensure or certification. It is the responsibility of the supervisor to be certain that supervisees understand the definition of a multiple relationship and avoid all such relationships with clients.

Multiple relationships between supervisors and supervisees have proved to be a much more difficult issue to resolve and have been a topic of significant discourse in the professional literature. Problematic multiple relationships with supervisees can include intimate relationships, therapeutic relationships, work relationships, and social relationships. Most authors concede that supervisors often have more than one professional relationship with a supervisee (e.g., supervisee and research assistant); these typically have been viewed as unavoidable (Gottlieb, Robinson, & Younggren, 2007). Additionally, a distinction has been made between boundary *crossings* and boundary *violations* (Gutheil & Gabbard, 1993; Gutheil & Simon, 2002). The former describes behavior that is outside the professional role (e.g., a supervisor and supervisee carpooling to a conference) but would not be considered unethical. Boundary violations, on the other hand, are the

outcome of problematic multiple relationships, whether professional or personal. It is because of the frequency and range of multiple relationships between supervisors and supervisees that supervisors need to be vigilant regarding boundary violations (Borders, 2001; Gottlieb et al., 2007). Scarborough, Bernard, and Morse (2006) raised similar concerns when doctoral students are involved in the supervision of master's students. Therefore, because multiple relationships are ubiquitous to graduate education, the focus of much of the supervision professional literature has been in clarifying when a multiple relationship is problematic (i.e., a boundary violation). Simply put, what makes a multiple relationship unethical is (1) the likelihood that it will impair the supervisor's judgment and (2) the risk to the supervisee of exploitation (Hall, 1988b).

Pearson and Piazza (1997) criticized much of the literature for treating multiple relationships as static rather than dynamic. Pearson and Piazza also asserted that most professionals are well meaning and attempt to behave ethically. However, they "are probably unaware or minimally aware of situations that may lead to the development of relationships with serious ethical implications" (pp. 91–92). Pearson and Piazza offered five categories of multiple relationships in an attempt to reflect some of the fluidity of human relationships in general: (1) Circumstantial multiple roles or multiple relationships that happen by coincidence (e.g., a supervisor's adult son begins dating a young woman who turns out to be a student in his mother's practicum class). (2) Structured multiple professional roles, when supervisor and supervisee have more than one professional role. This is what is usually being referred to when authors note that multiple relationships are ubiquitous to doctoral training programs. (3) Shifts in professional roles (e.g., when a doctoral student who was formerly a classmate in a course with a master's student becomes that student's practicum supervisor). (4) Personal and professional role conflicts, a category that includes preexisting professional relationships that are followed by a personal relationship or a personal relationship that is followed by the professional one. (5) The predatory professional, a category for those who deliberately seduce or exploit others for their personal gain. We will refer to Pearson and Piazza's categories as we discuss multiple relationships.

Multiple Relationships Between Supervisees and Clients.   The literature attending to therapist misconduct (though not necessarily supervisee misconduct) with clients is vast and cannot be fully addressed here. A few authors, however, have attended to multiple relationships as a supervision issue, that is, grappling with the importance of both monitoring relationships between supervisees and clients and assisting supervisees in ways that will reduce the likelihood of their involvement in exploitative relationships in the future. Hamilton and Spruill (1999) speculated that supervisee vulnerability to boundary violations included loneliness, prior paraprofessional or friendship "counseling" experiences in which levels of intimacy were higher than the professional norm, and failure to recognize ethical conflicts. They criticized supervisors for not addressing sexual attraction to clients as normative and for stereotyping the problem in a sexist manner.

Research conducted by Fly, van Bark, Weinman, Kitchener, and Lang (1997) confirmed that boundary transgressions (sexual and nonsexual) were indeed among the most common ethical transgressions among psychology supervisees, second only to violations of confidentiality. Furthermore, these two categories of ethical transgressions combined accounted for 45% of the total reported by training directors. Maki and Bernard (2007) stated that, because it is not uncommon for persons attracted to mental health fields to have unresolved personal issues, supervisors should not be surprised that supervisees may need assistance with boundary negotiation. This assumption is supported by research conducted by Celenza (1998), who found that problems with self-esteem and unresolved anger toward authority figures were included among precursors to therapist sexual misconduct. Similarly, Jackson

and Nuttall (2001) found that three out of five mental health practitioners in their sample who reported a history of severe childhood sexual abuse reported sexual boundary violations with clients. All in all, these data from the practitioner world suggest that supervisors are naïve to deny the possibility of boundary transgressions involving their supervisees.

Preventing Supervisee Ethical Transgressions.   Although there is no foolproof way to ensure the ethical behavior of supervisees, several authors have encouraged a proactive supervisor posture (Koenig & Spano, 2003; Ladany, 2004; Ladany, Friedlander, & Nelson, 2005). Most professional literature to date addressing supervisee transgressions has focused on sexual intimacies with clients. Among the most common strategies recommended are preventive education (Samuel & Gorton, 1998) and honest discussion between supervisors and supervisees about the possibility, if not the probability, of occasional sexual attraction to clients, of supervisors to supervisees, or the converse for each dyad (Bridges & Wohlberg, 1999; Hamilton & Spruill, 1999; Ladany, 2004; Ladany, O'Brien, Hill, Melincoff, Knox, & Petersen 1997; Ladany et al., 2005; Ladany & Melincoff, 1999). Furthermore, as with other sensitive issues, it is imperative that the supervisor accept responsibility for raising the topic. Ladany et al. (1997) found that, otherwise, only about half of supervisees who experience sexual attraction to clients will share this with their supervisors. Bridges (1999) further emphasized the importance of supervisor openness and candor in assisting supervisees to manage intense feelings. "Ethical supervision is embedded in a clearly articulated supervisor–student relationship that monitors misuse of power and boundary crossings, yet is capable of deeply personal discourse" (Bridges, 1999, p. 218). Despite these exhortations, Heru, Strong, Price, and Recupero (2004) found supervisees were more reluctant than supervisors to address sexual topics in supervision that included sexual attraction. These authors hypothesized that supervisors were more favorably inclined toward such topics because of their experience and appreciation of their importance. Heru et al. also found that females (supervisors and supervisees) were less inclined than their male counterparts to self-disclose regarding a variety of personal topics. This, then, would lead us to conclude that the most difficult context for initiating a discussion about sexual attraction within counseling or supervision would be when a female supervisor works with a female supervisee.

Hamilton and Spruill (1999) suggested that all supervisees receive instruction in the following areas prior to seeing clients: (1) the powerful effects on attraction of familiarity, similarity, self-disclosure, and physical closeness; (2) testimonials from well-respected clinicians about their encounters with sexual attraction in therapy; (3) specific actions to take when feelings of attraction arise, with emphasis on the importance of supervision; (4) suspected risk factors for and signs of client–therapist intimacy; (5) consequences of therapist sexual misconduct on the client; (6) social skills training to increase skill and decrease anxiety related to enacting ethical behavior; and (7) a clear explanation of program policy regarding ethical transgressions, with emphasis on a clear distinction between feelings that are to be expected and actions that are unacceptable (p. 320). Offering this kind of information in a group format might serve as an antidote to the reluctance of any individual supervisee to address the topic.

Ladany et al. (2005) suggested a preventive approach that includes introducing the topic of sexual attraction during the first stage of supervision. As has been emphasized by others as well, they argued that including topics such as these in an orientation to supervision normalizes them in a way that makes it easier to discuss them should they emerge during supervision. Once such groundwork has been established, Ladany et al. encouraged supervisors to recognize what they referred to as "markers" of a potential boundary vulnerability, both overt (e.g., supervisee shares strong feelings about a client) or covert (e.g., supervisee dresses more attractively on days a particular client is scheduled). Walker and Clark

(1999) noted similar cues and included inappropriate gift giving, off-hours telephone calls, and "overdoing, overprotecting, and overidentifying" (p. 1438), among others. Once supervisors have noted what might be markers, supervisors engage supervisees in discussion about their feelings, assess their knowledge of ethical standards, normalize the experience if indeed an attraction is experienced, focus on any potential countertransference issues that may be operating, and finally focus on how the attraction can be managed without negatively affecting the therapeutic process. Ladany et al. would suggest a similar process if the attraction was between the supervisor and supervisee.

Finally, the use of professional disclosure statements for both supervision (Blackwell, Strohmer, Belcas, & Burton, 2002; Cobia & Boes, 2000) and counseling or therapy are well advised as deterrents to boundary violations. A professional disclosure statement (PDS), which includes details about one's training and experience, as well as about issues such as confidentiality, has the potential of alerting both supervisee and client to the professional nature of the relationship. It also typically includes contact information for an outside authority should there be some concern about what has transpired in the relationship. This alone, it would seem, communicates a high regard for professionalism and integrity. (See the Supervisor's Toolbox and Fall & Sutton, 2004, for examples of a PDS.)

Multiple Relationships Between Supervisor and Supervisee. As with the literature regarding supervisees, by far the multiple relationship within supervision that has received the most attention is sexual involvement between supervisor and supervisee. Prior to reviewing all types of multiple relationships between supervisors and supervisees, we will review briefly a number of studies that have attempted to grasp how widespread this particular issue is. An early study (Pope, Levenson, & Schover, 1979) found that 10% of psychologists admitted to having sexual contact, as students, with their educators, and

13% reported having had a sexual relationship with their students now that they were educators. As might be expected, more female supervisees reported having had sexual contact with their educators than male supervisees. Furthermore, for those women who had graduated closer to the time of the study, the incidence was much higher (25%) compared to women who had graduated 20 years earlier (5%). Two other studies involving clinical psychologists (Glaser & Thorpe, 1986; Robinson & Reid, 1985) found similar results.

Bartell and Rubin (1990), in a follow-up to Pope et al. (1979), found that of those women who had sexual relationships as students, a striking 23% had similar relationships as educators. By contrast, only 6% of those educators who had not had such relationships as students had sexual relationships as educators. Bartell and Rubin, therefore, believed that there is an important modeling effect that may contribute to the perpetuation of unethical behavior in supervision.

A more recent study (Lamb & Catanzaro, 1998), however, found that having been involved in a sexual boundary transgression as a supervisee did not increase one's likelihood to be a transgressor as a professional. Their study also found a lower rate (8%) of sexual boundary violations by professional psychologists. Of these, 6% represented violations with clients. The authors speculated that these newer findings may reflect better documentation from the profession regarding the negative outcomes of such transgressions for clients, as well as clearer messages about the negative consequences, both legal and professional, for transgressors. One disturbing finding, however, was that, over time, sexual transgressions with supervisees and/or students were not viewed as negatively by the transgressors as those with clients. It is impossible to know whether these relationships fell into Pearson and Piazza's (1997) personal and professional role conflicts category or the predatory professional category. Lamb, Catanzaro, and Moorman (2003) returned to this topic later, asking psychologists to reflect upon sexual relationships they had had with clients, supervisees, or students. Of the 368 psychologists who returned the survey, 3.5% (i.e., 13 people) reported sexual relationships. Relationships with students were the most frequent. Of these, three were ongoing and ranged from a few months to 30 years in duration. Those in ongoing relationships reported positive feelings about them; however, for those relationships that ended, feelings were far less positive, especially in hindsight. Additionally, these relationships had typically been short in duration and at a time when the psychologist was struggling with personal issues. Despite all of this, 40% of these individuals did not see their boundary transgression as harmful to the other person involved. Interestingly, almost three times as many of these professionals had been involved in a sexual boundary violation when they were clients, supervisees, or students; therefore, a majority had not repeated their past in this regard. Perhaps this is further evidence that the mental health professions are becoming more vigilant about boundary transgressions. Also, all of those who sought collegial consultation during the period in their careers when they found themselves struggling with professional boundaries found it very helpful.

A study using a similar definition of sexual contact as studies done in psychology found a similar rate (6%) of sexual intimacy between counselor educators and their students (Miller & Larrabee, 1995). Thoreson, Shaughnessy, Heppner, and Cook (1993) surveyed male counselors and found that 16.9% admitted having sexual contact within professional relationships, with the majority occurring after the professional relationship had ended, a rate more similar to earlier studies involving psychologists. Additionally, Glaser and Thorpe (1986) investigated the issue of coercion. Of those individuals who reported sexual contact, the majority felt that they had not been coerced (72%). However, 51% saw some degree of coercion in retrospect. When asked their current opinion of sexual contact between educators and students, 95% considered it to be unethical and harmful, thus reflecting the wisdom of hindsight.

Despite percentages or hindsight reflections, whether with clients, supervisees, or students, sexual boundary transgressions involving supervisors are a documented occurrence in the mental health professions. All relevant ethical codes for the mental health professions make some reference to multiple relationships between supervisors and supervisees. Sexual issues between supervisors and supervisees have been addressed in several ways in the professional literature and will be separated here for discussion. These will be followed by nonsexual relationships that could involve boundary transgressions.

Sexual Attraction. Sexual attraction does not necessarily mean that a multiple relationship will develop. And yet, it is the wisdom of the profession, that, if not handled professionally, there is more of a chance that it will. In one study (Rodolfa, Rowen, Steier, Nicassio, & Gordon, 1994), one quarter of interns in postdoctoral internship sites reported feeling sexually attracted to their clinical supervisors. Ellis and Douce (1994) identified sexual attraction as one of eight recurring issues in supervision. Ladany et al. (1996) found that both counselor–client attraction issues and supervisee–supervisor attraction issues were among the topics that supervisees were unwilling to disclose in supervision (9% of study participants for each category). In a later study, Ladany and Melincoff (1999) found that 10% of supervisors also chose to be nondisclosive about their own attraction to their supervisees. Ellis and Douce further admonished that acting on sexual attraction in supervision results in "calamity."

Sexual Harassment. Unlike sexual attraction, sexual harassment is an aberration of the supervision process and is never acceptable. Sexual harassment clearly falls into Pearson and Piazza's (1997) category of the predatory professional. Those supervisors who expect or request sexual favors or who take sexual liberties with their supervisees are clearly in violation of all ethical codes for the helping professions. They have abused the power afforded them by to their professional status and serve as poor role models for future therapists (Corey, Corey, & Callanan, 2003). Sexual harassment can be insidious

and subtle, leaving the victims doubting themselves (Anonymous, 1991) and/or manipulated into the role of caretaker (Peterson, 1993).

DeMayo (2000) investigated the issue of sexual harassment from a different source. He looked at how supervisors reacted when supervisees reported sexual harassment by a client. In his study, 45% of experienced supervisors recalled at least one incident in which a supervisee had been harassed. A range of supervisor reactions followed such reports. Most supervisors discussed the incident in supervision, helped the supervisee to clarify events, and assisted the supervisee in establishing firm boundaries with the client. At other times, supervisors needed to be more directive, including having a joint session with the client, transferring the client to another therapist, or, in extreme cases, ensuring the safety of the supervisee. DeMayo suggested that all supervisees should have a conceptual framework for understanding harassment in therapy, ranging from understanding that sexualized feelings are commonplace to trusting their "gut" feelings of harassment. DeMayo also reiterated the suggestion of others that supervisors who are candid and self-disclose with their supervisees are more likely to hear about these important incidents from their supervisees.

Consensual (but hidden) Sexual Relationships. Results of national studies indicate that the majority of sexual relationships between supervisor and supervisees fall into this category. It is also assumed that the large majority of such relationships do not predate the supervision relationship. Therefore, they fall into Pearson and Piazza's role conflict category. It should be noted that the word "consensual" is used broadly. As reported earlier, in retrospect, many people believe that there was more coercion involved in a sexual relationship than they thought at the time. Furthermore, supervisors also tend to report that these transgressions occurred during times when they were struggling personally (Lamb et al., 2003). Because of the clear power differential between supervisor and supervisee, these relationships are both unethical and unwise. In the most measured of commentary, Bartell and Rubin (1990) advised that "[s]exual involvement may further a human relationship, but it does so at the expense of the professional relationship" (p. 446).

Intimate Committed Relationships. As Lamb et al. (2003) noted, a minority of intimate relationships that begin within supervision far outlive the supervisory relationship. In fact, most of us know at least one dual-career couple whose relationship began while one was in training and the other had supervisory status. In an acknowledgement of this reality, all mental health profession ethical codes, while advising caution, do not sanction relationships with former students or supervisees. The question, then, is not how to prevent such relationships from occurring, but how to assure that such a relationship poses no ethical compromise for the supervisor or supervisee and no negative consequence for the supervisee's clients.

An obvious characteristic of a healthy relationship is the fact that it is centered in respect and concern for all involved. Therefore, when either the supervisor or the supervisee becomes aware that feelings for the other are crossing a professional boundary, this is the time for a discussion to occur within supervision about the evolving relationship. Such a discussion will be made easier if the topic of sexual attraction has been normalized earlier in supervision (Ladany, O'Brien, Hill, Melincoff, Knox, & Petersen, 1997). If the outcome of the discussion is both people acknowledging that personal feelings are making a professional relationship difficult (and this would always be the case for intimate relationships), the supervisor and supervisee should begin a process of ending the supervisory relationship. It is never appropriate for a supervisor and supervisee to "try out" a personal relationship outside of supervision before taking steps to end their supervision relationship as this would be a clear case of an inappropriate multiple relationship.

Usually, another supervisor is easily available to take over the supervisory responsibilities. Consultation with the original supervisor may be

needed during a time of transition. If there are no other options, technology that may not have been available in the past offers possibilities for using a supervisor off-location. There is no reason for a professional couple to feel shame about an important relationship or to feel unethical because their feelings for one another began while one was supervisor and one was supervisee. It also is very important that those in administrative roles honor the attempt of the couple to be ethical and not treat the situation as an a priori ethical violation.

Nonsexual Multiple Relationships. Goodyear and Sinnett (1984) argued that it is inevitable that supervisors and their supervisees will have multiple relationships, an opinion shared by others (Aponte, 1994; Clarkson, 1994; Cornell, 1994; Gottlieb et al., 2007; Lamb, Catanzaro, & Moorman, 2004; Magnuson, Norem, & Wilcoxon, 2000; Ryder & Hepworth, 1990). The person who serves as a trainee's therapy supervisor could be a member of the same trainee's doctoral research committee, an instructor for another course, or the supervisor for an assistantship. In an agency or school, it sometimes happens that someone under supervision is the same person that the supervisor learned to count on in a crisis or is someone with a personal style that allows the supervisor to be more candid than he or she is with other professional peers. Some of these structured multiple professional relationships (Pearson & Piazza, 1997) are very gratifying, and we would not choose to avoid them. It seems to us, therefore, that we should approach this matter, as Aponte (1994) suggested, by attempting to differentiate between multiple relationships that abuse power, exploit supervisees, or harm the supervisee, and those that occur within the positive context of a maturing professional relationship.

Lloyd (1992) charged that some professional writings have created "dual relationship phobia" while simultaneously attempting to caution supervisors about unethical relationships. While Lloyd's point is well taken, Kolbert, Morgan, and Brendel (2002) found that, in general, students were more cautious about multiple relationships with faculty than were faculty. The authors of this qualitative study reported that students were concerned about special personal relationships between their peers and the counselor education faculty, fearing both the possibility of exploitation but also the possibility of favoritism. Kolbert et al. admonished faculty to be more sensitive to student reactions to multiple relationships. Similarly, Burian and Slimp (2000) cautioned supervisors of doctoral student interns about the potential risks involved when social multiple relationships emerge. These authors noted the intern's ability to leave the social relationship without repercussions, the probable impact on other interns, and the probable impact on other staff members as areas that supervisors needed to consider before encouraging such a relationship.

A unique study conducted by Lamb et al. (2004) asked psychologists the extent to which they discussed the issue of multiple relationships with their supervisees when these were imminent. They found that a large percentage of their respondents reported discussions about social interactions with their supervisees and additional collegial relationships. It would seem, therefore, that the conversations that have been called for by so many are occurring in certain contexts.

One area of multiple relationships for which there is particular agreement in the field, however, is the inappropriateness of doing therapy with one's supervisee. Because supervision can stimulate personal issues in the supervisee, it is quite likely that a supervisor will be faced with the challenge of determining where supervision ends and therapy begins (Whiston & Emerson, 1989; Wise, Lowery, & Silvergrade, 1989). In spite of some confusion, most authors (e.g., Bridges, 1999; Burns & Holloway, 1989; Green & Hansen, 1986; Kitchener, 1988; Patrick, 1989; Stout, 1987; Whiston & Emerson, 1989; Wise et al., 1989) recommend that supervisors be clear from the outset of supervision that personal issues might be activated in supervision and, if these issues are found to be substantial, that the supervisee will be asked to work through them with another professional. Normalizing the need to do one's own personal work is also advisable.

Preventing Supervisor Transgressions. Multiple relationships appear to exist on a behavioral continuum (Dickey, Housley, & Guest, 1993) from extremely inappropriate and unethical behavior; that is, from those included in Pearson and Piazza's (1997) predatory professional category, to behavior that could easily be construed as part of the mentoring process, such as taking a few students to a social occasion at a professional meeting. Neither end of the continuum causes much confusion among clinical supervisors. However, many situations in the middle represent "the murky pool of ambiguity" (Peterson, 1993, p. 1). Peterson cautioned that multiple relationship challenges abound in supervisory relationships and cannot be regulated out of existence. At the same time, Erwin (2000) found that supervisors displayed less "moral sensitivity" when things indeed were murky.

Gottlieb et al. (2007) also addressed the complexity of the issue. These authors made the salient point that supervisees frequently rate as their best supervisors those with whom they eventually developed positive personal relationships. In fact, we would argue that many students who seek training programs are looking for programs in which they will be mentored in a fashion that feels as personal as it does professional. Still, this fact does not alter the "slippery slope" about which supervisors must remain vigilant. Gottlieb et al. admonished that the greater the number of relationships, the more risk of boundary violation. Therefore, they suggested that supervisors ask themselves if any new relationship is really necessary. Would it be beneficial to the supervisee? Would it compromise the primary supervision relationship? They also advised supervisors to remain only in evaluative relationships with supervisees. Therefore, having a supervisee as a course teaching assistant should pose no serious issue. Finally, Gottlieb et al. suggested that "public" supervision (i.e., live supervision or group supervision) be used as well as individual supervision when multiple relationships exist so as to help reduce the risk of boundary violations.

Focusing on the supervisory relationship itself, Ladany et al. (2005) advised supervisors to take inventory of their own relationship biases.

What types of persons do they find attractive? Do they prefer supervisees who are dependent or who are autonomous? Are they pulled more by students who exhibit vulnerability or who are self-confident? Ladany et al. argued that such an a priori assessment will help to prepare the supervisor for attraction to a supervisee if it occurs.

Koenig and Spano (2003) proposed an educational approach similar to that suggested by Hamilton and Spruill (1999) to assist supervisees. Koenig and Spano criticized approaches to supervisor boundary violations that were psychodynamically oriented and looked for psychological problems within the supervisor and used psychotherapy as the sole solution. With sexual boundary violations in mind, Koenig and Spano echoed the thoughts of others that sexual attraction should be normalized. They also advised that supervisor training should include a comprehensive review of human sexuality and the interconnectedness of its various parts: sensuality, intimacy, sexual identity, reproduction, and sexualization. Their model is intuitively appealing as it is occasionally apparent that a person is attempting to use sexuality to influence another (sexualization) without the kind of openness that is essential for intimacy. Koenig and Spano not only argued that an increased awareness of human sexuality would serve them well in their work with supervisees, they asserted that through modeling and parallel process, improved ability to address sexual dynamics would be evident for supervisees as well.

Multiple relationships represent the broadest category of ethical challenges for the supervisor. Although the mental health professions have evolved in their understanding of multiple relationships, there is still much that calls for judgment one situation at a time.

Example: Vanessa has been a marriage and family therapist at an agency for 6 months. Gary, one of the other three therapists in the agency and the only other single therapist, is her clinical supervisor. It will take Vanessa 2 years under supervision to accrue the experience she needs to be eligible to sit for the state licensing examination for her LMFT. One evening Gary calls Vanessa to inquire whether she would like to go to a day-long workshop with him. The speaker for the workshop specializes in a kind of therapy in which Vanessa has expressed interest. Vanessa accepts and the workshop turns out to be an excellent professional experience. On the way home, Vanessa and Gary stop for dinner. Vanessa picks up the tab to thank Gary for including her.

The following day Vanessa is sharing some of the experiences of the workshop with Camille, another therapist at the agency. When Camille asks, "Isn't Gary your supervisor?" Vanessa feels defensive and misunderstood. Later that day, Vanessa decides to go to her agency director and ask his opinion of the situation. He tells her not to be concerned about it and that Camille "worries about everything." During her next supervision session, Vanessa chooses not to mention either conversation to Gary.

Is Gary in danger of violating the principle of avoiding multiple relationships? Has he already violated this principle? Was Camille's reaction appropriate? The agency director's? How do you evaluate Vanessa's choice to talk to her agency director? To not apprise Gary of the conversations with Camille and the agency director?

Example: Derek is a training director at a university counseling center. Gail is his new supervisee. Derek works hard to establish a positive working alliance with his supervisees. He believes it is important to establish a good relationship early in supervision. Gail ended the second supervision session asking Derek if he had a family. He told her that he was separated from his wife and had one small child. After the session, he was aware that his answer disclosed more than it needed to. He is also aware that he finds Gail very attractive and realizes that he will need to be careful about this. At the next supervision session, Gail arrives without any tape to review. She also seems to hold eye contact longer than in past sessions and is dressed in a manner that Derek finds extremely attractive. Derek decides not to push the issue of Gail coming without a tape and they spend the majority of the session continuing to get to know each other. After the session, hindsight again makes Derek feel uncomfortable about how the session transpired. He wonders if the attraction is mutual.

How should Derek proceed at this early juncture? How can he be sure that he is not projecting his own feelings onto Gail? What interventions should he consider? What if he is correct and he and Gail are mutually attracted to each other? Is this grounds for transferring Gail to another supervisor?

Example: Sharon is a good therapist. In her work with Jeanne, her supervisor, she has been very open and unguarded. Sharon had a very troubled past and she has struggled hard to get where she is. A couple of times Sharon has shared some of her personal pain with Jeanne during intense supervision sessions. Sharon and Jeanne feel very close to each other. In the past couple of weeks, Sharon has not looked well. She's jumpy and short with Jeanne. When Jeanne pursues this change in behavior, Sharon begins to cry and tells Jeanne that she has recently returned to an old cocaine habit. She begs Jeanne not to share her secret, promising that she will discontinue using the drug. She also asks that she be allowed to continue seeing clients.

How is power being negotiated in this example? How does each person stand to be damaged by this relationship? Has Jeanne been inappropriate up to this point? What should Jeanne do at this point to be ethical?

Example: Margaret is a school counselor who has been assigned a trainee from the local university for the academic year. As she observes Noah work with elementary school children, she is increasingly impressed with his skills. She asks him to work with Peter, a 9-year-old, who has not adjusted well to his parents' recent divorce. Again, she is impressed with Noah's skill, his warmth and understanding, and, ultimately, with the success he has in working with Peter. Margaret is a single parent who is concerned about her 9-year-old son. She decides to ask Noah to see him. Noah is complimented by her confidence in him. Margaret's son attends a different school, but she arranges to have Noah see him after school hours.

How is Noah vulnerable in this example? How is Margaret's son vulnerable? If Noah had had second thoughts about this situation, what are his recourses for resolution?

Competence

We all remember the feelings we had when we saw our first client. We might have doubted the sanity of

our supervisor to trust an incompetent with someone who had a problem. And if we were observed for that session, it was even worse. (One of us recalls a nightmare in which I am electrocuted by my audio recorder as I try to record my first counseling session!) For most of us, those feelings waned with time, helped by encouraging feedback from our supervisors, the accumulation of experience, and active reflection on both. The feelings also lessened as we grew to appreciate that counseling and therapy are at least part intuitive and probably a combination of many things, only some of which we control. Finally, the feelings diminished through the authenticity of the relationships that we shared with our clients and the positive results of those relationships. The issue of our own competence became less and less bothersome to us. Eventually, we felt good enough about our own abilities that we agreed to supervise the work of another. Now we are involved in the developmental process at two levels: We are overseers of the initial steps taken by our supervisees while we continue to develop ourselves and, at times, we can appreciate how far we have come by observing the tentative work of those under our supervision.

There is something very self-assuring about having some experience and being able to see from where one has come. There also is something seductive, and even dangerous, about being in such a position: Supervisors can forget to question their own competence. This is not to imply that it is admirable to remain professionally insecure, but that it is vital for supervisors to remember that the issue of competence is one of the most central questions in the process of clinical supervision. Supervisors must remain competent not only as therapists, but also as judges of another's abilities, while being competent in many facets of supervision itself (Falender & Shafranske, 2007; Knapp & Vande-Creek, 2006). In fact, the whole issue of competence, both for supervisors and supervisees, is central to the most pressing ethical responsibility of all, that of monitoring client welfare (Sherry, 1991).

Monitoring Supervisee Competence. By definition, most supervisees are not yet competent to practice independently. But if supervisees are to improve as practitioners, they must be challenged. Attending to the best interests of both client and supervisee simultaneously is the greatest clinical and ethical challenge of supervision (Sherry, 1991). Furthermore, monitoring supervisee competence begins with the assumption that the supervisor is a knowledgeable clinician.

The first of 11 core areas promulgated by ACES in the Standards for Counseling Supervisors (Supervision Interest Network, 1990) requires that the supervisor be an effective counselor. The supervisor must be more advanced than the supervisee in all areas in which the supervisee is practicing. This relates not only to the generic practice of counseling and psychotherapy, but to specific clinical problems as well. Most supervisors realize that they cannot be all things to all people. Yet they are tempted to ignore this bit of wisdom when a supervisee wants to gain some experience in an area in which the supervisor is unfamiliar. The helping professions, for better or for worse, have become fields with many specialties. At times it can be a difficult decision whether the supervisor's skills are sufficient to supervise in a particular area (e.g., Stratton & Smith, 2006). Supervisors would be wise to have a clear sense of the kinds of cases that they would either not supervise or would supervise only under certain conditions (e.g., for a limited number of sessions, for the purposes of referral, or, as suggested by Hall, 1988a; and Sherry, 1991, with the aid of a consultant).

As the field has become more aware of the importance of cultural factors in therapy, competence in cultural matters has been included as a significant area to be monitored by supervisors (ACA, 2005; D'Andrea & Daniels, 1997; Gonzalez, 1997; Lopez, 1997; Pack-Brown & Williams, 2003; Sherry, 1991; Vasquez, 1992). Again, such competence must first be acquired by the supervisor in order for the supervisor to assist the supervisee to work with persons representing diverse groups, as well as for the supervisor to be successful on this dimension in supervisory relationships. We will discuss this issue in greater detail in Chapter 5.

Finally, Vasquez (1992) noted that part of the responsibility of the supervisor is to help the supervisee become a self-evaluator. In other words, if one of the ethical mandates of all helping professions is to practice only within one's competence, supervisees must become able to make such determinations for themselves. The relevance of this admonition was confirmed by research conducted by Neukrug, Milliken, and Walden (2001), in which incompetence was found to be the second most frequent complaint made to counseling licensure boards. Yet, as we discussed in Chapter 2, the jury is still out regarding a supervisor's ability to influence the important skill of self-assessment.

Competence in the Practice of Supervision. As the knowledge and skill base for clinical supervision has increased, it has become more compulsory that supervisors be competent in the practice of supervision above and beyond their competence as a therapist. Although there are examples of professions already demanding such competence for clinical supervisors (e.g., AAMFT), this expectation is not yet uniform. At the same time, the expectation that clinical supervisors have training in supervision is growing. Borders and Cashwell (1992) surveyed legislation regarding supervisor criteria and conduct of supervision for counselor licensure applicants and found that few state boards recognized the need for specialized training in supervision. Several years later, however, Sutton, Nielson, and Essex (1998) found that 17 boards obligated supervisors to be trained in supervision, with other boards considering this requirement. Goodyear (2007) strongly asserted that at this point in the evolution of the mental health professions, a clinical supervisor must be trained in supervision in order to be considered competent.

If, as Rinas and Clyne-Jackson (1988) charged, training program faculty are too academic in their approach to supervision, it is sometimes the case that field supervisors are too caught up in their immediate context and do not stay abreast of changes in national standards for practice. Navin,

Beamish, and Johanson (1995) studied the ethics practice of field supervisors and compared them to the ACES Ethical Guidelines for Counseling Supervisors (Supervision Interest Network, 1993). Whether the problem was standards that are too lofty or field settings that lack adequate regulation, these authors found a good bit of disparity between standards and practice, at least for the supervision of master's level practitioners. Disney and Stephens (1994) noted that national standards (such as those for counseling supervisors) may represent the ideal and that liability is more likely to be determined using state standards. However, the court may refer to such standards as a guide. It would be an error, therefore, to assume that national standards are irrelevant for local practice (Guest & Dooley, 1999).

Remaining Competent. Many seasoned professionals become complacent with their degree of competence and wean themselves from the professional literature and/or attendance at professional meetings or workshops (Campbell, 1994). When licenses or certifications do not require continuing education, this separation from the evolution of mental health practice can be complete (Overholser & Fine, 1990). Although most professionals would probably agree with the necessity of continuing education for all practitioners, and for supervisors in particular, the task itself can be daunting. Not only should supervisors be current in their own professional specialties, but they should also be aware of the substantial developments that are being made in the area of clinical supervision (Falender & Shafranske, 2007). Some would add that supervisors should be at least minimally aware of specialties that coincide with their own. And, as has already been stated, awareness of current developments to assist an understanding of the impact of cultural phenomena in both therapy and supervision is also required.

In addition to continuing education, a liberal use of consultation with professional peers is important to prevent the kind of isolation that diminishes competence (Sherry, 1991). Supervision is a serious

activity and one with unforeseen challenges. It is important that a supervisor have a network of colleagues for consultation so that the demands of supervision can be met adequately.

Being able to consult with a colleague seems especially important when trying to balance the client's therapy needs with the supervisee's training needs (Upchurch, 1985). There can be a rather narrow band of case complexity that will challenge the supervisee without jeopardizing the client. Furthermore, interactions with another supervisor can increase a supervisor's skills in ways that may not have been predicted.

> *Example:* Dwayne has been a licensed psychologist in private practice for over 20 years. His therapeutic approach is primarily psychodynamic. Dwayne receives a call from a small group practice consisting of mental health counselors and marriage and family therapists. They are looking for a psychologist who wants to contract with them for supervision. Their interest is mostly that the psychologist be able to evaluate certain clients for possible referral to a psychologist or a psychiatrist. Dwayne has never supervised anyone and is ready for a new challenge. He makes an appointment to meet with the staff of the practice group.

What are the competency issues embedded in this example? If Dwayne decides to take this group on, what does he need to consider in order to be ethically sound? What conditions for supervision are advisable? As you understand it, is this arrangement legally defensible?

Confidentiality

Confidentiality is the ethical principle given the most attention in most training programs. In addition to liability concerns, we believe this is so because confidentiality represents the essence of counseling and therapy (a safe place where secrets and hidden fears can be exposed) and because much of our professional status comes from being the bearer of such private information. We earn our clients' respect and the respect of others by the posture we take toward confidentiality. In recent years, however, confidentiality has become the stepsibling to safety and judicial judgment. As a result, the issues surrounding confidentiality have become more complicated. Pope and Vetter (1992) surveyed more than 1,300 psychologists about incidents that they found ethically troubling. Of the 703 incidents reported, the greatest number (128) fell into the category of confidentiality. Similarly, Fly et al. (1997) found that the most frequent trainee ethical violation concerned confidentiality. Therefore, it seems that the most sacred trust in mental health practice is also the most vulnerable to insult. And as with all therapeutic components, the implications for supervision are more complex still.

The supervisor must be sure that the supervisee keeps confidential all client information except for the purposes of supervision. Because supervision allows for a third-party discussion of the therapy situation, the supervisee must be reminded that this type of discourse cannot be repeated elsewhere. In group supervision, the supervisor must reiterate this point and take the extra precaution of having cases presented using first names only and with as few demographic details as possible (Strein & Hershenson, 1991). When videotape or live supervision is employed with additional supervisees present, the only recourse for the supervisor is to emphasize and reemphasize the importance of confidentiality. When students are asked to tape their sessions, they must be reminded that they have in their possession confidential documents. Notes on clients should use code numbers rather than names and be guarded with great care.

To what extent supervisee information will be regarded as confidential is really an informed consent issue. Because supervision is essentially an evaluative relationship, information received in supervision is not typically considered confidential and ethical codes are silent on this issue. In fact, the gatekeeping responsibility of supervisors may require that supervisors share personal information of supervisees with others. Still, best practice would include clear guidelines that are presented to supervisees prior to the beginning of supervision. These guidelines should indicate that the goal of supervision is the professional development of the supervisee and that personal information will be

honored and treated as sensitively as possible. For example, the trainee might share some painful aspect of childhood as it relates to a client. The divulging of such information might come from the trainee's concern that personal history should not detract from therapy and with the request that the supervisor monitor the case more closely. As long as the trainee is successful in this goal, this information should be considered confidential. Most trainees understand that training in a mental health profession will include personal development that may involve grappling with personal issues. Still, knowing that evaluative information from supervision may be passed along to faculty and that any particular issue that troubles the supervisor may be discussed with faculty colleagues allows the supervisee to make an informed decision about what to reveal in supervision (Sherry, 1991). It has also been our experience that issues that ultimately need to be shared in evaluations are rarely about trainee secrets and more about patterns of behavior that are fairly obvious.

There is still some occasional confusion in the helping professions regarding the distinctions between confidentiality, privacy, and privileged communication. Confidentiality is defined by Siegel (1979) as follows: "Confidentiality involves professional ethics rather than any legalism and indicates an explicit promise or contract to reveal nothing about an individual except under conditions agreed to by the source or subject" (p. 251). Privacy is the other side of confidentiality. It is the client's right not to have private information divulged without informed consent, including the information gained in therapy. Privileged communication, on the other hand, is a legal concept based on state statute. It refers to the right of clients not to have their confidential communications used in open court without their consent. Therefore, "although all privileged communications are confidential communications, some confidential communications may not be privileged" (Disney & Stephens, 1994, p. 26).

Although these three terms are vital in therapy and supervision, they are not absolute. In fact, knowing the limits of each is as serious a responsibility for the clinician as honoring their intent. It is ultimately an individual decision as to when the therapist or supervisor will decide to overturn the client's (or supervisee's) right of privacy and break confidentiality. However, in a number of cases either legal precedent, state law, or a value of a higher order dictates such a direction. Those typically included as exceptions to privilege are reported by Falvey (2002) as follows:

- When a client gives informed consent to disclosure
- When a therapist is acting in a court-appointed capacity
- When there is a suicidal risk or some other life-threatening emergency
- When a client initiates litigation against the therapist
- When a client's mental health is introduced as part of a civil action
- When a child under the age of 16 is the victim of a crime
- When a client requires psychiatric hospitalization
- When a client expresses intent to commit a crime that will endanger society or another person (duty to warn)
- When a client is deemed to be dangerous to himself or herself
- When required for third-party billing authorized by the client
- When required for properly utilized fee collection services (p. 93)

Because privileged communication is a legal matter, it is always wise to receive legal counsel when confidential information is demanded. Outside court proceedings, many situations fall into gray areas.

The trend in the helping professions seems to be toward a less robust view of confidentiality. This professional obligation seems to be increasingly vulnerable to legal interpretation (Falvey, 2002). It is considered wise, therefore, to make a discussion of confidentiality and its limits a common practice in therapy and supervision.

Marketplace Issues

As more states pass legislation to regulate all the mental health professions, the need for clinical supervisors to supervise postacademic professionals is increasing (Magnuson, Norem, & Wilcoxon, 2000). At the same time, changes in mental health delivery systems require that supervisors stay informed so as to keep supervisees informed and to avoid any business arrangements that would prove to be unethical and/or illegal.

A common practice of the past involved the supervisor "signing off" for supervisees, often not because supervision was taking place but because the supervisor's credentials allowed for third-party payment, whereas the supervisee's did not. This practice is, of course, unethical and illegal. But other marketplace issues are more ambiguous ethically. For example, should a supervisor accept payment from a supervisee for supervision that will lead to certification or licensure? Under what conditions might this be acceptable? If one is a supervisor for someone outside one's place of employment, what kinds of protections are necessary for the clients of the supervisee? The supervisee? The supervisor? (Wheeler & King, 2000). How do particular third-party payers affect supervisory practice? What is the implication of supervising counseling services offered over the Internet (Kanz, 2001; Maheu & Gordon, 2000)? In short, the marketplace is changing dramatically as a result of legislation, changes in health-care systems, and advances in technology. It is the ethical and legal responsibility of clinical supervisors to stay abreast of relevant developments and to assure that supervisees' practice is consistent with ethical mandates and the law.

The Supervisee's Perspective

Most of the data we have regarding ethical issues come from therapists or supervisors. Furthermore, the ethical issues addressed are those that can manifest in either therapy or supervision (e.g., boundary violations). In contrast, Worthington, Tan, and Poulin (2002) conducted an exploratory investigation of supervisee ethical behavior that focused specifically on supervision issues. In their distinctive study, they conceptualized supervisee transgressions to include themes such as intentional nondisclosure (to supervisors) of important information, mismanagement of case records, actively operating at an inappropriate level of autonomy, failure to address (in supervision) personal biases that impact counseling, inappropriate methods of managing conflict with supervisors, and failure to engage in necessary professional development activities. The authors identified 31 questionable behaviors and asked more than 300 supervisors and supervisees (combined) to judge each item on its ethicality. Twenty-eight of their items were viewed as more unethical than ethical and there was relatively high agreement between supervisors and supervisees about these behaviors. The behaviors ranged from forging a supervisor's signature on case material (viewed as most unethical) to gossiping about a conflict with her/his supervisor without discussing the issue in supervision (considered mildly unethical). As a second function of the study, supervisees were asked to report how frequently they had engaged in each behavior. As might be expected, supervisees engaged in behaviors considered less unethical more often than the most egregious behaviors. Finally, supervisees were asked to identify reasons for engaging in ethically questionable conduct. Six reasons surfaced as most prevalent: (1) It is an indirect way of coping with or expressing my feelings toward my supervisor; (2) My personal problems sometimes affect my judgment; (3) I feel that I should be given more professional autonomy; (4) My relationship with my supervisor feels unsafe; (5) Sometimes I feel like I know more than my supervisor does; and (6) My workload is too heavy (pp. 342–343).

While the Worthington et al. (2002) study was descriptive in nature and based on self-report, it offers a unique glimpse into the many aspects of supervision that have ethical implications. The authors rightly concluded that their data contain implications for training as well as for monitoring supervisees. Future research in this area would be fruitful.

LEGAL RAMIFICATIONS FOR CLINICAL SUPERVISORS

Malpractice

An ethical violation becomes a legal issue when the aggrieved party makes such a claim (Maki & Bernard, 2007). In other words, the difference between a claim of an ethical violation and a claim of malpractice is not determined by the egregiousness of the behavior committed by the supervisee, counselor–therapist, or supervisor. Rather, it is determined by whether the aggrieved choose to bring their complaints to a regulatory body or to civil court. In fact, it is not uncommon for the same claim to be brought to both a regulatory body and to court as a malpractice lawsuit (Montgomery, Cupit, & Wimberley, 1999). That being said, it is safe to assume that there are far more complaints made to regulatory bodies than there are lawsuits. There are at least two reasons for this: (1) the cost of litigation is a deterrent and (2) whereas a regulatory body (peer review board) would investigate whether the professional breached relevant professional ethics, civil court is quite different. Briefly, a legal complaint is restricted by tort law; therefore, the defendant must be able to prove that the negligence claimed resulted in harm. Many complaints cannot meet such a level of proof.

There are two types of torts (i.e., civil wrongs other than breach of contract): intentional and unintentional (Swenson, 1997). It is highly unlikely that the therapist or supervisor would be sued for an intentional tort. For this to be the case, the intention of the supervisor or therapist would be to cause harm. As an example, a supervisor and therapist may decide to suggest to a client behavior that they believe will cause her to lose her job (thinking, perhaps, that she needs to experience such a crisis to face some intrapsychic issues). Such a case could be argued under intentional tort. Similarly, a supervisor could decide to be overly critical with a supervisee in order to force the supervisee out of a training program. Again, this kind of Machiavellian behavior would fall under intentional tort law.

Virtually all malpractice cases in the mental health professions, however, are unintentional torts, or negligence cases (Swenson, 1997). Malpractice is defined as "harm to another individual due to negligence consisting of the breach of a professional duty or standard of care. If, for example, a mental health professional fails to follow acceptable standards of practice and harm to clients results, the professional is liable for the harm caused" (Disney & Stephens, 1994, p. 7). Similarly, failure to act on serious concerns about a supervisee may be grounds for negligent supervision (Recupero & Rainey, 2007). Four elements must be proved for a plaintiff to succeed in a malpractice claim (Ogloff & Olley, 1998): (1) A fiduciary relationship with the therapist (or supervisor) must have been established. Within supervision, this means that the supervisor is working in the best interests of the supervisee and the supervisee's clients and not in his or her own interests (Remley & Herlihy, 2001); (2) the therapist's (or supervisor's) conduct must have been improper or negligent and have fallen below the acceptable standard of care; (3) the client (or supervisee) must have suffered harm or injury, which must be demonstrated; and (4) a causal relationship must be established between the injury and the negligence or improper conduct. We are not aware of any suits brought against supervisors by trainees for inadequate supervision. It is more likely that supervisors would be involved in legal action as a codefendant in a malpractice suit (Snider, 1985) based on the alleged inadequate performance of the supervisee.

Therapists' (and supervisors') vulnerability is directly linked to their assumption of professional roles. When they take on the role of therapist or supervisor, they are expected to know and follow the law, as well as the profession's accepted practice and ethical standards. Additionally, though it is not uncommon to hear professionals bemoan the increasing litigiousness of society, at least part of the problem seems to lie with faulty self-regulation within the mental health professions. Research seems to support that helping professionals have great difficulty in judging peers' or

sometimes even supervisees' competence (Forrest et al., 1999; Haas, Malouf, & Mayerson, 1986) and are reluctant to report known ethical violations of peers or supervisees (Bernard & Jara, 1986; King & Wheeler, 1999) or peers or supervisees who are professionally impaired (Forrest et al., 1999; Wood, Klein, Cross, Lammers, & Elliot, 1985).

Sociological factors also contribute to the increase in lawsuits against helping professionals. Cohen's (1979) claim seems even more relevant today that the three primary factors for the increase are (1) a general decline in the respect afforded helping professionals by clients and society at large, (2) increased awareness of consumer rights in general, and (3) highly publicized malpractice suits for which settlements were enormous, leading to the conclusion that a lawsuit may be a means to obtain easy money. All these factors increase the likelihood of potential lawsuits (however spurious) against the practitioner (however ethical). As M. H. Williams (2000) observed, there is little that therapists or supervisors can do to totally protect themselves from persons who attempt to use the court for disturbed or vengeful reasons. At the same time, there are some precautions that professionals can take, and these will be covered later in this section.

Although failure to warn accounts for a very small number of legal claims (Meyer et al., 1988), the Tarasoff case has made this issue highly visible. The Tarasoff case also involved a clinical supervisor and thus introduces the concept of vicarious liability or *respondeat superior* (literally, "let the master answer"). Following the discussion regarding the duty to warn, therefore, will be a review of salient direct and vicarious liability issues.

The Duty to Warn. The duty to warn is a prime example of a legal precedent becoming a direct influence on ethical codes. The duty to warn stems from the famous Tarasoff case (Tarasoff vs. Regents of the University of California, 1976). In the landmark case, a university therapist believed that his client (Poddar) was dangerous and might do harm to a woman who had rejected Poddar's romantic advances (Tatiana Tarasoff). Because Poddar refused voluntary hospitalization, the therapist notified police to have him taken to a state hospital for involuntary hospitalization. The police spoke to Poddar and decided that he was not dangerous. On the advice of his supervisor, who feared a lawsuit for breach of confidence (Lee & Gillam, 2000), the therapist did not pursue the matter further. Poddar did not return to therapy. Two months later Poddar killed Tarasoff. Although most mental health professionals believe that the Tarasoffs won this case based on the duty to warn, actually the court only determined that they could file a suit on these grounds. Rather, the case was settled out of court (Meyer et al., 1988). Furthermore, the Supreme Court of the State of California actually heard the Tarasoff case twice and articulated the duty to protect at this second hearing (Chaimowitz, Glancy, & Blackburn, 2000). Chaimowitz et al. argued that the duty to warn, therefore, must be assessed as it relates to the duty to protect. They further asserted that warning an intended victim may be insufficient to meeting the duty to protect. They also noted that there may be times that warning could actually exacerbate a tenuous situation. In short, these authors suggested that more than a knee-jerk decision to warn is called for; rather, a reasoned strategy that holds the duty to protect at its center is recommended.

In spite of the ambiguous outcome of the original case, the duty to warn and protect has become a legal standard for all mental health professionals and has become the law in several states. It remains an important case for supervisors as well as therapists, because the supervisor was implicated in the case.

It is imperative, then, for supervisors to inform supervisees of conditions under which it would be appropriate to implement the duty to inform for the protection of an intended victim(s). Two issues are embedded in the duty to warn and protect: assessing the level of dangerousness of the client and the identifiability of potential victims (Ahia & Martin, 1993; Lee & Gillam, 2000). The practitioner and supervisor are not expected to see

the unforeseeable. There is no foolproof way to predict all human behavior. Rather, there is an expectation that sound judgment is used and reasonable or due care is taken regarding the determination of dangerousness. For this reason, most authorities on such legal matters strongly advise that consultation with others and documentation of all decisions are vital in any questionable case.

The second embedded issue emerges when there is some indication that the client might be dangerous, but no potential victim has been named. In fact, there might not be a particular person in danger; rather, the client's hostility might be nonspecific. At present, ethical standards and legal experts seem to lean in favor of client privilege unless there is clear evidence that the client is immediately dangerous and there is an identifiable (or highly likely) victim (Ahia & Martin, 1993; Fulero, 1988; Lee & Gillam, 2000; Schutz, 1982; Woody and Associates, 1984). In other words, therapists and supervisors are not expected to, nor should they, read between the lines when working with clients. Many clients make idle threats when they are frustrated. It is the job of mental health practitioners to make a reasonable evaluation of these threats. In fact, in the eyes of the law, it is more important that reasonable evaluation be made than that the prediction be accurate.

Direct Liability and Vicarious Liability

Direct liability would be argued when the actions of the supervisor were themselves the cause of harm. For example, if the supervisor did not perform supervision adequate for a novice counselor or if the supervisor suggested (and documented) an intervention that was determined to be the cause of harm (e.g., suggesting that a client use "tough love" strategies with a child, which resulted in physical harm to the child). Results reported by Montgomery et al. (1999) suggested that direct liability is still rare for supervisors, though two reported malpractice suits involved supervision (evaluation of a supervisee and a billing issue). Potentially, all supervision practice standards, if violated, could lead to a supervisor being found to be directly liable. These include issues such as violation of informed consent, breach of confidentiality, inability to work with cultural differences, or an inappropriate multiple relationship (Maki & Bernard, 2007).

Vicarious liability, on the other hand, represents possibly the worst nightmare for the clinical supervisor; that is, being held liable for the actions of the supervisee when these were not suggested or perhaps even known by the supervisor. In such cases, the supervisor becomes liable by virtue of the relationship with the supervisee. Therefore, the supervisor generally is only held liable "for the negligent acts of supervisees if these acts are performed in the course and scope of the supervisory relationship" (Disney & Stephens, 1994, p. 15). Falvey (2002) outlined three conditions that must be met for vicarious liability to be established:

1. Supervisees must voluntarily agree to work under the direction and control of the supervisor and act in ways that benefit the supervisor (e.g., see clients who might otherwise need to be seen by the supervisor).
2. Supervisees must be acting within the defined scope of tasks permitted by the supervisor.
3. The supervisor must have the power to control and direct the supervisee's work. (pp. 17–18)

Disney and Stephens (1994) reported additional factors that might be used to establish whether an action fell within the scope of the supervisory relationship. These included the time, place, and purpose of the act (e.g., was it done during counseling or away from the place of counseling?); the motivation of the supervisee (e.g., was the supervisee attempting to be helpful?); and whether the supervisor could have reasonably expected the supervisee to commit the act (p. 16). Disney and Stephens (1994) observed that, should the supervisor be found guilty based on vicarious responsibility, then the supervisor, if found not to be negligent in subsequent court proceedings, could recover damages from the supervisee.

Despite these stated parameters, some court cases demonstrate a more far-reaching responsibility for supervisors. For example, Recupero

and Rainey (2007) reported one case (*Simmons vs. United States*) where respondeat superior was used to hold a social work supervisor liable for the sexual misconduct of the supervisee. The court argued that the supervisee had mishandled transference, which was ruled as a foreseeable supervision issue. Recupero and Rainey therefore advised that "prudent supervisors aware of this risk, may watch carefully for early warning signs of boundary violation" (p. 192).

Remley and Herlihy (2001) cautioned that each legal case is unique; therefore, generalizability from one situation to another may be limited. They stressed the importance of establishing the amount of control a supervisor had over a supervisee in order to arrive at a judgment of vicarious liability. Because of this, they indicated that supervisors at the clinical site are more likely to be held accountable for a therapist's negligence than off-site (e.g., university) supervisors. Recupero and Rainey (2007) also noted that direct contact with a supervisee's clients or patients increased supervisor vulnerability. While acknowledging the general principle that more control over the supervisee generally increases the risk of liability for the supervisor, Hall, Macvaugh, Meridith, and Montgomery (2007) argued that supervisor remoteness was not a protection. Rather, it may be asserted that supervisors must be as vigilant as their role would dictate. Going back to Remley and Herlihy's example, it stands to reason that a campus supervisor who is receiving information about a client seen elsewhere is not being remote but, rather, is fulfilling a role different from that of a supervisor on site. Still, if a campus supervisor should receive information that causes concern, the supervisor should act on the concern, which often entails contacting the site directly.

Moving to the contractual arrangements between supervisor and supervisee, Falvey (2002) speculated that supervisors who received part of a fee paid to a supervisee were more likely to be found vicariously liable, because such a situation clearly benefits the supervisor, meeting one of the conditions for vicarious liability. Finally, Knapp and VandeCreek (2006) observed that supervisors who have followed reasonable standards of practice may be unaware of a supervisee's actions that were contrary to what the supervisor had advised or instructed. In such a case, Knapp and VandeCreek advised that the supervisor might be exonerated. Still, these authors cautioned that supervisors should not count on such exoneration. In short, relatively close supervision may be the best antidote for a claim of vicarious liability.

Preventing Claims of Malpractice

Snider (1985) offered four guidelines to supervisors to reduce the likelihood of being named as a codefendant in a malpractice suit; the guidelines continue to be relevant today. First, maintain a trusting relationship with supervisees. Within a context of mutual trust and respect, supervisees will be far more likely to voice their concerns about their clients, themselves, and their work. Second, keep up to date regarding legal issues that affect mental health settings and the profession in general. Additionally, supervisors need to have a healthy respect for the complexity of the law and recognize the need for competent legal aid. Third, if the supervisor is the administrative head of an agency, it is essential that the supervisor retain the services of an attorney who specializes in malpractice litigation. If this is not the supervisor's decision, the supervisor should be sure that the organization has appropriate legal support. Fourth, supervisors should have adequate liability insurance and should be sure that their supervisees also carry liability insurance. Although this final precaution does not reduce the chances of being sued, it does, obviously, minimize the damage that could accrue from such an unfortunate experience.

In addition to these admonitions, supervisors are advised to stay current with professional standards of practice and to seek consultation with trusted colleagues when necessary (Ogloff & Olley, 1998). It is also wise to establish boundary expectations with supervisees (Recupero & Rainey, 2007). Another important risk-management strategy is record keeping (Falvey, Caldwell, &

Cohen, 2002; Recupero & Rainey, 2007; Woodworth, 2000). Methods of documenting supervision will be covered in Chapter 8. Finally, Woodworth (2000) also recommended that helping professionals (including supervisors) attend to their emotional and physical well-being. Being professionally or personally overextended is too often a precursor to making foolish errors.

Regrettably, there is little comfort to offer the timid supervisor who is afraid of the tremendous responsibility and potential legal liability inherent in supervision. Short of refusing to supervise, we believe protection for the supervisor lies in the same concepts of reasonable care and sound judgment that protect counselors and therapists. This includes an awareness of and command of the concepts and skills presented in this book. It also includes a commitment to investing the time and energy to supervise adequately and to document all supervisory contacts. Ultimately, the most fruitful approach to practice "involves a unique blend of professional wisdom and human wisdom. In addition to some distinct knowledge, skill, and good work habits, healthy, respectful relationships and keen, unencumbered self-knowledge add significant protection to the clinical supervisor. In short, insight, integrity, and goodwill are enormous barriers to professional difficulty" (Maki & Bernard, 2007, p. 363).

ETHICAL DECISION MAKING

As we already have conveyed, the relationship between ethics and the law is generally perceived to be very close. This is not only true for the human services, but also for society at large. The great danger of this perception is the pairing of what is "right" with "what I can get away with," leaving only "what I can't get away with" as "wrong." Knowing full well that most unethical behavior is not confronted, the practitioner becomes more vulnerable to losing sight of the moral constants. The potential consequence is that the helping professions become another example of the law dictating professional ethics or, at worst, professional behavior dictated by self-interest.

The only reasonable alternative to this approach is putting ethics in the foreground, in both training and practice, for therapists and clinical supervisors—a suggestion supported by research conducted by Cikanek, McCarthy Veach, and Braun (2004). Cikanek et al. conducted a qualitative investigation of advanced doctoral students in psychology and found their knowledge and understanding of supervision ethical responsibilities to be uneven. Therefore, approaches to mastery of supervision ethical issues should be proactive and not reactive. Waiting for ethical issues to emerge in supervision seems to set up the conditions for crisis training, not ethics training.

Ethical practice is a way of professional existence, not only a command of a body of knowledge. Handelsman, Gottlieb, and Knapp (2005) referred to the acculturation process whereby students entering mental health training programs are asked to become members of a professional culture. They warned that mishaps may occur in this acculturation process just as has been observed for other acculturation processes, leading to practitioners who are separated or marginalized from their profession's code of ethics. Viewing ethics training as an acculturation process may, in itself, enrich the discourse and sensitize supervisors to their own and their supervisees' development.

One aid to ethical development is for training programs to use experiential learning and/or case analysis (cf. Storm & Haug, 1997). Many ethical mishaps result from acts of omission, not intentional malice (Bernard, 1981). Such omissions are more likely if professionals have not had an opportunity to experience the ins and outs of a similar situation. The use of simulation and behavioral rehearsal is an excellent way to safely allow both trainees and supervisors to face difficult situations, try alternative resolutions, and evaluate their outcomes.

Hansen and Goldberg (1999) outlined a seven-category matrix of considerations that could be used to assess ethical and legal dilemmas, both in training and in actual situations. They rightly argued that a linear model of ethical decision making, one that begins by identifying an ethical dilemma and ends with a decision to act, belies the complexity of most situations with ethical and legal overtones. By considering multiple influencing variables as interfaced with a linear process, the mental health professional is more likely to arrive at a sound course of action.

Hansen and Goldberg reiterated the work of others (e.g., Kitchener, 1984) that moral principles are of primary importance when evaluating a difficult situation. The principles that Kitchener advocated are autonomy (both being responsible for one's behavior and having freedom of choice), beneficence (contributing to the well-being of others), nonmaleficence ("above all, do no harm"), justice (fairness in dealings with all people), and fidelity (the promotion of honesty and fulfilling commitments and contracts). Tarvydas (1995) noted that much of our influence on supervisees may lie in our ability to model these principles. In addition to these, Hansen and Goldberg (1999) asserted that professionals are influenced by personal (e.g., political or religious) values, what Handelsman et al. (2005) referred to as "ethics of origin" (p. 59). Training in ethical decision making that does not acknowledge the importance of personal values does trainees an injustice.

Hansen and Goldberg's second consideration involved clinical and cultural factors. For example, as stated earlier in our discussion about the duty to warn, the therapist and supervisor must make an assessment of a client's level of risk in order to make an informed decision about a course of action. What may be ethical in one situation may violate a client's rights in another. In addition to clinical assessment, cultural assessments must be made. Hansen and Goldberg noted, for example, that the boundaries of confidentiality can take on different meaning when viewed with cultural sensitivity.

Hansen and Goldberg's next four considerations are less fluid and include professional codes of ethics; agency or employer policies; federal, state, and local statutes; and rules and regulations that elaborate statutes. All these call for a certain amount of vigilance from the professional to stay informed about changes in professional and regulatory pronouncements. At the same time, it must be said that codes, statutes, rules, and regulations are not sufficient for all (even most) difficult situations. In fact, Pope and Bajt (1988, as referenced in Hansen and Goldberg) found that 75% of a sample of senior psychologists, all of whom were known for ethics expertise, believed that formal codes and statutes should sometimes be violated to ensure client welfare or because of personal values.

Finally, Hansen and Goldberg identified case law as an important consideration when making an ethical decision. Because case law calls for interpretation regarding its relevance for a particular ethical or legal dilemma, it could be viewed as more fluid than statutes and codes of ethics. Additionally, case law represents the history of our most dramatic struggles as mental health professionals, thus providing a rich context for deliberation.

Betan and Stanton (1999) added another dimension to ethical decision making that goes beyond personal beliefs and values. They studied the effect of concerns and emotions on willingness to implement ethical knowledge and found that anxiety or guilt interfered with action, whereas compassion (i.e., concern, empathy, and loyalty) and confidence that a situation can change (i.e., optimism) enhanced action. These findings need to be addressed adequately in training for ethical decision making. Betan and

Stanton concluded that awareness of how one's emotions may be influencing ethical decision making can lead to appropriate management of these emotions.

Finally, once we have carefully attended to the multiple factors already noted, we must eventually return to a process that will end in some form of resolution. This includes consideration of alternative courses of action (often weighing one aspect of the situation against another), an attempt to predict the consequences of each potential course (both short term and long term and for each of the parties involved), and making a decision about which course of action to take that includes a willingness to take responsibility for the consequences of the selected action (Hadjistavropoulos & Malloy, 2000).

CONCLUSION

As gatekeepers of the profession, clinical supervisors will continue to be heavily involved with ethical standards for practice. The most instrumental approach to this responsibility is to be well informed and personally and professionally sanguine. Both are accomplished by continually putting ethics in the foreground of discussion, contemplation, and practice. In this case, perhaps more than any other, supervisors' primary responsibility is to model what they aspire to teach.

CHAPTER 4

SUPERVISION MODELS

Theories enable us to make sense of what otherwise might be overwhelming amounts of information. As Schermer (2001) noted, "The facts never just speak for themselves. They must be interpreted through the colored lenses of ideas: percepts need concepts" (p. XI). Lewin (1951) was more direct in stating a similar point: "there is nothing so practical as a good theory" (p. 169). We noted in Chapter 1 that one characteristic of professionals is that they typically make decisions under conditions of uncertainty: It is *theory* that enables them to do so.

Schermer characterized theory as a lens, which is a useful metaphor. Such a lens helps to focus our attention on particular phenomena and therefore to make sense of the "blooming buzzing confusion" of our worlds (James, 1890/1981, p. 462). In supervision, that confusing world includes the behaviors, attitudes, and feelings of a client, of the supervisee, and of the supervisor, as well as interactions among them. It would be impossible for a supervisor to negotiate this complexity without the benefit of some theory.

Even a very rudimentary theory can help. An example can be found in Strupp and Hadley's (1979) study of college professors working as paraprofessional therapists. Significantly, they obtained treatment outcomes similar to those of the experienced clinical psychologists against whom they were being compared. Given this context, it is interesting that one professor tended to explain his male clients' problems in terms of "girl troubles." To a trained mental health professional, this theory would seem both naïve and inadequate. Yet it apparently provided a necessary and reassuring cognitive map for this particular professor–therapist.

That reassurance is a key aspect of theory, and more novice professionals rely heavily on the established models. As Woskett and Page (2001) noted:

> *The supervisor who is learning to venture out on his or her own has, in the core model, a safe and certain "parent" to return to and look back upon when a steadying presence is needed. Beginning supervisors will inevitably lose their footing on occasion and need to know that when this happens they can fall back on and be guided by a tried and trusted model.* (p. 14)

This chapter will summarize important aspects of the models supervisors use most frequently. Because it is but a single chapter, those summaries are necessarily brief. It is our hope, however, that they will provide the reader with a general map of the theories—a model of models, if you will—and enough information to help find necessary readings to flesh out the models that promise to be of most help to them.

Because most theorists and researchers have focused on supervision as an intervention that occurs in the context of a one-to-one relationship, that will be the primary focus of this chapter. We discuss models related to group and team forms of supervision in Chapters 10 and 11.

ATTRIBUTES OF THEORIES OR MODELS

Primarily, theories of practice must steer a course between being sufficiently comprehensive to cover the salient phenomena, but not so comprehensive that they overwhelm the practitioner. In fact, the need for comprehensiveness can create tension with another desired quality of theory: "Occam's razor," named after the 14th-century

English epistemologist, William of Occam. In keeping with Occam's razor, which states that the simplest explanation is preferable, a theory should employ only the minimum number of assumptions and interrelationships among the assumptions necessary to explain the domain that is the focus of the theory. Einstein (1933: pp. 10–11) seemed to have struck a middle stance, arguing for simplifying, but not to the point of *over*simplifying: "The supreme goal of all theory is to make the irreducible basic elements as simple and as few as possible without having to surrender the adequate representation of a single datum of experience."

A theory also should be falsifiable (Popper, 1935/1959). It is impossible for scientists ever to "prove" that a theory is correct or true. But the theory should be formulated in such a manner that its propositions can be *disproved*. By this criterion, some psychotherapy theories have fallen short. This is especially true of psychoanalysis, for some of its propositions have been set up so that they are virtually impossible to disprove (see, e.g., Popper, 1968).

It is important to know, especially in science, when a theory has been falsified. In the practice realm, though, there is the curious, but important, point that theories can be useful even when they are not actually "true." For example, Levenson (1984) noted that people in the Middle Ages were convinced that to avoid malaria they should build their houses on high land, make sure there was no stagnant water in or around the house, and close the windows at night. The *theory* guiding these behaviors concerned avoiding evil effects from the humors and the night air, whereas the more contemporary theory is that anopheles mosquitoes serve as disease-carrying agents. Nevertheless, the medieval and the modern theory each would lead people to engage in similar preventive behaviors.

Our final point about theories is that one of theory's positive attributes, the focusing of attention on particular phenomena, is at the same time a drawback. In return for reducing confusion by focusing our attention on particular phenomena, we then necessarily miss a great deal that might otherwise be useful to us.

There is a classic East Indian story of six blind men who, encountering an elephant for the first time, attempted to understand it. Each, having touched a different part of the elephant, made his own inferences about its nature. For example, the man who touched its side likened the elephant to a wall, the man who touched its tusk likened it to a spear, the man who touched its knee likened it to a tree, and so on (Saxe, 1865).

It is not difficult to see this parable's relevance to theory, whether that theory concerns therapy or supervision. The lens that the particular theory provides enables us to see only a part of the elephant that is therapy or supervision.

The organization we employ, depicted in Figure 4.1, recognizes three broad categories of supervision models: the first category of models is comprised of those based on psychotherapy theories; the other two categories are of models developed specifically for supervision. Our organization reflects Holloway's (1992) suggestion that models developed specifically for supervision generally can be typed as playing either a developmental or social role. Figure 4.1 also serves as something of an advance organizer for the chapter in that it depicts the order in which we will discuss the specific models.

Before beginning our discussion of the models, we want to note that whereas entire books are devoted to some of these models, our space is limited to such an extent that we are able to cover each of these at only a relatively general level. But to provide even this limited coverage is important for several reasons. One is that the development of many of these models is intertwined with the development of supervision itself and so is important to better understanding of the field. Another is that our coverage of these models establishes a context for discussing material in the following chapters. We will not necessarily link supervisor interventions to models in these discussions. But as the Friedlander and Ward conceptual model in Figure 4.2 shows, these interventions are affected by theoretical orientation. It is important, therefore, that the reader have at least some exposure to the more prominent supervision models.

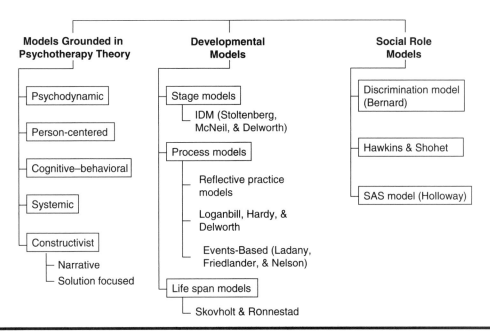

FIGURE 4.1   Models of Clinical Supervision

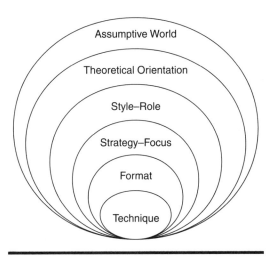

FIGURE 4.2   Successively Higher Ordered Determinants of Supervisor Behavior

Source: From "Development and Validation of the Supervisory Styles Inventory," by M. L. Friedlander and L. G. Ward, 1984, *Journal of Counseling Psychology, 31,* pp. 541–557. Reprinted with permission.

In the model in Figure 4.2, *assumptive world* refers to the person's past professional and life experience, training, values, and general outlook on life. It influences the person's choice of *theoretical orientation* (e.g., behavioral, psychoanalytic, or eclectic), which in turn influences his or her choice of style or role. *Style* or *role* determines *strategy–focus,* which in turn influences choice of *format* (or *method*; e.g., live supervision or group supervision), which in turn influences choice of *technique*. In short, then, the model assumes the following path of causal influence: assumptive world → theoretical orientation → style–role → strategy–focus → format → technique.

THEORY IN CLINICAL SUPERVISION

Clinical supervisors first were counselors or therapists. It is almost inevitable, then, that the lens they learned to use in understanding their work in that role would generalize to their work in the role of supervisor as well. By many estimates, there are several hundred such lenses (i.e., theories) through which to view therapy. Supervision has been described from a number of these perspectives, including Adlerian (e.g., Kopp & Robles, 1989), reality (e.g., Smadi & Landreth, 1988), Gestalt (Hoyt & Goulding, 1989; Resnick & Estrup, 2000), Jungian (Kugler, 1995), and integrative therapies (e.g., Tennen, 1988). In the interest of space, though, we will cover only five psychotherapy-based models of supervision: the psychoanalytic, client-centered, and cognitive–behavioral models, as well as systemic and constructivist approaches.

Before discussing these models, it is important first to contextualize this discussion, beginning with the inevitable continuity in how supervisors conceptualize their work as therapists versus work as supervisors. As Shoben (1962) argued some years ago and others (e.g., Arthur, 2000; Topolinski & Hertel, 2007) since have corroborated empirically, therapists work from an implicit theory of human nature that also must influence how they construe reality, including interpersonal behavior, normal personality development (or family development), and abnormal or dysfunctional development. This is another way of asserting that a therapist's assumptive world will affect theory, as depicted in Figure 4.2.

It is reasonable to assume that this assumptive world is constant across situations. Therefore, it would be manifest in professionals' work as both therapist *and* supervisor (see, for example, data from Friedlander & Ward, 1984; Goodyear, Abadie, & Efros, 1984; Holloway, Freund, Gardner, Nelson, & Walker, 1989). Moreover, many of the techniques used in therapy are used in supervision as well.

In their survey of 84 psychology interns from 32 sites, Putney, Worthington, and McCulloughy (1992) documented the extent to which theories of therapy affected supervisors' focus and behavior. They found that supervisees perceived cognitive–behavioral supervisors to employ a consultant role and to focus on supervisees' skills and strategies more than humanistic, psychodynamic, and existential supervisors (see, also, Goodyear & Robyak,

1982). Supervisees perceived supervisors who adhered to these latter models, though, as more likely to use the relationship, to employ something of the therapist role during supervision, and to focus on conceptualization of client problems. Findings of the Putney et al. study can be understood in terms of Figure 4.2, whereby theoretical orientation determines style or role.

It is inevitable, then, that supervisors will use their particular models of therapy as one of the lenses through which they view supervision. But supervisors who rely on this as their exclusive lens will miss important information about their supervisees and about the range and impact of interventions they might use to help those supervisees. Often, this single lens also can lead supervisors to think in "therapeutic" rather than educational ways about their supervisees.

Supervisors use psychotherapy theory as a lens through which to view supervision, typically also imposing that same lens on their supervisees (Guest & Beutler, 1988). This can occur unintentionally through what they model. But in most cases, supervisors intend deliberately to transmit a way of thinking and intervening.

Maher's (2005) discovery-oriented model of supervision is one exception; this model focused on helping supervisees to discover their own, implicit models of practice. This is a minority position—and one that would be absolute anathema to adherents of evidence-based practice whose focus usually is on helping the supervisee learn to deliver a particular treatment with fidelity. Interestingly, though, Maher was able to locate a statement from Rogers (1957) that is consistent with his position.

I believe that the goal of training in the therapeutic process is that the student should develop his own orientation to psychotherapy out of his own experience. In my estimation every effective therapist has built his own orientation within himself and out of his own experience with his clients or patients. (p. 87)

The constructivists adhere to the position stated in this quote. But that position is unique among the psychotherapy-based models we cover in this chapter.

PSYCHOTHERAPY-BASED MODELS OF SUPERVISION

We begin our coverage of the psychotherapy-based models of supervision with psychodynamic supervision. We then cover, in turn, person-centered, cognitive–behavioral, systemic, and constructivist approaches.

Psychodynamic Supervision

Psychoanalytic conceptions of supervision have a long history. Arguably, these conceptions have affected supervision theory and practice more than those of any other model. For example, the two psychodynamically derived concepts of working alliance and parallel processes, both of which we discuss in Chapter 6, are dominant supervision concepts that have informed the work of supervisors of all orientations.

Freud seems to deserve credit not only for developing the "talking cure," but also for being the first psychotherapy supervisor. Social work supervision had began at roughly the same time, with "the nineteenth century Charity Organization Societies in which paid social work agents supervised the moral treatment of the poor by friendly visitors" (Harkness & Poertner, 1989, p. 115). Freud, though, supervised actual therapeutic practice. He reported that supervision began in 1902 with "a number of young doctors gathered around me with the express intention of learning, practicing, and spreading the knowledge of psychoanalysis" (Freud, 1914/1986, p. 82).

Jacobs, David, and Meyer (1995) argued that the first *recorded* psychoanalytic supervision occurred in the treatment of 5-year-old Herbert Graf ("Little Hans"; Freud, 1909/1973). The boy had developed a fear that one of the large horses he saw pulling wagons might bite him and that one would fall down. In this case, Freud began working through the boy's father. "In an attempt to help his son, Max Graf began to interview him

and to report his sessions to Freud in detail" (p. 15). Freud began seeing in Little Hans's situation an example of the Oedipal complex that he previously had described theoretically.

Freud . . . demonstrated that the source of Herbert's phobia lay in his repressed erotic longings for his mother and his competitive and death wishes toward his father, whom he also loved. The little boy was trying to deal with these unacceptable wishes by erecting barriers of disgust, shame, and inhibition and by developing a phobia. (pp. 15–16)

Jacobs et al. reported that this is the first detailed account we have of a psychodynamically oriented supervision.

Freud seemed unaware of how tangled and intrusive an educational experience it was for everyone involved. At times, it is not clear who is treating Herbert—Freud or the boy's father. For the most part, Freud relied on suggestion and didactic instruction in his supervision of the treatment. But through this educational process, flawed as it may have been, the patient got better, the therapist developed a deeper understanding of his patient's dynamics, and the supervisor further developed and elaborated his own ideas. (p. 16)

Frawley-O'Dea and Sarnat (2001) noted that

Freud was the first supervisor and thus represents the archetypal supervisor to whom we all maintain a transference of some kind. In his model of supervision, he combined a positivistic stance analogous to his model of treatment with a personal insistence on maintaining a position as the ultimate arbiter of truth, knowledge, and power. (p. 17)

Psychodynamic Concepts and Practices. Supervision soon became an institutionalized aspect of the psychoanalytic enterprise. Frayn (1991) suggested that formal psychotherapy supervision was first instituted in the early 1920s by Max Eitingon at the Berlin Institute of Psychoanalysis. And Caligor (1984) noted that, in 1922, to standardize training, the International Psychoanalytic Society adopted formalized standards that stipulated formal coursework and the treatment of several patients under supervision.

During the 1930s, two competing views developed concerning the place of "control analysis," which was the psychoanalytic term for supervision. One group (the Budapest School) maintained that it should be a continuation of the supervisee's personal analysis (with the same analyst in each case) with a focus on transference in the candidate's therapy and countertransference in his or her supervision. The other group (the Viennese School) maintained that the transference and countertransference issues should be addressed in the candidate's personal analysis, whereas supervision itself should emphasize didactic teaching.

Ekstein and Wallerstein (1972) were the first to articulate a model of supervision that most psychodynamic (and many other) supervisors accepted. They portrayed supervision as a teaching and learning process that gives particular emphasis to the relationships between and among patient, therapist, and supervisor and the processes that interplay among them. Its purpose is not to provide therapy, but to teach, and the reason for working closely with the supervisee is to have him or her learn how to understand the dynamics of resolving relational conflicts between supervisor and supervisee (cf. Bordin, 1983; Mueller & Kell, 1972) for the benefit of future work with clients.

Because of the diversity within the psychoanalytic perspective and the richness of its conceptualizations, it has continued to provide ideas and concepts that have been infused throughout supervision. Psychoanalytic writers have been prolific contributors to the supervision literature. This continues, as illustrated by their many recent books, including those by Gill (2001), Frawley-O'Dea and Sarnat (2001), Jacobs et al. (1995), and Rock (1997).

Among these recent authors, the work of Frawley-O'Dea and Sarnat (2001) is sufficiently novel and well articulated to warrant specific mention. Although grounded in psychodynamic theory, theirs is a supervision model in its own right.

To set the stage for their model, Frawley-O'Dea and Sarnat reviewed the development of psychodynamic supervision. They observed, for example, that the earliest supervision was "patient centered," focusing on the client's dynamics and employing a didactic role. Later-psychodynamic supervisors, beginning with Ekstein and Wallerstein (1972), began to conduct "supervisee centered" supervision, giving greater attention to the supervisee's dynamics.

Both types of supervision place the supervisor in the role of an "uninvolved expert" on theory and technique. In contrast, the relational model that Frawley-O'Dea and Sarnat advocate allows the supervisor to focus either on the therapeutic or the supervisory dyad. The supervisor's authority stems less from his or her role as expert on theory and practice and more from his or her role "as an embedded participant in a mutually influencing supervisory process" (p. 41).

The framework Frawley-O'Dea and Sarnat proposed for describing supervisory models provides a useful conceptual map for all supervision. Its three dimensions are the following:

Dimension 1: **The nature of the supervisor's authority in relationship to the supervisee.** Supervisors' authority can be understood as existing somewhere on a continuum between two poles. On one end is authority that derives from the knowledge that the supervisor brings to supervision. His or her stance is that of the objective and uninvolved expert who helps the supervisee know "what is 'true' about the patient's mind and what is 'correct' technique" (p. 26). On the other end is authority that derives from the supervisor's involved participation. He or she certainly has more expertise than the supervisee, but makes no absolute knowledge claims. His or her authority resides in supervisor–supervisee relational processes.

Dimension 2: **The supervisor's focus.** This concerns the relevant data on which supervision is based. Specifically, the supervisor can focus attention on (a) the client, (b) the supervisee, or (c) the relationship between supervisor and supervisee.

Dimension 3: **The supervisor's primary mode of participation.** Despite its label, this is not actually a dimension. It concerns roles and styles that supervisors might adopt. Among those that the authors describe are didactic teacher, Socratic "asker of questions," a container of supervisee affects, and so on.

In summary, it is safe to assert that psychoanalytic or psychodynamic models have influenced supervision as have no other. They certainly have historical importance. But, as well, they have served as a rich source of observations and as a springboard for various conceptions of supervision.

PERSON-CENTERED SUPERVISION

Supervision was a central and long-standing concern of Carl Rogers, as it was for those who later identified with the person-centered model. Rogers (1942) and also Covner (1942a, 1942b) were among the very first to report the use of electronically recorded interviews and transcripts in supervision. Until then, supervision had been based entirely on self-reports of supervisees, as it still often is in psychoanalytically oriented supervision.

Rogers (1942) concluded from listening to these early recordings of therapy interviews that mere didactic training in what then was called nondirective methods was insufficient. Only when students had direct access to the content of their interviews could they identify their natural tendencies to provide advice or otherwise control their sessions. This is consistent with Patterson's (1964) contention two decades later that client-centered supervision was an influencing process that incorporated elements of teaching and therapy, though it was neither.

Rogers's own conception of supervision seemed to lean more toward therapy. In an interview with Goodyear, he stated

> I think my major goal is to help the therapist to grow in self-confidence and to grow in understanding of himself or herself, and to grow in understanding the therapeutic process. And to that end, I find it very fruitful to explore any difficulties the therapist may feel he or she is having working with the client. Supervision for me becomes a modified form of the therapeutic interview. (Hackney & Goodyear, 1984, p. 283)

Later, when he was asked how he differentiated supervision from therapy, Rogers answered:

> I think there is no clean way. I think it does exist on a continuum. Sometimes therapists starting in to discuss some of the problems they're having with a client will look deeply into themselves and it's straight therapy. Sometimes it is more concerned with problems of the relationship and that is clearly supervision. But in that sense, too, I will follow the lead, in this case, the lead of the therapist. The one difference is I might feel more free to express how I might have done it than I would if I were dealing with a client. (p. 285)

It is clear from Rogers's words that his counseling theory informed his supervision in a relatively direct way. He believed the facilitative conditions (i.e., genuineness, empathy, warmth) were necessary for supervisees and clients alike. Rice (1980) described person-centered supervision as relying on a theory of *process* in the context of *relationship*. The successful person-centered supervisor must have a profound trust that the supervisee has within himself or herself the ability and motivation to grow and explore both the therapy situation and the self. This is the same type of trust that the therapist must have (Rice, 1980). Patterson (1983), too, emphasized the similarity between the conditions and processes of therapy and those that occur during supervision.

Patterson and Rice both outlined the attitudes toward human nature and change and the attitude toward self that the supervisor must model for the supervisee. First and foremost is the belief in the growth motivation and in the person's ability to differentiate and move toward self-actualization. The supervisee who is unable to accept this as true will be unable to offer the kind of psychological environment necessary for clients to change. Other blocks to successful use of this theory are a strong belief in the dynamic unconscious and/or a basic need to control and be directive. Finally, the therapist and supervisor must accept themselves and be able to "prize" each other and the clients with whom they work.

Our own review of the literature reveals relatively little recent literature on person-centered supervision in the United States. But the model retains vitality in Britain, as witnessed by three recent edited books. One (Bryant-Jefferies, 2005) is practitioner oriented, with case descriptions and transcripts; chapters in the other two (Tudor & Worrall, 2004, 2007) provide a conceptual/theoretical consideration of person-centered supervision.

That virtually no new literature is being generated on this topic—at least in the United States—seems to corroborate Gelso and Carter's (1985) assessment that the Rogerian perspective has reached its upper limits in what it can offer counselors and practitioners. But even if they are correct, this does not diminish the profound and enduring influence the Rogerian perspective has had on supervision and, especially, training. Most counseling and psychology programs now train students in basic interviewing skills using procedures that have a direct lineage to Rogers. Rogers and his associates (e.g., Rogers, Gendlin, Kiesler, & Truax, 1967) developed rating scales to assess the level at which therapists demonstrated use of Rogers's (1957) relationship variables. To operationalize these relationship attitudes or conditions then enabled two of Rogers's research associates, Robert Carkhuff and Charles Truax, to propose procedures to teach these relationship attitudes as specific skills (e.g., Carkhuff & Truax, 1965). This skill-building approach and its variants are now in nearly universal use.

Cognitive–Behavioral Supervision

Behavioral therapy and the rational and the cognitive therapies had separate origins. The former focused on observable behaviors and a reliance on conditioning (classical and operant) models of learning; the latter was concerned with modifying clients' cognitions, especially those cognitions that were manifest as "self-talk" (e.g., Beck, Rush, Shaw, & Emery, 1979; Ellis, 1974; Mahoney, 1974, 1977; Meichenbaum, 1977). As the models have become more blended (see, e.g., most of the chapters in Barlow, 2001), the convention has become one of grouping them into the

broader category of *cognitive–behavioral* models. Moreover, as Rosenbaum and Ronen (1998) noted, "CBT is continuously developing and expanding on both the theoretical and applied fronts" (p. 221).

Cognitive–behavioral therapists operate on the assumption that both adaptive and maladaptive behaviors are learned and maintained through their consequences. It is probably no surprise that behavioral supervisors have been more specific and more systematic than supervisors of other orientations in their presentation of the goals and processes of supervision. Rosenbaum and Ronen (1998) noted, for example, that the cognitive–behavioral therapy (CBT) supervisor will negotiate with the supervisee an agreed-upon agenda at the beginning of each session. As well, the supervisor will continuously assess and monitor the supervisee's progress.

Leddick and Bernard (1980) reported that Wolpe, Knopp, and Garfield (1966) were among the first to outline procedures for behavioral supervision. During the past 30 years, a number of authors have discussed their particular perspectives on CBT supervision (e.g., Boyd, 1978; Delaney, 1972; Friedberg & Taylor, 1994; Jakubowski-Spector, Dustin, & George, 1971; Levine & Tilker, 1974; Linehan, 1980; Perris, 1994; Rosenbaum & Ronen, 1998; Safran & Muran, 2001; Schmidt, 1979) and the closely related Rational Emotive supervision (e.g., Ellis, 1989; Wes sler & Ellis, 1983; Woods & Ellis, 1996). Common to most of these is an endorsement of some variation on the following four propositions Boyd (1978) had proposed:

1. *Proficient therapist performance is more a function of learned skills than a "personality fit." The purpose of supervision is to teach appropriate therapist behaviors and extinguish inappropriate behavior.*
2. *The therapist's professional role consists of identifiable tasks, each one requiring specific skills. Training and supervision should assist the trainee in developing these skills, applying and refining them.*

3. *Therapy skills are behaviorally definable and are responsive to learning theory, just as are other behaviors.*
4. *Supervision should employ the principles of learning theory within its procedures.* (p. 89)

Rosenbaum and Ronen (1998) discussed the importance of supervisees using behavioral practice in both the counseling sessions they conduct and in the supervision they receive, using such means as imagery exercises, behavioral rehearsals, and role-playing. Milne and James (2000) found these interventions to be associated with positive supervision outcomes, as were careful assessment and close monitoring.

Assessment and close monitoring also are associated with the use of treatment manuals. Although CBT therapists are not alone in using manuals, they dominate the list of empirically validated treatments (see, e.g., Chambless & Ollendick, 2001), all of which employ treatment manuals. Moreover, CBT manuals tend to be much more specific and detailed than those of other models (cf. Barlow, 2001), because the essential premise of these models is that specific interventions result in specific client outcomes. Treatment fidelity (i.e., whether the therapist is adhering to what the manual dictates) is a very important matter. Assessment and monitoring become even more central to supervision. In these ways, the distinctions between *training* and *supervision* can become much more blurred in this form of supervision than in others.

Rosenbaum and Ronen (1998) noted that the CBT supervisor will rely heavily on Socratic questioning. Liese and Beck (1997) noted that they also employ the cognitive therapy approach of challenging supervisee cognitions and misperceptions, just as do Ellis and his associates when conducting supervision (e.g., Ellis, 1989; Wessler & Ellis, 1983; Woods & Ellis, 1996). Finally, it is important to acknowledge that CBT has continued to evolve and that its recent variants have begun to incorporate elements that previously would have been associated to a greater extent with other models of treatment. For example,

Safran and Muran (2000) have incorporated relational concepts into cognitive therapy, focusing on ruptures and repairs in the therapeutic alliance (their work informs our discussion in Chapter 6 of the rupture–repair process). The models of Hayes (2004), Linehan (Fruzzetti, Waltz, & Linehan, 1997), and Segal, Williams, and Teasdale (2002) incorporated meditation and even elements of Buddhist thinking. These changes are broadening the content of CBT supervision, and likely the process and focus of supervision.

In summary, behavioral supervisors define the potential of the supervisee as the potential to learn. Supervisors take at least part of the responsibility for supervisee learning, for they are the experts who can guide the supervisee into the correct learning environment. Perhaps more than most supervisors, they are concerned about the extent to which supervisees demonstrate technical mastery and that their work has fidelity to the particular mode of treatment being taught.

Systemic Supervision

Systemic supervision, characterized by attention to the interlocking family, therapy, and supervisory systems, is virtually synonymous with family therapy supervision, which has a literature dating back at least to the late 1960s (Liddle, Becker, & Diamond, 1997). In their review of the key publications and trends in family therapy supervision, Liddle et al. (1997) asserted that that these developments have occurred independently of psychotherapy supervision.

But, as is the case with psychotherapy, family therapy is characterized by a number of models. As a result, family therapy supervision has been focused on providing supervisees with the knowledge and skills appropriate to those particular models; those models also have affected how supervision occurs and what is emphasized. McDaniel, Weber, and McKeever (1983), for example, reviewed the structural, strategic, Bowenian, and experiential schools of systemic family therapy and argued that supervision in these schools should be theoretically consistent. Therefore, if the goal of the therapy was to maintain a clear boundary between therapist and family (and between parents in the family and the children), then there should be a clear boundary between the supervisor and the therapist. And like family therapy itself, family therapy supervision is "active, directive, and collaborative" (Liddle et al., 1997, p. 413).

The more recent trend has been for integration in family therapy theory and therefore also in supervision and training (Fraenkel & Pinsof, 2001; Kaslow, Celano, & Stanton, 2005; Lee & Everett, 2004). That integration almost certainly will include several hallmarks. One of those is a focus on the supervisee's family-of-origin issues. In fact, Montgomery, Hendricks, and Bradley (2001) elaborated on that point, noting that

> The activation of family-of-origin dynamics is a supervision issue because they affect the degree of objectivity and emotional reactivity that counselors have with their clients and hence their therapeutic capabilities. . . . Therefore, supervision should provide trainees with opportunities to attain higher levels of differentiation and emotional maturity. (p. 310)

This focus seems a more specific instance of the broader issue of whether supervisees should themselves participate in therapy as a means of better understanding themselves (cf. Orlinsky, Botermans, & Rønnestad, 2001). It also raises the sometimes-tricky issue of where the boundary is or should be between supervision and therapy for the supervisee.

Another hallmark is the use of paradoxical interventions or at the very least, those that do not rely for their impact on the insight of the recipient. Strategic supervisors have asked themselves, therefore, if strategic interventions are appropriate for supervisees. To date, at least as reflected in the scant literature on the topic, the answer seems to be yes. Storm and Heath (1982) reported that their supervisees expected their supervisors to use strategic interventions with them. But when

supervisors were caught using such an approach, the supervisees' reactions were negative. In other words, supervisees were comfortable with the notion that they might need to be manipulated in order to learn, but they expected the manipulation to be very clever and subtle. This begs the question about what to do as supervisees make gains in their own clinical skill.

Protinsky and Preli (1987) noted that "the best strategic supervisory interventions seem to be those that remain out of the awareness of the supervisee. This out-of-awareness prevents self-reflexive thinking and is useful in producing behavior change in the supervisee" (p. 23). They went on to suggest, however, that once a supervisee had made the breakthrough that the intervention called for, it was appropriate, if not desirable, for the supervisor to initiate a discussion aimed at supervisee insight.

Several other hallmarks of systemic supervision have been incorporated into the broader domain of clinical supervision. Therefore, whereas the debt to family therapy supervision needs to be acknowledged here, we will discuss *isomorphism* (that is, how two phenomena, particularly therapy and supervision, can be mapped onto one another, with between-phenomena similarities possible to observe) in Chapter 6; *live supervision* in Chapter 11; and *reflecting teams, also* in Chapter 11. Also, the constructivist approaches to supervision discussed in the section that follows often are embedded in a family therapy supervision context.

Constructivist Approaches

A significant development in the human sciences has been the emergence of a worldview that has been characterized as postmodern, postpositivist, or constructivist. The terms are not completely synonymous, but have in common the position that reality and truth are contextual and exist as creations of the observer. For humans, truth is a construction grounded in their social interactions and informed by their verbal behavior (Philp, Guy, & Lowe, 2007).

Mahoney (1991) pointed out that the term constructivism originates from the Latin *construere*, which "means 'to interpret' or 'to analyze,' with emphasis on a person's active 'construing' of a particular meaning or significance" (p. 96). Constructivism has been adopted as an approach to science, but also increasingly informs thinking about psychotherapy. George Kelly generally is credited as having developed (e.g., 1955) the most formal expression of constructivism in psychotherapy. But more recently a number of other models have been developed that are informed by a constructivist perspective.

> *What joins constructivists is their commitment to a common epistemology, or theory of knowledge. . . . [C]onstructivists believe that 'reality' . . . lies beyond the reach of our most ambitious theories, whether personal or scientific, forever denying us as human beings the security of justifying our beliefs, faiths, and ideologies by simple recourse to 'objective circumstances' outside ourselves. . . .* (Neimeyer, 1995, p. 3)

In short, constructivists assume that there are multiple truths that are understood in a contextual way. They also give strong emphasis to the use of language as the means by which we construct our realities.

Common among constructivist approaches to supervision is a heavy reliance on a consultative role for the supervisor, an attempt to maintain relative equality between participants (i.e., a downplaying of hierarchy; Behan, 2003), and a focus on supervisee strengths. Narrative and solution-focused approaches fall under the larger constructivism umbrella. In the sections that follow, we will briefly summarize each.

Narrative Approaches to Supervision. Therapists who work from a narrative model perspective assume that people inherently are "storytellers" who develop a story about themselves that serves as a template both to organize past experience and to influence future behavior (Bob, 1999; Parry & Doan, 1994; Polkinghorne, 1988). This story is populated with characters who are chosen for, or

who are influenced to perform, certain roles in the story.

The narrative approach seems an intellectual heir of Adler's ideas about lifestyle (Ansbacher & Ansbacher, 1956) and Berne's about life scripts (1972), but with the postmodern perspective concerning the relativism of truth. Family therapists (e.g., Hardy, 1993; Parry, 1991) have been especially, although not exclusively, interested in this approach (see, e.g., Gonccalves, 1994; Vogel, 1994).

Parry and Doan (1994) have developed what may be the most fully articulated version of the narrative approach. Clients come to therapy with a story about themselves that they have developed over a lifetime. The therapist's role is to help the person to tell his or her story, while being careful not to "be violent" with the client by insisting that she or he accept a particular point of view. The therapist serves as a story "editor." In this role, the therapist is careful to ask questions in the subjunctive ("as if") rather than the indicative ("this is the way it is") mode.

The client generally has a developed story of self that he or she is seeking to modify. However, the supervisee is just beginning to develop his or her own story of self-as-professional. The supervisors' role, then, is both to assist the supervisee in the editing of the client's story and also to help the supervisee to develop his or her own professional story. Supervision, from the perspective of these authors, is a process of revising stories that supervisees (1) tell about their clients (i.e., a *metastory*), (2) tell about themselves, and (3) tell about other therapists.

The role of the supervisor, then, is to serve as an editor or catalyst to help supervisees to write and revise the scripts that define who they are as therapists and what they do in that role (Clifton, Doan, & Mitchell, 1990). They contrast the stance of *knowing* (which is manifest as straightforward declarations of fact) versus the stance of *curiosity* (which is expressed in a questioning or wondering way). For example, "At that moment with the client, you seemed to be feeling overwhelmed" (knowing) versus "I am wondering what you were feeling at that moment with the client" (curiosity). In this way, the technique is similar to that of Kagan (e.g., 1980). That is, by expressing interventions as questions or implied questions rather than statements, the supervisee is invited to participate actively as an editor of the constantly evolving script of who she or he is as a therapist.

We also should note that narrative supervisors claim the live supervision technique of reflection teams (e.g., Landis & Young, 1994; Prest, Darden, & Keller, 1990), even though reflecting teams are not exclusive to this model. They are discussed in Chapter 11.

Solution-Focused Supervision.   Solution-focused therapy (e.g., Molnar & de Shazer, 1987) focuses on enabling clients to get what they want, rather than on what is wrong with them. It is grounded in the assumptions that: (1) clients know what is best for them; (2) there is no single, correct way to view things; (3) it is important to focus on what is possible and changeable; and (4) curiosity is essential. One of the best-known features of the model is what its adherents call the "miracle question," which has this basic form: "Imagine that a miracle has occurred: the problems for which you are seeking treatment magically disappear. What, specifically, will you notice that will tell you that this has occurred? What else (and so on)." This question has both a goal-setting intent and a focus on the positive.

An increasing number of authors have begun to discuss solution-focused supervision (see, e.g., Rita, 1998; Triantafillou, 1997). Juhnke (1996), Presbury, Echterling, and McKee (1999), and Thomas (1996) have provided some basic assumptions to guide the work of the solution-focused supervisor. These include: (1) rather than being didactic, the supervisor should help the supervisee to draw on his or her own resources, learn to behave independently, and make changes; (2) resistance is understood to reside in the supervisory relationship itself; the way to avoid or circumvent it is to establish a collaborative relationship; (3) focus on supervisees' strengths and successes rather than faults; (4) supervisors

should take advantage of the snowball effect and work toward small changes, rather than only the large ones; (5) rather than attempting dramatic or radical changes, supervisors work to achieve what is possible; and, (6) accept that there is no one correct way to understand or intervene.

To be true to this model, the supervisor will attend to the positive (i.e., positive changes rather than faults) in both the client and the supervisee. As with the narrative approach, the supervisor employs a consultant role (e.g., using questions to guide interactions) and gives particular attention to language usage. Presbury et al. (1999) distinguished between subjunctive and presuppositional language. The former supposes a possibility (e.g., "Can you think of a time when you were able to be assertive with your client?"), whereas the latter supposes an actuality (e.g., "Tell me about a time when you were able to be assertive with your client"). Supervisees are less likely to dismiss the latter. As well, in their use of presuppositional language, supervisors convey an assumption of the supervisee's competency.

Presbury et al. (1999) provided some possible examples of questions that a solution-focused supervisor might ask a supervisee. For example, in an effort to direct discussion toward supervisee achievements and competencies, he might ask, "What aspect of your counseling have you noticed getting better since we last met?" or "Tell me the best thing you did with your client this week" (p. 151).

Should the supervisee focus too heavily on problems that she or he is experiencing with the client, the supervisor might ask, "As you begin to get better at dealing with this situation, how will you know that you have become good enough at it so that you can take it on your own?" and then, later, "What will you be doing differently" or "When you get to the point at which you won't need to deal with this issue in supervision any more, how will you know?" (p. 151).

There is scant research on this model. Although his participants did not identify specifically as solution-focused supervisors, Koob (2002) did find that supervisors' endorsement of solution-focused ideas for their work significantly predicted supervisee self-efficacy.

DEVELOPMENTAL APPROACHES TO SUPERVISION

Developmental conceptions of supervision are not at all new. In fact, some date to the 1950s and 1960s (e.g., Fleming, 1953; Hogan, 1964). A small cadre of psychologists at the University of Iowa helped move them onto supervision's center stage. Stoltenberg, whose developmental model (1981) was published when he still was an Iowa doctoral student, was influenced by professor and Counseling Center Director, Ursula Delworth. A year later, Delworth herself coauthored a developmental model with two other University of Iowa Counseling Center staff members (Loganbill, Hardy, & Delworth, 1982). These articles, along with several other contemporary ones (e.g., Blocher, 1983; Littrell, Lee-Bordin, & Lorenz, 1979) struck a resonant chord in the supervision community, which responded enthusiastically. Evidence of this can be found in the fact that Stoltenberg's article is one of the 25 most-cited articles the *Journal of Counseling Psychology* has published whereas the Loganbill et al., article is one of the 25 most-cited articles *The Counseling Psychologist* has published.

By 1987, Holloway was able to comment: "developmental models of supervision have become the Zeitgeist of supervision thinking and research" (p. 209). That same year, Worthington (1987) found in his literature review 16 models of counselor supervisee development; in a later expansion of this review, Watkins (1995d) identified 6 more.

That level of interest could not be sustained, of course. In fact, attention to the topic of developmental models since has dropped off considerably. Goodyear and Guzzardo (2000) reported in their supervision chapter in *Handbook of Counseling Psychology* that little new theory or research had been reported since the previous *Handbook* chapter on supervision (Holloway, 1992); the most recent *Handbook* supervision

chapter (Ladany & Inman, 2008), reports no new research since the Goodyear and Guzzardo chapter.

However, developmental conceptions of supervision remain important. In fact, the Supervision Workgroup at the 2002 APPIC Competencies Conference identified knowledge of how supervisees develop as a core competency for supervisors (see Falender et al., 2004) as had NBCC for the Approved Clinical Supervisor (CCE, 2000).

Developmental models are not all of the same type. In fact, it is possible to discern model types that differ substantially. Holloway (1987), for example, suggested that they might be divided into: (1) those drawing on psychosocial developmental theory (Blocher, 1983; Loganbill et al., 1982; Stoltenberg, 1981) and (2) those that do not (Hogan, 1964; Littrell et al., 1979). Russell, Crimmings, and Lent (1984) also divided them into two categories, but theirs were: (1) models in the Eriksonian tradition that offer definitive linear stages of development (e.g., Hogan, 1964; Littrell et al., 1979; Stoltenberg, 1981) and (2) those that propose a step-by-step process for conflict resolution or skill mastery, a process that will be repeated as the supervisee faces more complicated issues (e.g., Ekstein & Wallerstein, 1972; Loganbill et al., 1982; Mueller & Kell, 1972).

Anderson, Rigazio-DiGilio, and Kunkler (1995) suggested three categories, the first two of which seemed to overlap with those of Russell et al. Their third type is what we will term here *lifespan developmental*. In our discussion of developmental models, we follow Anderson et al. and have organized the material that follows accordingly (see also Figure 4.1).

Stage Developmental Models: The Integrated Developmental Model (IDM)

A number of stage models warrant attention, including, for example, those of Friedman and Kaslow (1986), Hill et al. (1981), and Littrell et al. (1979), as well as others we already have cited. Because of space constraints, we will focus on the

IDM (Stoltenberg, McNeil, & Delworth, 1998), the best known and most widely used stage developmental model (see, e.g., Maki & Delworth, 1995). It has the virtue of being both descriptive with respect to supervisee processes and prescriptive with respect to supervisor interventions.

Stoltenberg's (1981) initial four-stage model was an integration of two others: Hogan's (1964), concerning stages through which supervisees progress; and Harvey, Hunt, and Schroeder's (1961) conceptual level model. Conceptual level is a construct concerning how people at different cognitive developmental levels will think, reason, and understand their environment.

This model stimulated a number of studies, though there also was criticism about how applicable the conceptual level model is to supervisee development (e.g., Holloway, 1987). Recently, Stoltenberg (2005) offered his own criticism:

Viewed through a contemporary lens, this initial model was simplistic and overly general, describing counselor and therapist trainees as moving through four stages of development from beginner through master. In addition to general descriptions of professionals at each stage of development, the model proposed variations in the type of supervision environments that would most effectively enhance growth, moving from a high degree of structure or directive supervision toward less structured and nondirective supervision. (p. 858)

Stoltenberg has continued to refine the model, adding a new collaborator with each of its iterations (Stoltenberg & Delworth, 1987; Stoltenberg et al., 1998) and dropping conceptual level in the Stoltenberg et al. (1998) version. The IDM still has a cognitive basis, but one that is less prominent and relies instead on Anderson's (1996) work on the development of expertise, as well as on others who have conceptualized the development of schemas.

The IDM describes counselor development as occurring through four stages, each of which is characterized by changes on "three overriding structures that provide markers in assessing professional growth" (Stoltenberg et al., 1998, p. 16). These three structures are:

- *Self–other awareness* ("where the person is in terms of self-preoccupation, awareness of the client's world, and enlightened self-awareness," p. 16)
- *Motivation* ("reflects the supervisee's interest, investment, and effort expended in clinical training and practice," p. 16)
- *Autonomy* (reflects the degree of independence that the supervisee is manifesting)

Table 4.1 summarizes the manner in which these three structures are reflected for the four supervisee developmental levels. Supervisors interested in assessing their supervisees' level of functioning on these three structures have available to them the Supervisee Levels Questionnaire–Revised (McNeill, Stoltenberg, & Romans, 1992), which is available in the Supervisor's Toolbox at the end of this book.

Stoltenberg et al. (1998) also specified eight domains of professional functioning in which the supervisee will develop. These are: (1) *intervention skills competence* (confidence and ability to carry our therapeutic interventions); (2) *assessment techniques* (confidence and ability to conduct psychological assessments); (3) *interpersonal assessment* (this extends beyond the formal assessment period and includes the use of self in conceptualizing client problems; its nature will vary according to theoretical orientation); (4) *client conceptualization* (diagnosis, but also pertains to the therapist's understanding of how the client's circumstances, history, and characteristics affect his or her functioning); (5) *individual differences* (an understanding of ethnic and cultural influences on individuals); (6) *theoretical orientation* (this pertains to the level of complexity and sophistication of the therapist's understanding of theory); (7) *treatment plans and goals* (how the therapist plans to organize his or her efforts in working with clients); and (8) *professional ethics* (how professional ethics intertwine with personal ethics).

TABLE 4.1   Supervisee Characteristics and Supervisor Behavior for Each
of the Four IDM-Specified Supervisee Developmental Levels

Level 1. These supervisees have limited training, or at least limited experience in the specific domain in which they are being supervised.

   Motivation: Both motivation and anxiety are high; focused on acquiring skills. Want to know "the correct" or "best" approach with clients.

   Autonomy: Dependent on supervisor. Needs structure, positive feedback, and little direct confrontation.

   Awareness: High self-focus, but with limited self-awareness; apprehensive about evaluation.

Level 2. Supervisees at this level are "making the transition from being highly dependent, imitative, and unaware in responding to a highly structured, supportive, and largely instructional supervisory environment" (p. 64). Usually after two to three semesters of practicum.

   Motivation: Fluctuating as the supervisee vacillates between being very confident to unconfident and confused.

   Autonomy: Although functioning more independently, he or she experiences conflict between autonomy and dependency, much as an adolescent does. This can manifest as pronounced resistance to the supervisor.

   Awareness: Greater ability to focus on and empathize with client. However, balance still is an issue. In this case, the problem can be veering into confusion and enmeshment with the client.

Stoltenberg et al. notes that this can be a turbulent stage and "supervision of the Level 2 therapist . . . [requires] considerable skill, flexibility, and perhaps a sense of humor" (p. 87).

Level 3. Supervisees at this level are focusing more on a personalized approach to practice and on using and understanding of "self" in therapy.

   Motivation: Consistent; occasional doubts about one's effectiveness will occur, but without being immobilizing.

   Autonomy: A solid belief in one's own professional judgment has developed as the supervisee moves into independent practice. Supervision tends to be collegial as differences between supervisor and supervisee expertise diminish.

   Awareness: The supervisees return to being self-aware, but with a very different quality than at Level 1. Supervisees at this level are able to remain focused on the client while also stepping back to attend to their own personal reactions to the client and then to use this in decision making about the client.

Level 3i (Integrated). This level occurs as the supervisee reaches Level 3 across multiple domains (e.g., treatment, assessment, conceptualization). The supervisee's task is one of integrating across domains. It is characterized by a personalized approach to professional practice across domains and the ability to move easily across them. This supervisee has strong awareness of his or her strengths and weaknesses.

The most recent version of the IDM speaks to interventions the supervisor might employ. These were the interventions originally described by Loganbill et al. (1982), who in turn had adapted them from the work of Blake and Mouton (1976).

Interestingly, Heron (1989), too, adapted Blake and Mouton's organization-level interventions to the individual level. The Heron and the Loganbill et al. interventions differ somewhat. But because of the general similarity of their work and because

Heron's (1989) six-category system of interventions has been widely adopted in Great Britain (Sloan & Watson, 2001) to conceptualize the work of both therapists and supervisors, we will summarize Heron's, which features two broad classifications of interventions, each with three specific interventions.

Facilitative interventions enable the client (or, in supervision, the supervisee) to retain some control in the relationship. The interventions in this category are:

- *Cathartic:* those that elicit affective reactions
- *Catalytic:* open-ended questions intended to encourage self-exploration or problem solving (e.g., Supervisor: "What keeps you from acting on what you are understanding about this client?")
- *Supportive:* those that validate the supervisee

Authoritative interventions provide more relational control to the therapist or supervisor. The interventions in this category are:

- *Prescriptive:* giving advice and making suggestions
- *Informative:* providing information
- *Confronting:* pointing out discrepancies the supervisor observes between or among supervisee (a) feelings, (b) attitudes, and/or (c) behaviors

We should note that Loganbill et al. and Stoltenberg et al. do not discuss using the catalytic or informative interventions. Also, they suggested one intervention that is missing from the Heron (1989) model: that of *conceptual interventions,* which help the supervisee link theory to practice. Loganbill et al. suggested that there are two primary ways to do this, depending on the learning style of the supervisee: (1) watch for the supervisee's use of a particular strategy, then help him or her develop a conceptual frame for what was just done; or (2) present the model, then suggest an intervention based on it.

It is interesting that several models employ this general framework for describing supervisory interventions, yet there has so far been no

research to examine its use. This would be a promising area to explore.

With respect to the IDM model itself, we concur with Stoltenberg's (2005) statement about its current status:

> *Although limitations exist in the research on supervision, my view is that the preponderance of evidence suggests the value of the developmental perspective. . . . Although the IDM has been elaborated over the years to reflect our more refined view of the supervision process, I agree with Ellis and Ladany (1997) that it has yet to be adequately empirically tested. I also agree that the field would benefit from more specific attention being paid to testing existing supervisory theory, including the IDM.* (p. 862)

Process Developmental Models

The second broad category of developmental models is those concerned with processes that occur within a fairly limited, discrete period. We address three models that each illustrate a different type of process. The first of the models focuses on reflectivity in practice. The second, that of Loganbill et al. (1982), is important for historic reasons, and the third, that of Ladany et al. (2005), is the newest and adds an important interpersonal perspective.

Reflective Models of Practice. Dewey (1933) is credited with the first formal statement about the use of reflection to improve practice. Many others—including, particularly, Schön (1983, 1987)—have offered more contemporary statements about reflection. Yet all continue to describe it as Dewey originally had. Reflection is a process that begins with a professional practice situation that is somehow upsetting, surprising, or confusing; Holloway (in Neufeldt, Karno & Nelson, 1996) referred to this as a "trigger event." That trigger event sets in motion a critical review of the situation that results in a new, deeper understanding of that situation. It is assumed that the person will employ this new understanding when similar situations arise in the future.

Hinett (2002) quoted Briggs (1999) as having observed that ". . . a reflection in a mirror is an exact replica of what is in front of it. Reflection in professional practice, however, gives back not what it is, but what might be; an improvement on the original" (p. 6).

Figure 4.3 graphically depicts the basic process of reflection as it occurs in supervision. The trigger event can be related to the supervisee's skills, to issues related to his or her personhood (countertransference and so on), or to the way the supervisee is conceptualizing the client or the therapeutic process (these are the foci of supervision Bernard, 1997, proposed; her model will be discussed later in this chapter). For example, a supervisee might try an intervention with a client that does not work even though he or she had been sure it would; the supervisee might find wonder what there is about a particular client that is so irritating; or, the supervisee might find that what she or he had understood to be going on with the client was simply wrong. Each of these is an example of a trigger event that might set in motion a reflective process that the supervisor would facilitate.

Authors such as Ward and House (1998) and Driscoll (2000) have discussed reflective approaches to supervision. As well, Neufeldt et al.'s (1996) qualitative study based on interviews with prominent experts on reflective practice provides important understandings of the nature of reflection. We believe, however, that Kagan's Interpersonal Process Recall (e.g., Kagan, 1976, 1980; Kagan & Kagan, 1997; Kagan & Krathwohl, 1967; Kagan, Krathwohl, & Farquahar, 1965) model provides an especially clear version of a reflective supervision model. We discuss it as an intervention in Chapter 9, but note here that it employs a protocol that uses audio- or videotaping of counseling sessions; the supervisee is to stop his or her audio- or videotape of a session whenever anything occurs to him or her—in other words, when some trigger event has occurred. The supervisor's role is to ask questions to guide the supervisee's reflections about the experience.

We close this brief discussion of reflective processes in supervision with three observations. The first is that it is likely that all supervisors facilitate some level of reflective processes with their supervisees. The extent to which they do this, though, will depend on their theory of therapy as well as the supervisee's level of experience.

Second, as supervisors facilitate supervisees' work-related reflections, they are also teaching those supervisees an important skill that they eventually can use on their own. This skill in reflecting on their work—paired with the related ability to self-monitor—becomes an important

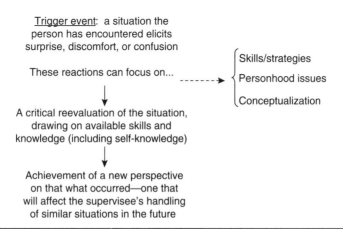

FIGURE 4.3   The Reflective Process in Supervision

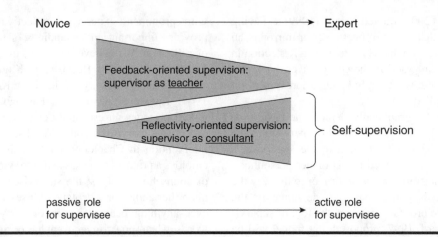

FIGURE 4.4   A Developmental Conception of the Reflective Process in Supervision

method of self-supervision (cf. Goodyear, 2006). Once a mental health professional is licensed, he or she typically no longer required to be formally supervised (at least in the United States). It is important, therefore, that she or he be able to self-supervise (see also Dennin & Ellis, 2003).

Our third observation is that reflection should be more than simply "discovery learning" (see, eg., kirschner et al, 2006). Otherwise, each of us might "discover" something quite unique and that discovery might or might not correspond to what others would understand to constitute good practice. The supervisee's reflections certainly should involve his or her own internal processes (e.g., confusions, discomforts), but ultimately be linked to some externally validated understandings of good professional practice. Therefore, the supervisee's level of experience will affect (a) the extent to which reflection is used as a supervisory process and (b) the quality of the reflections.

Figure 4.4 suggests how we believe these assumptions translate to practice. It shows, for example, that some level of reflection always is a part of supervision, but that supervision of a more novice supervisee has a greater teaching component. The intent is to help the supervisee accrue and master the essential practice skills and to develop an appreciation for what constitutes a good or effective skill or way of thinking. Gradually,

though, the proportion of time focused on teaching will drop as the proportion of time devoted to fostering reflection increases. The ultimate outcome is the ability to use those reflective skills to self-supervise.

The Loganbill, Hardy, and Delworth Model. Holloway (1987) observed that Loganbill et al. (1982) probably were the first to publish a comprehensive model of counselor development. Although there has been scant research follow-up on that model, it is sufficiently unique and important to warrant coverage.

Loganbill et al. used the language of stages. But these are process-related stages that are continually changing and recursive. The three supervisee stages and their relationships with each other are depicted in Figure 4.5. The stages are typified by characteristic attitudes toward (1) the world, (2) the self, and (3) the supervisor. In contrast to other developmental models, which assume a linear progression across stages, this model assumes that the counselor will cycle and recycle through the stages, increasing their levels of integration at each cycle. To explain, Loganbill et al. used the metaphor of changing a tire:

One tightens the bolts, one after another, just enough so that the wheel is in place; then the

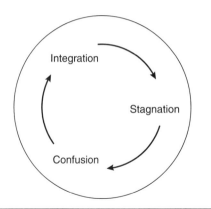

FIGURE 4.5   The Three Loganbill et al. (Repeating) Stages of Development

process is repeated. Each bolt is tightened in turn until the wheel is entirely secure. In a similar way, stages of the process can be gone through again and again with each issue receiving increasing thoroughness. (p. 17)

What makes the model complex is that Loganbill et al. asserted that there are eight supervisee developmental issues to which the supervisor should be attentive and that the supervisee could be at any one of the three stages for any one of the eight issues. The supervisor's role is to assess each supervisee's standing on each of the eight issues and attempt to move the supervisee to the next stage of development. This requires the supervisor to track the supervisee's progress through 24 different positions with respect to the model (eight issues times three stages). No one has tested supervisors' ability to do that; our understanding of the limits of working memory (see, e.g., Miyake & Priti, 1999) would suggest that it would be difficult. It is more likely that a supervisor will attend more selectively to a few of the eight issues in any given period.

Those eight issues, adapted from Chickering's (1969) earlier model of college student development, were those of: competence; emotional awareness; autonomy; theoretical identity; respect for individual differences; purpose and direction; personal motivation; and, professional ethics.

Loganbill et al. did not suggest a hierarchy of importance or salience within these issues, though Sansbury (1982) did in his reaction to the model. In a naturalistic study, Ellis (1991a) later tested Sansbury's assertions by coding critical incidents reported by supervisors and supervisees. He concluded that there *was* a hierarchy of frequency with which these issues occur in supervision and that the hierarchy was generally consistent with what Sansbury proposed. For example, issues of relationship and of competence occurred most frequently in his study, whereas those of motivation and identity were lowest.

More recently, Howard, Inman and Altman (2006) conducted a similar study of supervisees' critical incidents. They did not develop a hierarchy of incidents, but did find supervisees focusing on similar issues to those of Ellis (1991a). Specifically, the issues they identified were: professional identity, personal reactions, competence, supervision, and philosophy of counseling.

Stagnation Stage.   For more novice supervisees, this stage is characterized by unawareness of deficiencies or difficulties. The more experienced supervisee, though, is more likely to experience this stage either as stagnation (or "stuckness") or as a blind spot concerning his or her functioning in a particular area. The supervisee at this stage is likely to engage in cognitively simple, black and white thinking and to lack insight into his or her impact on the supervisor or client. He or she also may experience counseling as uninteresting or dull.

Supervisees at this stage may exhibit one of two patterns during supervision. In one, the supervisee will be especially dependent on the supervisor and idealize him or her. Alternatively, the supervisee may view the supervisor as somewhat irrelevant, at least with respect to the issue with which the supervisee is dealing. The tone, though, more likely is one of neutrality or unawareness.

Confusion Stage.   The onset of this stage can be either gradual or abrupt. Its key characteristics are "instability, disorganization, erratic fluctuations, disturbance, confusion, and conflict" (Loganbill et al., 1982, p. 18). It is a stage in which the supervisee "becomes liberated from a rigid belief system and from traditional ways of viewing the self and behaving toward others" (p. 18). This can be troubling, for the supervisee realizes that something is wrong, but does not yet see how it will be resolved.

In this stage, the supervisee recognizes that the answer will not come from the supervisor. The dependency that characterized the earlier stage is replaced by anger or frustration toward the supervisor, who either is withholding or incompetent, depending on the supervisee's particular perception.

Integration Stage. This stage, the "calm after the storm," is characterized by "a new cognitive understanding, flexibility, personal security based on awareness of insecurity and an ongoing continual monitoring of the important issues of supervision" (p. 19). At this stage, the supervisee sees the supervisor in realistic terms, as a person with strengths and weaknesses. The supervisee takes responsibility for what occurs during supervision sessions and has learned to make the best use of the supervisor's time and expertise. His or her expectations are consistent with what is possible from supervision.

The supervisory interventions that Loganbill et al. (1982) described were adopted by Stoltenberg et al. (1998) for their IDM. Those interventions were described as part of our presentation of the IDM.

Event-Based Supervision. Ladany, Friedlander, and Nelson's (2005) events-based supervision is grounded in the premise that most supervision focuses on the "smaller" events in the supervisee's work. They focus on the supervisor's handing of specific events as they occur, drawing on the strategy of task analysis that is being used by some psychotherapy researchers (e.g., Greenberg, 1984).

An event has an identifiable beginning, middle, and end. Although it often occurs within a particular session, it might also extend across sessions. In addition, there can be events within events. In all cases, though, an event begins with a marker. This can be the supervisee's overt request for a specific kind of help or it might be subtler and something the supervisor notices.

Once the marker occurs, supervision shifts to the task environment, which might consist of any number of what Ladany et al. (2005) referred to as interaction sequences. These are "comprised of various supervisor operations (interventions or strategies) and supervisee performances or reactions" (p. 14). Depending on the situation, these interaction sequences might include, but are not limited to: (1) focus on the supervisory alliance; (2) focus on therapeutic process; (3) exploration of feelings; (4) focus on countertransference; (5) attention to parallel process; (6) focus on self-efficacy; (7) focus on skill; (8) assessment of knowledge; (9) focus on multicultural awareness; and (10) focus on evaluation.

Any given task environment is likely to involve the use of multiple interaction sequences. Ladany et al. (2005) gave the example of the marker being the supervisee reporting feelings of sexual attraction for the client and then suggest that

The Task Environment proceeds through four stages: (a) exploration of feelings, (b) focus on the supervisory alliance, (c) normalizing experience, and (d) exploration of countertransference. (pp. 16–17)

Although many types of events can become the focus of supervision, Ladany et al. focused on the seven they believe occur most commonly, devoting one chapter to each: remediating skill difficulties/deficits; heightening multicultural awareness; negotiating role conflicts; working through countertransference; managing sexual attraction; repairing gender-related misunderstandings; and addressing problematic thoughts, feelings, behaviors (crisis in confidence, vicarious traumatization, impairment).

The progression of the supervisory event will depend on such factors as the supervisee's readiness to address the issue, his or her level of development, the supervisor's interventions, and the supervisee's response to them. The end point is the resolution, which Ladany et al. suggested is an increase or decrease in one or more of the following: supervisee knowledge, supervisee skills, supervisee self-awareness, or supervisory alliance.

Although the events-based model has some surface similarities to the reflective supervision model, these models differ in at least two important ways. The first is that whereas a trigger event in reflective supervision is identified exclusively by the supervisee, a marker can be identified by either the supervisee *or* the supervisor. The second, and perhaps more important, is that the supervisor using the events-based model has a broader range of interventions that she or he might apply.

Life-Span Developmental Models: The Rønnestad and Skovholt Model

Although most models of counselor development focus primarily on the period of graduate and internship training, professional development no more stops at graduation than does our personal development. The work of Rønnestad and Skovholt (1993, 2003; Skovholt & Rønnestad, 1992b) is therefore important for its articulation of the ways that therapists continue to develop across the life span. The life-span developmental model is not the only one to have originated inductively from data (see, e.g., Hill et al., 1981). It is, though, the first to derive from a qualitative study.

This model is based on interviews with 100 counselors and therapists who ranged in experience from the first year of graduate school to 40 years beyond graduate school. In their initial analyses of the data, Rønnestad and Skovholt identified eight stages of therapist development, each of which might be characterized along a number of dimensions (e.g., predominant affect, predominant sources of influence, role and working style, style of learning, and determinants of effectiveness and satisfaction). As well, they identified 20 themes that were not specifically stage related, but that characterized therapist development across time.

Rønnestad and Skovholt (2003) recently have offered a more refined and parsimonious model, based on reinterviews with some therapists, feedback obtained over the past decade, and their own reanalyses of the data. They have collapsed the model so that there now are only six phases (a term that they now believe is more technically accurate than stages) of development and 14 themes. Because of the importance of this model, we will summarize these phases and then the themes. It is useful to note that the early phases correspond well to stages that Stoltenberg et al. (1998) described.

Phase 1: The Lay Helper Phase. Novices already will have had the experience of helping others (e.g., as a friend, parent, or colleague). "The lay helper typically identifies the problem quickly, provides strong emotional support, and gives advice based on one's own experience" (Rønnestad & Skovholt, 2003, p. 10). Lay helpers are prone to boundary problems, tend to become overly involved, and express sympathy rather than empathy.

Phase 2: The Beginning Student Phase. Although this is an exciting time for students, they often feel dependent, vulnerable, and anxious, and have fragile self-confidence. Therefore, they especially value their supervisors' encouragement and support. Perceived criticism from either their supervisors or their clients can have a severe effect on their self-confidence and morale. They actively search for "the right way" to function, looking for models and expert practitioners to emulate.

Phase 3: The Advanced Student Phase. These students, usually at the advanced practica or internship stage, have the central task of functioning at a basic established, professional level. They feel pressure to "do it right" and therefore have a conservative, cautious, and thorough style (versus one that is relaxed, risk-taking, or spontaneous).

The opportunity to provide supervision to beginning students "can be a powerful source of influence for the advanced student" (Rønnestad & Skovholt, 2003, p. 15), who are able both to see how much they have learned and to consolidate that learning.

Phase 4: The Novice Professional Phase. The years immediately postgraduation can be a heady time, for the person now is free of the demands of graduate school and the constraints of supervision. Still, many find that they are not as well prepared as they had imagined. The new therapist increasingly integrates his or her own personality in treatment. As this occurs, the therapist becomes more at ease. He or she also uses this period to seek compatible work roles and environments.

Phase 5: The Experienced Professional Phase. Counselors and therapists with some years and types of experience have the core developmental task of finding a way to be authentic—specifically, developing a working style that is highly congruent with their own values, interests, and personality. Virtually all have come to understand ways in which the therapeutic relationship is crucial for client change. Techniques that they employ are used in flexible, personalized ways. As well, they have come to understand that it frequently is impossible to have clear answers for the situations that they encounter.

One characteristic of this phase is the ability to calibrate levels of involvement with clients so that they can be fully engaged when with the clients, but then can let go afterward. Clients are a valuable source of learning, as is the mentoring many therapists do with more junior professionals. Often they also begin looking outside the profession to areas such as religion or poetry or even theater or cinema to expand their knowledge of people.

Phase 6: The Senior Professional Phase. These professionals, usually with more than 20 years of experience, typically have developed very individualized and authentic approaches. Despite their felt-competence, they generally have become more modest about their own impact on clients. They also tend to have become skeptical that anything really new will be added to the field. Loss is a prominent theme in this phase. This is both anticipatory, as they look toward their own retirements, and current, for "their own professional elders are no longer alive and same age colleagues are generally no longer a strong

source of influence" (Rønnestad & Skovholt, 2003, p. 26).

Woskett and Page (2001) observed that it might be possible to think of the first phases as ones that, together, comprise a broad *learning* phase; and that the last of the phases might, together, comprise a broad *unlearning* phase. Significantly, this latter phase lasts for most of the practitioner's professional life! Most supervision literature has focused on the learning phase, with much less written about the supervision of experienced professionals. The Skovholt and Rønnestad model, though, suggests that the focus of this supervision will less on established models of practice and more on the individualized work of the particular practitioner.

Themes and Concluding Comments. Rønnestad and Skovholt's 14 themes are summarized in Table 4.2. When the label is not sufficient to fully express its meaning, we have added explanatory text. Together with the six phases, these themes provide supervisors with an important cognitive map. Like the other models, this suggests the importance to beginning students of having clear, direct models for practice and perhaps greater attention to a didactic approach early on. But it also adds support for providing a supervision course during graduate training (i.e., as a source of development for the supervisor-in-training) and makes clear how the mentoring of newer professionals is a source of professional development to therapists at phases 5 and 6.

In short, this is a unique and important model. Its applications to supervision, though, are not as direct as is true with some other models—or as likely will be true with continued development of this model. It was developed through a research study of therapist development and therefore remains more descriptive than prescriptive.

The 14 themes vary in their level of implication for supervisors. For example, whereas theme 3 concerning self-reflection has very important, direct implications for supervisors (who then can design interventions to foster the self-reflective process), other themes are more distantly related

TABLE 4.2   Rønnestad and Skovholt's 14 Themes of Therapist–Counselor Development

1. *Professional development involves an increasing higher-order integration of the professional self and the personal self.* Across time, a professional's theoretical perspective and professional roles become increasingly consistent with his or her values, beliefs, and personal life experiences.
2. *The focus of functioning shifts dramatically over time, from internal to external to internal.* During formal training, a person drops an earlier ("lay helper") reliance on an internal, personal epistemology for helping in order to rely on the professionally based knowledge and skills that guide practice. Later, during postdegree experience, professionals gradually regain an internal focus and, with it, a more flexible and confident style.
3. *Continuous reflection is a prerequisite for optimal learning and professional development at all levels of experience.* A straightforward observation, but its implications for supervision are substantial. It implies, for example, that supervisees should be taught self-reflection and self-supervision (cf. Dennin & Ellis, 2003).
4. *An intense commitment to learn propels the developmental process.* Importantly, Rønnestad and Skovholt found that, for most of their respondents, enthusiasm for professional growth tended not to diminish with time.
5. The cognitive map changes: Beginning practitioners rely on external expertise, seasoned practitioners rely on internal expertise. Early on, supervisees seek "received knowledge" of experts and therefore prefer a didactic approach to supervision. They later shift increasingly to developing "constructed knowledge" that is based on their own experiences and self-reflections.
6. *Professional development is a long, slow, continuous process that also can be erratic.*
7. *Professional development is a lifelong process.*
8. *Many beginning practitioners experience much anxiety in their professional work.* Over time, anxiety is mastered by most.
9. *Clients serve as a major source of influence and serve as primary teachers.*
10. *Personal life influences professional functioning and development throughout the professional life span.* "Family interactional patterns, sibling and peer relationships, one's own parenting experiences, disability in family members, other crises in the family, personal trauma and so on influenced current practice and more long term development in both positive and adverse ways" (Rønnestad & Skovholt, 2003, p. 34).
11. *Interpersonal sources of influence propel professional development more than "impersonal" sources of influence.* Growth occurs through contact with clients, supervisors, therapists, family and friends, and (later) younger colleagues. Rønnestad and Skovholt found that, when asked to rank the impact of various influences on their professional development, therapists ranked clients first, supervisors second, their own therapists third, and the people in their personal lives fourth.
12. *New members of the field view professional elders and graduate training with strong affective reactions.* It is likely that the power differences magnify these responses, which can range from strongly idealizing to strongly devaluing teachers and supervisors.
13. *Extensive experience with suffering contributes to heightened recognition, acceptance, and appreciation of human variability.* Through this process, therapists develop wisdom and integrity.
14. *For the practitioner there is realignment from Self as hero to Client as hero.* Over time the client's contributions to the process are better understood and appreciated, and therapists adopt a more realistic and humble appreciation of what they actually contribute to the change process. "If these 'blows to the ego' are processed and integrated into the therapists' self-experience, they may contribute to the paradox of increased sense of confidence and competence while also feeling more humble and less powerful as a therapist" (Rønnestad & Skovholt, 2003, p. 38).

to supervision. As a final note, it is our impression that the themes could be collapsed in the interest of simplifying. Goodyear, Wertheimer, Cypers, and Rosemond (2003) demonstrated, for example, that it is possible to cluster these 14 themes into 6.

Conclusions About Developmental Models

There is an intuitive appeal to all three types of developmental models. They are hopeful in that they suggest change with experience, whether that change occurs in a linear, stage-like manner or as a function of smaller, more idiosyncratic episodes.

Most research has focused, though, on only the stage developmental models. Virtually none has examined effects of a life-span developmental model, except insofar as it overlaps at the earlier stages with the stage models.

With one notable exception, the same absence of research is true with respect to the process developmental models. That exception is research on Kagan's IPR model (a reflective approach), which has been shown to be effective in supervisee skill development (Baker, Daniels, and Greeley, 1990). But as important as this is, it focuses on training of basic skills and so the results do not generalize to a broader supervision context. There is much that is compelling about the process models and so this absence of research is regrettable. The field would profit from an empirical examination of their processes and outcomes.

A great deal of research on developmental models occurred in the early 1980s and by the late 1980s, a sufficient body of research existed to allow meaningful critiques. Holloway (1987), for example, noted that supervision is only one process occurring in the supervisee's professional and personal life, perhaps not the most important. She noted as well that weakness in research methodologies had precluded any meaningful conclusions about the utility of such models.

Although researchers are interpreting their results as tentatively supporting a developmental model, lack of developmental-specific methodology, confinement to the supervisory experience as a source

of information, predominant use of structured self-report questionnaires, and lack of evidence of distinct, sequential stages in trainee's growth reflect the prematurity of such claims. (p. 215)

Writing at the same time, though, Worthington (1987) reached somewhat more sanguine conclusions on the basis of his literature review. Specifically, he suggested that:

- There is some support for general developmental models.
- For the most part, perceptions of supervisors and supervisees have been broadly consistent with developmental theories.
- The behavior of supervisors changes as supervisees gain experience.
- The supervision relationship changes as counselors gain experience.
- Supervisors do not become more competent as they gain experience.

In their follow-up to the Worthington (1987) review 7 years later, Stoltenberg, McNeill, and Crethar (1994) concluded: "evidence appears solid for developmental changes across training levels" (p. 419). They also noted that, whereas experience alone is a relatively crude measure of "development," it has been used in most studies. For this reason and given that most of this research had focused on a restricted range of experience (e.g., first practicum versus second practicum versus internship), Stoltenberg et al. found that "it is remarkable that so many differences have been found among trainees based on this categorization" (p. 419). We explore experience levels more fully in the next chapter.

Yet Ellis and Ladany (1997), echoing Holloway's (1987) conclusion a decade earlier, characterized their rigorous review of the developmental literature as "disheartening." In particular, they found that methodological problems and failures to eliminate rival hypotheses have so characterized this area of research that "data from these studies are largely uninterpretable . . ." (p. 474). Virtually no new studies of developmental conceptions of supervision have been published since the Ellis and Ladany (1997) review and so it stands as the most recent statement on the state of that research.

Probably the safest conclusion at this point is that there is some limited evidence to support some aspects of stage developmental models. Because the most prominent of these stage models were presented 20 or more years ago, there has been ample opportunity to demonstrate their utility and so this limited level of support is disappointing. Nevertheless, stage models of development do provide a useful heuristic to practitioners.

SOCIAL ROLE MODELS

In Chapter 1 we discussed some root metaphors that might influence expectations and behaviors of supervisors and supervisees. These are metaphors based on enduring, ingrained role behaviors that occur in parent–child, sibling, and mentor–apprenticeship relationships. Because these relationships are so very basic and indelible, they may affect supervision in ways that remain outside our awareness.

Another class of metaphors consists of the professional roles that supervisors already have mastered in their professional work. It is logical, then, that these would become templates for their work as supervisors. Ekstein and Wallerstein (1972) addressed this point in stating that

> The one confronted with something new will try at first to reduce the new to the familiar. The psychotherapist who becomes a teacher of psychotherapy will frequently be tempted to fall back on skills that represent prior acquisitions. He will thus try to convert the teaching relationship into a therapeutic relationship. (pp. 254–255)

This tendency of supervisors to draw on what they already know is complemented by the fact that it is possible to consider supervision a higher-order role that encompasses other professional roles. For example, we have heard colleagues state that supervision is more than teaching and less than therapy. Though this is only superficially accurate, it does suggest the point we intend to make. Perhaps Douce (1989) stated this even better when she pointed out that "supervision is a

separate skill similar to teaching—but different; similar to counseling—but different; and similar to consulting—but different" (p. 5). Ekstein (1964) was addressing a similar point when he titled his article, *Supervision of Psychotherapy: Is It Teaching? Is It Administration? Or Is It Therapy?*

But there are a number of factors that will affect the particular role or roles that a supervisor will employ at any given point. It therefore is useful to return for a moment to Friedlander and Figure 4.2, which visually depicts the determinants of the supervisory role. As well, it makes clear in a visual way that terms such as role, theory, focus, and technique are not interchangeable. Not all authors have been clear about these distinctions.

Supervisors, though, draw from only a relatively few roles. The ones most frequently mentioned in the literature are illustrated in Table 4.3, along with an indication of how some of the more influential supervision theorists have depicted supervisory roles. The table shows that there is greatest consensus around the two roles of counselor–therapist and teacher; these have been mentioned by virtually any author who has discussed the supervisory role. Most also suggest the role of consultant. The next most frequently suggested role is that of evaluator or monitor.

Holloway (1992) characterized those supervision models that have given particular attention to these roles as social role models. In the following sections, we will briefly summarize three of them. Supervisor roles are prominent in each, but they are not the sole aspect of the model.

The Discrimination Model

Bernard (1997) reported that she developed what she called the Discrimination Model in the mid-1970s as a teaching tool. She was assigned to teach a supervision course and "having recently received my doctorate, I was close enough to the experience of assuming the role of supervisor for the first time to understand my students' need for an aid to organize their initial supervision activities" (p. 310). The result of her efforts was "the simplest of maps to direct their teaching efforts"

TABLE 4.3   Supervisor Roles as Suggested by a Sample of Theorists

BERNARD (1979)	EKSTEIN (1964)	WILLIAMS (1995)	HESS (1980)	HOLLOWAY[1] (1995)	CARROLL[1] (1996)
			lecturer		
				relating	
teacher	teacher	teacher	teacher	instructing/ advising	teaching
				modeling	
counselor	therapist	facilitator	therapist	supporting/ sharing	counseling
consultant		consultant	consultant	consulting	consulting
		evaluator	monitor/ evaluator case reviewer/ master therapist	monitoring/ evaluating	monitoring evaluating
	administrator				administrating

[1] Holloway (1995) suggested making the tranformation from nouns (roles) to verbs (functions); Carroll (1996) followed that same convention.

(p. 310). Hers is an eclectic model with the virtues both of parsimony and versatility.

The Discrimination Model (Bernard, 1979, 1997; Luke & Bernard, 2006) attends to three separate foci for supervision as well as three supervisor roles:

Foci: Supervisors might focus on a supervisee's:
- *intervention skills* (what the supervisee is doing in the session that is observable by the supervisor);
- *conceptualization skills* (how the supervisee understands what is occurring in the session, identifies patterns, or chooses interventions, all covert pro cesses); and,
- *personalization skills* (how the supervisee interfaces a personal style with therapy at the same time that he or she attempts to keep therapy uncontaminated by personal issues and countertransference responses).

Roles: Once supervisors have made a judgment about their supervisee's abilities within each focus area, they must choose a role to accomplish their supervision goals. The available roles are those of

- *teacher,*
- *counselor* or
- *consultant*

As a consequence, the supervisor might be responding at any given moment in one of nine different ways (i.e., three roles by three foci). Table 4.4 illustrates how the model might operate in practice.

The model is situation specific. In fact, it is called the Discrimination Model precisely because it implies that the supervisor will tailor his or response to the particular supervisee's needs. This means that the supervisor's roles and foci should change not only across sessions, but also *within* a session.

Supervisors should attend to each focus as appropriate. The problems arise either when the supervisor attends to one focus at the expense of the supervisee's more salient needs or, relatedly, when the supervisor is rigid in a preference for one particular focus. There are many reasons to choose a role, but the worst reason is habit or personal preference independent of the supervisee's needs.

Theory and research concerning developmental approaches suggest that supervisors are more

TABLE 4.4   The Discrimination Model

FOCUS OF SUPERVISION	SUPERVISOR ROLE		
	Teacher	*Counselor*	*Consultant*
Intervention	S-ee would like to use systematic desensitization with a client but has never learned the technique	S-ee is able to use a variety of process skills, but with one client uses question-asking as her primary style	S-ee finds her clients reacting well to her metaphor and would like to know more ways to use metaphor in counseling
	S-or teaches the S-ee relaxation techniques, successive approximation, hierarchy building, and the desensitization process	S-or attempts to help S-ee determine the effect of this client on her that limits his or her use of skills in therapy sessions	S-or works with S-ee to identify different uses of metaphor in counseling and to practice these
Conceptualization	S-ee is unable to recognize themes and patterns of client thought either during or following therapy sessions	S-ee is unable to set realistic goals for her client who requests assertion training	S-ee would like to use a different model for case conceptualization
	S-or uses session transcripts to teach S-ee to identify thematic client statements (e.g., blaming; dependence)	S-or helps S-ee relate her discomfort to her own inability to be assertive in several relationships	S-or discusses several models for S-ee to consider
Personalization	S-ee is unaware that her preference for a close seating arrangement reflects her own cultural background and intimidates the client	S-ee is unaware that his female client is attracted to him sexually	S-ee would like to feel more comfortable working with older clients
	S-or assigns the reading of literature summarizing proximity studies	S-or attempts to help the S-ee confront his own sexuality and his resistance to recognizing sexual cues from women	S-or and S-ee discuss developmental concerns of older people

Note: S-or = supervisor; S-ee = supervisee.

Source: Compiled from "Supervisor Training: A Discrimination Model," by Bernard, 1979, *Counselor Education and Supervision, 19,* pp. 60–69.

likely to employ the teaching role with novice supervisees and the consultant role with those who are more advanced. Also, supervisors of beginning supervisees might expect to focus primarily on intervention skills, whereas supervisors of more advanced students might expect to offer more balance across foci.

But these are general predictions of what a supervisor might do. Bernard (1979, 1997) would argue that the effective supervisor will be prepared to employ all roles and address all foci for supervisees at any level.

Our own professional experience has been that the Discrimination Model is useful in training and supervising supervisors. Nevertheless, it merits some specific critical examination.

1. Because it suggests both roles and foci, this model is more inclusive than are most social role models. In fact, the Discrimination Model is rooted in a technical eclecticism. It frees the user to be broadly flexible in responding to the supervisee. The fact is, though, that supervisors never can or will divorce themselves totally from the influence of their theoretical beliefs. Moreover, they often will invoke theory as a rationalization for what actually is personal idiosyncrasy. But whether theory or rationalization, the net result is to block the supervisor's flexibility demanded to fully use the Discrimination Model.
2. The discrimination model is concerned specifically with interactions within the supervision session as these relate to immediate learning needs of the supervisee. Therefore, it does not speak to the role of evaluator or monitor, which is important as a means to ensure quality of client care. But, though that role is not spoken to in the model, its presence is assumed.
3. Russell et al. (1984) correctly noted that very little research has tested models of supervision that suggest supervisor roles. Their observation remains true today. However, a strength of the Discrimination Model is that it is among the most researched of these models. During the 1980s, a number of studies either explicitly tested the Discrimination Model or employed

it as a way to frame research questions (e.g., Ellis & Dell, 1986; Ellis, Dell, & Good, 1988; Glidden & Tracey, 1992; Goodyear et al., 1984; Goodyear & Robyak, 1982; Lazovsky & Shimoni, 2007; Stenack & Dye, 1982; Yager, Wilson, Brewer, & Kinnetz, 1989). The model seems generally to have been supported in the various findings of these studies.

Interestingly, the role of consultant has remained somewhat elusive in these studies. For example, Goodyear et al. (1984) found that a sample of experienced supervisors was able to differentiate among the supervision sessions of four major psychotherapy theorists according to their use of the teacher and counselor roles, but not the consultant role. Similarly, the counselor and teacher roles were validated, but the consultant role was not, in a factor analytic study by Stenack and Dye (1982). In multidimensional scaling studies by Ellis and Dell (1986) and Glidden and Tracey (1989), the teaching and counseling roles were found to anchor opposite ends of a single dimension; the consultant role did not clearly emerge from their data.

This is curious, because the idea of the consultant role for supervisors is intuitively appealing, especially in work with more advanced supervisees (e.g., Gurk & Wicas, 1979). One possible explanation is that the consultant role is "fuzzier" than the others. Though it is frequently endorsed, there is not the common understanding of it that is true of the counselor and teacher roles.

Styles versus Roles. Friedlander and Ward (1984; see Figure 4.2) equated supervisory styles with supervisory roles. In fact, their Supervisory Styles Inventory (SSI; in the Supervisor's Toolbox at the end of this book) measures three styles that correspond roughly to Bernard's three roles (i.e., teacher = task oriented; consultant = attractive; and counselor = interpersonally sensitive). The fairly substantial literature on the SSI therefore reasonably can be understood to have clear implications for the Discrimination Model as well.

Hart and Nance (2003) have offered a framework of supervisory styles that could be understood

TABLE 4.5   Hart and Nance's Framework for Supervisory Styles

	HIGH SUPPORT	LOW SUPPORT
High Direction	Supportive Teacher	Directive or Expert Teacher
Low Direction	Counselor	Consultant

according to a 2 (high versus low direction) by 2 (high versus low support) framework. That framework, depicted in Table 4.5, is a potentially useful way to consider supervisory roles. In this framework, there are two variants of the teacher role: although they can be differentiated from one another by their level of support, both are high in direction. In contrast, the other two of the Discrimination Model's roles are characterized by low direction, though the counselor role would have high support and the consultant role low support.

The Hawkins and Shohet Model

The orienting metaphor for Hawkins and Shohet (1989, 2000) is that of the "good enough" supervisor. The supervisor is there not only to offer support and reassurance, but also to contain the otherwise-overwhelming affective responses the supervisee might have. Theirs is a social role model in that the supervisor is expected to employ different roles or styles. However, Hawkins and Shohet maintained that the particular style is driven by the focus the supervisor employs. They therefore devoted relatively more attention to focus than to roles or style.

In fact, Hawkins and Shohet (2000) developed seven possible supervisory phenomena on which supervisors might focus at any given moment. This, which they describe colorfully as the "seven-eyed model of supervision," is depicted in Figure 4.6. Their model recognizes that two interlocking

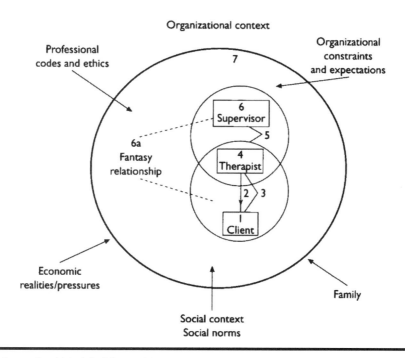

FIGURE 4.6   Seven-Eyed Model of Supervision

Source: From *Supervision in the Helping Professions,* Second Edition, by P. Hawkins & R. Shohet, 2000, Buckingham, UK: Open University Press. Copyright 2000 by Open University Press. Reprinted by permission.

systems occur in supervision: (1) the therapy system and (2) the supervisory system. These two systems exist "within a wider context which impinges upon and colours the processes within it" (p. 71). The various "modes of focus" (p. 71) are:

Mode 1: The content of the therapy session: The supervisee's narrative about the phenomena of the therapy session, including clients' verbal and nonverbal behaviors; examining how material from one session is related to that of other sessions.

Mode 2: Strategies and interventions: Attention to the supervisee's interventions with clients.

Mode 3: The therapy relationship: Attention to the system the supervisee and client create together (rather than on either as an individual).

Mode 4: The therapist's process: Attention to the internal processes of the supervisee, especially countertransference, and their effects on the counseling.

Mode 5: The supervisory relationship: Attention to parallel processes (which are discussed in Chapter 6).

Mode 6: The supervisor's own process: Attention to the supervisor's own countertransference reactions to the supervisee.

Mode 6a: The supervisor-client relationship: Attention to fantasies the supervisor and client have about one another.

Mode 7: The wider context: Attention to the professional community of which the supervisor and supervisee are members. This includes the organization in which they work, as well as their profession.

In an unpublished manuscript, Michael Ellis suggested that in making the decision about where to focus, supervisors should employ the following continuum: supervisor chooses focus → supervisor offers option of focus → supervisor helps supervisee review options → supervisee chooses focus. Ellis also suggested that the determinants of focus should include such matters as: the contract with the supervisee; the developmental stage of the supervisee; the supervisees' theoretical orientation; identified learning needs

from previous session/s; if the supervisee is a student, any tie-in to current course learning; the stage of the supervisee's work with the client; time constraints; the mood of the moment.

Attention to focus is central to the Hawkins and Shohet model. It is not, though, the only feature of that model. We do not have the space here to cover the five factors of their full model, but would note that they are: (1) the style or role of the supervisor; (2) the stage of development of the supervisee; (3) the counseling orientation of both the supervisor and supervisee; (4) the supervisor–supervisee contract; and (5) the setting, or what we would call modality (individual, group, etc.).

Holloway's Systems Approach to Supervision (SAS) Model

Holloway has been among the more prolific and influential supervision researchers and theorists. Her SAS model represents a culmination of that work and takes into account multiple factors as they work in dynamic relationship to one another.

Whereas Bernard (1997) proposed a 3 (roles) by 3 (foci) matrix of what might be occurring in supervision at any given time, Holloway provided an expanded version, with a 5 by 5 matrix (in her model, functions are generally equivalent to roles; tasks, to foci). That is, at any given time, the supervisor may be performing one of the following 5 functions with one of the following 5 tasks. Holloway (1997) noted, however, that "hypothetically a supervisor may engage in any [task] with any [function, but] . . . realistically there probably are some task and function matches that are more likely to occur in supervision" (p. 258).

FUNCTIONS	TASKS
1. Advising/ instructing	a. Counseling skills
2. Supporting/ sharing	b. Case conceptualization
3. Consulting	c. Emotional awareness
4. Modeling	d. Professional role
5. Monitoring/ evaluating	e. Evaluation

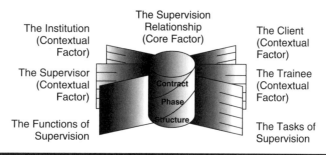

The Institution (Contextual Factor) — The Supervision Relationship (Core Factor) — The Client (Contextual Factor)

The Supervisor (Contextual Factor) — Contract Phase Structure — The Trainee (Contextual Factor)

The Functions of Supervision — The Tasks of Supervision

FIGURE 4.7 Holloway's Systems Approach to Supervision

Source: From *Clinical Supervision: A Systems Approach* (p. 58), by E. L. Holloway, 1995, Copyright, E. L. Holloway. Reprinted by permission of Sage Publications, Inc.

Functions and tasks are but two of the seven components of the SAS model. Four of the components are what Holloway terms "contextual" factors. These include not only the three principals in the supervisory relationship (the supervisor, the supervisee, and the client), but the institutional context in which supervision is occurring as well.

The supervisory relationship is conceptualized (see Figure 4.7) as the pillar on which rests the remainder of the model's components. The three elements to that relationship are: the *contract* that guides the supervisory work; the *phase* of the relationship; and the *structure* of that relationship. Holloway borrowed "structure" from the interactional and communication theorists (esp. Penman, 1980)—all of whose work has its foundation in the theories of Leary (1957). Structure, in this model, is concerned with the extent to which a relationship can at any given time be characterized by a certain level of interpersonal power (high to low) that each party has over the other, as well as the level of involvement (also high to low) each has with the other.

Holloway's (1995) SAS model is almost certainly the most comprehensive of the available supervision models, taking into account the key phenomena and the interrelationships between and among them. It is an important contribution to the literature.

CONCLUSION

Because therapy and supervision are so closely linked, developments in psychotherapy theory

inevitably will affect supervision models (cf. Milne, 2006). Psychotherapy theory itself is changing. A vivid reminder of this was the deaths of Albert Ellis, Jay Haley, and Paul Watzlawick during 2007, leaving almost none of the early, larger-than-life proponents of their own models. It useful, then to consider Norcross's (Lilienfeld & Norcross, 2003) observation that

> . . . *most of the founders of the traditional schools of psychotherapy are dead or quite old. And . . . there is not a new generation of "giants" replacing them. Instead, we are entering a second or third generation of psychotherapies, more integrative and empirically based than the traditional schools. . . . My friends who are philosophers of science reassure me that this is the typical evolution of a practice-science field. The "great figures" slowly die off, replaced by scores of lesser luminaries and more science.*

It is difficult to quarrel with this contemporary pressure to have professional practice supported by the best available evidence. Who would not want that? But as with most things, the devil is in the details. In this case, those details concern what evidence we use and the conclusions that we then draw from that evidence.

Wampold (2001) captured the tensions around these issues in his discussion of the two major ways of thinking about the evidence about what works in psychotherapy. One approach assumes that specific techniques are the primary source of client change. Adherents of this approach employ evidence obtained using the model of the U.S.

Food and Drug Administration's methods, with randomized clinical trials comparing a particular treatment with a control or comparison group. Treatment manuals are used to maximize the likelihood that people have treatment fidelity; that is, to provide treatments consistent with the espoused model. Evidence of efficacy is provided when one treatment outperforms another treatment or a control condition.

Adherents of the other approach assume that because no single study ever is definitive, the most reliable evidence comes from the aggregation of data across studies and it therefore relies on meta-analytic procedures. This approach illustrate that whereas psychotherapy itself is effective, it is difficult to show that one treatment model is more effective than another. This finding, which Rosenzwieg (1936) termed the "Dodo Bird Hypothesis" (from *Alice in Wonderland,* wherein the Queen, observing a foot race, asserted "all have one and all shall have prizes"), leads inevitably to the assumption that if all treatments are similar in effect, then all must have in common elements that would account for effective treatment. Rosenzweig termed these "common factors."

It is reasonable to expect that the next generation of supervision models will be drawn from each of these traditions (the specific effects versus the common factor). Although it has been difficult to do manual-based, randomized clinical trials of supervision (see Goodyear & Guzzardo, 2000), it is still possible to infer specific effects from supervision studies conducted with other methodologies. Milne and his associates take this position and have been pulling together those supervision practices and interventions for which there is evidence of effectiveness (Milne & James, 1999; Milne & Westerman, 2001), lately working toward a proposed model of supervision based on this research review (e.g., Milne & Aylott, 2006).

Meanwhile, those who adhere to a common factors perspective also have suggested their own common factors models (e.g., Lampropoulos, 2002; Morgan & Sprenkle, 2007; Skovholt & Jennings, 2004). But the range of possible common factors is fairly wide (see, e.g., Grencavage & Norcross,

1990) and so all of these authors have focused on different factors on which to build their models.

Whether theorists are constructing their models from the specific effects they infer from separate studies or from their understanding of what constitutes common factors, they ultimately will have to rely on their own rational processes to integrate the component parts. In this way, the models could be seen as integrationist models. In this, they are mirroring—albeit more formally—what most supervisors already are doing.

Norcross and Napolitano (1986) provided a useful culinary metaphor to suggest the nuances between eclecticism and integrationism, asserting that, whereas "the eclectic selects among several dishes to constitute a meal, the integrationist creates new dishes by combining different ingredients" (p. 253). We believe that most supervisors eventually develop their own, unique integrationist perspectives. Indeed, one central finding of Skovholt and Rønnestadt's (1992a, 1992b) model was that developing such an individualized perspective was a hallmark of the advanced practitioner; Stoltenberg et al. (1998) made a similar assertion.

Norcross and Halgin (1997) suggested that in developing an integrationist perspective supervisors should attend to what they called cardinal principles of integrative supervision. Among these were to customize supervision to the individual student; conduct a needs assessment; construct explicit contracts; blend supervision methods; address with supervisees their "relationships of choice"; operate from a coherent framework; match supervision to supervisee variables; consider the therapy approach (in general, "the 'how' of supervision [method] should parallel the 'what' of supervision [content]," p. 15), the developmental level of the supervisee, the cognitive style of the supervisee, and the supervisee's personal idiom; assess the supervisee' therapeutic skills; and evaluate the outcomes.

In short, we believe that to develop an integrationist perspective probably is inevitable. Perhaps the above mentioned suggestions of Norcross and Halgin (1997) will help this process.

CHAPTER 5

THE SUPERVISORY RELATIONSHIP
THE INFLUENCE OF INDIVIDUAL, CULTURAL, AND DEVELOPMENTAL DIFFERENCES

Striking similarities exist between the processes of counseling and of clinical supervision. Perhaps the most pronounced of these are the centrality and role of the interpersonal relationship. Just as a positive and productive relationship is critical to successful counseling, so too is a positive and productive relationship critical to successful supervision (Ramos-Sánchez et al., 2002; Rønnestad & Skovholt, 1993; Worthen & McNeill, 1996). Understanding relationship variables that affect the supervisory relationship and having the skill to establish a productive supervisory relationship have been cited as requisite for supervision preparation and practice (Borders et al., 1991; Falender et al., 2004). In fact, when supervision participants are asked to identify critical incidents in supervision, the most frequently cited incidents cluster around the supervisory relationship (Ellis, 1991a; Nelson & Friedlander, 2001) or find their resolution through that relationship (Ladany et al., 2005).

This chapter will examine the effect that individual, cultural, and developmental differences can have on the supervisory relationship. More specifically, we will discuss how these unique characteristics of the supervisee require the supervisor to behave in certain ways, often referred to as the *supervision environment*. Individual differences refer to those unique personal qualities that make up one's personality. Although the influence of most aspects of personality on either counseling or supervision represents unchartered waters, there is a small amount of literature that considers cognitive style and supervision. Cultural differences

include cultural identities and the meanings attached to these identities. The supervision literature addressing cultural identity has grown significantly in recent years. Finally, developmental differences refer to one's placement along the continuum of counseling skill acquisition. For example, many behaviors and perceptions of the first-year student will be different when the student is in the second or third year of training.

Whereas Chapters 6 and 7 will focus more directly on the *interpersonal processes* that may occur between supervisors and supervisees, this chapter focuses primarily on characteristics descriptive of the individual and how these have been found to affect supervision. Our goal, then, is to consider the following topics and how they should inform the supervisory process (environment): cognitive–learning style, cognitive complexity, cognitive development, experience level, and multiple cultural identities. We have depicted the interaction of these factors in Figure 5.1.

THE UNIQUENESS OF EACH RELATIONSHIP

Knowing some of the variables that have been considered in the professional literature as affecting the supervision relationship will arm supervisors with additional tools to make that relationship productive. Personal (or individual) variables include relatively stable attributes, such as cognitive–learning style, and attributes that change over time, including cognitive development and experience in the field. In addition, individual variables include the various ways that an individual identifies herself

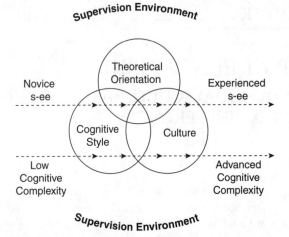

Supervision Environment

Supervision Environment

FIGURE 5.1 Supervisee Characteristics Calling for the Appropriate Supervision Environment

or himself culturally. The first half of this chapter addresses cognitive–learning style, cognitive complexity, cognitive development, and experience, and how these call for different supervision responses. The second half of the chapter addresses the complex topic of cultural differences.

COGNITIVE STYLE, COGNITIVE COMPLEXITY, THEORETICAL ORIENTATION, COGNITIVE DEVELOPMENT, AND LEVEL OF EXPERIENCE OF THE SUPERVISEE

Cognitive style and cognitive complexity have not received the same level of attention in the supervision literature as have developmental differences, including the developmental differences based on level of experience. This limit aside, we begin with a consideration of cognitive–learning styles and cognitive complexity. We also briefly consider the theoretical orientation of the supervisee as a subset of cognitive style.

Cognitive or Learning Styles

Cognitive or learning styles concern a person's particular ways of processing information and different preferences in learning. Specifically, they

represent ways in which individuals receive information, interpret data, make decisions, and structure their interactions with others (Moore, Dietz, & Dettlaff, 2004; Rigazio-DiGilio, 1998). Cognitive or learning styles, unlike cognitive complexity, are assumed to be nonhierarchical. Rigazio-DiGilio (1998) has noted that, although there are many classification systems for cognitive processing, few have been considered for their utility in clinical supervision. We will use the two different lenses to consider this topic that have surfaced in the literature: (1) the work using the Myers–Briggs Type Indicator (MBTI; Myers, 1962; Myers & McCaulley, 1985) to differentiate supervisees and (2) the contributions of Rigazio-DiGilio and her colleagues (e.g., Rigazio-DiGilio & Anderson, 1994; Rigazio-DiGilio, Daniels, & Ivey, 1997) in applying the work of Ivey (1986) to formulate systemic cognitive–developmental supervision. Taken together, these authors offer a relatively rich discussion of the importance of cognitive or learning style in establishing and monitoring the supervisory relationship. We will begin by considering the implication of MBTI.

The Myers–Briggs Type Indicator (MBTI) and Supervision. The MBTI produces a profile that addresses the following differences:

- Focus of interest or source of energy (*Extroversion,* E), drawing on the outer world of people and things, versus *Introversion* (I), directed toward the inner world of ideas
- Information gathering (*Sensing,* S), relying on facts and data, versus *Intuiting* (N), relying on intuition to understand meaning
- Information used in decision making (*Feeling,* F), focusing on subjective experience and analysis, versus *Thinking* (T), looking to objective facts and analysis
- Environment management (*Judging,* J), attempting to structure and regulate, versus *Perceiving* (P), looking to experience the environment and adapt to it

Although the study emerged from the discipline of communication disorders, Craig and Sleight

(1990) found significant differences between supervisors and supervisees on cognitive style. Supervisors were far more likely to have a psychological type profile of ENTJ, INTJ, or ESTJ. Not surprisingly, these same profiles have been found to be common among those drawn to college teaching. The most dramatic differences between supervisors and supervisees had to do with the T–F scale and the J–P scale.

Craig and Sleight (1990) addressed some of the implications of these findings. For example, a Thinking–Judging supervisor (i.e., assumed to be the most common profile among supervisors in academic settings) will find a supervisee who makes decisions based on subjective experience to be frustrating. Similarly, the well-organized supervisor (J) may be critical of the supervisee whose paperwork or general approach to learning seems too random. At the same time, FP supervisees may in fact be more capable of achieving empathy with clients than their supervisors.

Students who are Intuitive rather than Sensing have been found to receive far more regard from supervisors and were evaluated as significantly more competent than Sensing supervisees (Handley, 1982). Despite these findings, Handley also reported that the cognitive style of the supervisor did not affect supervisees' ratings of their relationship with their supervisors or their satisfaction with supervision. Carey and Williams (1986) attempted a partial replication of the Handley study and found no significant relationship between supervisees' cognitive style and supervisors' evaluations of them. At the same time, their findings were consistent with others that supervisors were more likely to score higher on the NT scales, whereas counseling students were more likely to demonstrate SF preferences. As a result of their literature review, Goodyear and Guzzardo (2000) concluded that the best assessment at this point is that the relationship between S–N and supervisee evaluations is inconclusive.

Lochner and Melchert (1997) asserted the importance of cognitive style by examining whether supervisees' cognitive style determined the type of supervision these supervisees preferred.

The authors hypothesized that supervisees with high scores on the Intuiting, Feeling, and Perceiving scales (and low scores on Sensing, Thinking, and Judging) would prefer relationship-oriented supervision, whereas those scoring high on Sensing, Thinking, and Judging would prefer task-oriented supervision. The results of their research supported these hypotheses. As we will discuss later, Lochner and Melchert used these results to challenge some of the assumptions of the developmental models of supervision.

While supervisee cognitive style may dictate preferences for supervision, Clingerman (2006) found that supervision tends to emerge with its own profile. Despite cognitive styles of either supervisors or supervisees in 78 supervisory dyads, Clingerman reported that supervisors of students in their first practicum were more likely to direct supervision toward strategies that had an Intuiting or Perceiving focus. For example, supervisees were consistently more likely to be encouraged to look beyond facts and to reflect on meaning and were equally more likely to be encouraged to remain open to the counseling process rather than be more directive. Only if supervisees appeared to strongly favor openness did the supervisor switch to a Judging (structured) posture. A corrective posture did not occur if the supervisee was highly Intuitive.

In summary, psychological type seems to play a role in supervision, though it must be viewed as only one factor of many that can affect the supervisory relationship. Moore et al. (2004) found the literature compelling enough to suggest that supervisee type differences be considered when delivering supervision and feedback strategies (see Table 5.1). In a complementary manner Kitzrow (2001) has focused on the supervisor and outlined strengths and weaknesses of supervisory styles based on each scale of the MBTI (see Table 5.2).

Although the psychometric adequacy of the MBTI occasionally has been challenged, the most recent meta-analytic data (Capraro & Capraro, 2002) are reassuring. With some appreciation of the strengths and deficits of their own profiles and

TABLE 5.1   Supervision Strategies and Feedback Strategies Based on Psychological Type

---

Extroverts

Supervision Strategies

Provide face-to-face supervision, in groups
if possible
Allow students to seek new experiences and opportunities
for early client contact
Provide opportunities for students to talk out issues
Provide variety and action

Feedback Strategies

Provide substantial encouragement
and feedback
Discuss ongoing performance

Introverts

Supervision Strategies

Provide individual supervision with additional input by
memos or e-mail
Allow students to adequately prepare before new
experiences and client contact
Provide opportunities for students internally process
issues before discussion
Provide orderly structure

Feedback Strategies

Provide feedback as needed
Allow time between feedback and
discussion of performance

Sensors

Supervision Strategies

Focus on practical application of theory
Provide experience before theory
Provide specific tasks and structured assignments
Encourage tried-and-true techniques
Encourage projects
Allow student to learn from experience of field
instructor

Feedback Strategies

Provide stability
Provide concrete information

Intuitives

Supervision Strategies

Focus on possibilities of theory
Provide theory before experience
Provide insights and opportunities for
independent learning
Encourage new ways of doing things
Encourage ideas
Allow opportunities to debate ideas and theories

Feedback Strategies

Provide change and variety
Praise creativity

Thinkers

Supervision Strategies

Provide constructive criticism
Allow debate and argumentation
Provide logical explanations
Provide the truth
Facilitate professional relationships
Encourage opportunities to analyze

Feedback Strategies

Give recognition to a good job
Recognize accomplishments
Give specific information on what needs
to be done or changed

Feelers

Supervision Strategies
Provide appreciation and concern
Facilitate harmony
Provide personal discussion of issues
Be tactful
Facilitate personal relationships
Encourage opportunities to help people

Feedback Strategies
Give recognition for good relationships
Appreciate as a person
Suggest changes or new tasks

Judgers

Supervision Strategies
Provide structure
Provide a plan for work and deadlines
Assign projects so they can be completed consecutively

Feedback Strategies
Structure feedback
Provide consistency

Perceivers

Supervision Strategies
Provide organization
Allow flexibility, but maintain firm deadlines
Assign multiple projects with demand for completion

Feedback Strategies
Show appreciation
Provide motivation

Source: From "Using the Myers-Briggs Type Indicator in Field Education Supervision," by L. S. Moore, T. J. Dietz, & A. J. Dettlaff, 2004, *Journal of Social Work Education, 40,* pp. 337–349. Reprinted by permission.

those of their supervisees, supervisors may be more effective in establishing strong working relationships within supervision.

Systemic Cognitive–Developmental Supervision (SCDS). Rigazio-DiGilio and her colleagues have extended the earlier work of Ivey (1986) to develop a model that encourages supervisors to track and intervene with supervisees based on the cognitive style of the supervisee (Rigazio-DiGilio & Anderson, 1994; Rigazio-DiGilio, 1997; Rigazio-DiGilio et al., 1997). Although it is referred to as a developmental model using Piagetian terms to describe different types of learners (supervisees), there is no assumption within the model that one type of learner is superior to another. Rather, each of the four world views has its advantages and disadvantages for conducting therapy. The task of the supervisor is to identify the primary orientation(s) of each supervisee and to assist each supervisee to become more flexible and to see the world from additional orientations to the one(s) that comes naturally.

When supervisees can access all four orientations, they can shift gears when necessary during therapy, thus enabling them to offer assistance that is more likely to be on target. What follows is a description of each cognitive orientation as described by Rigazio-DiGilio (1995). The descriptions reflect both the competencies and the constraints of each orientation when it is dominant.

The first type of orientation described by Rigazio-DiGilio (1995) is the sensorimotor. These supervisees are affected emotionally, if not viscerally, by their experiences. They can identify feelings easily and process them, permitting them to work through issues of transference and countertransference. If constrained by this worldview, supervisees can be overstimulated by their emotions and this can interfere with their conceptual skills. As can be the case for Feeling types on the MBTI, they may also rely on "what feels right" as the basis for interventions, rather than solid treatment planning. Rigazio-DiGilio suggested that the supervisor working with the sensorimotor supervisee use a directive style that provides the

TABLE 5.2   Supervisory Style Based on Psychological Type

The Extroverted Supervisor

Natural Strengths and Characteristics

Active approach

Helps students explore a broad range of interests and issues

Open, expressive, and energetic

Processes information and solves problems externally through interaction and discussion

Supervision Skills to Work on

Help students to explore issues and cases in depth

Slow down and allow time for reflection and processing

Talk less and listen more

The Introverted Supervisor

Natural Strengths and Characteristics

Allows students time to process information internally

Helps students explore issues and cases in depth

Reflective approach

Skilled at one-to-one communication

Supervision Skills to Work on

Help students focus on action as well as reflection

Talk more and make an effort to be more open and expressive

The Sensing Supervisor

Natural Strengths and Characteristics

Focuses on dealing with present issues and concerns

Good at details and facts

Helps students come up with practical, step-by-step action plans

Practical and realistic

Supervision Skills to Work on

Be open to a variety of approaches rather than just traditional, tried-and-true methods

Encourage students to use and value intuition and imagination, as well as facts

Step back to consider the big picture, patterns, and new possibilities

The Intuitive Supervisor

Natural Strengths and Characteristics

Encourages students to use and trust intuition and imagination

Enjoys abstract thinking, theory, and identifying patterns and meanings

Focuses on dealing with potential issues and concerns that may arise in the future

Skilled at helping students see the big picture and possibilities

Supervision Skills to Work on

Be more attentive to facts, details, and issues that need attention now

Integrate theory with practical applications

The Thinking Supervisor

Natural Strengths and Characteristics

Good at solving complex problems

Intellectually challenging

Logical

Objective, analytical approach

Supervision Skills to Work on
Balance theory with practical approaches and concrete examples
Be more subjective; take feelings and values, as well as logic and analysis, into consideration
Moderate the tendency to be overly challenging and critical
Remember to give positive feedback

The Feeling Supervisor

Natural Strengths and Characteristics
Empathetic, supportive, collaborative
Good at facilitating growth and development in others
Seeks harmony, avoids conflict
Subjective, interpersonal approach

Supervision Skills to Work on
Address conflicts and problems that may arise in the supervisory relationship, and help students address these issues with clients
Be more objective; take analysis and logic, as well as feelings and values, into consideration
Provide challenge as well as support

The Judging Supervisor

Natural Strengths and Characteristics
Attends to details, schedules, and deadlines
Helps students plan and implement therapeutic goals in a structured manner
Structured and organized; dislikes disruption in routine or last-minute changes

Supervision Skills to Work on
Be more flexible, spontaneous, and open to innovative approaches
Focus on process, not just on goals or deadlines
Remember to give positive feedback

The Perceiving Supervisor

Natural Strengths and Characteristics
May overlook schedules and deadlines
Open to new and innovative approaches; encourages students to try new approaches
Spontaneous, flexible, and tolerant; adapts to last-minute change or crisis well
Tends to procrastinate and put off tasks and decisions

Supervision Skills to Work on
Be aware of tendency to procrastinate and inattention to deadlines, details, and requirements of supervision, i.e., routine paperwork, viewing tapes, reading case notes
Conduct supervisory sessions in a more punctual and structured manner
Help students develop goals and structured treatment plans

Source: From "A Model of Supervisory Style Based on Psychological Type," by M. A. Kitzrow, 2001, *The Clinical Supervisor, 20*(2), pp. 133–146. Copyright 2001 by Haworth Press, Inc. Reprinted by permission.

supervisee with a safe environment to explore sensory data. The goal is to help the supervisee translate an abundance of emotional data into a viable framework for conducting therapy.

The second cognitive style is concrete, and these supervisees see the world (and their clients) through a linear, cause–effect lens. The concrete learner can describe the events described by the client, often in the same order as the client presented them. Because of their if–then reasoning ability, concrete thinkers can anticipate patterned behavior of their clients. At the same time, supervisees with a concrete orientation can fore-close regarding their understanding of the client and can have difficulty seeing alternative perspectives. They also have difficulty moving from the specific to the more nuanced in understanding the direction of counseling or therapy.

Rigazio-DiGilio's (1995) third orientation is the *formal*. These supervisees can analyze situations from multiple perspectives and are naturally reflective. They can easily modify their treatment plans based on supervisory feedback. They have no difficulty linking a specific session to the overall direction of therapy. If the formal orientation is too strong, supervisees will have difficulty translating their understanding of client themes to actual practice. They can also underestimate the role of feelings and behavior in counseling. Because they see their analytical abilities as their strength, they may have difficulty when these are challenged.

Finally, Rigazio-DiGilio (1995) described the *dialectic* orientation as one in which supervisees challenge their own assumptions that inform their case conceptualization. In other words, these supervisees are drawn to think about *how* they think. Because of their tendencies to conceptualize broadly, dialectic thinkers are more likely to consider the broader environment, including historical and cultural contexts. The supervisee with a strong dialectic orientation can become overwhelmed by multiple perspectives, unable to commit to one because competing perspectives appear equally valid (or invalid). Clients may have a difficult time integrating the complex thinking of a dialectic therapist.

In discussing supervision environments, Rigazio-DiGilio and Anderson (1994) suggested that there are advantages to *both* matched and unmatched supervisory environments; that is, matching or not matching the supervisee's primary orientation. Supervisors match the orientation in order to assist the supervisee to access the most positive characteristics within a particular orientation; at other times, the supervisor will attempt to mismatch in order to challenge the supervisee to acquire some of the skills of another

orientation. As might be expected, it is most feasible for a supervisee to understand an orientation that is only one orientation removed from the supervisee's orientation of choice.

The SCDS model, MBTI, and other learning-style models can probably offer all supervisors some additional understanding of their supervisees. (For example, it is not too difficult to figure out a supervisee's Myers–Briggs type and, with a little practice, whether the supervisee is concrete or dialectic in her orientation.) At the same time, a superficial application of these models may be a disservice to supervisees, leading to cognitive stereotyping, rather than a more sophisticated appreciation of what cognitive-style models can offer and what they cannot. Although the profession waits for additional empirical data regarding their utility, these models at the very least remind us that individual differences include how we process information, more specifically how we process the information received during the helping process and during supervision. Because of this, supervisors may need to operate from other than their own preferred style of thinking if they intend to be of service to a variety of supervisees.

Theoretical Orientation and Cognitive Style

There is a great deal of speculation and some evidence (e.g., Kennard, Stewart, & Gluck, 1987) that similarity of theoretical orientation between supervisor and supervisee is consequential for the relationship (Ramos-Sánchez et al., 2002). Guest and Beutler (1988) presented data to suggest that, several years after training, early supervisory experiences can still exert an effect on the supervisee's theoretical position. Even so, when compared to other relationship factors, such as respect for the supervisee, theoretical orientation has been found to be the lesser influence (e.g., Schacht, Howe, & Berman, 1989; Wetchler, 1989). Putney et al. (1992) have shed some light on this issue.

As others (e.g., Holloway et al., 1989) have observed, Putney et al. (1992) found that the supervisor's theory is much more likely to drive supervision than is the supervisee's. In other words, most supervisors direct supervisees based on their vision of psychotherapy and do not attend to the differences between their vision and the supervisee's. In light of this finding, it is understandable that theoretical compatibility would benefit the supervisee. These authors concluded, however, that *perceived* similarity was more important than *actual* similarity. Furthermore, for pairs who shared theoretical assumptions, weak adherence to theory by the supervisor led to increased supervisee autonomy.

As the heading of this section implies, however, we think that theoretical orientation is best placed within the realm of cognitive style. Andrews's (1989) thoughtful and provocative work is highly relevant here. Andrews proposed that standard theoretical orientations reflect the personal visions of the authors who formulated them. The theories of psychotherapy that are taught in most training programs, then, are just a handful of "personal visions" that resonate with enough consumers to keep them alive. Part of their attractiveness, of course, is their high degree of cohesiveness and better-than-average insight into the human condition. Yet, Andrews's point remains that these theories emerged from the vision of one person or several persons of "like mind." Andrews argued that psychotherapists needed to strive for high degrees of theoretical flexibility (so that they may be tooled to react to the various visions presented by clients). Although Andrews does not mention supervision, his position begs the question of acknowledging individual vision in supervision as well as therapy. The important point here, however, is that theoretical orientation may be more a matter of individual difference than an academic construct handed down from supervisor to supervisee.

Research conducted by Lochner and Melchert (1997) partially supports Andrews's premise. These authors found that theoretical orientation operated similarly to cognitive style (Myers–Briggs type) in predicting a preference for a particular supervisory style. It seems then that orientation to theory may be as idiosyncratic as whether one is a Perceiving type or a Judging type (perhaps similar to

Friedlander and Ward's, 1984, "assumptive world" as depicted in Figure 4.2). Supervisors may need to view alternative theoretical biases as true individual differences. This would put the findings of Putney et al. (1992) in a different light. The fact that supervisors chose the theoretical orientation within which supervision would occur could be viewed similarly to the supervisor who ignores learning style or cultural variables of supervisees. Rather than offering their supervisees theoretical consistency, these supervisors could be accused of requiring theoretical foreclosure (Bernard, 1992). Although we need additional empirical evidence regarding the rightful place of theoretical orientation in training and supervision, Andrews's seminal work may offer the most practical posture for practicing supervisors.

Cognitive Complexity, Cognitive Development, and Level of Experience

We have ample evidence that trainees with high cognitive complexity are more capable of several of the tasks of counseling, such as increased empathy and less negative bias (Stoppard & Miller, 1985), more sophisticated descriptions of client characteristics (Borders, 1989a), more parsimonious conceptualization of specific counseling situations (Martin, Slemon, Hiebert, Hallberg, & Cummings, 1989), and better ability to stay focused on counseling and less on themselves (Birk & Mahalik, 1996). Because of this, the mental health professions have been invested in determining (or confirming) how cognitive development can be nurtured so that supervisees will attain the desired level of conceptual competence by the end of their formal training and be poised for additional development after training.

Simultaneously, the supervision literature has been dominated by developmental assumptions about training and supervision, most of which assume that experience under supervision and cognitive development enjoy a symbiotic relationship. In the following pages, we will attempt to review pertinent literature in order to answer the following questions: How and to what extent are cognitive complexity and cognitive development related? To what extent does cognitive development occur during training programs? How does it occur? Is supervised experience the most potent training variable for assuring or accelerating cognitive development?

Although it is impossible to isolate these variables entirely, we will begin this section with a brief discussion of the relationship between cognitive complexity and cognitive development and follow this with a more elaborate discussion of the role of experience in supervisee development.

Cognitive Complexity and Cognitive Development. As is stated above, cognitive complexity has been found to be correlated with competencies that are important to successful counseling. The assumption of the mental health professions has been that training and supervision stimulate cognitive development among trainees that culminates in increased cognitive complexity by the end of training. In recent years, empirical scrutiny has found that, whereas development does indeed seem to occur as a result of training (e.g., Duys & Hedstrom, 2000), it could not be described as uniformly robust, nor does it cover all aspects of cognitive complexity (Fong, Borders, Ethington, & Pitts, 1997; Granello, 2002; Lovell, 1999; Stein & Lambert, 1995). In fact, to date, there is little to challenge the work of Skovholt and Rønnestad (1992a), which concluded that the majority of cognitive development for mental health practitioners occurred after formal training.

What is unknown at this point is the relationship between baseline cognitive complexity and cognitive development that occurs through training and supervision. In other words, although there is an assumption that baseline cognitive complexity is an advantage, little is known about its lasting advantage throughout training and beyond. Stoltenberg et al. (1998) asserted that, whereas all trainees begin at level 1 of their developmental model, the speed of transition between levels depends to some extent on the cognitive growth that they have attained in their individual lives.

As Stoltenberg (1981) implied in his earlier work, Granello (2002) speculated that persons of higher cognitive complexity must "re-progress" (p. 292) through earlier stages of development as they conceptualize the intricacies of counseling (a possibility that Holloway, 1987, had challenged), but that the learning for trainees of high cognitive complexity may be more accelerated. Although these assumptions make intuitive sense, Lovell (1999) found that the amount of supervised clinical experience accounted for more cognitive development than individual cognitive complexity, although the latter also contributed significantly. Similarly, Granello (2002) found that the bulk of cognitive development occurred between the midpoint and end of training; that is, when the trainee is under supervision. This finding is consistent with the study conducted by Fong et al. (1997).

As supervisees are gaining experience, Granello (2000) suggested the application of Bloom's Taxonomy (Bloom, Englehart, Furst, Hill, & Krothwohl, 1956) to assist them in their cognitive development. Bloom's work is a classification of cognitive operations familiar to educators. The taxonomy includes six competencies that increase in cognitive complexity: knowledge (which Granello reframed as "recall"), comprehension, application, analysis, synthesis, and evaluation. Granello translated the concepts to be used in clinical supervision and suggested that Bloom's work lends itself as a tool for assessing the supervisee's cognitive level around any particular issue. She also proposed that whenever a supervisee is floundering, the supervisor can use the taxonomy to propose questions to form interventions that will be helpful to the supervisee developmentally. Granello's application of Bloom's Taxonomy to counselor supervision is shown in Table 5.3.

In summary, it would seem that high cognitive complexity has a substantial role to play in cognitive development. At the same time, development as a counselor is multifaceted and integrative. Evidently, the role of supervised experience is the key to assisting supervisees to attain the level of cognitive complexity that will allow them to assimilate and analyze counseling information in

TABLE 5.3   Application of Bloom's Taxonomy to Counseling Supervision

COMPETENCY	SAMPLE SKILLS	QUESTION STEMS	SAMPLE QUESTIONS
Knowledge	Recall of information related to client or case. Knowledge of core classroom-based information.	What When Name List Define	When did the client enter treatment? What is the diagnosis? What are the stages of group? What does Adlerian theory say about family constellation?
Comprehension	Summarize facts related to cases. Predict consequences of interventions. Show comprehension of importance of data collection	Summarize Describe Why Paraphrase Interpret	Summarize the client's history with the legal system. How do clinicians make a diagnosis? What is the reason clinicians order assessments? What does the research say about the prognosis for personality disorders?
Application	Use research to make clinical decisions and decide on interventions. Apply theories to current cases. Problem solve difficult client issues.	Apply Demonstrate Construct Interpret Practice	What stage of group is your trauma recovery group in? How could you use cognitive interventions with this client? What evidence exists for the diagnosis that you made? How can you use what you know about assertiveness training to work with this client?
Analysis	Identify patterns of behavior in clients. Identify parts of client history that are relevant to presenting problem. Compare and contrast similar interventions with different clients.	Analyze Classify Compare Contrast Experiment	What secondary gains are there for this client? Analyze the relationship between the client's substance abuse and his anger. What components of the client's problem support this intervention? Compare and contrast the client's role in her family of origin versus the role that she is assuming in her family of procreation.
Synthesis	Combine information from different academic courses to apply to real-world problems. Conceptualize cases, bringing together all relevant information. Design intervention that uses all the client's resources.	Create Combine Integrate Design Generalize Hypothesize Construct Summarize	Taking into account what you know about the effects of racism and what you have learned about the client's trauma, how can you design an assessment program that accurately captures his current intellectual functioning? Could you predict the outcome if you used a cognitive-behavioral intervention? Construct a treatment plan based on the goals that you have developed.
Evaluation	Articulate a rationale for interventions. Assess the value or significance of a particular theory or intervention. Make choices based on reasoned arguments.	Appraise Assess Defend Evaluate Recommend Critique	Assess the effectiveness of your interventions with this client. What would you recommend to a counselor who might be taking over this case? Evaluate the client's progress to date. Which intervention has a better chance of success with this client?

Source: From "Encouraging the Cognitive Development of Supervisees: Using Bloom's Taxonomy in Supervision," by D. H. Granello, 2000, *Counselor Education and Supervision, 40,* pp. 31–46. Copyright 2000 ACA. Reprinted with permission. No further reproduction authorized without written permission of the American Counseling Association.

a productive manner (Granello, 2002). Furthermore, Ramos-Sánchez et al. (2002) found that higher developmental levels for supervisees were correlated with stronger working alliances with supervisors and more satisfaction with supervision. Thus, the costs for stalled cognitive development could be significant. Methods for increasing cognitive complexity proposed by Guiffrida (2005) and others will be addressed in Chapter 9 under the topic of increasing reflectivity.

Experience as an Indicator of Developmental Level. The supervisee's level of experience has been one of the more broadly researched areas of counselor development. Although there are a few exceptions (e.g., Friedlander & Snyder, 1983), the great majority of empirical studies have suggested that supervisees have different characteristics and different abilities based on the amount of supervised experience that they have accrued (e.g., Borders, 1990; Burke et al., 1998; Cummings, Hallberg, Martin, Slemon, & Hiebert, 1990; Granello, 2002; Ladany, Marotta, & Muse-Burke, 2001; Lovell, 1999; Mallinckrodt & Nelson, 1991; McNeill, Stoltenberg, & Pierce, 1985; McNeill et al., 1992; Murray, Portman, & Maki, 2003; Olk & Friedlander, 1992; Shechtman & Wirzberger, 1999; Swanson & O'Saben, 1993; Tracey, Ellickson, & Sherry, 1989; Tracey, Hays, Malone, & Herman, 1988; Wiley & Ray, 1986; Williams, Judge, Hill, & Hoffman, 1997; Winter & Holloway, 1991). Other reviewers of the empirical literature (Goodyear & Guzzardo, 2000; Holloway, 1992, 1995; Stoltenberg et al., 1994) also identified experience level as an important point of departure for understanding the developmental needs of the supervisee.

Several authors (Ellis & Ladany, 1997; Fong et al., 1997; Granello, 2002) have echoed Holloway's (1992) earlier caution, however, that there are multiple problems in interpreting the results of most developmental studies, one of these being the lack of longitudinal studies. That is, without tracking the same supervisees over time, it is very difficult to discern whether the significant results of various studies depict true *development* or cohort effects. But even without this and other issues fully resolved, there is still ample empirical evidence to support an examination of the supervisee's experience level as one indicator of developmental level.

Researchers have examined the relationship between amount of training and supervisee behavior. Looking at the beginning practicum student, Borders (1990) found significant change in supervisee self-reports for self-awareness, dependency–autonomy, and theory–skills acquisition over one semester. McNeill et al. (1985) obtained similar results when they compared beginning trainees to intermediate trainees. Examining prepracticum student growth over a period of one semester, Williams et al. (1997) found that trainees at the end of the semester decreased in anxiety and were better at managing their own transference and countertransference reactions.

Studies that considered larger experience differences have reported inconsistent and more complex results. Cummings et al. (1990) and Martin et al. (1989) found that experienced counselors were more efficient in their conceptualization, employing well-established cognitive schemata to conceptualize clients, although novice counselors seemed to require much more specific information about the clients to conceptualize the problem; they were more random in their information seeking, and their ultimate conceptualizations were less sophisticated.

Hillerbrand and Claiborn (1990) arrived at somewhat different conclusions. They found no differences in cognitive processes used by experienced and novice counselors when asked to diagnose client cases of different complexity. What they did find was that confidence and clarity in presenting cases were greater for the more experienced counselors. Hillerbrand and Claiborn's findings might be explained by the fact that they defined novice as doctoral students with one to three semesters of practicum; experts were defined as professionals with at least 5 years of postdoctoral experience.

Other researchers have also looked at a broader continuum of experience. Tracey et al. (1988) studied counselor responses across three experience levels: beginning counselors (0 to 1 year of practicum), advanced counselors (graduate students with more than 1 year of practicum), and doctoral counselors (at least 2 years of postdoctoral experience). When supervisee interventions (i.e., dominance, approach–avoidance, focus on affect, immediacy, breadth versus specificity, meeting client demands, verbosity and confrontation) were compared across groups, doctoral-level counselors were less dominant (yet confronted more), were less verbose, and yielded less to client demands than non-doctoral-level counselors (Tracey et al., 1988).

Burke et al. (1998) investigated the working alliance of 10 supervisor–supervisee dyads in terms of events that "weakened" and interventions that "repaired" the alliance. Even though all their supervisees had a master's degree in a mental health discipline, experience effects were found in the types of issues that were raised in supervision, as well as in the supervisee's approach to supervision. Less-experienced supervisees (i.e., 1 year or less of postdegree experience) raised issues that revolved around the development of professional skills (e.g., definitions of diagnostic terms or the delivery of particular techniques). Less-experienced supervisees also devoted considerable time to a single case and often did not meet previously established supervision goals. On the other hand, more-experienced supervisees were more active in prioritizing the supervision agenda. They also tended to treat their supervisors more as consultants. When issues emerged, they tended to be around differences in theoretical orientation, presentation style, and treatment planning. The Burke et al. results, therefore, support several assumptions of developmental models of supervision.

Finally, an investigation conducted by Ladany et al. (2001) involved supervisees who were seeking a master's degree in counseling and supervisees seeking a doctoral degree in a mental health discipline. Ladany et al. sought to determine if general experience (i.e., length of time engaged in the practice of counseling) was related to cognitive complexity or if number of clients seen was a better predictor. Results indicated that experience alone accounted for cognitive complexity around diagnostic and treatment conceptualization. Seeing a greater number of clients over a shorter time span did not produce similar gains in cognitive development. The authors hypothesized that too many clients may discourage the supervisee from reflective activity or may mean that supervision will be less intensive for any particular case, either of which might account for the diminished returns.

A final comment regarding experience is in order before we proceed. Most studies that demonstrate supervisee development over time have confounded experience with training. We have very little evidence that experience alone leads to developmental gains. Yet the changes observed within supervisees under supervision are promising. An inference one can draw is that experience obtained under close supervision and with specific feedback is necessary for learning to occur. The more direct methods of supervision that have been espoused in recent years, therefore, may account for some of the differences that have been observed among supervisees at different experience levels.

Experience Level and Moderating Variables. We have already indicated that cognitive complexity interacts with experience; that is, the trainee who has attained high conceptual ability will advance more quickly. Cultural factors may also enhance or interfere with the expected gains of supervised experience, and these are addressed in the second half of this chapter. We have examples of research that found experience level to be secondary to other individual characteristics in its effect on development. Although our examples are few, they raise the possibility that there may be other, perhaps many, variables that compromise or negate the effects of experience on professional development.

Winter and Holloway (1991) found that less-experienced trainees were more likely to focus on conceptualization of the client, whereas more-advanced trainees were more likely to focus on personal growth. Trainees with higher conceptual levels were more likely to request a focus on the development of counseling skills and to request feedback, thus indicating less concern about evaluation. Both level of experience and conceptual level (cognitive complexity), therefore, produced significant results in this study.

Borders, Fong, and Neimeyer (1986) found neither experience nor ego development related to perceptions of clients for trainees at three different levels within a master's program. Despite the nonsignificant findings, the authors noted that students at the higher ego levels "seemed to have a greater awareness of the interactive nature of the counselor–client relationship, perhaps thinking of their clients more often in terms of this process than did students at low ego levels" (p. 46). A later study by Fong et al. (1997) again found no measurable differences in ego development for master's-level trainees over the course of their program of study, thus prompting the authors to suggest that educators and supervisors need to attend more deliberately to the cognitive development of supervisees.

Swanson and O'Saben (1993) reported that supervisees' Myers–Briggs Type Indicator (MBTI) profile, amount of practicum experience (ranging from prepracticum to 15 completed semesters of practicum), and type of program (counseling psychology, clinical psychology, or counselor education) all produced significant differences in terms of supervisee needs and expectations for supervision. Program membership was the least-dramatic predictor of differences, and level of experience produced the greatest differences. Level of experience differences produced results similar to other experience studies, indicating that supervisees with less experience expected more supervisor involvement, direction, and support.

Finally, whereas Granello (2002) found evidence of cognitive development with experience, she also found that program concentration was a moderating variable. Granello used an instrument that tapped Perry's (1970) model of cognitive development. As expected, beginning counselors-in-training demonstrated dualistic thinking, whereas more-advanced trainees demonstrated multiplistic thinking. (As in Perry's 1981 research, relativistic thinking was not demonstrated.) However, in contrast to students majoring in mental health counseling, rehabilitation counseling, or marriage and family therapy, students majoring in school counseling became more dualistic in their thinking over the course of their training, not less. Granello also found that experience in human services prior to the training program, age, or GPA accounted for no differences in cognitive complexity.

Supervision Environment

Much research interest has been shown in the relative importance of matching supervisee developmental level with the appropriate supervisory conditions, typically referred to as the *supervision environment.* The assumptions regarding the appropriate environment have been based primarily on the work of early counselor development theorists, especially Stoltenberg and his colleagues (Stoltenberg, 1981; Stoltenberg & Delworth, 1987; Stoltenberg et al., 1998). As described in Chapter 4, the model asserts that during the initial stages of supervision the supervisee should be offered significant structure, direction, and support to assure movement in a positive direction. As supervisees gain some experience, expertise, and confidence, they are ready to have some of the structure diminished, to be challenged with alternative conceptualizations of the cases that they have been assigned, to be given technical guidance as needed, and to begin to look at personal issues that affect their work. In short, to accommodate the different developmental needs of supervisees, supervisors alter their interventions or the supervision environment.

By and large, research has supported, or partially supported, the supervision environment premises of counselor developmental models (Bear & Kivlighan, 1994; Borders & Usher, 1992; Dodenhoff, 1981; Fisher, 1989; Glidden & Tracey, 1992; Guest & Beutler, 1988; Heppner & Handley, 1982; Heppner & Roehlke, 1984; Holloway & Wampold, 1983; Krause & Allen, 1988; Lazar & Eisikovits, 1997; Miars et al., 1983; Murray, Portman, & Maki, 2003; Rabinowitz, Heppner, & Roehlke, 1986; Reising & Daniels, 1983; Stoltenberg, Pierce, & McNeill, 1987;

Usher & Borders, 1993; Wetchler, 1989; Wiley & Ray, 1986; Williams et al., 1997; Winter & Holloway, 1991; Worthington & Stern, 1985). The questions that have driven this body of research include: Has the matching of environment to development level of supervisee significantly enhanced supervisee learning, and do supervisees prefer a supervision environment that is developmentally appropriate?

The assumptions underlying these questions have received some support, although there certainly have been mixed results when the literature is examined closely. A study conducted by Ladany, Walker, and Melincoff (2001) produced results that challenged developmental models. As part of their research, Ladany et al. hypothesized that a relatively low level of cognitive complexity, limited experience, and unfamiliarity with a particular type of client would lead supervisees to seek supervision that was more task focused. Instead they found that all supervisees wanted supervisors to be moderately high on all supervision environments. Ladany et al. concluded that "the theoretical assumption that beginning supervisees need more structure is an overgeneralization or a misguided view based more on clinical lore than on research, which specifically attends to changes in trainees' conceptual understanding of clients" (p. 215). Sumerel and Borders (1996) obtained similar findings and concluded that it may not be the supervision environment (intervention) per se that matters, but the style of delivery. Although inexperienced supervisees are expected to find a focus on personal issues to be less helpful, Sumerel and Borders suggested that, when this is done in a manner that is warm, supportive, and instructional, supervisees can benefit. Barrett and Barber (2005), however, argued that the novice supervisee's inability to integrate emotional experience in a way that promotes growth is more to the point. Such integration takes insight and tolerance for ambiguity, both signs that the counselor has reached a higher level of development.

Despite arguments to the contrary, it seems that moderating variables operate to change the needs of trainees, making them occasionally inconsistent with the assumptions of developmental models. A case in point is an interesting study conducted by Tracey et al. (1989), in which they considered the interaction of level of experience (beginning or advanced counseling psychology doctoral students), reactance potential (an individual's need to resist or comply with imposed structure), supervision structure (low structure or high structure), and content of supervision (crisis or noncrisis), using Brehm's (1966) concept of reactance potential. The authors found that advanced trainees with high reactance (i.e., high need to resist structure) preferred supervision with less structure than did advanced trainees with low reactance. In noncrisis situations (i.e., when all things were equal), beginning trainees preferred structured supervision, whereas more experienced trainees preferred less structure. However, in crisis situations, *all* trainees preferred structured supervision regardless of their level of experience or reactance.

This last finding is reinforced by Zarski, Sand-Pringle, Pannell, and Lindon (1995), who noted that supervision must be modified based on the severity of individual cases. For supervisees working with difficult or volatile situations (e.g., family violence), more structure may be needed for advanced supervisees until they have attained a necessary level of comfort and competence. Similarly, when Wetchler and Vaughn (1992) surveyed marriage and family therapists at multiple levels, supervisor directiveness was the most frequently identified supervisor skill that therapists thought enhanced their development. This result may indicate that more advanced supervisees take more difficult cases to supervision, thus requiring more direction from the supervisor around these identified cases.

In summary, although supervisors seem to offer different environments when supervisees' developmental differences are pronounced, empirical findings do not as yet support some of the finer distinctions made by developmental theorists. It is difficult to determine if the problem is in the design of particular studies or with the developmental models themselves (Ellis & Ladany, 1997). It is important to recall, however, that development is multifaceted, and the ability to address different levels of competence at any one point in the supervision process is challenging indeed. Additionally, we do not know what stage of development might take precedence at any measuring point. It is likely that supervisees master particular aspects of the therapeutic process, thus reflecting more advanced developmental characteristics around these, while still faltering with other aspects of skill development. One group of supervisees, therefore, may represent several levels of development when measured on one variable; at the same time, if multiple variables are considered, each supervisee may offer a developmental profile in which the supervisee is more advanced on some variables than on others. If differing developmental levels require different supervision interventions, each supervisee may need a variety of interventions offered in a discriminating fashion. In short, it is probably best if the supervisor considers both development and environment to be dynamic and fluid, requiring astute observation and flexibility during all levels of training and for posttraining supervision as well.

DEVELOPMENTAL CONSTRUCTS: PULLING IT ALL TOGETHER

By now it is clear to the reader that "individual differences" covers a lot of territory. As supervisors approach a supervisory relationship, how do they weigh the different developmental contingencies we have addressed thus far? Some empirical findings are conflicting, yet some themes definitely warrant serious attention. Before we embark on what we know about cultural characteristics, we offer the following as guidelines to consider regarding the various constructs relevant to development.

• **Cognitive complexity matters.** High cognitive complexity (or conceptual level) is an important predictor of success for key counseling tasks, such as offering increased empathy (Deal, 2003; Stoppard & Miller, 1985) and developing accurate conceptualizations of client situations (Martin

et al., 1989). Supervisees with low cognitive complexity will need assistance in forming cognitive maps that can be used to assess client issues and in goal setting and strategy selection. Supervision interventions that challenge this supervisee to conceptualize in highly abstract ways will be counterproductive.

Supervisees with high cognitive complexity appear more confident and ask for more feedback to improve counseling skills and thus seemingly are less concerned about evaluation. It is likely that the process of counseling is more exciting to supervisees with high cognitive complexity because they are able to produce and weigh more options and choose the most appropriate intervention (Gordon, 1990; Holloway & Wampold, 1986).

• **Cognitive style matters.** Although conceptual level–cognitive complexity connotes a hierarchy of ability, cognitive style represents the way we think naturally (as opposed to how well we think!). Though the evidence is still modest, we have growing confirmation that cognitive style affects how supervisees organize data about clients, how they present these data to their supervisors, and how they interact with both clients and supervisors (Lochner & Melchert, 1997; Rigazio-DiGilio et al., 1997; Swanson & O'Saben, 1993).

• **Supervisors also exhibit cognitive styles.** As a key player in the supervisory relationship, the supervisor cannot be excluded in an assessment of cognitive styles (Clingerman, 2006). Supervisors who understand the importance of the supervisee's manner of making sense of the world will certainly understand that their cognitive style is equally relevant. If outside of one's awareness, differences in cognitive styles may serve to frustrate the supervision process (Craig & Sleight, 1990). Conversely, compatibility in cognitive style may lead to enhanced evaluation (Handley, 1982), but also potentially limited growth for the supervisee.

• **Theoretical orientation is intrinsically tied to individual differences.** Although the mental health professions have appreciated that theory represents a "worldview," they have been slow to view theoretical orientation as something that relates to cognitive style, if not cultural identity (e.g., feminist identity as fundamental to feminist supervision; Szymanski, 2005). We have evidence that perceived theoretical compatibility enhances clinical supervision (Putney et al., 1992), but the supervision literature has been relatively quiet about theoretical orientation, except to say that declarations of one's orientation should be made in places like the supervision contract. The discourse around theory may evolve quite differently if it were appreciated as an aspect of cognitive style.

• **Experience under supervision matters.** Because of the field-specific nature of conceptual level, Stoltenberg (1981) and Blocher (1983) were among those who initially suggested that, at least for novices, experience and conceptual level are highly correlated. Indeed, they suggested that it is possible to predict conceptual level from experience. It is not surprising, then, that much of the development of clinical supervision practice has been informed by this assumption.

Although we have a substantial body of research that supports the claim that supervised experience results in developmental advances for supervisees, the research has its critics (e.g., Ellis & Ladany, 1997). As we reviewed earlier in this chapter, the discourse regarding the relative strength of experience to increase the supervisee's competence has become more complicated and more interesting.

• **Experience may be trumped by cognitive style.** Although experience is a good predictor of supervision needs, cognitive style can be a powerful moderating variable. With a group of supervisees all at the same experience level, Lochner and Melchert (1997) found that Myers–Briggs Type Indicator predicted the type of supervision that supervisees preferred.

We should note that all supervision environments will appeal to some supervisees based on cognitive style. This could inadvertently contribute to mixed results when attempting to conduct developmental supervision research.

• **Experience may be trumped by circumstances.** As we discussed, despite the fact that research consistently suggests that the more advanced supervisee will want or require less structure in supervision, several variables can change this prediction, including a crisis situation (Tracey et al., 1989) or a particularly difficult client population (Zarski et al., 1995). This leads us to the conclusion that supervision of an advanced supervisee is more idiosyncratic than supervision of a novice supervisee. In other words, the novice supervisee will most likely need some structure across his or her client load, whereas the advanced supervisee may benefit from more autonomy with some clients, more structure with others, support with difficult clients, and challenge with those clients that may push the supervisee's personal buttons.

• **Experience level is typically paired with certain developmental characteristics. Supervisors should know these.** With experience, the supervisee should exhibit an increase in: (1) self-awareness of behavior and motivation within counseling sessions, (2) consistency in the execution of counseling interventions, and (3) autonomy (Borders, 1990; McNeill et al., 1992). If these developmental characteristics are not forthcoming, supervisors need to ask what might be blocking learning (e.g., cognitive complexity, personality, or cultural issues) and to consider this more carefully.

With experience, it is expected that supervisees will develop more sophisticated ways to conceptualize the counseling process and the issues that their clients present and be less distracted by random specific information (Cummings et al., 1990). Novice supervisees will be more rigid and less discriminating in their delivery of therapeutic interventions. An "exaggerated forcefulness" (Tracey et al., 1988) in the delivery of an intervention may indicate that the supervisee is at the front end of a learning curve regarding this intervention. A hallmark of more advanced supervisees is that they are more flexible and less dominant when delivering interventions such as confrontation.

• **Supervision environment matters.** Supervisee characteristics and developmental agendas must be met with appropriate supervisor interventions in order for growth to occur. Although there are a plethora of supervision techniques to consider, these need to be used in ways that are appropriate to the developmental stage of the supervisee. To date, the research would support using experience level as a determinant for supervision environment, at least initially.

• **Supervision environment should be adjusted based on awareness of cognitive complexity and cognitive style.** Even though experience level is an appropriate place to begin in establishing the supervision environment, it is overly simplistic as the sole variable to take into consideration. Because other supervisee characteristics can trump experience, the supervision environment must follow the predominant characteristic in order to be maximally successful.

• **Development only begins during formal training. It doesn't end there.** In their seminal longitudinal study of professional development (Skovholt & Rønnestad, 1992a) and in a recent reformulation (Rønnestad & Skovholt, 2003), Skovholt and Rønnestad established that development for the mental health professional was a long road with many intriguing complexities along the way. They also established that most of the development for serious professionals occurred after formal training. Similarly, Fong et al. (1997) and Granello (2002) found that counselor (cognitive) development occurred only in the latter half of training programs. All this underscores the importance of clinical supervision beyond training and the early years in the field.

• **Developmental concepts are important, but not sufficient.** We have noted the inconsistencies in the research about the relative predictive power of development versus more stable individual characteristics such as cognitive style. In the second half of this chapter, we address cultural variables that must also inform supervision. In short, although we find developmental assumptions to be compelling, we advise clinical supervisors to expand beyond them in their practice.

• **Development of the supervisee must be an intentional process.** Finally, we concur with others (e.g., Barrett & Barber, 2005; Deal, 2003; Fong et al., 1997; Granello, 2002; Guiffrida, 2005; Peace & Sprinthall, 1998) that, although some cognitive development occurs as a result of supervised experience, we may not be as intentional in promoting development as we could be. Fong et al. noted that skill development receives much more consistent attention than cognitive development in many training programs. Similarly, it is not uncommon for personal growth (intrapersonal and interpersonal) to serve as a hallmark of a training program. Overall cognitive development, however, has been a sidebar.

CULTURAL DIFFERENCES

When two people meet in supervision or counseling, there is a negotiation that always happens. First, similarities are assessed, then dissimilarities. [Race]might be one . . . being from the same region might be another . . . having parents with similar emphases on education might be yet another. We then look to see how many of those dissimilarities can be bridged. The greater the effectiveness we have in bridging those dissimilarities the greater the multicultural competence we have in supervision or counseling (Hird, Cavalieri, Dulko, Felice, & Ho, 2001, p. 117).

The influence of cultural phenomena on the helping process has received sustained attention in recent years. Pedersen's (1991) assertion that virtually all counseling is multicultural has become a mantra for the helping professions. Killian (2001) applied Pedersen's sentiment to supervision by stating, "Since we all inhabit various social locations on ecosystemic axes of race, gender, class, and culture, to name but a few, and these locations intersect in unique and sometimes contradictory ways, we are all multicultural, and our interactions with others must necessarily be so as well" (p. 63). Any discussion of individual differences, therefore, must include a serious discussion of cultural differences.

We wish to make two points at this transition between individual differences that are primarily cognitive in nature to those that are cultural. First, these may seem to some readers to be strange bedfellows. It is our contention that, rather, they must be considered together for each to be fully understood. In other words, culture influences and shapes what we consider individual characteristics, such as personality (Daniels, D'Andrea, & Kim, 1999), and may significantly affect cognitive style and developmental trajectories. For example, experience level must be viewed in the cultural context within which the experience was gained. Was the supervisee the only male in his supervision group? The only male of color? The only male of color from a working-class background? To separate the influence of experience from the cultural context represents an incomplete supervision paradigm.

Second, we are sensitive to the position that cultural topics are marginalized when they are treated in isolation from all the aspects of supervision they touch. However, we view this as a political position (albeit an essential one) rather than an academic position. It is not our intention to isolate the importance of culture any more than it is our intention to isolate ethics or evaluation. Instead, we hope to offer the reader a convenient way to review the most compelling literature in each of the topics presented in this text with the assumption that all topics are infused in supervision practice. It is with both dissonance and intentionality, therefore, that we review the literature that addresses cultural influences on supervision. And we follow the literature in dividing culture even further into more discrete topics. The real challenge for the reader (and for all supervisors) is to remain integrative and constructionist, even as the literature is presented in a way that is primarily reductionist!

Several authors have asserted that entry-level training in multicultural issues must precede supervision if the latter is to be productive (e.g., Bernard, 1994a; Constantine, 1997; Fong & Lease, 1997; Priest, 1994). Constantine (1997) found that 70 percent of the supervisees that she surveyed had received training in multicultural issues, whereas 70 percent of the supervisors in her study had received no such academic training. While these findings may represent a cohort issue, they nonetheless call for systematic training of clinical supervisors in the many dimensions of multicultural interactions.

Attending to supervisor multicultural competence has positive outcomes for supervisees. Both Constantine (2001) and Burkard et al. (2006) found that providing multicultural supervision to supervisees was associated with higher levels of multicultural counseling self-efficacy. Because of the importance of self-efficacy for the professional development of counselors, Constantine suggested that supervisors may, by offering multicultural supervision, serve as catalysts for increased attention to multicultural dimensions in the counseling offered by their supervisees. The fact that Gatmon et al. (2001) found a low frequency of supervisory conversations about culture may support Constantine's (1997) earlier research, which determined that supervisors are inadequately prepared for this aspect of supervision. Ford and Britton (2002) found greater discourse about cultural matters in supervision than did Gatmon et al.; however, supervisees reported that these discussions only concerned clients, rather than supervisor–supervisee interactions. Therefore, the readily accepted premise that culture interfaces with all supervision has yet to become fully operationalized.

Political Nature of the Helping Professions

Social justice literature underscores the fact that the helping professions are sociopolitical in nature (Katz, 1985). By ignoring cultural differences, the dominant culture has been able to ignore much injustice done to nondominant cultures. Supervision is as vulnerable to reflecting the "theoretical myth of sameness" (Hardy, 1989) by ignoring the enormous and evasive effects of power and privilege as they influence interactions across cultural groups. Katz described this insensitivity as an "invisible veil" that affects our interactions with others, often outside our awareness. This blind spot leaves supervisees and clients unacceptably vulnerable when diagnostic or evaluative conclusions are made that are culturally uninformed (Dressel, Consoli, Kim, & Atkinson, 2007). Recent research (Constantine & Sue, 2007) indicates that some cross-cultural supervision still is defined by an invisible veil.

In this context, all supervision is not only cultural, but also political. Because supervisors have position power, they, by definition, weigh in on one side or the other of the many cultural struggles that define one's place in society, whether the person affected is the supervisee or the client or both. Killian (2001) asserted that "it is important for us to anchor or locate supervisors in terms of their own privilege and power ecosystemically so that they can more fully understand how that social location informs what happens in supervision" (p. 85). Porter (1994) stated that the final stage of multicultural supervision must be social justice for clients, supervisees, supervisors, and institutions. To have a lesser vision significantly compromises the ability of supervisors to have influence that might actually make a positive difference around the values espoused by the helping professions.

Culture Treated Holistically

Whereas most of the theoretical and empirical contributions regarding multicultural supervision continue to discuss discrete cultural factors (e.g., gender or race), a small amount of empirical work has considered multicultural supervision in a more integrative fashion.

Inman (2006) investigated the effects of the supervisor's multicultural competence (as perceived by their supervisees) on the supervisory working alliance, the supervisee's multicultural competence in case conceptualization (problem etiology and treatment plans), and supervisee satisfaction with supervision. Two interesting findings emerged from this study. First, while working alliance and satisfaction were positively affected by the supervisor's perceived multicultural competence, case conceptualization was negatively affected. Second, additional analyses determined that working alliance was a mediator variable between supervisor multicultural competence and satisfaction with supervision.

Because the majority of Inman's subjects were trainees in master's programs, the first of these findings may point to the complexity of incorporating new levels of awareness into one's work as a counselor. In other words, it may be that trainees who are invited to increase their awareness of how culture is operating in their work with clients may exhibit less cognitive complexity when asked to integrate this awareness into analytical tasks. Therefore, these findings may be more about the cognitive development of the supervisees used in the study than about the true effects of multicultural supervision over the longer term.

The revelation that the working alliance between supervisor and supervisee is key in setting the stage for productive encounters around the topic of culture is an important contribution to our knowledge base. While it has been argued that the working alliance is reduced for supervisees of color when multicultural issues are bypassed (Hays & Chang, 2003), Inman's results suggest that the shared goals and mutual trust that define the working alliance are foundational to successful multicultural supervision rather than an outcome of it. (See Chapter 6 for a more complete discussion of working alliance.)

Another study underscored the importance of the working alliance. Toporek, Ortega-Villalobos, and Pope-Davis (2004) conducted a qualitative investigation of critical incidents that occurred within multicultural supervision. Seventeen supervision dyads reported important critical incidents. While half of the incidents reported led to a positive increased awareness of culture for the participants, 15 percent of the incidents were considered to have a negative outcome. The authors noted that in these latter cases, the supervisory relationship may have been too fragile to benefit from a discussion of cultural issues.

Taylor, Hernández, Deri, Rankin, and Siegel (2006) reported a qualitative study of ethnic minority marriage and family therapy supervisors who asserted their felt responsibility to mentor future generations of therapists in multiple aspects of cultural identity. Yet these supervisors also acknowledged that their supervision was much more likely to include discussions of racial and ethnic identity, gender, and social class as each related to social location than it was the topics of sexual orientation or religion. This study serves as one example of the difficulty of attending to diversity variables in their entirety, even when there is an acknowledgement of the importance of doing so.

Assistance for supervisors who aspire to provide competent multicultural supervision is provided by Dressel et al. (2007), who used a Delphi method to survey counseling center supervisors with extensive multicultural experience regarding those behaviors that correlate with successful multicultural supervision. Dressel et al. found 35 behaviors that supported multicultural supervision, most of which addressed culture directly (see Table 5.4 for behaviors listed in rank order). Both this list and the Multicultural Supervision Competencies Questionnaire (Wong & Wong, 2003), found in the Supervisor's Toolbox, can be used as assessment tools or as a guide for practice.

As we stated earlier, while it is generally accepted that multiple cultural identities interact within supervision, much of the professional literature focuses on discrete aspects of cultural identity. In the following sections, we review this literature. We begin each section with a review of evolving critical thought and follow with a discussion of the modest amount of empirical work to date.

Racial and Ethnic Issues Within Multicultural Supervision

In his seminal work, Bradshaw (1982) addressed the implications of race in the supervisory relationship, stating that race is a highly charged catalyst in our society, one that is bound to emerge, even if not addressed, in supervision. Helms and Piper (1994) magnified this assumption when they claimed that racial identity has evolved to occupy the greatest percentage of self-concept. Killian (2001) cited Carter and Qureshi (1995) as asserting that race is considered the most significant difference between people because other cultural characteristics are often more fluid and flexible. In short, we continue to be a society within which we are often defined, and divided, by the social construction of race. As a result, supervisory interactions that are cross-racial represent some of our most challenging moments as supervisors (Ladany et al., 2005).

Fong and Lease (1997) provided a comprehensive overview of the issues salient to the White supervisor attempting to provide culturally sensitive cross-racial supervision. They asserted that most of the challenges facing the White supervisor can be categorized by one of the following: (1) unintentional racism, (2) power dynamics, (3) trust and the supervisory alliance, and (4) communication issues. Basic to both unintentional racism and power dynamics, it seems to us, is the power and privilege of the supervisor to address the topic of race. In fact, we now have evidence that if supervisors do not initiate discussions about cultural issues in supervision, very few discussions will occur (Duan & Roehlke, 2001; Gatmon et al., 2001).

TABLE 5.4 Supervisory Behaviors in Successful Multicultural Supervision

RANK	BEHAVIORAL STATEMENT
1.	Creating a safe (nonjudgmental, supportive) environment for discussion of multicultural issues, values, and ideas
2.	Developing my own self-awareness about cultural/ethnic identity, biases, and limitations
2.	Communicating acceptance of and respect for supervisees' culture and perspectives
4.	Listening [to] and demonstrating genuine respect [for] supervisees' ideas about how culture influences the clinical interaction
4.	Providing openness, genuineness, empathy, warmth, and nonjudgmental stance
4.	Validating integration of supervisees' professional and racial/ethnic identities and helping to explore potential blocks to this process
7.	Discussing and supporting multicultural perspectives as they relate to the supervisees' clinical work

(Continued)

TABLE 5.4   Continued

RANK	BEHAVIORAL STATEMENT
7.	Tending to feelings of discomfort experienced by supervisees concerning multicultural issues
7.	Supporting supervisees' own racial/ethnic identity development
10.	Presenting myself nondefensively by tolerating anger, rage, and fear around multicultural issues
11.	Providing supervisees a multiculturally diverse caseload to ensure breadth of clinical experience
12.	Attending to racial/ethnic cultural differences reflected in parallel process issues (supervisor/supervisee and supervisee/client)
13.	Discussing realities of racism/oppression and acknowledging that race is always an issue
14.	Acknowledging, discussing, and respecting racial/ethnic multicultural similarities and differences between myself and supervisees, and exploring feelings concerning these
15.	Addressing a broad range of differences (e.g., learning styles, interpersonal needs, sexual orientation, religious/spiritual beliefs, race)
16.	Checking out the supervisory expectations with supervisees
17.	Initiating discussions about the importance of culture
18.	Acknowledging and discussing power issues in supervision that may be related to racial/ethnic multicultural differences
19.	Encouraging supervisees to share, within supervision, their personal and professional cultural background and experiences
20.	Consulting colleagues willingly about my own reactions to racial/ethnic concerns from supervision
21.	Acknowledging my own lack of knowledge on racial/ethnic multicultural differences and inviting supervisees to give me feedback and teach me
22.	Testing hypotheses about my supervisees, not accepting just one view
22.	Self-disclosing aspects of my own cultural background
24.	Implementing knowledge and awareness of supervision theory by attending to supervisees' process and stage of development
25.	Engaging supervisees in peer review with each other's cases through case conferences
26.	Seeking understanding of supervisees' culture through both didactic and experiential means on my own
27.	Providing written and verbal feedback regarding supervisees' multicultural interactions with staff and clients
28.	Providing multicultural readings and related training experiences for supervisees
29.	Being willing to confront supervisee's inadequate skills, listening if that is challenged on grounds of cultural insensitivity, but not backing away from my own standards and values
30.	Allowing supervisees to see my clinical work in cross-cultural counseling and/or consultation through tapes or live observation
31.	Letting supervisees take responsibility
32.	Providing supervisees with information about various cultures
33.	Offering supervisees mentorship and other collaborative professional opportunities with me (e.g., co-led presentations, coauthored papers)
33.	Departing from Western theoretical perspectives in supervision
35.	Having supervisees keep a journal that documents personal reactions to interactions with seminar facilitator and intern colleagues

Source: From "Successful and Unsuccessful Multicultural Supervisory Behaviors: A Delphi Poll," by J. L. Dressel, A. J. Consoli, B. S. K. Kim, D. R. Atkinson, 2007, *Journal of Multicultural Counseling and Development, 35,* pp. 51–64. Reprinted by permission.

White privilege is endemic to the social construction of race in the United States and has been viewed as not receiving adequate attention in the supervision literature (Hays & Chang, 2003). Indeed, addressing the oppression that is embedded in privilege is most likely to be the most challenging aspect for most White supervisees in their counseling. Embracing cultural differences while ignoring privilege, however, is anathema to multicultural counseling and supervision. Hays and Chang suggested that supervisors begin the task of addressing privilege by sharing their own grappling with these issues and how the issues have affected them as counselors and supervisors.

As an acknowledgement of the challenge in addressing White privilege, D'Andrea (2005) suggested that White students would benefit from a special orientation prior to commencing their training as mental health professionals. This orientation would include an overview of the evolution of the multicultural counseling movement in the United States, a review of some of the implications of the rapid cultural, racial, and ethnic changes in the United States for the practicing counselor, the pervasiveness of cultural dynamics, and some of the typical reactions of White students to multicultural training.

In a similar vein, Cook (1994) addressed power in two ways: the power inherent in the role of the supervisor and the power of being a member of the dominant culture in a sociopolitical context that is overtly and covertly racist. The latter is central to the concern of privilege and unintentional racism. Though inexcusable at this point in the evolution of the mental health professions, it is sadly conceivable that supervisors may remain ignorant of their racism due to their own limited racial identity development (Chang, Hays, & Shoffner, 2003; Constantine & Sue, 2007; Cook, 1994; Fong & Lease, 1997).

Racial Identity Development.   To the extent that one accepts that racial identity development is stage-like and linear, development has been described for both persons of color and Whites (Helms, 1990). Theoretically, the former begin

with a preference for values and norms of the dominant culture (Conformity), move through a questioning period (Dissonance), become ethnocentric within their racial/ethnic group (Resistance and Immersion), become secure in their racial identity such that they can question rigid Resistance attitudes (Introspection), and finally, arrive at a point of both secure racial identity and sensitivity to all forms of oppression, as well as be open to constructive elements of the dominant culture (Integrative Awareness).

Whites have a longer road to travel in arriving at a balanced racial identity, primarily because of the comfort of being in the dominant group. Theoretically, Whites begin with no awareness of being a racial being and are oblivious to racism (Contact), become conflicted as they become more aware of racism and some of the moral dilemmas it poses for them (Disintegration), pull back from that new awareness through increased discomfort (Reintegration), move to an intellectual understanding of race issues and seek contact with persons of color who are similar to them (Pseudo-Independence), confront their own White privilege and explore self as a racial being in ways that include the affective (Immersion/Emersion), and finally exhibit more comfort with the experiential reality of race and are committed to work toward abandonment of White entitlement (Autonomy). The matching up of these similar, though distinct, racial identity paths for supervisors and supervisees has been reflected in the literature.

Chang et al. (2003) adapted these models to chart the hypothetical responses of the White supervisor and a supervisee of color based on their racial identity development (see Table 5.5). As Fong and Lease stated, supervisors are ill equipped to conduct multicultural supervision if they are below the immersion–emersion stages of development. Additionally, Chang et al. developed Cook's (1994) understanding of the supervision as parallel, progressive, or regressive based on the White supervisor's racial identity development in relation to that of the supervisee of color. Because of the power and privilege of the White supervisor, it is that person's sophistication regarding

TABLE 5.5   A Developmental Approach: White Supervisors Working with Supervisees of Color

Supervisee of Color's Racial Identity Development Status

WHITE SUPERVISOR'S RACIAL IDENTITY STATUS	CONFORMITY	DISSONANCE	RESISTANCE AND IMMERSION	INTROSPECTION	INTEGRATIVE AWARENESS
Contact	Parallel: Unawareness of racial/cultural issues; neither the supervisor nor supervisee increase multicultural competence; myth of sameness	Regressive: Supervisor unaware of racial/cultural issues; supervisor could unconsciously push the supervisee into self-depreciating attitudes and beliefs	Regressive: Supervisor unaware of racial/cultural issues; supervisee may attempt to reform supervisor; short, conflictual relationship	Regressive: Supervisor unaware of racial/cultural issues; supervisee frustrated with supervisor's obliviousness to race; supervisory relationship ends in frustration	Regressive: Supervisor unaware of racial/cultural issues; premature termination because supervisee views supervisor as inexpert
Disintegration	Parallel: Supervisor attempts to protect and nurture supervisee; supervisee idealizes supervisor	Parallel: Supervisee attempts to protect and nurture supervisee; supervisee has conflictual feelings	Regressive: Supervisee mistrusts supervisor and views supervisor as part of the oppressive group	Regressive: Unproductive relationship; supervisee may become frustrated with supervisor and view supervisor as patronizing	Regressive: Unproductive; supervisee may attempt to reform supervisor; premature termination with supervisee perceiving supervisor as inexpert
Pseudo-Independence	Progressive: Supervisor recognizes racial/cultural issues; may discuss racial differences; supervisee will find racial/cultural issues anxiety provoking	Progressive: Supervisor recognizes racial/cultural issues; open discussion of racial differences	Progressive: Supervisor recognizes racial/cultural issues; supervisee may mistrust supervisor	Parallel: Open discussion of racial/cultural issues; supervisor still lacks working knowledge of how to adapt skills and knowledge to supervisee of color	Regressive: Supervisee may become frustrated with supervisor's inability to adapt skills and knowledge to supervisee of color; supervisor may improve multicultural competence while working with this supervisee

Immersion/ Emersion	Progressive: Supervisor willing to confront racial/cultural issues; supervisee may find this very threatening	Progressive: Supervisor can assist supervisee in resolving racial/cultural conflict	Progressive: Supervisor can dispel supervisee's view of dominant culture; supervisee may be distrusting of supervisor	Parallel: Mutually enhancing relation-ship; awareness of racial/cultural issues in supervisor	Parallel: Cultural issues are openly recognized and discussed
Autonomy	Progressive: Supervisor recognizes racial/ cultural issues; provides a culturally sensitive approach to supervision	Progressive: Supervisor recognizes racial/ cultural issues; provides a culturally sensitive approach	Progressive: Supervisor recognizes racial/ cultural issues; supervisee may be resistant to working with a white supervisor	Progressive: Supervisor recognizes racial/ cultural issues; can assist supervisee in resolving ethnic identity conflict	Parallel: Both recognize race/ethnicity as an important part of each person's identity; culturally sensitive approach to supervision; movement by both towards advocacy

Relationship Types:
Parallel Relationship—the supervisor and the supervisee exhibit similar racial identity status
Cross-Regressive—the supervisor and supervisee exhibit opposite racial identity status where the supervisee is more advanced than the supervisor
Crossed-Progressive—the supervisor and supervisee exhibit opposite racial identity status where the supervisor is more advanced than the supervisee

Adapted from: (Atkinson, Morten, & Sue, 1998; Cook, 1994; Helms, 1984).
Source: From "Cross-Racial Supervision: A Developmental Approach for White Supervisor Working with Supervisees of Color, by C. Y. Chang, D. G. Hays & M. F. Shoffner, 2003, *The Clinical Supervisor, 22*(2), pp. 121–138. Reprinted by permission.

cross-racial interactions that will drive supervision. Therefore, the helping professions can only begin to claim that competent multicultural supervision is the norm when supervisors are required to demonstrate adequate racial identity development as a prerequisite for assuming the role of supervisor (Bernard, 1994a). In our discussion of key empirical work, we will return to racial identity development as a critical factor.

International Supervisees.   Although most discussions about cross-racial supervision are centered around persons who share the complicated racial history of the United States, Killian (2001) collected interviews with supervisors who had supervised international students as well. One White male supervisor had this to say about his experience supervising a female student from Japan:

> *Looking back . . . I don't think I was able to speak her "language." I did broach the subject of culture, and we did discuss some cultural concepts explicitly, and we were comfortable. But I did not take into account her own background in terms of education system and how that might influence her expectations of the training she would receive from me as a . . . supervisor. And so, I was . . . trying to be collaborative and non-hierarchical and just "getting together to talk about some clinical scenarios." And now, I think that's not at all what she was expecting. These differences had an impact on our relationship, but, unfortunately, they were not always processed or made explicit during supervision. For example, I think that now we would be much more likely to talk about our respective values around indirect communication, saving face, training style, and power.* (p. 75)

One Russian male supervisee explained his experience as a cross-ethnic international supervisee in the United States:

> *I felt like sometimes they didn't know what to do with me, like they didn't know how to approach me. They were very cautious. It felt like they had to go an extra mile and I felt like a burden. I could see that they were having to make an extra effort. I couldn't help thinking that they would prefer to have an American student as a supervisee because it makes life easier.* (pp. 74–75)

This last example underscores the complexities that are included in the terms *multicultural* or *diversity*. Killian (2001) quoted a Jewish female supervisor who stated, "As trainers, we want to be sensitive to gender, ethnicity, race, culture, class, but we tend to see one of these more clearly than the others, possibly because it's been experienced as crucial to our own sense of being, possibly because we tend to look at only one thing at a time" (p. 78). This supervisor addresses the difficulty of sustaining the complexity of multicultural supervision because we "tend to privilege or resonate with a particular ecosystemic axis of power more than others" (Killian, 2001, p. 78). We will review empirical work regarding the supervision of international students in the next section.

Before moving to the research, we want to reflect the thoughtful contribution of Estrada, Frame, and Williams (2004) who acknowledged the issues we have already raised, but also caution supervisors about making common errors in multicultural supervision. Estrada et al., for example, noted that the word "culture" is often used loosely and to moderate the effect of a more direct (and more uncomfortable) reference to race. We might add that the word "culture" is sometimes used so loosely as to be meaningless. Conversely, Estrada et al. (2004) cited earlier work (Leong & Wagner, 1994) and cautioned that our zeal to become culturally competent quickly can translate to overindulgence in discussions of race, especially for our novice supervisees with their clients. They suggested that supervisors invite conversations about race and privilege within supervision first, so supervisees can wrestle with nuances there rather than engaging in overly simplistic discussions with clients. In short, Estrada et al. remind us that errors can be made by the enthused as well as the negligent. This admonition seems important to remember as we address this important area of competence.

Empirical Results.   The vast majority of research addressing race within supervision has studied the perceptions of supervisees (Burkard et al., 2006; Constantine & Sue, 2007; Cook & Helms, 1988;

Fukuyama, 1994; Gatmon et al., 2001; Hilton, Russell, & Salmi, 1995; Kleintjes & Swartz, 1996; Vander Kolk, 1974). Though methodologies and sample sizes are quite varied, a picture of the experiences of supervisees does emerge. Studies that focused on supervisees of color exclusively reported distinct feelings of vulnerability, especially when their supervisors were White. Supervisees of color remain guarded (Cook & Helms, 1988) and reported either fear of not being respected (Kleintjes & Swartz, 1996; Vander Kolk, 1974) or incidences of cultural insensitivity (Constantine & Sue, 2007). One noteworthy finding from the Constantine and Sue qualitative study was that Black supervisees experienced a reluctance on the part of their White supervisors to give them critical feedback as a "microaggression" (that is, an indignity that communicates a negative message). Anticipating a "damned if I do and damned if I don't" reaction from White supervisors, Constantine and Sue noted that the "same underlying process or issue, namely . . . racism" (p. 149) is involved when supervisors hold back, and communicates to the supervisee "that feedback is influenced or tied to their racial group membership" (p. 149). The Constantine and Sue findings underscore an important dimension to cultural competence.

Despite an overall profile that seems to elevate the importance of race in supervision, Cook and Helms (1988) found that the perception that their supervisors liked them was much more important to supervisees of color than the race of the supervisor in contributing to satisfaction with supervision. Additionally, Fukuyama (1994) found that supervisees of color reported more positive critical incidents than negative with White supervisors, noting openness and support, and culturally relevant supervision as key to their postive experience. Because none of these studies included a sample of White supervisees, we are reminded of Leong and Wagner's (1994) caution that we must not overinterpret the results. We espeically want to distinguish between studies that considered supervisees' fears (e.g., VanderKolk, 1974) versus those that tracked actual experiences of supervisees of color.

When both supervisees of color and White supervisees are surveyed, the picture is more complex. Burkard et al. (2006) reported that both White supervisees and supervisees of color found that supervisors are sometimes unresponsive to cultural issues, whether or not they are themselves persons of color. Thirteen White supervisees and thirteen supervisees of color were interviewed regarding their cross-racial supervision experiences to explore the effects of supervision that was culturally responsive or unresponsive. Culturally responsive supervision was perceived to be of great benefit to the supervisee, the supervision relationship, and client outcome (that is, clients benefitted from counseling that was culturally appropriate). As might be expected, supervisees of color reported unresponsive supervision more often than White supervisees who had supervisors of color. Supervisees of color also reported being more harmed by unresponsive supervision and were less willing to self-disclose with their supervisors after such events. It should be noted that those supervisees of color who experienced culturally unresponsive supervision were more likely to have had a tenuous relationship with their supervisors before the unresponsive supervision occurred. These findings refer to the importance of the working alliance as a basis for multicultural supervision.

Two other studies that focused on supervisee perceptions reflected mixed results regarding the role race plays within supervision. Hilton et al. (1995) investigated the effects of supervisor support and race on counselor anxiety, perceived performance, satisfaction, and perceptions of the supervisory relationship. All supervisees were White; supervisors were either White or African American. Whereas supervisor support emerged as a main effect, supervisor race did not. Finally, Gatmon et al. (2001) explored the effect of conversation around the cultural variables of gender, ethnicity, and sexual orientation on the supervisory working alliance and satisfaction with supervision. They reported that only the discussion of differences and similarities regarding ethnicity significantly enhanced the supervisory working alliance, though not satisfaction with supervision.

Interestingly, matching supervisor and supervisee for all variables studied did not improve working alliance or satisfaction. It should also be emphasized that the incidence of discussion of cultural variables was low overall, leading the authors to reiterate the concerns of Constantine (1997).

It makes sense intuitively that supervisees would be the focus of the bulk of research addressing race and ethnicity as supervisees are consumers of supervision, good or bad. A handful of studies have extended beyond this focus and looked at supervision from the supervisor's perspective or from both supervisee and supervisor.

Following the theme of the importance of the supervision relationship, Duan and Roehlke (2001) found that perception of the relationship was significant in cross-racial supervision. These researchers surveyed 60 supervision dyads, all of which were cross-racial. Interestingly, results revealed similar patterns whether supervisors were White or a racial minority. Findings were that supervisees were more sensitive to cultural and racial issues than were supervisors, supervisors reported making greater efforts to engage in multicultural supervision than supervisees perceived, and satisfaction with supervision was related to supervisees' self-disclosure and both members of the dyad perceiving positive attitudes toward each other. Once again, these results seem to support the concern stated by others that supervisors are not carrying their weight in the process of multicultural supervision (Constantine, 1997; Ford & Britton, 2002).

Hird, Tao, and Gloria (2004) studied the perception of supervisors only. They reported that racial–ethnic minority (REM) supervisors took a broad view of culture and were more likely to discuss culture with both REM supervisees and White supervisees. White supervisors, on the other hand, focused primarily on language, racial identity, sexual orientation, and religion and were more likely to address these when they supervised someone who was racially different than they. These findings, then, seem to indicate that we are making progress on multicultural supervision when differences are visible or known, but that we still have work to do to assist all supervisory

dyads to acknowledge the importance of discourse about cultural identity.

As most cross-racial studies are focused on satisfaction and relationship variables, little is known about how racial differences affect other aspects of supervision. Chung, Marshall, and Gordon (2001) studied 76 supervisors who were identified as either White or Black and were asked to evaluate hypothetical supervisees who were either similar to them or different on race and gender. Chung et al. found no main effect for race in studying bias in evaluation and feedback, though they did find gender was a factor. These kinds of discriminating studies, which weigh the effect of race against other factors, are essential for understanding the complexity of multicultural supervision.

Racial Identity Development. Another important line of research has used racial identity models (Atkinson, Morten, & Sue, 1998; Cook, 1994; Helms, 1984) to assess interactions between supervisors and supervisees. Ladany, Brittan-Powell, and Pannu (1997) found that, whereas racial matching between supervisor and supervisee did not affect the supervisory working alliance in a positive manner, racial identity similarity was predictive in some instances. Specifically, those dyads who shared higher racial identity attitudes (parallel–high interactions) had the strongest supervisory working alliance; they also were found to have positive feelings of liking and trust for each other. Progressive interactions (i.e., a supervisor with higher racial identity development than the supervisee) had the next-most-positive interactions. The authors speculated that, in these relationships, the supervisor was able to provide both a safe and challenging context for supervisees that benefited the relationship. Regressive interactions (for which the supervisee's racial identity development is higher than the supervisor's) predicted the weakest supervisory alliance. Finally, both parallel–high interactions and progressive interactions were correlated with supervisee perception of supervisor influence on multicultural development. A later study (Bhat & Davis, 2007) also found parallel–highs to have the strongest working alliance. However, their weakest group was parallel–lows, not those in regressive relationships. The authors speculated that supervisors in regressive relationships may have viewed the working alliance "in an artificially elevated manner" (p. 89). Finally, as in other studies, race itself was not a significant factor.

Ladany, Inman, Constantine, and Hofheinz (1997) shed additional light on the topic of racial identity development and supervision. This study found that for both White supervisees and supervisees of color, racial identity development was related to self-reported multicultural competence. Specifically, White students at the pseudo-independence stage and ethnic minority supervisees at the dissonance and awareness stages reported higher levels of multicultural competence. In light of the definitions of both dissonance and pseudo-independence, the pairing of these levels of racial identity with perceived multicultural competence is not particularly comforting. Additionally, Ladany, Inman, Constantine, and Hofheinz found that perceived competence was not correlated with multicultural case conceptualization ability; however, supervisor intervention was found to ameliorate supervisees' ability to infuse cultural information into the conceptualization of treatment.

Constantine, Warren, and Miville (2005) have continued this line of research by studying White dyads to determine how racial identity influenced self-reported multicultural competence. Both progressive supervision dyads and parallel–high dyads resulted in higher supervisee self-report of multicultural counseling competence and higher ratings for multicultural case conceptualization than those within parallel–low dyads. Results for those involved in regressive supervision were not significant. The authors noted that this last finding may be the result of the low numbers of pairs that were regressive. It may also be the case that supervisees whose racial identity development is more advanced than their supervisors find other contexts to further increase their skills. The most alarming result, however, was that 18 percent, or nine dyads, were parallel–low. While the racial awareness of White supervisees has increased in recent years

due to concerted efforts of training programs in mental health disciplines, Utsey, Gernat, and Hammar (2005) reported a considerable range in comfort among these supervisees in discussing racial issues. Without supervisors who are advanced in their racial identity development, these supervisees will most likely enter the profession with unacceptably low multicultural competence.

Ethnic Differences.   Finally, in a relatively rare cross-ethnic study, Haj-Yahia and Roer-Strier (1999) reported results from two samples of Arab supervisees working with Jewish supervisors in Israel. This would seem to be a poignant example of what Killian (2001) referred to as politics encroaching on the supervisory process. Results having to do with the supervisory relationship revealed that, similar to studies done in the United States with cross-racial populations, supervisees in this study were far more likely to be attuned to cultural differences than were supervisors. Only 15 percent of the supervisors felt that relationship difficulties were attributable to supervising students "from a different cultural background in a complicated sociopolitical environment" (p. 27). By contrast, all Arab students could recall at least one cultural misunderstanding between them and their supervisors. Difficulties included different expectations about the supervision process, supervisor's lack of familiarity with the Arab students' cultural norms and values, differences in perception regarding clients' problems, and different styles of communication (e.g., supervisors noted that students would not "speak up"). By far the most frequent issues raised by supervisees revolved around cultural difference. Surprisingly, however, the authors reported that "supervisors hardly related to this aspect and only one of them expressed her interest in learning more about norms in Arab culture" (p. 28). Finally, and despite the difficulties this study brought to light, the vast majority of Arab supervisees preferred Jewish supervisors whom they described as "more open and liberal, better at expressing emotions and more professional" (p. 31). This study, it seems to us, is an excellent example of the competing and complex variables that contribute to the supervisory relationship, not the least of which is cultural difference. It also indicates that ethnic identity development is as crucial as racial identity development in particular geopolitical contexts.

International Students. Another sizable population that has received very little attention in the supervision literature is that of international students who seek an education in the helping professions in the United States. These students often speak English only haltingly and struggle with the cultural nuances and assumptions embedded in their training programs. Nilsson and her colleagues (Nilsson & Anderson, 2004; Nilsson & Dodds, 2006; Nilsson, 2007) have served as key contributors to our present understanding of international students within supervision. Nilsson and Anderson (2004) surveyed 42 international students in APA programs and found that low level of acculturation to U.S. culture was significantly related to a low working alliance with one's supervisor, less counseling self-efficacy, and more role ambiguity. On a positive note, it was also found that additional discussions of cultural issues occurred for these students with their supervisors. Nilsson and Anderson stressed the importance of inviting a discussion that compares and contrasts U.S. culture to culture of origin for international students. This would include discussing how relationships are negotiated in different cultures, how mental illness is perceived, and how race and ethnic relations are handled. As with all cross-cultural interactions, it also is important for the supervisor to communicate the limits of his or her understanding and openness to learning about the student's cultural context.

Understandably, students who were less acculturated to the United States reported more discussion of cultural issues in their supervision (Nilsson & Dodds, 2006). Using a sample of 115 counseling and psychology students, Nilsson and Dodds found that these discussions led to more satisfaction with supervision and to rating their supervisors as more sensitive to diversity issues. The exception to this was if, like U.S. supervisees, the international students felt more culturally

knowledgeable than their supervisors. In this case, satisfaction and regard for the supervisors decreased. There was no difference found between White supervisors and supervisors of color.

Finally, in a study of 73 counseling students, Nilsson (2007) found that lower academic self-efficacy was correlated with more cultural discussions in supervision. These same supervisees valued these conversations more than students with higher self-efficacy. Additionally, and again consistent with other multicultural research, students with a more favorable view of their supervisors also reported having more cultural discussions with them. Taken together, these studies underscore the importance of cultural sensitivity in working with supervisees from other countries, whether or not these students are different racially.

In summary, a review of the literature to date would seem to indicate that, although racial and ethnic diversity play a key role in supervision, other supervisor attributes are equally, if not more, important. The willingness of the supervisor to open the cultural door and walk through it with the supervisee is perhaps the single most powerful intervention for multicultural supervision. Secondly, it is key for supervisors to continue to revisit identity models in order to challenge themselves and stimulate increased development. Whether one is a therapist or a supervisor, multicultural competence is not easily attained; the will to attain such competence and the trust that can be engendered by such a commitment may be the most powerful operative variable within the supervisory relationship to move both supervisor and supervisee toward increased cultural competence.

Gender Issues Within Multicultural Supervision

The status of women in our society has been a tenacious problem that has affected them economically and psychologically. Just as with racial and ethnic identities, it is important that both supervisees and supervisors enter the supervision relationship having spent some time and energy addressing their own gender identities and assumptions and having been sensitized to the many ways in which gender affects them in relationships, including relationships with clients (Stevens-Smith, 1995). Nelson (1991) advised supervisors to remain vigilant regarding their own gender biases prior to engaging in supervision.

Some types of dilemmas involving gender are fairly predictable:

- A female supervisee does not think her male supervisor takes her seriously.
- A male supervisee states that he expected his female supervisor to be more supportive.
- A male supervisor finds it easier to evaluate the strengths of his males supervisees than his female supervisees.
- A female supervisor gives her male supervisee feedback that he is treating his female client in a sexist manner. The supervisee feels ganged up on.

These are only a few of the complications around the issue of gender in the supervision process. The themes that seem to emerge with consistency, both in practice and in the supervision literature, have to do with the different voices of female versus male supervisors and supervisees, the different ways that power is awarded and used depending on the supervisor's or supervisee's gender, and the implications of matching gender in supervision or not. To the extent possible, these themes will be addressed separately. Whereas gender identity development may prove to be as fruitful as racial and ethnic identity development for informing supervision, studies using identity development rather than gender have not yet emerged (Barnes & Bernard, 2003).

We will attempt to look at gender from several different angles, but we will not pay particular attention to the ethical issues that are covered in Chapter 3, specifically overt sexism, sexual harassment, and sexual exploitation. Such abuses of power are quite different from legitimate (if uninformed) cultural differences based on gender and represent a perversion of the supervision process (Bernard, 1994a).

Different Voices.   Carol Gilligan (1982) is usually credited with the "voice" metaphor, suggesting that women and men are socialized to approach interpersonal relationships differently; women take on the voice of care, which focuses on "loving and being loved, listening and being listened to, responding and being responded to" (Brown & Gilligan, 1990, p. 8), and men take on the voice of justice, which focuses on "a vision of equality, reciprocity, and fairness between persons" (Brown & Gilligan, 1990, p. 8). Twohey and Volker (1993) argued that, because the supervisory role has more often been held by men, the voice of justice has been the predominant voice in supervision, emphasizing objective and scientific perspectives.

Twohey and Volker (1993) asserted that the Western tradition of splitting intellectual and emotional events has been perpetuated by diminishing the care voice in supervision. By contrast, when the voice of care is included, some of the most pertinent issues in the supervision relationship can be addressed openly and in the context of support. Jordan's (2006) research found that, indeed, "care and concern" were of key importance to master's level supervisees.

Bernstein (1993) and Ellis and Robbins (1993) stressed the error in assuming that male supervisors (and supervisees) consistently speak from the voice of justice and that female supervisors (and supervisees) represent primarily the voice of care. They noted that this assumption is not supported empirically, a position ardently emphasized by Osterberg (1996). Furthermore, Ellis and Robbins addressed both the gains and disadvantages of matching the supervisee's voice. In other words, although Twohey and Volker seemed to indicate that the care voice is unrepresented in supervision and should be attended to more consistently, Ellis and Robbins took a more strategic approach and suggested that the supervisor choose the voice that will either challenge or support the supervisee, depending on the supervision goal at the time.

Although Bernstein (1993) and Ellis and Robbins (1993) put forth a convincing argument for androgynous supervision, gender stereotypes may confound the outcome. Ault-Riche (1988), for example, noted that capable female supervisors are often misinterpreted despite which voice they deliver. "Those supervisors who present as primarily nurturant are devalued for not being clear thinkers; those who present as primarily task-focused are experienced as dangerous" (p. 188). Ault-Riche's discussion implies that it would be naive for supervisors of either gender to think that their supervisees are not influenced by gender bias. These biases are, after all, the product of life-long socialization.

Gender Role Conflict. Whereas much of the supervision literature on gender has focused on the issues of female socialization, more recent contributions (Wester & Vogel, 2002; Wester, Vogel, & Archer, 2004) have alerted us to the training and supervision issues for male supervisees based on the extent to which they reflect traditional male socialization. Male gender role conflict (GRC) occurs when the current situation calls for behaviors that confront previously held assumptions about appropriate male norms. Drawing on the work of O'Neil and his colleagues (O'Neil, 1981; O'Neil, Helmas, Gable, David, & Wrightsman, 1986; O'Neil, Good, & Holmes, 1995), Wester and Vogel suggested that the learning required to become a good therapist could exacerbate GRC for some supervisees. As one example, these authors noted that the male pattern of excelling through competition is incompatible with the important skill of seeking feedback about skill deficits. Similarly, the restricted emotionality (RE) demanded of traditional norms, especially for men in their relationships with other men, would be confronted in many counseling and supervisory contexts. Wester and Vogel admonished supervisors to use the skills endemic to all multicultural supervision in their work with GRC males. Their empirical work will be reviewed in the next section.

Differences Between Male and Female Supervisors. The supervision literature regarding differences between male and female supervisors, as well as distinguishable reactions to supervisors

because of their gender, draws both from conjecture and scientific investigation. Watson (1993), for example, warned that female supervisors might be more prone to find themselves in therapy-like dual relationships with their supervisees as an extension of their inclination or desire to be nurturant. Male supervisors might arrive at their perceptions more quickly, but employ less data to do so. Female supervisors might also take feedback from supervisees more to heart (Reid, McDaniel, Donaldson, & Tollers, 1987) than would their male counterparts. We suggest that these gender stereotypes would be moderated by other factors; for example, whether one is a Feeling or Thinking type on the MBTI.

Granello (1996) suggested that, because supervision is largely a conversational process, findings regarding the different conversational styles of men and women are relevant. As examples, Granello surveyed authors and researchers who have noted that males are not socialized to be listeners (Hotelling & Forrest, 1985); that males have been found to respond differently in conversations when they are in positions of power, whereas women do not (Sagrestano, 1992); and that males have been found to execute 75 percent of all conversational interruptions (Kollock, Blumstein, & Schwartz, 1985). Certainly, if unchecked, these gendered behaviors would interfere with a supervisory conference.

Empirical Results. Empirical support for gender differences related specifically to supervision is growing and, in recent years, has expanded into several aspects of supervision, including the supervisory relationship, evaluation, the use of power in supervision, and interaction styles. What follows is a discussion of this research.

Sells, Goodyear, Lichtenberg, and Polkinghorne (1997) studied gender-related differences for both supervisors and supervisees. These authors found that female supervisors had a greater relational focus than did male supervisors, spending more time in supervision focused on the supervisee. Male supervisors, on the other hand, spent a significantly greater amount of time focused on the supervisee's client. When male supervisors worked with male supervisees, these supervisees rated their technical skills higher; when female supervisors worked with female supervisees, the latter rated their personal awareness higher. Perhaps the most important finding of the Sells et al. study (from the perspective of the supervisee) was that gender was not related to the reported impact of supervision by either supervisor or supervisee, nor was it related to the supervisor's evaluation of the supervisee. Goodyear (1990) also found no differences in how male and female supervisees were evaluated according to (a) skills, (b) conceptualization, and (c) personhood variables.

Research conducted by Chung et al. (2001) unfortunately did not support the gender-free conclusions of previous research in terms of evaluation. Chung et al. found that male participants in their study (all of whom had served as clinical supervisors) rated hypothetical supervisees more negatively when the supervisee was depicted as being female than when the supervisee was male. Their rating difference approached one standard deviation. Female respondents, however, did not show this same kind of gender bias.

The Chung et al. (2001) study might shed some light on a finding reported by Anderson, Schlossberg, and Rigazio-DiGilio (2000). Anderson et al. asked marriage and family therapists to recollect "best" and "worst" supervision experiences. Although "best" supervision was conducted by both male and female supervisors somewhat evenly, almost two-thirds of "worst" experiences were when the supervisor was male. Because most respondents were female, it is possible that their reactions might have reflected the critical evaluations of their male supervisors during their supervision.

Looking at evaluation from the supervisee's perspective, Warburton, Newberry, and Alexander (1989) reported that female supervisees tended to underestimate their accomplishments, whereas male supervisees overestimated them. It would seem, then, that attention to gender during the evaluation process is warranted.

Wester et al. (2004) studied 103 male supervisees and found that male supervisees with higher levels of restricted emotionality (RE) used a turning-against-self defensive style and reported lower self-efficacy as counselors. These results contradict findings that males tend to be kinder self-evaluators than females. It is quite possible that males with low RE respond more like females than males with high RE.

Finally, Heru, Strong, Price, and Recupero (2004, 2006) found male and female supervisors and supervisees to differ on their level of comfort with boundary negotiations, discussions about sexual topics, and self-disclosure within supervision. In all cases, females were more conservative than males. In summary, it seems clear that gender, like race, is not a monolithic construct. More research is warranted to determine within-gender differences as well as cross-gender differences.

Use of Power Within Supervision.   Social or interpersonal power is a critical factor in supervision; power, or the capacity to influence the behavior of another person, is also endemic to gender interactions. This combination makes it a consequential variable to be acknowledged within the supervision relationship (Turner, 1993; Watson, 1993).

Robyak, Goodyear, and Prange (1987) considered the topic of power and whether male and female supervisors were different in their use of power as it had been conceptualized by French and Raven (1959). They categorized power as either *expert* (the display of such resources as specialized knowledge and skills, confidence, and rationality), *referent* (derived from interpersonal attraction and based on supervisees perceiving that they hold in common with supervisors relevant values, attitudes, opinions, and experiences), or *legitimate* (a consequence of perceived trustworthiness because the supervisor is a socially sanctioned provider of services who is not motivated by personal gain). Contrary to what one might expect, male supervisors reported greater preference for referent power than did female supervisors.

In a similar study that focused on supervisee behavior (Goodyear, 1990), both supervisees and their supervisors perceived female supervisees as more likely to employ a personal–dependent influence style in a conflict situation with their supervisors. This was the only significant finding of the study, which examined eight different influence strategies for supervisees of both genders interacting with supervisors of both genders. It is interesting to note that both male and female supervisors perceived the female supervisees similarly.

Nelson and Holloway (1990) provided an intriguing look at messages and interaction patterns within supervision for the manipulation of power. Using all gender and role combinations possible, Nelson and Holloway found that both male and female supervisors were less likely to encourage the assumption of power in female supervisees than in male supervisees; furthermore, female supervisees deferred to the power of the supervisor significantly more often than did male supervisees. As explained by the authors,

> It appears that individuals in the expert role, regardless of gender, may assume more power in interaction with their female subordinates than with their male subordinates, either by withholding support for the female subordinates' attempts at exerting power or by simply exerting stronger influence with female subordinates. In the supervisory relationship the female trainee may respond to this stance on the part of her supervisor by declining opportunities to assert herself as an expert. (p. 479)

Granello, Beamish, and Davis (1997) reported findings similar to those of Nelson and Holloway (1990) in a study with counselors in training. On average, male supervisees were asked for their opinion in supervision more than twice as often as female supervisees. Female supervisees were more often told what to do. This was the case whether the supervisor was male or female. Furthermore, these patterns remained constant over time. Granello et al. noted that the supervision given to male supervisees, therefore, reflected developmental models, whereas that for females did not. "With less external direction given over time, the male supervisees were encouraged to develop healthy internal supervisors by making more decisions on their own . . . the experiences

provided the female supervisee did not allow for their natural development to occur" (p. 313).

In a follow-up study (Granello, 2003), male supervisees were again asked their opinions more often and offered more suggestions than female supervisees, regardless of the gender of the supervisor. An unanticipated finding of this study, however, was that the ideas of female supervisees were more often accepted and built on by supervisors. It may be that, intuitively, supervisors began to experience male supervisees as being able to "take care of themselves," while female supervisees were perceived as needing more encouragement. Granello also studied the interactional effects of age and gender by separating groups into those in which the supervisee was older than the supervisor and those in which the supervisee was younger than the supervisor. While the gender differences held (i.e., both older and younger males were asked their opinions more often and made suggestions more often than older and younger females), age seemed to exacerbate the situation. Thus, the greatest differences were found between older male supervisees and older female supervisees. We need to reiterate that these differences are not only displayed by the supervisees themselves but reinforced by supervisors of both genders. Granello's results call for serious deliberation among supervisors regarding their reactions to both the gender and age of the supervisee.

In yet another similar study, Sells et al. (1997) reported that, when the supervisor was male, the influence over the structure of supervision was attributed to the supervisor; when the supervisor was female, the structure of the supervision session was more often attributed to the supervisee. These results were replicated by Lichtenberg and Goodyear (2000).

Finally, in a study with marriage and family therapy supervisees, Moorhouse and Carr (2002) found that the supervisors' collaborative behavior (i.e., consultative rather than directive) was highest when males were supervising males and lowest when males were supervising females. Although the authors found these results surprising, because they expected males to be more directive with other males, the results point to the differential (preferred) status given to male supervisees. Miller and Ivey (2006), however, found male marriage and family therapy supervisors to be regarded as more affiliative by both male and female supervisees. These authors speculated that male supervisors may be advantaged by their affiliative behaviors while female supervisors are not, but that female supervisors are devalued by any behaviors that are not viewed as affiliative.

Clearly, supervision is a relationship that includes a power dynamic that is endemic. Given the complexity of gender relationships, it is not surprising that power is manipulated differently in supervision for men and women. Although research has shed some light on how gender and influence interact, more empirical efforts are clearly warranted.

Same-Gender and Cross-Gender Pairs in Supervision. There is some evidence that, when given a choice, supervisees prefer to work with a supervisor of the same gender (McCarthy et al., 1994). Behling, Curtis, and Foster (1988) found that female–female pairings resulted in the greatest satisfaction with supervision, and the most negative combination for supervision in the field occurred when a female supervisee was supervised by a male supervisor. Worthington and Stern (1985) found that the closest relationships occurred in male–male pairings, whereas Wester et al. (2004) found that male–male dyads reported the poorest supervisory working alliance, and Jordan (2006) reported that gender-matching did not emerge as an important variable to the novice counselors in her study. In trying to make sense of these disparities, it may be helpful to review the work of Thyer, Sower-Hoag, and Love (1988). These researchers found that same-gender pairs produced the most favorable ratings of supervision, but the authors made the point that gender accounted for only 5 percent of the variance. Therefore, the argument for matching supervisee and supervisor by gender may be tenuous.

Androgenous supervisors of both genders may be more advantageous to the supervisee than working exclusively with a person of one's own gender. In support of this assumption, Putney et al. (1992) found that cross-gender pairs resulted in increased autonomy for the supervisee. Developmentally, such an outcome might be critical for positive professional growth. In short, the ways in which gender affect supervision appear to be complex and call for both additional research and supervision practices that attend specifically to gender (Barnes & Bernard, 2003; Nelson, 1991).

Feminist Supervision. Following the lead of feminist family therapies, the concept of feminist supervision has begun to take hold (Nelson, Gizara, et al., 2006; Prouty, 2001; Prouty, Thomas, Johnson, & Long, 2001; Szymanski, 2005). Prouty et al. conducted extensive interviews with clinical supervisors who considered themselves to be informed by feminist ideology. Their findings indicated that supervisors were intentional about their feminism throughout the supervision experience. For example, supervision contracts were approached in a manner that attempted to give maximum voice to the supervisee. Supervisee-identified goals were of paramount importance. This emphasis on the supervisee's voice continued in the methods chosen by the supervisors. For the most part, they preferred collaborative methods and providing options for supervisees, rather than directives. Even though subjects in the Prouty et al. study indicated that there were times when collaboration was not appropriate, they remained highly concerned about the use of "expert power" in supervision, returning as soon as possible to a more egalitarian posture. Szymanski (2005) emphasized power analysis as well, but also stressed the importance of feminist advocacy for the elimination of oppression of women. Nelson, Gizara, et al. (2006) also reported that power imbalances, privilege, and oppression were important themes among feminist supervisors.

Reporting on the same data as Prouty et al. (2001), Prouty (2001) emphasized that the relationship was central to feminist supervisors and served as the cornerstone of their activity. As indicative of their emphasis on relationship, supervisors identified commitment, availability, respect, and a willingness to talk about the relationship as central values driving their work. When supervisees needed to be challenged, feminist supervisors attempted to do this in a way that empowered them; they refrained from exerting supervisor power. "Challenging the therapist was reflective of a deeper ability to join with the therapist in order to help them push their limits" (Prouty, 2001, p. 182).

Finally, Prouty's subjects emphasized the larger themes of socialization, gender, power, diversity, and addressing emotion as key to their supervision. Their worldview focused on multicultural issues, not on women's issues exclusively, a somewhat different outcome than Szymanski's (2005) research, which found that feminist supervision practice was positively related to anger about sexism and commitment to feminist activism. We would note that the approach described by Prouty's subjects is wholly compatible with the suggestions proposed by Wester and Vogel (2002) for working with male supervisees who experience gender role conflict. For both, the importance of allowing the supervisee's voice to be heard and affirmed is essential. From the research we have to date, it seems that male supervisors in particular would be well served by attempting to adopt key tenets of a feminist model of supervision. The Supervisor's Toolbox includes Szymanski's (2003) feminist supervision assessment instrument.

Sexual Minority Issues Within Multicultural Supervision

As the mental health professions grapple with greater inclusion of cultural variables within supervision, they still lag behind in their attention to lesbian, gay, bisexual, and transgender (LGBT) issues. The available supervision literature continues to be largely theoretical or anecdotal (e.g., Bruss, Brack, Brack, Glickauf-Hughes, & O'Leary, 1997; Buhrke, 1989; Buhrke & Douce, 1991; Gautney, 1994; Halpert & Pfaller, 2001; Pfohl, 2004; Russell & Greenhouse, 1997; Schrag,

1994; Woolley, 1991), though there is some empirical evidence that LGBT supervisees have experienced discrimination during supervision (Messinger, 2004, 2007; Pilkington & Cantor, 1996). Murphy, Rawlings, and Howe (2002) found that, of those clinical psychologists who reported having at least one sexual minority client, 46 percent identified supervision as a place where training for working with LGBT clients occurred. However, only half found their supervisors to be knowledgeable about the concerns of LGBT clients. Murphy et al. noted that this low percentage raises the issue of the quality of supervision and the likelihood of propagating poor practice.

Buhrke and Douce (1991) maintained that supervisees should enter supervision with at least initial skills in recognizing sexual minority identity development stages, a readiness to assist clients in addressing intimacy issues within a gay or lesbian relationship, and a readiness to confront their own sexual identity assumptions. Bruss et al. (1997), while reiterating Buhrke and Douce's assertion, also advised that supervisors be clear about their expectations with supervisees who are working with LGBT clients. One expectation, then, could be that a supervisee "get educated" about sexual identity development and be prepared to discuss one's own affect and assumptions if knowledge and/or awareness were lacking in the supervisee. Bruss et al. also included supervisor self-awareness as the third "foundation" for supervision around sexual minority issues.

Both Buhrke and Douce (1991) and Russell and Greenhouse (1997) addressed some of the intrapsychic dimensions for multicultural supervision involving one or more persons with an LBGT identity. Buhrke and Douce considered transference and countertransference issues that might emerge when the supervisee counsels the same-gender coming-out client. Noting the strong emotions present throughout the coming-out process, it is quite likely that the client will experience attraction for the counselor, especially if that person is lesbian, gay, or bisexual. From the perspective of both gay and nongay supervisees, dealing with same-gender attraction is a topic that supervisors must be willing to address without disapproval. If supervisors shut down the supervisee by communicating distaste for the topic, the supervisee is far more vulnerable to handling the attraction inappropriately. Buhrke and Douce also noted that LGBT supervisees working with LGBT clients or supervisors are perhaps more vulnerable to multiple relationships than nongay supervisees and supervisors because of the advocacy required in working with disenfranchised populations, as well as the reality of overlapping social circles common to the LGBT community. Buhrke and Douce advised that a strict definition of multiple relationships may not be appropriate in this situation; at the same time, the supervisee will need assistance in determining appropriate boundaries that allow the supervisee to practice ethically and productively.

Russell and Greenhouse (1997) focused on the dynamics within supervision itself when the supervisor is a female heterosexual and the supervisee is lesbian. Among the most glaring errors the supervisor can make, according to Russell and Greenhouse, is assuming that sexual orientation is a nonissue for supervision. The authors addressed reasons for resistance to the topic from both supervisor and supervisee vantage points. Among the reasons for supervisor resistance, Russell and Greenhouse included the supervisor's discomfort in moving beyond the area within which she feels comfortable (competent), wanting to avoid the pain of truly understanding the experiences of an oppressed supervisee, and protecting herself against potential negative feedback from the supervisee. The therapist has her reasons for resisting the topic as well, including internalized homophobia, wanting to view her sexual orientation as a "private matter," and wishing to avoid any additional vulnerability within supervision. Despite reasonable reluctance for either party, Russell and Greenhouse maintained that allowing these resistances to dictate the relationship represents an unfortunate collusion for ignoring an important cultural influence, one not only affecting their relationship, but those between the supervisee and her clients as well.

These sentiments were echoed by Schrag (1994), who noted that when the supervisor has a positive view of alternative lifestyles, the supervisor can be an important role model for supervisees, gay and nongay alike. Furthermore, when the supervisor takes such a posture, it is more likely that LGBT supervisees will come out to the supervisor. As Schrag (1994) stated, "my openness models a method of moving from shame to self-empowerment, from abuse to compassion, and from secrecy to taking care of myself. These are pivotal for all therapists to acquire" (p. 7). Similarly, one lesbian supervisee who was "out" in supervision, but who never received supervision specific to her sexual orientation, now regrets the conspiracy of silence between her and her supervisor and made this appeal:

The advice I am about to give is strictly from the perspective of a lesbian supervisee to supervisors: Bring it up. Talk about it. Whether your supervisee or her clients are heterosexual or homosexual, sexual orientation is a relevant issue that may be avoided unless you attend to it. Take the responsibility, because you probably have less to risk than your supervisees. And if your supervisee is gay or lesbian, believe me, they are already thinking about it. (Gautney, 1994, p. 7)

These concerns are supported by Messinger's (2004, 2007) qualitative research in which 30 gay and lesbian social work students were interviewed about their field experiences working with heterosexual site supervisors. Twelve themes emerged from the data including homophobic attitudes at field sites and general feelings of lack of safety or anxiety. As a whole, students reported that the field placements presented challenges that were different from their experiences in their training programs and that placements posed both personal and professional challenges for them as lesbian or gay persons. A subset of students (18) allowed Messinger (2007) to contact site supervisors to determine the level of agreement between the perceptions of students and those of the supervisors. Supervisors were more likely to view the field sites as gay-friendly than did students. The second most common area of disagreement between site supervisors and students was whether students had experienced problems as a result of their sexual orientation. Factors that contributed to supervisors and students agreeing on critical matters included the supervisor's style, quality of the supervisory relationship, supervisor knowledge, and the willingness of the supervisor to discuss sexual orientation issues, among others. In short, students and site supervisors who were able to engage in open and informed conversations about matters related to sexual orientation and the issues that were arising in the site, reported things similarly. Open and respectful communication emerges once again as a hallmark of successful supervision.

Following a similar theme, Pfohl (2004) noted that there is a clear parallel between the prerequisites for good supervision that crosses race and good supervision that crosses sexual identity, including paying attention to sexual minority identity models such as that of Cass (1979, 1984). Pfohl also stressed the importance of supervisors attending to their own identity development as advocates of LBGT counselors. Once supervisors and supervisees have put sexual identity on the table, Pfohl reminded supervisors that the supervisor roles used to address other supervision issues are relevant to the discussion of sexual identity issues as well. For example, Pfohl noted that if the issue of self-disclosing sexual identity comes up in supervision, supervisors can ask the same kinds of questions of the supervisee that would be asked about self-disclosure in general. In short, as with other cultural issues, worldview and a strong working alliance are the most critical ingredients to successful cross-sexual identity supervision.

Spirituality Issues Within Multicultural Supervision

As the mental health disciplines have become more inclusive in their definition of culture, spirituality has emerged as a culturally determined subject of interest (Berkel, Constantine, & Olson, 2007). Like all cultural topics, spirituality is both unique as a point of interest yet intersects with each of the topics we have discussed in this chapter and other cultural dimensions we have not discussed.

Bishop, Avilla-Juarbe, and Thumme (2003) appropriately challenged supervisors to ensure that clients (and we would add supervisees) with strong belief systems do not encounter counseling contexts that are unfriendly to their worldviews. Others have challenged training programs to include curriculum that addresses spirituality and its importance for the helping professions (e.g., Bava, Burchard, Ichihashi, Irani, & Zunker, 2002; Brawer, Handal, Fabricatore, Roberts, & Wajda-Johnston, 2002; Prest, Russel, & D'Souza, 1999).

Historically, the training and practice literature will embrace a subject before it fully emerges into the clinical supervision literature. This is the case with spirituality, which only recently has surfaced in the supervision literature and, as yet, has led to limited empirical work. Contributions to this initial stage of development include Frame (2001) who suggested the use of genograms to track spiritual history within supervision; Polanski (2003) who applied Bernard's (1979, 1997) discrimination model for working with supervisees attempting to address spirituality in their counseling; and Aten and Hernandez (2004) who suggested the use of Stoltenberg's (1981) developmental model to track supervisees' developmental level in the area of spirituality in their work.

Thorell (2003) found that supervisors were more likely to be trained in spirituality issues than their supervisees, a reversal of the case for other cultural topics. She also found that supervisors who perceived that spirituality was important to their supervisees were more likely to infuse it into supervision. Rosen-Galvin (2005) reported research that is consistent with findings in other areas of multiculturalism. Specifically, Rosen-Galvin found that supervisors were much more likely to report having discussed spirituality in supervision than were their supervisees. Furthermore, the reasons reported by Rosen-Galvin that prevented supervisees from discussing issues of spirituality (e.g., feeling unsafe) were also similar to results from other multicultural studies. Similarly, Gubi (2007) reported that British counselors in his qualitative study were reluctant to report their use of prayer in counseling to their supervisors. These counselors feared losing respect and credibility, even condemnation and dismissal if they did. Once again, a positive working alliance was suggested by the author as an antidote to counselors avoiding an important part of their work in supervision. These combined results would indicate that this area of multiculturalism must continue to be seriously addressed by the mental health professions.

We have covered those cultural areas that have at least the beginnings of a "critical mass" of professional literature and research attesting to their role in the supervisory relationship. Other cultural categories may be as important to consider, but the professions have not evolved to the point of including them in their inquiry. For example, social class has not yet emerged in the supervision literature and disability is only barely represented (e.g., Borg, 2005). Therefore, we hope that the literature we have reported and our comments serve to inform discourse about culture within supervision, but not to define it.

MULTICULTURAL CONSTRUCTS: PULLING IT ALL TOGETHER

In many ways, we have only scratched the surface of culture and the ways that cultural differences play out in our interactions with others, including those interactions that transpire within supervision. Whereas our assumptions and fears often run unchecked, our knowledge is actually quite limited. What follows is an attempt to encapsulate what we consider to be the most dominant guidelines that are justified by what we know:

• **All interactions are multicultural.** Multicultural supervision is not only about working with persons whom Helms and Cook (1999) refer to as VREGs (visible racial or ethnic groups). Instead, it is a constant and dynamic force in all supervisory interactions. If not defined broadly, we will

forget to check our assumptions too often and we will be awkward (if not incompetent) when cultural differences are significant.

• **Supervisors tend to lag behind supervisees in multicultural awareness and knowledge.** By virtue of changes in training programs, supervisees come to supervision with training in multicultural concepts that their supervisors often lack (Constantine, 1997). Supervisors who acknowledge this discrepancy can do something about it. There are ample opportunities for continuing education and training. Cultural competence must be included in the supervisor's definition of supervisory efficacy.

• **Power and privilege are key to understanding multiculturalism.** It is not difference that matters. It is the power and privilege assigned to that difference. Ryde (2000) discussed the accumulated power of the supervisor when the supervisor represents a powerful cultural group, has a strong personality, and is in the role of supervisor. Power has many sources, and these must be attended to in the supervisory relationship.

• **Identity development seems to be key.** It seems that, whether we are talking about race or ethnicity, gender, sexual orientation, or spirituality, our relative development in that area of identity may be more important in the long run than identification with a particular group. Referring to the research on race (Ladany et al., 1997), racial identity development of supervisor and supervisee appears to be a promising construct with more predictive power than race in cross-race supervision. Gender research also seems to be implying this distinction. We would speculate that, overall, cultural group membership will become a weak second to development within that identity as a factor affecting supervision. The potential for this kind of development is, of course, the basis for education and training in multiculturalism.

• **The supervisor is key.** Regardless of the cultural differences within the supervisory triad, it is the supervisor's cultural competence and openness that will dictate whether the experience will be positive. Although the research we have is limited, the evidence is clear that an uninformed or biased supervisor has instrumental power when cultural differences emerge within the supervision process. Furthermore, the supervisor must initiate the dialogue around cultural matters. Position power dictates this (Ryde, 2000).

• **A strong working alliance is a prerequisite to productive multicultural supervision.** It is not enough for a supervisor to be informed; the supervisor must work to establish shared goals and a positive working relationship as part of multicultural supervision. This prerequisite is not outside of multicultural competence, but endemic to it in that cultural competence includes an ability to determine those dimensions of worldview that are likely to be highly charged for the individual. Supervisors must become accustomed to seeing their power and influence through the eyes of their supervisees.

• **Avoid stereotypes.** When it works, multicultural supervision allows us to respect a particular worldview and to understand how it matters to the individual. Although the worldview may be representative of others from a particular cultural group, it may not. This is the hard part. But like other complex domains, the more sophisticated we become as multicultural supervisors, the more within-group distinctions we will discern. Stereotypes emerge when they loosely describe some members of a particular cultural group. They often fail us when we attempt to build a relationship with an individual from that same group.

• **Our cultural selves should enrich and energize supervision, not deplete it.** Because cultural identities are intertwined with assumptions about power and privilege, supervisors can become ineffectual in their supervision due to hypersensitivity to cultural differences (Constantine & Sue, 2007). This kind of depleted supervision robs the supervisee of feedback that is necessary to become competent. It is incumbent upon supervisors to be increasingly sensitive to cultural factors while still meeting their present responsibilities as supervisor to the best of their abilities.

CONCLUSION

This chapter surveyed a variety of topics relevant to the formation of a supervisory relationship. The developmental status of the supervisee may be determined by level of experience or by other variables, but, though a reliable predictor of supervisee needs and expectations in many circumstances, developmental level can be secondary to cognitive and interpersonal style. Likewise, cultural variables are key to understanding within the supervision relationship.

More than any other, the point of this chapter is that each supervisee brings to supervision a rich blend of experience, insight, habit, and beliefs that will affect supervision with or without the supervisor's knowledge. In this respect, the topics covered in the chapter are only examples of the types of issues that might interest the supervisor in assessing where to begin with a supervisee. Broad themes of lifelong learning (developmental level), uniqueness (personal style, belief systems, and cultural identity), and privilege and oppression (social location) will affect how both the supervisor and the supervisee interact with the supervision process. In short, this chapter has attempted to explain what every supervisor knows: the experience with each supervisee is different.

CHAPTER 6

THE SUPERVISORY RELATIONSHIP
PROCESSES AND ISSUES OF THE SUPERVISORY TRIAD AND DYAD

In all aspects of our lives, relationships provide us both with emotional nourishment and opportunities to learn about interacting with others and about ourselves. In fact, we use feedback that we receive in the context of relationships to define who we are (see especially the work of symbolic interactionists such as Mead, 1913, and Stryker & Statham, 1985). These relationship dynamics all are present in supervision relationships.

Gelso and Carter (1985) provided a definition of therapeutic relationships that applies also to supervisory relationships. In their definition, relationships concern "the feelings and attitudes that [supervision] participants have toward one another, and the manner in which these are expressed" (p. 159). Relationships are not static; nor are they the same across any two subsets of people.

In fact, supervisory relationships are multilayered and complex and to examine them is akin to scanning a forest through a telescope: Each focal range will reveal different aspects and details of the forest, with any number of features that might be the object of attention. Fiscalini's (1997) term "supervisory ecology" (p. 43) suggests the complexity of the interactions among people and phenomena that occur at the various focal ranges.

In examining the figurative forest that is supervision, we will focus our telescope at three different ranges:

1. Supervision as a triadic system (the broadest focal range)
2. The supervisory dyad
3. Individual participants' contributions to the relationship (the most restricted range)

In this chapter, we will give attention to the first two—the broader—of these three focal ranges. In the next chapter, we will consider phenomena related to the most restricted of the focal ranges, that which considers the supervisee and supervisor individual contributions to the relationship.

SUPERVISION AS A THREE-PERSON SYSTEM

In pyramid fashion, the supervisory relationship is a relationship about a relationship about other relationships. (Fiscalini, 1997, p. 30)

It is important to be aware that the supervisory room is crowded with all sorts of "persons" who create anxieties for both the supervisor and the supervisee. It is often more crowded than the analytic one. (Lesser, 1983, p. 126)

These two observations underscore the complexity of the supervisory relationship system. Not only does that system involve the supervisor, supervisee, and client, but it also is possible for other people in the client's life to have effects that reverberate throughout the system. But to keep our discussion manageable, we will limit it to only the three principals in the supervisory relationship: the client, the therapist/supervisee, and the supervisor. This triadic relationship is illustrated in Figure 6.1, which makes clear that the supervisee is the pivot point in this system (Frawley-O'Dea & Sarnat, 2001). It shows that there are two manifest relationships (client–supervisee and supervisee–supervisor) and that the person common to both those relationships is the supervisee. He or she serves as a conduit of both information and processes between the dyads.

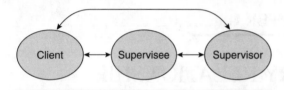

FIGURE 6.1 Supervisee as Relational Pivot Point in the Supervisory Triad

Although Figure 6.1 might seem simple, the processes it captures can be complex as the three involved parties influence each other. This chapter is about that complexity. In the section that follows, we will discuss supervision as a three-person system, addressing first parallel processes and isomorphic phenomena, and then triangulations that occur among the members of the supervisory triad.

Parallel Processes and Isomorphism

Friedlander et al. (1989) described parallel process as a phenomenon in which: "supervisees unconsciously present themselves to their supervisors as their clients have presented to them. The process reverses when the supervisee adopts attitudes and behaviors of the supervisor in relating to the client" (p. 149).

Parallel processes have their conceptual roots in psychodynamic supervision (Friedman, 1983; Grey & Fiscalini, 1987; Schneider, 1992). Searles (1955) apparently was the first to write about the phenomenon, describing the "reflection process" between therapy and supervision. Others (e.g., Ekstein & Wallerstein, 1972; Mueller, 1982; Mueller & Kell, 1972) began soon after to employ the concept, but using the current term, parallel process, instead. This now has become perhaps the best-known phenomenon in supervision; perhaps even the signature phenomenon.

Structural and strategic family therapists have employed the related concept of isomorphism, for which Haley (1976) has been given credit (Liddle & Saba, 1983). In choosing the term *isomorphism,* systemic supervisors have focused on the interrelational and structural similarities between therapy and supervision.

These concepts initially were described and promoted by adherents of specific models of treatment (i.e., parallel process by psychodynamic supervisors; isomorphism by family systems theorists), but can be useful to any supervisor. They seem in many respects to be two sides of the same coin. Abroms (1977) came as close as anyone to blending the concepts of parallel process and isomorphism in his introduction of the term *metatransference:* "To think in terms of metatransference is to think in parallel structures at different levels of abstraction, that is, to recognize the multilevel, isomorphic mirroring of interactional processes" (p. 93).

Nevertheless, these two phenomena are distinct enough to warrant separate treatment. We discuss each in the sections that immediately follow.

Parallel Process.   Russell et al. (1984) suggested two ways that parallel processes can be useful in supervision:

First, as the supervisee becomes aware of the parallels in the relationships with the client and the supervisor, understanding of the client's psychological maladjustment is increased. Second, the supervisee's understanding of the therapeutic process grows in that the supervisee learns how to respond therapeutically to the client just as the supervisor has responded to the supervisee. (p. 629)

Initially, supervisors assumed that parallel process was a bottom-up phenomenon in which some characteristic of the client is displayed by the supervisee during supervision. Therefore, a supervisee working with a depressed client might present in supervision in an uncharacteristically depressed manner. Or the supervisee working with a particularly confused client might present in supervision in an uncharacteristically confused manner.

Parallel process dynamics have been explained in various ways. The following seven explanations all emphasize a bottom-up process that (a) is triggered either by the client or by some aspect of the client–supervisee relationship; (b) occurs outside awareness of the participants; and for which (c) the supervisee serves as the conduit of the process from the client–therapist relationship to that of the supervisor–supervisee:

1. Because of their identification with their clients, supervisees produce reactions in their supervisors that they themselves had felt in response to their clients (Russell et al., 1984).
2. The parallel the supervisee (unconsciously) chooses to exhibit reflects the initial impasse formed between the client and the supervisee (Mueller & Kell, 1972).
3. The supervisee selects part of the client's problem that parallels one that the supervisee shares (Mueller & Kell, 1972).
4. The supervisee identifies unconsciously with some aspect of the client's psychological functioning. Because the supervisee is unaware of this identification, she or he "cannot verbally discuss this aspect of the patient in supervision but, rather, enacts the patient's dynamic with the supervisor" (Frawley-O'Dea & Sarnat, 2001, p. 171).
5. Through lack of skill, the supervisee is prone to those aspects of the client's problem that parallel the supervisee's specific learning problems in supervision (Ekstein & Wallerstein, 1972).
6. Parallel process has "similarities with the repetition compulsion, namely, that what is not understood is enacted" (Arkowitz, 2001, p. 53).
7. When supervisor, therapist, and/or client represent different cultural backgrounds, some parallel processes are likely to reflect cross-cultural issues (Vargas, 1989).

Ekstein and Wallerstein (1972) commented that parallel process is a "never-ending surprise," based on the "irrational expectation that the teaching and learning of psychotherapy should consist primarily of rational elements" (p. 177). The flavor of their comment, however, is that the supervisee is the root of that irrationality—the bottom-up perspective to which we already have alluded; what Frawley-O'Dea and Sarnat (2001) characterized as the traditional view of parallel processes.

The more contemporary view of parallel processes is that the supervisor is as likely to initiate a dynamic that would then be played out in the supervisee's therapy as is the reverse. This expanded perspective began with Doehrman's (1976) dissertation research findings that parallel processes were bidirectional. For example, she observed that a supervisor–supervisee relationship impasse was mirrored by a supervisee–client impasse; when the supervisor–supervisee impasse was resolved, so too was that between supervisee and client.

Frawley-O'Dea and Sarnat (2001) discuss this bidirectional conception as "symmetrical parallel processes:"

> The central conceptualization of symmetrical parallel process is that a transference and countertransference configuration arises in either the supervised treatment or the supervision. At this point, the relational pattern in play is out of the conscious awareness of the members of the dyad. It is not available for conscious elaboration, discussion, meaning making, or negotiation because it has not been linguistically formulated yet by either party to the dyad. The supervisee, however, the common member of both dyads, nonverbally exerts relational pressure on the member of the other dyad to enact a similar transference and countertransference matrix with the supervisee, in the often unconscious hope that someone can contain, enact, process, and put words to what is transpiring now in both dyads. The key to symmetrical parallel processes is that both the treatment and the supervisory dyads play out similar relational constellations. (p. 182)

This statement makes clear that, regardless of direction, "the conduits for parallel processes are supervisees: they are members of both systems (though with different roles) and carry one system into the other" (Carroll, 1996, p. 107). This is what we have illustrated in Figure 6.1.

There is, though, a type of pseudo parallel process that Mothersole (1999) describes. This is the situation in which either unresolved problems or lack of skills in the supervisee are "'beaming out' in both directions and affecting the therapeutic and supervisory relationships" (p. 118). This might have the appearance of a parallel process, but actually is not.

Implications for Supervisors.   Virtually all theorists who discuss parallel processes now embrace the more contemporary, symmetrical view. Yet most discussions of possible interventions for the supervisor focus only on the traditional view in which the supervisee is transmitting client material to the supervisory dyad. It may be that this is because it is easier for the supervisor to observe this phenomenon than it is to observe phenomena that originate with him or her. Heidegger's observation that "Fish are the last ones to discover water" perhaps is apt in this situation.

Neufeldt, Iverson, and Juntunen (1995) pointed out that, whereas a supervisor might anticipate many interventions in advance, opportunities to address parallel processes typically will occur serendipitously. They also noted that, whereas psychodynamic supervisors are likely to point out or interpret parallel processes to more-advanced supervisees as they observe them, this can be confusing to less-advanced students. Moreover, for a supervisee simply to have awareness of a particular parallel process does not make it disappear (Carroll, 1996).

Neufeldt et al. (1995) recommended instead that the supervisor respond less directly and serve as a model for the supervisee about how to respond to the client issues that the supervisee is mirroring in the supervisory sessions. For more intractable situations, Carroll (1996) recommended that the supervisee role-play the client in order to gain a clearer perspective.

McNeill and Worthen (1989) cautioned that too much focus on the process of supervision might become tiresome for supervisees and that, in general, more advanced supervisees are most likely to benefit from a discussion of transference and countertransference.

Research Concerning Parallel Processes.   Two circumstances have hampered research on parallel processes. One is that the concept is sufficiently "fuzzy" that it has been difficult to operationalize meaningfully. The other is that it is hard to predict when parallel processes will manifest themselves and therefore be available for study.

In response to these factors, the relatively few studies of parallel processes have employed primarily a case-study design (e.g., Alpher, 1991; Doehrman, 1976; Friedlander et al., 1989; Jacobsen, 2007), though these have varied in sophistication. McNeill and Worthen (1989) concluded from their review that, whereas empirical support for parallel process is sparse, there is some. Not much had changed a decade later when Mothersole (1999) concluded from his review that "parallel process is a concept with a long history and is widely used, yet there is very little empirical evidence for its existence" (p. 117). Nevertheless, he asserted that the concept itself is robust and has utility for supervisors.

Other researchers have used designs other than case studies that provide data that linked the functioning of the supervisory dyad with that of the therapy dyad. One of those studies was that of Patton and Kivlighan (1997), who found that the week-to-week fluctuations in the quality of the supervisor–supervisee working alliance predicted the week-to-week fluctuations in the supervisee–client working alliance. Williams (2000) used 44 supervisory triads, having clients complete a measure of their counselors' interpersonal style and supervisees complete that same measure with respect to their supervisors. She found that the greater the supervisors' affiliative interpersonal style, the less controlling or dominant the supervisees' style in their work as therapists with their clients.

Another type of study has examined which supervisors attend to parallel processes and how they perceive its effects. Perhaps unsurprisingly, Raichelson, Herron, Primavera, and Ramirez (1997) confirmed that psychodynamic supervisors and supervisees were more likely than their rational–emotive or cognitive–behavioral counterparts to recognize the existence and importance of parallel processes. In a qualitative study, Ladany, Constantine, Miller, Erickson, and Muse-Burke (2000) found that supervisors of unspecified theoretical orientations frequently identified parallel processes as sources of countertransference reactions that they had experienced toward supervisees.

Concluding Comments about Parallel Processes. Parallel process often has been presented as a nearly mystical phenomenon. McWilliams (1994) acknowledged that this apparent mysticism can be particularly troublesome for someone with the skepticism that can characterize the scientist–practitioner. She suggested, though, that parallel processes become more comprehensible when one realizes that in the earliest years of life most communication with others is both nonverbal and complex and that we then continue to employ this mode throughout life without necessarily understanding the extent to which we do so.

> *People relating to babies figure out what they need largely on the basis of intuitive, emotional reactions. Nonverbal communication can be remarkably powerful, as anyone who has ever taken care of a newborn or been moved to tears, or fallen inexplicably in love can testify.* (McWilliams, 1994, p. 34)

McWilliams was arguing against a too-skeptical perception of parallel processes. But the complementary issue is one of invoking it too frequently and uncritically without considering alternative explanations for what may be occurring within the supervisory system. Schimel (1984), for example, acknowledged that, although the concept of parallel processes can be quite useful in supervision, it can be invoked in an irresponsible and possibly trivial manner to frame in psychological terms a matter that actually is one of skill and competence.

> *The basic observation is a simple one. The patient wants something from the therapist that is not forthcoming. He or she is displeased. This troubles the therapist, who, in turn, looks to the supervisor for help that may or may not be forthcoming. The therapist is displeased with the supervisor, who, in his turn, may be troubled and displeased with the supervisee and himself. This is a common situation. One has reason to expect, however, that with the increasing skill of the supervisee and the accumulating experience of the supervisor that this kind of situation will be recognized early and dealt with by putting it into an appropriate perspective.* (p. 239)

Feiner (1994) is another who urged caution in putting too much credence in the parallel process as a supervision phenomenon:

> *The supervisor is allegedly "put" (not deliberately) in the position of a proxy therapist with the supervisee playing the part of the patient. Although out-of-awareness, the enactment is not taken by sophisticated supervisors as a simple, mechanistic repetition, but as more likely representing some sort of homology. It's as though the student were saying, "Do it with me and I'll know what to do with my patients." But . . . while the issues that belong to the patient may seem similar to the issues that the therapist-as-student brings into supervision . . . the similarity is more apparent than real. It's sort of like the descriptions of a spouse by a patient. The image of the described other cannot be taken as objective truth.* (pp. 61–62)

Feiner pointed out that one risk of a too-heavy reliance on parallel process thinking is that it may ignore, obscure, or even deny the supervisor's or the supervisee's own contributions to the interactions occurring between them. Finally, we would point out that parallel processes can manifest in supervision-of-supervision as well (Ellis & Douce, 1994; see Chapter 12). In this case, the supervisory relationship system involves four people: client, supervisee, supervisor, and the supervisor's supervisor. Despite the added complexity of this situation, the material we have covered in this section should extrapolate readily to it.

Isomorphism

> *Isomorphism refers to the phenomenon whereby categories with different content, but similar form, can be mapped on each other in such a way that there are corresponding parts and processes within each structure. When this occurs, these parallel structures can be described as isomorphic, and each is an isomorph of the other. Therefore, when the supervisory system is mapped onto the therapeutic system, the roles of supervisor and supervisee correspond to those of the therapist and client, respectively.* (White & Russell, 1997, p. 317)

For systems therapists, isomorphism refers to the "recursive replication" (Liddle, Breunlin,

Schwartz, & Constantine, 1984) that occurs between therapy and supervision. The focus is interrelational and not intrapsychic. As Liddle and Saba (1983) suggested, the two fields (therapy and supervision) constantly influence and are influenced by each other; both are interpersonal systems with properties of all systems, including boundaries, hierarchies, and subsystems, each with its own distinct characteristics. There is no linear reality in this construct, only reverberation. Content is important, but not nearly as important as repeating patterns.

Because supervision is viewed as an isomorph of therapy, Liddle et al. (1984) suggested that many of the same rules apply to both. These rules include the need to join with both clients and supervisees, the need for setting goals and thinking in stages, the importance of appreciating contextual sensitivity, and the charge of challenging realities. "It suggests that trainers would do well to understand and intentionally utilize with their supervisees the same basic principles of change employed in therapy" (Liddle et al., 1984, p. 141).

The supervisor who is aware of this process will watch for dynamics in supervision that reflect the initial assessment that the supervisor has made about what is transpiring in therapy. In this way, the assessment is either verified or called into question. Because the client (family) is usually a group, and many systemic supervisors prefer team supervision (see Chapter 11), the interactions are easily replicated. For example, an overwhelmed parent will appeal to the supervisee for help (while other family members sit expectantly), which will be followed by an overwhelmed supervisee appealing to the supervisor for help (while other team members sit expectantly). When intervening into the therapeutic system (supervisee plus family), it is important that there be consistency down the hierarchy. For example, Haley (1987) recommended that if the goal is for the parents to be firm with their teenager the therapist must be firm with the parents. And to complete the isomorph, the supervisor must be firm with the therapist. In this way, content and process are matched and communicate the same message throughout the interconnected systems.

Liddle and Saba (1983) argued that live supervision, by requiring risk taking and experiential behavior on the part of the therapist, parallels structural family therapy during which family members are actively put in direct contact with each other. Therefore, live supervision is an isomorphically correct form of supervision for structural family therapy.

White and Russell (1997) found that authors who had written about isomorphism had focused on four phenomena or "facets" related to it:

• **Facet 1:** *Identifying repetitive or similar patterns.* This refers to the replication of patterns across systems. Often this is the replication from another system (client–therapist system; family of origin for either the supervisor or supervisee; etc.) into the supervisory system. But it also can manifest as a replication of supervisor–supervisee pattern onto other systems, especially the therapist–client system. White and Russell (1997) noted that the concept of parallel processes could just as well describe this facet of isomorphism.

• **Facet 2:** *Translation of therapeutic models and principles into supervision.* As we noted in Chapter 5, it is impossible for a person's therapeutic model not to affect his or her approach to supervision. To the extent that this occurs, this facet of isomorphism is operating.

• **Facet 3:** *The structure and process of therapy and supervision are identical.* Certainly, there are many structural similarities between supervision and therapy, at least with respect to individual therapy. For example, both typically involve two people isolating themselves in a room with a closed door to discuss sensitive material in private; in both, one person is to disclose material to another whose task is to examine and perhaps take action on some aspect of that material.

• **Facet 4:** *Isomorphism as an interventive stance.* The supervisor can alter the sequences in supervision with the purpose of influencing a corresponding alteration of sequences within therapy.

The following illustrates the first of these four facets of isomorphism between therapy and supervision, the facet that is most difficult to differentiate from parallel process (White & Russell, 1997).

> *Ted is seeing the Doyles for marital therapy with a supervision team observing the session. The Doyles, married for 20 years, have no children and Mr. Doyle has fought depression most of his adult life. Mrs. Doyle reports how hard it has been to help him, only to have her efforts go nowhere, and she cries intermittently. It is obvious watching Ted that he is feeling this couple's plight. In the supervision room, there is virtually no movement. The team mirrors the sadness and despair of the couple. Halfway through the session, Ted excuses himself to consult with the team...As Ted is seated, JoAnn turns around and says, "Boy, what do you do for them at this point?" Ted shrugs and looks around for help.*

This type of isomorphism most resembles parallel processes. On the face of it, the several other types of isomorphism would seem easier to operationalize and study than parallel processes. Interestingly, this area seems to have no empirical research. Given the potential utility of the concept, it seems a fertile area to explore. At the same time, supervisors should be aware of the caution by Storm, Todd and Sprenkle (2001) that a too-heavy emphasis on isomorphism can obscure the important differences between therapy and supervision.

Interpersonal Triangles

It seems customary, at least in our culture, to think of the dyad as the basic social unit. But Bowen (e.g., 1978) did a great deal to sensitize mental health professionals, especially family therapists, to the notion that the interpersonal triangle actually is the more fundamental unit of relationship. This conception has important implications for how supervisors, supervisees, and clients all interrelate with one another.

To think of relationships in terms of triangles is not new. Since at least the 1890s there have been theorists who have maintained that triangles constitute a type of social geometry (Caplow, 1968). Within any given triangle, two members will tend to be in a coalition, with the third either more peripheral or even perceived as antagonistic to them. Caplow (1968) maintained that the most distinctive feature of triadic social systems is "the transformation of strength into weakness and weakness into strength" (p. 3), according to the particular alignments occurring within the triangle.

Triangles occur in many ways in our day-to-day lives. Psychoanalytic therapists have been concerned with Oedipal triangles and family therapists have been concerned with the broader spectrum of possible triangles that can occur in a family system. Political scientists have been concerned with the triangles that occur within governments (e.g., with liberal, moderate, and conservative groups) and even among nations. We all can describe childhood (and current!) relationships in which, within a group of three friends, there were two who were particularly close: During times of tension between these two, however, the less-involved third member was drawn into an alliance with one of those two; the other then becomes more peripheral.

One especially interesting characteristic of triangles is that they seem to have a catalytic effect on participants' behavior. That is, although coalitions can occur between two members of a triangle without the third member present, his or her presence almost always modifies the relationship of the other two. To illustrate, Caplow offered as an example the common playground situation in which the presence of a mutual antagonist enhances (1) the affection between two friends and (2) their felt hostility toward the antagonist. It is not difficult to see how variants of this same scenario play out in the professional lives of adults as well.

One manifestation of a coalition (and therefore of triangulation) is the circumstance of two people secretly discussing a third. Most of us also have experienced this in our families and in work settings. But this occurs in counseling as well.

For example, triangulation is one reason it is so difficult for counselors to begin with an individual client and then later to include that person's spouse in the treatment. The initial client already will have discussed ("in secret") the spouse with the counselor, who almost inevitably will have adopted at least some of that person's perspective about the spouse. This situation has all the characteristics of the coalition of which Bowen spoke, making it very difficult for the spouse to enter a neutral situation.

Interpersonal Triangles in Supervision. In supervision the most obvious triangle is that of the client, counselor, and supervisor. This particular triangle has characteristics that constrain the possible coalitions that will occur. Two of these are (1) the way in which power is arrayed (the least powerful member of this group is the client; the most powerful, the supervisor) and (2) the fact that the supervisor and client rarely will have an ongoing face-to-face relationship with each other.

Within this triangle, the discussion between two people of the third person most often occurs between supervisee and supervisor. This, of course, suggests a counselor–supervisor coalition with the client as the third member. It is possible, though, for the counselor and client to discuss the supervisor. In this instance, it is possible to develop a coalition between counselor and client against the supervisor.

Strategically oriented family therapists sometimes employ this latter coalition possibility to their advantage, using the supervisory relationship for therapeutic purposes. The supervisor is deliberately set up in the "oppressor" role as a means to catalyze the client–counselor bond and steer the client toward a desired behavior. For example, the supervisor might direct the counselor to say something like this to the client: "My supervisor is convinced that your problem is _____ and that I should be doing _____ about it. Just between us, though, I think she's off base. In fact, I think she's pretty insensitive to the issues you are facing." The goal of such a strategy is for the client to improve in order to prove the supervisor wrong.

But because supervision occurs in a larger context, not all the possible triangles of which the supervisor and supervisee might be a part necessarily will involve the client. For example, the supervisee might "triangle in" another current or past supervisor by saying to his or her supervisor something like this: "I'm feeling confused: You are telling me this, but the supervisor I had last semester [or, the supervisor I have in my other setting] has been telling me something really different."

A statement such as this establishes a coalition between the supervisee and another supervisor who may not even realize that he or she has become a member of this particular triangle. Coalitions—even with a phantom member such as this—redistribute power. Whether or not the supervisee is doing this with deliberate intent, it has the effect of putting the current supervisor in the situation of being "odd person out."

In summary, interpersonal triangles are ubiquitous in human interactions. It is unsurprising, then, that they would occur between and among professionals. Our intent in this discussion was not to suggest that triangles are necessarily always to be avoided. We are convinced, though, that it is essential for supervisors to be aware of interpersonal triangles and their effects. With this knowledge, supervisors are better equipped to avoid problematic triangles and to manage others in a strategic manner.

Lawson (1993) made helpful suggestions about how supervisors might assist supervisees to avoid being triangulated. He noted Bowen's position that the more differentiated (roughly equivalent to emotional autonomy) the supervisee, the less likely she or he will be vulnerable to being triangulated. This suggests the importance of providing opportunities for the supervisee's personal growth so that they can increase their levels of differentiation. And, more simply, Lawson suggested teaching supervisees about triangles as a way to help successfully negotiate them.

SUPERVISION AS A TWO-PERSON SYSTEM

In the foregoing section, we had set our figurative telescope at a focal range that permitted the broadest view of the supervisory relationship: that of a three-person system that included the client, supervisee, and supervisor. In this next section, we restrict the range of that telescope to focus only on the supervisor and supervisee working together as a dyad.

The Working Alliance as a Means to Frame the Supervisory Relationship

The supervisory dyad often has been understood in terms directly extrapolated from the client–therapist relationship. For example, during the early 1970s, Carkhuff's (1969) extension of the Rogerian model became a dominant relationship paradigm, both for counseling and supervision. Carkhuff's (e.g., 1969) assertion that the level and quality of the supervisor's interpersonal skills may establish a ceiling for the supervisee's own skills for a time seemed to be the "received view" among many. This meant, for example, that the supervisee could be no more empathic, on average, with clients than the supervisee's supervisor was with him or her.

This hypothesis drove studies such as those of Pierce and Schauble (1970, 1971) and of Lambert (1974), which examined the extent to which supervisors' levels of empathy, regard, genuineness, and concreteness (i.e., facilitative conditions) influenced the development of these same conditions in their supervisees (for summaries of this and related research, see Lambert & Arnold, 1987; Lambert & Ogles, 1997; Matarazzo & Patterson, 1986). Based on their review, Lambert and Ogles concluded that

> there exists little empirical evidence supporting the necessity of a therapeutic climate for the acquisition of interpersonal skills . . . and it appears that learning these skills can occur without high levels of empathy, genuineness, and unconditional positive regard, as long as the supervisee perceives the supervisor is indeed trying to be helpful. (p. 426)

In short, although Rogerian-defined relationship dimensions are too important to ignore, they seem to have greater salience in the practice of therapy than in the practice of supervision.

But even in the domain of therapy, the Rogerian-based paradigm seems to have reached a ceiling in

terms of what it can add to conceptualizations of the processes. In acknowledging this, Gelso and Carter (1985) found promise in Bordin's (1979) working alliance model as a means to conceptualize therapeutic relationships. They anticipated what now has become a major focus of psychotherapy theorists and researchers; a trend substantially helped by the development of reliable and valid measures with which to assess it (Horvath & Luborsky, 1993).

Psychodynamic theorists offered the initial conceptions of the working alliance. But it increasingly has been accepted as a phenomenon of interest to virtually all therapists, independent of their theory. That is, it is pantheoretical. Bordin suggested that the working alliance is a "collaboration to change" (p. 73). In his conception, the working alliance is composed of three elements: the extent to which the therapist and client agree on *goals,* the extent to which they agree on the *tasks* necessary to reach those goals, and the *bond* that develops between them (see Figure 6.2). Bordin (1983) asserted that relational bonds develop as a result either of working together on a common task to achieve shared goals or on the basis of shared emotional experiences. These bonds "will center around the feelings of liking, caring, and trusting that the participants share."

Although Bordin's initial work concerned therapeutic relationships, he later extended his working alliance model to include supervision

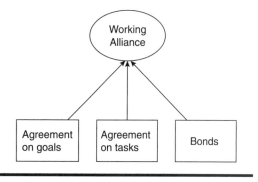

FIGURE 6.2   Model of the Working Alliance
Source: Based on Bordin (1979)

(Bordin, 1983). In this, he had been foreshadowed by Fleming and Benedek (1966), who had introduced the term *learning alliance* to describe the supervisory relationship.

As in the case of psychotherapy research, research on the supervisory alliance has been facilitated by the development of instruments to measure it. One strategy has been to modify the best-known measure of the therapeutic alliance, the Working Alliance Inventory (Horvath & Greenberg, 1989), for use in supervision research (e.g., Bahrick, 1990; Baker, 1990). Another was that of Efstation, Patton, and Kardash (1990), who developed an alliance measure specific to supervision, the Supervisory Working Alliance Inventory (the Efstation et al. instrument is available in this text as part of the Supervisor's Toolbox).

Goals and Expectations.   We want to elaborate here on one of the three components of the alliance: shared goals. Although goals and expectations are not completely the same, they overlap sufficiently for us to treat them interchangeably in this section.

Bahrick, Russell, and Salmi (1991) and Olk and Friedlander (1992) addressed expectations in supervision. Ellis et al. (1994), who made supervisor–supervisee expectations an explicit focus of their work, defined expectations as "a person's anticipatory beliefs about the nature (i.e., roles, behaviors, interactions, and tasks) or outcome of a particular event" (p. 3). Ellis et al. cited counseling and psychotherapy literature showing that *congruence* of expectations (i.e., shared goals) between or among people in a relationship is at least as important, and likely more important, than the expectations of any one person.

Sometimes a supervisor and supervisee will have differing expectations because the supervisee simply is uninformed about the appropriate role(s) that she or he is to assume as supervisee. To maximize the likelihood of supervisor–supervisee congruence in expectations for supervision, it is useful for the supervisor to ensure that initial negotiation or contracting between them

occurs (see Chapter 8 for a discussion of supervision contracts). When the issue is that the supervisee simply does not know role options, as might be the case with a beginning supervisee, it is possible to educate him or her about expected behaviors and roles through, for example, discussions and audio- or videotape modeling.

Although little research has been done to investigate the effectiveness of this educational procedure, generally referred to as *role induction,* in supervision, its effectiveness with therapy clients has been demonstrated (see, e.g., Garfield, 1986; Kaul & Bednar, 1986). Bahrick et al. (1991) developed a 10-minute audiotaped summary of Bernard's (1979) supervision model and then administered it to 19 supervisees at one of several points in the semester. They found that after supervisees heard the tape they reported having a clearer conceptualization of supervision and being more willing to reveal concerns to their supervisors. This effect occurred regardless of when in the semester supervisees heard the tapes. In a more recent study, Ellis, Chapin, Dennin, and Anderson-Hanley (1996) found that a role induction that they conducted significantly decreased supervisee anxiety compared to a control group.

Role induction can occur in multiple formats. One is through assigned readings. To this end, there is at least one book now available to supervisees that has a role-induction intent (Carroll & Gilbert, 2005). As well, a chapter in Holloway and Carroll (1999) speaks to how to prepare supervisees for their role.

Another potentially useful supervision strategy would be to assess participants' expectations. Tinsley and his associates (e.g., Tinsley, Workman, & Kass, 1980; Tinsley, Bowman, & Ray, 1988) have conducted programmatic research on clients' expectations for counseling, and their instrument for assessing counselor–client expectations has been frequently employed in counseling research. But because supervision and counseling are different activities, it is important to be able to evaluate expectations for supervision. To that end, Ellis et al. (1994) did the field a service in developing parallel, 52-item scales (one for supervisees, another for supervisors) to examine expectations for supervision.

Finally, the importance of having mutually agreed upon goals suggests the importance of developing a supervision contract such as we address in Chapter 8. A useful example is the Supervision Agreement section of the Supervisee Bill of Rights (Giordano, Altekruse, & Kern, 2000), which is available in our Supervisor's Toolbox at the end of this book.

Antecedents and Consequences of Effective Supervisory Alliances

We propose that a key task in early supervision is building a strong working alliance (Bordin, 1983) that can serve as a base from which future dilemmas in supervision can be managed. Ongoing mainte-nance of the alliance should be the supervisor's responsibility throughout the course of the relation-ship. (Nelson, Gray, Friedlander, Ladany, & Walker, 2001, p. 408)

To maintain that alliance, though, requires that the supervisor appreciate the variables that affect the alliance, as well as the outcomes of effective alliances. Figure 6.3 visually depicts a conceptual model of this, buttressed by available studies. Before we discuss the model, though, a few caveats about the figure are in order.

- The studies used to develop this figure were correlational and therefore do not permit strict causal inferences. It is possible, for example, that supervisee self-efficacy results in the supervisee's perception of a stronger alliance, rather than the opposite. The causal direction-ality that we imposed in this figure is based on what seemed theoretically justified (in virtu-ally all cases this was the causal direction that the authors themselves had assumed).
- There was no common measure of alliance across these studies. Some used either the Bahrick (1990) or Baker (1990) adaptation of the Working Alliance Inventory (Horvath & Greenberg, 1989); others used the Efstation et al. (1990) measure.

- Working alliance measures have multiple sub-scales. In some cases, we indicate a relation-ship if not all subscales were statistically linked to the antecedent or outcome. For example, Ladany, Ellis, et al. (1999) found that super-visee perceptions of bond predicted efficacy, but that shared tasks and bonds did not. But bond seems so central to the concept of alliance that we included this study in the figure.
- We address only studies for which significant results were obtained, though in some cases similar studies did not obtain these results. For example, Efstation et al. (1990) found a rela-tionship between alliance and supervisee self-efficacy, whereas Ladany, Ellis, et al. (1999) did not; Renfro-Michel (2006) found supervisee attachment style predicted working alliance, but White and Queener (2003) did not.

Despite these caveats, the figure provides important information about supervisory alliances. It also provides us with a means for organizing the following discussion.

We should note, too, that the following discus-sion foreshadows Chapter 7 to some extent. Although that chapter also focuses on the supervi-sory relationship, its specific emphasis is on the attributes and reactions of the supervisor and of the supervisee as individuals. But it would be dif-ficult to discuss working alliance in this chapter without examining some of the supervisor and supervisee factors that affect the working alliance.

Supervisor Factors That Predict Alliance. Six supervisor attributes or behaviors have been shown to affect the supervisory alliance. These are the supervisor's (1) style, (2) use of expert and referent power, (3) use of self-disclosure, (4) attachment style, (5) evaluative practices, and (6) ethical behavior.

The Supervisor's Style. Ladany et al. (2001) found that use of an attractive supervision style (i.e., roughly equivalent to a consultant role) pre-dicted all three working alliance scales (bond, agreement on tasks, and agreement on goals), whereas use of either an interpersonally sensitive

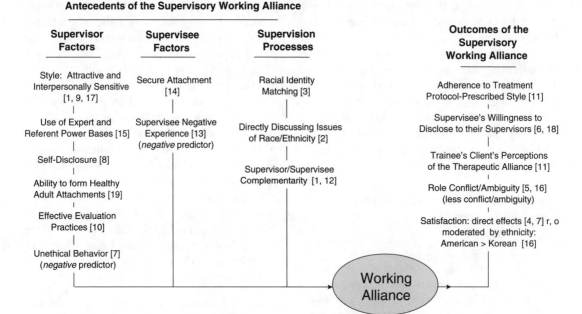

Antecedents of the Supervisory Working Alliance

FIGURE 6.3   Antecedents and Consequences of Positive Supervisory Alliances

Sources: Studies Cited: [1] Chen & Bernstein (2000); [2] Gatmon et al. (2001); [3] Ladany, Brittan-Powell, & Pannu (1997); [4] Ladany, Ellis, & Friedlander (1999); [5] Ladany & Friedlander (1995); [6] Ladany et al. (1996); [7] Ladany, Lehrman-Waterman, et al. (1999); [8] Ladany & Lehrman-Waterman (1999); [9] Ladany et al. (2001); [10] Lehrman-Waterman & Ladany (2001); [11] Patton and Kivlighan (1997); [12] Quarto (2002); [13] Ramos-Sánchez et al. (2002); [14] Renfro-Michel (2006); [15] Schultz, Ososkie, Fried, Nelson, & Bardos (2002); [16] Son, Ellis & Yoo (in press); [17] Spelliscy, Chen, & Zusho (2007); [18] Webb & Wheeler (1998); [19] White & Queener (2003).

style (i.e., counselor role) or a task-oriented style (i.e., teacher role) predicted agreement on tasks only. Spelliscy et al. (2007) found that supervisees who perceived their supervisors to employ both attractive and interpersonally sensitive supervisory styles reported better working alliances. Similarly, in their comparative case study, Chen and Bernstein (2000) found that the attractive and interpersonally sensitive styles were more prominent in the dyad with the stronger alliance than in the dyad with the weaker alliance.

In short, three studies now show interpersonal style to predict supervisory alliance. The attractive and interpersonally sensitive styles seem most

predictive; when the task oriented style (that is, a teaching approach) is linked to alliance, it is only to the task agreement component.

The Supervisors' Use of Expert and Referent Power. Schultz et al. (2002) had rehabilitation counselors rate both the types of interpersonal influence that their supervisors used and the quality of their supervisory alliances with these supervisors. Interpersonal influence (or social power) was defined in terms of French and Raven's (1959) taxonomy, wherein one person is assumed to exert influence over another to the extent that she or he uses one or more of five means of persuasion: reward power, coercive power, legitimate power, referent power, and expert power.

Schultz et al. found that the greater the supervisor's use of the expert (i.e., the perception that the supervisor had knowledge and expertise) and referent power bases (i.e., the perception that the supervisor is similar to the supervisee on some dimensions important to the supervisee), the stronger the supervisory alliance. This seems consistent with the social influence research (e.g., Heppner & Claiborn, 1989), which shows that referent power (also referred to as "attractiveness") is related to the client's liking of the therapist.

These findings can be seen as overlapping with those concerning supervisory style described immediately above. In particular, supervisor "attractiveness" again emerges as an important attribute.

The Supervisor's Use of Self-Disclosure. In their review of the literature on self-disclosure in therapy, Hill and Knox (2002) noted that, although there were relatively few studies of the immediate outcomes of self-disclosure in therapy, moderate levels of therapist self-disclosure tended to have a positive effect on the therapeutic relationship. Because supervisors are better known to their supervisees than counselors are to clients, and because they serve as role models, it stands to reason that supervisor self-disclosures would have at least as great an impact. In fact, Ladany and Lehrman-Waterman (1999) found that level of supervisory disclosures (which primarily concerned personal issues, neutral counseling experiences, and counseling struggles) predicted the strength of the supervisory alliance.

The Supervisor's Attachment Style. We address attachment styles in Chapter 7. Therefore, we simply will acknowledge at this point that at least one study (White & Queener, 2003) found that healthy adult attachments predicted alliance quality.

The Supervisor's Evaluative Practices. Ladany, Lehrman-Waterman, et al. (1999) found that a third of the ethical violations that supervisees reported concerned the manner in which supervisors evaluated them. This corroborates the importance of supervisors attending to their evaluative practices.

Importantly, then, Lehrman-Waterman and Ladany (2001) reported the development of a measure to assess evaluation practices in clinical supervision, the Evaluation Process within Supervision Inventory (EPSI) (available in the Supervisor's Toolbox). Two EPSI scales were used:

1. *Goal Setting—Sample items: The goals my supervisor and I generated for my training seemed important; My supervisor and I created goals that were easy for me to understand.*
2. *Feedback—Sample items: My supervisor welcomed comments on his or her style as a supervisor; The feedback I received was directly related to the goals we established.*

This was an instrument-development study. But, as part of the validation process, Lehrman-Waterman and Ladany compared scores on the new measure with scores on measures that would be theoretically linked. Scores on both EPSI scales predicted supervisees' ratings of supervisory alliance (all three alliance elements: tasks, goals, bonds). As well, scores on these scales predicted satisfaction with supervision. It is logical to wonder about the extent to which the EPSI's Goal Setting scale and the Goal scale of the Working Alliance Inventory might actually be measuring the same construct, though (e.g., the correlation between the two was .78).

Reasonably, the clearer and fairer the evaluative process is perceived to be, the less supervisee anxiety and greater the level of trust. Both would have positive effects on the supervisory alliance.

The Supervisor's Ethical Behavior. Ladany, Lehrman-Waterman, et al. (1999) examined the prevalence of 15 ethical behaviors that are particular to supervision. These included issues related, for example, to Performance Evaluation and Monitoring of Supervisee Activities, Confidentiality in Supervision, and Supervision Boundaries and Respectful Treatment. Some of the behaviors that they examined (e.g., "My supervisor allowed our sessions to be interrupted unnecessarily by people or events") would not rise to the level of ethical breaches that would warrant complaints to professional associations' ethics committees. The breadth of these authors' definition of ethical behavior is suggested by the fact that more than half the supervisees in the study reported that their current supervisors had not adhered to at least one of the ethical guidelines that Ladany et al. had developed.

Ladany, Lehrman-Waterman et al. (1999) found that the greater the frequency with which supervisees reported unethical behaviors, the lower the supervisees rated supervisory bonds and agreement on tasks and goals. They also found that the greater the number of unethical behaviors, the less satisfied the supervisees were with supervision. To put this in a more colloquial way, the more the supervisor had let down the supervisee, the less strong the supervisee felt a connection to the supervisor.

Supervisee Factors that Predict Alliance.   The supervisor has the greater responsibility for maintaining the alliance and so it probably is fitting that less attention has been given to supervisee variables. Nevertheless, we find it surprising that there have been so few. To date, only two have been investigated: the supervisee's (1) attachment style, and (2) experience of negative supervision.

The Supervisee's Attachment Style.   Renfro-Michel (2006) found that a secure attachment style predicted rapport (on the Efstation et al. measure). On the other hand, White and Queener (2003) found no relationship between supervisee attachment style and working alliance. Therefore, as intuitive as that relationship might seem, it has yet to be established empirically.

The Supervisee's Experience of Negative Supervision.   Ramos-Sánchez et al. (2002) confirmed the intuitive link between negative supervisory experiences and the resulting, weaker supervisory alliances. From a national sample of supervisees, they compared those who reported at least one

negative supervisory event with those who had not. The former group reported weaker alliances. Also, those who reported negative experiences reported (1) being less satisfied with supervision, (2) being at a lower developmental level as measured by the Supervisee Levels Questionnaire–Revised (SLQ–R; McNeill et al., 1992; see the Supervisor's Toolbox), and (3) having less positive relationships with their clients.

There are many ways, of course, for the supervisory experience to be made negative for the supervisee. Both Magnuson et al. (2000) and Nelson (2002) have cataloged ways for supervisors to provide what they termed "lousy" supervision. Table 6.1 lists the 22 ways Nelson found in her review of the literature. Regardless of how obvious items on this list might seem, to have this list in writing provides an important reminder to supervisors of behaviors to avoid.

Supervision Processes that Predict Alliance.   Three supervisor × supervisee interaction variables have been found to be related to working alliance. Interestingly, two of those are related to issues of race and ethnicity.

Racial Identity Matching.   Although we addressed in Chapter 5 the impact of race and ethnicity on supervision, one study warrants specific attention here. Ladany, Brittan-Powell, et al. (1997) found that racial matching of supervisors and supervisees had no relationship to strength of working alliance. Significantly, though, they found that racial identity matching (Helms, 1990) was a predictor of alliance. Specifically, supervisors and supervisees who shared high levels of racial identity had the highest agreement on goals and tasks. They also had the strongest emotional bonds.

Discussions of Ethnic Differences.   Racial identity matching focuses on attributes of the participants. But this does not speak to the behaviors that might be effective.

Gatmon et al. (2001) examined the extent to which frank discussions of differences in ethnicity, gender, and sexual orientation affected working alliance. Interestingly, they found that

TABLE 6.1   How to Be a Lousy Supervisor: Lessons from the Research

From Worthen and McNeill (1996)

1. Don't establish a strong supervisory alliance with your supervisee.
2. Don't reveal any of your own shortcomings to your supervisee.
3. Don't provide a sense of safety so that your supervisee can reveal his or her doubts and fears about competency.

From Kozlowska, Nunn, and Cousins (1997)

4. Place the importance of service delivery above your supervisee's educational needs.
5. Ignore your supervisee's need for emotional support in a new and challenging context.

From Wulf and Nelson (2000)

6. Involve your supervisee in the conflicted dynamics among professional staff in your setting.
7. Don't support your supervisee's strengths. Only point out weaknesses.
8. Don't take an interest in your supervisee's interests.
9. Talk mostly about your own cases in supervision.

From Nelson & Friedlander (2001)

10. Don't conduct a role induction process with your supervisee that involves being explicit about his or her and your own expectations about how supervision will proceed.
11. Allow yourself to feel threatened by your supervisee's competencies.
12. Retaliate against your supervisee for being more competent than you are in one or more areas or more mature than you are chronologically.
13. Insist that your supervisee work from the same theoretical orientation that you do.
14. Demand that your supervisee "act like a student rather than a colleague."
15. Criticize your supervisee in front of his or her peers.
16. Deny responsibility for interpersonal conflicts that arise between you and your supervisee.
17. If you sense the presence of conflict in the relationship, don't bring it up.
18. If your relationship with your supervisee becomes difficult, don't consult with someone else about it. It might reveal your lack of competence.
19. Treat your supervisee as a confidante. Use her or him as your counselor.
20. Be sexist, ageist, multiculturally incompetent, and the like.
21. Don't take your supervisee's expressed concerns about any of the above issues seriously.
22. Reveal intimate details about your own sexual experiences to your supervisee.

Source: From table based on a paper, *How to Be a Lousy Supervisor: Lessons from the Research,* by M. L. Nelson, October, 2002, presented at the convention of the Association for Counselor Education and Supervision, Park City, UT.

supervisor–supervisee discussions of gender or sexual orientation did not predict working alliance, but discussions of similarities and differences in ethnicity did. Specifically, these discussions predicted higher levels on the bond subscale of the Working Alliance Inventory (Horvath & Greenburg, 1989). This does not resolve the question of who should initiate these discussions. It does, though, indicate that such discussions are important.

Supervisor–Supervisee Complementarity. In Chapter 7 we will more fully address the issue of interpersonal complementarity and its implications for supervision. Briefly, though, complementarity is based on the assumptions that (a) in any relationship there are power inequities and that (b) relationships are smoother when each person's behavior complements the other on that power dimension. For example, a complementary interaction sequence might occur with one person requesting help and the other responding by providing that help.

That premise was confirmed by Chen and Bernstein (2000), who compared two supervisory dyads over their first three sessions. The one with the stronger alliance also demonstrated greater complementarity. That complementarity was determined through coding of actual within-session behaviors of each participant.

Quarto (2002) also was interested in complementarity, but used a questionnaire to determine the extent to which supervisors and supervisees characterized their supervisory relationship as one that (a) was conflictual, (b) was characterized by supervisor control of what happened in the relationship, or (c) was characterized by supervisee control of what happened in the relationship. Unsurprisingly, perceptions of conflictual relationships negatively predicted working alliance, whereas control by either of the other parties did not (one caveat: the supervisors tended not to see supervisee-control over the sessions, whereas some supervisees did).

Unfortunately, neither of these studies was designed to permit an analysis of fluctuation in complementarity across time and how that might affect working alliance. Tracey and Sherry (1993) hypothesized that supervision will be characterized by an initial stage with high complementarity, followed by a stage of lower complementarity, and then ending with a stage of high complementarity. If such stages were demonstrated to occur, would such fluctuations in complementarity be matched by fluctuations in the alliance? Or, alternatively, would the fact that an alliance was established earlier in the relationship be the factor that *allows* there a phase of lower complementarity to occur?

Supervisory Alliance Outcomes.   The assumption implicit in the discussion so far is that the working alliance is not an end it itself: Better alliances will result in better outcomes of one kind or another. In psychotherapy, for example, the working alliance predicts client outcomes (e.g., Horvath & Symonds, 1991; Orlinsky et al., 1994). In supervision, there are at least five outcomes that have been observed.

Adherence to Treatment Protocols.   Manualized treatments have been greeted with suspicion or even disdain by many mental health professionals who regard adherence to a protocol as an unnecessary constraint on their use of professional judgment and creativity. However, as Lambert and Arnold (1987) have pointed out, the use of treatment manuals is an excellent way for supervisees to learn a particular approach. Importantly, then, Holloway and Neufeldt (1995) suggested that the quality of the supervisory relationship should affect the level of supervisees' adherence to a treatment manual.

Therefore, the results of Patton and Kivlighan's (1997) study are significant. In their examination of supervisees' adherence to a particular treatment model (Strupp and Binder's, 1984, time-limited psychodynamic therapy), they found that week-to-week fluctuations in the supervisory alliance accounted for a substantial portion of the week-to-week fluctuations in adherence to general psychodynamic interviewing skills. The supervisory alliance did not, however, predict the use of specific manualized techniques.

Supervisees' Willingness to Disclose.   Slavin (1994) posed this rhetorical question: "How often have we heard clinicians joke, privately and guiltily, about what they don't tell their supervisors?" (p. 256). In so doing, he highlighted a significant problem in supervision: Supervisees vary in their willingness to reveal both what Sarnat and Frawley-O'Dea (2001) playfully call "crimes and misdemeanors" and more personal material.

Supervisees' failure to disclose relevant information to supervisors hinders their learning. It also puts the supervisor at risk legally, for the supervisor is liable if the supervisee is engaged in unethical or illegal activities.

For these reasons, we believe that the Ladany et al. (1996) study should rank as among the more important in the supervision literature. They examined what supervisees had failed to disclose to their supervisees and why. We have summarized their results in Table 6.2.

As these results indicate, supervisees report a number of reasons for having failed to disclose material. Although a poor alliance is only one of these, it was reported by half the supervisees. One indicator that these nondisclosures were not trivial is the fact that these supervisees report that 66% of what was not disclosed to supervisors was disclosed elsewhere.

Webb and Wheeler (1998) conducted a related study, focusing on psychodynamically oriented supervisees in Britain. They found that scores on the Rapport scale of the Supervisory Working Alliance Inventory (Efstation et al., 1990) predicted supervisees' willingness to report sensitive material to their supervisors.

Therapeutic Alliances of Supervisees with Their Clients   As we discussed earlier with respect to parallel processes, Patton and Kivlighan (1997) found that week-to-week fluctuations in the supervisory alliance predicted week-to-week fluctuations in the supervisee–client working alliance. This is an important finding, for it permits an inferential link between quality of supervision and client outcomes. That is, (1) client–therapist working alliances have been shown to predict therapeutic outcome (Horvath & Symonds, 1991; Orlinsky et al., 1994), (2) the Patton and Kivlighan study established a link between supervisory and therapeutic alliance, and (3) it is therefore possible to infer that supervisory alliances indirectly affect client outcomes through

---

TABLE 6.2   What Supervisees Fail to Disclose and Why

In their sample of supervisees, Ladany et al. (1996) found the following:
What they had failed to disclose:
- negative feelings toward a supervisor (90% of supervisees who had failed to disclose material)
- their own personal issues (e.g., thoughts about themselves; experiences; problems) (60%)
- clinical mistakes (44%)
- uneasiness or concerns about the supervisor's evaluations of them (44%)
- general observations about the client (e.g., diagnosis; appearance; interventions; or counseling process) (43%)
- negative (critical, disapproving, or unpleasant) reactions to the client (36%)
- thoughts or feelings of attraction toward the client (25%)
- positive feelings toward the supervisor (23%)
- countertransference reactions to client (22%)

Why they had not disclosed:
- perceived to be too personal (73%)
- perceived to be unimportant (62%)
- negative feelings such as shame, embarrassment, or discomfort (51%)
- feelings of deference (i.e., it was not his or her place to bring up material that would be uncomfortable to the supervisor) (55%)
- poor alliance with the supervisor (50%)
- impression management (i.e., to avoid being perceived negatively) (46%)

Note: Percentages were of those supervisees who reported having failed to disclose material. Supervisees could indicate multiple categories of what they had not disclosed and of why they had not.

the therapeutic alliances between supervisee and client.

Role Conflict and Ambiguity.   Olk and Friedlander (1992) suggested that at various points the supervisee may be required to function in the roles of student, client, counselor, or colleague. Then, drawing from organizational psychology literature, they suggested role ambiguity or role conflict as two role-related problems that a supervisee might face.

Role ambiguity occurs when the supervisee is uncertain about the role expectations that the supervisor and/or agency has for him or her. Role conflict occurs either (1) when the supervisees are required to engage in two or more roles that may require inconsistent behavior or (2) when the supervisees are required to engage in behavior that is incongruent with their personal judgment. Ladany and Friedlander (1995) provided illustrative examples of each. In the first case, supervisees may be required to reveal personal weaknesses and potential inadequacies while *also* needing to present themselves to the supervisor as competent so that they will pass the practicum. This might be understood as a conflict between the supervisee-as-client and supervisee-as-counselor. In the second case, the supervisor might give directives to behave in a manner that is inconsistent with the supervisee's ethical or theoretical beliefs. Here the conflict is between the roles of supervisee-as-student and supervisee-as-counselor.

To study these two types of supervisee role difficulties, Olk and Friedlander (1992) developed the Role Conflict and Role Ambiguity Inventory (RCRAI). Readers interested in using it in their own research or in monitoring supervisee role difficulties will find the RCRAI (labeled the *Supervisee Perceptions of Supervision* scale) in the Supervisor's Toolbox at the end of this book.

Olk and Friedlander (1992) found that many supervisees did not report role difficulties. Those who did, however, were more likely to report work-related anxiety and dissatisfaction as well as dissatisfaction with supervision. They also found that supervisees reported less role ambiguity when they perceived themselves to have been offered clear statements from their supervisors about their expectations for supervision.

In a subsequent study in which they used both the RCRAI and a version of the Working Alliance Inventory (WAI; Horvath & Greenburg, 1989), Ladany and Friedlander (1995) found that the greater the strength of the supervisor–supervisee emotional bond, the less role conflict the supervisee experienced. This finding was supported by the path-analytic study of Son et al. (in press), who found that better working alliances predicted lower levels of role conflict and ambiguity.

Note, however, that the data in both the Ladany and Friedlander and the Son et al. studies were correlational. Therefore, even though they interpreted their findings as meaning that better relationships predicted less role conflict and ambiguity, the opposite could just as well be true. That is, the relationship could be stronger *because* there is less role conflict or ambiguity.

Finally, we would note the work of Nelson and Friedlander (2001). They did not specifically examine working alliances in their qualitative study of conflictual supervision that 13 supervisees had experienced, but their results provide additional data to suggest that role conflict and ambiguity negatively affect the working alliance. In their study, all but one of the supervisees scored substantially above the norm group means for both role conflict and role ambiguity. In addition, these supervisees rated their supervisors substantially below norm group means for the Attractive and Interpersonally Sensitive scores on the SSI (Friedlander & Ward, 1984).

Satisfaction.   It is intuitive to believe that a better supervisory alliance would predict greater satisfaction with supervision. In fact, Ladany, Ellis, et al. (1999) found this to be true in their sample of supervisees as did Ladany, Lehrman-Waterman, et al. (1999).

Interestingly, though, that relationship between working alliance may not be the same across different nationalities. In their cross-national study, Son et al. (in press) found that the relationship between working alliance and satisfaction was stronger for American than for Korean supervisees. This finding provides a useful reminder that the predictors and outcomes of supervisory working alliance that are depicted in Figure 6.3 were obtained in Western—primarily American—studies and so should be generalized with caution to supervisory relationships in Eastern and other parts of the world.

The Dynamic Nature of the Supervisory Alliance

Sullivan's statement, "God keep me from a therapy that goes well!" can be extended to "Keep me from a supervisory relationship that goes well!" Going well may mean that there is more superficiality in the relationship, but less anxiety; a more comfortable atmosphere, but limited interpersonal engagement; a greater sense of certainty, but complexities are dissociated; more interpretations, but little structural change in the relatedness between the participants . . . disappointments and struggles have more likely been avoided, but the potential richness and joy of a significant relationship [are] lost. (Lesser, 1983, p. 128)

The conception of the working alliance in the immediately preceding section was that it is relatively stable. Whereas its quality or strength will be affected by factors such as those we have discussed, changes in that alliance will occur in a relatively predictable way over time.

However, there is a dynamic nature to the alliance that would be overlooked if we were to stop with what we have presented in the section above. The supervisory alliance fluctuates in quality and intensity. In understanding those fluctuations and how they might be managed, it is useful to consider Betcher and Zinberg's (1988) discussion of the ways they perceived supervisory and therapeutic relationships to be similar.

One of those similarities is that participants have the capacity to undo the human errors that they make, especially with one another. This is a particularly important aspect of the supervisory relationship. In fact, a central thesis of Mueller and Kell's (1972) now classic supervision book,

Coping with Conflict, was that in any relationship, whether personal or professional, conflict inevitably will occur between or among the parties. This conflict can stem from conflicting goals that the two parties entertain, from a "mistake" that one party in the relationship has made, or through the repetition of a maladaptive interpersonal pattern.

The manner in which the parties resolve, or fail to resolve, this conflict will dictate whether the relationship continues to grow and develop or stagnates. This is similar to Bordin's (1983) assertion that (1) alliances undergo a continual "weakening and repair" (also referred to as "tear–repair," "rupture–repair," or "disruption–restoration") process and (2) this process constitutes a vehicle for therapeutic change.

It is likely that most supervisory relationship weakenings or conflicts are resolved within a single session. But some last longer. In a relatively informal study of supervision with psychiatric residents, Nigam, Cameron, and Leverette (1997) examined supervisory "impasses" as stalemates that lasted at least three to four weeks. Interestingly, 40% of the respondents reported having experienced at least one such impasse as supervisees. The usefulness of this descriptive study was in its cataloging of types of interpersonal problems between the supervisor and supervisee that led to impasses including: boundary violations; lack of acceptance of a supervisee's sexual identity; and inhibition of disclosure of pertinent information.

Finally, we should note that a few supervisor–supervisee conflicts never are resolved. When these are serious in nature, the supervisee can suffer lasting consequences (cf. Nelson & Friedlander, 2001) and clients, too, can be affected. Arkowitz (2001), invoking a parallel process framework, noted that "A supervisee injured in supervision will act out these injuries with the patient, in confused attempts to repair them" (p. 59). Some support for this is provided by the finding of Ramos-Sánchez et al. (2002) that supervisees who had experienced problematic supervision experienced less-strong relationships with their clients.

Figure 6.4 visually models how the resolution—or nonresolution—of episodes of conflict will affect the quality of the supervisory relationship across time. If the conflict is resolved, the relationship is strengthened and grows; if the conflict is *not* resolved, the relationship suffers and is diminished. Because there are likely to be multiple conflictual episodes, there will be multiple opportunities to strengthen or weaken the relationship. In one way, this is a hopeful model in that it shows that if one episode is not resolved well, there likely will be other episodes that will provide the opportunity to correct the trajectory of the relationship.

This figure oversimplifies, of course, for it is unlikely that a supervisor–supervisee conflict will be either resolved or not in a dichotomous manner. In real life, the resolution can be understood as occurring in some degree. But this figure is useful in making the point that relationships have a history of a series of conflict–resolution

sequences and that the overall course of a particular supervisory relationship will be affected by the successes in resolving these conflicts.

Supervisee–supervisor conflicts can arise from many sources, some of which are more problematic than others. It is useful to consider them as types that occur on a continuum from (1) those that occur as a function of either a supervisor mistake or a miscommunication between the two, (2) those that occur because of normative processes, and (3) those that occur as a function of interpersonal dynamics and expectations of the supervisee. Each provides a learning opportunity. In the section that follows, each of these types is discussed in turn.

Conflicts Arising from Miscommunications or Mismatched Expectations. Evaluative feedback seems to make the supervisory relationship particularly vulnerable to conflict (Robiner et al., 1993). We already have noted that Ladany, Lehrman-Waterman, et al. (1999) found that a third of supervisee-reported ethical breaches were related to evaluation and that Lehrman-Waterman and Ladany (2001) found that the clearer the evaluation process, the less supervisee anxiety and the stronger the supervisory alliance.

These findings were confirmed in the only study yet to examine the weakening–repair process in supervisory alliances. In their observations of within-session tear–repair processes within 10 consecutive sessions of 10 supervisory dyads, Burke et al. (1998) found that the more affect-arousing and difficult to repair weakenings occurred as supervisors assumed evaluative roles. They also observed that the type of weakening events varied according to the experience level of the supervisees. For example, alliance-weakening events with more advanced supervisees were more likely to involve disagreements about theoretical or treatment-planning issues.

The February 2000 issue of the *Journal of Clinical Psychology—In Session: Psychotherapy in Practice* was devoted to the therapeutic alliance. Many of the alliance conflicts or ruptures that the articles described were a function of

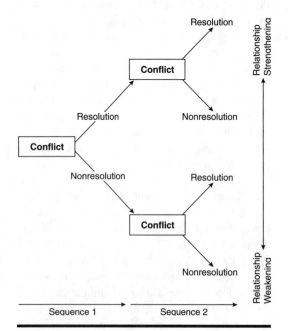

FIGURE 6.4   Relationship Trajectory as Conflictual Episodes Are Resolved or Not Resolved

either misunderstandings or disagreements about the goals or tasks of therapy (or, by extension, supervision). In their response to these articles, Safran and Muran (2000) discussed interventions that the therapist (or supervisor) could use in response to these misunderstandings or disagreements. Among them were:

1. **Direct intervention.** This involves (1) clarifying to the client (or supervisee) the rationale for the intervention and (2) addressing any misunderstandings that he or she might have.
2. **Indirect intervention.** This involves giving particular attention to the tasks and goals that have relevance to the client (or supervisee), rather than trying to address the underlying conflict.

In supervision, direct intervention is the better option in most cases in which a supervisory conflict has arisen because of either a misunderstanding or incongruent expectations.

Normative Conflicts. Some supervisee–supervisor conflict is normative and occurs in response to the supervisee's developmental level. In particular, Rønnestad and Skovholt (1993) suggested that both supervisor–supervisee tension and dissatisfaction with supervision may be at its greatest with more advanced students. Like most adolescents, supervisees at this level vacillate between feelings of confidence and insecurity. Rønnestad and Skovholt note that "The student has now actively assimilated information from many sources but still has not had enough time to accommodate and find her or his own way of behaving professionally" (p. 400). This is not, in itself, a matter for concern, particularly if the supervisor is able to understand and anticipate this particular developmental phenomenon.

Conflicts Arising from Participants' Interpersonal Dynamics. Safran and Muran's (1996, 2000) is probably the best-known research program to focus on the resolution of therapeutic alliance ruptures. Many of their observations apply as well to supervisory alliances, with one important

caveat: In most cases, the maladaptive interpersonal cycle to which they refer is less prominent in supervision, for most supervisees will have less rigid or negative expectations about others than will clients and therefore are less likely to elicit a complementary response from their supervisors.

With this caveat, it is useful to consider Safran and Muran's observations. Although we will use their language and discuss client–therapist interactions, it is reasonable in most cases to understand that these same observations apply as well to supervisee–supervisor interactions.

Safran and Muran note that there are two major subtypes of alliance ruptures, though they often work in some degree of combination with one another. In one, the *confrontation rupture,* the client will directly express unhappiness or even anger at some aspect of the therapy or the therapist. In *withdrawal ruptures,* the client disengages from the therapist or some aspect of the therapeutic process.

Therapists' initial attempts to resolve the ruptures often are complementary to the client's response, putting them into the role of perpetuating the "maladaptive interpersonal cycle" (Safran & Muran, 2000, p. 240). That is, therapists often respond to confrontation ruptures defensively or with their own anger and to withdrawal ruptures with their own controlling behavior. These responses generally replicate those of other people in the clients' lives.

To be effective, it is essential that the therapist be (1) aware of his or her own reactions that the client has elicited, and then (2) rather than participating further in the maladaptive interpersonal cycle, begin metacommunicating (i.e., to communicate about their communications).

> *The process of extricating oneself from the dysfunctional dance that is being enacted is facilitated by inviting the client to take a step back and join with the therapist in a process of examining or metacommunicating about what is currently going on between them. The therapist's task is to identify his or her own feelings and to use these as a point of departure for collaborative exploration.* (Safran & Muran, 2000, p. 238)

The therapist's purpose is to help clients to learn that they can express their needs without endangering the therapeutic alliance. To do this, therapists have at least the following options in metacommunicating about an alliance rupture for tailoring their response to the specific client.

• Share his or her personal reactions and feelings by giving specific examples of client behaviors that might elicit them. "I feel dismissed or closed out by you, and I think it's because you don't seem to me to pause and reflect in a way that suggests you are really considering what I am saying" (Safran & Muran, 2000, p. 238). The therapist should then follow up with an inquiry such as "How does this match your perceptions?" to elicit the client's response.

• In response to the client's withdrawal or confrontation, offer an empathic statement as means both to convey understanding and to invite the client to explore the issue.

• Offer a more interpretive response, especially to clients who have limited access to their inner experience or who find it too anxiety provoking or chaotic to explore.

These seem useful strategies for the supervisor as well. Of the three, the last strategy is least likely to be of use in supervision to resolve impasses. That is, we can assume that most supervisees have reasonable access to their inner experience.

Mental health professionals generally acknowledge that therapists may not be expected to form an effective working relationship with every client that they see: Why should we have a different expectation for supervision? In the (fortunately rare) cases of intractable personality conflicts, the responsible supervisor will transfer the supervisee to another supervisor or otherwise work to protect the supervisee's interests. However, to be sensitive to the issues that we have raised here is likely to minimize the frequency with which such conflicts happen.

In summary, conflict occurs in any relationship, including that between supervisor and supervisee. The manner in which it is resolved affects the overall course and strength of the relationship and also provides useful learning opportunities for both supervisor and supervisee. In other sections of this book, we address the resolution of conflict. However, this section has given particular emphasis to the importance of the process.

CONCLUSION

More than any other, this chapter demonstrates just how complex the supervisory relationship is. That complexity is most evident when the relationship is considered as a three-person system, with its attendant parallel processes, isomorphism, triangulations, and so on. But even when supervisory relationships are scrutinized at the level of a two-person system, with only the supervisor and supervisee interactions, there is ample complexity. In short, this material has illustrated how important it is that supervisors receive the formal training that will help them address this complexity.

CHAPTER 7

THE SUPERVISORY RELATIONSHIP
SUPERVISEE AND SUPERVISOR CONTRIBUTING FACTORS

We began Chapter 6 by suggesting that to examine the supervisory relationship is akin to examining a forest through a telescope. At each focal range there are different levels of detail and complexity. Chapter 6 was focused on two telescopic "focal ranges": the supervisory triad and the dyad. In this chapter, we refocus that telescope to examine contributions of the individual supervisee and supervisor to the quality and effectiveness of the supervisory relationship.

Chapter 5 shares similarities with this chapter in that it focuses on individual differences and factors of supervisees and supervisors that certainly affect the supervisory relationship. But, whereas Chapter 5 stresses between-supervisee and supervisor differences, our concern here is with more dynamic processes that affect the nature and the quality of the dyadic relationship.

We have organized the chapter into two sections. The first focuses on factors specific to the supervisee. The second focuses on factors specific to the supervisor. Because this book is intended to improve the work of supervisors, we discuss implications for supervisors in both sections. The supervisor and supervisee factors that we cover in this chapter are depicted in Figure 7.1.

SUPERVISEE FACTORS

Supervisee issues such as attachment style, shame, anxiety, need for competence, and transference all affect the effectiveness and quality of the supervisor–supervisee relationship. As Figure 7.1 indicates, though, we are anchoring our discussions of these several supervisee variables to the concept of resistance. It may seem in so doing that we are attending only to negative issues in the relationship. But, in fact, we understand supervisee behavior to exist on a continuum, with fully resistant behavior on one end and, on the other, an ideal relationship in which the supervisee feels and acts fully engaged.

Supervisee Resistance

The concept of client resistance in psychotherapy originated with psychoanalysis, but has found much broader application. The February 2002 issue of the *Journal of Clinical Psychology—In Session: Psychotherapy in Practice* was comprised of articles that each offered a different theoretical perspective on client resistance. Beutler, Moleiro, and Talebi (2002a) wrote an integrative response to these articles, beginning it with this assertion:

> *While they disagree with one another in many ways, the 400+ theories of psychotherapy that are practiced in contemporary society converge on the curious observation that some painfully distressed patients seeking assistance from expensive and highly trained professionals reject their therapists' best advice, fail to act in their own best interests, and do not respond to the most effective interventions that can be mustered on their behalf. . . . [But whereas] the descriptions offered of resistant behavior by different theories are similar, they offer dramatically different explanations and intervention methods.* (p. 207)

These observations about resistance in therapy also extend to supervision (cf. Bradley & Gould, 1994; Pearson, 2000), despite its educational rather

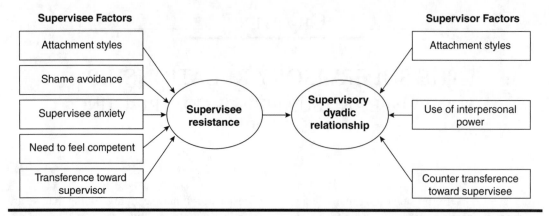

Supervisee Factors

- Attachment styles
- Shame avoidance
- Supervisee anxiety
- Need to feel competent
- Transference toward supervisor

Supervisee resistance

Supervisory dyadic relationship

Supervisor Factors

- Attachment styles
- Use of interpersonal power
- Counter transference toward supervisee

FIGURE 7.1   Supervisee and Supervisor Factors That Affect the Nature and Quality of the Supervisory Dyad

than therapeutic purpose. Whether supervisors intentionally employ the concept of resistance, the phenomenon is there to be addressed. McColley and Baker (1982), for example, found that most novice supervisors identified their primary difficulty to be that of not knowing how to intervene effectively with supervisee resistance.

Liddle (1986) suggested that supervisees' resistance should be understood as self-protective behavior that they employ in the face of some threat. It is likely that this dynamic accounts for many or even most instances of supervisee resistance. But that resistance can originate from other sources as well, including the supervisee's need to individuate from the supervisor (i.e., a developmental issue), supervisor–supervisee conflict, and disagreements about tasks and goals.

Before going further, we want to assert that we introduce this discussion of supervisee resistance with some trepidation. Specifically, we recognize how readily terms like "resistance" can be heard as pejorative and blaming of supervisees. Such blaming is wrong at a conceptual level, because resistance can arise from a number of sources and often is a healthy response by the supervisee to a perceived threat. It also is wrong at a practical level, because it invites supervisor irritation or even anger toward the supervisee, which almost certainly will be counterproductive. Moreover, blaming inappropriately absolves supervisors of

interpersonal consequences of their own behaviors (see, e.g., Beutler, Moleiro, & Talebi, 2002b). Therefore, we hope the material in this chapter will be read with the understanding that supervisee resistance is a challenge to be addressed, but for which blame in inappropriate.

Manifestations of Supervisee Resistance.   The term resistance implies that supervisees are resisting something. But both the target and style of supervisee resistance can vary substantially. The following four categories of resistance that we developed are imprecise and overlapping, but give some sense of the scope of supervisee resistance. Supervisees can:

1. *Resist the supervisor's influence* (e.g., by being nondisclosive about his or her behaviors or experiences; by deflecting discussions away from particular topics, or from a focus on some aspect of his or her behavior; by engaging in what the supervisor experiences as power struggles).

2. *Resist the supervisory experience itself* (which may be difficult to differentiate from the above). This is exemplified by Epstein's (2001) comment that "I operate on the assumption that persisting negative behaviors, such as lateness or missing sessions, are resistances signifying negative reactions to supervision" (p. 150).

3. *Be noncompliant with tasks related to the supervisory process.* A frequent example is that of supervisees' use of audio- or videotaping. Although we later will discuss the study by Ellis, Krengel, and Beck (2002), who found otherwise, we still find taping to raise supervisees' anxiety levels. Therefore, they often will resist doing so, sometimes overtly, sometimes through more indirect means such as projecting their fear on the client ("it will upset the client too much and therefore disrupt the therapy"), or by forgetting to bring equipment or tapes.
4. *Be noncompliant with mutually agreed upon plans with respect to clients.* This would apply, especially, to the implementation of particular interventions.

Circumstances that Elicit Supervisee Resistance.
Many factors affect supervisee resistance. Those we discuss in the material immediately below all concern interpersonal processes. We follow that with a discussion of supervisee attributes.

Supervisee Trust Levels. There is an old aphorism, "trust is efficient." That is, in interpersonal relationships, to trust another means to relax vigilance, thereby conserving energy and time. In general, the higher the supervisee's level of trust in the supervisor, the less he or she will need to exhibit the self-protective behavior that occurs as resistance; and, the less supervisee resistance, the more effective the supervisory relationship.

Trustworthiness, as discussed by Strong (1968), accrues to the counselor (or, here, the supervisor) as the client (or the supervisee) is able to believe that he or she is acting professionally and not in a way to exploit the relationship to meet his or her own needs. It creates an atmosphere of safety.

One characteristic of trust is that it always exists in some degree: It is not an all-or-nothing phenomenon. Another characteristic of trust is that it is earned over the course of many interactions and interpersonal risks taken together; it is not something that can occur instantaneously. Therefore, no single supervisor intervention or technique will earn a supervisee's trust. Trust is simply one of those broad goals that supervisors must work to achieve and maintain.

Client Issues Transmitted by Parallel Processes. Ekstein and Wallerstein (1972) were among the first authors to discuss supervisee resistance. They noted that it can arise by parallel processes, so that supervisee resistant behavior is a mirroring of the client's attitudes and behaviors, such as we discussed in Chapter 6.

Disagreement About Supervision Tasks and Goals. Supervisees are likely to become resistant when they do not agree with the tasks and goals of the supervisor. Resistance in this case can be understood as relationship rupture and is handled as we discussed in Chapter 6.

Supervisor Directiveness. Proctor and Inskipp (1988) made the useful distinction between *must* and *can* supervisory interventions. *Must interventions* are those that supervisors employ when they want to ensure that the supervisee will take some very specific action, for client welfare and other reasons. *Can interventions,* though, are ones in which the supervisee has the choice about whether and when she or he might take a particular action.

Must interventions are more likely to arouse resistance. This is especially true when the supervisee does not understand or agree with the rationale for the intervention and therefore perceives the supervisor's intervention as an arbitrary directive. Brehm and Brehm (1981) discussed the concept of reactance as opposition that manifests itself when people perceive their freedom of choice and/or action being constrained: The less voice people (supervisees included) are given, the more oppositional they will behave. This concept is useful in understanding how it is that *must* interventions that are misunderstood or perceived as being arbitrary will elicit resistance.

Supervisee Trait Reactance. Brehm and Brehm (1981) conceptualized reactance as situation specific. However, Dowd (1989) and others later conceptualized reactance as a trait that each person possesses to a greater or lesser degree. A highly reactant person is hypersensitive to losses of freedom and is especially vigilant in the presence of people of authority. Reactant supervisees will seem resistant.

Developmental Level. Various developmental models have shown supervisees to differ in their levels of resistance according to their levels of development (Rønnestad & Skovholt, 1993; Stoltenberg et al., 1998). Much as an adolescent who needs to begin individuating, supervisees at particular levels will begin to assert themselves.

Interventions. Various interventions we discuss throughout this chapter are useful in addressing supervisee resistance. However, we want to highlight some selectively here.

Supervision Focus. Supervisory focus can affect supervisees' felt vulnerability, which in turn elicits reactance. Specifically, vulnerability is least when the supervisory focus is on the client (i.e., on case conceptualization issues), rather than on the supervisee's personhood or behavior. Therefore, case conceptualization might be given greater initial emphasis with supervisees whom the supervisor perceives to feel especially vulnerable.

In the following, Epstein (2001) is speaking as well to supervisor style:

> *I favor, whenever possible, the use of what Spotznitz (1969) has termed "object-oriented questions" as contrasted with "ego-oriented questions." These questions direct the supervisee's attention to faults of the other, to myself, or to the patient rather than to his own faults. This technique might appear to further the supervisee's tendency to externalize responsibility for his own contribution to the failure of the supervision or of the treatment situation. Actually, it has the opposite effect. Object-oriented questions establish an atmosphere in which the supervisee becomes increasingly free, with a minimal sense of risk, to contact and directly communicate all of his feelings vis-à-vis both the supervision and his patient.* (p. 298)

Supervisor Style. To the extent that the supervisee feels in control, his or her resistance will be minimized. This is especially true of those supervisees who are highly reactant. Beutler et al. (2002b) noted that it is useful for therapists to use one of the available scales to assess client reactance and then to calibrate their levels of directiveness accordingly. That is, the greater the client's reactance, the less directive and authoritative the therapist. In fact, with highly reactant clients, therapists might consider using defiance-based paradoxical techniques.

Although supervisees are unlikely to demonstrate the range of reactance that clients do, they will differ in their levels of it. Therefore, these guidelines reasonably can apply in supervision as well. Of the several supervisory styles or roles (Bernard, 1997), that of the consultant is probably least threatening and maximizes supervisees' sense of control. Interpersonal process recall (IPR; Kagan & Kagan, 1997) for example, is a technique that is almost entirely consultive in style and therefore useful.

Supervisee Countertransference. Epstein (2001) noted that in some cases what may seem like resistance to the supervision may actually reside elsewhere. For example, it could be that failure to carry through with agreed-upon interventions with the client stems from some particularly strong countertransference reaction to the client. In this case, the supervisor's intervention is one of helping the supervisee identify and express whatever those reactions might be.

Summary Comments About Supervisee Resistance. Supervisee resistance can be thought of as the supervisee applying the brakes when he or she perceives the vehicle that is supervision to be moving too fast, in the wrong direction, or on a too-bumpy road. In most instances, the resistance will be akin to gently tapping the brakes. There are some instances, though, in which the supervisee will figuratively "lock-'em-up." For the supervisor to be effective, she or he should create a climate that minimizes supervisees' felt need to put on the brakes. As well, she or he must be alert to instances of resistance and then make informed decisions about the best response. In general, the best supervision will be that in which the least resistance occurs.

Patton, Kivlighan, and Multon (1997) report a pattern of resistance in counseling whereby the client initially displays low levels of resistance, then high levels, and then ends with low levels again. It is unclear how well this might apply to supervision. However, it would be useful for supervision process researchers to examine such possible patterns.

For the remainder of this supervisee-focused portion of the chapter, we will address specific supervisee factors that affect resistance and therefore the quality of the dyad relationship. We begin with attachment and then examine, in turn, shame, anxiety, the need for competence, and finally transference.

Supervisee Attachment

From their review of the literature, Baumeister and Leary (1995) concluded that the evidence is strong in both that "the need to belong is a powerful, fundamental, and extremely pervasive motivation" (p. 497). Put another way, people are "hardwired" to be relational.

Attachment theory suggests ways in which a person expresses his or her need to belong. Bowlby (1977), attachment theory's primary developer, stated that "Briefly put, attachment behavior is conceived as any form of behavior that results in a person attaining or retaining proximity to some other differentiated and preferred individual, who is usually conceived as stronger and/or wiser" (p. 203).

Watkins (1995c; Pistole & Watkins, 1995) suggested that supervision is an attachment process that involves the development and eventual loosening of an affectional bond. The supervisory relationship has many similarities to both parent–child relationships and many adult–adult relationships. Watkins argued, therefore, that attachment theory has useful implications for understanding supervisor–supervisee relationships.

Bowlby (1977, 1978) described two primary pathological attachment patterns or styles. One is anxious attachment; the other, compulsive self-reliance. A third, which is something of a variant on the second, is compulsive caregiving. Bowlby argued that a person's style (i.e., the way he or she approaches and maintains relationships) is learned

during childhood, based on experiences with parents and other caregivers. The style then persists throughout life in relationships with important others, regardless of the style's current appropriateness. It endures across people and situations.

A supervisee with an anxious attachment style is likely to be very dependent and even "clingy," to call the supervisor constantly for help, to want to be the supervisor's favorite, and to resent the supervisor for not needing him or her in a reciprocal way. A supervisee who is a compulsive caregiver is likely to "rescue" clients, working to immediately lessen their concerns and problems (often at the expense of letting them fully grapple with and find resolution to their issues); this supervisee also is likely to be uncomfortable and even anxious in the supervisory context where she or he is the recipient of the supervisor's help and support. And a compulsively self-reliant supervisee is likely to refuse, resist, or even resent the supervisor's attempts to help.

Watkins (1995c) suggested that when supervisors encounter a supervisee with a pathological attachment style, they will feel caught up in something they may not initially understand. That is, they may be concerned about what they may have done to provoke the supervisee's responses, wonder about their competence, and feel quite exasperated. Watkins suggested that, for the relatively rare supervisee who actually does meet criterion for one of these three pathological attachment styles, psychotherapy is the appropriate intervention.

Watkins (1995c) noted that even though many supervisees may exhibit features of one or another of these three patterns, most have a sufficiently secure attachment style to allow supervision to occur in a satisfactory manner. Nevertheless, it is useful for supervisors to have these behavioral styles in mind as ways to conceptualize problematic bonding between them and their supervisees.

Data to support these hypotheses about supervisee attachment remain scant. In Chapter 6, we noted two studies that examined supervisee attachment style and supervisory alliance. One (Renfro-Michel, 2006) found a link between healthy supervisee attachment and supervisory alliance, but the other (White & Queener, 2003) did not.

Foster (2002), though, found that, compared to supervisees who rated themselves as having a secure attachment to their supervisors, those with fearful or preoccupied attachment were less interested in their work, less able to use self-referential perceptions to understand their clients, and less advanced in their overall development. None of these relationships was obtained, however, when the supervisor (as opposed to the supervisee) was rating supervisee attachment and level of supervisee development.

This led Foster to conclude that supervisors and supervisees have differential perceptions of supervisees' attachment style and its relationship to supervisee development, a result later confirmed by Foster, Lichtenberg, and Peyton (2007). Notably, though, Foster et al. found that supervisees' own ratings of an insecure attachment style predicted their having lower levels of professional development.

Supervisee Shame

Although some people are especially shame prone (e.g., those who are narcissistic; Miller, 1996), it is an emotion we all experience. Moreover, it is one that supervision is especially likely to elicit in supervisees because of its evaluative components and the requirement that supervisees expose themselves and their work. Yet, as Hahn (2002) pointed out, only a little (e.g., Alonso & Rutan, 1988; Lidmila, 1997) has been written about the role of supervisee shame in supervision. Because of its potentially detrimental effects on both the supervisee and the supervisory relationship, supervisee shame warrants more attention than it has so far received.

Shame, embarrassment, and guilt are self-conscious emotions. Of the three, guilt and shame seem the two that are most often confused. Lewis (1971) made what has become the generally accepted distinction between the two: That is, in shame, the focus of evaluation is the self (i.e., "I am flawed"), whereas in guilt, it is some thing

(act, thought, etc.) that the person has performed ("I have done something wrong").

Tangney, Wagner, Fletcher, and Gramzow (1992) noted that

in guilt, behavior is evaluated somewhat apart from the self. There is remorse or regret over the "bad thing" that was done and a sense of tension that often serves to motivate reparative action. . . . Whereas guilt motivates a desire to repair, to confess, apologize, or make amends, shame motivates a desire to hide—to sink into the floor and disappear. (pp. 669–670)

Shame requires that the person experiencing it have a basic notion of the self and that she or he engage in some form of self-evaluation (Lewis, 2000). As well, shame has two other attributes that are particularly important to supervision. One is that it involves a sense of exposure or of being exposed; the other is that for it to occur there must be some level of bond between the person and the "observing other" (Retzinger, 1998).

Supervisee Responses to Shame. Gilbert (1998) suggested that there are two basic categories of response to shame: submissive and aggressive. In his discussion of shame in supervision, Hahn (2002) drew from Nathanson (1992) to identify four common supervisee reactions to shame. Summarized below, the first two of these four reactions would fit Gilbert's passive category; the second two, the aggressive category.

Withdrawal. Withdrawal can occur as a momentary response to shame (e.g., by pulling back, breaking eye contact). But, depending on the strength and pervasiveness of the shame reaction, supervisees can manifest withdrawal across time as forgetfulness, coming late to sessions, and even the adoption of a passive, noncurious style of interaction with the supervisor.

Avoidance. Whereas withdrawal is a more passive way to "minimize shame, avoidance reactions are relatively active efforts to prevent exposure and condemnation" (Hahn, 2002, p. 276). Among the many avoidance strategies that supervisees might employ are diverting the supervisor's attention away from their mistakes and failures and encouraging the supervisor to provide his or her own observations and wisdom about a particular case (versus exposing their own knowledge, feelings, or skills). In fact, shame can prompt supervisees to withhold information from their supervisors (Yourman, 2003), which can be understood as a form of avoidance.

Attack on Others.   This externalizing behavior can vary in intensity from mild dismissiveness and devaluing of the supervisor (Yerushalmi, 1999) to more overt, hostile criticism. It is most likely to occur as a response to shame that is triggered by feeling devalued or in some way diminished by the supervisor (a feeling that can be based on an actual supervisor behavior or by some supervisee's unmet expectation of which the supervisor is unaware).

Attack on Self.   This internalizing behavior "also occurs on a continuum and may be manifested as deference on one end of the continuum to excessive self-criticism on the other" (Hahn, 2001, p. 280). Hahn notes that in supervision this defensive style can be used as a "preemptive strike": By criticizing himself or herself, the supervisor is deflected from doing so. A primary motivation for this strategy often is for the supervisee to maintain emotional connection with the supervisor.

Supervisor Responses.   The supervisor's role in addressing supervisee shame probably can be clustered into two types. The first is to create an environment that is minimally shame inducing. There is no single way to accomplish this. Among other things, it involves the supervisor creating a climate of trust and respect and employing a style and providing feedback in a way that is least likely to arouse shame (see, e.g., the Claiborn, Goodyear, & Horner, 2002, review of feedback in psychotherapy and the Hoffman et al., 2005 study of supervisors' perspective on the feedback they provide).

The second supervisor role is to recognize signs that the supervisee is or has been experiencing shame. For this second role, to be aware of these four major responses to supervisee shame

provides supervisors with a conceptual tool to guide their responses.

Alonso and Rutan (1988) offered supervisory suggestions to enable the supervisee to examine "secret failures that [he or she] was too horrified to admit" (p. 580). One is that the supervisor contribute to the supervisee's sense of dignity and security by offering consistent support and backing. Another is that supervisors take the risk of disclosing to supervisees embarrassing moments in their own work.

Bridges (1999) argued for creating a "shame free learning milieu." She suggested that this would have several elements. One is to "normalize the trainee's shame, powerlessness, and self-consciousness about not knowing, being a trainee, and struggle with personal, painful feelings . . . helps create an interpersonal environment where self-exposure, risk taking, and clinical curiosity are possible" (p. 220). As one means to accomplish this normalization, she suggests that the supervisor be willing to share his or her own "mistakes, humiliating clinical moments, and examples of countertransference domination with attention to how to understand and manage these dilemmas" (p. 220).

Hemlick (1998) developed a measure of supervisee shame as her dissertation research. Perhaps with it and other such instruments, it will be possible to learn more about the role of shame in supervision—and then possible appropriate responses by supervisors.

Supervisee Anxiety

Supervisees experience anxiety on two fronts: in their work with the client and with the supervisor. With respect to the latter, there are many possible sources of anxiety, the most prominent of which is ambiguity—about expectations and roles and about the criteria and procedures of evaluation. Moreover, anxiety is related to experience level, with beginning students more vulnerable to it (cf. Chapin & Ellis, 2002).

One of the really striking findings in Skovholt and Rønnestad's (1992a, 1992b) qualitative study of therapists across the life span was the intense anxiety experienced by graduate students. Interestingly, though, Skovholt and Rønnestad were less able to access this anxiety from their graduate student informants than they were from more senior practitioners who were reflecting back on their experiences in graduate school.

Whereas anxiety is a fact of life for the supervisee, there is no simple or uniform way to characterize it. This is so because a supervisee's anxiety may arise from a number of sources and is moderated by such factors as the supervisee's maturity, experience level, personality, and relationships with clients and the supervisor. In the material that follows, we will address, in turn, the (1) effects of supervisee anxiety, (2) sources, and (3) possible supervisor responses.

Effects of Anxiety on the Supervisee. In general, it is possible to think of three effects of supervisee anxiety. It may affect the supervisee's: (1) ability to learn, (2) ability to demonstrate already present skills, and (3) manner of responding to the supervisor. This is depicted visually in Figure 7.2. The first two are not necessarily related to the issue of resistance, which is the primary concept driving this section of the chapter, but are important and warrant attention.

Supervisee Learning. Although all learning processes begin with observation, a person's capacity to observe is reduced during states of high anxiety (Dombeck & Brody, 1995). For this reason, supervisee anxiety is a factor that can interfere with how much supervisees can profit from supervision.

This is not to suggest, though, that supervisee anxiety is always something to ward off. As counselors or therapists, we know that much of the time it is unhelpful to rush in with attempts to diminish a client's anxiety. The same rule pertains to supervisors' response to supervisee anxiety. Rioch (in Rioch, Coulter, & Weinberger, 1976) is among those who have observed that, within limits, the more anxiety counselors are able to allow themselves, the more they will learn. In part, this is because being able to "stay with" anxiety can be useful in identifying problem areas, either in what the client is presenting or in the supervisee's own history and characteristic ways of responding.

Supervisee Performance. Supervisee performance is concerned with what the supervisee actually has learned. When discussed in the context of anxiety, it certainly overlaps heavily with the process of supervisee learning. However, there is enough difference that we treat them distinctly here.

Friedlander, Keller, Peca-Baker, and Olk (1986) found that supervisees' performance was inversely related to their anxiety levels. This is not to suggest, though, that supervisee anxiety always is to be minimized. Despite some conceptual and empirical questions about it (e.g., Matthews, Davies, & Lees, 1990; Neiss, 1988), Yerkes and Dodson's (1908) inverted-U hypothesis, depicted visually in Figure 7.3, remains a useful way to think about anxiety. This is one of psychology's most famous hypotheses: that anxiety is an arousal state that, in moderate amounts, serves to motivate the individual and to facilitate task performance. Performance suffers, however, when the individual experiences either *too little* or *too much* anxiety: too little, and one lacks sufficient motivation to perform; too much, and one is debilitated.

If there is an optimal level of anxiety for supervisees to experience, then supervisors logically have the simultaneous goals of (1) helping to keep their supervisees from engaging in anxiety-avoidant behaviors and of (2) helping to keep supervisee anxiety in bounds so that it works in

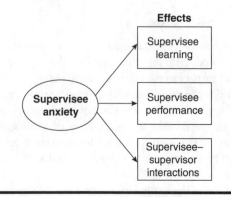

FIGURE 7.2 Consequence of Supervisee Anxiety

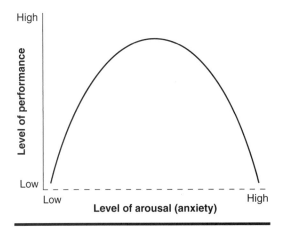

FIGURE 7.3 Depiction of the Yerkes–Dodson Inverted-U Hypothesis Regarding the Relationship Between Level of Arousal and Level of Performance

the service of performance. Kell and Burow (1970) noted, for example, that they worked "not only to facilitate . . . an awareness of the anxiety associated with the seriousness of learning, but also to leaven and help control the anxious experience" (p. 184).

One factor that affects supervisee anxiety, and therefore performance, is the fact that their work is observed and evaluated. To understand these effects on performance, it is useful to turn to social facilitation theory, which "focuses on changes in performance that occur when individuals perform in the presence of others versus alone" (Aiello & Douthitt, 2001, p. 163). Although this theory has a 100-year history, Aiello and Douthitt credit Zajonc (1965) for developing its contemporary version.

Zajonc distinguished between dominant responses (those it is easiest for the person to perform) and nondominant responses (those that are part of the person's skill repertoire, but are less likely to be performed). He noted that increases in arousal will facilitate performance of dominant responses, but impede performance of nondominant responses.

Athletics is a useful domain from which to draw to illustrate this effect. Olympic athletes have overlearned their particular athletic skill

through thousands of hours of practice. Under conditions of competition and close scrutiny, their performance is enhanced and may attain record-breaking levels. In contrast, people who still are working to master their skills are much more prone to "clutching" when under conditions of observation.

Supervisees are akin to these beginning athletes in that they still are working to develop skills that have not yet become automatic (cf. Bargh & Chartrand, 1999). When observed or monitored by a supervisor, their performance is vulnerable to deterioration. That is, they are vulnerable to clutching.

But, despite consistent findings in support of this model in other domains, its applications to supervision are called into question by the results of studies by Ellis and his colleagues. From the Chapin and Ellis (2002), the Ellis et al. (2002), and several instrument development studies, Ellis (personal communication, October 15, 2002) has concluded that the role of supervisee anxiety may have been overstated in the supervision literature. He asserted that "It looks like less than 10 percent report even moderate anxiety in high anxiety supervision or training situations (e.g., first video-tape review supervision in pre-practicum)." It appears, therefore, that more research is needed. In the meantime, it is useful for supervisors to be sensitive to the possible effects of observation on the supervisee.

Supervisee Interactions with Supervisor. Supervisee anxiety affects supervisor–supervisee interactions in a number of ways. One of those is in what the supervisee reveals during supervision (see, e.g., Ladany et al., 1996). Rønnestad and Skovholt (1993) noted that "the anxious student may tend to discuss in supervision only clients who show good progress, choose themes in which he or she is functioning well, or choose a mode of presenting data that allows full control over what the supervisor learns" (p. 398). They suggested that the supervisor may therefore, in the beginning, allow the student to select or even distort data until some of that anxiety dissipates.

The wish to manage supervisors' impressions of them is motivated at least in part by supervisees' anxiety and certainly affects interactions. All of us are concerned about how others perceive us (e.g., Schlenker & Leary, 1982). That is, we want to convey a certain impression, but worry about how well we are accomplishing it. Supervisees, however, deal not only with these "ordinary" concerns about creating a desired social impression, but also with the added concern of creating the impressions necessary to earn them satisfactory evaluations from their supervisors.

Social psychologists have discussed the strategies that people use to cope with these concerns as *impression management* (or strategic *self-presentation*). This is the person's attempt to deliberately project a certain image. It is possible to use the perspective of the theater and think of any person's social behavior as being a performance given to create a desired effect on others.

A person's motivation to manage impressions can be influenced by a number of factors (Leary & Kowalski, 1990). One is the importance to the person of a particular goal (a supervisee, for example, is likely to want to present himself or herself as having the characteristics and skills that the supervisor believes necessary to be an effective mental health professional). Another motivator is the circumstance of being evaluated in some manner, a condition which *absolutely* applies to supervisees. Leary and Kowalski cited studies, for example, showing that a person is more likely to want to impression manage with teachers and employers than with friends.

Still another motivation to impression manage is the person's desire to resolve discrepancies between his or her desired versus current image. People will use impression-management strategies to gain respect and admiration after their social image has been damaged. For example, when individuals believe that they have failed at an important task, they tend to behave in a more self-enhancing manner in order to repair their image (Schlenker, 1980). They also are likely to become more self-enhancing about their task performance after they have received negative evaluations of their work.

Despite the clear relevance of the concept of impression management to supervision, only a couple of studies so far have examined directly supervisees' self-presentation motivations and impression-construction strategies (Friedlander & Schwartz, 1985; Ward et al., 1985). It is important to note, however, that a number of supervision studies that have not been framed as ones in impression management actually have implications for that model of behavior. Ladany et al.'s (1996) study of what supervisees choose not to disclose to their supervisors is an excellent case in point. In summary, to understand behaviors that the supervisor otherwise might label "defensive" or even "manipulative" as impression management can open up new response possibilities for the supervisor.

Impression management is one supervisee response to anxiety. A complementary strategy is to engage in the psychological games that Berne (1964) first described and that Kadushin (1968) extended to supervision.

Although McWilliams (1994) was not using this framework, the following describes this type of psychological game:

> *Therapists in training who approach supervision in a flood of self-criticism are often using a masochistic strategy to hedge their bets: If my supervisor thinks I made a major error with my client, I've already shown that I'm aware of it and have been punished enough; if not, I get reassured and exonerated.* (p. 263)

If the supervisor does respond to this "invitation" to behave in a sympathetic manner and therefore mutes the criticism that she or he otherwise would offer, this would seem to illustrate a classic interpersonal game (and one that is observed frequently in supervision). A game, then, is understood as a series of transactions that are to some extent stylized and that emanate from the interlocking or complementary roles that the participants adopt. This assumes that each participant understands and accepts these roles with greater or lesser degrees of conscious awareness. One person may initiate the particular game, but it always requires the collusion of *both parties* to make it a game.

Although the concept of games can be useful, it easily can be understood as pejorative (as in the observation that someone is "gamy"). So we introduce it here, but invite those who might want to learn more to consult Kadushin (1968) or Bauman (1972).

Supervisor Management of Supervisee Anxiety. To the extent that supervisee anxiety is minimized, so too is supervisee resistant behavior. Fortunately, there is evidence that supervision itself lessens supervisee anxiety. In a meta-analysis, Whittaker (2004) found that the average effect of supervision on supervisee anxiety was .46, which approximates the .5 level that Cohen (1992) had identified as a "medium" effect size in the social sciences.

So there is evidence that supervisors can reduce supervisee anxiety. It is useful, therefore, to consider some specific strategies they might use for that purpose.

Optimizing Levels of Supervisor Challenge versus Support. All supervisees approach supervision expecting to be judged and, therefore, inevitably are anxious to some degree. The experience of positive supervision, however, is such that the supervisee's anxiety does not rise to such a level that the work of supervision is hindered. This occurs because the supervisor is able simultaneously to be supportive and encouraging, which seems to us to echo Blocher's (1983) argument that effective supervision demands an optimal balance between *support* (including structure) and *challenge* (reflected also in the findings of Worthington and Roehlke, 1979, whose factor analysis of supervisors' behaviors yielded two factors that they labeled *support* and *evaluation,* which certainly is a form of challenge).

Too much support robs the supervisee of initiative and the opportunity to try new behaviors. By the same token, the level of supervisor challenge needs to be optimized: too little and the supervisee will not have the external push to try new behaviors; too much and the supervisee may become overwhelmed and incapacitated.

We recognize that this mention of support versus challenge is abstract rather than concrete. We hope, however, that it will provide a useful conceptual frame to guide supervisors' thinking about their styles of interactions and their interventions with supervisees.

Supervision Structure. Theory (e.g., Stoltenberg & Delworth, 1987) and research (e.g., Tracey et al., 1989) suggest that supervisees desire more structure in conditions of greater anxiety (e.g., when the context of counseling arouses anxiety, when the client presents "in crisis," when the supervisee is relatively inexperienced). Freeman (1993) observed that supervisors can lessen supervisee anxiety by providing structure, and she suggested, along with others (e.g., Friedlander & Ward, 1984; Sansbury, 1982; Usher & Borders, 1993), that the provision of structure is more important to the inexperienced counselor than to one who is more advanced.

Supervisees' experience levels moderate the amount of structure that they perceive themselves to need. That is, beginning supervisees perceive themselves as needing more structure than those who are more advanced (e.g., Heppner & Roehkle, 1984; McNeill et al., 1985; Reising & Daniels, 1983; Stoltenberg et al., 1987; Tracey et al., 1989; Wiley & Ray, 1986). But across all levels of supervisee experience, ambiguity in the supervisory context apparently is a root cause of supervisee anxiety.

Interestingly, Lichtenberg, Goodyear, and McCormick (2000) found no relationship between supervisee anxiety and level of session structure. Perhaps the reason for this seemingly discrepant finding was the manner in which structure has been operationalized. Lichtenberg et al. defined it in terms of moment-to-moment verbal interaction patterns. Most others who have written about structure, though, have operationalized it in terms of supervisor directiveness and control of session content and process. Perhaps it would be useful for the field to develop a general understanding of this commonly used term.

Role Induction. Supervisees' uncertainty about roles and expectations is a common cause for their anxiety. Therefore, there is utility in specifically educating them about roles and expectations through, for example, discussions and audio- or videotape modeling. Generally referred to as *role induction,* this has had demonstrated effectiveness with counseling clients. In a meta-analysis of 28 studies, Monks (1996) found that for clients role induction had significant positive effects on (1) treatment outcome, (2) attendance, and (3) dropout rates.

Less research has been done on role induction in supervision. However, what *has* been done has shown positive effects. For example, Bahrick et al. (1991) developed a 10-minute audiotaped summary of Bernard's (1979) supervision model and administered it to 19 supervisees at one of several points in the semester. They found that after supervisees heard the tape they reported having a clearer conceptualization of supervision and being more willing to reveal concerns to their supervisors. This effect occurred regardless of when in the semester supervisees heard the tapes.

Ellis et al. (1996) found that a role induction that they conducted significantly decreased supervisee anxiety compared to a control group. More recently, Chapin and Ellis (2002) again confirmed the utility of role induction. Moreover, they found in their multiple case study design that a role induction workshop interacted with supervisee level. That is, practicum students showed a decrease in anxiety following a role induction procedure, whereas interns either showed no difference or a brief *increase* in anxiety before it again decreased.

Supervisees' Need to Feel and Appear Competent

Whereas the need for felt competence is especially important at particular stages of childhood (e.g., White, 1959), it remains an important, lifelong need for all of us. Felt competence is similarly important to supervisees. And, just as is the case with children, its salience varies according to the supervisee's level of (professional) development. This is explicit in Loganbill et al.'s (1982)

developmental model. And Rabinowitz et al. (1986) found that beginning practicum students, compared to intern-level supervisees, rated as significantly more important to them this issue: *Believing that I have sufficient skills as a counselor or psychotherapist to be competent in working with my clients.*

Bordin (1983) noted that, when he would contract with supervisees about goals that they wished to accomplish during supervision, he found that their overt request typically was for fairly limited and focused goals, such as "learning to deal more effectively with manipulative clients" or "becoming more aware of when my own need to nurture gets in my way of being therapeutic." Yet he found that his supervisees' unspoken agenda almost always seemed to be the wish for him to provide global feedback about their overall level of functioning.

> At first, I thought that this goal would be satisfied by the feedback I was giving in connection with the more specifically stated ones. But I soon learned such feedback was not enough. Despite our reviews of what the therapist was doing or not doing and of its appropriateness and effectiveness, the supervisee seemed uncertain how I evaluated him or her. Only as I offered the remark that I saw him or her as typical of (or even above or below) those of his or her level of training and experience was that need satisfied. (p. 39)

Stoltenberg (1981) hypothesized that supervisees at level 2 (of a four-level model in which level 4 is the most advanced) move from the strong dependency characteristic of beginning-level supervisees to a dependency–autonomy conflict. Correspondingly, "there is a constant oscillation between being overconfident in newly learned counseling skills and being overwhelmed by the increasing responsibility" (p. 62). This is very similar to the struggle that adolescents experience as they enter the middle ground between childhood and adulthood. Kell and Mueller (1966) vividly captured this struggle around adequacy by employing what they referred to as a topographic analogy. According to them, the supervisee's struggle can be characterized as *an effort to stay on a highway which is bordered on one side by the beautiful and inviting "Omnipotence Mountains" and on the other side by terrifying "Impotence Cliff." Clients can and often do tempt counselors to climb to the mountain tops. Sometimes the counselor's own needs and dynamics can push him into mountain climbing. More often, the complex, subtle interaction of counselor and client dynamics together lead to counselor trips into the rarified mountain air. Yet the attainment of a mountain top may stir uneasy and uncomfortable feelings. From a mountain top, what direction is there to go except downward? The view to the bottom of the cliff below may be frightening and compelling. The trip down the mountain may well not stop at the highway. The momentum may carry our counselor on over the cliff where he or [she] will experience the crushing effects of inadequacy and immobilization. . . . It seems that either feeling state [omnipotence or impotence] carries the seeds of the other. . . . Rapid oscillation between the two kinds of feeling can occur in such a short time span as a five minute segment of an interview.* (pp. 124–125)

Another competence-related supervisee phenomenon is that of experiencing themselves as impostors (Harvey & Katz, 1985) who are vulnerable to being found out. This occurs when their level of actual competence exceeds that of their felt competence. Although they behave as therapists, they worry that they are acting a charade, that it will be only a matter of time before they are found out to be the impostors that they believe themselves to be. Significantly, then, Kell and Mueller (1966) contended that supervision is "a process of mobilizing [the supervisee's] adequacy" (p. 18). To the extent that they feel adequate or competent, supervisees will be less vulnerable to feeling like imposters.

Another way to frame this discussion of competence is in terms of self-efficacy, which Bandura (1994) defined as "people's beliefs about their capabilities to produce designated levels of performance that exercise influence over events that affect their lives" (p. 71). Self-efficacy usually is understood to be domain specific so that one of us might have high self-efficacy for one thing (say, our athletic ability) but low self-efficacy for another (e.g., singing).

Larson has been central to the work on self-efficacy in counselor supervisees. She and her colleagues (Larson et al., 1992) developed the Counseling Self-Estimate Inventory, which has been perhaps the most widely used instrument in studying counselor self-efficacy. With Daniels (Larson & Daniels, 1998) she reviewed the 32 studies on counselor self-efficacy that then were available, establishing that it is a crucial variable in understanding supervisee development.

Authors such as Barnes (2004) have described specific strategies supervisors might use to increase supervisor self-efficacy. Whittaker's (2004) meta-analysis of the several available studies shows that supervision has a robust effect size of .65 on self-efficacy.

Supervisee Transference

In a nontechnical sense, transference is a phenomenon in which a person transfers to someone in the present the responses and feelings that he or she has had to someone in the past. It is understood that clients develop transferences to their therapists. But, as well, supervisees develop transference-based responses to their supervisors (cf. Fiscalini, 1985). To illustrate, consider Lane's (1986) example of how supervisee transference can affect the supervisory process:

The supervisor becomes the father who died or who left them or the mother who was never there for them, and is accused of taking something from them. This gives them the right of refusal to take in anything from the supervisor parent (p. 71)

Supervisee transference can take numerous forms. At the broadest level, they can be categorized as either negative or positive. To illustrate the former, the supervisee can develop a negative transference in which he or she perceives the supervisor to be more critical or punitive than actually is the case. Lewis (2001) suggested that one mechanism by which this occurs is the supervisee's projection of their own punitively self-critical evaluations of themselves onto the supervisor.

A frequently occurring positive transference is that in which supervisees idealize their supervisors (Allphin, 1987). To do so can fill an important need, especially at the very early stages of training. Specifically, it can be important for the neophyte to have a relationship with someone who seems more competent and therefore capable of guiding their learning and development, someone to serve as a model.

Sexual attractions can constitute a specific type of positive transference. Attractions toward the supervisor can have various origins, including such reality-based considerations as shared interests. Such feelings, however, often derive at least in part from supervisee transference (Frawley-O'Dea & Sarnat, 2001).

Frawley-O'Dea and Sarnat (2001) also asserted that at least some supervisee transference can originate in parallel processes. This speaks to the origin rather than the valence of the transference. The following example that they gave is one of negative transference, but positive ones are just as possible.

> For example, a patient may experience his male therapist as a persecutory, demanding father who is never pleased. The therapist who is uncomfortable with the patient's transference may not become consciously aware of it and therefore ignores [it]. . . . Rather than consciously working with the patient's transference, the therapist resists awareness of it and instead begins to experience the supervisor as a persecutory figure who never can be satisfied. (p. 173)

Implications for Supervisors. In therapy, transference is most likely to occur when the therapist remains relatively anonymous to the client. In his discussion of transference in supervision, Lewis (2001) contrasted supervision with therapy, noting that in the former

> you are not anonymous or abstinent. Here you are a real person. Here you show your warmth and openness and acceptance. Here you praise, support, encourage, and advise. Here you show empathy to the vulnerability of the learner. Here you share your own experiences, your own mistakes. Here you share your own doubts and anxieties as a learner. (pp. 76–77)

This is consistent with Carl Rogers's observation that in supervision he shared more of his own thoughts and reactions than when he was in the role of therapist (Hackney & Goodyear, 1984). To the extent that the supervisor is known as a "real" person, supervisee transference is minimized.

Supervisee transference is yet another reason for supervisors to avoid providing therapy to their supervisees. To blur this "teach versus treat" distinction not only is ethically problematic (Ladany, Lehrman-Waterman, et al., 1999; Neufeldt & Nelson, 1999), but also invites supervisee transference.

But even in an optimal supervisory environment, supervisees still will develop transference reactions to their supervisors. How to handle them depends on the nature, intensity, and origin of the transference.

For example, with idealizing transference, the supervisor should steer a careful course. On the one hand, it can be important to respect the supervisee's need to idealize the supervisor (e.g., it can be very important to the supervisee to be reassured with the "knowledge" that the supervisor has it all under control). But the flip side is to not allow the idealization of the supervisor to cheat the supervisee of the chance to develop his or her own sense of competence. As an additional matter, the type and timing of supervisor interventions in the face of supervisee idealization should be moderated by the supervisee's developmental level (e.g., Stoltenberg et al., 1998).

Negative transference responses can be more difficult, both because of the greater difficulty in addressing them productively and because of their consequences to the supervisory relationship and to supervisee learning. To address them, as we discussed in Chapter 6 concerning relationship ruptures, can be one avenue.

SUPERVISOR FACTORS

So far in this chapter, we have been discussing supervisee factors and dynamics that affect the dyadic relationship. For the remainder we will focus on the supervisor. We will continue using Figure 7.1 to organize our discussion.

Before addressing the supervisor factors in Figure 7.1, we want to acknowledge two other factors that we addressed with respect to supervisees but that also have application to supervisors. For example, we discussed supervisee trust; trust is important to the supervisor as well. Unless the supervisor can trust that supervisees are being honest and straightforward about material from their sessions, he or she will be especially vigilant because of liability and other issues. This can lead to attempts to constrain supervisee behaviors in a way that will affect not only their relationship but also the supervisee's learning.

We also discussed supervisee anxiety at some length. But the supervisor's anxieties also are a factor in supervision. Lesser (1983) discussed possible sources of supervisor anxiety. Among these are the anxieties that arise in evaluation and the feelings of responsibility both to supervisees and to the public that they will serve if successful in training; criticism or praise, whether overt or covert, may elicit anxiety; anxiety can arise when a client is in crisis and the supervisor has some doubts, however small, about the supervisee's ability to handle it (that the supervisor is vicariously liable [see Chapter 3] certainly can amplify this feeling); and anxieties can occur at times when the supervisor may feel no longer needed. The anxieties that supervisees express in response to these circumstances can affect the dyadic relationship.

Although we were not able to give more space to matters of supervisor trust and anxiety, we thought it important at least to acknowledge their importance. In the remainder of the chapter, we will address, in turn, supervisor attachment, power, and countertransference.

Supervisor Attachment

To date, attention to attachment style in supervision has been concerned primarily with that of the supervisee. Yet supervisors, too, have particular relational styles that they bring to supervision.

White and Queener (2003) did not find that supervisees' attachment styles predicted either supervisor or supervisee ratings of working alliance. Interestingly, however, supervisors' attachment styles predicted strength of alliance, as rated by both supervisor and supervisee. The authors noted that

> Most models of supervision do not explicitly consider the individual characteristics of the supervisor and supervisee in understanding the dynamics of the supervisory relationship. This study suggests that supervisors' ability to make positive–affiliative attachments with others play[s] an important role in understanding the supervisory relationship. (p. 214)

Foster, Heinen, Lichtenberg, and Gomez (2006) found that supervisors with a preoccupied attachment style were more likely to give their supervisees lower professional ratings than their colleagues with other attachment styles. That is, their accuracy in evaluating supervisees seemed to be impaired.

Although we so far have only these studies, their results are important and suggest that more research attention to supervisor attachment is warranted. Not only does supervisor attachment seem to predict the quality of the supervisory alliance, but it could affect how supervisees are evaluated.

Interpersonal Power

Supervisory relationships are characterized by power inequality. Of course, this exists in psychotherapy; several aspects of the therapeutic context contribute to it. For example, the person in a relationship who needs the other more (i.e., the client) typically has less power than the person who is needed; and the person who has permission to comment on the other's behavior also has the greater power. Not only are these factors similarly present in supervision, but so too is the supervisor's power of expertise and role, including that of evaluator.

Supervisors can be oblivious of the full extent to which they have that interpersonal power, for in hierarchical relationships the person with greater power often is able to remain less consciously aware of it than is the person with less power. But interpersonal power permeates supervisors' work and their awareness of having it may elicit uneasiness. It is useful, then, to consider Holloway's (1995) caution:

> In the helping professions, power often has been viewed pejoratively because the concept of control and dominance has seemingly been antithetical to the tenets of mutuality and unconditional positive regard. This interpretation limits the ability of power in constructing a mutually empowering relationship. (p. 43)

Effective supervision requires that the supervisor recognize the sources, manifestations of, and ways to use the power that they have in the relationship. Eventually, supervisor–supervisee power discrepancies will dissipate, as Acker's (1992) observation suggests: "The supervisory relationship is a relationship between unequals, the objective of which is equalization. This would seem to be an inherent contradiction, a paradox, and is the challenge in supervision"

The "objective of equalization" does suggest that power and hierarchy differ in level according to supervisee developmental levels. But they remain nevertheless. This section deals with the challenge that Acker posed.

Two conceptions of interpersonal power have been especially important for supervisors and supervision researchers: social influence theory and the interactional perspective. We will address each in turn.

Social Influence Theory. Power can be understood as the ability to influence others' behaviors and attitudes. Heppner and Claiborn (1989) asserted that literature applying social psychological concepts of interpersonal influence and attitude change to counseling and therapy probably began with the publication of Frank's (1961) *Persuasion and Healing*. Further articulation of that point of view occurred in such other works as those of Goldstein, Heller, and Sechrest (1966) and Strong (1968). In fact, Strong's article presenting a two-stage model of change probably was most directly

instrumental in stimulating what now has become a substantial research literature.

In Strong's view, we individuals give interpersonal power (or the ability to influence) to those in our lives whom we perceive to have the resources necessary to meet our needs. This is consistent with social exchange theory, which posits that if A has what B wants, A has power over B. The extent of this power depends on the access that B has to alternative resources.

Strong (1968) adopted three of French and Raven's (1959) five types of interpersonal power to conceptualize counselors' influence. Strong asserted that a counselor will have interpersonal power or influence to the extent that the client perceives him or her to have *expertness, attractiveness* (i.e., perceived similarities in values, goals, etc.), and *trustworthiness*. This same model applies as well to supervision.

During the first of Strong's posited two stages, the supervisor's task is to establish himself or herself to the supervisee as a credible resource (i.e., a person who is perceived to possess the requisite expertness, attractiveness, and trustworthiness). Once the supervisor has established credibility, the second stage is one in which he or she begins using these sources of power to influence the supervisee to make behavioral or attitudinal changes. This is the actual social influence process.

Appropriately, Strong (1968) had not employed in his model of counseling a fourth of French and Raven's types of interpersonal power, that of *coercion*. But, as we have noted repeatedly throughout this book, supervisors have an evaluative function. This suggests that supervisors have coercive power, even though counselors do not. Because supervisors were trained first as counselors or therapists, to have this type of power can be uncomfortable. Yet it is important for the supervisor to understand that this power, however latent it might be, is real to the supervisees.

Corrigan, Dell, Lewis, and Schmidt (1980) and Heppner and Dixon (1981) reviewed the first decade of research on this model. Heppner and Claiborn (1989) later reviewed the second decade of that work. In the meantime, a distinct body of literature had developed in which that model was employed in supervision research. Dixon and Claiborn (1987) reviewed that research. With a few exceptions, most research on this model has been analog in nature. The real-life applications that exist suggest that attractiveness (which we understand as relational bonding) probably is the greatest of the French and Raven power sources.

Petty and Cacioppo's (1986) elaboration likelihood model (ELM) is a more recent and complex model of attitude change and might be considered the "second-generation" social influence model. This model suggests that people can be influenced through two information-processing routes: either *central* (involving an effortful elaboration of information) or *peripheral* (greater reliance on cues or on simple rules) for information processing. Influence that occurs through the central route is considered more enduring and has more effect on subsequent behaviors.

However, the route by which persuasion occurs depends on characteristics of the person who is the source of the information (e.g., credibility and attractiveness), message variables (i.e., the subjective strength of the arguments supporting a position), and recipient characteristics (e.g., degree of motivation to process the message). When people are motivated and able to consider messages that they perceive to have compelling arguments, they can then be influenced by a central route; otherwise, influence might occur through more peripheral means, such as the perceived expertness of the communicator. Claiborn, Etringer, and Hillerbrand (1995) and Stoltenberg, McNeill, and Crethar (1995) have discussed the promise of the ELM for research in supervision. Significantly, too, Stoltenberg et al. have attempted to incorporate what we already know about supervisee development into applications of the ELM.

The two models of social influence that we have reviewed both have a more formal and "scientific" language and structure than much of what we discuss in this book (see Blocher, 1987, and Martin, 1988, for discussions of distinctions between models to guide practice versus those to guide inquiry). But they are important models for supervisors to understand because they provide supervisors with valuable explanations of how power operates in their relationships with supervisees. Supervisors interested in learning more about their practice implications should consult articles such as those of Claiborn et al. (1995), Kerr, Claiborn, and Dixon (1982), and Stoltenberg et al. (1995).

An Interpersonal Perspective.   A second perspective on interpersonal power is more explicitly interactional. This perspective, concerned especially with the more dynamic give and take that occurs between people, is grounded in the assumption that people always are negotiating their status (i.e., relative power) with respect to one another.

Gregory Bateson and Timothy Leary made two of the seminal contributions to this perspective. Bateson (1936/1958) proposed that status (which also has been referred to variously as dominance, control, or power) is a construct that influences all human relationships and communication. Leary (1957) later employed Sullivan's (1953) interpersonal theory of personality to develop a circumplex model in which behavior can be plotted according to its placement on a circle with two orthogonal dimensions. One of those dimensions is that of *power* (dominance versus submission). In this way, his model was similar to that of Bateson.

But Leary's inclusion of *affiliation* as the second dimension (i.e., hostility versus nurturance) was a significant additive step. Leary's assumption that any given behavior can be described according to how it maps on these two dimensions has come to inform a great deal of current personality research. The model has proven to be robust (cf. Tracey, Ryan, & Jaschik-Herman, 2001); most people tend to organize their perceptions of their interpersonal worlds along those two dimensions.

This model can be used to describe the characteristic interpersonal behavior of any one person,

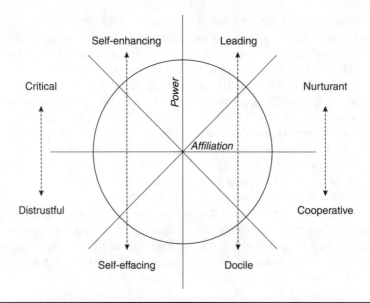

FIGURE 7.4   Complementary Behaviors of the Interpersonal Circle

Note: Arrows connect behaviors hypothesized to be complements.

Source: From "The Interpersonal Process of Cognitive-Behavioral Therapy: An Examination of Complementarity Over the Course of Treatment," by T. J. G. Tracey, P. Sherry, & J. M. Albright. 1999, *Journal of Counseling Psychology,* 46, pp. 80–91. Copyright 1999 by the American Psychological Association. Reprinted with permission.

often in ways that correspond to diagnostic categories. But the model also provides a way of understanding how any two people might interact with one another.

Bateson (1936/1958) proposed that interpersonal interactions can be characterized as of two basic types:

> *complementary (where there is an unequal amount of status) and symmetrical (where there is equal status). In a complementary interaction, each person is agreeing on the relative status positions (i.e., who determines what is to occur and who is to follow along). If the behaviors of the actors complement each other, there is a smooth interaction that is productive as the dyad agrees on what is to be done. In essence, one actor initiates and the other follows. However, if the behaviors of the two actors indicate equal status, resulting in a symmetrical interaction, there is more tension in the interaction and there is less accomplished.* (Tracey, 2002, p. 268)

Tracey (2002) characterized the degree of complementarity in a relationship as one index of between-participant "harmony." It indicates that the two individuals are similarly defining their relative power within that relationship. Variants of Leary's circumplex model (e.g., Benjamin, 1974; Carson, 1969; Kiesler, 1983; Strong & Hills, 1986; Wiggins, 1985) have been used in studies of complementarity. For example Figure 7.4 reproduces the Tracey, Sherry, and Albright (1999) variant.

Using this figure, an example of complementarity would occur if a supervisor were to make a leading statement (e.g., "Would you turn on your tape so that we can listen to some of what you have been describing?") to which the supervisee responds with a docile behavior (e.g., "Sure, let me pull out my tape recorder"). As the figure indicates, leading behaviors are high on dominance, whereas docile behaviors are low; both leading and docile behaviors are moderate in level of friendliness. The figure also indicates that nurturant behavior elicits cooperative behavior; self-enhancing behavior elicits self-effacing behavior; and critical behavior elicits distrustful behavior.

One variant of Leary's model that has been especially important to supervision researchers is that of Penman (1980). Although this model was not organized as a circumplex, it employed the same two dimensions of *power* and *involvement* to characterize interpersonal behaviors. At least four studies (Abadie, 1985; Holloway et al., 1989; Martin, Goodyear, & Newton, 1987; Nelson & Holloway, 1990) have employed Penman's system to analyze supervisory interactions. This model was useful, for example, in the Nelson and Holloway (1990) finding that supervisors were more likely to reinforce high power statements by male supervisees than those by their female counterparts, thereby demonstrating that gender role affects how power is utilized in supervision. Holloway's (1995) model of supervision is grounded in this interplay between the dimensions of supervisor power and involvement.

Drawing from his and others' research, Tracey (1993) proposed a three-stage model of counseling based on the notion of complementarity. In the initial phase, level of therapist and client complementarity is high; in the middle or working phase, it becomes lower as the relationship becomes more conflictual; and in the final stage the relationship returns to a situation of higher complementarity. But, although there seems to be generally solid support for this model in therapy, the one supervision study of this type (Tracey & Sherry, 1993) found no support for it. The authors speculated that their results might call into question the application of therapy models to supervision. It was, though, but a single study, so the question about whether Tracey's (1993) stage model of counseling applies to supervision is yet to be fully considered.

Implications for Supervisors. Power often is thought to involve dominance or control by one person over the other. But to employ social psychological conceptions of power as the social

influence by one person of another importantly broadens understandings of it. All behavior is communication, and communication is an act of influence (Watzlawick & Beavin, 1976). This perspective allows for mutual influence: that the supervisee also can influence the supervisor, even though the latter continues to have the greater possibility to influence the supervisee.

We recently heard a conference presenter assert that the person with greater power in a relationship is able to define reality for the other person. This does seem strong as an absolute statement. Yet, through the sorts of power that we have discussed in this section (e.g., expertness, attractiveness, and trustworthiness), the supervisor is able to persuade the supervisee to look through a particular theoretical lens to evaluate behavior and to adopt particular attitudes. In this sense, the supervisor is using interpersonal power to define (or at least shape) the supervisee's reality.

It is likely that the person with less power in the relationship will be more conscious of this fact. Yet, precisely because of his or her greater power, the supervisor has a responsibility to be aware of it and to use it both effectively and nonabusively.

In short, the fact of the supervisor's greater power in the relationship is not in itself problematic. This power (in its multiple forms) is a tool that the supervisor uses in the service of both protecting the client and enhancing the learning of the supervisee. It can, though, invite supervisee resistance, depending on (1) how the supervisor uses the power and (2) the supervisee's response to it (either by virtue of developmental stage or level of reactance). It also can invite transference responses, either positive or negative. The challenge for the supervisor is to be aware of the power that he or she has and to use it in a way that maximizes effectiveness.

Supervisor Countertransference

[S]upervisor countertransference has been viewed as a complex and inevitable process that involves unconscious and exaggerated reactions stemming from a supervisory interaction customarily related to the supervisor's unresolved personal issues or internal conflicts. (Ladany et al., 2000, p. 102)

Strean (2000) noted that mental health professionals generally recognize that therapist countertransference is as ubiquitous as client transference. He then suggested that, by analogy, supervisor countertransference is likely as ubiquitous as supervisee transference. Ekstein and Wallerstein (1972) noted that the mutual evaluation and reevaluation that occur in supervision do not occur at a strictly intellectual level. They will "be accompanied by interactions on every level, which would be described, were they to occur in a therapeutic context, as transference reactions of the one and countertransference reactions of the other" (p. 284).

Literature on this topic is relatively scarce. Ladany et al. (2000) noted that Balint (1948) and Benedek (1954) apparently were among the earliest authors to acknowledge supervisor countertransference and its potentially harmful effects on supervisees. A number of authors have offered their observations about supervisor countertransference. For example, Lower (1972) observed that "the learning alliance . . . is threatened continuously by resistances that derive from immature, neurotic, conflict-laden elements of the personality" (p. 70). Teitelbaum (1990) suggested the term "supertransference" to characterize the reactions of the supervisor to the supervisee and to the supervisee's treatment.

But we know of only two studies of supervisor countertransference, one published (Ladany et al., 2000) and one unpublished (Walker & Gray, 2002). Each was a qualitative study designed to describe countertransference events.

Walker and Gray (2002) obtained 144 instances of supervisory countertransference during 70 postsupervision session interviews. In their preliminary clustering of these events, they identified four sources of supervisor countertransference: external stress from workload; disappointment that supervisee is not taking work seriously; overidentification with what it is like to be a beginning counselor; and, wanting the supervisee to be a better therapist.

An important aspect of this work was that the authors not only were interested in problematic countertransference reactions, but also in those that in one way or another facilitated the supervision. Other work has treated countertransference almost exclusively as problematic. For example, even positive countertransference is considered problematic when it has erotic overtones (e.g., Ladany et al., 2000).

Ladany et al. (2000) have conducted the single published investigation of supervisor countertransference. Their findings provide the most comprehensive knowledge to date about this phenomenon. Therefore, we devote more space than usual to summarizing this study's findings.

Theirs was a qualitative study of 11 supervisors at university counseling center internship sites. Raters coded the structured interviews with these participants, all of whom believed that this had affected the supervisory relationship in either positive or negative ways. Ladany et al. (2000) found that most supervisors reported the countertransference lasted more than 2 months. To deal with it, most reported having pursued one or both of two courses: (1) consulting with a colleague (coworker, the training director, a supervision group) and/or (2) discussing it with the supervisee as it was appropriate. A few reported using either personal therapy or developing increased awareness through self-reflection as a means to resolve it.

A particularly useful feature of the Ladany et al. (2000) study was their examination of cues that led the supervisor to become aware of his or her countertransference. There was no one type of cue that all 11 supervisors reported. However more than half reported each of the following types of cues:

- Having particularly strong positive or negative feelings when they interacted with the supervisee
- Experiencing feelings toward the supervisee that were uniquely different from those toward other supervisees with whom she or he had worked
- Experiencing a gradual change in feelings toward the supervisee or their sessions together
- Discussions with colleagues (especially their own supervisors)

Ladany et al. (2000) were able to identify six sources of supervisor countertransference. Two of these were reported by all respondents:

1. *Countertransference triggered by the interpersonal style of the supervisee.* In some cases, this was a defensiveness or guardedness; in others, an assertiveness; in others, passivity, shyness, or vulnerability; and finally, such positive qualities as warmth and being engaging (this last was especially true for erotic countertransference).
2. *Countertransference stemming from some aspect of the supervisor's own unresolved personal issues.* In some cases, this concerned personal and family issues; in others, concerns about his or her competency; his or her own interpersonal style (e.g., having unduly high self-expectations; strong need to be liked); or experiences in the past from work with other supervisees.

To have these two sources identified through an inductive, empirical technique is important. But because this literature still is small, we also will summarize next the four categories of supervisor countertransference that Lower (1972) suggested some years ago.

1. *Countertransference stemming from general personality characteristics.* This type of countertransference stems from the supervisor's own characterological defenses, which then affect the supervisory relationship.
2. *Countertransference stemming from inner conflicts reactivated by the supervisory situation.* Lower's (1972) first category of supervisor countertransference focused on supervisors' characteristic ways of expressing themselves. The second category focused on supervisors' inner conflicts that are triggered by the supervision. Although some of the supervisor behaviors might resemble those of the first category, they have different origins.

   The following list of other supervisor responses suggests the myriad ways that supervisors' own inner conflicts can be manifest in supervision. Lower (1972) suggested that they may

   - Play favorites with the supervisees;
   - Covertly encourage the supervisee to act out his or her own conflicts with other colleagues or encourage rebellion against the institution;
   - Compete with other supervisors for supervisees' affection;
   - Harbor exaggerated expectations of the supervisee that, when unmet or rejected by the supervisee, lead to frustration and perhaps even aggression;
   - Have narcissistic needs to be admired that divert the supervisor from the appropriate tasks of supervision.

3. *Reactions to the individual supervisee.* The types of supervisor countertransference discussed so far have been triggered by the supervisor's response to the supervisory situation. In addition to these, there may be aspects of the individual supervisee that stimulate conflicts in the supervisor; for example, if the supervisee seems brighter (or more socially successful, or financially better off, etc.) than the supervisor.

   Sexual or romantic attraction is a specific instance of this type of supervisor countertransference (Frawley-O'Dea & Sarnat, 2001). Ellis and Douce (1994) have argued that issues of supervisor attraction to supervisees have been too little emphasized during supervision training.

   Another specific instance of this type of supervisor countertransference (i.e., reaction to the individual supervisee) is cultural countertransference. Vargas (1989) differentiated between this and prejudice: "Whereas prejudice refers to an opinion for or against someone or something without adequate basis, the sources and consequences of cultural countertransference are far more insidious and are often repressed by the therapist" (p. 3).

   Vargas (1989) noted that cultural countertransference reactions can originate in either of two ways. The first, and more common instance, occurs when the supervisor has limited experience with members of the ethnic minority group to which the supervisee belongs. The second is the consequence of potent feelings associated with nonminority people in the supervisor's past with whom the current minority supervisee is associated.

Regardless of the source, however, these cultural countertransference reactions, like many social perceptions, occur at an automatic level, outside the observer's awareness (see, e.g., Bargh & Chartrand, 1999). Research such as that of Abreu (1999) illustrated how this applies in a mental health context. He showed that with subliminal priming (i.e., words flashed at 80 milliseconds, a speed that would preclude conscious recognition of them), using 16 words or stereotypes ascribed to African Americans (e.g., Negroes, Blacks, lazy, blues, rhythm, etc.), therapists would rate a client described in a vignette as more hostile. This was even though most indicated that they understood the client probably was White. This suggests the importance of ongoing attention to cultural sensitivity, even when at a conscious level the supervisor is not aware of stereotyping.

4. *Countertransference to the supervisee's transference.* Perhaps the area in which supervisors are at the greatest risk of experiencing countertransference reactions to the supervisee is when the supervisee manifests transference responses to the supervisor. As a vivid illustration, Lower (1972) offered the following example.

A resident had been working in psychotherapy with a . . . young woman for about six months when a new supervisor questioned his formulations and treatment goals and suggested that they follow the patient in supervision over a period of time. The resident responded as though the supervisor were intruding on his relationship with the patient and became more and more vague in his presentation of material. In reaction, the supervisor became increasingly active in suggesting what the therapist should pursue with the patient and at last asked to see the patient together with the resident in order to make his own assessment. Only after the supervisor began the interview by asking the patient "Well how are you and Doctor what's his name here getting along" did he recognize the Oedipal conflict within both himself and the resident that had interfered with the learning alliance. (p. 74)

CONCLUSION

Whereas Chapter 6 focused on triadic and dyadic supervision processes, this chapter was concerned more specifically with dynamic individual factors that affect the relationship. Each of the several factors we addressed has implications for, or even direct influence on, the dyadic supervisory relationship. Our intent in presenting these factors was to better equip supervisors with knowledge that would permit greater sensitivity to these features in the supervisory process and allow them to offer more prescriptive intervention (e.g., to minimize supervisee anxiety or transference or supervisors' countertransference).

We also are aware that the factors we presented in this chapter do not exhaust the range of individual factors and characteristics that might affect supervision. However, they are those that have received particular emphasis in the supervision literature.

CHAPTER 8

ORGANIZING THE SUPERVISION EXPERIENCE

It is tempting to begin our supervisor tasks section of the book (see Figure 1.2) by delving into supervision interventions. Certainly, most supervisors envision themselves conducting individual, group, or live team supervision when they think of the actions of a clinical supervisor. Instead, we want to begin the section where we believe supervision must begin, with a process of assuring that supervision is organized with clear parameters and expectations. We will begin by looking at the available data that underscore the importance of organized or intentional supervision. We will then consider institutional characteristics that are supervision friendly. Mostly, we will discuss some of the activities and tools that add consistency and predictability to supervision. We see the content of this chapter as including many of the activities that often get neglected in supervision or are performed in a pro forma manner. While nothing in the chapter deals with the essence of clinical supervision (e.g., relationship issues, intervention selection, supervision models), the topics discussed here create the framework that makes it easier to attend to issues such as these. We refer to much in the chapter as the *organizational responsibilities* of the supervisor (which we sometimes refer to as *managerial competence*). We include what we consider essential for the process of mapping out the supervision experience before it begins and monitoring the experience for the duration of the relationship.

Traditionally, roles and responsibilities held by supervisors have been described as either administrative or clinical. Although there is almost always some overlap and, indeed, some supervisors fulfill both clinical and administrative duties for the same supervisees, these terms have helped to differentiate supervisory functions within an organization. The clinical supervisor has a dual investment in the quality of services offered to clients and the professional development of the supervisee; the administrative supervisor, while obviously concerned about service delivery and staff development, must also focus on matters such as communication protocol, personnel concerns, and fiscal issues, to name just a few. The administrative supervisor will, by necessity, need to view supervision in the larger context of institutional expediency (Falvey, 1987; Tromski-Klingshirn, 2006); the clinical supervisor will view supervision and service delivery quite differently. In fact, the argument has been made that the tasks demanded of each role are divergent enough to make them essentially incompatible (Erera & Lazar, 1994).

Our position is that there is a strong and necessary component to clinical supervision that is managerial in nature, thus requiring organizational skills that are similar to those used by administrative supervisors. One would have a difficult time accepting the information presented in either the chapter on ethics and legal considerations or the chapter on evaluation without recognizing that these issues must be managed adequately within the supervisory relationship. Therefore, our goal in this chapter is to address some of the most essential managerial aspects of clinical supervision.

We have chosen the words *managerial* and *organizational* in order to avoid the word *administrative*. Borders and Fong (1991) used the term *executive* to refer to the same set of behaviors and skills. All these terms imply some choreography within an institutional system(s) to achieve clinical supervision goals.

At least three matters complicate a discussion of the organizational tasks of clinical supervision. The first is a bias among many mental health practitioners (clinical supervisors included) that such matters are tiresome—a necessary evil that detracts from, rather than enhances, one's clinical supervision. This bias is supported, in part, by Kadushin and Harkness (2002), who reported results from an earlier study conducted by Kadushin that the most highly ranked source of dissatisfaction reported by clinical supervisors was "dissatisfaction with administrative 'housekeeping'" (Kadushin & Harkness, 2002, p. 316). Additionally, Kadushin (1992a–c) sampled a large number of social work supervisors and supervisees about supervisor strengths and shortcomings. Both supervisors and supervisees identified enacting managerial responsibilities as the major shortcoming of supervisors.

The second complicating matter is an assumption that clinical perceptiveness and organizational skill are rarely found in the same individual. This is similar to the assumption about absentminded professors, that they can be brilliant in their field but have little ability to navigate the real world. Rather than accept this stereotype, we believe that a lack of organization often is the result of neglect, rather than a deficit of inherent individual ability. In other words, if the managerial aspects of clinical supervision are isolated for the purpose of strengthening these skills, such scrutiny will lead to increased managerial competence among clinical supervisors. On the other hand, if the myth is accepted that clinical skill and organizational skill are incompatible, little change will occur.

The third complicating factor to our discussion is the reality that in some organizations there is no distinction between clinical supervision and administrative supervision. Supervisors are asked to wear one blended hat without the luxury of a clear focus in either direction. Several authors have commented on the inherent challenges of blending administrative and clinical supervision (Erera & Lazar, 1994; Henderson, 1994; Kadushin, 1992a; Kadushin & Harkness, 2002; Rodway, 1991; Tromski-Klingshirn, 2006; Tromski-Klingshirn & Davis, 2007). We acknowledge this dilemma as a real one and hope that having some clarity about the types of managerial activities that directly affect clinical supervision will somehow help the blended supervisor with both sets of responsibilities to be more deliberate in all activities.

With these complications in mind, we begin by arguing for the importance of managerial–organizational competence in the delivery of clinical supervision. We then underscore the importance of understanding a particular institution's culture and how this can provide either a positive or negative context for clinical supervision. We follow with a consideration of the differences when supervision is offered within a graduate program (i.e., on campus) versus when supervision is conducted in the field. An examination of various tasks follows and a variety of tools to assist with those tasks are described. Finally, we suggest some ways to assist a clinical supervisor in achieving organizational competence.

THE IMPORTANCE OF COMPETENCE IN ORGANIZING SUPERVISION

Even though there are many references to the importance of being organized in one's delivery of clinical supervision, until recently very few direct data have supported the importance of organizational skills for clinical supervisors. Perhaps because the field has only recently begun to address and codify ineffective, conflictual, or "lousy" supervision, the importance of managing clinical supervision remained in the background. While the centrality of the supervision relationship to satisfactory supervision is clear (e.g., Magnuson, Wilcoxon, & Norem, 2000; Nelson & Friedlander, 2001; Worthen & McNeill, 1996), it is equally apparent that a significant amount of dissatisfaction can result from supervision that is poorly organized.

Nelson and Friedlander (2001) found that supervision had a negative impact when supervisees entered the relationship without a clear sense of what was expected of them or how supervision would proceed. They also found that unstable relationships between the site and home program had negative consequences. Gross (2005) also found that a sizable number of supervisees had negative feelings about their practical experiences because they were not what the supervisees had expected, as did those subjects in a study conducted by Ramos-Sanchez et al. (2002) who reported negative supervisory events that included unclear expectations. Kozlowska, Nunn, and Cousins (1997) surveyed psychiatric trainees and found that they were dissatisfied when their educational needs were neglected by their supervisors, pointing to supervision that is reactive, rather than organized and deliberate.

A key study indicating the importance of organizational factors in supervision came from Magnuson, Wilcoxon, and Norem's (2000) qualitative study of "lousy" supervision. While the number of supervisees interviewed was small ($N = 11$), organizational–administrative issues emerged as one of three general spheres of lousy supervision (the other two being technical–cognitive and relational–affective). Specifically, subjects reported six areas in which organizational–administrative competence was lacking to their detriment: (1) failure to clarify expectations, (2) failure to provide standards for accountability, (3) failure to assess the supervisee's needs, (4) failure to be adequately prepared for supervision, (5) failure to provide purposeful continuity, and (6) failure to provide an equitable environment in group supervision. Reporting from the vantage point of graduate students, Martino (2001) similarly found undesirable supervisor behaviors to include lack of interest in the supervisee's professional development, lack of availability, unreliability, and lack of structure in the supervisory process.

From the site supervisor's perspective, Bennett and Coe (1998) found that satisfaction with their role was significantly related to both quality and frequency of contact with the program liaison and to their agencies providing adequate release time for conducting supervision. Similarly, in a study of social work field supervisors in Israel, Peleg-Oren and Even-Zahav (2004) found that the primary reason for field supervisors dropping out of supervision was less-than-functional communication with the graduate training program.

Other studies have indicated that a lack of regular supervision during field placements is a common problem (Giddings, Vodde, & Cleveland, 2003; Gross, 2005; Ramos-Sanchez et al., 2002; Sommer & Cox, 2005), that orientation to sites is often neglected (Gross, 2005), that supervision is sometimes not performed by the site supervisor identified by the training program (Gross, 2005), and that field sites are often unclear about the training program's expectations (Lewis, Hatcher, & Pate, 2005). We should note that the research that reports negative supervision experiences also finds that most supervisees are satisfied with the supervision they have received. However, it is clear that some of the negative experiences have had lasting effects on those who have experienced them. One exception to supervisee angst was reported by Giddings et al. (2003) who found that social work supervisees in their study were not particularly concerned by the lack of overall supervision on-site. The authors found this alarming and stated " . . . students are not in a position to evaluate the potential impact of a lack of supervision on their careers, the profession, or future clients" (p. 209).

We do not assume that any of these research findings were the result of intentional malice on the part of supervisors. Rather, it seems to us that it is the result of structures that have not been thought out thoroughly for the purpose of providing adequate supervision. It is also not lost on us that the importance of organizational or management skills for the practice of clinical supervision becomes evident through a negative lens, rather than a more affirming lens. Our hypothesis is that well-organized supervision allows for other aspects of supervision to emerge; therefore, the organizational backdrop is likely to remain invisible. When a supervisee is given clear guidelines for supervision by a well-prepared supervisor, this is experienced as the norm. If, however, the supervisor confuses the supervisee, offers little or no structure for the experience, and seems unable to manage supervisory duties, the supervisee is more likely to become aware of the organizational skills requisite for good supervision.

Another body of literature that indicates the importance of well-managed supervision is that of practitioner burnout (again, a view of organizational skill through a negative lens). Several authors have asserted that practitioner burnout may indeed be related not only to service demands, but also to a poor administrative structure (Bogo, 2005; Brashears, 1995; Hyrkäs, 2005; Kaslow & Rice, 1985; Malouf, Haas, & Farah, 1983; Murphy & Pardeck, 1986; Raiger, 2005; Sommer & Cox, 2005; Stoltenberg & Delworth, 1987). Murphy and Pardeck noted that either authoritarian or laissez-faire styles of management (supervision) add to burnout and that burnout may be more organizational than psychological. They asserted the importance of appreciating that "a lack of planning is not understood to be the only method for encouraging individualism" (Murphy & Pardeck, 1986, p. 40). Brashears similarly noted that, when the administrative tasks of supervision are viewed as too distinct from service delivery, this false dichotomy contributed to job stress, burnout, and turnover.

We wish to underscore the idea that burnout may be organizational as well as, if not rather than, psychological. From the supervisee's perspective, it makes intuitive sense to us that the best of supervisory relationships or the finest of clinical insights can be sabotaged by weak managerial skills (Bernard, 2005). This can be seen in training situations or in work situations when supervisees are no longer patient or tolerant of inconveniences or frustrations caused by the supervisor who cannot maintain some level of mastery of the supervisory plan. Supervisees often realize that a lack of organization not only leaves them vulnerable but also leaves the client and agency vulnerable as well. When messages are inconsistent, communication is erratic, procedures are unclear or not adhered to, and conferences are rushed, the entire experience of service delivery under supervision becomes compromised. Because of lack of experience, supervisees or new employees are hard pressed to distinguish their feelings about service delivery from their feelings about supervision. Supervisors must realize, therefore, that signs of frustration or burnout may be feedback *to* the supervisor rather than *about* the supervisee.

As we have said, the focus on burnout or unsatisfactory supervision is a focus on the negative effects of managerial incompetence. Managerial competence, however, enhances positive experience or, as Lowy (1983) stated, "[T]he learning and teaching transactions in supervision require an organizational structure in order to become implementable" (p. 60). Edwards et al. (2005) found that supervision quality was rated higher when regular and predictable. And the host of studies that pointed to a poor organizational context as part of the problem by inference certainly supported the importance of a strong organizational context.

Finally, certain supervisory functions are inextricably tied to managerial competence. Specifically, evaluation of supervisees and maintaining a clinic or agency that meet minimal ethical standards require organizational skill. Because a deficit in these areas can become threatening to supervisors and supervisees alike, we hope that the importance of organizational competence becomes self-evident. But with the minimal attention given to this topic in clinical supervision literature, it is understandable that these skills remain underdeveloped.

Once the supervisor appreciates the importance of supervision that is thoughtful, organized, appropriate for the supervisee, and well executed, the supervisor will also appreciate the importance of a work environment that will support exemplary supervision. Even if the environment is one in which supervision is expected to be an integral part, the institutional culture will play a role, often an enormous role, in either assisting or hampering the supervisor. It is important, then, to assess institutional culture as one task in managing clinical supervision.

THE ROLE OF INSTITUTIONAL CULTURE

Supervision is an integral and time-consuming aspect of the delivery of mental health services. When taken seriously and conducted properly, clinical supervision demands institutional support. It behooves supervisors to assess the culture of the organization to determine if it is supervision friendly. Otherwise, the most organized supervisor with the best-laid plans will soon be frustrated by an institutional culture that works against supervision goals. Furthermore, because supervisors are persons of some authority, they have an opportunity and a responsibility to influence their organization's culture if it reflects characteristics that are anathema to clinical supervision. This is so whether their organization is a training program, a school or university, or a mental health agency. Therefore, we hope to provide some food for thought as supervisors assess their institutions and the underlying characteristics of those institutions.

Osborn (2004) used the acronym STAMINA to describe a series of characteristics or behaviors that can assist counselors in remaining fully engaged in the demanding contexts within which they find themselves. Emphasizing the positive, she encouraged mental health professionals to develop stamina, rather than "resisting burnout." Using Osborn's acronym, we will look at institutional culture and describe some of the essentials that must be in place if clinical supervision is to be managed optimally.

Selectivity

Organizations cannot be all things to all constituents. Clinical supervision is often squeezed out because organizations are overburdened with heavy client loads, grant applications, new programs, and bureaucratic demands. There is probably no more an essential characteristic than selectivity for an organization to emulate. For clinicians to become increasingly competent (and more valuable to the organization), clinical supervision must be selected in, not out. When this is the case, it is unlikely that supervisees will feel like a supervisee interviewed by Sommer and Cox (2005) who stated, "My supervisor is just being pulled in too many directions with too many responsibilities, so I'm just put on a list of things to do" (p. 129).

Temporal Sensitivity

Osborn described this characteristic as both a realistic understanding of the limits of time and a respect for the time that one is given. Organizations that value clinical supervision demonstrate this value by allocating the precious resource of time to it. There is no apology necessary in a supervision-friendly organization when adequate time is blocked out for supervision. Furthermore, this commitment to supervision is viewed as seriously as commitments to clients. Kadushin and Harkness (2002) reported a study of 885 supervisors and supervisees and found the time given to supervision to be a serious problem. Both supervisors and supervisees complained that there was too little time to conduct adequate supervision. Inadequate amounts of time committed to supervision leading to reports of dissatisfaction with supervision is a theme that continues to be reported in the literature (Bogo, 2005; Giddings et al., 2003; Gross, 2005; Ramos-Sanchez et al., 2002; Sommer & Cox, 2005). It is impossible to discern whether the problem is too little time to do too much or the status of supervision among competing duties. Regardless, supervisees across several mental health disciplines report feeling shortchanged in their field placements.

Just like individuals, organizations that are effective and efficient about time can accomplish more. These organizations are never frenetic, a characteristic more often associated with institutional cultures in which time is perceived as the enemy and often managed poorly.

Accountability

Osborn was quick to state that she was not using the term accountability in its more reactive sense;

that is, as a word to stifle creative practice. Rather, consistent with Osborn's definition, the organization that values accountability is credible, both internally and to its constituents. Implicit in this kind of accountability is some ownership of the work that takes place within the organization and a desire to improve. Used in this way, clinical supervision is key to accountable counseling and therapy. Organizations that welcome accountability embrace the evaluative and developmental aspects of clinical supervision. Copeland (1998) stated that organizations that create a context conducive to supervision expect more accountability from the supervisor. If framed in the way Osborn framed the term, this could only be a good thing.

Measurement and Management

As used by Osborn, measurement and management come closest to describing the kinds of activity necessary to organize effective supervision. While selectivity more broadly defines the mission of the organization, measurement and management reflect the day-to-day operations and the skills necessary to complete them effectively. An organization with this characteristic will be clear about assigned roles, will have good record-keeping practices, and so on. It is a real advantage for the supervisor when clinical supervision is grounded in an efficient and effective organization.

Inquisitiveness

Osborn stated that the importance of a spirit of inquisitiveness for the long-term stamina of the individual counselor cannot be overstated. If one does not remain curious about one's work, stagnation can quickly set in. As an organizational trait, inquisitiveness is often translated as a respect for professional development and is viewed as essential for building and maintaining vibrant organizations (Frohman, 1998; Hawkins & Shohet, 2000). Clinical supervision is integral to professional development. Ongoing supervision can enhance the process of reflectivity (a form of inquisitiveness) that Skovholt and Rønnestad (1995) found

was essential for professional development. Furthermore, the organization that reflects inquisitiveness will encourage professional development for the supervisor as well as for supervisees.

Negotiation

Osborn's inclusion of negotiation is essential for the supervisor-friendly organization. In this context, negotiation is defined as the ability to give and take without giving in. In other words, organizations that reflect the value of negotiation give their members voice. Others refer to the importance of trust and collegiality within an organization (e.g., Frohman, 1998; Raiger, 2005; Sparks & Loucks-Horsley, 1989). As Chapters 6 and 7 made clear, clinical supervision is highly sensitive to relationship. While a positive supervisory relationship can limp along within a caustic institutional context, it is unlikely that this could be sustained indefinitely. Organizations that value negotiation and collegiality are a great support to clinical supervisors.

Agency

Finally, Osborn advanced the concept of agency which she defined as "an intangible, dynamic force" (p. 326). She viewed agency as coming close to the essence of stamina and including several empowering characteristics, such as having a sense of one's impact and being aware of one's resourcefulness. Translated to the institution, agency is a quality of those organizations that refuse to be dragged down by complications, unresponsive bureaucracies, or demanding client loads. These organizations are fed by their work, not depleted by it. They are the organizations that view clinical supervision as a building force, not a time drain. In short, they are defined by a vision that is fundamentally optimistic.

Although these descriptions of organizational stamina may not include all that is necessary in an institution to support the functions of clinical supervision, they give the clinical supervisor one viable frame for such an assessment. Additionally, they can provide a handle for the supervisor in determining what feels wrong in an organization when attempting to meet supervisory responsibilities. For example, Congress (1992) noted that ethical decision making is controlled by agency culture, rather than individual input (perhaps reflecting the agency's view of accountability and management). The supervisor who has not attempted to evaluate organizational context may be unprepared for a discrepancy between a supervision goal and the culture within which supervision is occurring. Most likely, it is the supervision, not the culture, that will be compromised when there is such a discrepancy.

THE ESSENTIAL INGREDIENT: A SUPERVISION PLAN

Before we look at the places in which supervision occurs and the tasks that must be accomplished, we need to stress the importance of arriving at a general framework for supervision even before one meets the supervisee for the first time. In fact, it could be argued that the source of all sustained influence is planning and foresight (Covey, Merrill, & Merrill, 1994) and that these allow for other dimensions of supervision to emerge, such as the supervisory relationship (Bernard, 2005). To some extent, planning includes methods for assuring accountability, and we will cover the importance of record keeping later in this chapter. But the driving force for the supervisor should be to plan an effective and efficient supervision experience that will culminate in the emergence of a capable and grounded practitioner, while safeguarding client welfare. This goal will be frustrated if supervision is random or repetitious. In other words, the antithesis of planning occurs when a supervisor accepts a supervisee, sets weekly appointments with the supervisee, and lets things just happen, or when a university instructor places students in field sites and then conducts weekly group supervision sessions that are based on self-report and little else. In both of these instances, there is no evidence of an awareness of supervisees' developmental needs or of the desirability of some variety of learning modes. This is supervision as you go, not planned supervision.

In preparation for supervision, therefore, the supervisor might be well advised to answer the following questions:

- What do I know about the supervisee I will work with? How do learning style, cultural worldview, experience level, and so on, affect my thinking about working with this supervisee?
- In light of what I know about my supervisee, is there any additional preparation I need to do in order to be most helpful to this person?
- As I understand the supervisee's goals, which are most likely to be met in this experience? Which are less likely to be met? Is the supervisee clear about this?
- What supervision modalities are available to me? Can I supplement those that are provided by the organization? What is my rationale for beginning where I intend to begin? What supervision schedule will we adhere to?
- How and when will I orient the supervisee to the organization within which clients will be treated? How will I determine if the supervisee is adequately aware of ethical and legal imperatives? When will I introduce my evaluation plan?
- Have I adequately structured matters to ensure client flow for my supervisee? Have I made plans for other important experiences, including integration into the organization?
- Knowing the institution as I do, what are the predictable challenges that will face the supervisee? How can I make these productive learning opportunities?
- Whom will I turn to for consultation when I am challenged in my work with this supervisee?

With a general idea of the importance of organizational skill, institutional culture, and a framework that defines clinical supervision broadly, we can now turn to more specific topics. We begin by looking at two different contexts within which supervision occurs.

CONTEXTS FOR SUPERVISION: TWO DIFFERENT WORLDS

Predominately, there are two different contexts for supervision: graduate programs and agencies (used generically to include schools, hospitals, mental health agencies, and the like). The fundamental difference between these two contexts, of course, is that one is organized around education and the other is organized around service delivery. Most students in graduate training programs will receive clinical supervision within the training context and in a field site (i.e., an agency) where they complete clinical hour requirements. Postdegree supervision is more contained (and therefore less complicated) within the agency. The challenges for postdegree supervision will be referenced later when we refer to field sites as the context for supervision. This section, however, will focus primarily on counselors and therapists in training and the contexts within which they will receive their clinical experiences.

The Graduate Program as Context for Supervision

While navigating back and forth between the graduate training program and the field site is normative for most graduate students, some training programs run counseling centers or other service delivery training clinics on campus so that students receive clinical supervision and didactic education within the same context (Myers, 1994). Graduate programs often prefer such a setup for the very reasons that we will discuss in this chapter: It is much easier to negotiate one system than it is to react to two. Furthermore, because these training clinics are focused on training as their primary mission, supervision is central to their culture. As a result, neither faculty nor students need to spend time advocating for the importance of clinical supervision, leaving more time for the process itself.

Because of the educational advantages of program-based training clinics, these are usually viewed enviably by supervisors working in contexts with less of an emphasis on supervision.

Beavers (1986) noted that training clinics were usually less hurried and supervisees could expect individual attention, facilities that are usually more than adequate, and supervisors that are typically well grounded theoretically. With pressures at universities increasing (Bogo, 2005), these conditions may be partially compromised though it is still likely that they are more controlled than in agencies without a primary training function. Although they tend to offer strong organizational structures for training, training clinics have unique challenges as well and include balancing training responsibilities with the responsibilities of service delivery (Bernard, 1994b; Myers & Hutchinson, 1994); identifying, or perhaps recruiting, appropriate clients and matching clients with supervisees (Leddick, 1994; Scanlon & Gold, 1996); managing client expectations (Leddick, 1994); bridging the gap between the academic calendar and client needs (Scanlon & Gold, 1996); and clarifying roles of professional staff, especially when a tiered system exists, that is, master's-level students supervised by doctoral students who are themselves supervised by faculty supervisors (Dye, 1994; Scanlon & Gold, 1996; West, Bubenzer, & Delmonico, 1994).

As the above implies, there may be downsides to being supervised in a training facility. Beavers (1986) noted that, even though the staff may attempt to recruit a wide range of clients, it is most often the case that university settings offer a rather narrow and limited client population. Additionally, university supervisors may have less clinical experience than supervisors found in off-campus settings and are not as "street savvy." In other words, university settings may confront the supervisee with fewer dilemmas resulting from bureaucratic protocol, but this can be reframed as offering the supervisee fewer experiences in negotiating complex systems to achieve service delivery and professional development goals. This view was echoed by Gross (2005), who noted that the shortfalls of field sites might indeed help students come to terms "with the realities of service provision and training in the imperfect world of mental health" (p. 304).

The Field Site as Context for Supervision

Often the supervisee in a graduate training program completes clinical experiences off campus and is supervised by a site supervisor. This, of course, is by design. Departments of social work and psychiatry were perhaps the first to realize the importance of field instruction to supplement academic instruction. Counseling, psychology, and marriage and family therapy, as well as a host of other clinical professions, also require the student to successfully complete a supervised field experience while still in a degree program. The site supervisor typically accepts the supervisee because the supervisor enjoys the supervision process (Globerman & Bogo, 2003), including influencing trainees about real client issues and agency circumstances (Copeland, 1998; Holloway & Roehlke, 1987). Often the site supervisor would also like to influence the training program in terms of the preparation offered to trainees prior to field experience. Therefore, both contexts have an investment in one another that is both practical and educational. Yet the differences between these two types of organizations and their separate goals often are not acknowledged in a way that allows the principals to work them through (Peleg-Oren & Even-Zahav, 2004). Additionally, adequate communication between the two is often wanting (Bogo, Regehr, Power, & Regehr, 2007; Elman, Forrest, Vacha-Haase, & Gizara, 1999; Holtzman & Raskin, 1988; Igartua, 2000; Kahn, 1999; Lewis et al., 2005; Olsen & Stern, 1990). We will address goals and communication separately.

Goals. Dodds's (1986) delineation of the major difference between the training institution and the service delivery agency as a difference in population to be served remains unchanged. As depicted in Figure 8.1, the training institution is invested in the education and training of its students, whereas the mental health agency is primarily invested in the delivery of quantity and quality services to a target population. Dodds warned, however, that to stereotype each system by these goals is to lose sight of each unit's investment in the other's mission. That

notwithstanding, the basic goals of each system will drive some of the decision making within the system. As Figure 8.1 illustrates, the university and site supervisors have the responsibility for interfacing these two systems. But if they default on this responsibility due to time constraints, disinterest, or the absence of managerial acumen, it is left to the supervisee to interface the two systems. When difficulties emerge, this leaves the least powerful individual (in both organizations) to negotiate and attempt to find a resolution.

As an example of one of the many differences that grow out of each system's goals, Dodds (1986) noted the "common source of stress [that] arises when the student participates simultaneously in two institutions with differing time rhythms" (p. 299). For instance, the trainee must perform the role of junior staff member on the agency's timetable, turning in reports and so on, regardless of whether the training institution is on semester break. Furthermore, the regularity of demands at the site will not be sensitive to pressure increases from the training institution, such as during midterm or final exams.

The first step in mastering the interface between the two systems is in understanding that there will be complications whenever two systems are simultaneously involved with a trainee because of each unit's systemic properties, including their different goals and even different calendars. Once this fact is accepted, supervisors can begin to predict issues that may arise. A primary strategy for reducing problems either within each system or especially between them is to increase the quantity and quality of communication.

Communication. The university supervisor is often very clear about what kinds of communication are expected from the site supervisor; however, a reciprocity of information often is lacking. Authors of empirical studies have reported frustration among field site supervisors when expectations of training programs exceeded what was initially understood (Shapiro, 1988) or when expectations in general are not clearly communicated (Lewis et al., 2005; Peleg-Oren & Even-Zahav, 2004). Another

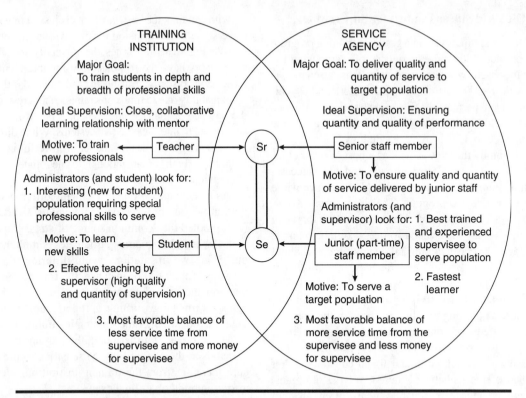

FIGURE 8.1   Overlapping Systems of a Training Institution and a Service Agency

Note: Sr, supervisor; Se, supervisee

Source: From "Supervision of Psychology Trainees in Field Placements," by J. B. Dobbs, 1986, *Professional Psychology: Research and Practice, 17,* pp. 296–300. Copyright 1986 by the American Psychological Association. Reprinted with permission.

error both sides make is to keep information too limited in its focus. For example, there can be ample information about placement expectations from both sides. But university programs do not always keep their field sites current with program growth or curriculum changes and agencies do not let university programs know when administrative, fiscal, or programmatic changes are being planned or implemented. Programs do not always communicate clearly about the evaluation criteria that they adhere to (Elman et al., 1999). The result of such incomplete communication can be conflict that could have been avoided or two systems growing less and less relevant to each other without being aware of it. We will consider the types of communications that are

desirable between graduate program and field site later in the chapter.

The remainder of this chapter will outline some of the tasks of supervision and some of the issues that can either enhance or detract from the goal of offering exemplary clinical supervision. We attempt to delineate which tasks are primarily the responsibility of the training program supervisor and which fall to the site supervisor. We also caution the reader that, in and of itself, well-organized supervision is not necessarily good supervision. But if clinical supervisors have addressed the tasks that follow, they can have some confidence that supervisory efforts will not be undermined by a crumbling structural base (Bernard, 2005).

FOUNDATIONAL TASKS FOR ORGANIZING SUPERVISION

While we have discussed several ways in which supervisors prepare themselves to approach a productive supervision experience, we now turn our attention to tasks that involve the supervisor with the supervisee. While much of our discussion focuses on the trainee in a graduate program, many of the tasks outlined can be applied to all supervision relationships. As with many enterprises, it is also the case that most of the organizational activity is concentrated at the front end of the supervisory relationship. The reward for getting organized comes later, when supervision is well under way.

Advising Supervisees for Clinical Instruction

While all students in clinical training programs realize that there is a point at which they will begin seeing clients under supervision, students vary greatly in their awareness of the preparation process for this aspect of their education. For those graduate programs that use off-campus clinical sites, the first task is an advising one. Unless a training program has the luxury of a full-time (or even part-time) director of training or field placement coordinator, university faculty supervisors must coordinate a placement system. In the absence of some system to manage the flow of clinical placements, some degree of chaos may reign. Among the consequences of random advising are rushed or inappropriate placements and rattled students. When matters are rushed, the field supervisor may think that the university program is slightly out of control and may feel less accountable to the program and the student as a result.

A key advising issue, then, is how much lead time a student should allow in finding an appropriate field placement. This will be determined by the following:

1. *The amount of local competition for field sites.* If there are other universities nearby or if other programs within the university are seeking the same sites, the student must start looking earlier than if the market is wide open.

2. *The specificity of the student's interests.* If the student has a very specific interest not represented in a variety of sites (e.g., hospice work), then more lead time will be required.
3. *The policy of the specific agency.* Some agencies will only accept interns during a certain time period or may require a résumé and more than one interview, all of which are time consuming. To be assured enough time to find a site, the student should assume that there will be some hurdles to negotiate in the selection process.
4. *The relationship established between the university and a particular site.* Some sites not only want, but expect, students every semester. Because of their past dealings with the program, they require only minimal contact with the student prior to starting the field experience.

Selecting Sites

There is a good deal in the professional literature to assist doctoral students in selecting an appropriate practicum internship (e.g., Brill, Wolkin, & McKeel, 1987; Gloria & Robinson, 1994; Stewart & Stewart, 1996), with little attention given to this topic for the more common placement of premaster's-level mental health trainees. In some academic programs it is the training director or the faculty supervisor who makes the initial contact with a potential field site. In other programs it is the student who makes the first contact. In either case, the graduate program must assume a role in helping the student to determine the appropriateness of a particular site based on three categories of variables: program factors, student factors, and agency factors.

Program factors are those baseline conditions that must be met before a site can be accepted as meeting training goals. For example, the program may require that students not only see a variety of clients, but also have continuity in their work. Therefore, a crisis center that revolves around single-client contacts would not be an appropriate placement. Or the program may require that audiotaping be allowed for the purposes of campus supervision. This may be a nonnegotiable item for some sites and one that eliminates them.

Student factors can be introduced either by the student or observed by the supervisor. The student's career goals must be the most important variable in finding an appropriate site. Many other conditions can be survived if the site will increase the student's chances of pursuing a desired career path. Other student characteristics include whether the student is a self-starter or someone who needs a more structured atmosphere. The student's readiness for the demands of a particular site also must be of paramount importance. Developmentally, a desired site may not be appropriate for a particular student because of the difficulty of the clinical cases or the unavailability of close supervision (e.g., live observation) that would ensure client protection. In addition to these, a variety of individual characteristics can be discussed to assist the student in identifying a site that will be both challenging and realistic for the student.

Agency factors are the third consideration and include the atmosphere of the work environment (Stoltenberg & Delworth, 1987), the interest of the agency to work with students, the variety of opportunities within the agency, and the value placed on clinical supervision, to name a few. The agency factors may or may not be known by the campus supervisor or the student if the site has not been used before. Therefore, the student should be assisted in determining a list of things to look for when making contact with the site.

Despite a program's best efforts to find a site that meets the student's and the program's expectations, it should also be noted that the advantage to the trainee of gaining clinical experience in the field is directly related to its untidiness (Beavers, 1986); in other words, mental health delivery systems are imperfect organizations, and the trainee who learns to navigate such organizations is better prepared to enter the job market. The challenge for graduate training programs is to weigh each organizational deficit with the opportunities afforded to trainees. Is it better for the trainee to be provided with a steady flow of diverse clients or to have closely monitored supervision? Is it better for the trainee to work within one strong framework or to be challenged to work from a variety of perspectives? Is it more important to bow to accreditation standards or to go with one's judgment of an exemplary experience? These kinds of questions must constantly be raised and resolved. It must be understood, however, that all but the most unique field placements represent some compromise for the training program.

Initial Communication Between Graduate Program and Site

The reader will note that communication surfaces regularly in this chapter as a task for organizing supervision. While lip service is given to the importance of communication between all parties involved in a trainee's clinical supervision, a functional plan for communication is called for.

It is up to the university supervisor, not the student, to communicate the program's expectations to the site supervisor (Lewis et al., 2005). Under the best of circumstances, this is done both in writing and in person. Manzanares et al. (2004) described the development of a CD-ROM for site supervisors that included key information about the training program, training expectations, and video clips of the faculty. Face-to-face contact allows the university supervisor to determine whether there is any resistance to meeting the program's requirements. It has been our experience that student supervisees are typically not good judges of a site when the site is ambivalent about meeting program requirements. Perhaps they are too eager to find an appropriate site to be discriminating. Even when they do discern ambivalence, they are in a vulnerable position regarding the site and are uncertain about asserting themselves with potential site supervisors. Clearly, this is something the university supervisor can and should do. While we believe it is primarily the graduate program's responsibility to orient the site to the program's expectations, Roberts, Morotti, Herrick, and Tilbury (2001) addressed the site's responsibility and urged site supervisors to seek full clarification of what is expected of them when they agree to take a supervisee.

Once a site has been chosen, it is important that the campus supervisor stay in touch with the site supervisor. A phone call or e-mail a couple of weeks after the student has been placed is a good idea to be sure that things are going reasonably well. Additionally, there should be a plan for formal contacts in order to evaluate the student's progress. The site supervisor should know when these will occur and what form they will take (i.e., face-to-face meeting or written evaluations).

The Interview

The goal of the university training program is to place all students; the goal of the site supervisor is to make a judgment about the individual student's fit with the goals and work of the agency. Although background information is sometimes requested, the basis for the decision is usually the placement interview. It is essential that the site supervisor have a grasp of the attributes that are necessary for the student to take full advantage of the placement.

Trainees should receive feedback about this interview whether or not the site accepts them. Hearing the supervisor's perception of why one was seen as appropriate is a good beginning for a working relationship with the site supervisor. When the trainee is not accepted, it is important to know if the decision was made based on a negative evaluation of the student's competence or because of a perceived lack of fit. If the feedback is not given directly to the student, it should at least be given to the campus supervisor.

The interview may also serve as a metaphor for the agency. In other words, if the agency is unstructured and requires a great deal of creativity from staff, the interview should mirror this situation. If, on the other hand, the agency is highly structured with clear guidelines for each staff member's role, the interview should be handled similarly. This type of consistency serves two purposes: it becomes a first-level orientation for the student to the agency and its expectations, and it allows the site supervisor the opportunity to gain relevant data about the student on which to base a decision.

Orientation

Because of the relatively short duration of both practicum and of many internship situations, the trainee must be oriented to the organization and service delivery issues as efficiently as possible. There are some lessons that only a learn-as-you-go approach can accomplish. But many more things can be learned through an orientation. Unfortunately, many trainees feel that they are just getting a handle on procedures and policy issues as they wrap up their field experience. At least some of this can be attributed to an inadequate orientation process.

If an agency accepts trainees on a regular basis, the site supervisor would be wise to develop a trainee manual covering the major agency policies that must be mastered. (A good resource for such a manual is the trainees who are at the end of their field experience; they can usually be precise about what information would have made their adaptation easier.) If written orientation materials are not available, the site supervisor might schedule more intensive supervision the first week or so to cover orientation matters with the trainee.

While orienting a supervisee to a particular site is essential, another intervention that should be considered for grounding supervisees and preparing them for the supervisory experience is the supervision contract.

The Supervision Contract

Supervision contracts or agreements of understanding have traditionally been good-faith documents between the training institution and the field site, stipulating the roles that would be played by the supervisee, the program supervisor, and the field site supervisor. Such agreements would also spell out the responsibilities for all parties and the opportunities that would be afforded to the supervisee for the duration of the contract. While such contracts are not binding in a legal sense, they serve the purpose of increasing accountability for those concerned.

More recently, emphasis has been placed on the supervision contract as a supervisory intervention (e.g., Studer, 2005). These more individualized supervision contracts should be created (usually with the supervisee) by the supervisor (either program or field) who will be the primary supervisor. The supervision contract typically acts not only to orient the supervisee to supervision, but as a method of ensuring informed consent (Thomas, 2007). Hewson (1999) also hypothesized that contracts can have the positive effects of increasing mutuality of goals between supervisee and supervisor and minimizing covert agendas. Even so, supervision contracts can lean toward agency structure (i.e., how the supervisee must conform in order to be successful), toward reducing legal vulnerability by outlining in detail ethical mandates and record-keeping imperatives (Falvey, 2002; Sutter, McPherson, & Geeseman, 2002), or toward the developmental learning goals of the supervisee (i.e., how supervision will be organized to maximize supervisee professional development).

Munson (2002) offered a supervision contract outline that reflects an emphasis on agency structure. Munson suggested that contracts include reference to the following:

1. *Timing element.* Frequency of supervision, length of session, and the duration of the supervision experience should be made clear.
2. *Learning structure.* Items that would fall under this heading have to do with approaches that the supervisor might use to enhance learning, including audiovisual techniques, cotherapy, assigned reading, and the like.
3. *Supervision structure.* Munson suggested that a contract include not only supervision modality (e.g., individual supervision, group supervision, or a combination), but also clear information about any change of supervisor, required rotation through different agency units, and explicit information about lines of authority.
4. *Agency conformity.* Items such as work hours, dress codes, agency rules regarding sharing phone numbers or e-mails, and record-keeping format would be covered in this section.

5. *Special conditions.* Finally, Munson suggested that any requirements unique to a particular site should be delineated, as well as how the agency expects the supervisee to acquire the knowledge and skills listed. Among such requirements could include expertise in the DSM–IV, familiarity with a particular assessment tool, or familiarity with medications.

Thomas (2007) suggested similar items to those outlined by Munson (2002). Thomas included a more direct reference to supervisor and supervisee responsibilities as part of the contract, as well as a statement of risks and benefits of supervision. Thomas also suggested the inclusion of items that we will cover under professional disclosure statements.

Osborn and Davis (1996) and Luepker (2003) developed contract guidelines that veer more toward the supervisee's professional development, while still covering necessary structural elements. Osborn and Davis argued that contracts not only help to clarify the supervision relationship, but, as later asserted by others (Luepker, 2003; Thomas, 2007), can also be used to promote ethical practice by itemizing important ethical standards (e.g., informed consent) and their implementation within supervision. Osborn and Davis suggested that supervision contracts include the following:

1. *Purpose, goals, and objectives.* This category includes the obvious purpose of safeguarding clients, as well as promoting supervisee development. Putting this in writing, however, is an important ritual for both supervisor and supervisee. Additionally, the more immediate goal of, for example, completing the clinical requirements for a training program is listed as well. Luepker (2003) suggested that a category such as this also include the type of clients that are needed for the supervisee's professional goals to be attained.
2. *Context of services.* The contract must include where and when supervision will take place, what method of monitoring will be in place,

and what supervision modalities will be used. We would add to this item a description of the clientele to be served.

3. *Method of evaluation.* Both formative and summative evaluation methods and schedules should be included. Any instrument that will be used for evaluation should be given to the supervisee at this time.

4. *Duties and responsibilities of supervisor and supervisee.* In this section, both persons outline the behaviors that they are committed to in order that supervision evolve successfully. For the supervisor, this may include challenging the supervisee to consider different treatment methods; for the supervisee, this may include coming to each supervision session with a preset videotaped sample of one's use of a particular technique.

5. *Procedural considerations.* Part of the contract must address issues such as emergency procedures and the format for record keeping required by the agency. Osborn and Davis also advised that the contract include a procedure that is to be followed if either party feels that a conflict within supervision has not been resolved.

6. *Supervisor's scope of practice.* Finally, Osborn and Davis suggested that the supervisor's experience and clinical credentials be listed to "make explicit to themselves and their supervisees their professional competence" (p. 130). A sample supervision contract adhering to Osborn and Davis's guidelines is presented in the Supervisor's Toolbox.

Supervisee Bill of Rights

While supervision contracts establish tasks and responsibilities for both supervisees and supervisors, the *Supervisee's Bill of Rights* (Giordano, Altekruse, & Kern, 2000; Munson, 2002) has emerged in professional literature and clearly places the supervisee at the center of the contractual relationship. While these documents can include responsibilities of supervisees, they emphasize the rights of supervisees to be the

recipients of quality supervision. For example, Munson (2002) included five conditions in the bill of rights for the supervisee:

1. a supervisor who supervises consistently and at regular intervals;
2. growth-oriented supervision that respects personal privacy;
3. supervision that is technically sound and theoretically grounded;
4. evaluation based on criteria that are made clear in advance, and evaluations that are based on actual observation of performance; and
5. a supervisor who is adequately skilled in clinical practice and trained in supervision practice. (p. 43)

Giordano et al. (2000) have developed a comprehensive supervision document that outlines the nature of the supervisory relationship and clarifies expectations as part of the bill of rights. This is followed by a delineation of relevant ethical standards that regulate supervision. The authors subsequently offered a supervision contract template based on the bill of rights and an evaluation form to document the extent to which the supervisee experienced supervision as consistent with the bill of rights. The contribution of Giordano et al. offers a synthesis of intent and outcome that is still relatively rare in the profession. The full Giordano et al. document can be seen in the Supervisor's Toolbox.

Professional Disclosure Statements

While statements about the supervisor's credentials, supervision approach, experience, and the like, are often included in supervision contracts (e.g., Giordano et al., 2000; Osborn & Davis, 1996; Thomas, 2007), some supervisors develop separate statements to educate the supervisee about them and about their supervision. This practice of preparing professional disclosure statements has become more common as states have increasingly required them for mental health practitioners. Because therapists have experienced the advantage of preparing such statements for their clients, they began preparing statements specific to supervision for their supervisees.

Professional disclosure statements provide a slightly different slant than the supervision contract. Because they tend not to be individualized for each supervisee, they provide a look at the constants that a particular supervisor offers. If they go beyond the nuts and bolts type of statements, they can also be used as a handout to help to orient the supervisee to a particular supervisor. We have found that putting one's beliefs, policies, and approaches on paper is good grounding for both supervisor and supervisee and is much more productive than attempting to convey an equal amount of information verbally.

A professional disclosure statement is required as part of the application process for the Approved Clinical Supervisor (ACS) credential (Center for Credentialing and Education [CCE], 2001). CCE, an affiliate of the National Board for Certified Counselors, Inc., requires that applicants for the ACS submit a professional disclosure statement that addresses the following:

1. Name, title, business address, and business telephone number
2. A listing of degrees, credentials, and licenses
3. General areas of competence in mental health practice in which the applicant can supervise
4. A statement documenting training in supervision and experience in providing supervision
5. A general statement addressing a model(s) of or approach to supervision, including the role of the supervisor, objectives and goals of supervision, and modalities
6. A description of the evaluation procedures to be used in the supervisory relationship
7. A statement indicating the limits and scope of confidentiality and privileged communication within the supervisory relationship
8. A statement, when applicable, indicating that the applicant is under supervision and that the supervisee's actions may be discussed with the applicant's supervisor

9. A fee schedule (when applicable)
10. A way to reach the applicant in an emergency situation
11. A statement indicating that the applicant follows a relevant credentialing body's Code of Ethics and CCE's Standards for the Ethical Practice of Clinical Supervision.

See the Supervisor's Toolbox for a sample of a professional disclosure statement created by a faculty supervisor for distribution to master's-level practicum supervisees, and Fall and Sutton (2004) for additional examples of professional disclosure statements.

As we stated at the beginning of this section, the organizational suggestions described above are foundational; that is, they provide the framework for supervision and continue to reap benefits for the supervisor and supervisee throughout the time they work together. Documents such as supervision contracts and professional disclosure statements should be used in conjunction with criteria for evaluation that were discussed in Chapter 2. Together, they give the supervisees a good sense of what is about to transpire and how their work will be assessed.

What we have discussed thus far is foundational; that is, these aids can help to lay the groundwork for supervision that is not distracted by the "white noise" of a chaotic supervisory context (Bernard, 2005). It is very difficult later in a supervisory relationship to recover from a disorganized beginning. The few tasks that follow fall in the category of maintenance and are much less onerous when foundational tasks have received adequate attention.

ONGOING ORGANIZATIONAL TASKS

Communication, Communication, Communication

We have already discussed the importance of initial communication among all parties in establishing field placements; supervision contracts and professional disclosure statements are organized around the value of clear and open communication. The balance of supervision must reflect adequate communication as well. "Communication is the heart and soul of the counseling profession, yet, too often, communications among site supervisor, the intern, and the [training] program get garbled" (Roberts et al., 2001). As we mentioned at the beginning of this chapter, the need for increased communication between the field and graduate programs has been echoed by others as well (Bogo, 2005; Bogo et al., 2007; Kahn, 1999; Lee & Cashwell, 2001; Lewis et al., 2005).

While communication among several parties once meant a number of phone calls, site visits, or clearly crafted memos, the Internet significantly reduces the effort that must be expended to keep everyone abreast of changes. A site supervisor Listserv would allow the training program to communicate efficiently regarding program developments (an area that almost always gets neglected, at least in the short run). Chat rooms could invite site supervisor input to campus supervisory discussions. With very little technological expertise or effort required, the communication between the training program and site could be vastly improved.

Although technology serves an important purpose in communication, it cannot replace site visits or contact by phone. Meetings on campus for site supervisors are also essential in allowing a forum for discussion and professional development. Training programs should attempt to communicate new developments in the area of supervision to their site supervisors. Although site supervisors have a wealth of practical knowledge, traditionally they have not stayed as current as university types in terms of the research on supervision, new models and techniques, and supervision literature in general. Therefore, in-service training for site supervisors or seminars in which both campus and site supervisors share their ideas and experiences comprise a special kind of communication activity (Beck, Yager, Williams, Williams, & Morris, 1989; Brown & Otto, 1986; Roberts et al., 2001).

Just as it is critical for the university supervisor to keep the site supervisor abreast of programmatic developments, it is equally important for the site supervisor to keep the university current.

Political, organizational, and fiscal developments may affect trainees both in their field experiences and employment search. When campus supervisors are kept current about what is going on in their sites, they are better able to advise students about the professions that they are entering.

An invaluable contribution that site supervisors can make to training programs is to communicate their opinion of the training that the students have received prior to their field placement. Once a site supervisor has overseen several trainees from the same program, the supervisor is in a position to see thematic strengths and weaknesses. To do this, however, site supervisors must have a template that allows them to view the trainee in a variety of ways so that this type of appraisal can be accomplished in a valid and consistent manner. This template can emerge from either the site or the training program, though it is more likely to come from the latter.

Finally, as specified by Hardcastle (1991), the site supervisor must organize communication within the agency to benefit the trainee. It happens occasionally that a trainee has contact only with the supervisor and feels isolated from the rest of the agency. In some instances, trainees are made to feel disloyal if they happen to ask advice from another employee other than their primary supervisors. This always leads to a negative outcome. The supervisor should have a plan as to how the trainee will be integrated into the agency, including attendance at staff meetings and joint projects with other staff members.

Communication and Evaluation. It is the prerogative and responsibility of the university supervisor to develop an evaluation plan and to conduct all summative evaluations that lead to course grades. The extent to which the site is being asked to evaluate the supervisee must be clearly communicated (Bogo et al., 2007; Olsen & Stern, 1990). As Rosenblum and Raphael (1987) noted, however, site supervisors often dread evaluating university students. Kadushin (1992c) offered empirical support that evaluation was among field supervisors' least favorite responsibilities. When the site supervisor's experience with a trainee has been positive, evaluation tends to be glowing; when the trainee has not met expectations, the evaluation is sometimes avoided. It is our belief that site supervisors, because their relationships with trainees are short-term and because their relationships with the universities are rarely mandated, should not be asked to carry out discriminating summative evaluations. For example, the site supervisor should not be asked to grade the student except to give a pass or fail recommendation. On the other hand, it is important for site supervisors to give feedback, both to the trainee and to the university supervisor. But the task of translating feedback into a final grade is clearly the charge of the program faculty. (Evaluation procedures were delineated in Chapter 2.)

The above notwithstanding, occasionally the site supervisor alerts the training program about some conflict with the supervisee or concern about the performance of the supervisee (Elman et al., 1999; Igartua, 2000; Leonardelli & Gratz, 1985). It is important that training programs encourage sites to contact the training program if a supervisee shows any signs of unprofessional behavior, impairment, or developmental stagnation. It goes without saying that training programs must be responsive to such contact. Peleg-Oren and Even-Zahav (2004) found that a primary reason for site supervisors dropping out was disenchantment over the lack of a functional way to negotiate with the training program when there were differences of opinion about a student. Additionally, field supervisors interviewed for Bogo et al.'s (2007) qualitative study reported feeling isolated in their roles as gatekeepers and were not confident that academic programs would in fact support their negative evaluations of trainees when these occurred.

Occasionally, it is the supervisee who raises concerns with the training program about the site. Although it is important for students to have experience in resolving conflict, the power differential between them and their site supervisors may make this difficult in some cases. In such instances, the program supervisor has a legitimate role to play.

Supervisor as Agency Representative. Another communication function, but one that the site supervisor is less likely to perceive as such, is to serve as a liaison or advocate between supervisees and agency administration. (Even if the supervisor wears two hats, when in the role of clinical supervisor, the supervisor must communicate administrative parameters to trainees.) This function is unique enough to be addressed separately and is critical to the trainee's professional development. Often, the site supervisor fulfills this role in an informal manner, sharing bits and pieces of both spoken and unspoken rules, agency politics, and the like. When done in an informal fashion, however, the trainee is more likely to get incomplete information and/or become triangulated in organizational power struggles. It is far better for the interface between service delivery and organizational realities to be covered in supervision in a deliberate way. Perhaps part of each supervision session could be reserved for "organization as system" discussions, not as a gripe session but as a learning process.

Another liaison function of the site supervisor is to structure some way that other agency personnel can give input about the performance of the trainee. Again, it is common for this to occur informally and therefore inconsistently. The site supervisor can devise a short form and ask colleagues to complete it once or twice during the field placement. This kind of overture can have several positive effects.

1. It lessens the trainee's isolation by involving additional personnel in the trainee's experience.
2. It can provide the trainee with additional feedback from different perspectives or role positions.
3. It can confirm or confront the supervisor's own evaluation of the trainee.

Managing Time

Time management has become a cliché, even as the challenge to "find time" seems to increase. Supervisors are busy people. Whether at the university or in the field, many obligations compete with supervision. Because supervision is an enjoyable role for many professionals, they often take it on when they really have little extra time. Yet almost without exception, those studies that have surveyed supervisees about past unsatisfactory supervision found having insufficient time for supervision as a primary complaint.

Time management, therefore, becomes a crucial skill for clinical supervisors; one that needs to be exercised and modeled for supervisees who themselves are juggling several roles. Falvey (1987) listed several simple time-management strategies for administrative supervisors, which include coordinating activities to maximize one's productivity (e.g., tackling difficult tasks when one's energy is high), avoiding escapist behaviors (e.g., doing an unpleasant task first thing in the morning, rather than allowing it to weigh on one's mind all day), and dividing difficult tasks so that they do not appear overwhelming.

A central time-management skill is the ability to set priorities and keep to them. It is virtually impossible to end one's work day with absolutely no work leftover for the following day. Rather, supervisors who can manage time have addressed the most important concerns immediately and have learned to pace themselves in accomplishing less-pressing tasks. For some supervisors, it is a seemingly natural ability to take control of one's schedule; for others, it is a constant struggle that can be supplemented by time-management strategies suggested in the literature. Covey et al. (1994) warned against falling into an urgency mentality; that is, what is immediate is always treated as urgent, even when it is not. They also cautioned against using time-management strategies to fit an unreasonable amount of activity into one's schedule, a sentiment echoed by Osborn (2004). In other words, time management can become part of the problem, not the solution. Regardless of how the supervisor accomplishes the goal of finding and protecting time for supervision, the supervisor must realize that making time must be a deliberate choice and is not something that will take care of itself.

Time Management and Burnout. The site supervisor has considerable control over the atmosphere within which the trainee (and all supervisees) works. The trainee is not likely to refer to an initial experience as one of burnout, but trainees have often referred to being overwhelmed and too busy to be able to integrate the experience (Kaslow & Rice, 1985). All mental health practitioners need time to regroup and consult if they are to remain vital in their direct-service responsibilities. Structuring time so that supervisees have a variety of activities and the opportunity for collegial support in their day will raise not only the quality of the work environment, but also the quality of service delivery (Falvey, 1987; Osborn, 2004). Protecting supervisees from overload communicates a respect for the *practitioner* and also respect for the work that needs to be done, work that should be done by persons who can perform at their optimal level.

The issue of supervisor burnout is relevant to this discussion. Managing from a perspective that protects supervisees must encompass a respect for the supervisor's multiple responsibilities as well. In their survey of clinical supervisors, Nichols, Nichols, and Hardy (1990) found that supervisors were less invested in doing supervision than supervisors were a decade earlier. Though the reasons for this decline in interest were not reported, the demands of supervision in organizations that do not provide adequate resources for this demanding role have been documented (Bogo, 2005). It seems imperative, therefore, that supervisors take themselves into consideration when developing a plan for supervision, a plan that allows them the time and support that they need to conduct clinical supervision in a manner that adds to the quality of their work environment.

Time Management and Choosing Supervision Methods. Chapters 9, 10, and 11 outline a variety of ways in which the process of supervision can be conducted. Deciding on the form that supervision will take and implementing the desired process can be an organizational task of significant proportion. For example, the supervisor might decide that using interpersonal process recall (IPR; Kagan, 1976; Kagan & Kagan, 1997) would be desirable with a particular supervisee because of difficulties the supervisee is having with one of her clients. Using the technique, however, will require that video or DVD equipment be made available and that arrangements be made for taping the next therapy session. It is understandable, though regrettable, that supervisors often default on their supervision plans because the method that supervision should take becomes logistically too complicated. If the supervisor is convinced that a particular process (e.g., IPR or live supervision) is essential for the supervisee's learning, it is incumbent on the supervisor to work out the logistical details. This is even more the case when using technology for distance supervision (e.g., Schultz & Finger, 2003; Watson, 2003). When supervisors continue to put aside their teaching instincts because of the time and care required, the quality of supervision eventually deteriorates. Perhaps there is no organizational responsibility so essential to clinical supervision as the choreography required to ensure that the method of supervision matches the learning needs of supervisees.

Record Keeping

In a litigious era, the process of record keeping has gained in importance for helping professionals of all disciplines. Falvey and Cohen (2003) asserted that from a legal perspective "if it isn't documented, it didn't occur." Others have concurred that good clinical records serve as a desirable defense against litigation (Brantley, 2000; Snider, 1987; Soisson, Vandecreek, & Knapp, 1987; Swenson, 1997).

Whether supervising from campus or on-site, it is the supervisor's responsibility to be sure that client records are complete. Most agencies and university professors have established record-keeping procedures that have evolved over time. But with an ever-changing professional and legal climate, the wise supervisor reviews the record-keeping system occasionally to be sure that it is current with national trends. Among the items that should be considered for inclusion in client records are the following (Mitchell, 1991; Munson, 2002; Schultz, 1982):

1. Written and signed informed consents for all treatment, as well as signed informed consent for all transmissions of confidential information
2. Treatment contracts, if used
3. Notes on all treatment contacts made, either in person or by telephone, including descriptions of significant events and interventions made
4. Notes on all contacts or consultation with significant others, including correspondence
5. A complete history and symptom picture leading to diagnosis, with regular review (every 90 days) and revision of the diagnosis, as well as treatment direction based on diagnosis
6. A record of all prescriptions and current drug use profile
7. Any instructions, suggestions, or directives made to the client that he or she failed to follow through on
8. Records relevant to supervision, including permission to tape sessions, and consultations sought by either supervisee or supervisor regarding a case
9. A record of termination and an aftercare plan (Beis, 1984)

Research conducted by Worthington, Tan, and Poulin (2002) underscored the wisdom of supervisor vigilance regarding supervisee documentation of work with clients. Of the behaviors viewed by supervisees and supervisors as unethical, one of the most frequently committed (as reported by supervisees about their own behavior) was failure "to complete documentation of client records within the required time frame" (p. 335). Additionally, while both supervisors and supervisees found this behavior to be problematic, supervisees found it less so than supervisors. The authors concluded that:

> ... *documentation is one of the most important protections against legal liability because of its importance in establishing whether a given liability claim meets the criteria for malpractice, and failure to complete documentation may increase exposure to liability if harm comes to a client—a set of circumstances that may be more salient to supervisors than it is to supervisees.* (p. 345)

Most supervisors are far more careful about client records than about supervision records. Yet, as the Tarasoff case pointed out (*Tarasoff* v. *Regents of the University of California,* 1976), supervision records can be equally important in a malpractice suit. On a more optimistic note, supervision records discipline supervisors to pause and consider their supervision with each supervisee, offering moments of insight that would not otherwise occur. Luepker (2003) found parallel benefits between good psychotherapy records and good supervision records (see Table 8.1). Therefore, for legal, instructional, and best-practice reasons, supervisors are strongly encouraged to keep accurate and complete supervision records.

Munson (2002) suggested that supervision records include seven components. Luepker (2003) added another component:

1. the supervisory contract, if used or required by the agency;
2. a brief statement of supervisee experience, training, and learning needs;
3. a summary of all performance evaluations;
4. notation of all supervisory sessions;
5. cancelled or missed sessions;
6. notation of cases discussed and significant decisions;
7. significant problems encountered in the supervision and how they were resolved, or whether

TABLE 8.1   Parallel Between Benefits of Psychotherapy Records and Benefits of Clinical Supervision Records

BENEFITS OF PSYCHOTHERAPY RECORDS	BENEFITS OF CLINICAL SUPERVISION RECORDS
Help clarify presenting problems and histories of patients	Help clarify supervisees' professional strengths, weaknesses, previous professional training, experience
Help psychotherapists clarify treatment goals for clients that logically flow from clients' presenting problems and history	Help clinical supervisors establish supervisory goals and learning plans that logically flow from assessment of supervisees' learning needs
Assist psychotherapists and patients to formulate and mutually agree upon treatment plans, including treatment goals and procedures	Assist clinical supervisors to formulate and mutually agree upon learning plans, including supervision goals and procedures
Help assess progress or lack of progress in meeting treatment goals	Help assess progress or lack of progress in meeting supervisory goals
Help foster treatment alliance	Help foster collaboration in supervisory relationship
Help evaluate efficacy of treatment	Help evaluate efficacy of supervision
Provide summary of progress and outcomes of treatment and recommendations that can be used later for continuity of care	Provide summary of progress and outcomes of clinical supervision and recommendations for supervisory evaluations and letters of reference
Help psychotherapists show what they did so they can respond to a financial audit	Help clinical supervisors show what they did so they can respond to a financial audit
Help psychotherapists show that their services met the standard of professional care for psychotherapists in their professional community in the event of a regulatory board or legal complaint of psychotherapist negligence	Help clinical supervisors show that their supervisory services met the standard of professional care for clinical supervisors in their professional community in the event of a regulatory board or legal complaint of supervisory negligence

Source: From *Record Keeping in Psychotherapy and Counseling,* by E. T. Luepker, 2003, New York: Brunner-Routledge. Reprinted by permission.

they remain unresolved and why (Munson, 2002, p. 256); and

8. appropriate consent forms (informing clients and supervisees of supervison parameters) (Luepker, 2003).

We offer the Supervision Record Form (SRF), which asks the supervisor to focus on goals for supervision and subsequent supervision inter-

ventions (including a rationale for each). While the primary purpose of the SRF is to assist the supervisor in reflecting upon his or her supervision, the form also includes a section directed at supervision risk management (see Figure 8.2). Risk management issues can include a host of topics, including a need for parental consent, risk of harm, concerns about substance abuse, need for medical consultation, possible boundary issues, suspected

FIGURE 8.2   Supervision Record Form

Date: _____

SUPERVISOR: _____   SUPERVISEE:_____

First name (pseudonym) of client(s) discussed:

For the names of clients listed, indicate whether you heard/saw a portion of the counseling session:

_____

Pre-session goals for the supervision session:

_____
_____
_____
_____

Extent to which pre-session goals were met: (comment)

_____
_____
_____
_____

Major topics that emerged during the supervision session (either supervisor-initiated or supervisee-initiated):

_____
_____
_____
_____

List client(s)-focused supervision interventions (including a rationale for each):

_____
_____
_____
_____

List supervisee-focused supervision interventions (including a rationale for each):

_____

_____

_____

_____

Goals for next supervision session:

_____

_____

_____

_____

RISK MANAGEMENT REVIEW. Note any concerns based on review of supervisee's entire caseload. Include (a) 1st name [or case number] of client, (b) Nature of the concern, and (c) Supervision intervention at this time.

_____

_____

_____

_____

_____

Signature

abuse, required supervisee or supervisor expertise, and so forth (Falvey, Caldwell, & Cohen, 2002). Once risk management issues are identified, it is encumbant upon the supervisor to document interventions that have been executed to address these.

Planning for the Exceptions

It is frustrating, if not frightening, for a trainee to face an emergency with a client—for example, the need to hospitalize—and have no idea how the situation is to be handled. While it may be the supervisor's intention or assumption that a supervisee will never handle an emergency alone, the unexpected happens, and emergency procedures should be in written form, given to the trainee during orientation, and placed in a convenient place for reference should an emergency occur.

Another time when planning ahead is crucial is when the supervisor will be away. For example, it is not unusual for all clinical supervisors in a training program to attend the same conference, leaving a university-based clinic either in the hands of doctoral students or fill-in supervisors. With the rush to prepare the paper that will be presented at the conference or the arrangements that must be made to cover one's classes, it often happens that a colleague from the field or another department is asked to cover supervision with little or no information about the operations of the clinic, the status of any worrisome clients, or the student staff. This could easily be a case for which the lack of managerial foresight takes on the characteristics of questionable ethical practice.

By planning ahead we do not mean to suggest that the supervisor compulsively worry about every possible way that things may go wrong. "The sky is falling" is not a productive supervisory posture. Rather, we urge supervisors to take reasonable care regarding their responsibilities and, especially, to give themselves the time to plan well and to put their plans into action.

EVALUATION AND DEBRIEFING

The many dimensions of evaluation were covered in Chapter 2; therefore, at this point, we only remind the supervisor that evaluation is both an ongoing activity and a summative and gatekeeping task for the supervisor. Chapter 2 offered many ways to organize the evaluative aspect of supervision, and these should be reflected in the supervision contract and the record-keeping system.

While most supervisees receive some sort of final evaluation, many do not experience a quality debriefing of their time under supervision. This is unfortunate, because many worthwhile insights could be offered by both supervisor and supervisee during a debriefing session. In fact, debriefing is a perfect context for the supervisor to receive feedback about the supervision package that was offered to the supervisee, including how well supervision was organized. A debriefing can also include comments about how the supervisee might approach future supervision experiences in ways that build on the experience just ended. It is best if debriefing occurs in the placement site, but at the very least, training programs should conduct some form of debriefing for trainees.

SOME FINAL THOUGHTS

Short of receiving training in time management or developing training manuals, what can the clinical supervisor do to achieve organizational competence (not that the former wouldn't be a good idea)? This chapter has presented many of the goals that the clinical supervisor might set for himself or herself. The following are five additional guidelines that can be of use as one sets out to achieve these goals.

Get Support

Before clinical supervisors commit themselves to the substantial task of supervising either on or off a university campus, they should be sure that they have administrative support for this responsibility because, without it, they are vulnerable to a host of difficulties that are bound to affect their supervision (Copeland, 1998; Globerman & Bogo, 2003; Sommer & Cox, 2005). Likewise, an academic program director must appreciate the time it takes to develop good field sites, to organize the operation of practicum and internship, and to serve as an ongoing liaison with sites. If, as most accrediting bodies suggest, the faculty supervisor also offers to train site supervisors, the responsibilities can begin to grow exponentially. The greater the support offered by superiors, the more that can be accomplished and the better the quality of the supervision. If support is limited, the clinical supervisor must decide if minimal standards can be met. If they cannot, the supervisor must decline an offer to supervise on ethical grounds.

Know Yourself

As simple as it sounds, there seems to be a relatively high degree of unawareness among clinical supervisors about their ability to organize themselves and those under their supervision. Perhaps supervisors assume that they should already have the organizational skills to manage the supervisory process and therefore resist admitting that this is an area in which they need to grow.

Organization comes far more naturally to some than to others. When supervisors believe that they fall in the latter category, they should find a member of their staff or a professional colleague whom they believe can help to develop a plan or, more likely, help to implement a plan. (For example, a highly intuitive thinker on the Myers–Briggs Type Indicator would benefit from consultation with a more sensing type.) The beginning of implementation is a critical juncture that calls for different abilities than those required for arriving at the original plan. This is the point at which many clinical supervisors could use assistance.

Gather Data

There is nothing particularly virtuous about reinventing the wheel. As supervisors approach the task of organizing a training program or the clinical operation of an agency, they might contact other training programs or agencies and ask for samples of policy statements, supervision forms, and other materials relevant to their tasks. When a specific issue arises, consulting with colleagues and determining how they have managed a similar issue is a sound strategy. Isolating oneself is a common supervisor flaw, both in terms of clinical work and organizational tasks. Supervisors have a tremendous amount to learn from each other, and they need to model for their supervisees the ability to consult with others as part of good clinical practice. The development of a supervision portfolio of criteria for evaluation, templates for supervision contracts and record keeping, and the like, may save valuable time for supervisors who intend to continue in this role.

Get Feedback

Any new procedure should be considered a pilot study of sorts. An organizational strategy may work well from the supervisor's vantage point, but be untenable for supervisees. The competent supervisor knows how to manipulate procedures to work for people and the program or agency, not the other way around. Part of this competence is demonstrated by seeking the opinions of others. The result is an organizational style that is always being fine tuned without continually starting over from scratch.

Be Intentional

One way to avoid having to scrap one plan for another (and thereby keeping those under supervision in a state of turmoil) is for supervisors to give themselves permission to build their organizational plan slowly, but deliberately. No one who is supervising for the first time will be totally organized in the first year. Rather, one should begin with those aspects of supervision that are most critical for ethical and safe practice and eventually pay heed to items that add to convenience and expediency of communication and a variety of training goals, among other things. In addition to being practical, being intentional encourages the supervisor to immediately home in on those things that are absolutely essential to any supervisory operation. Discriminating between issues that are essential and those that are desirable is the beginning and the core of organizational competence.

CONCLUSION

Although organizational issues tend to fall to the bottom of the list of motivational forces for clinical supervisors, the manner in which they are handled may be more predictive of long-term success as a supervisor than clinical expertise. Organizational tasks are tedious only when they are viewed as distractors. When viewed as building blocks for the essential work of supervision, organizational challenges can tap the energy typically reserved for activities such as establishing a working relationship with a supervisee. Paradoxically, the energy invested in the organization of clinical supervision may produce the greatest payoff in terms of protecting time and providing a context for exemplary supervisory practice.

CHAPTER 9

SUPERVISION INTERVENTIONS
INDIVIDUAL SUPERVISION

Having described the major parameters of supervision and the supervisory relationship, we are finally prepared to consider with some specificity the delivery of a variety of supervision interventions, most often referred to as methods or techniques. This chapter on individual supervision is only one of three chapters that will look at methods and techniques of supervision. It will be followed by chapters on group supervision and live supervision. It should also be noted that, in a way, most of the chapters in this text have supervision intervention implications. Individual differences, interpersonal issues, ethical dilemmas, delivering evaluative feedback—all require specific supervision interventions. This chapter serves a more targeted purpose, a template so to speak, for how supervision takes place in a one-on-one context.

Individual supervision is still considered the cornerstone of professional development. Although most supervisees will experience some form of group supervision in their training and some may have an opportunity to work within a live supervision paradigm, virtually all supervisees will experience individual supervision sessions. Whether these individual conferences will produce memories and insights that will linger long into the supervisee's career or will frustrate, bore, or even outrage the supervisee has something to do with the supervisor's skill in choosing and using a variety of supervision methods. At this point in the history of the helping professions, there are many different approaches and techniques from which the supervisor can choose to conduct an individual case conference. This chapter will describe the most common of these

assorted approaches and discuss their advantages and occasional disadvantages. Although all the supervision interventions described in this chapter are appropriate for individual conferences, many also could be applied within a group supervision context. Chapter 10 on group supervision, however, focuses on strategies that rely specifically on group dynamics for their implementation. Finally, we have also chosen to include in this chapter a discussion on the reflective process and issues surrounding the use of technology in supervision. Although both of these topics can transcend individual supervision, it seemed appropriate to include them here.

In summary, we return to our previous comment about the connectedness between this chapter (as well as the two following) and the rest of the book. When writing a textbook of this sort, each chapter becomes an artificial compartmentalization of one aspect of the whole. The gestalt, so to speak, is violated. Although this cannot be avoided, it seems particularly problematic as we consider methods and techniques of supervision. It is possible to conduct supervision using a great many different formats without stepping back to consider the bigger picture—a conceptual base, an evaluation plan, ethical constraints, cultural differences, and so on. We urge the reader, therefore, to view this chapter not in isolation, but in the context of other concepts presented in this book.

INITIAL CRITERIA FOR CHOOSING SUPERVISION INTERVENTIONS

A supervisor's initial choice of method is influenced by a number of factors, both rational and irrational in nature. The supervisor might believe that without an audiotape or videotape of counseling or therapy there is no real way to know what has transpired between supervisees and their clients. Or the supervisor might be adamant that self-report is the only form of supervision that provides a glimpse at the supervisee's internal reasoning. The list can, and indeed does, go on. Borders and Brown (2005) listed six reasons for choosing specific supervision methods: (1) supervisor preferences (influenced by worldview, theoretical orientation, and past experience); (2) supervisee developmental level (see Chapter 5); (3) supervisee learning goals; (4) supervisor goals for the supervisee; (5) supervisor's own learning goals as a supervisor (which may include becoming more comfortable with a particular supervisory intervention); and (6) contextual factors (such as site policies or facility capabilities, client difficulty, and so on). Each of these criteria and all of them in unison will influence the choice of a supervision method.

Supervision is best placed somewhere on the continuum between training and consultation. In other words, the supervisee should come to supervision with some ability to articulate learning goals based on initial experiences in training, but cannot be expected to function autonomously with only an occasional need for consultation. Supervision methods, therefore, must take into account the supervisee's stated goals and known supervision needs, as well as how far down the training–supervision–consultation axis the supervisee has traveled. By and large, however, supervision methods tend to reflect the supervisor's preferences for supervision more than the supervisee's, with the exception perhaps of the more advanced supervisee.

As described in Chapter 4, supervision has grown significantly in terms of options available to the supervisor. While increased attention has been given in the recent past to more interactive forms of supervision (e.g., live supervision, teleconferencing), there is a new emergence of authors calling for supervision methods that will increase supervisees' thoughtfulness and ability to reflect on their work as they increase in skill (Carroll,

2001; Deal, 2003; Guiffrida, 2005; Knowles, Gilbourne, Tomlinson, & Anderson, 2007; Koch, Arhar, & Wells, 2000; Nelson & Neufeldt, 1998; Neufeldt, 1997; Skovholt & Rønnestad, 1992a–b, 1995). Neufeldt (1997) argued that the supervisor may choose to deliberately ignore empirical findings that indicate that novice supervisees prefer structured supervision interventions in order to encourage reflectivity in the supervisee. But if the supervisee is not only a novice but concrete in conceptual style, some structured intervention may be necessary to guide the supervisee into a process that may lead to reflectivity.

Methods and techniques, therefore, must be malleable and conducive to reaching a variety of supervision goals. Technical eclecticism may be as important to supervisors as it has been argued to be for therapists. Supervisors (and supervisees) may be best served when creative alternatives are utilized to accomplish immediate goals, as well as goals that are more long range.

Lastly, an additional frame for deciding what method to use in a given situation is to determine the function of supervision at a given point in time. There are three general functions of supervision interventions (Borders et al., 1991): (1) *assessing* the learning needs of the supervisee; (2) *changing, shaping,* or *supporting* the supervisee's behavior; and (3) *evaluating* the performance of the supervisee. Although the majority of supervision falls within the second function, supervisors are continually reassessing their supervisee's learning needs and evaluating their progress. As these separate functions are being addressed, the supervisor might find that different methods serve one function better than others. For example, a supervisor might choose to watch a videotape of a supervisee to assess that person's skills, but rely on process notes to accomplish the second function of attempting to change, support, or redirect the supervisee's work.

STRUCTURED VERSUS UNSTRUCTURED INTERVENTIONS

Much of the literature addressing developmental issues, cognitive style of the supervisee, and numerous other topics refers to the relative need for structure in supervision. Rarely, however, do authors describe specifically what is meant by structure or the lack of it. Highly structured supervision can be viewed as an extension of training, while unstructured supervision can be viewed as approaching consultation. Although methods of supervision are often associated with a particular degree of structure, it is the supervisor's use of the method that will determine the level of structure. For example, Rigazio-DiGilio and Anderson (1994) noted that a structured use of live supervision might entail the use of the bug-in-the-ear, thus coaching the supervisee through a therapy session, while a less structured form might rely on presession planning, mid-session consultation, and postsession debriefing. (See Chapter 11 for a complete description of these options.) Similarly, individual supervision based on audiotape may be directed by the supervisor and follow the supervisor's instructional agenda, or the use of audiotape may be used to encourage the supervisee to reflect on a moment in a counseling session that appears to have had special meaning for the supervisee.

In short, structure or the lack of structure is not dictated by the modality used. Rather, structured interventions are supervisor directed and involve a reasonably high amount of supervision control; unstructured interventions may be supervisor or supervisee directed and require more discipline on the part of the supervisor to allow learning to take place without directing it. For the supervisor who is impatient or who dislikes ambiguity, unstructured interventions will be more challenging; for the supervisor who has difficulty planning ahead and organizing learning, structured interventions will be more challenging. The great majority of supervisees will benefit from both types of interventions at different junctures in their professional development.

METHODS, FORMS, AND TECHNIQUES OF SUPERVISION

With technology and computer capabilities becoming more sophisticated every day and with the

helping professions exhibiting a heightened interest in supervision, different techniques, methods, and paradigms for conducting supervision continue to evolve. Because of the dynamic nature of the field, therefore, we do not presume to present an inclusive list of supervision interventions. Rather, we hope to reflect the diversity of choices that has been spawned as clinical supervision continues to evolve, to give some rationale for using different methods, and to report the findings on their frequency of use and relative strengths and weaknesses.

The remainder of this chapter has been designed to review supervision methods, advancing from those methods that allow the least direct observation by the supervisor to those that allow the most. Therefore, self-report begins our list as a supervision format that relies on the supervisee's recollections of counseling or therapy as the source of information to be used for supervision.

Self-Report

Although it is a simple form of supervision in one sense, we consider self-report to be a difficult method to perform well. In fact, some of the best and the worst supervision can be found within the domain of self-report. Under the best of conditions, supervisees will be challenged conceptually and personally and will learn a great deal. Many supervisors relying on self-report, however, have fallen into stagnation; supervision becomes pro forma, with little difference evident from session to session or from supervisee to supervisee. Also, much of what is viewed in the field as self-report supervision is, instead, restricted to case management.

Professional literature has given relatively little attention to self-report in the recent past, focusing much more on forms of supervision that include direct samples of the supervisee's work. Self-report, however, continues to be a commonly used form of supervision, especially for postgraduate supervision (e.g., Goodyear & Nelson, 1997; Magnuson, 1995). At its best, self-report is an intense tutorial relationship in which the supervisee fine-tunes both case conceptualization ability and personal knowledge as each relates to therapist–client and supervisor–supervisee relationships. At its worst, self-report becomes a perfect modality when the supervisee is experiencing the pressure to distort (rather than report) his or her work, whether or not this is conscious (Noelle, 2002). Self-report is generally viewed as far less appropriate for novice supervisees for reasons delineated by Holloway (1988), who doubted the wisdom of a supervision model that excludes direct observation. Holloway stated that supervision without direct observation forfeits "the opportunity for (a) independent judgment regarding the client's problem, and (b) illustrating directly with the case in question how to draw inferences from client information" (p. 256). Holloway's point is still well taken and underscores one of the key vulnerabilities of the self-report method: As a supervision strategy, it is only as good as the observational and conceptual abilities of the supervisee and the seasoned insightfulness of the supervisor. It seems, therefore, that self-report offers too many opportunities for failure if it represents the complete supervision plan.

Campbell (1994) supported this contention on ethical and legal grounds. He referred to an early study conducted by Muslin, Thurnblad, and Meschel (1981) in which more than 50% of the important issues evident in videotapes of therapy sessions of psychiatric supervisees were not reported in supervision; furthermore, some degree of distortion characterized more than 50% of supervisees' reports. Campbell described such supervision as supervision in absentia and stated that

As a result of their inexperience, trainees find it difficult to comprehend the problems of their clients. Because they do not observe trainees, supervisors find it difficult to correct their errors. Thus, trainees struggle with what they do not understand; and supervisors labor with what they cannot see. (p. 11)

A more recent study further indicted the memories of therapists when a group of licensed psychologists was asked to recall the molar (main) and molecular (supporting) ideas from specific segments of actual therapy sessions. Wynne, Susman, Ries, Birringer, and Katz (1994) reported only a 42% recall rate for molar ideas and 30% recall for molecular ideas. It seems reasonable to ask whether such a rate is adequate for the purposes of supervision, especially when the supervisee is relatively inexperienced.

Because self-report is the grandparent of supervision forms, there also is a tendency to return to it when other supervisory processes become tiring or tiresome. In fact, studies that investigated the frequency of methods used in supervision have found self-report as a relatively dominant method and often the most frequently used method (Anderson, Schlossberg, & Rigazio-DiGilio, 2000; Borders, Cashwell, & Rotter, 1995; Coll, 1995; Romans, Boswell, Carlozzi, & Ferguson, 1995; Wetchler, Piercy, & Sprenkle, 1989). When these same supervisees (and sometimes supervisors) were asked to identify the most valuable form of supervision, self-report dropped in its primacy (e.g., Wetchler et al., 1989). In a study that compared perceptions of best and worst supervision, Anderson et al. (2000) found that their subjects were far more likely to consider self-report as representing their worst supervision experiences than their best supervision experiences. Supporting a cautious stance toward self-report as the supervision modality of choice, Rogers and McDonald (1995) found that when supervisors used more direct methods of supervision they evaluated their supervisees as less prepared for the job than when they used self-report. Such results reinforce the argument that self-report is weakest when used with supervisees who have not reached a minimally acceptable level of professional competence.

Finally, an interesting investigation conducted by Wetchler and Vaughn (1992) homed in on the supervision method used during what, in retrospect, was identified as a critical supervisory incident that had a positive developmental impact on the supervisee. For both supervisors and supervisees, the method most frequently noted was an individual conference without reference to the use of any technology. Although this study may seem to contradict other findings, it may be viewed as underscoring our earlier statement that self-report includes some of the best as well as some of the worst supervision experiences. When a situation is highly charged for the supervisee, it may take the more open-ended context of a conference based on self-report to help the supervisee to process the meaning of what is occurring. At times, information does not enlighten, but rather detracts from the issues. (Our discussion of encouraging reflective practice later in this chapter will pick up on this theme.) Knowing when to limit the information flow in order to take a more introspective approach to supervision requires both experience and a posture of keen attentiveness on the part of the supervisor.

Process Notes and Case Notes

Process notes are the supervisee's written explanation of the content of the therapy session, the interactional processes that occurred between supervisee and client, the supervisee's feelings about the client, and the rationale and manner of intervention (Goldberg, 1985). As such, process notes can be very extensive and therefore time consuming. It is unlikely that a supervisor would require complete process notes for each session that a supervisee conducts. They may, however, be a worthwhile endeavor on occasion, especially if the supervisor believes that the supervisee would benefit from a more intensive review of supervisee–client interactions and the outcomes of these. Lee, Nichols, Nichols, and Odom (2004) found that process reports were the most frequently used method of supervision for American Association for Marriage and Family Therapy (AAMFT) approved supervisors when their data were collected in 2001. These authors offered no definition of process reports; therefore, it is unknown if they were referring to a method as labor intensive as process notes.

Case notes, on the other hand, are a normative aspect of counseling and supervision (see record keeping in Chapter 8). Case notes should include all pertinent information from a counseling session, including the interventions used. As such, case notes are the professional, institutional, and

legal record of counseling. This being said, case notes can also be used deliberately as part of the supervision conference. While some information should be apparent in all therapy case notes, a supervisor may ask the supervisee to reflect on and answer specific questions that meet supervision goals. For example, questions could be posed to assist the supervisee in a reflective process (discussed later in this chapter), to assist the supervisee in linking conceptualization to intervention, or to be vigilant regarding cultural dynamics. When used in this way, case notes become a supervision intervention that can direct the conference. Case notes can and perhaps should be used in conjunction with any other supervision modality. (See Table 9.1 for sample case conference leads that may be helpful to supervisees in preparing for supervision.)

Audiotape

Although live observation and videotape have led to some of the more dramatic breakthroughs in the supervision process, the audiotape was the first to revolutionize our perceptions of what could be accomplished in supervision, and Rogers (1942) and Covner (1942a,b) are attributed with this development (Goodyear & Nelson, 1997). Without the facilities of a training clinic or easily accessible video equipment, the audiotape allows supervisees to transport an accurate (albeit partial) recording of counseling or therapy to a supervisor who was not present at the time that the session occurred. With the exception of marriage and family therapy supervisors, who prefer videorecordings (Lee et al., 2004), the audiotape is one of the most widely used sources of information for supervisors who expect to have some sort of direct access to the work of their supervisees (e.g., Borders et al., 1995; Coll, 1995). Furthermore, this supervision method finds support among those who investigated its effectiveness. As one example, when Magnuson, Wilcoxon, and Norem (2000) asked experienced counselors to reflect on exemplary supervision that they had received, the review of audio- or videotapes with

TABLE 9.1 Leads to Assist the Supervisee in Preparing for the Supervision Case Conference

1. A. Briefly describe the client's presenting problem.
   B. What were your objectives for this session?
2. Describe the dynamics in the session (your own reactions to the client and the interactions between you and the client). Be sure to attend to dynamics that may be based on cultural differences/similarities.
3. A. Describe other important information that was learned during the session, including contextual information.
   B. Summarize key issues discussed during the session.
4. Describe relevant cultural or developmental information as it relates to the presenting problem(s).
5. A. What is your initial conceptualization of the client's issue(s)? (Be sure that your comments are theoretically sound.)
   B. Explain changes (or expansions) of your conceptualizations of the presenting problem(s).
6. List relevant diagnostic impressions, including DSM code and axis.
7. A. To the extent possible, describe initial treatment plan for this client.
   B. Explain changes (or expansions) of your treatment plan for this client.
8. Based on your treatment plan, what are your objectives for the next session?
9. To what extent were your objectives for this session met?
10. Does any aspect of this case raise ethical concerns for you?
11. Share any personal reflections on the session.
12. What specific questions do you have for your supervisor?

Leads relevant to (A) initial counseling session and (B) subsequent counseling sessions.

their supervisors surfaced as examples of supervision that led to strong positive recollections.

When an audiotape is first required of supervisees (especially if they have been relying on self-report or process notes), there is often some resistance that takes the form of "My clients won't be comfortable." This reaction is occasionally echoed at practicum or internship sites when a training institution asks for audiotapes of the supervisee's clinical work. Although client resistance to taping may be real and must be addressed in a sensitive and ethical manner, it is often not the client but the supervisee who is experiencing the greatest amount of discomfort at the prospect of being taped (and therefore scrutinized). In fact, the majority of clients are open to having their sessions audiotaped if the supervisee's demeanor is professional when presenting the topic of audiotaping and they have an assurance that confidentiality will not be compromised. Additionally, once over their initial reactions, Ellis, Krengel, and Beck (2002) found that taping (audio or video) did not cause significant anxiety in supervisees. In

fact, any aversive reactions to taping as a supervision method were negligible.

Planning Audiotape-Based Supervision. The least productive way to use an audiotape in supervision may be that which is depicted in the following example: The supervisee arrives with two or three audiotapes of recent counseling sessions, without having reviewed any of them privately. Because the supervisee has made no decision about which session to discuss during supervision, the supervisee spends several minutes telling the supervisor about the different cases represented on tape. The supervisor eventually picks one tape, which the supervisee must then rewind. The counseling session is played from the beginning until something strikes the supervisor as important.

Our point is simple: The process of supervision must be based on a plan, and it is the supervisor's responsibility to outline that plan. We do believe that spontaneity is important, but it is unlikely to emerge when the supervision process is tedious. Listening to an audiotape for 20 minutes with a supervisee saying, "Gee, I guess the part I was talking about was further into the session than I realized" is one sure way to add to the tedium of supervision.

Audiotaped segments of counseling can be used in several ways for supervision. West, Bubenzer, Pinsoneault, and Holeman (1993) noted that delayed reviews of audiotapes (and videotapes) are best used to facilitate the supervisee's perceptual–conceptual skills. Goldberg (1985) identified several teaching goals that can be accomplished using audiotape, including focusing on specific therapy techniques, helping the supervisee see the relationship between process and content, focusing on how things are said (paralanguage), and helping the supervisee differentiate between a conversational tone and a therapeutic one. Audiotape can also be used to provide an experiential moment for the supervisee if a segment of tape is chosen where it is obvious that the supervisee is struggling personally or interpersonally in the taped session.

During the initial phase of a supervision relationship, it may be advisable for the supervisor to listen to an entire counseling session prior to supervision in order to get an overview of the supervisee's ability and have control over what segment of tape will be chosen for supervision (Borders & Brown, 2005). It is important also to help the supervisee understand the rationale behind the choice of a taped segment if this is not apparent. Preselected segments can be chosen for a variety of reasons:

1. To highlight the most productive part of the session
2. To highlight the most important part of the session
3. To highlight the part of the session where the supervisee is struggling the most
4. To underscore any number of content issues, including metaphors and recurring themes
5. To ask about a confusing part of the session, perhaps because paralanguage contradicts content
6. To focus attention on the point in the session where interpersonal or cross-cultural

dynamics were either particularly therapeutic or particularly strained, or where cultural encapsulation is evident (Cashwell, Looby, & Housley, 1997).

In other words, supervisors will almost always have in mind a teaching function when they preselect a section of audiotape for supervision.

This process should evolve, however, as the supervisee develops in conceptual ability and experience. Relatively quickly the supervisee can be preselecting the section of tape that will determine the direction of supervision. Often supervisees are just asked to choose a part of the session where they felt confused, lost, overwhelmed, or frustrated. The supervisor will then listen to the segment with them and proceed from there. If this format is used, the supervisee should be prepared to

- State the reason for selecting this part of the session for discussion in supervision
- Briefly state what transpired up to that point
- Explain what he or she was trying to accomplish at that point in the session
- Clearly state the specific help desired from the supervisor

Although audiotaping is a valid supervision format, any format used repeatedly may contribute to supervision becoming stagnant. When the supervisee is repeatedly asked to select a troublesome tape segment, for example, the supervision may become skewed toward problems in counseling sessions, with little opportunity for the supervisee to enjoy successes in supervision.

As an alternative method of using audiotapes, the supervisor might assign a theme for the next session and ask the supervisee to be responsible for producing the segment of tape. For example, the supervisor might suggest that reframing would be of great help for a particular client or family and that the supervisee should try to reframe as often as possible in the next session and choose the most successful of these attempts to present in the next supervision session. In addition to using supervision to sharpen a skill, this strategy also allows the supervisor to connect technique to a counseling situation and to get data on the supervisee's self-evaluation ability. The types of assignments that can direct the use of audiotape are potentially limitless and can focus on the process of therapy, the conceptual issues in therapy, personal or interpersonal issues, and ethical dilemmas, among others; it can also reflect different supervisee developmental levels. In summary, careful preselection of an audiotape segment is perhaps most crucial in making the audiotape a powerful supervision tool.

Although the use of direct supervision methods is not usually associated with psychodynamic approaches to therapy, Aveline (1992) and Brandell (1992) addressed the unique advantages of using audiotaped segments in supervision. In a particularly adroit description of the benefit of hearing a supervisee's session, Aveline stated:

> I am stimulated by the way in which words are used, the metaphors deployed and the images evoked. Snatches of interaction often vividly illustrate the central dilemmas of a person's life. . . . The medium is particularly well placed to identify such phenomena as the patient filling all the space of [the] session with words so as to leave no room for the therapist to say anything for fear that what might be said will disrupt the inner equilibrium; the nervous laugh that as surely indicates that there is an issue of importance at hand as does the bird with trailing wing that the nest is nearby; the therapist whose words of encouragement are belied by his impatient tone or gesture; and the patient whose placatory dependence is shot through with hostility. (p. 350)

Despite his convincing and poetic arguments in favor of the use of audiotaping for supervision, Aveline also cautioned that there are significant disadvantages. Primarily, Aveline argued that a tape recorder *always* has an effect on therapy, and its meaning to the client (and the therapist) must be explored. He cautioned that taping might even be abusive to a client who is in too weak a position to refute its use. Similarly, Aveline saw the possibility that taping could hurt the supervisory relationship if the exposure that the tape allowed led to humiliation for the therapist. In all cases,

Aveline stressed that the supervisor must be willing to address the consequences that the audiotape has produced. "Taping is a supervisory aid; it is servant, not master" (Aveline, 1992, p. 351). Aveline's insights notwithstanding, we assert that direct samples of supervisee work may be an ethical necessity in some instances and most assuredly is so for the novice supervisee.

Written Critique of Audiotapes. For supervisees who are more visual than auditory, the supervisor can combine a written analysis of an audiotape with individual supervision. Many supervisors choose to listen to tapes between supervision sessions rather than during them. This is especially so during the beginning stages of supervision. Rather than taking notes to use in a subsequent supervision session, the supervisor writes feedback regarding the session that can be given to the supervisee. This exercise forces the supervisor to conceptualize the feedback before the supervision session. Additionally, the critiques automatically become a record of supervision; they allow the supervisee to review comments made by the supervisor; and they can become a way of coordinating supervision if other supervisors are involved (e.g., a site supervisor could be sent a copy of the feedback prepared by the university supervisor). In fact, the written critiques serve as excellent instructional material for the training of supervisors in the planning and giving of feedback. It must be noted, however, that such written feedback does not replace either individual or group supervision.

Transcripts. Finally, supervisors occasionally ask supervisees to transcribe their audiotapes (or their videotapes) and submit these for supervision. Arthur and Gfoerer (2002) argued that transcripts were especially helpful for supervisees in early stages of training (e.g., a first practicum). They proposed that basing supervision on transcripts of sessions facilitates a collaborative style of feedback and becomes a building block toward supervision that is more helpful for an intermediate or advanced intern. In other words, because the sessions are in print form, it is more likely that supervisees will be able to notice faulty interventions, such as multiple questions or a run of incomplete statements, than might be possible using audiotape alone. This, then, allows the student greater opportunity to critique their own work (at this early stage) than taping alone might afford. Additionally, because transcripts utilize a more familiar educational modality (a paper document), it may be helpful for students who seem to be having a particularly difficult time making the transition from traditional classroom contexts to clinical supervision.

Arthur and Gfoerer (2002) gathered survey data from 30 graduates of a training program, all of whom had been supervised by the same supervisor using transcription as the focus of supervision. For the questions regarding the value of the transcripts, 11 of 12 were answered positively by the vast majority of the respondents. Only the item "The use of transcripts made me anxious" caused mixed results. While 16 of the 30 disagreed with this statement, 13 agreed (and 1 gave no response). It is unknown, however, if those who found this form of supervision anxiety provoking would have found another form to be less so.

Arthur and Gfoerer (2002) also asked their respondents to identify positive and negative attributes that they associated with transcript use in supervision. Positive attributes included the facts that the supervisor reviewed the whole session, that transcripts gave supervisees a visual reminder of the session, and that transcripts were concrete and allowed for equally concrete examples of what they needed to work on, thus making it easier for them to critique their own work. Negative attributes associated with the transcripts were that they were so time consuming for both intern and supervisor, that nonverbal cues and all paralanguage were not included in supervision, that mistakes were even more visible than they may have been through other supervision modalities, and that they were too focused on the content of a session, rather than the overall development of the supervisee.

Transcripts of counseling sessions provide an enormous amount of material for a subsequent supervision session. They seem to result in several positive outcomes, at least for novice interns. In light of the time-consuming nature of this form of supervision, however, as well as its other limitations, perhaps an intermittent or abbreviated (i.e., transcription of a certain number of minutes of a session) use of this supervision method represents its optimal use.

Videotape

Although the audiotape is still our backup, the videotape has certainly taken center stage as the technology of choice in supervision (e.g., Carlozzi, Romans, Boswell, Ferguson, & Whisenhunt, 1997; Lee et al., 2004; Romans et al., 1995; Wetchler et al., 1989). Those who use videotape have tended to be firm about its superiority over audiotape (e.g., Broder & Sloman, 1982; Stoltenberg & Delworth, 1987). We want to emphasize, however, that many of the process variables that we mentioned for using audiotape could be used with videotape, as well as the reverse.

With no intention of insulting our readers, we will point out that the videotape has one major advantage, the addition of the picture, and two major disadvantages, its expense and its relative bulk (though costs are reasonable and better equipment continues to reduce the latter issue as well). To say that a picture is worth a thousand words is less trite when one sees a client that one has heard but not seen up to that time. A voice that is gruff matched with an expression that is gentle, a precise presentation of plot when the physical presentation is disorganized, the smiles, the nods, the looking away, the hand gestures—all comprise a wealth of information. When the client is a family, the phenomenon grows exponentially (which may explain why Lee et al., 2004, found that marriage and family therapy supervisors prefer videotape over audiotape). In fact, experiencing an overload of data is one of the reasons that Goldberg (1985) suggested using videotape at later stages of supervision. Or, as Rubinstein and Hammond (1982) once aptly put it, "[p]aradoxically, the greatest limitation of videotape may result from what it best provides the supervisor—a wealth of material about the recorded session" (p. 161).

Munson (1983) once made an observation that still merits consideration. He speculated that the associations that supervisees may make between videotaped supervision and commercial television can present a problem. Because television connotes entertainment, Munson saw the dual problem of observers not finding others' sessions entertaining enough and supervisees feeling they must "perform" on videotape, thereby suffering from excessive "performance anxiety." The supervisor's role, according to Munson, includes structuring supervision so that observers are stimulated cognitively (usually by means of a specific task related to the videotaped segment), while at the same time attempting to safeguard the integrity of the supervisee on tape. Munson's admonition has been supported by empirical findings that videotape review of counseling sessions caused a shift from positive mood about a counseling session to a lowered mood for therapists and therapists-in-training after videotape review (Hill et al., 1994). It seems, therefore, that the obvious advantage of videotape can become a liability and must be monitored carefully by the supervisor. As one of our supervisees put it, "[v]ideotape is a little like some hotel room mirrors; the reflection is *too* accurate."

Despite valid cautions regarding the use of videotape in supervision, there is no question that our knowledge base and experiential alternatives have increased greatly as a result of this technology. With videotape, supervisees can literally see themselves in the role of helper, thus allowing them to be an observer of their work, which is not possible with audiotape.

In an excellent discussion of the use of videotape in the supervision of marriage and family therapy, Breunlin, Karrer, McGuire, & Cimmarusti (1988) argued that videotape supervision should not only be focused on the interaction between supervisee and clients but also on the far more subtle internal processes experienced by the supervisee during both the therapy session and the supervision session. To focus on one to the exclusion of the other would be an error, according to Breunlin et al. Furthermore, they stated that therapists can never be objective observers of their own roles separate from the family (or individual) client, as this is an interactional impossibility. Breunlin et al., therefore, recommended six guidelines for working with both the cold accuracy of the videotape and the dynamic reality experienced by the supervisee (pp. 199–204). These guidelines, when followed, help to alleviate some of the dangers noted by Munson (1983) and Hill et al. (1994). (We should note that the guidelines outlined by Breunlin et al. also apply to other methods of supervision.)

1. *Focus videotape supervision by setting realistic goals for the supervised therapy session.* This has two advantages: It reduces the sense of information overload by narrowing down the field to those interventions that are connected to goals, and it increases the possibility that the supervisee will emerge from the session moderately satisfied because realistic goals are attainable.

2. *Relate internal process across contexts.* The point here is that what the supervisee experiences in the session is important to discuss in supervision. Furthermore, Breunlin et al. emphasized that supervisors should allow supervisees to disclose their perceptions first, rather than supervisors offering their observations. Most important, however, is the issue of validating the internal processes of the supervisee, rather than forfeiting such a discussion in favor of "strategy review." Interpersonal process recall (Kagan, 1976, 1980; Kagan & Kagan, 1997), as described later in this chapter, is an excellent technique for meeting this guideline.

3. *Select tape segments that focus on remedial performance.* The authors explained this guideline as providing corrective feedback about performance that the supervisee has the ability to change. In other words, focusing on aspects of the supervisee's personal style or on skills that are too complex for immediate attainment will be nonproductive.

4. *Use supervisor comments to create a moderate evaluation of performance.* The authors relied on the research of Fuller and Manning (1973) to arrive at this guideline. The latter found that a moderate discrepancy between performance and the target goal is optimal for learning. Therefore, the supervisor must find videotape segments that are neither exemplary nor too far from the stated goal. We can begin to appreciate the kind of supervisor commitment that is required to use the suggestions of Breunlin et al. (1988).

5. *Refine goals moderately.* This guideline underscores the fact that videotape review must be seen in the larger context of supervisee development. Sometimes the multitude of possibilities that a review can generate are irrespective of the skill level of the supervisee. Additionally, Breunlin et al. reminded us that what appears easy when viewing a session can be far more difficult to pull off in therapy. Small increments of improvement, therefore, should be targeted by the supervisor.

6. *Maintain a moderate level of arousal.* The authors posited that attending to the first five guidelines will take care of the sixth. The supervisor, however, must always be cautious that the supervisee is stimulated to grow without becoming overly threatened. Therefore, the supervisor, as always, must be alert to multiple levels of experience.

Also addressing supervisee internal processes, Rubinstein and Hammond (1982) maintained early on that the supervisor who uses videotape must have a healthy respect for its power. There is no hiding from the stark reality of one's picture and voice being projected into the supervision room. Therefore, Rubinstein and Hammond cautioned that videotape should not be used unless there is a relatively good relationship between supervisor and supervisee. We would concur up to a point, but also postulate that a good relationship can be formed in the process of using videotape with sensitivity. In addition, the supervisee will

be far less camera shy if videotape was used in training prior to supervision. Rubinstein and Hammond made one fine suggestion that supervisors appear on videotape prior to having their supervisees do the same. More recently, Kaplan, Rothrock, and Culkin (1999) also suggested this kind of modeling. Providing samples of one's own counseling can serve many purposes, but especially attractive is dispelling the myth that supervisors conduct perfect therapy sessions. As all supervisors know, the insight and cleverness that are evidenced in supervision are rarely matched in one's own therapy, at least not without the occasional misstep.

Finally, Rubinstein and Hammond suggested that the use of the videotape remain technologically simple. They are not in favor of split screens, superimposed images, or other such equipment capabilities, believing that it detracts from the lifelike experience of watching the taped session. Of course, decisions about using videotape reflect the supervisor's comfort, or lack thereof, with this type of technology, as well as the supervision goals. And yet, as we stated earlier, supervisor comfort and technological expertise may need to increase as the present technological revolution continues. Each supervisor ultimately will find a viable comfort level with technological advances, but the supervisor would still be wise to remember Rubinstein and Hammond's caution lest technology and its multiple uses become the center of supervision.

Interpersonal Process Recall. Perhaps the most widely known supervision method using videotape is interpersonal process recall (IPR) (Kagan, 1976, 1980; Kagan & Kagan, 1997; Kagan & Krathwohl, 1967; Kagan, Krathwohl, & Farquahar, 1965; Kagan, Krathwohl, & Miller, 1963). An earlier national survey of counselor education programs (Borders & Leddick, 1988) found that, at that time, IPR was one of only two clearly delineated methods of supervision taught in supervision courses, the other being live supervision. IPR began as a therapy model and occasionally is still used as such; for our purposes here, however, we will confine ourselves to the use of IPR in supervision. Kagan (1980) asserted that there are many psychological barriers to open, honest communication and that these operate in counseling and therapy as they do in other daily interactions. Primary among these is the strongly socialized habit of behaving diplomatically. As a result, much of what a supervisee thinks, intuits, and feels during counseling and therapy is disregarded almost automatically, because allowing such perceptions to surface would confront the predisposition to be diplomatic.

The purpose of IPR, then, is to give the supervisee a safe haven for these internal reactions. Kagan (1980) strongly maintained that all persons are "the best authority of their own dynamics and the best interpreter of their own experience" (pp. 279–280). Starting with this assumption, therefore, the supervisor's role becomes that of a facilitator to stimulate the awareness of the supervisee beyond the point at which it operated during the counseling session.

The process of IPR is relatively simple. The supervisor and supervisee view a prerecorded videotape of a counseling session together. Any point at which either person believes that something of importance is happening on tape, especially something that is not being addressed in the counseling session, the videotape is stopped (dual controls are helpful, but it is easy enough to signal the person holding the controls to stop the tape). If the supervisee stops the tape, the supervisee will speak first, saying, for example "I was getting really frustrated here. I didn't know what she wanted. We had been over all of this before. I thought it was resolved last week but here it is again." At this point, it is essential that the supervisor refrain from adopting a teaching role to instruct the supervisee about what might have been done. Rather, the supervisor needs to allow the supervisee the psychological space to investigate internal processes to some resolution. At the same time, the good facilitator, or "inquirer," as Kagan preferred to call the role, can ask direct questions that are challenging to the supervisee. Some possibilities for the above example include:

What do you wish you had said to her? How do you think she might have reacted if you said those things to her? What kept you from saying what you wanted to say? If you had the opportunity now, how might you tell her what you are thinking and feeling? Once it is felt that the dynamics for the chosen segment of tape have been sufficiently reexamined, the tape is allowed to continue.

Table 9.2 lists a variety of lead statements that reflect different supervision goals. Specifically, leads are listed that inspire affective exploration, check out unstated agendas, encourage cognitive examination, get at images, or help to search out expectations. As one can certainly discern, this process is slow. Only a portion of a therapy session can be reviewed in this manner unless supervision is extended significantly. Therefore, choosing the most interpersonally weighted or most metaphorically meaningful segment of videotape will be most productive for supervision purposes.

One caution is advisable: Because IPR often puts interpersonal dynamics under a microscope, it is possible that they will be magnified to the extent of distortion (Bernard, 1981). In other words, what is a perfectly functional helping relationship can come to look somehow dysfunctional when overexposed, and as all persons in the helping professions know, some relationship dynamics are best left underexposed. We need not be in perfect sync with all our clients to be of help to them. The clinical skill comes in determining which interactions are important and which are not. IPR is not a method to guide what is to be examined. Therefore, it is up to the supervisor and supervisee to decide which interactions warrant exploration and which do not. Because the supervisee is usually more reticent than the supervisor, the supervisor will most often be left to make such decisions. Answering the following two questions may be useful in selecting segments for IPR: From what I can observe, does this interaction seem to be interrupting the flow of counseling? From what I know of the supervisee, would focusing on this interaction aid in his or her development as a mental health professional?

TABLE 9.2 Supervisor Leads for Use with Interpersonal Process Recall

Leads That Inspire Affective Exploration
• How did that make you feel?
• How did that make you feel about him or her?
• Do you remember what you were feeling?
• Were you aware of any feelings?
• What do those feelings mean to you?
• Does that feeling have any special meaning to you?
• Is it a familiar feeling?
• What did you do (or decide to do) about that feeling you had?
• Did you want to express that feeling at any time?
• Did you have any fantasies of taking any risk?

Leads That Check Out Unstated Agendas
• What would you have liked to have said to her or him at this point?
• What's happening here?
• What did you feel like doing?
• How were you feeling about your role as counselor at this point?
• What had that meant to you?
• If you had more time, where would you have liked to have gone?

Leads That Encourage Cognitive Examination
• What were you thinking at that time?
• What thoughts were you having about the other person at that time?
• Something going on there?
• Anything going on there?
• Had you any ideas about what you wanted to do with that?
• Did you fantasize taking any risks?
• Were you able to say it the way you wanted to?
• Did you want to say anything else then?
• Did you have any plan of where you wanted the session to go next?
• Did you think that the other person knew what you wanted?
• What kind of image were you aware of projecting?
• Is that the image you wanted to project?
• Can you recall what effect the setting had on you or the interaction?
• Can you recall what effect you thought that the setting had on the other person?
• Did the equipment affect you in any way?
• (If reaction to the recorder) What did you want, or not want, the recorder to hear from you?

Leads That Get at Images
• Were you having any fantasies at that moment?
• Were any pictures, images, or memories flashing through your mind then?
• What was going on in your mind at that time?
• Did it remind you of anything?
• Did you think that you had "been there before"? Is that familiar to you?
• Where had that put you in the past?

Leads That Explore Mutual Perceptions Between Client and Counselor
• What did you think that she or he was feeling about you?
• How do you think that she or he was seeing you at that point?

- Do you think that she or he was aware of your feelings? Your thoughts?
- What message do you think that she or he was trying to give you?
- Did you feel that he or she had any expectations of you at that point?
- What did you think that she or he wanted you to think or feel or do?
- Do you think that your description of the interaction would coincide with her or his description?
- Was she or he giving you any cues as to how she or he was feeling?
- How do you think that she or he felt about talking about this problem?
- How do you think that she or he felt about continuing to talk with you at this point?

Leads That Help Search Out Expectations
- What did you want her or him to tell you?
- What did you want to hear?
- What would you have liked from her or him?
- Were you expecting anything of her or him at that point?
- Did you want her or him to see you in some particular way? How?
- What do you think that her or his perceptions were of you?
- What message did you want to give to her or him?
- Was there anything in particular that you wanted her or him to say or do or think?
- Was she or he "with you"? How did her or his responses hit you?
- What did you really want to tell her or him at this moment? What prevented you from doing so?
- What did you want her or him to do?
- Did you want her or him to do something that would have made it easier for you?
- What would that have been?

Finally, it is important that the supervisor refrain from asking questions to make statements. Loaded questions will very quickly be discerned by the supervisee and will most assuredly shut down the process as it was intended. For this reason, it is not advisable to use IPR when direct feedback is warranted. As an example, cultural encapsulation may need to be addressed initially in a different manner. Once a learning goal around cultural competence has been established, IPR can serve the purpose of assisting the supervisee to process internal filters operating during a counseling session.

The Reflective Process

Encouraging reflective practice is an overriding supervision goal. We place our discussion here because some authors (e.g., Goodyear & Nelson, 1997) described efforts to develop reflectivity in supervisees as an elaboration on some of the tenets of IPR. Neufeldt et al. (1996) provided the following description of the reflective process:

> *The reflective process itself is a search for under-standing of the phenomena of the counseling session, with attention to therapist actions, emotions, and thoughts, as well as to the interaction between the therapist and the client. The intent to understand what has occurred, active inquiry, openness to that understanding, and vulnerability and risk-taking, rather than defensive self-protection, characterize the stance of the reflective supervisee. Supervisees use theory, their prior personal and professional experience, and their experience of themselves in the counseling session as sources of understanding. If they are to contribute to future development, reflections must be profound rather than superficial and must be meaningful to the supervisees. To complete the sequence, reflectivity in supervision leads to changes in perception, changes in counseling practice, and an increased capacity to make meaning of experiences. (p. 8)*

As was discussed in Chapter 5, Neufeldt et al. (1996) noted that supervisee personality and cognitive capacities, as well as the supervision environment, must be considered when attempting to move the supervisee toward reflectivity. As might be surmised by the reader, producing a reflective practitioner may be the most challenging task of the clinical supervisor and requires deliberate models of intervention (Guiffrida, 2005).

Prior to discussing ways to encourage reflectivity, we should note that the focus on reflectivity is paired with the knowledge that expertise in counseling or psychotherapy is not a brief process. Skovholt, Rønnestad, and Jennings (1997) concluded that it takes a minimum of 10 years to move from novice to expert in any specific area of therapy practice. Referring to this conclusion, Nelson and Neufeldt (1998) emphasized the short amount of time that supervisors typically have with supervisees and the importance, therefore, that reflective tools are established so that supervisees can contribute to their own subsequent development. Nelson and Neufeldt also specified what needs to occur in order for reflection to occur:

> *there must be a problem, a dilemma—something about which the learner feels confusion or dissonance and intends to search for a solution. The problem should revolve around an issue of consequence, one that is important to good practice. Reflection occurs in a context of the learner's capacity to tolerate the ambiguity of not knowing and an educational setting in which the learner has space to struggle with ideas as well as the safety to experience not knowing as acceptable.* (pp. 81–82)

Therefore, the first task of the supervisor is to establish a context for reflection. To do this, they must at the very least provide time, encouragement, and psychological space for this activity, as well as a supervisory relationship that is built on trust (Nelson & Neufeldt, 1998; Osborn, Paez, & Carrabine, 2007; Ward & House, 1998). Guiffrida (2005) suggested that theory should be de-emphasized as novices become familiar with counseling practice; he suggested that supervisors assist counselors-in-training to identify their conceptual

orientations to practice by providing supervision that is organized around reflective interventions. Several authors have offered suggestions for such interventions (Borders, 2006; Deal, 2003; Griffith & Frieden, 2000; Guiffrida, 2005; Knowles, Gilbourne, Tomlinson, & Anderson, 2007; Koch et al., 2000; Neufeldt, 1999).

Griffith and Frieden (2000) argued the usefulness of four supervision interventions to facilitate reflective thinking among supervisees, all of which have been supported by others as well. The first of these is Socratic questioning, emphasizing the role of the supervisor as the source of important questions, rather than the source of all the answers. This age-old method of stimulating reflection is highly relevant to clinical contexts. Griffith and Frieden encouraged primarily "how" and "what" questions to help dualistic thinkers to broaden their horizons. While Socratic questioning may be best used in group supervision contexts, it certainly has a place in individual supervision as well. Guiffrida's (2005) Emergence Model of counselor development seems to support a Socratic approach as a process for helping supervisees to identify their instincts and preexisting knowledge as it relates to their present interventions with clients. Deal (2003) concurred that the quality of supervisor questions is key to supervisee development as reflective, discriminating thinkers.

A second suggestion is that supervisors require supervisees to engage in journal writing (Griffith & Frieden, 2000; Guiffrida, 2005; Knowles et al., 2007). While journals are often used early in the training program, they are less likely to be used as part of supervision. The advantage of journaling is that it not only helps supervisees to critically evaluate their counseling and external conditions, but to focus on their internal reality, including painful emotional experiences that are stimulated by either the therapeutic or supervisory context. Additionally, journal writing can be used to assist students to move beyond a description of events in counseling to identifying themes and patterns, thus assisting them in the necessary cognitive development from concrete thinking to that which is more complex and abstract (Rigazio-DiGilio et al., 1997).

The third strategy suggested by Griffith and Frieden (2000) is IPR, which has already been described in this chapter. Griffith and Frieden agreed with Kagan that well-constructed reflective probes could stimulate new insight for the supervisee regarding internal processes that may have been outside the supervisee's consciousness, but nevertheless influenced the direction of counseling.

Griffith and Frieden's last strategy is the use of a reflective team (Anderson, 1987) which they described within a group supervision format. The reflective team technique is primarily used during live supervision (see Chapter 11). More recently, however, Stinchfield, Hill, and Kleist (2007) have described the use of a reflective process for triadic supervision. In their model, supervisees are allowed an opportunity to reflect on their own work as they listen to a peer and their supervisor discuss their presentation of their counseling; alternatively, they engage in an observer–reflector role when it is their peer's turn to present a case. Stinchfield et al. argued that this model allows for the benefits of more traditional individual supervision as well as stimulating inner dialogues that "occur only within oneself, informed by the ideas constructed while engaging in or listening to outer dialogues" (p. 174). Stinchfield et al. further asserted that inner dialogues—when matched with the insights of a peer and a supervisor—are reflective in nature and potentially formative. Reporting on their qualitative investigation, Lawson, Hein, and Stuart (in press) supported the notion that vicarious learning is a key component of triadic supervision. They also found, however, that successful triadic supervision was dependent on the level of compatibility between supervisees. Here, then, is an excellent example of the interface of one supervision dynamic (relationship) with another (increasing reflectivity using triadic supervision). Methods and techniques, therefore, must constantly be considered within the larger contexts of relationship variables, ethical mandates, and so forth.

While presented for implementation as a group supervision activity, Koch et al. (2000) described an approach to engaging students in reflective practice that spans an entire semester of supervision. Each supervisee is first invited to reflect on a dilemma that resonates for them, consistent with Nelson and Neufeldt's (1998) conditions for reflectivity. Typical examples would include these: How can I prevent clients from manipulating me? How do I keep focused on a client's concerns and keep my personal issues from clouding my judgment? How can I know when racism is affecting my behavior? Once they have been challenged to reflect, supervisees are asked to spend a couple of weeks identifying their own dilemma while the supervisor stays alert to the same for them during supervision. Several weeks into the semester, supervisees are asked to present their dilemma to their peers. The other students in the supervision group are advised to ask open-ended questions to gain clarity (and are discouraged from giving advice). Following this session, which includes debriefing for the supervisee involved, the supervisee is asked to develop an action plan to help him or her to address the dilemma. Koch et al. cautioned that supervision after this point must continue to encourage reflectivity through assignments such as a reflection journal. They also emphasized the importance for the supervisee to follow contemplation with "making informed decisions and taking action in a way that addresses the dilemmas in a socially and ethically responsible manner" (pp. 263–264). In this way, the supervisee experiences a complete process from problem identification through reflection and growth to some resolution. Supervisees should also be aware that this process can and should be revisited at more profound levels.

Inspired by the work of Skovholt and Rønnestad (1995), who determined the importance of continuous professional reflection, Neufeldt (1999) advanced the importance of helping supervisees learn to self-reflect. Supervisees are directed to respond to a number of questions (see Table 9.3) immediately after a session in which they encountered a puzzle or dilemma. Although time

TABLE 9.3   Self-Reflection Activity: Questions to Answer Regarding a Therapy Session Dilemma

1. Describe the therapy events that precipitated your puzzlement.
2. State your question about these events as clearly as you can.
3. What were you thinking during this portion of the session?
4. What were you feeling? How do you understand those feelings now?
5. Consider your own actions during this portion of the session. What did you intend?
6. Now look at the interaction between you and the client. What were the results of your interventions?
7. What was the feel, the emotional flavor, of the interaction between you? Was it similar to or different from your usual experience with this client?
8. To what degree do you understand this interaction as similar to the client's interactions in other relationships? How does this inform your experience of the interaction in session?
9. What theories do you use to understand what is going on in session?
10. What past professional or personal experiences affect your understanding?
11. How else might you interpret the event and interaction in the session?
12. How might you test out the various alternatives in your next counseling session? (Be sure to look for what confirms and what disconfirms your interpretations.)
13. How will the clients' responses inform what you do next?

Source: From "Training in Reflective Processes in Supervision," by S. A. Neufeldt, 1999, in *Training Counselling Supervisors* (p. 101), by E. Holloway and M. Carroll (Eds.), London: Sage Publications.

consuming, challenging supervisees to complete such an assessment independently is essential for helping them to claim ownership of reflective skills. Of course, this exercise can become the subject of a subsequent supervision session as well.

Finally, Borders (2006) and Borders & Brown (2005) advanced a supervisor approach that she described as "thinking-aloud." In this approach, the supervisor models a reflective, decision-making process that can occur during a counseling session. Borders emphasized the importance that supervisors "think aloud" in ways that are developmentally appropriate for the supervisee and challenge the supervisee to stretch their thinking about clients and about their work with them. Supervisor's statements often include observations regarding the client; reflections about the client's behavior across sessions; awareness of the supervisee's internal processes in reaction to the client; and some attempt to integrate the information presented to the supervisee, including information that has been presented to them externally as well as insights that have surfaced from internal processes (Borders & Brown, 2005). This

technique provides a mirror to IPR in that the supervisor offers reflective observations for the benefit of the supervisee rather than asking questions in a manner that requires the supervisee to reflect upon their internal reality. Osborn et al. (2007) concurred that this modeling of reflective thinking by supervisors was very important for supervisees to experience.

Nonlinear Strategies.   A perusal of recent literature in clinical supervision finds that two topics seem to have special currency: the use of technology for supervision and a cluster of contributions that might be summarized as nonlinear or relying on "right-brain" strategies to enhance supervision (Bernard, 2005). Those authors who describe the use of nonlinear strategies for supervision consistently claim that they increase reflectivity (Dean, 2001; Fall & Sutton, 2004; Guiffrida, Jordan, Saiz, & Barnes, 2007; McNamee & McWey, 2004; Mullen, Luke, & Drewes, 2007; Sommer & Cox, 2003, 2006; Ward & Sommer, 2006). For example, the use of the sandtray technique (Dean, 2001; Fall & Sutton, 2004; Guiffrida et al., 2007;

Mullen, Luke, & Drewes, 2007) allows the supervisee to symbolically represent counseling dynamics using a variety of small figures in sand. The choice of figures to represent each person in the counseling system and the use of space to depict relationship dynamics, often offer insights that were beyond the supervisee's awareness when describing a case verbally. Additional insights are possible if the technique is used by someone else listening to the supervisee's case presentation (either the supervisor or a peer). And the creative use of the figurines to symbolize people, events, and relationship dynamics give the supervisee a great deal of "new" information to reflect upon. In the same way that "a picture equals a thousand words," drawing a "picture" of dynamics using a variety of symbols can be profound for some supervisees. For this reason, Dean (2001) suggested that the technique be used only after a comfortable relationship between supervisor and supervisee has been established. A full description of this technique is described in Fall and Sutton (2004) for use in group supervision.

Sommer and her colleagues (Sommer & Cox, 2003, 2006; Ward & Sommer, 2006) described the use of the rich themes of mythology and fairy tales to help supervisees make meaning of their own development as counselors and of the supervision process. They argued that stories ranging from classics to children's stories can be chosen by supervisors to address a multitude of developmental tasks, thus bringing home the universality of issues that supervisees often believe are unique to them. In short, just as film and literature has been used to embellish counseling, Sommer and her colleagues argued that the arts can assist supervisees to reflect on their development within supervision.

Guiffrida et al. (2007) reviewed the use of metaphor in supervision to assist the supervisee in understanding the process of becoming a mental health professional and to facilitate case-conceptualization skills. They concluded that it was important for supervisees to be amenable to activities such as using metaphoric drawing activities in order for them to be effective, and that the

success of such techniques also depended on supervisor comfort in using them. Guiffrida et al. also reported that, to date, the efficacy of such techniques is primarily anecdotal. Still, it seems to us that the use of metaphor is probably underutilized in most clinical supervision. Although a direct question such as "How do you experience your client?" may have a brief impact on the supervisee, a question such as, "If you were to describe your experience of your client from the animal kingdom, would she be a possum, a porcupine, a kitten, a tiger, or yet some other animal?" might not only open up new insights but linger beyond a supervision session. When creative juices are activated, their life span can be longer than their more logical counterparts.

We conclude this section on reflective practice by referring to Carroll's (2001) use of the concept of the "philosophy of supervision." Carroll drew a distinction between "functional" supervision (supervision as technology) and a philosophy of supervision that focused on the "being" of people and the meaning supervision has for the supervisor. That is, supervision is not something someone *does,* but something that someone *is.* In short, supervisors who have a philosophy of supervision reflect on their supervision; they view reflective behavior as something to engage, not something to teach. Only through their own reflection can the supervisor continue to pair functional supervision with a maturing philosophy of supervision. Clearly, Carroll implied that a nonreflective supervisor would be hard-pressed to create a reflective context for others. Perhaps concerning this issue, more than around many other activities, "do as I do" is the only credible posture.

Live Observation

Live observation is a frequent form of supervision in many training programs; it is used less frequently in the field because of scheduling difficulties and structural constraints. We differentiate between live observation and live supervision, the former being a method of observing the supervisee, but not interacting with the supervisee during the session (except in the case of an emergency) and the latter being a combination of observation and active supervision during the session. Because the involvement of the supervisor in live supervision represents a paradigm shift from all other supervisory methods, we treat it separately in Chapter 11.

Live observation offers several advantages over all other forms of supervision, with the exception of live supervision. First, there is a high safeguard for client welfare when live observation is employed because the supervisor is immediately available to intervene in case of emergency. A second advantage of live observation is that it affords the supervisor a more complete picture of clients and supervisees than is attainable through the use of audiotape or videotape. When using videotape, for example, the camera position is often fixed throughout a session, giving only side views of both client and supervisee or focusing on one or the other exclusively. Supervisors who have used both live observation and taping can certainly attest to the more firsthand experience that live observation provides.

A third, and perhaps most utilized, advantage of live observation is that it offers the utmost flexibility regarding the timing of the case conference. Should the supervisor choose to conduct supervision immediately after the counseling session, the supervisee has the maximum amount of time available to use supervision in preparing for the next counseling session. Certainly, the use of live observation will reduce the chances of a most frustrating situation when the supervisor is watching a videotape of a session only to be told that the supervisee has seen the client again since the video was made. It is difficult to make supervision fresh when the therapy session is stale. Because the timing of a supervision session affects all individual supervision, we will address this topic separately.

One advantage of live observation must be monitored carefully. When other supervisees are present in the observation room, there is an opportunity to offer instruction based on the session that is transpiring. This instruction can become overly candid, and the supervisor might point out dynamics that he or she might be less likely to share with the counselor conducting the session. This, of course, is inappropriate and will affect the level of trust among all the members of the supervisory group. Whenever other supervisees are present during an observation, a protocol must be established, such as that all comments will be shared with the counselor either in individual or group supervision.

Technology and Supervision

Generally speaking, there are three different uses of technology within clinical supervision: (1) To provide the supervisor with samples of the supervisee's work; (2) to bridge distance between the supervisee and the supervisor; and (3) to influence the process of supervision.

Up to this point in this chapter, we have discussed technology as a means of providing the supervisor with samples of the supervisee's work (e.g., use of the audiotape, the videotape, or capability for live observation). And as we have already stated, even the most commonplace form of technology (e.g., the audiotape) should be used with its advantages and disadvantages in mind. Manosevitz (2006) reported on a round table discussion regarding the use of the telephone for supervisees of psychoanalysis. As cell phones have become ever present in our lives, even the use of the telephone for supervision may need serious assessment.

Using technology to bridge distance between the supervisee and the supervisor is, in effect, using technology to conquer geography (Bernard, 2005). Several authors have reported use of technology for this purpose (e.g., Court & Winwood, 2005; Dudding & Justice, 2004; Kanz, 2001; Panos, 2005; Schultz & Finger, 2003). Among the many arguments made for using technology to bridge distance include serving rural and other sparsely populated areas, providing supervision within specific clinical settings which are not replicated nearby, serving the needs of international students who are completing internships in their home countries, supplementing supervision in settings where within-agency supervision may be inadequate or where a particular expertise is missing, and serving supervisees with disabilities. Typically, supervision for the purpose of reaching supervisees who are located in a different geograhic area relies on more advanced forms of technological capability. Several authors who have conducted supervision using these newer technologies offer information regarding set-up conditions, required software, and admonitions regarding ethical safeguards (e.g., Borders & Brown, 2005; Dudding & Justice, 2004; Panos, 2005; Schultz & Finger, 2003; Watson, 2003).

Despite the principal goal of serving broader audiences, some have reported advantages of using distance technology that goes beyond reaching supervisees in other vicinities. For example, Dudding (2004) reported that some speech–language pathology students were more positively disposed torward videoconferencing than face-to-face supervision, finding it led to "a greater sense of autonomy and control when the supervisor was not physically present" (p. 149). Participants in this study also commented that videoconferencing was less intrusive and that they found the supervisor more transparent when using this form of supervision. Perhaps most importantly, students reported no differences in what they gained from supervision when using videoconferencing versus being in face-to-face supervision. These findings are similar to psychotherapy research reported by Day and Schneider (2002) who found that clients actually had higher scores on activity level, trust, spontaneity, and disinhibition when psychotherapy was offered using distance technologies. Furthermore, no significant treatment differences were found overall when contrasting face-to-face therapy with distance modalities.

Advantages of distance technologies notwithstanding, there are still barriers to their use including cost for real-time technologies (though these are steadily decreasing), unequal availability of technology, the loss of all nonverbal cues with technologies such as e-mail, fears regarding informed consent and breaches of confidentiality, lack of training in the use of technology, and the

ramifications of technological failure (Borders & Brown, 2005; Dudding & Justice, 2004; Jerome et al., 2000; Kanz, 2001; Olson, Russell, & White, 2001; Panos, 2005; Panos, Roby, Panos, Matheson, & Cox, 2002; Sampson, Kolodinsky, & Greeno, 1997; Schultz & Finger, 2003; Vaccaro & Lambie, 2007; Watson, 2003).

The third use of technology is to influence the process of supervision directly. A good example of this is live supervision, which relies on technology as endemic to its process. (Live supervision is the focus of Chapter 11 and all pertinent literature regarding the use of technology for live supervision will be reported in that chapter.) It should also be noted that some technologies that bridge geographical distance (e.g., chat rooms) may also be used for pedagogical reasons as well.

The literature that addresses technology for the purpose of changing or supplementing supervision exclusively is modest. This category also includes the small amount of research that has attempted to track effects of specific technological interventions on supervisee development. Two studies have investigated the use of e-mail as a supplement to traditional, individual, and group supervision (Clingerman & Bernard, 2004; Graf & Stebnicki, 2002).

Graf and Stebnicki reported on data collected on three practicum students in a rehabilitation counseling program. These students had been asked to communicate by e-mail at least once weekly with the first author, who served as their practicum supervisor over the course of one semester. Messages were analyzed and found to fall into three categories: messages about clients, messages about the on-site supervisors, and messages about themselves. While messages about clients stayed positive throughout the practicum (though increasing in complexity), messages about the site supervisors seemed to follow a more predictable developmental path, moving from highly positive to becoming more critical and ending with a more balanced view of their supervisors. The students' messages about themselves reflected the following pattern: an initial sense of anticipation and lack of confidence, a period of boredom when responsibility was withheld from them, increased confidence paired with increased responsibility, a sense of frustration over inability to make sufficient changes, and, finally, a more reflective place of increased awareness and more realistic goals.

Although these data were not compared to interactions using another form of supervision, and represent a very small sample size, they seem to support developmental models of supervision and, for our purposes here, seem to indicate that e-supervision can at least document, if not stimulate, development for a supervisee. (It is, of course, impossible to know the relative role that individual and group supervision played for these supervisees.)

Clingerman and Bernard (2004) also tracked the use of e-mail with practicum students. Specifically, the authors asked whether e-mail would encourage a personalization (intrapersonal) focus and if this would increase over the course of one semester. Nineteen students in three sections of practicum (taught by three different instructors) were asked to e-mail their instructor once a week in addition to the individual and group supervision they were receiving. Instructors were asked to respond to each e-mail but to refrain from responding in a way that encouraged a follow-up e-mail. Once the 15-week practicum was over, all messages were divided into three time periods (first 5 weeks, second 5 weeks, and final 5 weeks) and trained raters coded each message using the Discrimination Model (Bernard, 1979, 1997) (see Chapter 4 for a discussion of the model's focus areas) and Lanning's (1986) additional focus area of professional behavior. Messages were coded as addressing interventions, conceptualizations, personalization, professional behavior having to do with the practicum class, and professional behavior having to do with the practicum off-campus site. Because the frequency of messages sent declined significantly across time periods, no developmental trends were found. However, the question regarding the fit between e-mail and a personalization focus was answered in the affirmative. A full 40% of all student messages addressed a personalization focus and this pattern was maintained across all three time periods. The second most frequent category, professional issues having to do with the practicum class, accounted for another 24% of the messages. Unlike the students monitored by Graf and Stebnicki (2002), only 7% of messages dealt with the site or the site supervisor and patterns were the same for students in all three sections of practicum. Clingerman and Bernard concluded that further investigation is warranted regarding the benefit of e-mail for tapping personalization issues. They also noted that their data did not offer insight about the degree of reflectivity embedded in personalization comments sent by students. That is, no judgment was made about e-mails regarding their relative superficiality or depth. Because reflectivity is regarded as an essential developmental issue for persons in supervision, the compatibility of e-mail with a reflective process is worthy of investigation as well.

Finally, Guth and Dandeneau (2007) reported on a technological advance for clinical supervision based on the Landro Play Analyzer (LPA), a sophisticated software package originally designed to assist football coaches to review and analyze game videos. The LPA requires digital video capability and an adequate technological infrastructure, and allows supervisors and supervisees to analyze counseling sessions on a multitude of dimensions. Using such a system virtually eliminates randomness from session review. Though start-up costs are high, the system can be designed to fit different developmental levels of supervisees, to reflect any conceptual model the supervisor adopts, and offers a multitude of possibilities for process research.

In conclusion, the explosion of technological capacity has, and will continue to affect supervision. As we move forward it is essential for supervisors to be vigilant that the relationship dynamics of supervision are not overly compromised by the use of distance technologies and that ethical safeguards are ensured (Vaccaro & Lambie, 2007).

Timing of Supervision

Regardless of the methods used to produce the material for the case conference, an additional matter—the timing of the conference—must be considered. Little has been said in professional literature about the timing of supervision except to warn that supervision that is scheduled for convenience only (e.g., every Tuesday at 10:00 for 1 hour) may invite legal liability if there are no provisions for the occasion when the supervisee experiences a more pressing need for supervision (Disney & Stephens, 1994).

A single study (Couchon & Bernard, 1984) examined how several variables were influenced by the timing of supervision. Among the variables that were considered were supervisor and counselor behavior in supervision, follow through from supervision to counseling, client and counselor satisfaction with counseling, and counselor satisfaction with supervision. Three treatments were introduced: supervision within 4 hours prior to an upcoming counseling session, supervision the day before a specified counseling session, and supervision occurring more than two days before a specified counseling session.

Some provocative results emerged from this study. Perhaps the most surprising result was that the timing of supervision seemed to affect supervisor behavior in the supervision session more so than counselor behavior. Supervision the day before a specified counseling session was very content oriented. Perhaps because the counseling session was still one day away, supervisors felt the permission to offer several alternative strategies for counselors to consider. The supervisor was more likely to adopt an instructional mode and therefore was doing more of the work in the supervision session. We do not know how much the supervisee actually learned in these supervision sessions, but follow-through to the subsequent counseling session was low. In other words, strategies discussed and approved by the supervisor in the supervision session were not acted on in counseling to any significant degree. We can hypothesize that because information was so voluminous in supervision, the counselor was not able to prioritize or translate supervisory information into counseling strategies.

Supervision conducted within 4 hours of a subsequent session was very different. With the press

of the upcoming session, the supervisor was far less likely to offer content and, instead, adopted a more consultative role. Fewer strategies were discussed, more of the strategies were offered by the counselor than by the supervisor, and those that were suggested met with supervisor approval. Furthermore, there was far more follow through from supervision to counseling for this treatment condition. Therefore, we can view supervision immediately before counseling to be more of a work session for the counselor, with support from the supervisor as needed.

The third time frame for supervision, more or less midway between counseling sessions, had no strong effects. Because other counseling sessions with other clients intervened and there was no immediate pressure to prepare for an upcoming session, the supervision conference was simply more diffuse in its content and follow-through.

The Couchon and Bernard (1984) study highlighted the importance of timing of supervision. Depending on the developmental and learning needs of the supervisee, different timing of supervision might be appropriate. For example,

> *a counselor who conceptualizes well but who implements ideas poorly might benefit more from supervision immediately before counseling. On the other hand, a counselor who performs well but who lacks conceptual ability might benefit from supervision conducted the day before counseling.* (p. 18)

Contrary to the assumptions of many supervisors, the counselors in the Couchon and Bernard (1984) study were equally satisfied with supervision regardless of when supervision was offered. (Timing also did not affect client or counselor satisfaction with counseling.) It should be noted, however, that an important time for supervision, immediately after counseling, was not studied. We hypothesize that if there is a time that would get an elevated satisfaction rating it would be immediately after counseling when the supervisee might benefit from support and reinforcement. This hypothesis was supported by Ray and Altekruse (2000). Though we know that supervisee satisfaction is high when feedback is delivered immediately, the amount and kind of learning resulting from this timing of supervision is still unknown. Additional research regarding the effects of the timing of supervision is warranted.

Beyond Methods

For the most part, our discussion thus far has focused on the methods used by the supervisor to conduct supervision. Although important, specific methods do not automatically translate into a productive supervision session. IPR, for example, uses videotape as the method for obtaining supervision data, but the technique is intended to increase supervisee reflectivity regarding the interpersonal and intrapersonal dynamics that were present during the session. If the supervisor had concerns about the supervisee's ability to be reflective at the level that IPR requires, this technique should be avoided and a less challenging form for stimulating reflectivity (e.g., journal writing) should be considered.

As part of their seminal developmental model (discussed in Chapter 4), Loganbill, Hardy, and Delworth (1982) described five supervisor techniques/strategies that would assist supervisees to get beyond stagnation or confusion and move toward integration for any of Chickering's (1969) eight vectors. These interventions are not limited to a specific format for supervision (e.g., the use of audiotape) but are important to consider across methods.

1. *Facilitative interventions* are as much a set of assumptions and attitudes as direct interventions (similar to Carroll's philosophy of supervision). They are supervisee centered and help to promote the natural developmental process. Inherent in this category is the belief that with support and reflective activity the supervisee can learn and change.

2. *Confrontive interventions* are a type of intervention that "brings together two things for examination and comparison" (Loganbill et al., 1982, p. 33). The discrepancy can be internal to the supervisee—for example, a conflict between feelings and behavior—or it can be a discrepancy between the supervisee and an external actuality—for example, the supervisor seeing client dynamics in a way very different from how they have been perceived by the supervisee. When the discrepancy is internal, it provides the dissonance necessary for reflective activity (Nelson & Neufeldt, 1998).

3. *Conceptual interventions* occur whenever the supervisor is asking the supervisee to think analytically or theoretically. Loganbill et al. (1982) cautioned the supervisor to take learning styles into consideration because some supervisees grasp theory through experience, whereas others need a theoretical grounding prior to experience.

4. *Prescriptive interventions* take the form of coaching the supervisee to either perform certain behaviors or to delete certain behaviors. This is the most direct intervention category described by Loganbill et al. (1982). Therefore, they warned that prescriptive interventions could thwart supervisee development if used too liberally or when a more conservative approach might be substituted. (We will find a similar caution in our discussion of live supervision in Chapter 11.) Client welfare is a frequent rationale for using prescriptive interventions.

5. *Catalytic interventions* include those supervisor statements that are "designed to get things moving" (Loganbill et al., 1982, p. 35). Although the authors noted that in one sense all supervision interventions are catalytic, they also argued that catalytic interventions are qualitatively different from each of the other four. When a supervisor uses a catalytic intervention, the supervisor is seizing the moment to bring additional meaning to the supervisory process. Loganbill et al. offered two examples of catalytic interventions: helping the supervisee to appreciate realistic client potential for change and thereby setting appropriate goals (a buffer, the authors asserted, from burnout) and encouraging the supervisee to experiment with new roles in the therapeutic relationship. Both examples given by Loganbill et al. should also stimulate introspection within the supervisee as part of reflective practice.

To summarize, the process of developmental supervision using the Loganbill et al. (1982)

model begins by assessing the supervisee on eight dimensions as either stagnant, confused, or integrated. (These eight dimensions were expanded to ten by Ellis, 1991a, and are reported in Chapter 4). The supervisor then relies on combinations of the five supervisor intervention categories to bring the supervisee to integration on as many dimensions as possible. The source of supervision information on which the supervisor relies would depend on the issue, some needing direct observation, others being more contemplative in nature.

Johnson and Moses (1988) followed Loganbill et al. (1982) by also relying on Chickering's (1969) vectors as the criteria for supervisee development. Rather than the five interventions proposed by Loganbill et al., however, Johnson and Moses reduced supervisor input to either *challenge* or *support*. If the supervisor offers too little challenge, the supervisee might slip into stagnation (borrowing from the Loganbill et al. model); with too much challenge and too little support, the supervisee may get discouraged or defensive. The choice between challenge and support was seen by Johnson and Moses as the most critical decision that the supervisor makes. Once this decision is made, Johnson and Moses referred to the Bernard (1979, 1997) schema of roles (teacher, consultant, counselor) as being the primary choices for the supervisor to help the supervisee to attain the desired growth. Although Johnson and Moses did not imply that either support or challenge interventions should constitute the majority of supervisor interventions, McCarthy et al. (1994) found that the most frequent supervisor technique was the offering of support and encouragement, while confrontation and the assignment of homework were rarely used. Supervisors, therefore, need to reflect upon their own work to determine if their avoidance of confrontation is meeting their own needs or that of their supervisees.

In conclusion, supervision techniques are much the same as those used in counseling or therapy. The goals of the supervisor, however, are more complex, because techniques must not only serve the developmental needs of the supervisee,

but indirectly must assure that the therapeutic needs of the client are met as well. Approaches used by supervisors must allow them adequate data for the central task of supervisee evaluation, while simultaneously allowing for a productive relationship between supervisor and supervisee.

PUTTING IT ALL TOGETHER

Reviewing each supervision method is a bit like reviewing theories of psychotherapy. While in the process of considering a particular method, it may seem attractive and worthwhile; but, like psychotherapy, the use of supervision formats and techniques requires an acceptable level of expertise and a sound rationale that is compatible with the supervisor's vision and the supervisee's needs. In general, technical eclecticism among supervisors is desirable because it allows the supervisor to help a variety of supervisees to attain a variety of supervision goals.

At the beginning of the chapter, we discussed initial criteria for choosing an intervention. Here we will attempt to draw on the information in this chapter, as well as broader topics, to form a list of questions to ask when selecting format and technique within individual supervision.

1. *How will this method of supervision be received?* No method is appropriate if the supervisee cannot become more expert as a result of the method. At times this may be a developmental issue only. For example, a supervisee may be too novice and/or too concrete to be able to benefit from the advantages of self-report. Occasionally, a particular method of supervision may simply be a bad fit for the supervisee as an individual. For example, is e-supervision a perfect fit for an introvert supervisee or a method that will retard growth? Not only developmental level and learning styles, but also temperament and cultural norms will determine the receptivity to particular supervision delivery systems.

2. *Am I being true to my beliefs about how one learns to be a mental health practitioner?* As stated earlier, if the supervisor believes that reflectivity is the cornerstone to becoming an expert therapist, then the supervision modality must achieve reflectivity. In such cases, supervisee behaviors will be viewed in the context of the larger dynamics of interpersonal or intrapersonal processes and meaning, not the other way around. Other supervisors will assume that supervisees will become more competent with a series of successes and will therefore focus more on therapeutic interventions. The larger point is that, if the supervisor doesn't accept the outcome of a supervision method as crucial to the supervisee's development, the method will most likely be used in a perfunctory manner.

3. *Am I considering the three functions of supervision (i.e., assessing learning needs; changing/shaping/supporting; evaluating performance)?* Using a different format to evaluate clinical competence from one used to promote supervisee development may make the supervision process clearer to the supervisee. Furthermore, a change of method can help the supervisor to maintain boundaries between different supervisor roles.

4. *Am I considering the timing and/or relative structure of my supervision?* Busy professional schedules often dictate the timing of supervision. But for the supervisee who is floundering, timing may be a relatively easy and potentially important variable to manipulate to assist a breakthrough in learning. Similarly, the relative use of structure may be manipulated to allow a different and potentially potent learning opportunity for the supervisee.

5. *Are administrative constraints real or am I not advocating with a strong enough voice?* It is not uncommon to hear that a piece of media equipment is too expensive or that a method of supervision is too time-consuming for a particular setting. Yet, a strong supervision program can energize a setting so that what is accomplished is more efficient and of higher quality. Supervisors must advocate for the kind and level of supervision that they believe must be present. As models to supervisees, it is imperative that supervisors work in ways that are productive and credible.

6. *What does this particular supervisee need to learn next? Am I using the best method for this purpose?* There are times when the supervisor must realize that the method being used is simply not accomplishing the desired outcome. One supervisor reported that, after spending several frustrating weeks in supervision with the supervisee making little progress conceptualizing client issues, the supervisor began to assign homework that required the supervisee to come to the conference with three different avenues to take with each client to be discussed, one of which had to be unconventional. This assignment seemed to energize the counselor and she started to make significant gains in her area of weakness.

What the supervisee needs may also challenge the comfort level of the supervisor. It may be more comfortable to remain supportive when the supervisee needs to be challenged. It may be more natural to continue a highly structured approach to supervision when the supervisee is ready for the supervisor to be more of a consultant in approach. If supervision is fairly standard from supervisee to supervisee, the supervisor should question whether it is the supervisor that needs to be stretched.

7. *Am I skilled in the use of this particular method or technique?* Ultimately, supervision will fall flat if the method is used poorly. IPR is a good example of a technique that can easily deteriorate if the supervisor is not skilled at asking probing questions without loading them with the supervisor's opinion. As we stated earlier, self-report can be a highly charged method of supervision, but only when the supervisor is expert and knows how to use the method to challenge the supervisee. Some form of cybersupervision may be attempted before the supervisor is adequately skilled, leading to frustration and failure.

8. *Have I considered ethical safeguards?* Supervision is based on the premise that the supervisee is not yet expert enough to handle a wide range of clients autonomously. An important criterion for choosing a method of supervision, therefore, must be some judgment about the level of competence of the supervisee. This is one reason why self-report is considered foolhardy for novice counselors. The ethics of supervision also include the supervisor's responsibility to the supervisee. Supervision that does not assist the supervisee in learning, the helping process could be considered unethical. As was stated earlier, technology introduces a whole new array of ethical concerns (Vaccaro & Lambie, 2007).

9. *Is it time to try something new?* Even if the supervisor is adamant about the centrality of one aspect of therapeutic practice (e.g., establishing an empathic relationship with the client), there are different ways to help the supervisee to reach the goal. For example, Sterling and Bugental (1993) suggested using role-play to help the supervisee to make phenomenological gains, Guiffrida et al. (2007) reviewed different techniques using metaphor to assist in conceptualization, and Deacon (2000) advocated the use of visualization to help supervisees to think more creatively. Training literature is replete with examples of specific techniques to arrive at a variety of areas of competence. Trying something new is as important for the supervisor as the supervisee. The goal is to stay fresh or to use a new method or technique to stimulate new and sometimes unexpected learning.

10. *Can I document the success of my method?* It would be nice if supervisors had hard data to support their work with each supervisee. (Some methods, e.g., transcription, taping, or e-supervision, lend themselves to the possibility of data collection.) In the absence of data, it is still important that the supervisor glean a sense of accomplishment from the method or techniques being used. Each method chosen translates to

alternative methods rejected. Therefore, supervisors must seek some justification for the continuation of a particular approach to supervision. At the very least, supervisors should seek feedback from supervisees about what they experienced as most helpful to their learning.

11. *Am I willing to confront my own assumptions?* Good supervisors can revisit familiar tenets with new scrutiny. No vision is complete. No supervision method has been found to be indispensable. Supervision at its best is a healthy balance of authority and humility. Supervisors who opt for confusion over stagnation model the essence of professional growth for their supervisees.

CONCLUSION

As the supervisor conducts individual supervision, many options are available regarding the form that supervision will take. Much of this will be determined by prior experience, interest in experimenting with different methods, and perceived supervisee need. All methods carry with them opportunities—and opportunities bypassed. The quality of supervision we offer is intimately related to the decisions we make about methods. But, presently, there is insufficient empirical evidence to either encourage or reject the use of any of the available methods for any particular supervisee. Clearly, supervisors need not only to expand their repertoire, but also to systematically study their methods and techniques, to examine both the process and meaning of what they do (Carroll, 2001; Holloway & Carroll, 1996). In this way, they can best serve both their supervisees and their profession.

CHAPTER 10

SUPERVISION INTERVENTIONS
GROUP SUPERVISION

Most mental health professionals' first thought of clinical supervision is of *individual* supervision. Yet much supervision also occurs in a group format; so much so that virtually all supervisees eventually will have participated in group supervision.

Most university training programs employ group supervision at some point in their curricula and at least one accrediting body—the Council for Accreditation of Counseling and Related Educational Programs (CACREP)—requires programs it accredits to provide supervisees with group supervision (CACREP, 2001). Group supervision is widely used in other training settings as well. Riva and Cornish (1995) found that 65% of predoctoral psychology internship sites reported using group supervision. And both university counseling center supervisors (Goodyear & Nelson, 1997) and family therapy supervisors (Lee & Everett, 2004) reported that although individual supervision was the more frequently used modality, group supervision came in a close second.

Significantly, in several studies that have directly compared them, neither group nor individual supervision has been shown to be superior to the other with respect to training outcomes (Averitt, 1989; Lanning, 1971; Ray & Altekruse, 2000). At least one study (Ray & Altekruse, 2000) did find, though, that supervisees *preferred* individual over group supervision.

Neither supervision modality has any historical advantage over the other. In fact, both can claim origins with Freud. With respect to group supervision, Rosenthal (1999) observed that:

> The Wednesday Evening Society, which met weekly in Freud's home from 1901 to 1906 (and then

became the Vienna Psychoanalytic Society), has been identified as the first recorded instance of analytic group psychotherapy. . . . However, since its members had avowedly gathered around Freud for instruction in psychoanalysis and for supervision on their cases, this historic group might more fittingly be seen as constituting the first recorded example of group supervision. Members presented their cases, their ideas, and their written papers to Freud and to each other. The final comments in any discussion were always reserved for Freud. (p. 197)

In short, group supervision is prevalent, appears to rival individual supervision's effectiveness, and is a long-established form of supervision. The remainder of this chapter will build on these grounding observations to address definitional, conceptual, and practical issues related to group supervision.

GROUP SUPERVISION IN BROAD STROKES: DEFINITION, ADVANTAGES, LIMITATIONS

The definition of supervision we provided in Chapter 1 applies to all formats of supervision. But the group format warrants its own, more specific definition to complement that more generic one. We suggest that

> Group supervision is the regular meeting of a group of supervisees (a) with a designated supervisor or supervisors, (b) to monitor the quality of their work, and (c) to further their understanding of themselves as clinicians, of the clients with whom they work, and of service delivery in general. These supervisees are aided in achieving these goals by their supervisor(s) and by their feedback from and interactions with each other.

This definition does not suggest how many supervisees might constitute a group. Therefore, we note that the group should be sufficiently large to avoid the disruptions caused by dropouts or absences, yet it should not be so large that members are shortchanged in the attention they receive. Authors who have spoken on this issue have differed in their recommendations, but it is possible to see some convergence of opinion at around six or seven members as optimal. Aronson (1990) recommended five to six as optimal, whereas Proctor (2000) recommended four to six; Chaiklin and Munson (1983) recommended six to twelve; and Schreiber and Frank (1983) recommended at least seven. Interestingly, the single available study of the differential training effects of supervision group size (supervisor–supervisee ratios of 8–1 versus 4–1; Ray & Altekruse, 2000) was inconclusive.

In practice, institutional factors affect group sizes. Riva and Cornish (1995, 2008) found in two surveys of psychology internship sites that the typical size was three to five supervisees, corresponding to the number of interns at that site. In university training programs, on the other hand, practicum groups typically range in size up to 10 members, which also is the maximum CACREP (2001) permits in programs it accredits: The actual number often is guided by course enrollment constraints of the particular university in which the given practicum is offered.

Benefits and Limitations of Group Supervision

As with any supervision format, there are both benefits and limitations to group supervision. We address some of the more important ones in the material that follows.

Benefits. A number of authors (e.g., Carroll, 1996; Hawkins & Shohet, 1989; Hayes, 1989; Proctor, 2000; Riva & Cornish, 1995, 2007) have discussed the advantages of a group format. The nine we give particular emphasis to are:

1. *Economies of time, costs, and expertise.* Perhaps the most obvious advantage of group

supervision is that it offers many of the same economies that are afforded by group counseling or therapy, particularly those of time, costs, and expertise (Hawkins & Shohet, 1989).

2. *Opportunities for vicarious learning.* Important vicarious learning can occur as supervisees observe peers conceptualizing and intervening with clients. In fact, Proctor and Inskipp (2001) suggested that "Perhaps the true 'economy' of group supervision lies in the 'free learning' opportunity of observing and participating in the supervision of other supervisees" (p. 160).

Significantly, novices who observe their peers performing a particular skill are more likely to exhibit skill improvement and increased self-efficacy than those who instead observed an expert (Hillerbrand, 1989). That vicarious learning also can be personal, as other group member discuss their experiences and feelings (Hawkins & Shohet, 1989).

3. *Breadth of client exposure.* During group supervision, supervisees are exposed to and learn about the clients with whom the other group members are working. This enables them to learn about a broader range of clients than any one person's case load would afford.

4. *Supervisee feedback of greater quantity and diversity.* Other supervisees can offer perspectives that are broader and more diverse than what a single supervisor could provide. The range of life experiences and other individual differences (age, gender, sexual orientation, race, and culture) that other group members bring can enrich the feedback supervisees receive (Hawkins & Shohet, 1989). For example, a supervisee of a particular ethnic background might provide important information to the group when the discussion concerns treatment of a client of that background. Supervisors must, of course, remain vigilant against putting one person in the position of representing an entire cultural group.

5. *Supervisee feedback of greater quality.* As people become expert in any domain their knowledge becomes more "proceduralized" (e.g., Ericcson & Lehmann, 1996). Their work will occur at an increasingly automatic level, with less conscious awareness. Therefore, "although experts are able to perform cognitive skills, they . . . are generally poor at post hoc descriptions of their actual cognitive processes" (Hillerbrand, 1989, p. 294).

By contrast, novices—in this case, fellow supervisees—are more likely to employ language that is more understandable to other novices than is the language used by the supervisor (i.e., expert). Moreover, they may be better able to decode nonverbal cues that other novices use to indicate their confusion.

6. *A more comprehensive picture of the supervisee.* The group format enriches the ways the supervisor is able to observe a supervisee. A particular supervisee might, for example, seem blocked when discussing his or her own work and yet be an intelligent and insightful contributor to group discussions. The opportunity to see this can allow the supervisor to view the supervisee's difficulties in a different way (e.g., as a function of fear, isomorphism, etc.) than might be the case if the supervisee were seen only in individual supervision. This feature of the group format also can moderate potentially deleterious countertransference reactions the supervisor might develop (Aronson, 1990).

Hawkins and Shohet (1989) suggested that the supervisor is able to gain important information by observing reactions supervisees are having to (a) material being discussed, (b) one another, and (c) the supervisor. Counselman and Gumpert (1993) expanded this point by noting that parallel processes can be especially transparent in groups: "Group member reactions such as boredom, anger, anxiety, and excessive helpfulness can serve as important clues to the case dynamics" (p. 26). Moreover, they suggested that for a supervisee to receive feedback about these processes from a number of peers often has more impact than similar feedback delivered by a single supervisor.

7. *The opportunity for supervisees to learn supervision skills.* In Chapter 1, we noted how important it is that mental health professionals be formally prepared to provide supervision. Participation in supervision groups should not substitute for that formal training but it can play a significant role in preparing mental health professionals for a supervisory role. In the group they have an opportunity both to observe the supervisor and other group members provide supervision and actually to engage in it themselves.

8. *Normalizing supervisees' experiences.* Supervisees can find themselves troubled by a number of experiences, including their own feelings of anxiety and doubt and their personal reactions to client material. To know that they are not alone in those reactions can be important and reassuring.

9. *Mirroring the supervisees' intervention.* A final advantage pertains specifically to the supervision of supervisees who are offering counseling or therapy in a group format. Supervisees and the supervisor alike can benefit by having a supervision format that mirrors that of the treatment being supervised (Hart, 1982; Hawkins & Shohet, 1989). For example, parallel processes and isomorphism are more likely to be observed, and supervisees can apply what they have learned from group processes in their supervision group to their counseling groups.

Limitations. The advantages of group supervision outweigh the limitations. Otherwise, there would be no reason to provide group supervision! Nevertheless, there are limitations to be considered. The following limitations are those suggested by Carroll (1996), supplemented as well by other sources and our own observations.

1. *The group format may not permit individuals to get what they need.* This can occur for several reasons. For example, supervisees with heavier caseloads may not have sufficient time to review their case loads adequately. In groups that are heterogeneous with respect to group members' skill levels, the less-skilled members may receive attention at the expense of their more-skilled peers. And if time is not managed well, some members may find during any particular session that the time has run out before they are able to present and get necessary feedback.

2. *Confidentiality concerns.* Confidentiality is less secure in group supervision with respect to (a) the clients who are the focus of attention and (b) the supervisees in the group. Most supervisees will readily understand the issues related to client confidentiality but they may be less clear about the importance of protecting the privacy of their fellow supervisees. In university training programs, supervisees interact with one another in multiple contexts. So they may be in a supervision group during the morning and then in the afternoon sitting in a class that includes group members, and then in the evening participating in social events with them. Though confidentiality about other supervisees can be difficult to maintain, it is an important rule to impress on the group members.

3. *The group format is not isomorphic with that of individual counseling.* We already have noted that it is an advantage that the group supervision of group counseling or therapy is isomorphic with what is being supervised. However, most group supervision focuses on individual counseling and so has the opposite problem: The form and structure of the supervision does not mirror that of the treatment being supervised, and therefore there is more limited opportunity to observe isomorphic and parallel processes.

4. *Certain group phenomena can impede learning.* Some group phenomena, especially between-member competition and scapegoating, can interfere with learning. It is even possible for one or more of the supervisees to experience harm in the face of those phenomena. Ögren, Jonsson and Sundin (2005) demonstrated that supervision focus can affect learning.

5. *The group may devote too much time to issues of limited relevance to or interest for some group members.* Aronson (1990) pointed out that the supervisor is responsible for ensuring that all members perceive they are getting something from the group. Meeting that responsibility, though, is a challenge that is not always reached. In the section that follows, we will note that the level of that challenge will depend on the leadership style the supervisor adopts.

A CONCEPTUAL MODEL FOR GROUP SUPERVISORS: SUPERVISEE DEVELOPMENTAL LEVEL, SUPERVISOR STYLE, AND GROUP STAGE

The tasks of the group supervisor significantly affect the group processes and outcomes. Foremost among those tasks is to be in charge. As Proctor (2000) noted:

> *Running supervision groups is a managerial enterprise. . . . I encounter many supervisors who are confused about this. . . . [A]ppearing to take charge is felt to be disrespectful and unempathic. Covert management may work (just) in individual supervision, but it is unhelpful in setting up group supervision.* (p. 59)

Proctor and Inskipp (2001) suggested other supervisory tasks as well. Among those are that group supervisors should:

1. assume an active stance in the group; one that steers a careful course between over- and under-control;

2. assert themselves as necessary to redirect the group, impose time limits, and so on;

3. listen to and then following the group, changing direction as necessary;

4. be able to choose the right fights when the inevitable conflicts emerge between supervisees or within the group itself;

5. communicate clearly just what they want to happen, using what Proctor and Inskipp termed "confident enough" communication. Himsel's (2003) fanciful use of the fictitious mob boss,

Tony Soprano, to provide lessons for leaders, addresses this clarity of communication:

Many times, leaders fail to be explicit about what they expect from the team. . . . [L]eaders fall short . . . when their people don't know what's expected of them or harbor false expectations. Tony makes sure his people know what's required of them, and his lieutenants in turn insist their people also are clear about what's needed. (p. 70)

To the above five tasks, we would add another that Sansbury (1982) had suggested. This sixth task is to process the group's interaction and development. Whereas the third task listed above concerned listening to and understanding group members, this sixth more active task, is one of synthesizing information and using that to intervene with the group.

To be effective in these tasks is an important step toward providing the helpful experiences—and avoiding the hindering experiences—that are listed in Table 10.1. The two studies (Carter et al., in press; Enyedy et al., 2003) are linked in that they drew from the same sample and used the same methodology. In both studies supervisees reported that the supervisor and the group itself *both* are important sources of impact, whether positive or negative. In their qualitative study of the perceptions of one group's members, Linton and Hedstrom (2006) obtained complementary findings; specifically, that supervisees perceived that group cohesion, the chance to observe others, and feedback from the supervisor and fellow supervisees all were important factors to their experiences in the group. And, like Enyedy et al., Linton and Hedstrom found that intermember conflict and time management were issues that interfered with the group's effectiveness.

Of course, successful execution of the six tasks is not sufficient to ensure that these helpful factors are addressed. Other skills are necessary are well. And with them, the supervisor should be able to ensure that supervisees are provided an optimal balance of challenge versus support (cf. Blocher, 1983). Challenge can have multiple forms, including confrontation and also the encouragement to stretch to try out new behaviors. Support, too, can have multiple forms, including encouragement and positive feedback. In group supervision, those challenges and supports will come from both the supervisor and the group itself. Regardless of the source, the supervisor's job is to manage the process to ensure that supervisees receive enough challenge to propel them forward to try new behaviors, but not so much that they feel overwhelmed, and to ensure that they receive support, but not so much that supervisees are infantilized or come to believe that they are too fragile or inept to handle honest feedback or work tasks.

Mastery of these six tasks is an essential starting point for these processes. For the supervisor to know when and how to execute each of them requires that she or he have a conceptual model from which to work. Figure 10.1 presents one such model. It suggests that three factors affect how a group supervisor might think about intervening at any particular point: *supervisor style,* the *stage of group,* and *supervisee developmental level.* Each factor is important, both alone and in combination with the other factors.

Supervisee developmental level is addressed in Chapter 4 and so will not be covered here. We will, though, address the other two elements of that model: Supervisor style and stage of the group.

Supervisor Style

Proctor and Inskipp (2001) identified three essential supervision styles that vary in the extent to which the group itself is used as part of the supervisory process. (Proctor and Inskipp identified peer-group supervision as a fourth style, but we have covered it in a later section of the chapter because it does not involve a formal leader.) The supervisor who uses *authoritative supervision* conducts supervision *in* the group rather than *with* the group (Proctor & Inskipp, 2001) and applies an individual supervision template to his or her work. This minimizes the extent to which other supervisees participate in the supervision. This can occur, for example, with supervisors who are newer to the group format.

TABLE 10.1   Helpful and Hindering Phenomena in Group Supervision

HELPFUL PHENOMENA	HINDERING PHENOMENA
Supervisor Impact (supervisor openness, sense of humor, competence, making the group feel comfortable, sharing past experiences, feedback)	**Problems with Supervisors** Subcluster a: **Negative Supervisor Behaviors** (lack of focus, dominating the group, either not listening or misunderstanding material presented, being overly critical, bragging about knowledge in nonhelpful ways, going on tangents) Subcluster b: **Supervisor's Lack of Experience/Clinical Focus** (insufficient expertise, lack of a theoretical focus, more wrapped up in administrative processes than clinical issues) Subcluster c: **Problems in Cosupervision** (cosupervisors had conflicting theoretical orientations or did not in their interactions "practice what they preached")
Peer Impact (getting peer feedback, hearing feedback given to others, critiquing other's audio- or videotapes, observing differences in presentation styles)	**Between-Member Problems** Subcluster a: **Negative Supervisee Behaviors** (within-group competition, between-supervisee conflict, bossy and controlling group members, members who did not engage or participate) Subcluster b: **Personal Reaction to Negative Behaviors** (compared to the first subcluster, this concerns the participants' personal reactions, including "the group criticized me for not doing it their way")
Support and Safety (the group was a safe place to ask questions and to vent about site concerns; there was camaraderie and mutual support; it felt safe to share fears, successes, and questions)	**Supervisee Anxiety and Other Negative Affects** (feeling unsafe, alienated, unsupported, or anxious; pressured to self-disclose; being the only male or female, African-American, etc.)
Specific Instruction (being given reading assignments, going over legal and ethical issues, attending lectures on clinical issues, watching videos that showed client and counselor interactions)	**Logistical Constraints** (lack of variety in cases; room size; group scheduled too late in the day; main supervisor out sick)
Self-understanding (learning from my own mistakes in counseling, being able to process my own countertransference, self-reflection in preparation for the group, the opportunity to explore differences/difficulties)	**Poor Group Time Management** (not enough time to discuss cases or to get questions and issues addressed, one person dominated the group's time, some cases were lengthy and time was not allotted to other cases, too many people needing time, too much time spent on things other than supervisees' cases)
Validation of Experience (therapeutic interventions and skills were validated, the supervisee felt affirmed, experiences were normalized)	

Note: The list of helpful phenomena is from Carter et al. (in press); the list of hindering phenomena is from Enyedy et al. (2003). This table reorganizes the order in which phenomena are presented in those studies.

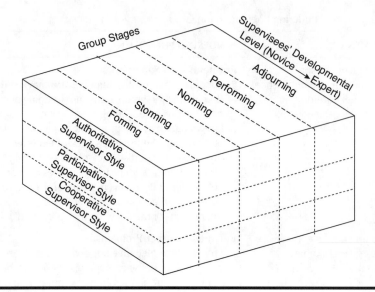

FIGURE 10.1   Group Supervision Conceptual Model

Proctor and Inskipp note that this authoritative style has some important advantages, including especially the greater ease it affords in managing group time and the sense of safety it can afford those members who distrust groups. However, there are significant disadvantages to this style as well. In particular, the expertise remains with the supervisor and the other members are neither utilized nor given the opportunity to develop their own supervisory skills. Moreover, the supervisor who uses this style does not develop group skills.

Supervisors who use the second of these styles, *participative supervision,* capitalize on the richness of the group as they encourage members to participate actively. It is a style that fosters commitment to a shared task and therefore interest and even excitement. Its disadvantages include the possible change of focus from client issues to group process and the difficulties the supervisor can have in managing either the equitable sharing of time or the maintaining of reflective space within the group. For some members, it can feel unsafe and therefore cause them to hedge what they tell the group.

Cooperative supervision is the third of the Proctor and Inskipp styles. In this case, the group itself provides supervision. The supervisor's tasks are to facilitate the group and share the actual supervision. For supervisees who are experienced practitioners, this style offers both a collegial experience and the opportunity to receive supervision that is informed by a variety of therapy models and styles. Proctor and Inskipp (2001) also note that the "freer interaction allows for serendipity—parallel process, group surprises" (p. 104).

This style of group supervision requires both the supervisor and the group members to have higher skill levels. There also are some risks, for although the group members may be experienced practitioners, they may not have well-developed group skills; and because the group processes are riskier, some members may feel unsafe. Also, it is more difficult to keep the group focus on supervision (versus on group processes and between-member interactions).

It is worth noting that these three styles correspond generally to the three types of group that Wilbur, Roberts-Wilbur, Morris, Betz, and Hart (1991) and Wilbur, Roberts-Wilbur, Hart, Morris, and Betz (1994) identified. Specifically, the *authoritative* style corresponds roughly to the task-process group; the *participative* style corresponds roughly to the psychoprocess group; and the *cooperative* style corresponds roughly to the socioprocess group.

These styles interact with the other two aspects of the model depicted in Figure 10.1. For example, the cooperative style of leading a group is more likely to occur with fairly advanced supervisees and so would be located in this figure on the expert end of the developmental spectrum. Also, the salience of the group's stage will vary according to the supervisor's style. If the supervisor employs an authoritative style, for example, then many of those stages will have considerably less relevance because group processes will be minimized.

What this model does *not* include is supervisory focus. We will address that point here and invoke Bernard's (1997) Discrimination Model, which alluded to three foci: supervisee skills and strategies; supervisee personhood issues; and conceptualization (see also Rubel & Okech, 2006 for an application of this model to groups). In group supervision, there is a fourth possibility, which is focus on the group processes. This focus can affect what supervisees report having learned. In particular, Ögren et al. (2005) found that a theory and conceptualization focus was least predictive of students' self-reported learning.

Stages of Group Supervision

Some group process experts would assert that there is little support for the generally held assumption that groups follow a predictable, linear sequence. Nevertheless, the assumption that there is linearity can provide a useful heuristic to therapists and supervisors. Tuckman's (1965) (later refined by Tuckman & Jensen, 1977) is the best-known model of group processes. Tucker's model suggests that groups of any type will proceed through five stages, each with characteristic goals for its members:

1. *Forming.* Members work to become comfortable with one another.
2. *Storming.* Members work to resolve issues of power; in a supervisory context; this is the stage at which between-member competitiveness is likely to be in its most direct and obvious form.
3. *Norming.* Members work to set norms for appropriate within-group behavior. Norms concern what is expected of those who are participating in the group (Hayes, 1989). Although these norms may develop and function outside group members' conscious awareness, they still exert powerful influences on behavior. Sanctions for their violation can be strong. Supervisors have a particular responsibility both (a) to be aware of emerging norms and (b) to shape them by, for example, modeling behaviors that should become normative (e.g., starting the group on time) and helping the members to identify the norms that are developing. In the next section our discussion of establishing ground rules and structure addresses this stage.
4. *Performing.* This is the stage at which members tackle work-related tasks. It is the group's most productive stage.
5. *Adjourning.* Members work on saying goodbye to one another.

Tuckman's model assumes that though different types of groups might move through the stages in different ways and with varying levels of intensity, all will conform to this sequence to some degree. Therefore, whereas it is important that group supervisors be sensitive to these stages, they should also keep in mind that supervision is a task oriented rather than a therapy experience and that movement through the stages will reflect this difference.

In summary, the Tuckman (1965) and Tuckman & Jensen (1977) stages provide a useful, albeit imperfect framework for thinking about supervisors' roles, tasks, and strategies. In the material that follows, we address these issues as they may occur in the forming, performing, and adjourning stages.

Preliminary Work. We begin by discussing the work of the supervisor *before* the group is convened. The primary task here is that of screening group members. In many cases, the supervisor will have relatively little discretion in this matter (e.g., in the case of teaching a university-based practicum or a predoctoral internship). Nevertheless, some issues related to member screening merit attention. Perhaps the most important of these concerns is the extent to which a group could or should be homogeneous or heterogeneous with respect to such matters as supervisee ability, experience level, theoretical orientation, and characteristics of field site.

For novice supervisees, there seems to be a case for ensuring that the group members are relatively homogeneous. When that homogeneity is with respect to experience level, supervisees are likely to have greater empathy for one another and to more easily build trust. Furthermore, one's relative strength can be more readily appreciated in a homogeneous group because experience level does not cloud perceptions of individual talent.

Supervisees are more likely to find themselves in heterogeneous supervision groups in field training sites. More-experienced supervisees, though, are the ones likely to be shortchanged when the group is mixed (Chaiklin & Munson, 1983). Differing experience levels means that supervisees bring different expectations to supervision and the group supervisor inevitably will make compromises in a mixed group that will risk supervisee dissatisfaction with the experience.

More positively, heterogeneous groups do allow group members to adopt more responsible roles as they are ready (Wendorf, Wendorf, & Bond, 1985), taking appropriate leadership positions and modeling higher-level functioning for those who are less experienced. But because there seems no simple resolution to the homogeneity versus heterogeneity issue, the supervisor must consider the makeup of the group carefully and attempt to compensate for the disadvantages of either situation through group structure and ground rules.

Forming Stage. The supervisor has a particular responsibility to establish expectations with respect to group rules and structure. In fact, if the supervisor does not exert leadership in setting these expectations, the group members will.

We noted above that one task Proctor and Inskipp (2001) had identified for group supervisors was that of communicating clearly. This is important, for example, in the development of a contract with the group (whether this is done as an informal discussion or, more formally, with a written document that participants sign). To have a contract makes the management of the group easier; it also minimizes supervisee role conflict and ambiguity, which has been shown to have deleterious effects on supervisees (cf. Nelson and Friedlander, 2001); it also goes a long way toward establishing the sense of safety and trust that is so essential in group supervision (see, e.g., Sussman, Bogo, & Globerman, 2007).

A useful contract will cover both the supervisees' and the supervisor's expectations and responsibilities. One essential aspect of the contract should concern the contract itself: monitoring how people adhere to it. An early expectation should be set up that violations of the contract will be processed openly and immediately.

Supervisees should have the opportunity to state their expectations for the group. This can include expectations about both process (e.g., how members behave toward one another) and outcomes (e.g., what each person hopes to leave the group having gained). Each supervisor can approach this process of helping members articulate expected outcomes. Williams (1995) described an action technique he uses for the contracting process:

> *[For example, in an initial session, the supervisor might] ask the supervisee [Tina] to imagine a line in the room, one end of which represents 0 and the other 10. Let us suppose that one of Tina's selected training needs is "more strength in hypothesizing about cases," and she stands at a "3" on her present strength. The supervisor interviews her as she stands on that spot to find out what "3" means in terms of hypothesizing strength. She then is asked where she will be (rather than "would like to be") at the end of the year . . . let us say that she goes to a "7," wavers, and ends up at "6." Again, the supervisor interviews her as if she is that "6 person." . . . After a couple of demonstrations, the supervisor might ask those who have already been interviewed to interview the remainder of the group using [this] physical scaling. (pp. 215–216)*

It is useful to preface discussions of supervisee expectations, though, with a statement of the supervisor's own expectations, for these can have a real effect on what the supervisees then state as their own. The supervisor should make clear his or her preferred style (i.e., authoritative, participative, cooperative) and the implications of that style for expected member behavior. The supervisor's expectations also will include an articulation of the ground rules that will guide group and individual behavior.

Ground rules will include, of course, expectations about supervisee (a) participation (sharing their own material, but also giving honest feedback to others), (b) confidentiality, and (c) boundaries. Ground rules also concern such matters as frequency of meetings, attendance, and manner of case presentation. We will discuss each in turn. Although we are attempting to convey what we understand to be conventional clinical wisdom with respect to these matters, we realize that not all supervisors would agree on these points. What is important, though, is that supervisors be clear about how they intend to handle these matters and convey that clearly to group members.

Frequency of Meetings. How often the group meets will affect group process: meeting once a month, for instance, might make it difficult to develop a viable atmosphere, whereas, on the other extreme, to meet twice a week might be untenable for some members. Marks and Hixon (1986) found that members of groups that met weekly (as opposed to biweekly) had greater trust of other members and less anxiety. By contrast, groups that met biweekly were more cognitive and formal.

In each of their two studies of psychology internships, Riva and Cornish (1995, 2007) asked about frequency of group supervision sessions. The majority reported that they met weekly (88% of the respondents in the earlier study; 86% of those in the later study). For those who reported meeting every two weeks, those respective proportions were 6% and 9%; for those meeting once per month "or other," those proportions were 6% and 8%.

Attendance. Regular attendance is an especially important expectation to convey and enforce. Absences affect the group in multiple ways, including members' sense of cohesion that members feel, as well as the energy and vitality experienced during the meeting. Emphasize that, group members essentially are committing to be there for one another. As well, members will attach meaning to absences of other supervisees. For example, the supervisee who does not come the week after she presents a difficult case might cause others to worry that their feedback might have been too confrontive. This not only will affect the group session with the missing member, but, if not addressed in the group, will affect the quality of feedback given to this member when she returns.

Manner of Case Presentation. It is important to have ground rules concerning the manner of case presentations. These can include rules regarding confidentiality and each member's expected responsibilities and level of participation. But they also include expectations about how clinical material will be presented and processed. For example, Munson (2002) offered the following guidelines for case presentations:

1. The supervisor should present a case first.
2. The supervisee should be granted time to prepare the case for presentation.
3. The presentation should be based on written or audiovisual material.
4. The presentation should be built around questions to be answered.
5. The presentation should be organized and focused.
6. The presentation should progress from client dynamics to supervisee dynamics. (p. 156)

Munson went on to suggest that supervisors avoid:

1. presentation of several cases in a short session,
2. presentation of a specific problem rather than the case in context,
3. presentation of additional problems in a single case,

4. therapist dynamics preceding case dynamics during discussion, and
5. intervention expectations beyond the capabilities of the therapist. (p. 156)

Wilbur and Roberts-Wilbur (1983) and also, Wilbur et al. (1994) have devised a structure that distracts supervisees from some of their more personal issues and it seems, in our experience, to work very well with groups that approach the task of case conferences in an overly cautious fashion. Their structured group supervision model (SGS), presented in Table 10.2, begins with a supervisee making a "plea for help" that includes relevant information about the case and concludes with a request for specific feedback and then proceeds through the intervention of the group.

Storming. Supervisees need to feel and to seem competent. In group supervision, this can fuel

---

TABLE 10.2   Steps of the Wilbur et al. Structured Group Supervision Model

Step 1: Plea for Help. The supervisee states what assistance is being requested from the supervision group. The supervisee provides the group with summary information relating to the request for assistance. Information may be in the form of audio- or videotaped material, a written summary, or verbal communication. Following the presentation of the summary information, supervisee makes Plea for Help statement, e.g., "I need your help with. . . ."

Step 2: Question Period. The supervision group members ask the supervisee questions about the information presented in step 1. This step allows group members to obtain additional information or clarify any misperceptions concerning the summary information. One at a time, in an orderly manner, group members ask one question at a time of the supervisee. The process is repeated until there are no more questions.

Step 3: Feedback or Consultation. Group supervision members respond to the information provided in steps 1 and 2 by stating how they would handle the supervisee's issue, problem, client, etc. During this step, the supervisee remains silent but may take notes regarding the comments or suggestions. When giving feedback, group members again proceed one at a time, stating how they would handle the supervisee's dilemma. First person is used, e.g., "If this were my client, I would. . . ." The process is repeated until there is no additional feedback.

Pause or Break. There is a 10- to 15-minute break between steps 3 and 4. Group members should not converse with the supervisee during this break. This is time for the supervisee to reflect on the group's feedback and to prepare for step 4.

Step 4: Response Statement. The group members remain silent and the supervisee, in round-robin fashion, responds to each group member's feedback. The supervisee tells group members which of their statements were helpful, which were not helpful, and why they were beneficial or not.

Step 5: Discussion (optional). The supervisor may conduct a discussion of the four-step process, summarize, re-act feedback offered, process group dynamics, etc.

Source: From "Structured Group Supervision (SGS): A Pilot Study," by M. P. Wilbur, J. Roberts-Wilbur, C. M. Hart, I. R. Morris, and R. L. Betz, 1994, Counselor Education and Supervision, *33*, pp. 262–279. Copyright 1994 ACA. No further reproduction authorized without written permission of the American Counseling Association.

between-supervisee competition, especially over which one the supervisor will perceive as the best or perhaps even become the supervisor's favorite. This likely will be a continuing issue throughout the group experience, even if it remains latent. However, it is most prominent during the storming phase.

When between-supervisee competition is appropriately channeled, it can stimulate group members to stretch to be the best that they can. Moreover, some degree of competition seems actually to be good for group process (e.g., Boëthius, Ögren, Sjøvold, & Sundin, 2005). It falls to the supervisor, though, to contain and channel that competition.

In some educational contexts, educators actually encourage an openly competitive atmosphere. Aronson (1990) pointed out that one of the clearest examples occurs in some law schools: Because legal practice is adversarial, to encourage the development of combative skills is to prepare the students for practice. But no such demand exits in the mental health professions and too much competition can only interfere with learning.

Competition must be acknowledged in order for group members to put it into proper perspective. The following is one supervisor's intervention to accomplish that end:

> Could it be that the seminar is skirting around the question of who is the best therapist here? That is no doubt a hot potato, and what is even hotter is the question of who is the worst therapist. The issue of competition can contribute to the work of the group (everyone tries to do the best he [sic] can ... it may also interfere (people become too afraid of being rejected or envied)). (Rioch, Coulter, & Weinberger, 1976, p. 24)

Norming. By imposing an optimal level of structure, the supervisor provides group members with the sense of safety they need in order to risk exposing their clinical work—and themselves—to their peers. Yet the key word here is *optimal,* for if structure is too rigid, it can create its own tension by stifling spontaneity. The supervisor, therefore, needs not only to create an initial struc-

ture, but also to monitor its effect on the group and be prepared to alter or abandon part of the group's structure based on group feedback (in fact, to request the group's feedback is itself important).

Norming is an evolving process that occurs most heavily during one period of the group. But supervisors will have laid essential groundwork for the group's norming when they established structure and ground rules during the forming stage.

Performing. Keith, Connell, and Whitaker (1992) suggested that group therapists initially adopt a maternal role, providing nurturance, being solicitous of group members' feelings, and inviting the group members to be comfortable. The leader gradually then shifts to a paternal role, setting limits on topics and making demands on group members. Then, as the members' emotional investment in the group increases, the therapist gradually turns more and more of the leadership over to them. Keith et al. noted, though, that

> the supervision group passes through similar stages, but the maternal and paternal periods are usually brief. And to the extent the supervisor is either maternal or paternal, the parenting model is that of parent and older teenager; that is, it is very limited, acknowledging the freedom and maturity of the second generation. . . . The early 4 to 6 sessions require guidance; like learning to drive a car. Then the teacher becomes less active . . . (the driving instructor chooses to move to the back seat). (p. 98)

This observation would suggest, then, that Keith et al. would expect the supervision group to be into the performing stage by the fourth to the sixth session. In what they have described, the supervisor would be employing Proctor and Inskipp's (2001) *participative* style of supervision.

By the time the group reaches the performing stage, much important work already will have occurred. If this work has been effective, group members will have assumed appropriate levels of shared responsibility for the group and for one another. Individually, they will have begun to trust and will have become energized by a commitment to explore and examine their own therapeutic efforts. Supervisees will present cases that show them stretching the upper limits of their skill, rather than cases that either are too clear or are too impossible to elicit critical comments.

But for the group to be at the performing stage implies that something is being performed. Prieto (1998) investigated what that was with respect to one specific context and type of group supervision: the practicum class as taught in primarily master's-level counseling programs. His survey participants reported that, on average, more than half the group time (56%) was devoted to case presentations. The remainder of the time was apportioned for lectures and discussions on clinical topics (15%), supervisees' professional or personal issues (11%), administrative or practicum site issues (9%), and dynamics in the supervision group (8%). Interestingly, 62% of the supervisors required supervisees to read a textbook and 69% required them to read scientific journal articles.

Notably, case presentations predominated. Likely this would be true across most supervision groups, regardless of setting or supervisee level.

During the performing stage, the supervisor will continue to have issues and tasks to address, though these will be of a somewhat different form than was true in the earlier stages. The supervisor will be watching, for example, for signs of "nonwork" occurring and will change direction, ask the group for feedback, or offer the group some process feedback if this occurs. On the other hand, the supervisor must understand the importance of recycling some issues in order to permit them to be understood and confronted at new levels. What might feel like an old theme revisited might be a theme that finally is understood.

Borders (1991) proposed a model in which the supervisor employs the roles of both *moderator* and *process commentator*. As moderator, the supervisor keeps the group on task, choreographs the experience, and summarizes feedback. As process commentator, the supervisor attends to immediate group dynamics. For both roles, Borders emphasized the need for the supervisor to be cognizant of the developmental level of supervisees (e.g., novice counselors needing more direction and structure and more advanced supervisees being able to take on more responsibility). The model, therefore, requires a good deal of supervisor flexibility.

Borders (1989b) also described a structured group exercise that might breathe life into group processes when they become stagnant. This exercise relies on videotape for the presentation of cases and requires supervisees to present specific questions about the client or the session and to ask for specific feedback. Other group members then are assigned one of four tasks to direct their observation of the videotape segment, depending on the issues raised by the supervisee.

The first task is to engage in focused observation. A peer might be asked to focus on the use of one type of skill (e.g., confrontation) or one aspect of the session, such as the relationship between the counselor and client. Borders pointed out that a particular observation task could be used to develop specific skills of the observer. For example, the observer who has a tendency to quicken the pace of his or her sessions might be asked to observe the pace of the videotaped session.

The second task is that of role taking. An observer might be asked, for example, to take the role of the counselor, of the client, or even of some significant person in the client's life (e.g., a parent or a spouse). For family sessions, the assignment could be to represent the family member who refuses to come to therapy. After the videotape has been shown, the observer gives feedback from the perspective of the person that he or she represents.

The third task is to observe the session from a particular theoretical orientation. One observer could be assigned this task, or several observers could be looking at a session from different theoretical perspectives. For example, one supervisee could be asked to observe another supervisee's counseling session from a systemic perspective; another, from a cognitive–behavioral perspective. Not only does this exercise help supervisees to apply theory to practice, but it also helps to elicit underlying assumptions about problem formation and resolution.

The fourth task is for an observer to watch the session with the assignment of developing a descriptive metaphor. Borders reported that this approach has been particularly helpful when the issue is the interpersonal dynamics between the client and counselor or the counselor feeling "stuck." For example, an observer might be asked to think of a road map and describe the direction that counseling is taking or to view the counselor–client relationship within the context of a movie and describe each person's part in the drama.

Final Observations about the Performing Stage

We have two additional observations about the performing stage in group supervision. The first of these is that individual differences should be more salient at this stage. Because there is more group cohesion, each person's style of humor should be more evident, as should personal philosophies of life and of helping. When a supervision group is working well, there are no stars (including the supervisor) and no dunces. Rather, each supervisee is known for his or her particular talents, idiosyncratic way of viewing clients, and personal supervision goals. Everyone has something to gain from and to offer the group.

Some groups may never get fully to this performing stage, and probably all groups have some periods of "nonwork" throughout their life span. Shulman (1982) argued that the supervision group's "culture" is an important phenomenon to keep in mind. The culture is the gestalt that makes the group feel different from all other groups; these are the norms and rules that the group has adopted. Many of these are outside of members' conscious awareness, but powerful nevertheless. One such rule might be "give feedback, but don't make anyone angry." Although such a rule might be benign enough in the initial stages of group supervision, it would adversely affect the work of the group if it were to persevere and override the injunction to be honest.

It is rewarding when supervisees call into question nonproductive aspects of the supervision group's culture. But should this not occur, it ultimately is up to the supervisor to be aware of and to confront the limitations brought about by certain aspects of the group's culture.

The second of our concluding observations about the performing stage is that the supervisor should be open in all stages of the group—but perhaps especially during this stage—to feedback from the group about his or her own work. This allows the opportunity to change course if necessary, but also provides an important experience to the supervisees:

> *Therapists tend to have perfectionistic defenses that are reinforced by regular admonitions about appropriate behavior and professional responsibility. They need models and mentors who can keep their self-esteem despite acknowledged limitations and who concede that some clinical situations are inherently defeating, regardless of good intentions and proper training.* (McWilliams, 2004)

Our third concluding comment is that optimal group functioning at this stage depends on mutual trust and support among group members. Earlier we mentioned the importance of balancing challenge and support. This particular comment focuses specifically on support; feeling supported depends on trust of the person giving it.

Keith et al. (1992) and Nicholas (1989) have suggested that the supervisor provide "nurturant" energy in the early stages of the supervision group. As group members begin to invest emotionally in the group and in each other, primary responsibility for this nurturant energy shifts from the supervisor to the group members. This process corresponds with the development of group cohesiveness, which Yalom (1985) asserted is the group equivalent of empathy.

These processes, then, lead to an atmosphere of support between and among group members. And as support levels increase, so too do levels of between-member trust and therefore the extent to which supervisees are willing to become vulnerable with one another and to reveal their mistakes and weaknesses. All this contributes to the increasing value of the supervisory group to members.

Support might be understood as a counterbalance to between-member competitiveness. In fact, competition typically is more manifest in the early stages of the group but then becomes moderated as group cohesiveness and mutual support develop.

One interesting supportive phenomenon that we have observed concerns the situation in which a particular member of the supervision group clearly is faltering badly and the group rallies to protect that person. This protectiveness takes the form of giving softened and nurturing feedback and often even worrying that the supervisor may be behaving in an unduly harsh manner with this group member (despite objective evidence to the contrary).

Adjourning.   Most supervision groups probably are time limited. Some, however, are ongoing. Therefore, it is appropriate to discuss separately the termination processes of each type of group.

The Time-Limited Group.   Training calendars determine the time frames for many supervisory relationships. These calendars typically are linked to a semester, an academic year, or an internship rotation.

For practicum and internship groups, the supervision experience can be one of weeks, rather than months or years. Especially when the life of the supervision group is across a single semester, the ending of the group may feel premature to almost everyone. In addition, toward the conclusion of the semester, the urgency that supervisees may experience in managing the termination of their clients might override any consideration of the closure issues in the group itself.

It would be a mistake, though, to end a supervision group without allowing the group to process this phase. Moreover, because the ending of the supervisees' therapeutic relationships usually coincide with the ending of the supervisory group, the parallels become a useful tool and provide important material to process.

Virtually all brief therapy models have a particular structure, an emphasis on a treatment plan, and a particular emphasis on the process of termination. In a sense, this is a model that applies as well to time-limited supervision in any format. The goals of the supervision group should be specific enough that supervisees notice when those goals have been achieved so that they can feel a sense of accomplishment. At the same time, the supervisor needs to help supervisees to contextualize their learning—especially among less-experienced supervisees—to help allay panic at finding that they still are not the totally competent practitioners that they imagined they might or should be.

A time-limited experience inherently limits what supervisees will have the opportunity to learn. It is important, therefore, that they leave the supervision experience with a plan for self-improvement. One part of this plan for each supervisee most likely will be the securing of additional supervision. An important culminating experience, therefore, would be to crystallize what can be learned from supervision and how one goes about securing this type of supervision for oneself.

One aspect of time-limited supervision that can be frustrating for the supervisor is the nearly universal tendency of supervisees to begin withdrawing from the group when the end is in sight. Supervisees who are simultaneously approaching closure with their clients will complain that their clients have stopped "working." Often these same supervisees will be unaware that, in a type of parallel process, they are working less with each other in the supervision group. The need for psychological distance in order to cope with the loss both of people and of a valuable process is important to address in the group as supervisees handle multiple closure experiences.

The Ongoing Supervision Group.   A danger of the ongoing supervision group is that it might fizzle out, rather than end in a clear fashion. Like a relationship that fizzles out, the group that terminates in this manner is left with more unfinished business and perhaps an inadequate understanding of what caused the ending to occur. One strategy to avoid this is to schedule an ending from the outset of the group. Like all social systems, groups need markers in order to appreciate their development. An ending can provide this kind of marker, even if the group should reconstitute itself immediately with no change of membership.

The kind of ending that we suggest may be an appointed time when the group reviews the assumptions and decisions that were made in the pregroup phase. It is a time when as many things as possible become negotiable, including ground rules and the process of supervision itself. The ending allows supervisees to evaluate their individual development and their level of commitment and contribution to the goals of the group. Also, it is a time for the supervisor to evaluate the amount of responsibility that has been shared with group members, the process that has been in place, and the feasibility of continuance.

Endings can be added to the life of a group in several ways. One way is to freeze membership for a certain amount of time, say one year, at the end of which some members might leave and others might enter. In a sense, the change of membership gives the group a chance to start over. Another way is for the process of the group itself to change. For example, a supervisor might decide that it is time for the group to change from a supervisor-led group to a peer supervision group. This juncture could be planned as an ending.

Time can also be manipulated to produce a marker. A break of 4 to 6 weeks could be planned to occur every 6 months to encourage an evaluation and renegotiation period prior to or immediately after the break. Each group will find its own way to end once it appreciates the importance of ending.

Evaluation of the Supervisory Experience. The ending of the group also presents an opportunity for both supervisees and the supervisor to evaluate the experience. One key focus should be on what new knowledge and skills each supervisee obtained from the experience (from both their own and the supervisors' perspective), linking this back to the contract that was developed at the outset. It is equally important to assess what each supervisee had expected to get, but did not—and why they believed that was the case.

This is an opportunity, too, for the supervisor to obtain feedback about how the group perceived his or her work. If the group is offered as a practicum class, most universities will ensure that students complete end-of-term course evaluations. But these typically indicate more global information, such as how much the students learned and how prepared they believed the instructor to have been. But course evaluations typically do not provide information specific to effectiveness in supervising a group. Moreover, not all group supervision occurs in that context so the supervisor should be prepared to ask specific questions that will yield the type of feedback that will be helpful to him or her.

Researchers are beginning to recognize the need for instruments that will help to provide group supervisors with more systematic feedback. Supervisors now have available for their use at least three:

- White and Rudolph (2000) developed the *Group Supervisory Behavior Scale,* which has six subscales developed by rational means (Facilitation of an Open Climate; Demonstration of Professional Understanding; Clear Communication; Encouragement of Self-Evaluation; Efficiency and Clarity of Evaluation; Overall Quality of Behavior).
- Arcinue (2002) developed the *Group Supervision Scale* (available in the Supervisor's Toolbox). Its three factor-analytically derived scales are Group Safety, Skill Development and Case Conceptualization, and Group Management.
- Getzelman (2003) developed the *Group Supervision Impact Scale,* which measures impact of (a) the supervisor, (b) peers, and (c) the group environment. To have group members use instruments with established psychometric qualities to provide their supervisor with feedback about his or her performance can be very useful, not only during the adjourning stage of the group, but at other points as well.

PEER SUPERVISION GROUPS

Peer supervision has an important role in the life-long development of mental health professionals. Anyone who has been in the helping professions for a while knows—either firsthand or through observations of others—about problems of isolation and practitioner burnout, as well as that of becoming stale. Also, professional organizations have begun highlighting the need for continuing supervision, often incorporating the expectation for posttraining supervision into certification requirements; and, of course, this is an ongoing expectation in Britain and other countries.

Peer group supervision can help meet these needs. But we include peer supervision in its own section of the chapter because it has unique features that set it apart from supervisor-led groups. Most importantly, it is not hierarchical and includes no formal evaluation. In this sense, it really is consultation rather than supervision (see, e.g., McWilliams, 2004). But, at the same time, it is ongoing, and group members feel more accountable to each other than they might in a consulting relationship. It is difficult, therefore, to properly categorize it as being either supervision or consultation. But, however categorized, peer supervision seems to be a growing phenomenon and an important ingredient to the vitality of the mental health professions. Therefore, it is an important topic to address.

Although peer supervision has received only modest coverage in the professional literature, Lewis, Greenburg, and Hatch (1988) found, at least among psychologists in private practice, that 23% of a national sample were currently members of peer supervision groups, 24% had belonged to such a group in the past, and 61% expressed a desire to belong to a group if one were available. Among the reasons for joining peer groups (in rank order by importance) were: (1) recieving suggestions for problem cases, (2) discussing ethical professional issues, (3) countering isolation, (4) sharing information, (5) exploring problematic feelings and attitudes toward clients, (6) learning and mastering therapeutic techniques, (7) receiving support for stress in private practice, (8) countering burnout, and (9) gaining exposure to other theoretical approaches.

Wiley (1994) reported results of a survey of members of the American Psychological Association's Division of Counseling Psychology who were in private practice. She found that the proportion of those who reported participating either weekly or biweekly in peer supervision groups were as follows:

- Those who were 3 to 7 years postdoctorate; 25%
- Those who were 8 to 15 years postdoctorate: 38%
- Those 16 or more years postdoctorate: 32%

Her samples were small, but the findings were generally consistent with those of Lewis et al. (1988). Moreover, they were relatively consistent over time, even for very experienced practitioners.

Peer supervision groups can either develop from supervisor-led groups to peer groups or can be conceived as peer supervision groups from the outset. In either case, at the point that peers attempt to offer each other supervision (or consultation, as some authors prefer to designate it), certain conditions must exist if the process is to be successful. Chaiklin and Munson (1983) noted that a sincere desire to improve one's clinical skills is, of course, the primary condition for peer supervision. They also favored the model of a peer group beginning with a supervisor whose role is to work him- or herself out of a job. For practitioners working in mental health agencies or institutions, the second major condition is administrative backing (Chaiklin & Munson, 1983; Marks & Hixon, 1986). If administrators do not view peer supervision as valuable and cost-effective and if this is not communicated by the provision of space and time to conduct supervision meetings, the within-agency peer group will certainly falter.

The independent peer group (i.e., outside any employment setting) has probably the greatest potential for compatibility among its members because such a group tends to be formed by professionals who already know and respect each other. For the peer group formed within an institution, there may be some history to overcome among some of the members, such as political entanglements, competitiveness, or personality issues (Hamlin & Timberlake, 1982). In addition, lack of homogeneity of experience is far more likely for the within-agency group, which means that the group will most likely veer toward either the more-experienced or least-experienced members, to the potential frustration of the other members of the group.

Regardless of the initial compatibility of the peer group, however, the group stages outlined by Tuckman and Jensen (1977) will still occur and need attention. It is a common error of professionals who are already comfortable with one another to forego the planning stage for the group until issues begin to arise. Another potential for all supervision groups, but more so with peer groups, is differential contact among its members outside supervision. Ground rules may need to be outlined regarding any processing of supervision outside the group so as not to drain off energy that legitimately belongs within the group.

The Process of Peer Supervision Groups

Peer supervision groups tend to be more informal than other types of supervision groups (Lewis et al., 1988). This though, might be an error, at least in the beginning. Without the direction of a designated leader, structure can give the group some measure of stability while it is finding its particular rhythm. In fact, Counselman and Weber (2004) insist that a contract is essential in a peer supervision group.

Part of the structure must be, in fact, a plan for handling the leadership of the group. Although peer supervision groups are leaderless by definition, to ignore the issue of leadership gives rise to competitiveness (Schreiber & Frank, 1983). Therefore, many groups rotate the leadership role, with one person directing each meeting. The

leader may concern himself or herself with group leadership issues only, or may also be asked to take responsibility for secretarial issues arising as a result of the meeting, including communicating with absent members about the next meeting, keeping records of supervision meetings and actions taken, and the like.

On the other hand, Counselman and Weber (2004) present an alternative view:

> We believe that the successful, truly leaderless PSG shares the tasks of leadership. These include adherence to contract, gatekeeping and boundary management, and working with resistance. A successful PSG stays on task; i.e., it does not deviate from the original idea of being a PSG. . . . A PSG does not allow a de facto leader to emerge [nor do we] . . . recommend appointing a leader for each meeting. We believe in the value of everyone having equal responsibility for the group process. (p. 133)

The process also includes a plan for case presentation. Typically, one or two cases are the maximum that can be reasonably discussed at one meeting. Marks and Hixon (1986) suggested that the presenter come prepared with two or three questions about the case to direct the group's discussion. They also suggested that a process observer be appointed (different from either the presenter or the designated leader). This person would give feedback at the end of the supervision meeting about the group process that he or she observed, including "a statement regarding the group's ability to stay task-oriented, its adherence to ground rules, what group building may have occurred and the participation level of the group members" (p. 421).

Advantages and Disadvantages of Peer Supervision Groups

Those practitioners who participate in peer supervision groups tend to rate them very favorably. There is every reason to assume, therefore, that the number of peer supervision groups will grow. Among the advantages ascribed to peer supervision groups are the following (Counselman & Weber, 2004; Hamlin & Timberlake, 1982; Lewis et al., 1988; Marks & Hixon, 1986; Schreiber & Frank, 1983; Wendorf et al., 1985):

1. They help clinicians to remain reflective about their work and offer clinicians options beyond their individual frameworks. Skovholt and Rønnestad (1992b) found in their qualitative study of therapists across the life span that one theme that predicted therapists' ongoing professional development was their willingness to engage in reflective activity. Peer supervision groups serve this purpose.
2. They offer the type of environment that is especially attractive to adult learners.
3. They provide a forum for the reexamination of familiar experiences (e.g., early terminations or working with one particular ethnic group).
4. They provide a peer review process that maintains high standards for practice, thus reducing the risk of ethical violations.
5. They provide a forum for transmitting new information, thus providing continuing education for members.
6. They provide the continuity necessary for serious consultation.
7. They can provide some of the therapeutic factors often attributed to group process, including reassurance, validation, and a sense of belonging. As a result, they can reduce the potential for burnout.
8. They enable clinicians to become more aware of countertransference issues and parallel process.
9. Because peers, rather than experts, offer feedback, supervision is less likely to be compromised by conflicts with authority figures.

The major limitation reported by members of peer supervision groups came from within-agency groups (Marks & Hixon, 1986) because group members might form their own coalitions and interagency communication might not be facilitated. Also, when group members must work with each other outside the group, they may be reticent to self-disclose and are less trustful in the group.

But for some group members, the peer supervision group can be a vehicle for obtaining support or even some level of therapy. Counselman and Weber (2004) note that "one reason many therapists join a PSG is because they feel isolated in their professional lives" (p. 135) and so it is important that the group provide a mechanism to permit socializing, but not at the expense of the overall task, which is case presentation and discussion.

The structure of the group may be inflexible in dealing with crisis situations that are bound occasionally to occur in agencies. And, finally, Allen (1976) mentioned one additional disadvantage of peer groups: they may limit the amount of individual supervision sought by the group members. However, Marks and Hixon (1986) found that peer group supervision strengthened individual supervision by "pointing out its gaps" (p. 423).

CONCLUSION

Group supervision is an effective form of supervision that offers the supervisee the benefits of peer relationships, exposure to a greater number of cases, and vicarious as well as direct learning. There is little doubt that group supervision will continue to be an important supplement to individual supervision. Therefore, supervision practitioners would be well advised to give this vital form of supervision more empirical attention as practitioners develop and test group supervision models.

CHAPTER 11

SUPERVISION INTERVENTIONS
LIVE SUPERVISION

In Chapters 9 and 10 we reviewed the supervision interventions that typically transpire in individual case conferences and in the context of group supervision. That material addressed supervision as it is practiced by the majority of mental health professionals. A significant number of supervisors, however, rely on and often prefer the use of live supervision interventions. For obvious reasons, live supervision is especially popular in training programs where facilities are more conducive to its application (Carlozzi, Romans, Boswell, Ferguson, & Whisenhunt, 1997).

Live supervision represents a paradigmatic shift from either individual supervision or group supervision; therefore, it cannot be considered a subgroup of either. This shift essentially consists of two components: (1) the distinction between counseling or therapy and supervision is less pronounced than in traditional supervision, and (2) the role of the supervisor is significantly changed to include both coaching and cotherapist dimensions. As a result of these essential differences, the process of live supervision and its advantages and drawbacks are different from other forms of supervision. This chapter will address the evolution of live supervision, describe its process both with and without a supervision team, note the advantages and disadvantages for these two forms of live supervision, and address the available empirical findings about its effectiveness.

At one time, live supervision was considered the "hallmark of family therapy" (Nichols, 1984, p. 89). Marriage and family therapy training programs still rely heavily on live supervision (Nichols, Nichols, & Hardy, 1990; Wark, 2000), but its use has infiltrated other mental health professions (Bubenzer, West, & Gold, 1991; Carlozzi et al., 1997; Kivlighan, Angelone, & Swafford, 1991), and Saba (1999) reported the use of live supervision in medical training. Live supervision began as an intensive method for working with an individual supervisee (or perhaps two supervisees working as cotherapists). In more recent years, the team form of live supervision has gained in momentum. The team is a group of therapists (with or without a supervisor) or supervisees (with a supervisor) who work together on their cases. Because of the significantly different dynamics between live supervision without a team and team supervision, we will begin with the former and address team supervision later in the chapter. Furthermore, because "the literature suggests that the one-way mirror may be as basic to family therapy as the couch was to psychoanalysis" (Lewis & Rohrbaugh, 1989, p. 323), our discussion will follow suit and assume, in most cases, that the client is a family. Finally, we will not attempt to make clear distinctions between training or supervision (with the supervisee as the focus) and intervention (with the family system as the focus), even though we are aware that such distinctions sometimes are made in the literature on live supervision.

Live supervision was initiated by Jay Haley and Salvadore Minuchin (Simon, 1982) in the late 1960s as a result of a rather singular project. At the time, both were invested in treating low-income families, but were not enamored with the idea of trying to teach middle-class therapists what it was like to be poor. Therefore, they decided to recruit people with no more than a high school education from the communities being served and train them to work with other similar families. Because of the real need to protect the families being treated, Haley and Minuchin devised a live supervision model in which they could guide these inexperienced and untrained therapists as they worked. The result? In Haley's words: "Actually they did very well. We worked with them in live supervision, 40 hours a week for two years. Nobody has ever been trained that intensely" (Simon, 1982, p. 29).

Live supervision combines direct observation of the therapy session with some method that enables the supervisor to communicate with and thereby influence the work of the supervisee during the session. Therefore, the supervisor is simultaneously in charge of both training the therapist and controlling the course of therapy (Lewis, 1988). Because of the dual agenda of both observing and interacting with the supervisee, much has been written about the technology of live supervision, especially about different methods for communicating with the supervisee. We begin, therefore, by reviewing the different technologies used to communicate with the supervisee(s); we also consider the messages that are given by the supervisor during live supervision, as well as the function of presession and postsession deliberations. Once we have explored how live supervision is conducted, we will back up to consider some of the guidelines for the use of live supervision.

METHODS OF LIVE SUPERVISION

Bubenzer, Mahrle, and West (1987) listed six methods used to conduct live supervision: *bug-in-the-ear, monitoring, in vivo, walk-in, phone-in,* and *consultation.* We will explain each of these briefly, as well as *using computer and interactive television technology* to communicate with the therapist (Johnson & Combs, 1997; Kinsella, 2000; Klitzke & Lombardo, 1991; Miller, Miller, & Evans, 2002; Neukrug, 1991; Rosenberg, 2006; Smith, Mead, & Kinsella, 1998; Smith et al., 2007).

Bug-in-the-Ear

The bug-in-the-ear (BITE) consists of a wireless earphone that is worn by the supervisee through

which the supervisor can coach the supervisee during the therapy session. It has three major advantages: First, it allows the supervisor to make minor adjustments (e.g., "Get them to talk to each other") or to briefly reinforce the therapist (e.g., "Excellent") without interrupting the flow of the therapy session. In fact, much of what can be communicated through BITE might not warrant a more formal interruption of the session. Second, it has been established that BITE works as a behavioral strategy on the part of the supervisor to increase supervisee behaviors through such reinforcement (Gallant, Thyer, & Bailey, 1991). Third, BITE protects the therapy relationship more fully than other live supervision technologies because clients are unaware which comments are the direct suggestions of the supervisor (Alderfer, 1983, as cited in Gallant & Thyer, 1989). Recently, BITE has been found to be effective even when delivered through teleconferencing (Smith et al., 2007).

The disadvantages of BITE emerge from its advantages: Because BITE is seemingly so nonintrusive, it can be overused by the supervisor and can be a distraction to the supervisee who is trying to track the family, as well as take in advice from the supervisor (Smith et al., 1998). Similarly, there is a danger of "echo therapy" (Byng-Hall, 1982, as cited in Adamek, 1994): the supervisee simply parrots the words of the supervisor with little or no assimilation of the therapeutic implications of what is being said, thus encouraging supervisee dependence. Finally, because it is a less visible form of live supervision, it can produce awkward moments. For example, the supervisee who is attempting to listen to a supervisor comment might need to interrupt the family in order to focus on the supervisory input. Furthermore, because family members do not know when the supervisee is receiving input, the device itself can produce ambivalent feelings because of the secrecy it symbolizes.

Monitoring

The second form of live supervision, monitoring, is used minimally. Monitoring is the process whereby the supervisor observes the session and intervenes directly into the session if the therapist is in difficulty (Minuchin & Fishman, 1981). By implication, therefore, monitoring can be either a way to safeguard client welfare (in which case it is really not live supervision per se, but something that many supervisors might do if they felt a sense of urgency) or a form of live supervision that is less sensitive to the dynamics between therapist and clients. Conversely, an advantage of monitoring, assuming that the supervisor takes over when entering the room, is that it allows the supervisor to directly experience the family dynamics. A final advantage of monitoring is that it allows the supervisee to benefit from the modeling provided by the supervisor working with the family.

For more experienced therapists, supervisors can be called into an ongoing case as a consultant–supervisor (Richman, Aitken, & Prather, 1990). The supervisor is briefed ahead of time about the case and the difficulties that the therapist is having. The supervisor then conducts a session with the therapist present, typically referring particularly to the impasse that is being faced in therapy. Richman et al. remarked that using supervision in this way models and normalizes appropriate help-seeking behavior for the clients, as well as providing a helpful alteration to the therapy system that has been established.

In Vivo

In vivo has some similarity to monitoring in that it allows clients to see the supervisor in operation. Rather than taking over for the therapist, however, the supervisor consults with the therapist in the presence of the clients. With in vivo supervision, there is an assumption that the family deserves to have access to all information, including a discussion of interventions. Seen from a different angle, the conversation between supervisor and therapist can itself constitute an intervention by heightening the family's awareness of particular dynamics, especially when dynamics are therapeutically reframed for the benefit of the family. In vivo supervision has some similarity to the reflecting team that will be discussed later in the chapter.

The Walk-In

A form of live supervision that has similar characteristics to the two previous ones is the walk-in. The supervisor enters the room in order to interact with both the therapist and the clients, and then leaves. The walk-in does not imply an emergency, nor does it imply the kind of collegiality that is evident with in vivo supervision. A walk-in, therefore, can be used to redirect therapy and to establish certain dynamics between the supervisor and the family or the therapist and the family. As a result, it can be viewed as more of a therapy intervention than either monitoring or in-vivo supervision. All three methods of supervision that involve having the supervisor enter the therapy room are more intrusive in the therapy relationship than the methods that follow.

Phone-Ins and Consultation Breaks

The most common forms of live supervision are phone-ins or consultation breaks. These methods are similar in that both interrupt therapy for the therapist to receive input from the supervisor. There is little opportunity for the therapist to react to the intervention, however, when it is phoned in using an intercom system. In the consultation break, the therapist leaves the therapy room to consult with the supervisor (when the supervisor alerts the therapist by, for example, knocking on the door, when the therapist feels the need to consult, or at a predetermined point in the therapy hour). The therapist then has an opportunity to clarify what the supervisor is suggesting prior to returning to the therapy room. While both of these methods have documented training and supervision advantages, they have the disadvantage of intruding into the therapy system by virtue of the interruption.

Using Computers and Interactive Television for Live Supervision

First coined as "a bug-in-the-eye" by Klitzke and Lombardo (1991), this alternative to BITE uses a monitor in the therapy room in a fashion similar to how teleprompters are used in broadcast journalism. Rather than speaking into the ear of the supervisee, supervisors can unobtrusively make suggestions by typing them from a keyboard in the observation room to be read on the monitor placed behind the client.

Proponents of this method argue that it retains all the advantages while eliminating the disadvantages of BITE (Miller et al., 2002). Because the supervisee controls when it is an opportune time to read the supervisor's message, the supervisee feels less distracted by the method. Supposedly, this translates to a smooth session from the client's perspective. Neukrug (1991) added that the ability to save supervisor feedback on a disk in order to print it out for the supervisee is an additional advantage that allows the supervisee to review the feedback (along with an audiotape or videotape of the session) or the supervisor and supervisee to discuss the feedback at length in supervision. Rosenberg (2006) developed a system where text-based feedback is sent to supervisees observing a session while this same feedback is recorded on the session videotape (in a manner similar to subtitles) for the therapist to review after the session. The immediate beneficiaries of this method, therefore, are the peers of the therapist supervisee. Rosenberg asserted that this method is based on cognitive science that emphasizes vicarious learning for therapy situations that will most likely occur for these peer supervisees in the future.

Despite the arguments for using a monitor for supervision comments, this method also has been criticized for potentially overwhelming the supervisee with input. Follette and Callaghan (1995) proposed a significantly simpler cue of a graph line, heading up or down, to alert the therapist about his or her progress in the session. Tracey et al. (1995, as cited in Smith et al., 1998) used a monitor and a 14-icon system to offer the supervisee live feedback. In an attempt to find a "happy medium" between the minimal feedback offered by a graph line and the monitor methods that potentially deliver more information than the therapist can use during a session, Smith et al. (1998) developed a method that they have labeled Direct Supervision. Direct Supervision uses

software developed by Smith and Mead (1996) to give supervisees feedback about the supervisor's perceptions about the clients' and therapist's behavior, the expected therapeutic behaviors, and the therapist's "on target" behaviors. Direct Supervision uses a numbering system (1 to 4) in each of four quadrants on the monitor to alert the therapist during the session. Like the system proposed by Neukrug (1991), a permanent record of supervision input is kept and can be used to enhance postsession supervision. Smith et al. claimed that supervisees find the method to be nonintrusive and helpful.

Finally, Johnson and Combs (1997) advocated for two-way video transmission in order to conduct live supervision from campus to off-campus sites. Because live supervision tends to be more popular in training settings than clinical settings, the authors argued that this would allow trainees to benefit from live supervision while also benefiting from "real life" clinical settings. The disadvantages of this model include its cost; the time and training required to use the model; and potential trust, safety, and ethical issues. Because these disadvantages will be viewed as daunting by most clinical settings, it is unlikely that this model will be widely used in the field.

Although some supervisors are firmly committed to one method of live supervision, most of the literature on live supervision plays down the method used for live supervision, focusing instead on guidelines for the intervention or directive, parameters that must be respected when using live supervision, the acculturation of supervisees and clients to live supervision, and supervisee issues while working within the live supervision framework.

THE LIVE SUPERVISION INTERVENTION

Supervisor to supervisee communications during live supervision are typically referred to as the *supervisory intervention* or *supervisor directives*. For our purposes here, the terms are interchangeable. We will discuss interventions delivered by means of the bug-in-the-ear, phone-ins, and consultation breaks, as these are the most commonly used methods of live supervision. Consultation breaks also are a commonly used intervention when a team is involved in live supervision. Consultation within the context of team supervision will be discussed later in the chapter.

Prior to implementing a live supervision intervention, the supervisor should ask: (1) Is redirection necessarily called for in the session? (2) Might the therapist redirect the session without an intervention? (3) Will the therapist be able to carry out the intervention successfully? (4) Is the driving force of the intervention to attend to the needs of the therapist and the client or on the supervisor's desire to do cotherapy? (Frankel & Piercy, 1990; Heath, 1982; Liddle & Schwartz, 1983). Additionally, the supervisor must consider the strengths and limitations of the intervention modality to be used.

Bug-in-the-Ear Interventions

There is no question that this form of sending a supervision directive is the most limited for the reasons already discussed. In particular situations and for specific reasons, however, BITE may still be the intervention method of choice. BITE is especially recommended for novice supervisees (Adamek, 1994) when relatively frequent, yet brief, suggestions are warranted. The new supervisee would also benefit from the reinforcing potential of BITE (e.g., "Nice question") that might be lost using other methods of supervision. It stands to reason that the use of BITE implies that the supervisor will be focusing on basic observable skills during the therapy session. Additionally, it follows that if BITE is the method of delivering interventions the major part of supervision must occur either before or after the session. Finally, because BITE is inherently distracting, the supervisor must be sensitive to its effect for each supervisee. There may be instances, for example, when the use of BITE has no benefits at all because of the reactivity of the supervisee to the supervisor's interventions.

It might be appropriate to use BITE for a more advanced supervisee if the supervisee has a specific goal for a particular session. For example, if a supervisee has been consistently sidetracked by a particular client, the supervisor could alert the supervisee when this was occurring in the session using BITE. As this example demonstrates, BITE interventions take the form of *coaching,* whether they are delivered to novice supervisees or more experienced therapists.

Telephone Interventions

Unlike BITE, telephone interventions have the advantage of stopping the therapy session. This allows the supervisee to listen to the directive without having to attend to the client at the same time. The phone-in has another advantage in that the client is alerted simultaneously that the therapist is being advised and will be prepared for a change in direction in the session. Furthermore, because the client knows that the therapist is receiving feedback, the supervisor directive can be the intervention itself. For example, if the supervisor believes that a member of the family is getting lost, the therapist might be advised to continue the session with "My supervisor thinks that we women (referring to herself and the mother) have been doing all the talking and we're not letting John (the father) have a say. My supervisor would like to hear what you think is going on between your wife and your son."

As is the case for all live supervision interventions, telephone directives should be used conservatively; furthermore, they should be brief, concise, and generally action oriented (Haley, 1987; Lewis & Rohrbaugh, 1989; Mauzey & Erdman, 1997; Rickert & Turner, 1978; Wright, 1986). Depending on the developmental level of the supervisee, a verbatim directive might be given (e.g., "Ask the mother 'What is your worst fear about Thomas if he continues with his present crowd?'"), or, for the more advanced supervisee, a more flexible directive might be given (e.g., "Reframe Mom's behavior as concern") (Rickert & Turner, 1978; Wright, 1986). Other generally accepted guidelines when phoning in interventions include avoiding process statements (or keeping them very brief) and refraining from complex directives, not exceeding two instructions per phone-in, being sensitive to the timing of the intervention and avoiding interventions during the first 10 minutes of the therapy session, limiting phone-ins to a maximum of five per therapy session, and communicating that it is the supervisee's decision when a suggestion can be worked into the session (unless the supervisor has clearly stipulated a time for the intervention) (Frankel & Piercy, 1990; Lewis & Rohrbaugh, 1989; Wright, 1986).

Wright asserted additionally that it is sometimes strategically wise to begin an intervention with positive reinforcement of what has transpired in the session up to the present. In other words, taking the time to say "You're really doing a terrific job keeping Dad from taking over" might be worth the time and increase the supervisee's investment in carrying out future interventions. This advice was supported by research that found that supervisees experienced phone-ins that included support components as "most effective"; conversely, supervisees were twice as likely as their supervisors to judge phone-in interventions without support as "least effective" (Frankel, 1990). Unfortunately, Frankel found that supervisors using phone-ins employed supportive interventions only about one third as often as they used directive behaviors.

Mauzey and Erdman (1997) conducted a phenomenological study of the effect of phone-in interventions on supervisees that confirmed these earlier suggestions as valid. In addition, they found that well received phone-ins focused on the welfare of the client more than on training, were "on track" rather than suggesting that therapy go in a new direction, flowed from a trusting relationship with the supervisor, and considered both the anxiety level and developmental level of the supervisee.

In summary, the phone-in is a sound live supervision method when the message is relatively brief, uncomplicated, and action oriented. It is less effective for more complicated process issues. When the supervisee needs more clarification than can be provided with a phone directive, the supervisee should leave the room for a consultation break (Haley, 1987).

Consultation Break Interventions

Even if BITE or a phone system is available to the supervisor, a consultation break may be the method of choice. In addition to the supervisee's need for clarification, consultation will be preferred if it is the opinion of the supervisor that

1. the intervention will be lengthy and the supervisee will need some extra time to absorb it (Rickert & Turner, 1978);
2. the supervisee will need a rationale for the intervention, which is not accomplished well using the phone-in (Rickert & Turner, 1978);
3. the supervisee will profit from the opportunity to react to the intervention, perhaps to be sure that it is understood or compatible with how the supervisee is experiencing the family; and
4. there is a need to check out some impressions with the supervisee as part of forming the intervention.

When consultation is used, it is essential that the supervisor is attentive to the amount of time that the conference takes away from therapy. There is a momentum to the therapy session that is diluted by a live supervision conference. This momentum must be considered as part of the formula for successful live supervision. If the therapist remains out of the therapy room too long, the intervention that is carried back to the client might be moot. A partial exception to this admonition is if the client system has been forewarned that a lengthy consultation is part of the therapy hour. In fact, when strategic family therapy is being implemented, the consultation may take place somewhere near the halfway mark of the therapy hour and the supervisee might return to the session only to deliver the final directive, usually in the form of a homework assignment. That being said, Locke and McCollum's (2001) findings that clients were satisfied with live supervision as long as its perceived helpfulness outweighed its perceived intrusiveness remains important guidance.

Dimensions of Live Supervision Interventions

Heppner et al. (1994) studied live supervision interventions delivered during individual therapy. Using the walk-in mode of live supervision, this study found six identifiable dimensions, each being bidirectional (pp. 230–232):

1. *Directing–instructing versus deepening.* At one end of this dimension, the supervisor offered the supervisee explicit suggestions or direction. At the opposite end of this dimension the supervisor offered minor adjustment to deepen an emotional process occurring in the session.

2. *Cognitive clarification versus emotional encouragement.* On one side, the supervisor focused on the content of the session or a task and attempted to help the therapist come to a better understanding of what was transpiring. The opposite side for this dimension was described as supervisors attempting to get supervisees to express the feelings that they were having in the session, especially as they related to the client.

3. *Confronting versus encouraging the client.* At one end, the supervisor was identifying how the client was impeding the supervisee and how this could be altered; on the opposite end of this dimension, the supervisor attempted to make the client more comfortable and willing to take risks.

4. *Didactic–distant versus emotionally involved.* At one end of this dimension, the supervisor seemed to be taking a detached, expert stance, while at the other end the supervisor seemed emotionally involved with both supervisee and client and appeared highly invested in the outcome of therapy.

5. *Joining versus challenging the supervisee.* For this dimension, it was the relationship between supervisor and supervisee that seemed to vary from reinforcing the supervisee and attempting to help the client understand what the supervisee was trying to accomplish to the supervisor challenging the supervisee to examine his or her approach and perhaps consider a different approach.

6. *Providing direction versus resignation.* On one end of the continuum, the supervisor was highly invested in the session and worked hard to get the process to move forward, while on the other end the supervisor communicated that there was little that could be done from the supervisor's standpoint to move the session forward.

The Heppner et al. (1994) study offered no guidance about what constitutes optimal live supervision interventions. Still, the study offers a rubric by which interventions can be assessed. If, for example, most interventions challenged the supervisee (dimension 5), admonitions from other authors would suggest that leaning toward challenge rather than support may pose problems (Frankel, 1990; Mauzey & Erdman, 1997).

In summary, during-session interventions are far more complex than they may appear. A good directive must be succinct and add clarity, not confusion, to the supervisee's deliberations. Even consultation breaks must be efficient in their use of therapy time and should focus primarily on the supervisee's executive (behavioral) skills (West, Bubenzer, Pinsoneault, & Holeman, 1993). Additionally, supervisees must experience live supervision as constructive, not critical, if the interventions are to be successful. For the supervisee to have an opportunity to process more reflectively, thus developing perceptual and cognitive skills, presession and postsession conferences are requisite.

PRESESSION PLANNING AND POSTSESSION DEBRIEFING

Although the interaction between the supervisor and the therapy system is the crux of live supervision, what comes before and after are the foundation for the successful implementation of the model. Especially because of the level of activity involved in live supervision, there is a necessity for groundwork to be done in order for the activity during the session to remain meaningful.

As one might suppose, the goal of the presession is to prepare the supervisee for the upcoming therapy session. There will be some speculation about what the family might bring to this session. The supervisor will have two goals in the presession: to prepare the supervisee for the upcoming session and to focus on the supervisee's own learning goals as they pertain to the upcoming session. Piercy stated that he wanted his supervisees to show evidence of having a "theoretical map" and then to be able to "tie it to a practical understanding of how to bring about change" (West, Bubenzer, & Zarski, 1989, p. 27). Additionally, supervisees are often asked to attempt a particular technique (e.g., to raise the intensity of the interactions between family members), or they may be asked if they have something particular that they would like the supervisor to observe. In other words, it is important that both the supervisee and supervisor complete the presession with some clarity about their roles for the therapy session.

On the other hand, Okun argued that family therapy "cannot be organized like a lesson plan" (West et al., 1989, p. 27). Families will force both supervisees and supervisors to be spontaneous even if they are adequately prepared for the session. The developmental level of the supervisee must be reflected in presession planning. The supervisor will be more active with the novice supervisee in terms of both helping to provide a conceptual overview and planning for immediate interventions. Once the supervisee has gained in experience, it is expected that the supervisor will take a more consultative position (West et al., 1989; West et al., 1993).

The postsession debriefing allows the supervisee and the supervisor to discuss what transpired in the session. Because they were both involved in the therapy but held different vantage points, this is an important time to share perceptions, review the effectiveness of interventions, offer feedback, and address any unfinished business from the session as a precursor to planning the next session.

If homework has been assigned to the family, this is also a time to consider ways in which the family might respond to the assignment and to begin to consider future interventions based on the family's response. In other words, the successful postsession will leave the supervisee with some food for thought to consider prior to the next presession (West et al., 1989).

Although the presession conference is an important coaching session, the postsession debriefing is the optimal time for the conceptual growth of the supervisee. This conference, therefore, should not be rushed. If there is no opportunity to meet immediately after the therapy session, it should be scheduled at another time, but far enough prior to the next therapy session so it does not feel like another presession conference. Couchon and Bernard (1984) found that supervisor behaviors are significantly influenced by the timing of a supervision session in relation to the next counseling session for the supervisee. Specifically, when a supervisee is facing an upcoming session, the supervisor will become far more directive in order to help the supervisee to prepare, even if the last session has not been previously critiqued with the supervisee. Therefore, the postsession must occur at a time when the next session with the same client is not imminent and when there is ample time to move beyond intervention issues to larger conceptual and relationship issues.

Now that the overall process of live supervision has been described, we turn our attention to conditions for the effective use of live supervision.

IMPLEMENTING LIVE SUPERVISION

In his seminal article, Montalvo (1973) listed six guidelines for live supervision that continue to be relevant today.

1. *Supervisor and supervisee agree that a supervisor can either call the supervisee out, or that the latter can come out for feedback when he [sic] wishes.* [Elizur, 1990, later asserted that supervisees needed to buy into the model before its use, suggesting that this be negotiated as part of a supervision contract.]

2. *Supervisor and supervisee, before settling down to work, agree on defined limits within which both will operate.* [For example, the supervisor outlines under what conditions, if any, the supervisee can reject the supervisor's intervention.]

3. *The supervisor endeavors not to inhibit the supervisee's freedom of exploration and* *operation too much, but, if he does so, the supervisee is expected to tell him.*

4. *The mechanism for establishing direction is routine talks before and after the session.* [Montalvo felt strongly that the family should not be privy to these discussions and that efforts to "democratize" the therapy process have not proved useful. To date, there is no uniform opinion among family therapy theorists about this issue.]

5. *The supervisor tries to find procedures that best fit the supervisee's style and preferred way of working.*

6. *The beginner should understand that at the start he may feel as if he is under remote control.* (pp. 343–345)

These guidelines reflect Montalvo's structural family therapy bias. The wisdom of the guidelines, however, lies in both their clarity regarding the supervision hierarchy and their respect for the integrity, if not the ego, of the supervisee. Insufficient attention to one of these issues can result in an unsatisfactory experience with live supervision. More recently, Lee and Everett (2004) compiled their own list of conditions for effective live supervision. Reflecting the increasing focus on relationship variables within supervision, their admonitions are paraphrased as follows:

1. Supervisors, respecting the presence of isomorphism, need to attend to the supervisory relationship and relate to their supervisees as they would have their supervisees relate to their clients.
2. Supervisors must use active listening with their supervisees, validate them, and remain flexible as part of live supervision.
3. Supervisors should understand that offering criticism in a live setting, particularly with other supervisees present or in front of a clinical family, can be emotionally devastating to the supervisee.
4. Supervisors should not offer directions that are inappropriate to the supervisee's level of development and should take into account the

supervisee's ability to tolerate risks in this public setting.

5. Supervisors should be personable, acknowledge their mistakes, use concrete suggestions, explain the rationale for their suggestions, and be open to supervisee feedback.
6. Supervisors should demonstrate respect and support and, when appropriate, humor, enthusiasm, and humility.
7. Supervisors should remember that when supervisee anxiety gets too high or if criticism is combined with disrespect, the entire training experience can become toxic. (p. 71) (McCollum, 1995, addressed the supervisor's own anxiety during live supervision and posed the question: "How do I keep my own anxiety under control and curb my own oldest-brother wish to take over and make things 'right' versus letting the [supervisee] and clients stew with their troubles?" [p. 4].)

Bubenzer et al. (1987) made four suggestions to help desensitize supervisees to live supervision. Using phone-ins as their method, they suggested that supervisors first show new supervisees videotapes of family sessions during which the phone rings and the session is interrupted. By doing this, supervisees are able to observe how clients react when the phone rings and how things proceed afterward. This is often one of the first concerns for new supervisees. Second, new supervisees are allowed to be observers while live supervision is being conducted with other counselors. They are encouraged to ask the supervisor any questions as things proceed. Third, hypothetical cases are presented to the supervisees for them to practice the consecutive stages of pretreatment (or presession planning), counseling during session, and posttreatment (or postsession debriefing). At this time the possible use of phone-ins is discussed. Finally, again through role-play of hypothetical cases, the supervisees conduct sessions, following through on their plans and experiencing phone-ins during the session as previously discussed. With the amount of anxiety that can surround supervision of any type, the idea of allowing a trial run as described by Bubenzer et al. makes intuitive sense and has been implemented elsewhere (e.g., Neukrug, 1991). It should also be noted that this type of careful and caring orientation to the use of live supervision is consistent with the comments made by supervisees in the Mauzey and Erdman (1997) study when describing positive experiences with live supervision.

Once the therapist becomes used to the idea of the inevitability of being interrupted during therapy and knows what form this will take, the pressure is on the supervisor to be concise and helpful. Berger and Dammann (1982) offered two astute observations about the supervisor's reality versus the supervisee's reality during live supervision. Because of the one-way mirror separating them, the supervisor "will see patterns more quickly and will be better able to think about them—to think meta to them—than the therapist will" (p. 338). Second, "the supervisor will lack accurate information as to the intensity of the family affect. This becomes readily apparent if the supervisor enters the room to talk with the family" (pp. 338–339).

There are outgrowths to each of these perceptual differences. Because of the advantage that the supervisor enjoys by being behind the one-way mirror, a common reaction for the therapist, according to Berger and Dammann (1982), is to "feel stupid" (p. 338) once something is called to the therapist's attention. The reason, of course, that the supervisee feels stupid is because what is pointed out seems painfully obvious, but is something that eluded the supervisee during the therapy session. The wise supervisor will prepare supervisees for this reaction and allow them opportunities to experience firsthand the cleverness that comes from being at a safe distance from the therapy interaction.

Regarding the intensity issue, the supervisee might rightfully feel that the supervisor does not understand the family if the supervisor is underestimating the intensity of family affect. It is for this reason, that is, the direct contact with the family experienced primarily by the supervisee, that Berger and Dammann (1982) supported others who believed that, except for an emergency, "the supervisor proposes and the therapist disposes" (p. 339).

Gershenson and Cohen (1978) also noted that the relationship between supervisee and supervisor can begin on rocky ground because of the vulnerability felt by the supervisee. This vulnerability can be experienced as anxiety and resistance, persecutory fantasies, and anger. It could be conjectured that at this stage the supervisee is reacting to the unfair advantage of the supervisor (behind the one-way mirror), along with extreme embarrassment at the mediocrity of his or her own performance. Fortunately, this initial stage seems to be short-lived for most supervisees and, indeed, Mauzey, Harris, and Trusty (2000) found that both anger and anxiety diminished with more exposure to live supervision. According to Gershenson and Cohen, a second stage follows, characterized by having high emotional investment in the process and perceiving the supervisor as a supporter rather than as critic. We can assume that this stage also represents a heightened dependence on the supervisor. Finally, a third stage emerges in which "the directions of our supervisor became less important as techniques to be implemented and instead served as a stimulus to our own thinking . . . [we] reached a point at which we were able to initiate our own therapeutic strategies" (p. 229).

ADVANTAGES AND DISADVANTAGES

Advantages

The advocates of live supervision have been ardent (Bubenzer et al., 1991). The well-documented advantage of live supervision is that through this form of coaching by a more experienced clinician there is a much greater likelihood that counseling and therapy will go well. There is also an assumption and some empirical evidence (Kivlighan et al., 1991; Landis & Young, 1994; Storm, 1994) that the supervisee will learn more efficiently and, perhaps, more profoundly as a result of these successful therapy sessions. To return to our coaching metaphor, it is better to be coached and to win the game than to be playing independently and suffer defeat.

In addition to the training function of live supervision, there is a built-in safeguard for client welfare. Because the supervisor is immediately accessible, clients are protected more directly. This also allows trainees to work with more challenging cases, which might be too difficult for them if another form of supervision were being used (Cormier & Bernard, 1982; Jordan, 1999; Lee & Everett, 2004). Of course, the difficulty of the case must be considered carefully. Too difficult a therapy case will mean that the trainee is simply the voice of the supervisor and little more. The supervisor must be astute regarding the developmental level of the trainee and determine which cases are within the trainee's grasp (Lee & Everett, 2004).

A similar advantage to live supervision is that the supervisee is more likely to risk more in conducting therapy because of the knowledge that the supervisor is there to help with interventions (Berger & Dammann, 1982). Furthermore, because of the direct involvement of the highly skilled supervisor, clients assigned to supervisees will receive better treatment (Rickert & Turner, 1978).

Another set of advantages related to live supervision has to do with the supervisee's relationship with the supervisor. Because the supervisor often will share responsibility for interventions, the supervisor is far more active than in other forms of supervision. This level of involvement increases the credibility of the supervisor because supervisees experience the clinical skills of the supervisor directly (Lee & Everett, 2004). Furthermore, because the supervisor's assistance is direct and immediate, there is great potential for enhancement of the supervisory working alliance.

The supervisee's view of the process of therapy will also be affected by live supervision, because it should unfold more systematically due to the input from the supervisor. When the supervisor gives a rationale for an intervention, predicts reactions, and proves to be right, the supervisee experiences firsthand the predictability of some client patterns. This is an exciting moment for the supervisee; fortunately, it is balanced by those moments when clients react unpredictably, thus ensuring a sense of our fallibility as helpers.

Finally, supervisors often enjoy supervision more when engaged in live supervision (Lee & Everett, 2004). Because supervisor investment is central to good supervision, this advantage is a powerful one.

Disadvantages

The most noted disadvantages of live supervision are the time it demands of supervisors (Bubenzer et al., 1991; Lee & Everett, 2004), the cost of facilities, the problem of scheduling cases to accommodate all those who are to be involved, and the potential reactions of clients and supervisees to this unorthodox form of supervising (e.g., Anonymous, 1995). Additionally, Schwartz, Liddle, and Breunlin (1988) returned to one of Montalvo's (1973) initial concerns and alerted supervisors to the tendency of "robotization" in using live supervision. Unless the supervisor is highly systematic in giving the supervisee more and more autonomy, live supervision can produce clinicians who show little initiative or creativity during therapy and who conceptualize inadequately. This potential disadvantage of live supervision has been echoed by others (e.g., Adamek, 1994; Kaplan, 1987; Lee & Everett, 2004; Lee et al., 2004; Montalvo, 1973; Rickert & Turner, 1978; Storm, 1997; Wright, 1986). Lee et al. (2004) speculated that the practical challenges endemic to live supervision, as well as some pedagogical concerns, might have contributed to its relative decline in recent years.

> *Because live supervision historically has been highly associated with directive models of therapy, such as structural and strategic, the postmodern and integrative movements may be a contributing factor to the increasing use of other modalities. The decline of live supervision and the popularity of videotape and case presentation methods also may be a combination of the practical difficulties and financial costs of getting supervisor, therapists, and clients together in the same time and place, and the fact that live approaches, for all their benefits, do not address important training needs.* (pp. 67–68)

Schwartz et al. (1988) noted that both critics and proponents of live supervision are concerned about how live supervision potentially undercuts the therapist's own observations and intuitions in favor of the supervisor's. Lee and Everett (2004) similarly viewed a disadvantage of live supervision as potentially stalling the supervisee's self-sufficiency and self-confidence. Additionally, Lee and Everett have underscored a concern that all the focus on the present session can endanger a broader assessment of clients, as well as limit the supervisee's theory development and professional growth.

Focusing on the supervisor's influence on the supervisee, Moorhouse and Carr (2001) found that isomorphism between the two was met with resistance more often than cooperation from the client. These authors hypothesized that if therapist and supervisor were highly attuned to one another they may generate more creative, novel interventions, thus stimulating resistance in their clients. Therefore, Moorhouse and Carr seemed to be suggesting that, while the professionals are taking pleasure in their ingenuity, they may be losing sight of the immediate needs of the clients or their readiness to experiment with unorthodox strategies.

Finally, there is virtually no evidence in professional literature that skills learned within a live supervision context generalize to other counseling situations (Gallant et al., 1991; Kivlighan et al., 1991). This is a serious gap in our knowledge for both supervisee and client welfare, especially in cases for which supervision is limited to the live supervision modality.

TEAM SUPERVISION

To this point we have focused on the supervisor–therapist (supervisee) relationship in live supervision. More and more, however, live supervision has become synonymous with team supervision, that is, live supervision with other supervisees (in addition to the supervisor) behind the one-way mirror. Although team therapy was originally developed by seasoned practitioners (peers) as a means to study and improve their trade, it has become increasingly popular as

a method of training even novice practitioners (e.g., Haley, 1987; Heppner et al., 1994; Landis & Young, 1994). Briefly described, the process of team supervision involves a group of supervisees present with the supervisor behind the one-way mirror during the therapy session while another supervisee serves as the therapist with the clients. As with supervisor-only live supervision, the technology most frequently used in team supervision is the phone. The other common method of communication is consultation in the observation room.

Therefore, while the therapist is working with the family, the team is observing family interactions, metacommunication, and so on, to arrive at some sort of decision regarding the direction that therapy should go. The observation room is as busy, if not busier, than the therapy room. The team members have the luxury of being one step removed, allowing them to see the entire therapeutic system, including the therapist. The assumption is that this more objective posture will aid the conceptualization process, as will the synergy of ideas as the family is discussed. Team supervision also allows the supervisor to do a great deal of teaching while therapy is being conducted and to culminate an important clinical lesson with a timely intervention sent to the family through the therapist. Team supervision, therefore, becomes therapy, supervision, and classroom all in one.

To facilitate the activity and efficiency of the team, it is sometimes helpful to assign specific tasks to different team members (West et al., 1989). These tasks can be assigned by the supervisor or, if the therapist is looking for specific feedback, by the therapist. For example, the therapist supervisee who is concerned about her ability to maintain appropriate boundaries within the session might ask one team member to observe only this aspect of the session.

Bernstein, Brown, and Ferrier (1984) presented a model describing what they considered essential roles in team supervision: the *therapist,* the person who will sit with the family during the session and will remain attuned to the mechanics of running the session; the *taskmaster,* the member of the team assigned to direct the conference and keep the team from deviating from the previously agreed on structure for analyzing the information being produced by the family, while ensuring an atmosphere conducive to creativity and spontaneity; and the *historian,* the person responsible for maintaining the threads of continuity across and within treatment sessions.

The supervisor can organize the team to accomplish any number of goals. One member could be asked to observe one member of the family or one relationship (e.g., father–child) or to track one theme, such as what happens in the family when feelings are introduced. Such assignments allow the supervisor to teach the importance of particular dynamics for progress in therapy. Furthermore, the supervisor can assign tasks to specific team members that represent their unique training goals. For instance, the team member who has a difficult time joining with children in counseling sessions can be asked to observe another supervisee's joining style with children. The team, therefore, offers not only the advantage of in-session assistance but also numerous and rich possibilities for learning and postsession feedback.

The Reflecting Team

In his seminal work, Anderson (1987) described a novel team approach to working with families. His *reflecting team* represented a way to demystify the team approach to therapy for the family. Rather than leaving the family to their conjectures when the therapist joined the team for consultation, Anderson proposed that light and sound be switched from the therapy room to the observation room and that the family and therapist listen to the team reflect on what they have heard during the session to that point. Anderson suggested that the team's reflections could either be sought by the therapist (e.g., "I wonder if the team has any ideas that might be helpful at this point") or could be offered by the team (e.g., "We have some ideas that might be useful to your conversation"). As a therapy model, the reflecting team approach

is embedded in the work of Bateson (1972) and others, and the team's deliberations are carefully formed to reflect communication patterns within the family's repertoire. Because our interest in the reflecting team is as a supervision model, we will not focus on this aspect of the model.

By having the team's deliberations observed by the family, a certain egalitarianism was added to the live supervision model that seemed to be an advantage in accomplishing therapeutic goals. Rather than receiving one central message delivered by a spokesperson for the team, the family was able to hear the deliberations themselves and draw from them as they wished. Reflections could represent competing, yet equally sound, alternatives that allowed the family to reflect on others' impressions of their options. The input from the team, therefore, was far richer from the family's perspective.

For the team, the reflecting team model made all deliberations public. Because there could be no throwaway comments within this model, team members were more attentive as observers and more disciplined in their reflections. Guidelines for framing comments became more important than they were with confidential consultation breaks.

Anderson suggested that there be three team members who would participate in the model (not counting the therapist who stayed with the family). This way a third person could react to the deliberations of the other two. If the team was larger than this, Anderson advised that additional members be observers, participating only if called on by the team. Additionally, Anderson noted that persons could change rooms if it was not possible to reverse lights and sound within a facility. In the original discussion of reflecting teams, supervisees were mentioned only tangentially. Anderson stated that supervisees were invited to participate as reflecting team members as they felt ready, and most became increasingly active with experience.

Since Anderson's introduction of the reflecting team approach, the model has received attention as a supervision model (e.g., O'Connor, Davis, Meakes, Pickering, & Schuman, 2004; Roberts,

1997; Shilts, Rudes, & Madigan, 1993; Young et al., 1989). Young et al. offered a strong rationale for the reflecting team based on the disadvantages of the more standard live supervision team. The disadvantages of nonreflecting teams, according to Young et al., were at least four in number: First, regardless of the espoused support of the team, the supervisee in the room filling the role of therapist felt anxious and on the spot, not only with the family, but also in relation to the observing team. By contrast, the reflecting team spreads out the spotlight. The therapist is no longer the sole representative of the team of experts. The experts can speak for themselves and may look no more impressive than the therapist. Second, supervisees found it very difficult to disengage from the family, join the team in any meaningful way, and reengage with the family in the short time available for consultations. With the reflecting team, the therapist stays with the family, both physically and systemically. The therapist hears the team's thoughts as the family does and is in a position to facilitate the family's response to the team's comments from the vantage point of a neutral position. Third, the message delivered back to the family in traditional team approaches was often construed under time pressures and with uneven contributions from team members. With the reflecting team, the reflections themselves become the intervention and therefore need only develop as far as they can logically in the time allotted. The value is in the musings themselves as team members attempt to view the family's situation from different angles. Also, because of the structure of the team, the likelihood that one member will dominate is greatly diminished. Finally, Young et al. cited the relationship between clients and the team as a problem that the reflecting team addresses. In the more traditional model, the team becomes a cause for suspicion, "spies" from on high, persons of dubious motives. This apprehension is erased when clients hear the team members firsthand, not with slick interventions to transmit, but with their spontaneous interactions on the family's behalf. Despite the optimistic view of Young et al.,

O'Connor et al. (2004) found some therapists and clients were overwhelmed by the amount of information generated by reflecting teams. Therefore, it may be safe to say that reflecting teams that get overstimulated by therapy data may suffer from diminishing returns at some point in the reflection process.

Young et al. (1989) suggested the following guidelines for all comments made by reflecting team members:

1. *All remarks or comments are made in terms of positive connotations and genuine respect for family members.*
2. *Ideas and speculations are put in terms of the family's beliefs, not the team member's beliefs.*
3. *The team's beliefs about the family's beliefs are couched in "possibilities" or "maybes."* [Still, O'Connor et al., 2004, would recommend caution regarding the amount of information generated.]
4. *As a result, as many sides as can be seen of a situation are argued, by different team members.*
5. *Team members should enjoy trust and respect for each other.* (p. 70)

Young et al. (1989) sought feedback from supervisors, supervisees, and clients about the use of the reflecting team. Supervisors expressed initial nervousness that team members would say negative, unhelpful things (as they had done in confidential team meetings). When this did not occur, they found themselves trusting the process more and ultimately feeling liberated. Supervisees felt rudderless at the thought of the process, but found the experience itself to be affirming. Of 20 responses received from clients, 18 found the reflecting team to be either extremely helpful or moderately helpful; the remaining 2 were unsure of their reactions. In a separate study of clients' reaction to the reflecting team, Smith, Yoshioka, and Winton (1993) found that clients also reacted positively to the reflecting team's ability to offer them multiple perspectives. They determined that these multiple perspectives were most helpful "when they contained dialectic tensions. Clients who are confronted with two or more credible explanations of the same event benefited from teams able to articulate the differences between positions and hence their dialectic" (p. 40).

In spite of the many strengths claimed about reflecting teams as a therapy model and a method of supervision, some reasonable questions may be posed. Is the egalitarianism this model espouses an evolution of training and supervision (Hardy, 1993) or is it a model that fuses therapy and supervision to a point that supervision is compromised? Does the model diffuse individual contributions in its focus on the collective? Does the therapist lose the feeling of control over the outcome of therapy (Young et al., 1989)? Does the model produce too much information for the supervisee therapist to process in the limited time available (Kruse & Leddick, 2005)? Fine (2003) asked if the philosophy of the reflecting team runs counter to the competitiveness of the American culture. He suggested, therefore, that the issues of power dynamics and competition among team members be discussed openly. He also recommended that the supervisor acknowledge rejected reflections. This, it seems to us, will reduce the likelihood of the "winner" (in terms of insight) taking over the team. Finally, Fine advised that team members remain silent behind the mirror in order to enhance each member's individual creativity and minimize distraction. We would also suggest that silence can be a form of respect for clients and therapist while they are working; this might translate to team member respect for each other as well. Despite the potential vulnerabilities of the model, it seems that the reflecting team will continue to contribute to our understanding of live supervision.

Team Dynamics

As noted by Fine (2003), a team approach to live supervision involves some initial issues and complications not typically associated with other forms of supervision. The most central of these is the cohesion of the group that will form the team. Wendorf (1984) suggested that, before the team attempts to work as a unit in offering therapy, they come together as a group through a careful examination of group process. To help the team understand each member's needs and agendas, Wendorf recommended that the group alternate between meetings with a supervisor and meetings with peers only. His experience was that team members will relate to each other differently depending on whether the supervisor is present and that prior to doing therapy the team needs to know as much as possible about each member. Not surprisingly, Wendorf's recommendations are not universally accepted.

Theoretical compatibility among team members has been viewed as another essential ingredient for success (Cade, Speed, & Seligman, 1986). Although another type of supervision group might be enhanced by participants coming from widely varying assumptions about therapy, this would be far less so with a therapeutic team. Because there is a limited amount of time within a session for the team to confer and recommend an intervention, there needs to be enough theoretical compatibility to allow the team to work efficiently. Furthermore, the supervisee cannot be expected to integrate different theoretical assumptions within such a complex supervision process.

In-Session (Mid-session) Dynamics. The therapist's right to accept or reject the intervention (i.e., supervision) is a chronic supervisory issue and one that is exacerbated with a team. Unlike the situation with a solitary supervisor, for which a supervisee might be asked to carry out an intervention even though not totally committed to it, the dynamic is more complicated when a group of peers is primarily responsible for the intervention. Even if the supervisor is supportive of the team's direction, it is more important for the supervisee to be in agreement with the directive than it is when no team exists. If not, the therapist will eventually feel manipulated by his or her peers, and team dynamics might eventually override the goal of providing sound therapy. This concern is supported by the research of Mauzey and Erdman (1997), who found that directives initiated by the supervisor were received more favorably by supervisees than directives coming from team members.

Heath (1982) asserted that it is the supervisor's responsibility to choreograph the input from the team to the therapist and to be sure that the intervention is compatible with the therapist's style "unless the style has become part of the problem" (p. 192). Similar to Fine's (2003) position, Heath also acknowledged that prior to the in-session conference, the supervisor may be confronted with competitiveness among team members, an understandable phenomenon when the role of therapist is curtailed in favor of the team approach to therapy and training.

A final issue that should receive attention prior to the actual therapy session is which and how many team members will be allowed to formulate interventions for the therapist. When consultation is the method used, this is less of an issue, especially if there is a designated taskmaster to translate the group discussion into an intervention. However, when directives are phoned in or the therapist is called into the consultation room to receive the directive, rather than to confer with the team, will several members of the team be allowed to be involved in the interchange or just one? This may seem like a minor issue, but it is probably one of the most critical process issues for a team if relations between the therapist and the team are to remain intact and to avoid having the therapist become overwhelmed by a barrage of team opinion (O'Connor et al., 2004). Once again, it is up to the supervisor to monitor the activity level of the observation room and the readiness of individual team members to participate in a more direct fashion.

Pre- and Postsession Dynamics. Because of the complexity and intensity of team supervision during the therapy session, it is vital for planning sessions and debriefing sessions to occur. Liddle and Schwartz (1983) maintained that the presession conference should address family, supervisee, relationship, and teaching considerations. If the team goes into the session knowing pretty well what is to be accomplished with the family and what the supervisee will be working on personally, the during-session consultations should serve

the function of "mid-course corrections to the general session plan" (p. 478). Additionally, giving time in the presession to team dynamics, taking time to convey a respect for the position and perspective of the therapist, and addressing how this particular session reflects overall training goals will prepare the team for the intensity and activity of team supervision.

The postsession conference is equally important. Regardless of the amount of planning that has occurred, team members, especially the therapist, will have a need to debrief. Furthermore, Adams (1995) reported that supervisees ask their best questions during the postsession. Heath (1982) suggested that the supervisor allow the therapist to suggest a format for the discussion. In addition to a general discussion of the session, including a discussion of hypotheses and goals, the postsession should include some feedback to the therapist and to the team (Heath, 1982). Heath also maintained that emotional reactions on the part of different team members can be appropriate to address if they enhance the process, but that criticism be offered only if paired with alternative action. In a similar vein, Cade et al. (1986) stated that

> [t]he therapist will often need time to "disengage" mentally and emotionally from the family before feeling able to consider what the team has to offer. The advantages of multiple perspectives can become a disadvantage if the therapist becomes swamped with ideas, particularly where these are conflicting ideas arising out of conflicting frameworks. (pp. 112–113)

Once more immediate session issues have been processed, the supervisor should help the team to address the session that just occurred as it fits in the larger context of training (Adams, 1995; Liddle & Schwartz, 1983) and direct team members' thinking for the next scheduled presession.

Advantages and Disadvantages of Team Supervision

Advantages. We stated earlier that advocates of live supervision tend to be enthusiastic in their support. This is true of working with the team model of live supervision as well. Among the advantages enumerated are the following (Cade et al., 1986; Elizur, 1990; Hardy, 1993; Landis & Young, 1994; Quinn, Atkinson, & Hood, 1985; Speed, Seligman, Kingston, & Cade, 1982; Sperling et al., 1986):

1. Team work appears to be highly satisfying. "Family therapy is always difficult, sometimes nerve-wracking and sometimes depressing; working in teams can be creative, highly supportive, challenging and very often fun" (Speed et al., 1982, p. 283).
2. When a crisis occurs within a case, the therapist can attend to the immediate needs of the client, while the team wrestles with conceptual issues.
3. As with other forms of group supervision, the therapeutic team reinforces the value of case consultation. Because the team must brainstorm during the session, the criticism that live supervision is primarily a model for executive skill development is canceled.
4. The model requires that team members work on their feet, thus training them to arrive at therapeutic interventions more quickly.
5. The team model automatically multiplies the numbers of interesting cases with which each team member has the opportunity to work.
6. The team itself can be used to enhance therapeutic goals. For example, a team split can be used as the intervention (Sperling et al., 1986). Using this intervention, the team is said to be in disagreement behind the mirror and sends in two opposing courses of action. This allows the therapist to stay in a neutral position and help the family to look at alternatives while acknowledging that there is more than one valid way to proceed.
7. A group of therapists is more likely to take greater risks and operate at a more creative level than an individual therapist. For highly intransigent cases, creative approaches to intervention are called for if the client system is to improve.

8. When the supervisor is clearly directing the team and the team is stuck, the supervisor must assess whether he or she is part of the problem (Elizur, 1990). As a result, supervisors are less insulated from their own blind spots, and team members benefit from realizing that challenge is part of therapy regardless of the expertness of the therapist.
9. Because the team will present different cultural backgrounds, the therapy process is more likely to reflect a sensitivity to culture, as will training (Hardy, 1993).

Disadvantages. Although the team model is intriguing and dynamic, certain disadvantages and pitfalls must be considered and avoided (Cade et al., 1986; Kruse & Leddick, 2005; O'Connor et al., 2004; Smith et al., 1998; Todd, 1997; Wendorf, Wendorf, & Bond, 1985):

1. Because of the intensity of the team's efforts, the group can find itself engaged in unproductive interactions with members unable to extricate themselves.
2. It is very difficult for competitive team members to resist using the therapy sessions to prove their conceptual superiority. This not only means that team members are competing with each other instead of supporting each other, but also that sometimes interventions sent in to families are unduly complicated or clever and not necessarily the most productive for accomplishing therapeutic goals.
3. Team supervision may not prepare therapists adequately for other, more common, forms of supervision. Therefore, team supervision may inadvertently contribute to a difficult transition from training to a practice setting.
4. Because of the high level of group cohesiveness that typically is associated with therapeutic teams, members can become overprotective and fail to challenge each other. For peer team groups, members might drop from the team, rather than pursue a different line of thinking.
5. Teams can produce too much information in a limited amount of time for the supervisee

therapist or the family to assimilate in a productive manner.

6. If a team is a subunit of an agency or a training program, the members of the team can pose a threat to other staff members. "A mystique can develop around what a particular team is 'up to.' Other staff feel 'put down' or patronized when in discussion with team members who can somehow convey that they are in possession of 'the truth'" (Cade et al., 1986: pp. 114–115). At the very least, team members will share a common experience not available to others, thus promoting an atmosphere of an in group and an out group.

7. For a team that has a long span of time to work together, there is a danger of becoming the "other family." We believe, as did Cade et al., that every group has a limited creative life span, at least without the impetus of new members or a change of context. Supervisors need to be sensitive to systemic and developmental dynamics within teams as well as within client groups.

8. For some cases, the team approach is more intensive than is needed and may distort client dynamics through unnecessary scrutiny. One way to compensate for this pitfall is to vary one's approaches to supervision. We think the Quinn et al. (1985) "stuck-case clinic" is an excellent approach to team supervision. Rather than having the team consider all cases (and thereby running the risk of overkill for some cases), each team member is charged with bringing his or her most difficult case to the team. As a result, the team's time is spent efficiently, and the risk of client distortion is diminished.

9. Finally, it seems to us that team supervision is as much a closed system as some other forms of supervision. By this we mean that there is definitely some self-selection among those supervisors who choose team supervision as their method of choice. They might, for example, be somewhat more theatrical than other supervisors, or perhaps they enjoy therapy more than supervision. Whatever the reasons, training

programs that wed themselves entirely to team supervision might be discriminating against some of their trainees unknowingly—trainees who are equally talented but more traditional in their approach to therapy. Supervisors should be challenged to vary their approaches to supervision, just as trainees are challenged to vary their approaches to therapy.

RESEARCH RESULTS AND QUESTIONS

Live supervision has been found to be effective in training supervisees in initial counseling techniques (Gallant et al., 1991; Heppner et al., 1994; Kivlighan et al., 1991; Klitzke & Lombardo, 1991) and marriage and family therapy skills (e.g., Fennell, Hovestadt, & Harvey, 1986). To date, however, in spite of the ardor of those supervisors who prefer a live supervision model, there is no evidence that live supervision is better than, or weaker than, any other method of supervision.

Because live supervision breaks many normative canons of psychotherapy having to do with privacy and the centrality of relationship to therapy, there has been a good deal of interest in the reaction of clients and supervisees to the model. Piercy, Sprenkle, and Constantine (1986) conducted a follow-up study of both groups and found that almost one third (32%) of trainees would have preferred no observers to their therapy, and family members reported discomfort with the model in certain situations. Although comfort level was impeded, it is important to note that for these therapists and families the outcome of therapy did not seem to be affected by their negative feelings. Liddle, Davidson, and Barrett (1988) found that novice supervisees were most sensitive to evaluation issues during live supervision, while more experienced therapists focused on power and control issues. Reactions of both groups, however, minimized with continued use of live supervision, a result supported by Wong's (1997) subsequent research. In a study focusing on client reactions only, Locke and McCollum (2001) found that clients were satisfied with live supervision as long as perceived helpfulness outweighed perceived intrusiveness. Finally, Smith et al. (1993) conducted a qualitative study to determine client reactions to reflective teams. Clients were asked about their reactions at three different times during therapy (fourth week, seventh week, and eighth week), and the questions became more sophisticated as the clients gained more experience with the model. The results indicated that clients had a reasonable grasp of the process, found much of the process to be beneficial, and were able to articulate some limitations (e.g., feeling overwhelmed by the additional team members, the team going off on its own tangent, and the abruptness experienced when a session had some emotional content and the team interrupted). Interestingly, O'Connor et al.'s (2004) qualitative study tracking therapists' reactions to using reflecting teams revealed the same range of responses; that is, from exciting and challenging to overwhelming. One therapist in their study noted that, as an introvert, it was particularly difficult to use the team's insights without having an opportunity to process them. We are aware of no research that has attempted to investigate the fit for individuals having any particular personality characteristics with the use of different forms of live supervision.

Perhaps because of the labor intensity of live supervision, the relative frequency of the use of this method of supervision has received empirical attention (Carlozzi et al., 1997; Lee et al., 2004; Lewis & Rohrbaugh, 1989; McKenzie et al., 1986; Nichols et al., 1990). Although marriage and family therapy supervisors in particular have often defended live supervision as the most productive form of supervision, its actual use has peaked and waned over the years. Lee et al. (2004) conducted a survey of American Association for Marriage and Family Therapy (AAMFT)-approved supervisors in 2001 that used the same methodology as studies conducted in 1976 and 1986. Although live supervision was only beginning to be used in 1976 (6% of the time), it rose to the most regularly used method by 1986 (26% of the time). However, as we noted earlier, the method has declined in its use since that time and

in 2001 was the third most frequently used method (15% of the time) after video recordings and process reports.

Carlozzi et al. (1997) tracked methods of supervision in Council for the Accreditation of Counseling and Related Educational Programs (CACREP)-accredited counseling programs and programs accredited by the Commission on Accreditation for Marriage and Family Therapy Education (COAMFTE). Programs with either accreditation relied most heavily on videotape review for supervision. Live supervision was the second most frequent supervision modality for marriage and family therapy programs and the third most frequent for CACREP programs. The difference between this study and that conducted by Lee et al. (2004) is easily explained by the populations studied. Lee et al. investigated supervision of supervisors who practiced both in the field and in training institutions whereas Carlozzi et al. surveyed only graduate training programs. Live supervision is a more realistic supervision modality for graduate programs than for clinical settings because of the presence of training facilities.

Taking a slightly different approach, Anderson et al. (2000) surveyed marriage and family therapists regarding the modality used for their "best" supervision experiences and their "worst" supervision experiences. Similar to the frequency studies, videotape and live supervision were most often referenced for best supervision experiences. Because of their frequency, they were also frequently referenced as the modality for worst supervision, although self-report led in this category. Therefore, it would seem that modality per se is independent from the factors that determine whether supervision will be viewed as exemplary or deficient.

As live supervision has become less novel to the mental health professions and as its overall tenability as a supervision modality has been established, there has been more interest in understanding the discrete contributions of different aspects of this supervision approach. Mauzey et al. (2000) investigated the power of delayed supervision, phone-ins, or the bug-in-the-ear to increase supervisee anxiety and anger. Their results indicated that modality was not correlated with these affective states; rather, having a predisposition to anxiety and/or anger was predictive of having these states increase during the initial stages of supervision.

We have already reported the work of Frankel (1990) and Frankel and Piercy (1990) that investigated types of supervisor directives and their different effects. Kivlighan et al. (1991) conducted a similar study that focused on supervisee intentions, rather than supervisor intentions. Supervisees in this study were learning an interpersonal–dynamic approach to individual psychotherapy. Kivlighan et al. were interested in the difference between supervisees exposed to live supervision versus those using videotaped supervision. The dependent variable was the intention motivating each therapist response. Overall, the intentions for those in the live supervision treatment were consistent with the interpersonal approach to therapy (i.e., more support and relationship intentions). Therefore, the authors concluded that the live supervision approach allowed supervisees to learn more quickly. In addition to types of intentions, the authors hypothesized that live supervision would lead to stronger working alliances with clients and to therapy sessions that were *deeper* and *rougher* (i.e., more uncomfortable and difficult) (Stiles, Shapiro, & Firth-Cozens, 1988). The working alliance was considered stronger by clients for the live supervision condition than for the videotape condition, and sessions were viewed as rougher. Sessions were not experienced as deeper, however, a characteristic typically associated with interpersonal–dynamic therapy.

Although Lee (1997) found that therapist cooperation increased when phone-ins were longer than 30 seconds, Moorhouse and Carr (1999) found that frequency of phone-ins seemed to be more important than length in relation to particular supervisor and therapist behaviors. Fewer phone-ins led to more collaboration between supervisor and therapist and more cooperation (less resistance) from clients. (One would assume that a collaboration posture would take more than 30 seconds to establish, thus supporting Lee's

earlier findings.) Moorhouse and Carr also found that fewer phone-ins led to a less collaborative interaction between therapist and client. Therefore, although clients cooperated with therapy goals, therapists did not engage them as often in collaborative discourse. A separate analysis of these same interactions (Moorhouse & Carr, 2001) found that no particular supervisor style (i.e., support, teaching, or collaboration) was associated with increased client cooperation. What their results did determine was that isomorphism between supervisor and therapist (i.e., therapist using the same style with the client as had been used by the supervisor with the therapist) led to decreased client cooperation. The Moorhouse and Carr results raise interesting questions about the supervisory system and the relationships within it (i.e., therapist and supervisor, therapist and client, supervisor and client). Their results also differ from earlier research conducted by Wark (1995), who found that supervisees receiving live supervision using a combination of a nonegalitarian supervisory hierarchy (involving instruction and support) paired with adequate autonomy to be the most helpful to them. Obviously, more research is required before we can come to any definitive conclusions concerning these important relationship matters.

Though the research base regarding live supervision is growing, it is still relatively small. There are many questions to be asked; among them are the following:

1. Thus far, most live supervision experience and observation have been done with supervisees conducting family therapy. Although live supervision has become popular outside of family therapy, we know very little about its utility across theoretical approaches (Bubenzer et al., 1991). The requisite interruptions of therapy when conducting live supervision may discourage levels of the interpersonal depth required of some therapies.

2. Some authors have argued for an increased egalitarianism within live supervision (e.g., Hardy, 1993; Moorhouse & Carr, 1999; Woodside,

1994). The relationship between egalitarian supervision and the ability of the supervisor to evaluate supervisees must be measured.

3. There has been virtually no study of the generalizability or continuity of the therapist behaviors exhibited as a result of live supervision (Gallant et al., 1991; Kivlighan et al., 1991).

4. Hardy (1993) proposed that live supervision may change dramatically to reflect changes in our understanding of cultural variables, especially as they relate to power. To date, these variables have not been isolated within live supervision research.

5. Finally, with the exception that BITE is best used with more novice supervisees, the developmental level of the supervisee has received little empirical attention within live supervision research. Especially in terms of team activity, the developmental needs and abilities of supervisees are unknown.

CONCLUSION

The introduction of live supervision to the mental health professions represents a blending of skills training and the more contemplative forms of clinical supervision. Its primary advantage is the closing of the gap between the supervisee's experience and the supervisor's review of that experience; the assumed outcome of this advantage is accelerated learning and improved service to clients. The disadvantages of the model revolve around the time commitment required of the supervisor, the need for specific facilities, and the intrusion into the therapy relationship. Team approaches to live supervision offer additional training possibilities, as well as additional challenges and potential disadvantages. The reflecting team moves live supervision to a point that it may likely be called live consultation (Lewis, 1988).

Live supervision has moved from its identity as a family therapy training model exclusively, to increased use within the other mental health professions (Carlozzi et al., 1997; Schroll & Walton, 1991). Empirical investigation of live supervision has commenced and shows promise of ultimately assisting clinical supervisors in determining the optimal conditions for the use of live supervision, as well as its most necessary components.

CHAPTER 12

TEACHING AND RESEARCHING SUPERVISION

This chapter has two broad purposes. One is to discuss the training and supervision of supervisors. This includes a discussion of the stage models of supervisor development. The second is to discuss the nature and status of supervision research. We cover each of those topics in turn.

PREPARING AND SUPERVISING SUPERVISORS

Ethical codes (e.g., American Psychological Association [APA], 2002) are very explicit about the need to practice only in the areas in which one has competence. Pope and Vasquez (2007) applied this general principle to the domain of supervision when they asserted that "[I]t would be no more ethical to 'improvise' supervision if one lacked education, training, and supervised experience than if one were to improvise hypnotherapy, systematic desensitization, or administration of a Hallstead–Retan Neuropsychological Test Battery without adequate preparation" (pp. 282–283). In short, those who supervise should have formal preparation for that work.

Fortunately, as we noted in Chapter One, supervisor training is becoming increasingly common, even if it is not yet universal. It has helped that accreditation and regulatory bodies now encourage that training. Lagging behind this growing consensus that supervision training *should* occur, though, is agreement about what that training should include or when it should occur (Scott , Ingram, Vitanza, & Smith, 2000).

In the material that follows, we will discuss the training of supervisors and then the supervision of

supervisors. Following the convention suggested by Hoffman (1990, 1994), we will use the acronym SIT to refer to the "supervisor in training."

Training Supervisors

Supervisor training is offered in several contexts, for audiences of different types. For example, it might be provided as one or more formal university courses for graduate students; as a component of an internship training program; or, as a training program for practitioners, which has been more typical in Britain. It might also be provided as a workshop or series of continuing education workshops for practitioners.

Regardless of how such training occurs, we believe that it will be characterized by at least the two following elements if it is to be effective:

1. It should have both didactic and experiential components. Each is insufficient without the other.
2. It should occur as a series of graded sequential experiences that provide learners the opportunity to get consistent feedback on their practice.

Note that whereas continuing education workshops can be an important training vehicle, they are alone an insufficient mechanism for preparing supervisors because they typically provide neither of these two elements. In fact, our discussion of supervisor training is written with university-based supervision courses specifically in mind, though much of it should generalize to other contexts as well.

When to Begin Supervisor Training. Because supervision involves not only the professional development of the supervisee, but also the monitoring of client welfare, it seems logical that those who are to function autonomously as supervisors must be licensed in their own discipline and they should receive formal training before they assume supervisory responsibilities. But the field is not in complete agreement about when that training should begin. For example, Scott et al. (2000) found that training directors of psychology internship programs were more likely than their counterparts in academic programs to believe that training should occur after doctoral coursework has been completed. Our own stance, like that of the Association of Psychology Postdoctoral and Internship Centers (APPIC) supervision competency group (Falender et al., 2004), is that supervision training should begin during graduate training.

Common sense would dictate that SITs have more experience as counselors or therapists than the supervisees they are to supervise. Ellis and Douce (1994) suggested 1 to 2 years of supervised practicum training as a counselor; Russell and Petrie (1994) suggested at least 1 year of practicum. For the SIT to have at least this level of supervised experience is not only a matter of having the requisite skills, but also of having reached an appropriate level of professional identity, experience, and professional maturity.

SIT Assessment: The First Step in Training. SIT training should begin with some form of assessment. In this case, it would be of SIT (1) competencies and (2) training needs. This helps the trainers but also may usefully stimulate SITs' reflections about their own experiences, thereby constituting an important, initial aspect of their training (cf. Bonney, 1994; Borders & Leddick, 1988; Hawkins & Shohet, 1989; Hoffman, 1990, 1994). The flowchart depicted in Figure 12.1 provides Hawkins and Shohet's (2000) suggested sequence of steps in becoming supervisor. Notably, their beginning point is self-assessment.

As part of that self-assessment, it is useful to ask SITs to remember and discuss their own first clinical experiences with clients and then to consider ways in which these feelings might resemble their current feelings about beginning to supervise (Bonney, 1994). Borders and Leddick (1987) report having new supervisors begin by constructing a "résumé" of past supervision-relevant experiences. Their purpose was to stimulate a systematic review of the multiple relevant experiences that the SIT will have had as counselor, teacher, consultant, researcher, and peer supervisor; each contributes to the SIT's new role of supervisor. SITs often enter supervisor training with substantial life and professional experiences that can be generalized to their work as supervisors.

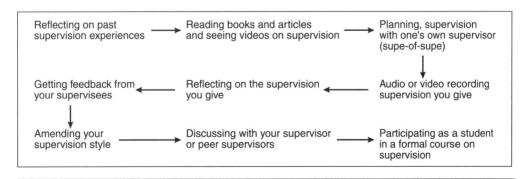

FIGURE 12.1   Supervision Learning Cycle.

Source: From *Supervision in the Helping Professions*, Milton Keyes, Second Edition, by P. Hawkins & R. Shohet (2000), Buckingham, U.K: Open University Press. Copyright © 2000 by Open University Press. Reprinted by permission.

Hoffman (1990) described a procedure that encourages SITs to reflect on their prior experiences as supervisees. She asked them to complete a Supervision Life Line (SLL), which lists past experiences of being supervised. For this task, they drew a vertical line down which they arrange their previous supervised experience in chronological order. The SITs are directed to list each of their experiences as a supervisee, with the first one at the top, the next directly below it, and so on. For each experience, the SIT is asked to jot down on the left side of the vertical line demographic information about the former supervisor. This includes the supervisor's professional discipline, gender, age, and years of experience. On the right side of the line, directly opposite this listing of supervisor demographics, SITs are to note the year of the particular supervision and its duration (e.g., "1995, 6 months") and to rate the value of this experience to their professional development (using a scale of 1 to 10, where 1 = *worst* and 10 = *best*).

Once SITs have done this, Hoffman suggested assigning their two follow-up tasks:

1. *Fleshing out the various supervisory experiences in narrative form.* For example, SITs might be asked to describe for each listed experience the client population that was served, the theoretical orientation that seemed to influence the supervisor's approach to supervision, the supervisor's approach to supervising, the most salient learnings from this supervisory experience, the aspects of the experience that were particularly easy and particularly difficult, and, finally, anything that was felt to be missing from the supervisory experience.

2. *Writing a discussion of what they have learned from both the SLL and their narrative material.* This discussion would include such observations as their conclusions regarding their preferred styles of learning, differences in how they appreciated didactic versus experiential learning at various stages in their development, lessons from the way(s) conflict was handled during supervision, the various barriers to learning that they encountered, and their preferences with

respect to such supervisor attributes as age, gender, and discipline. Hoffman reported that she concludes this exercise with a discussion among group members about what they had learned from it and how this might be useful to them as they begin adopting the role of supervisor themselves.

The Academic Component of Supervisor Training. Green and Dye (2002) conducted a Delphi study to identify the relative level of importance of 50 possible components of a supervision training course or program, using an expert panel of 50 British psychologists chosen to represent various perspectives on supervision. The panel had particularly strong agreement on the importance of matters best described as ethical in nature. But because the panel rated the majority of the components as at least "probably important," this study is most useful as a checklist of possible training components, rather than a prioritization of training goals.

Several key articles, though, have provided suggested training priorities. In the earliest of these, Borders et al. (1991) suggested that supervisor training should address the following seven core areas:

1. Models of supervision
2. Counselor development
3. Supervision methods and techniques
4. Supervisory relationship
5. Evaluation
6. Executive skills
7. Ethical, legal, and professional regulatory issues

Borders et al. (1991) also suggested three sets of learning objectives for each of these seven areas: (1) self-awareness, (2) theoretical and conceptual knowledge, and (3) skills and techniques. The result is therefore a 7 by 3 matrix with 21 types of learning objectives, which the authors then supplemented with a list of more than 200 specific learning objectives. Russell and Petrie (1994) characterized this as the "most extensive set of recommendations for supervisor training" (p. 38), but then also suggested that the model "falls victim to its own complexity" (p. 38). Russell and Petrie then suggested what they believed to be three essential areas for supervision training:

1. *Theoretical models of supervision.* They suggested that these be covered both with available books on supervision and with videotapes demonstrating supervision from several approaches. They recommended, for example, Goodyear's (1982) videotape series that illustrates supervision from five different theoretical perspectives: Albert Ellis (rational–emotive), Carl Rogers (client centered), Erving Polster (gestalt), Rudolph Ekstein (psychodynamic), and Norman Kagan (interpersonal process recall).

2. *Supervision research.* To familiarize students with the empirical literature, Russell and Petrie suggested two complementary strategies: (a) to assign students to read specific empirical articles that examine research issues in supervision; among these are selected research reviews and critiques (e.g., Avis & Sprenkle, 1990; Ellis, 1991b; Ellis, Ladany, Krengel, & Schult, 1996; Ellis & Ladany, 1997; Holloway, 1984; Holloway & Neufeldt, 1995; Lambert & Ogles, 1997); and (b) to develop a research proposal as their primary written product for the course. In doctoral programs and those master's degree programs that require a thesis, this paper might prove a springboard for some students' dissertation or thesis.

3. *Ethical and professional issues.* A review of ethical and legal issues that affect their work is important, especially as this is the first time that students have been responsible for both the client and the trainee. Moreover, Russell and Petrie pointed out that there is a broader training opportunity in reviewing ethical and legal issues at this level. That is, it is a chance to revisit the issues at a time when the trainees are developmentally ready to consider them in a less rule bound and more critical manner than when they were first exposed to those issues earlier in training.

More recently, the APPIC supervision competencies task group (Falender et al., 2004) has proposed minimal knowledge and skills that a supervisor should acquire. Their list overlaps considerably with that of Borders et al. (1991), though with two notable differences: Falender et al. suggested that supervisors should acquire (1) awareness and knowledge of diversity "in all of its forms"; and (2) knowledge of supervision research (which echoes a recommendation by Russell & Petrie, 1994). These seem important additions to the list of competencies.

The recent proliferation of books on supervision provides a wealth of possible resources SITs might use to acquire these several areas of knowledge. Our own bias is that a supervision course should include the use of at least two books: (1) one that provides broad coverage of the field and its key literature, as this one does; and (2) one that provides an elaborated model the SITs can learn in some depth (e.g., Ladany, Friedlander, & Nelson, 2005; Stoltenberg, McNeill, & Delworth, 1998). As well, we believe supervision courses or programs should provide SITs with the opportunity to read both current research and articles that are in some way "supervision classics" (such as, for example, Searles, 1955; Stoltenberg, 1981).

Basic Skills Training for SITs. Knowledge is essential, but, alone, insufficient; it must be complemented by actual skills. And, as with the training of beginning therapists, it is useful to start with basic skills onto which other, more advanced skills can be scaffolded.

In preparing SITs, we often begin their skills training by having them work in groups of three or four to develop skits in which they depict "absolutely awful" supervision. This and the discussions that follow can have an icebreaking role for a new group (and usually it is fun, for the nature of the task is really nonthreatening). But in addition, it begins to define for the group what supervision should *not* be. To define what something is not is a developmental step for beginning to define what it *should* be.

We provide SITs with early exposure to Kagan's IPR technique (see Chapter 9 for a description).

In his workshops, Kagan often would discuss the "inquirer" role as one that would enable even a "supervisor paraprofessional" to function effectively in supervision. Like the supervisor role that Williams (1995) advocates, the supervisor using IPR is to ask simple questions from a position of naive curiosity.

Early training in IPR techniques empowers the SIT, who now is equipped with some skills on which to fall back. Moreover, it helps him or her to set aside the teacher role, which often is difficult for beginning SITs to do.

Drawing from the microcounseling model that Allen (1967) originally developed, Richardson and Bradley (1984) suggested a "microsupervision" model for the training of supervisors. It provides an excellent complement to the IPR model and therefore can be used after SITs have become comfortable using IPR.

Richardson and Bradley (1984) suggested three stages in microsupervision training: (1) *assessment* (to assess the SIT's skills and skill deficits and then to rank the deficits in a hierarchy), (2) *modeling* (to use videotape for modeling of each supervisory skill to be taught by microsupervision), and (3) *transfer* (to transfer the skill to real practice settings through supervision role plays and self-evaluations of performance).

Supervising Supervisors

[T]he first prerequisite for being a good supervisor is being able to actively arrange good supervision for yourself. (Hawkins & Shohet, 2000, p. 35)

Supervision of supervision ("supe-of-supe") occurs in training programs in which supervisors are prepared. There, it is a central aspect of a practicum in supervision. But supe-of-supe also can occur with licensed practitioners who are providing supervision. In Britain, for example, the mandatory lifelong supervision of counselors extends to supervisors as well, and data suggest that they value it. Wheeler and King (2000) found 80% of the supervisors they surveyed reported that this supervision was helpful to them; almost as many (77%) reported they would obtain supervision even if it were not required.

Most of what follows will focus on supe-of-supe as part of a practicum experience for SITs. However, some of this material will apply as well to the supervision of experienced supervisors.

The institutional context will determine the point at which SITs actually begin their practicum experience. For example, if their training is occurring in a university that offers a sequence of two or more supervision courses, the practicum component usually will begin after at least one term of didactic and laboratory skills preparation. On the other hand, if there is only a single course, the practicum might begin much earlier and coincide with the didactic portion. Still another scenario is practicum at an internship training site where it might begin very early, perhaps after an orienting workshop or two.

Very much like the novice counselor, the novice supervisor will want direction and structure. Watkins (1994) made several suggestions for meeting the needs of novice supervisors, including:

(1) very closely monitoring the cases the trainee works with (which can . . . contribute to a feeling of being held, secured, and stabilized in the supervision relationship; "I am not alone in this"); (2) having a "setness" about the supervision of the supervisor trainee (i.e., having regularly scheduled meeting times that are clearly set as to place, time, frequency, and duration, which further grounds and stabilizes the supervision context); and (3) having a policy established about supervisory crises (i.e., if something comes up that the supervisor trainee feels unable to handle and which seemingly demands immediate attention, how can he/she then go about talking with the supervisor?), with which both the supervisor trainee and his/her supervisor feel comfortable. (p. 422)

Another step in providing structure and prescriptions for the beginning SIT concerns what to do during the first session(s) with a newly assigned supervisee. Both Bonney (1994) and Borders and Leddick (1987) suggested that this first session be scheduled, if possible, before the supervisee actually begins to see clients (if this is not possible, the session should address clients only in general terms).

The primary agenda for supervisor and supervisee in this session should be the development of a mutual understanding of the nature and process of supervision, establishing immediate and long-range goals, reviewing their respective theoretical or philosophical orientations, and a discussion of the supervisee's relevant past experiences. A discussion of role expectations and a beginning of mutual role definitions would also be helpful. If all this proves to be overwhelming for one interview, some of it may be delayed until a later time (Bonney, 1994, p. 32).

As SITs begin to work with supervisees their experience of themselves gradually will begin to change as they make the cognitive shift from thinking like a counselor to thinking like a supervisor. One simple indicator is when SITs no longer slip and inadvertently refer to their supervisees as "my client(s)."

Although this shift often will occur simply as a function of experience, Borders (1992) suggested some strategies to encourage it. A simple one is to have SITs review and take notes on a supervisee tape as if they were going to meet with that counselor for supervision during the following hour. After watching (or listening to) 10 to 15 minutes of the tape, SITs are stopped and asked to review their notes. They are to count the number of statements about the client versus those about the supervisee.

> *Typically, participants report few if any statements about the counselor. This has been especially true of experienced clinicians in inservice workshops. Then they are reminded that they will be meeting with the counselor, not the client: What will they do to help the counselor? They are to keep this question utmost in their minds as they review the remainder of the session.* (Borders, 1992, p. 139)

A second of Borders's strategies is to encourage SITs to employ deliberate educational planning for their supervision sessions. This is guided by two types of data: (1) SITs' own assessment of supervisees' strengths and weaknesses, based on a review of one or more of the supervisees' counseling tapes, and (2) the three to five learning goals for the supervisory experience that SITs have supervisees develop during the initial supervisory session. SITs are then to use both supervisees' learning goals and their own assessment of the supervisees' work to guide the feedback that they give the supervisee.

Group Supe-of-Supe. The techniques and format for supe-of-supe mirror those that are used in the supervision of counseling or therapy. These include videotape review of the supe-of-supe (Wilcoxon, 1992), live supe-of-supe (Constantine, Piercy, & Sprenkle, 1984), and even role reversals in which the SIT then supervises his or her own supervisor.

We speculate, however, that group may be the most frequently used modality. Supe-of-supe often is a component of a graduate-level course in which there also is simultaneous seminar-type didactic coverage of supervision-relevant material.

Ellis and Douce (1994) described one model of group supe-of-supe they developed on the basis of their experience with approximately 35 groups and 175 SITs over 13 years. In that model, the supe-of-supe group meets 2 hours weekly and typically consists of five to eight SITs and two trainers. During each session the first 30 to 60 minutes is spent monitoring the supervisory work of the various group members and then one SIT presents a supervisory case, supplementing that presentation with the playing of audio- and/or videotapes. Each SIT presents in this manner at least twice during the term.

Hoffman (1994) suggested that supervision (and therefore supe-of-supe) might be thought of as having three phases: (1) beginning, (2) middle, and (3) end. Within each stage are certain associated tasks. We already have discussed some of the tasks of the beginning stage and therefore now will address the latter two.

Middle Phase of Supervision Training. This is the longest of the stages and the one during which most of the work of both supervision and supe-of-supe will occur. During this period, SITs are likely to have to address at least the following five issues Ellis and Douce (1994) had observed to be common in supe-of-supe.

Balancing Responsibility. As SITs move into the role of supervisor, their responsibility for the client continues. But they now face the sometimes frustrating fact that they do not have the same direct access to the client that they are used to having. Moreover, as supervisors they now have the additional responsibility of facilitating the supervisee's development. Attaining a balance between these responsibilities is often difficult for the new supervisor. And sometimes these responsibilities can be at odds, or at least seem to be. Ellis and Douce (1994) suggested two interventions to address this: (1) assign and then discuss relevant literature (ethical, legal, and professional role related) and (2) suggest that SITs use an IPR technique with their supervisees.

Parallel Processes. SITs will most likely encounter and find themselves responding to parallel processes (e.g., Ekstein & Wallerstein, 1972; Mueller & Kell, 1972) during this middle phase. What we would add to our discussion in Chapter 6 is that supe-of-supe adds yet another level through which parallel processes may reverberate: Whereas in supervision the supervisor must be aware of paralled processes between the client–counselor and the supervisor–supervisee relationships, in supe-of-supe these processes might find expression at the additional level of the SIT and his or her supervisor. As Ellis and Douce (1994) pointed out, it is during supe-of-supe that parallel processes are most likely to be noticed. Noticing the patterns at this level gives a unique opportunity not only for teaching, but also for modification of that pattern.

Power Struggles. Most counselors understand that it is counterproductive to attempt to assert their wills against those of the client. There are characteristics of supervision, though, that make power struggles more likely to occur here than in therapy. These include the fact that the relationship

is evaluative, that it has a teaching function, and that supervisors ultimately are responsible for ensuring that the client's welfare is protected (and therefore are likely occasionally to adopt a directive stance when they believe that they know what is best for the client).

The already-present characteristics are compounded among beginning SITs who are more likely than their more-advanced colleagues to behave in a structured, controlling manner, while also remaining especially sensitive to any perceived threats to their authority. It is important, therefore, that SITs learn to recognize and address power struggles in order to minimize their effects.

Individual Differences. Ellis and Douce (1994) suggested that attention to individual differences (especially race, culture, gender, sexual orientation, and religion) is important during supe-of-supe. SITs should watch for opportunities to help their supervisees address these issues in counseling. As well, they should be prepared to address them as they are salient in the supervisory relationship itself. And then there is the third level, which is supe-of-supe: Ellis and Douce suggested that supervision trainers have particular responsibility for ensuring that individual differences are addressed at this level.

Sexual Attraction. Sexual attraction, either between counselor and client or between supervisor and supervisee, is likely to be an issue during supe-of-supe. Such attraction can pose particular challenges for the SIT and/or the supervisor trainer. This problem is compounded by the fact that sexual attraction remains somewhat taboo, and therefore the involved professionals may feel uncomfortable addressing it openly when it occurs.

Ellis and Douce (1994) suggested that the supervisor trainer has a particular obligation to watch for instances of sexual attraction and then to address them openly. That is, sexual attraction is natural: In surveys, Pope, Spiegel, and Tabachnik (1986) found 95% of men and 76% of women psychologists reported having felt sexually attracted to a client. In another study, Pope, Tabachnik, and Spiegel (1987) found that 91% of psychologists reported this experience. However, although SITs generally are clear that sexual contact between either counselor and client or supervisor and supervisee is unethical, they often are given too little training in the management of these naturally occurring feelings.

End Phase of Supervision Training. Two primary issues confront the SIT during the end phase of supervision. One is dealing with termination issues (certainly, dealing with the termination of the SIT–supervisee relationship, but often also helping the supervisee to deal with termination issues as they are occurring with clients); the other is to address the matter of providing a summative evaluation of the supervisee (Chapter 2).

To those earlier discussions, we would add that it is important for the SIT to have had some role in evaluating the supervisee (and for the supervisee to have been fully apprised of this SIT role and its nature from the very beginning). This gives ecological validity to the supervisory experience. That is, supervision occurs in an evaluative context; without having had evaluative responsibilities, the SIT will have missed a crucial aspect of the supervisory experience.

Of course, the SIT is also terminating supe-of-supe at this stage, while dealing with his or her own evaluation issues as well. These processes then provide an opportunity for the SIT to reflect on and integrate the experiences that she or he has had as a novice supervisor. One way we have fostered this process has been to require that SITs end the term by making a formal presentation that summarizes their work across the term with at least one supervisee. This is a chance to review the course of their work together, including (1) interventions that worked and did not, (2) the nature of any conflicts that occurred and how they were resolved, (3) transference and countertransferences that seemed to have affected their work, and (4) any parallel processes that might have affected the work.

In making such a presentation, SITs have the chance to obtain summative feedback from their supervisor, as well as from other group members.

In addition, they can reflect on feedback their supervisees have given them. This feedback should have been available in several forms.

1. During the summative evaluation of the supervisee, the SIT should have solicited feedback from him or her about aspects of the supervision experience that were especially useful or not.

2. The SIT should have looked for informal ways to obtain feedback during the course of the relationship. For example, the regular use of an IPR technique with supervisees is one means by which the SIT might get ongoing feedback.

3. We also believe it is important for the SIT to have used paper and pencil measures to obtain regular and systematic feedback from the supervisee (after every session if possible). This is consistent with a scientist–practitioner orientation and has at least the following benefits:

   a. Obtaining repeated measures from supervisees by using one or more specific questionnaires allows SITs to obtain feedback that is systematic and that can be compared across sessions. They can look back over the supervisory experience and regard it essentially as $n = 1$ research. For example, which session(s) was rated especially high and what was occurring during that session? Which session(s) was rated low and why? (In fact, we encourage this process by asking that the SIT, during the end-of-term summary presentations, provide session evaluation data, plotted across sessions if possible, with discussions of possible supervisory processes that might explain these data trends.)

   b. It may be more comfortable for both supervisee and SIT to have the supervisee give constructive feedback in written form, rather than in a face-to-face meeting.

   c. By making the solicitation of feedback a regular expectation, it can defuse potential conflicts that otherwise might arise as the supervisee "sits on" grievances or other bad feelings.

d. As SITs might receive negative feedback, it allows them the opportunity to reflect on it in private (as well as in supe-of-supe) and to consider what they will do with constructive feedback (e.g., Williams, 1994). There are a number of possible measures that SITs might use to obtain feedback from supervisees. Some of them, like the *Supervisory Styles Inventory* (Friedlander & Ward, 1984) and other measures are included in the Supervisor's Toolbox.

Research on Supervision Training Outcomes

Recognition of the importance of supervision training is growing, but remains far from universal. Given the almost-nonexistent research literature, we will group here the few studies that have examined the effects of supervisory training and supe-of-supe.

Training. The single study we located was that of McMahon and Simons (2004), who provided an intensive, four-day (6 hours per day) supervision workshop for experienced counselors. They found that, compared to a control group that did not receive this training, these supervision trainees showed greater supervisory confidence, self-awareness, and knowledge and skills. Moreover, these gains were retained across 6 months.

Supe-of-Supe. We found several studies in this category. Milne and James (2002) and Milne and Westerman (2001) conducted small-n, multiple case studies in which they demonstrated that "consultancy" (what we would call supe-of-supe) is effective in shaping these supervisor's (coded) behaviors. And the already-cited Wheeler and King (2000) study provides evidence of satisfaction among those whose supervision is supervised.

Conclusion. Supervision training, including supe-of-supe, is increasingly seen as necessary for anyone who aspires to supervise. A number of models have been developed for that training,

along with the competencies that should be taught during training. So far, little attention has been given to evaluating that training. The few available studies are a beginning and the fact that they have occurred during the past few years is encouraging. Yet there is so much more to learn about the effectiveness of supervisor training and evaluation. For example, supe-of-supe also occurs with experienced supervisors and apparently that supervision is appreciated (Wheeler & King, 2000). But, its effectiveness is wholly unexplored.

Several authors or groups of authors have suggested the necessary knowledge that SITs should acquire during training. The suggestions of these authors overlap heavily, although imperfectly. There seems to be some momentum toward the credentialing of supervisors by some professional associations or credentialing groups (American Association for Marriage and Family Therapy [AAMFT]; National Board for Certified Counselors [NBCC]; British Association for Counselling and Psychotherapy [BACP]). This is helping to standardize training. However, this is not uniform across professions. Ellis (2001), for example, suggested that the American Psychological Association (APA) come up with standards for supervisory training. The APPIC supervision competencies work group (Falender et al., 2004) has since taken a step in that direction on behalf of psychology, though those recommendations still do not have broader endorsement by the APA.

SUPERVISOR DEVELOPMENT

To become a supervisor involves shifts in identity that in many ways these shifts are as substantial as those experienced by the person who moves into the professional world of the counselor or therapist for the first time. Moreover, the shift in perception of self and role is not a one-time event, but rather a process that unfolds as new supervisors gain experience.

Several theorists have described these relatively normative changes in terms of developmental

TABLE 12.1   Summary of Supervisor Development Stages Suggested by Developmental Theorists

ALONSO	HESS	RODENHAUSER	STOLTENBERG, McNEIL, & DELWORTH (IDM MODEL)	WATKINS
Novice	Beginning	Emulation Conceptualization	Level 1	Role shock Role recovery and transition
	Exploration		Level 2	
		Incorporation		Role consolidation
Midcareer	Confirmation of supervisor identity	Consolidation	Level 3	Role mastery
Late career			Level 3 integrated	

Source: From Alonso (1983), Hess (1986, 1987), Rodenhauser (1994), Stoltenberg et al. (1998), Watkins (1990a; 1993).

stages that are similar in type to the counselor stage-developmental models we discussed in Chapter 4. Table 12.1 concisely summarizes the stages of five models that we discuss in the sections that follow.

Alonso's Model

Alonso (1983) proposed one of the earliest supervisor development models; one that was influenced both by psychodynamic and life-span developmental perspectives. Because of the latter perspective, her model encompasses the person's entire professional life as a supervisor. This is in contrast to the several other supervisor development models, which each suggest three or four stages that all might be traversed in a matter of only a few years, perhaps a decade or less. Each of Alonso's supervisor developmental stages can be characterized in terms of three themes: (1) self and identity, (2) relationship between supervisor and therapist, and (3) relationship between the supervisor and the administrative structure within which the supervisor works.

During the *novice* stage, supervisors are developing a sense of self-as-supervisor. In so doing, they also must cope with the anxiety that comes from needing to deal with narcissistic develop-

mental needs (e.g., for validation, for approval, and for role models) that emerge in response to the need to defend themselves as novices once again after already having achieved some sense of mastery as therapists. These issues are exacerbated by the fact that their supervisees typically are about the same age and are themselves novices who are taking on new levels of responsibility.

In the *midcareer* stage, supervisors generally conform to Levinson's (1978) description of the ideal mentor. That is, they are moving from a focus on self to more of a focus on others.

Late-career supervisors are often faced with the need to maintain self-esteem in the face of our culture's tendency to devalue older people. But they also are in a position to enjoy the status of the village elder, using the supervisory role as a medium to exhibit their wisdom and expertise. This role provides an opportunity to work through conflicts regarding integrity versus despair. There is a close correspondence between this stage and the last phase Rønnestad and Skovholt (2003) describe in their model (see Chapter 4).

Alonso also gave attention to the role of institutional context, recognizing that supervision usually takes place in the context of an institution and that this inevitably will affect the supervisor. For example, novice supervisors are likely to feel a greater need to be recognized by the institution and therefore may respond to supervisees more harshly and critically than their more advanced colleagues. Conversely, because of their own still unresolved issues as former supervisees, they might overidentify with their own supervisees when they struggle with institutional rules and procedures.

Hess's Model

Hess (1986, 1987) suggested that supervisor development occurs across three stages. In the *beginning* stage, the person changes both roles (i.e., from supervisee to supervisor) and reference groups (i.e., from novices to more experienced clinicians). This shift into new terrain, along with its attendant ambiguity about roles and technique renders the supervisors vulnerable to self-consciousness and sensitivity to peer and supervisee criticism. They compensate by (1) employing a concrete structure in supervision and (2) focusing on the client and the teaching of technique.

As supervisors gain experience, they develop both competence and confidence, along with an internalized belief in the professional value of supervision as an intervention. This characterizes the second or *exploration* stage. Hess suggested, though, that supervisors at this stage are prone to two potentially problematic response sets. One is to be too restrictive in their supervisory roles; the other is to become too intrusive with the supervisee, addressing issues that are unrelated to the supervisee's work as a therapist. The supervisee is likely to respond to either with resistance.

When supervisors reach the third stage, *confirmation of supervisor identity,* they find more of their gratification and professional pride in their supervisees' successes and, consequently, feel less dependent on receiving validation from others that they are "good supervisors." They are able to respond more to the supervisee's learning agenda and actually to be in the relationship with the supervisee, rather than dealing with the relationship at a cognitive level. Their sense of professional identity is strong and established.

Rodenhauser's Model

Rodenhauser (1994, 1997) observed that the newest supervisors will emulate their previous role models (*emulation stage*). This identification establishes an essential foundation on which to begin developing competence and identity as a supervisor. Gradually, though, new supervisors will encounter the limits of emulation and begin to search for their own methods and guidelines (*conceptualization stage*). Much of this search typically will occur in discussions with peers. This process of interacting with peers has the additional advantage of establishing alliances that reduce supervisors' likelihood of overidentifying with their supervisees.

The *incorporation stage* occurs as supervisors begin to develop an increasing awareness of the importance of the supervisory relationship. This awareness comes with increased sensitivity to the impact of their personal style on supervisees and, ultimately, on the supervisee–client relationship. Related to this is supervisors' heightened awareness of individual differences (gender, race, culture, etc.) that affect the supervisory triad.

Finally, in the *consolidation stage,* supervisors consolidate their learning and experience. One aspect of this stage is an increasing ability to use the supervisee's countertransference reactions in supervision, but also to balance this against the supervisees' need for privacy. Without deliberate effort, the supervisor at this stage is able to continually monitor parallel processes for instructional cues.

Stoltenberg et al.'s Integrated Developmental Model (IDM)

Stoltenberg et al. (1998) suggested that supervisors move through a series of stages analogous to those suggested in their counselor development model. In fact, they assume a sort of interlocking of counselor development and supervisor development stages. That is, Stoltenberg et al. assert that the level 1 supervisor first should have reached the stage of at least a late level 2 counselor (see Chapter 4 for our summary and discussion of these counselor stages).

Level 1 supervisors, like level 1 supervisees, feel characteristically anxious and are eager to "do the right thing." They frequently have a mechanistic and structured way with supervisees, are likely to assume an "expert" stance, and often are eager to push their own theoretical orientation and techniques on supervisees. In turn, they are relatively dependent on their own supervisors for support.

SITs at level 1 are often very effective when they are responsible for supervising beginning supervisees—who, in a complementary way, *want* the structure and "expertness" beginning supervisors will tend to offer. Stoltenberg et al. (1998), in fact, noted that level 1 supervisors who also are at level 2 in terms of their development as counselors frequently will be "far better" (p. 161) as supervisors than as counselors.

Level 2 is characterized by confusion and conflict. Fortunately, this stage tends to be short-lived. SITs now understand supervision to be more complex and difficult than they originally had thought it would be. They may tend to focus heavily on the supervisee, with a consequent risk of losing objectivity and, with it, the ability to guide and confront. But, at the same time, SITs at this level may vary in their motivation to be supervisors, with the consequence that they may then blame supervisees for their own problems as supervisor and become angry and withdraw. Stoltenberg et al. (1998) noted that level 2 SITs need their own supervisors to be expert and consistent with them.

Level 3 is characterized by a consistent motivation toward the supervisor role, which they approach as but one of the many that they have as professionals. Supervisors at this level function with relative autonomy, though they may seek consultation or even regular supervision as needed. They are able to engage in honest and relatively accurate self-appraisals. Level 3 integrated supervisors might be called master supervisors. They can work well with supervisees at any level of development and are unlikely to have strong preferences about supervisee level. In their agencies, they often are in the role of supervising less-advanced supervisors.

Watkins's Model

In a series of articles, Watkins (Watkins, 1993, 1994, 1995b, 1995c, 1995d, 1995e; Watkins, Schneider, Haynes, & Nieberding, 1995) reviewed the several conceptions of developmental stages through which supervisors progress. Based on those reviews, Watkins (1993) suggested a model of supervisor development that is based on counselor development models originated by Hogan (1964) and enhanced by Stoltenberg (1981). Because of this very direct lineage, Watkins called his the *supervision complexity model* (SCM; Watkins, 1990a, 1993).

Watkins's (1994) basic concept is that development occurs as a response to increased challenge along several dimensions as the supervisor gains experience. Although there are many potential developmental issues across the stages, Watkins suggested four as being "central to much developmental thought." These principal developmental issues are: (1) *competency versus incompetency*, (2) *autonomy versus dependency*, (3) *identity versus identity diffusion*, and (4) *self-awareness versus unawareness*.

Stage 1, *role shock*, is marked by the feeling of being an imposter. Watkins (1990a) described the supervisor at this stage as "playing the role of supervisor." Supervisors are more likely to experience general, unresolved conflict at this stage than at any other time. They typically employ a concrete, rules-oriented approach, with little attention paid to the processes occurring between them and their supervisees. Novice supervisors are likely either to withdraw from supervisees or to impose a too-rigid structure.

Supervisors at stage 2, that of *role recovery and transition*, are beginning to develop a supervisory identity, along with self-confidence and a more realistic perception of strengths and weaknesses. Nevertheless, supervisors at this level are prone to wide fluctuations in self-appraisals, vacillating rapidly from feeling good about their performance to feeling bad. Their tolerance of ambiguity is greater, as is their ability to recognize supervisory processes such as transference and countertransference (though their ability to address these processes is not yet at a commensurate level).

Supervisors at stage 3, *role consolidation,* are increasingly consistent in their thinking and acting as supervisors and in both self-confidence and accuracy of self-appraisal. They have begun to feel generally qualified for their role and, in fact, have begun to solidify a consistent and definably supervisory role. They are less controlling and leading with supervisees and instead are more encouraging and supportive. Transference and countertransference issues no longer pose a significant threat. These and similar process issues become considerations during supervision.

Supervisors at stage 4, *role mastery,* have developed a consistent, solid sense of confidence as well as an integrated and well-elaborated sense of identity. Their supervisory style is well integrated, theoretically consistent, and personalized.

Baker, Exum, and Tyler (2002) compared a small group of doctoral students who participated in a supervision course with those who did not. Using a model-specific measure that Watkins had created, they concluded that differences between the two groups of students provided some support for the supervisor complexity model.

Conclusions Regarding Supervisory Development Models

Fifteen years ago, Worthington (1987) concluded from his review of the literature that empirical research on ways that supervisors change with experience was "at a rudimentary level" (p. 206) and that relatively few researchers had yet made this a focus of their research. As a consequence, there was little understanding of how supervisors' conceptual abilities or cognitive styles might change as they gain experience.

Most of the supervisor development models summarized in this chapter have been published since Worthington's article appeared. But as Russell and Petrie (1994) observed, these models are in their formative stages and consequently are not yet supported by empirical data. In fact, research on these models, with an occasional rare

exception (e.g., Baker et al., 2002) is virtually nonexistent.

Russell and Petrie's (1994) conclusions about these models are as apt today as when they wrote them:

1. *There is considerable similarity among the theories of supervisor development. The theoretical models presented offer slightly different perspectives; however, all appear to describe a general process through which supervisors move from a new role in which they are overwhelmed, self-conscious, anxious, and insecure to an integrated identity where they feel comfortable, secure, and competent. Given these similar descriptions, there appears to be at least clinical, if not empirical support. What currently is needed, however, is model testing and not further model building.*

2. *The models of supervisor development provide preliminary guidelines for creating effective supervisory dyads in training environments. To develop the most effective training environments (i.e., supervisory dyads) for supervisees, training directors should pay attention to not only the developmental level of the supervisee, but also the level of the supervisor.*

3. *These models provide guidelines for developing training environments for supervisors. Awareness of the supervisor's developmental level may be helpful in guiding supervisor trainers in their interactions with their student supervisors.*

4. *These models provide directions and hypotheses for research on supervisor development. Although research examining supervisor developmental models has been virtually nonexistent, these models allow for specific hypotheses concerning supervisors' behaviors, thinking styles, emotions, and perceptions to be proposed and tested.* (pp. 34–35)

We offer two additional comments: (1) We have little more research-based knowledge of supervisor development now than we did two decades ago when Worthington wrote his review; and (2) interestingly, the models described here were developed within a 15-year period, and no new models have been developed in the past decade. It is easy to speculate that this lack of activity is related to the lack of any new interest in counselor stage developmental models.

SUPERVISION PROCESS AND OUTCOME RESEARCH

Although the conceptual and practitioner-based literature on supervision has provided rich insights into its processes, it is formal research that can provide essential depth of understanding and confidence in our knowledge. But whereas counseling and psychotherapy research has a relatively short history that dates only from approximately the end of World War II (Garfield, 1983), supervision-related research has an even shorter history.

Harkness and Poertner (1989) reported that the first published study of social work supervision appeared in 1958. At about that time also, *Counselor Education and Supervision* was founded (1961) to provide a journal outlet for articles on counselor training and supervision (this journal, along with the *Journal of Counseling Psychology* and *Professional Psychology: Research and Practice,* consistently has been among the several journals in which supervision research is most likely to be found; though the new journal, *Training and Education in Professional Psychology,* devoted to supervision and training, is a spin-off of *Professional Psychology* and likely will divert many supervision-related articles that previously would have been published there). More recently, *The Clinical Supervisor* was founded as an interdisciplinary journal to respond to the growing supervision literature in multiple disciplines.

Many researchers have conducted an occasional study of supervision. A number have been doctoral students who choose a dissertation topic just as they are learning about supervision and so find themselves curious about supervision processes or outcomes. Perhaps only a score of researchers, though, are engaged in programmatic investiga-

tions of supervision. This seems generally consistent with Price's (1963) law, which is that

If k is the number of persons active in a discipline, then the square root of this number approximates the size of that subset who produced half of the contributions. Thus, about 250 composers are responsible for the music played in the classical repertoire. The square root of this number is 15.8. It turns out that a mere 16 composers put their names on half of all the pieces performed and recorded. (Simonton, 1994, p. 140)

In any case, the volume of supervision research has grown steadily, creating a literature sufficiently large to justify a number of published reviews of it. Ellis et al. (1996) noted, for example, that there had been at least 32 reviews of empirically based studies of supervision and others have been published since. Anyone seriously interested in conducting supervision research should begin by reading some of these available commentaries (e.g., Borders, 1989b; Ellis et al., 1996; Goodyear & Guzzardo, 2000; Holloway, 1984, 1992; Holloway & Hosford, 1983; Lambert, 1980; Lambert & Arnold, 1987; Lambert & Ogles, 1997; Russell, Crimmings, & Lent, 1984; Wampold & Holloway, 1997; Wheeler & Richards, 2007; Worthington, 1987).

One privilege of seeing this book through multiple editions has been the opportunity it has afforded to monitor the supervision literature across time. We find ample reason for optimism in what we have observed yet there remains considerable room for growth in both the volume and overall quality of that literature.

Our optimism stems from the increasing recognition being accorded supervision as an essential aspect of the larger mental health enterprise. This is reflected in accreditation and licensure statutes, in the increasingly international nature of the supervision literature, and in the burgeoning number of supervision books. All that is good news.

Curiously, though, the level of supervision-related research activity seems not to have changed even as interest in the topic has increased; it even is possible that research productivity has decelerated to some extent. Goodyear, Bunch, and

Claiborn (2005), for example, recently identified supervision articles that had occurred during the previous 5 years in psychology journals (including those from Australia, Britain, Canada, and New Zealand). Of the 49 articles they found, 22 reported research of some kind (quantitative, qualitative, survey, or instrument development), for an average of approximately 4 articles per year. Psychology is, of course, only one discipline conducting research on supervision and so this underestimates overall productivity. (Ladany and Inman, 2008, put the annual rate of supervision research articles at about 10.) On the other very conservative end of the spectrum—using very stringent inclusion criteria—Wheeler and Richards (2007) identified only 18 articles that have measured the impact of supervision on supervisees. Regardless of which of these several indices of productivity are used, there can be no question that the volume of supervision research is dwarfed by the volume of research on counseling or psychotherapy.

This relative dearth of research articles is somewhat disquieting. It is made the more so by the assessment of Ellis et al. (1996) and others that the quality of supervision research too often has been deficient.

Studies with deficient methodology are hardly unique to supervision, of course. The perfect study is rare in any area of psychological research. Gelso's (1979) "bubble hypothesis" is a vivid reminder of why that is. His metaphor is that of applying a sticker to an automobile windshield: No matter how careful the application, the sticker typically will have at least one bubble under it. When a person pushes down on that bubble in an attempt to eradicate it, the bubble simply reappears elsewhere under the sticker. An analogous phenomenon occurs in designing research studies, wherein the attempt to solve one design problem often will result in the creation of a different problem.

In short, there always will be "bubbles" of some size in the social sciences studies we conduct. Supervision is not unique in that respect, though it does have some unique challenges with respect to the type of "bubbles" its researchers need to address. Some years ago, Russell et al.

(1984) singled out four of them, all of which remain today. Specifically:

- theory too often has been insufficient to offer researchers clear direction;
- the number of supervisees and supervisors at most sites typically is small, which creates difficulty for researchers hoping to obtain adequate sample sizes;
- to manipulate independent variables in real-life training settings has presented both practical and ethical challenges;
- the "criterion problem" has been thorny; that is, it has been difficult to resolve what standard should be used in assessing the effectiveness of supervision.

Fortunately, none of these challenges is insurmountable. The recent efficacy study by Bambling, King, Raue, Schweitzer, and Lambert (2006) illustrates that point, for they managed to overcome three of these four challenges: problems with sample size; the ethics of randomly assigning some supervisees to a no-supervision condition (i.e., they used credentialed therapists); and criterion (i.e., actual client change). So quality research in supervision is not only possible, it is occurring in studies such as this.

Trends

The above comments set the stage for our observations about some trends we have observed, many of which parallel trends summarized by Bernard (2005). We hope that the perspective this permits may be useful to those planning future supervision research.

Trends in Research Topics. One type of trend we have observed has concerned supervision research topics. What we offer is very much a broad-brush look and so we acknowledge up front that we are not acknowledging many research topics that have been covered.

The first real period of supervision research, during the late 1960s and into the 1970s, was characterized by attention to Rogerian-related relationship skills; particularly those informed by Carkhuff's model. In her review of the studies of that era, Holloway (1984) provided a table that the outcome measures used in each study. It is striking how many of those measures were relationship measures.

Developmental models become the dominant research topic during the 1980s; so much so that Holloway (1987) characterized this emphasis as the prevailing zeitgeist. That research stopped during the early 1990s, but its effects on supervision have been pervasive and ongoing: It would be rare now to find a supervision theorist who did not at least acknowledge supervisee development as a factor, as we have in this book (see Figure 1.1).

The social influence model, as articulated by the seminal writings of Strong (1968) and Strong and Matross (1973), dominated much of counseling psychology research during the late 1970s and 1980s. Unsurprisingly, interest in that model extended to supervision (see, e.g., Dixon & Claiborn, 1987), helped by the availability of instruments (e.g., Corrigan & Schmidt, 1983) to measure social influence. As interest in that topic waned in the broader counseling psychology literature, supervision research invoking that model also waned.

Attention to multicultural issues has grown during the recent past. Supervision research has reflected this shift to some extent, although less so than the topic otherwise would warrant. In their 2000 review of supervision literature, Goodyear and Guzzardo were able to identify only eight such studies; more recently, Ladany and Inman (2008) identified five more that since have been published.

The supervisory relationship once again has become a primary focus of researchers. But whereas the relationship research of the earlier era was driven by a Rogerian conception, the working alliance now provides the conceptual framework, with a subset of studies also examining attachment as a predictor of relationship type. The studies summarized in Figure 6.3 show the range of predictors of alliance that so for have been examined, as well as of the outcomes it has been found to predict.

Many other topics have been addressed by supervision researchers, of course. These few we have mentioned represent only the broad trends. Seeing these trends noted in this way is a reminder of how social science researchers in all disciplines typically will rally around a particular topic that then becomes hot for a while. They then move on to another topic, which itself becomes exhausted after a while, and so on.

To see these broad supervision trends also is a reminder of how yoked supervision research remains to research on therapy (see, e.g., Milne, 2006). That is, with the exception of the developmental research in supervision (which is relatively domain specific), the ebb and flow of topics that we noted corresponds to what also was occurring in counseling or therapy research.

We conclude this subsection by noting that there are some topics that should have received more attention from supervision researchers than they have. One of the clearer examples is parallel processes, which generally are regarded as one of the phenomena that define supervision (see Chapter 6 for a summary of that research).

Methodological Trends. Holloway and Hosford (1983) asserted that we should expect supervision research to proceed through three stages, in accordance with the usual way science progresses: (1) a stage of descriptive observation in which a phenomenon is observed in its natural environment, (2) a stage in which important, specific variables are identified and relationships between and among them are clarified, and (3) a stage in which a theory is developed based on the empirically derived evidence about variables and their interrelationships.

It is interesting, though, just how much of supervision research has remained at that first, descriptive phase. That descriptive research has, though, taken multiple forms. Qualitative research is one; it is increasing in volume. Goodyear and Guzzardo (2000) noted that, whereas there had been virtually no qualitative research just a decade before, they had identified at least 10 studies that had some qualitative features. But momentum has continued to pick up and there now are a number of such studies. In reviews of 5 years of supervision articles in psychology (Goodyear et al., 2005) and counseling (Borders, 2005), qualitative research was a prominent subset of scholarship, though somewhat more so in counseling than in psychology.

In some cases, these descriptive studies have been important simply in bringing to our attention particular phenomena such as categories of supervisee nondisclosures (e.g., Ladany et al., 1996). In other cases, they are important in suggesting hypotheses to be followed up in subsequent research. For example, Nelson and Friedlander's (2001) finding that supervisees who experienced conflictual supervision also experienced higher-than-usual levels of role conflict is one that easily can be followed up on in quantitative research.

One area that has represented stage-two research is that which examined supervision processes, especially those focusing on supervisor–supervisee interactions. There were some such studies in the late 1980s and early 1990s (e.g., Martin, Goodyear, & Newton, 1987; Nelson & Holloway, 1990; Sells, Goodyear, Lichtenberg, & Polkinghorne, 1997; Tracey & Sherry, 1993). Interactional research is quite labor-intensive for it involves breaking interactions down into units and then having trained raters code them. But though they yield rich information, such investigations have largely disappeared, perhaps reflecting the lessening emphasis on process research in psychotherapy as well.

One area in which later-stage supervision research occurred was in the social influence research alluded to above. That research was typified, though, with analogue research so what it gained in internal validity, it often lost in external validity (see, e.g., Heppner & Claiborn, 1989).

One area of supervision research that has been too infrequent has been instrument development. As Ellis et al. (1996) noted, supervision researchers have tended to rely on instruments developed for psychotherapy research, but adapted

for supervision with just the change of a few words (e.g., substituting "supervisee" for "client"). Lambert and Ogles's (1997) review of 50 different instruments that have been used in supervision research vividly illustrates the extent to which this is true. Ellis et al. (1988) recommended that when using such measures the researcher should, at minimum, conduct a pilot study to examine the psychometric properties of the measure in the new setting and report internal consistency (e.g., Cronbach's alpha) based on the entire sample. Better yet, though, is the development of instruments specific to supervision (e.g., *Supervisory Working Alliance Inventory,* Efstation, Patton, & Kardash, 1990; *Supervisory Styles Inventory*, Friedlander & Ward, 1984; *Role Conflict and Role Ambiguity Inventory,* Olk & Friedlander, 1992).

Supervision Research as Increasingly Global
Clinical supervision is of interest to mental health professionals in a number of countries. Britain, in particular, has been home to a dynamic community of supervision scholars. Historically, though, empirical research on supervision has been primarily done in the United States (Wheeler & Richards, 2007).

It is important to note, therefore, that this is changing and supervision research is becoming increasingly international. For example, in Sweden, Ögren has been engaged in a research program on group supervision (http://www2.psychology.su.se/staff/mlon/indexeng.html); in Denmark, Jacobsen (http://vbn.aau.dk/research/ (2438)|publications?language=pri) has been engaged in work on parallel processes; in Britain, Milne (http://www.ncl.ac.uk/nnp/myprofiles-linked/milne-a.pdf) has focused on supervision definitions, models, and outcomes; and Wheeler (http://www.le.ac.uk/ad/counselling/staff/wheelerpub.html) has both conducted in her own research and written important reviews. In Australia, Bambling's recent dissertation and then subsequent article (Bambling et al., 2006) was ambitious, employing a clinical trial that used client improvement as a key outcome variable. This is a single study but it marks a sufficiently strong entrance of a new researcher to warrant attention. At Ewha Women's University in Korea, Eun Jung Son and Sung-Kyung Yoo are beginning promising supervision research programs (see, e.g., Son, Ellis, & Yoo, 2007).

In addition, whereas the literature we cite in this book is from English-language sources, we note that supervision publications are available in other languages, and there are supervision-specific journals in other languages. One, for example, is the online, German-language journal, *Supervision: Theorie-Praxis-Forschung,* which can be accessed at: http://www.fpi-publikationen.de/supervision/.

Issues on Which to Focus in Future Research

We end this chapter by addressing two particular challenges for supervision researchers. One concerns the outcome criteria to employ; the other a particular research strategy.

Client Change as the Outcome Criterion.
Protection of the public has been a primary rationale for codifying supervision in licensure laws. This is the belief that supervised therapists will provide a better service, or at least one that poses less risk. Therefore, it is important to establish that this is the case. To establish that supervision positively affects the clients being served by supervisees is, as Ellis and Ladany (1997) note, "the acid test" (p. 485). Or, to invoke another metaphor, we believe it should be the gold standard.

Yet that research so far has been scant. Ellis and Ladany (1997) identified nine such studies published since 1981; Freitas (2002) identified three more. However, researchers primarily have focused on session impact, rather than on client symptom reduction or other treatment outcomes. Moreover, Ellis and Ladany (1997) concluded that methodological and other problems made it possible to draw "few justifiable conclusions" (p. 488).

There is one notable, recent exception. The Bambling et al. (2006) study we reported above established that clients of therapists who received supervision had better outcomes than those who received no supervision. Such a study was possible because the therapists were fully qualified professionals; it would not be possible to do such a study with prelicensure supervisees for ethical reasons. But the results are very encouraging and perhaps the study will promote more like it; these studies are needed.

While we are addressing possible outcome measures, we also will note one that probably has been overused: supervisee satisfaction. Satisfaction does have value, but its link to outcomes such as supervisee skills, attitudes, and cognitions is quite imperfect. We recently heard an analogy to illustrate that. Consider patrons who are just leaving a pastry shop: If they were asked whether they liked the product and would return for more, they very likely would affirm that they would. This is very different, though, from evaluating the nutrition they obtained from the pastries they had consumed.

Mediators and Moderators.
Supervision can be conceptualized as having particular direct effects on supervisees. But supervision also can work through mediation or moderation of other factors (for excellent discussions of mediation and moderation, see Baron & Kenny, 1986; Frazier, Tix, & Barron, 2004; Holmbeck, 1997).

Moderation is probably the more familiar concept to most researchers, even if the term itself is unfamiliar. "A moderator variable is one that affects the relationship between two variables, so that the nature of the impact of the predictor on the criterion varies according to the level or value of the moderator" (Holmbeck, 1997, p. 599). It speaks to interaction effects. Therefore, if a researcher were examining a particular impact of supervision and believed that it was moderated by supervisor sex, he or she would look for gender-by-intervention (supervision) interaction effects on outcomes (i.e., whether men and women differentially responded to supervision).

Mediators, though, are mechanisms through which an independent variable influences a particular dependent variable. For example, it might be possible to hypothesize that supervisees' level of anxiety mediates supervision's effects on supervisees' self-efficacy. This would mean that supervision could be understood to affect supervisee anxiety levels and that anxiety levels in turn affect self-efficacy.

Although they may not have used the term, supervision researchers have been conducting research with moderators for some time. But research on mediation of supervision-related variables upon one another has been infrequent. Noting this, both Goodyear and Guzzardo (2000) and Wampold and Holloway (1997) have suggested its use in supervision research. A drawback, though, is it often requires relatively large samples, especially if structural equation modeling (Hoyle, 1995) is employed for the analyses—and large samples often are difficult to obtain in supervision research. Such studies, though, will provide more complete modeling of the very complex process that is supervision.

CONCLUSIONS

In the report of psychology's famous Boulder Conference, Raimy (1950) wrote with some irony that "[p]sychotherapy is an undefined technique applied to unspecified problems with unpredictable outcomes. For this technique we recommend rigorous training" (p. 93).

Fortunately, circumstances now are much different. We have a substantial empirical literature to undergird both the practice of counseling and therapy; the "rigorous training" of which Raimy spoke is also evolving at a healthy rate.

The recent growth in the quantity and quality of supervision research is heartening to those concerned with improving the practice of supervision. But, though growing, the empirical foundation for supervisory practice is still relatively small. Moreover, it is also not uniform across the various supervision modalities and models. The body of research on family therapy training and supervision, for example, remains especially small. But this very unevenness in professional literature is an opportunity for those interested in conducting supervision research. Because supervision is a young field, practitioners and researchers alike have much yet to learn. It is our hope that this book will play a small role in contributing to this discovery process.

In concluding this chapter, we also conclude the book. In doing this, we want to borrow from Keith, Connell, and Whitaker (1992), who ended their article by expressing the worry that they had not accomplished exactly what they set out to do. But they then invited readers to think of them as cooks who were offering elements of a recipe that other cooks might follow to produce their own "uniquely flavored result" (p. 109). This useful metaphor characterizes our intentions as well. In this book, we have tried as best we could within space and other constraints to characterize the existing practical, theoretical, and empirical literature concerning supervision. Moreover, we have attempted to do so by drawing from the literature of the various mental health professions. We conclude, then, by expressing our hope that in reading this book you have found some essential recipe(s) that can help you to concoct your own, unique perspectives on the nature and practice of supervision.

THE SUPERVISOR'S TOOLBOX

This toolbox offers resources to support the research, practice, and teaching of supervision. Its contents are listed below in the order in which they are presented.

Documents for Use in Supervision

- Sample Counseling Supervision Contract
- Example of a Professional Disclosure Statement
- Supervisee's Bill of Rights
- Supervision Agreement
- Descriptive Criteria for Professional Performance Review Policy Standards
- The Practicum Competencies Outline

Measures for Supervision Research and Practice

Measures of Supervision Impacts

- *Supervisory Satisfaction Questionnaire*. A supervision outcome measure.
- *Group Supervision Scale*. A measure of group supervision effects, with three subscales: Group safety; Skill development and Case conceptualization; and Group management.

Measures of Supervisee Attributes and Experiences

- *Supervisee Levels Questionnaire–Revised*. Measures three supervisee attributes: Self and other awareness, Motivation, and Dependency–autonomy.
- *Anticipatory Supervisee Anxiety Scale* (ASAS).

Process Measures

- *Role Conflict and Role Ambiguity Inventory*. Measures (a) Role ambiguity and (b) Role conflict.
- *Evaluation Process Within Supervision Inventory*. This measure's two scales are (a) Goal-setting and (b) Feedback.
- *Supervisory Working Alliance–Supervisor Form*. Its three scales measure (a) Rapport, (b) Client focus, and (c) Identification.
- *Supervisory Working Alliance–Supervisee Form*. Its two scales measure (a) Rapport and (b) Client focus.

Measures of Supervisor Styles, Efficacy, and Competencies

- *Supervisory Styles Inventory*. Has one scale for each of three supervision styles: Attractive, Interpersonally sensitive, and Task oriented.
- *The Feminist Supervision Scale*. Assesses collaborative relationship, Power analysis, Diversity and Social context, Feminist advocacy and activism.
- *Counselor Supervisor Self-Efficacy Scale*. Assesses supervisors' self-efficacy in six domains: Theories and techniques, Group supervision, Supervisory ethics, Self in supervision, Multicultural competence, Knowledge of legal issues.

- *Multicultural Supervision Competencies Questionnaire.* Assesses (a) Attitude and beliefs, (b) Knowledge and understanding, (c) Skills and practices, and (d) Relationship.

Supervision Ethics Codes

- *The Approved Clinical Supervisor Code of Ethics,* National Board for Certified Counselors
- *Ethical Guidelines for Counseling Supervisors,* Association for Counselor Education and Supervision

SAMPLE COUNSELING SUPERVISION CONTRACT

This contract serves as verification and a description of the counseling supervision provided by Jane Doe, Ph.D., LMHC ("Supervisor"), to _____ ("Supervisee"), Counselor Trainee enrolled in Practicum in the Community Counseling Program at Exemplar University for _____ semester 20__. (For doctoral student supervisors, need to identify self as such, and need to mention name of practicum instructor as "Faculty Supervisor.")

I. *Purpose, Goals, and Objectives:*
   a. Monitor and ensure welfare of clients seen by Supervisee
   b. Promote development of Supervisee's professional counselor identity and competence
   c. Fulfill academic requirement for Supervisee's Practicum
   d. Fulfill requirements in preparation for Supervisee's pursuit of counselor licensure (when applicable)

II. *Context of Services:*
   a. One (1) clock hour of individual supervision weekly
   b. Supervision will revolve around counseling conducted with _____ (population[s] to be served)
   c. Individual supervision will be conducted in Humdrum Hall, Exemplar University on _____ (day of week), from _____ to _____(time), where monitor/VCR is available to review videotape
   d. The Discrimination Model, interpersonal process recall, progress notes, and tape review will be used in supervision

III. *Method of Evaluation:*
   a. Feedback will be provided by the Supervisor during each session, and a formal evaluation, using the Program's standard evaluation of student clinical skills, will be conducted at mid-term and at the conclusion of the semester. A narrative evaluation will also be provided at mid-semester and at the conclusion of the semester as an addendum to the objective evaluations completed.
      Specific feedback provided by Supervisor will focus on Supervisee's demonstrated counseling skills and clinical documentation.
   b. Supervisee will evaluate Supervisor at mid-semester and at the close of _____ semester, using the Program's standard evaluation form for evaluating supervisors. A narrative evaluation will also accompany the objective evaluations.
   c. Supervision notes will be shared with Supervisee at Supervisor's discretion and at the request of the Supervisee.

IV. *Duties and Responsibilities of Supervisor and Supervisee:*
   a. **Supervisor:**
      a. Examine client presenting complaints and treatment plans

    b. View videotapes of Supervisee's counseling sessions outside of regularly scheduled supervision sessions

    c. Sign off on all client documentation

    d. Challenge Supervisee to justify approach and techniques used

    e. Monitor Supervisee's basic attending skills

    f. Support Supervisee's development as a counselor

    g. Present and model appropriate directives

    h. Intervene when client welfare is at risk

    i. Ensure ethical guidelines are upheld

    j. Maintain weekly supervision case notes

  b. Supervisee:

    a. Uphold ethical guidelines

    b. View counseling session videotapes in preparation for weekly supervision

    c. Be prepared to discuss all client cases—have client files, current and completed client case notes, and counseling session videotapes ready to review in weekly supervision sessions

    d. Justify client case conceptualizations made and approach and techniques used

    e. Complete case notes and place in appropriate client files

    f. Consult with field placement staff and Supervisor in cases of emergency

    g. Implement supervisory directives in subsequent sessions

V. *Procedural Considerations:*

  a. Supervisee's written case notes and treatment plans and videotapes will be reviewed and evaluated in each session.

  b. Issues related to Supervisee's professional development will be discussed.

  c. Sessions will be used to discuss issues of conflict and failure of either party to abide by directives outlined here in contract. If concerns of either party are not resolved in supervision, _____ (practicum instructor of Supervisee's practicum section), will be consulted.

  d. In event of emergency, Supervisee is to contact Supervisor at the office ( ) _____ or at home, ( ) _____.

VI. *Supervisor's Scope of Competence:*

Dr. Doe received her Ph.D. in counselor education, is a National Certified Counselor, and is licensed in __ as a Mental Health Counselor and Marriage and Family Therapist. She is an NBCC Approved Clinical Supervisor and AAMFT Approved Supervisor. Dr. Doe is a Professor at Exemplar University and teaches clinical courses on a regular basis, as well as the doctoral level supervision course. She has written several articles in the areas of clinical supervision, children's adjustment to divorce, and eating disorders. Dr. Doe presently sits on the mental health counselor licensure board for the state of _____.

VII. *Terms of the Contract:*

This contract is subject to revision at any time, upon the request of either the Supervisor or Supervisee. A formal review of the contract will be made at the mid-term of

_____Semester 20__, and revisions will be made only with consent of Supervisee and approval of the Supervisor.

We agree, to the best of our ability, to uphold the directives specified in this supervision contract and to conduct our professional behavior according to the ethical principles of our professional association.

Supervisor:_____/Date:_____

Supervisee:_____/Date:_____

Community Counseling Program

                       522 Humdrum Hall

                       Exemplar University

This contract is effective from _____ (start date) to _____(finish date).

(Date of revision or termination)

_____

Adapted with permission from C. J. Osborn & T. E. Davis (1996). The supervision contract: Making it perfectly clear. *The Clinical Supervisor, 14*(2), 121–134.

EXAMPLE OF A
PROFESSIONAL DISCLOSURE STATEMENT
Prepared by Course Instructor for Practicum Supervision

As your Practicum instructor, I am responsible for the individual and group supervision you receive this semester. This statement is to be used in conjunction with your syllabus, which spells out all the requirements of Practicum. My purpose in presenting this to you is to acquaint you with some of my goals for supervision, to provide you with an overview of the supervision process, and to outline some of the conditions under which we both must operate.

Prior to addressing the points listed above, I'd like to review my qualifications for conducting supervision. (Includes degrees in counseling, licenses and certifications.)

I have been engaged in clinical supervision for over (number) years, mostly through my department responsibilities at (name of university(ies). (List areas of specialization that will inform and/or limit one's supervision. List other activity that qualifies one to supervise, e.g., publications in supervision, workshops conducted, etc.) I adhere to the NBCC Code of Ethics (attach for supervisee) and to the NBCC Clinical Supervision Standards of Practice (attach for supervisee).

Clinical supervision has two goals: the development of the counseling skills of the supervisee (counselor-in-training) and the protection of the client. These are always operating simultaneously when supervision is occurring. Most of the time, it will seem that primary attention is being paid to your developing skills. When this is so, it is because a judgment has been made that your client(s) is receiving adequate counseling services. When there is any question about the adequacy of the counseling your client(s) is receiving, supervision will become more active and, perhaps, more intrusive.

You will work with two supervisors this semester. You will have weekly hour-long individual sessions with a doctoral student supervisor. This weekly session will occur at your mutual convenience. The individual supervisors receive weekly supervision-of-supervision by me. On occasion, I will observe your individual supervision sessions. All supervision sessions will be audiotaped or videotaped. The Practicum class (or group supervision) will be conducted by me and will be a weekly 3-hour session. Group supervision allows you to learn from your peers as well as from your supervisors. Both individual and group supervision are explained in greater detail in your syllabus.

You are required to submit a *minimum* of one audiotaped counseling session per week to your individual supervisor. Additionally, you will be required to submit audiotapes as part of group supervision (on average, one every 3 weeks). You will also be required to submit case notes on all individual, family, and group counseling sessions that you conduct each week. It is your responsibility to turn in the required tapes and paperwork. It is my responsibility to coordinate your supervision from me, your individual supervisor, and in some cases, your site supervisor. Your case notes and records of all individual supervision sessions will be maintained by the Department for 7 years.

Your supervisors may draw from different supervision models. You can count on the following, however: You will be encouraged to consider your thoughts, your behaviors, and your feelings as you conduct counseling sessions. Your supervisors will draw from the roles of teacher, consultant, and counselor to assist you in doing this. The supervision you will be offered will be developmentally appropriate (that is, the supervision will be matched to your level of experience and your relative ability). The supervision you receive will include discussions about cultural context—your own, the supervisor's, and the client's—and how these affect the counseling and supervision relationships of which you are a part. The supervision you receive will be sensitive to your personal goals for yourself as a counselor and will be consistent with how you conceptualize client issues theoretically. You will be challenged and supported throughout supervision. You will be treated with respect.

Although one of your supervisors may draw on a counselor role, it is important for you to understand that this is only to help you understand any personal reactions you may be having that are diminishing your positive effect as a counselor. The resolution of personal difficulties cannot be attained through supervision. A referral list of counseling services is available in campus publications and can also be obtained through any Department faculty member. It is not unusual for a student to seek personal counseling while working toward a counseling degree.

You will receive a copy of an Evaluation Instrument on the first day of class. This will be used by me and by your individual supervisor throughout the semester to track your progress and to give you specific, formative feedback. You will receive two formal feedback sessions, one slightly before the mid-point of the semester and one at the end. At this time, you will receive written feedback. If I have any serious concerns about your progress in practicum, I will inform you of these concerns as soon as possible, preferably at the first formal feedback session.

Because you are a student in a counselor training program, I cannot guarantee confidentiality of information gained in supervision if it is relevant to your overall progress in the program. I can, however, commit to honoring and respecting all information I receive in supervision about you and/or your clients and keeping all such information confidential to the degree possible. Occasionally, there are situations that occur that make confidentiality impossible. These include: 1. Threats to harm self or others; 2. Reasonable suspicion of abuse of a child or other vulnerable persons; 3. When ordered by the court. Confidentiality may also be broken in one's defense against legal action before a court.

Please feel free to call me at home whenever you have any concern about a client for the duration of the practicum. My home number is _____. For regular communications, please call me at the office (_____) or e-mail me at [email address]. In case of emergency when I am out of town, you will be advised regarding who is the most appropriate contact person in my absence.

Although it is rare, occasionally a student does not feel that he or she has received adequate supervision or a fair evaluation. If this should occur, your first step is to attempt to resolve the issue with me. If you remain dissatisfied, this course is protected by the same appeal procedure as any other course as is outlined in Department materials and the SOE catalogue. If you believe I have acted unethically in any way, you may report your complaint to:

NBCC Ethics Officer (phone number)

Although the many parameters of the Practicum course listed in this document may make the experience sound tedious or intimidating, I assure you that on the contrary, this is a most exciting time in your development as a professional counselor. I look forward to working with you and to celebrating your progress as you take the next step in your goal of entering a noble profession.

Please sign, date and return one copy of this form.

_____   _____
Practicum Instructor Signature   Student Signature

DATE: _____   DATE: _____

SUPERVISEE'S BILL OF RIGHTS

Introduction

The purpose of the Bill of Rights is to inform supervisees of their rights and responsibilities in the supervisory process.

Nature of the Supervisory Relationship

The supervisory relationship is an experiential learning process that assists the supervisee in developing therapeutic and professional competence. A professional counselor supervisor who has received specific training in supervision facilitates professional growth of the supervisee through:

- monitoring client welfare
- encouraging compliance with legal, ethical, and professional standards
- teaching therapeutic skills
- providing regular feedback and evaluation
- providing professional experiences and opportunities

Expectations of the Initial Supervisory Session

The supervisee has the right to be informed of the supervisor's expectations of the supervisory relationship. The supervisor shall clearly state expectations of the supervisory relationship that may include:

- supervisee identification of supervision goals for oneself
- supervisee preparedness for supervisory meetings supervisee determination of areas for professional growth and development supervisor's expectations regarding formal and informal evaluations supervisor's expectations of the supervisee's need to provide formal and informal self-evaluations supervisor's expectations regarding the structure and/or the nature of the supervisory sessions
- weekly review of case notes until supervisee demonstrates competency in case conceptualization
- The supervisee shall provide input to the supervisor regarding the supervisee's expectations of the relationship.

Expectations of the Supervisory Relationship

A supervisor is a professional counselor with appropriate credentials. The supervisee can expect the supervisor to serve as a mentor and a positive role model who assists the supervisee in developing a professional identity. The supervisee has the right to work with a supervisor who is culturally sensitive and is able to openly discuss the influence of race, ethnicity, gender, sexual orientation, religion, and class on the counseling and the supervision process. The supervisor is aware of personal cultural assumptions and constructs and is able to assist the supervisee in developing additional knowledge and skills in working with clients from diverse cultures.

Since a positive rapport between the supervisor and supervisee is critical for successful supervision to occur, the relationship is a priority for both the supervisor and supervisee.

In the event that relationship concerns exist, the supervisor or supervisee will discuss concerns with one another and work towards resolving differences. Therapeutic interventions initiated by the supervisor or solicited by the supervisee shall be implemented only in the service of helping the supervisee increase effectiveness with clients. A proper referral for counseling shall be made if appropriate.

The supervisor shall inform the supervisee of an alternative supervisor who will be available in case of crisis situations or known absences.

Ethics and Issues in the Supervisory Relationship

1. **Code of Ethics & Standards of Practice:** The supervisor will insure the supervisee understands the *American Counseling Association Code of Ethics and Standards of Practice* and legal responsibilities. The supervisor and supervisee will discuss sections applicable to the beginning counselor.
2. **Dual Relationships:** Since a power differential exists in the supervisory relationship, the supervisor shall not utilize this differential to their gain. Since dual relationships may affect the objectivity of the supervisor, the supervisee shall not be asked to engage in social interaction that would compromise the professional nature of the supervisory relationship.
3. **Due Process:** During the initial meeting, supervisors provide the supervisee information regarding expectations, goals, and roles of the supervisory process. The supervisee has the right to regular verbal feedback and periodic formal written feedback signed by both individuals.
4. **Evaluation:** During the initial supervisory session, the supervisor provides the supervisee a copy of the evaluation instrument used to assess the counselor's progress.
5. **Informed Consent:** The supervisee informs the client she is in training, is being supervised, and receives written permission from the client to audiotape or videotape.
6. **Confidentiality:** The counseling relationship, assessments, records, and correspondences remain confidential. Failure to keep information confidential is a violation of the ethical code and the counselor is subject to a malpractice suit. The client must sign a written consent prior to counselor's consultation.
7. **Vicarious Liability:** The supervisor is ultimately liable for the welfare of the supervisee's clients. The supervisee is expected to discuss with the supervisor the counseling process and individual concerns of each client.
8. **Isolation:** The supervisor consults with peers regarding supervisory concerns and issues.
9. **Termination of Supervision:** The supervisor discusses termination of the supervisory relationship and helps the supervisee identify areas for continued growth and explore professional goals.

Expectations of the Supervisory Process

The supervisee shall be encouraged to determine a theoretical orientation that can be used for conceptualizing and guiding work with clients.

The supervisee has the right to work with a supervisor who is responsive to the supervisee's theoretical orientation, learning style, and developmental needs.

Since it is probable that the supervisor's theory of counseling will influence the supervision process, the supervisee needs to be informed of the supervisor's counseling theory and how the supervisor's theoretical orientation may influence the supervision process.

Expectations of Supervisory Sessions

The weekly supervisory session shall include a review of all cases, audiotapes, videotapes, and may include live supervision.

The supervisee is expected to meet with the supervisor face-to-face in a professional environment that insures confidentiality.

Expectations of the Evaluation Process

During the initial meeting, the supervisee shall be provided with a copy of the formal evaluation tool(s) that will be used by the supervisor.

The supervisee shall receive verbal feedback and/or informal evaluation during each supervisory session. The supervisee shall receive written feedback or written evaluation on a regular basis during beginning phases of counselor development. Written feedback may be requested by the supervisee during intermediate and advanced phases of counselor development.

The supervisee should be recommended for remedial assistance in a timely manner if the supervisor becomes aware of personal or professional limitations that may impede future professional performance.

Beginning counselors receive written and verbal summative evaluation during the last supervisory meeting. Intermediate and advanced counselors may receive a recommendation for licensure and/or certification.

References

American Association for Counselor Education & Supervision. (1995). Ethical guidelines for counseling supervisors. *Counselor Education & Supervision, 34,* 270–276.

American Counseling Association. (1997). *Code of Ethics and Standards of Practice.* Alexandria, VA: American Counseling Association.

Bernard, J. M., & Goodyear, R. K. (1998). *Fundamentals of clinical supervision.* (2nd ed.). Boston: Allyn & Bacon.

Borders, L. D., & Leddick, G. R. (1987). *Handbook of counseling supervision.* Alexandria, VA: Association for Counselor Education and Supervision.

Rønnestad, M. H., & Skovholt, T. M. (1993). Supervision of beginning and advanced graduate students of counseling and psychotherapy. *Journal of Counseling and Development, 71,* 396–405.

Supervision Interest Network, Association for Counselor Education and Supervision. (Summer, 1993). ACES ethical guidelines for counseling supervisors. *ACES Spectrum, 5*(4), 5–8.

Maria A. Giordano, Michael K. Altekruse, & Carolyn W. Kern (2000). Unpublished manuscript. Reprinted by the permission of the authors.

SUPERVISION AGREEMENT

Based on the Supervisee's Bill of Rights

The supervisory relationship is an experiential learning process that assists the supervisee in developing therapeutic and professional competence. This contract is designed to assist the supervisor and supervisee in establishing clear expectations about the supervisory process.

Supervisee

Read the *Supervisee's Bill of Rights* and this agreement. Complete the sections on skills, goals, and professional opportunities and bring this agreement to the initial supervisory session.

Prior to the first supervisory session, read the American Counseling Association's *Code of Ethics and Standards of Practice*.

Introduction and Expectations of the Supervisory Experience

Supervisor

1. Introduce yourself: discuss your credentials, licenses, academic background, counseling experience, and your supervisory style.
2. Describe your role as a supervisor: teacher, consultant, counselor, evaluator.
3. Discuss your responsibilities: monitoring client welfare, teaching therapeutic skills, providing regular verbal and written feedback and evaluation, and insuring compliance with legal, ethical, and professional standards.
4. Ask the supervisee about his or her learning style and developmental needs.

Supervisee

1. Introduce yourself and describe your academic background, clinical experience, and training.
2. Briefly discuss information you want to address during the supervisory meetings.
3. Describe the therapeutic skills you want to enhance and professional development opportunities you want to experience during the next three months.

List three therapeutic skills you would like to further develop.

1. _____
2. _____
3. _____

List three general goals you would like to attain during the supervisory process.

1. _____
2. _____
3. _____

List three specific counseling or professional development experiences you would like to have during the next three months. (Attending a conference, facilitating a group, presentation, etc.)

1. _____

2. _____

3. _____

Expectations of the Supervisory Relationship

Supervisor and Supervisee
1. Discuss your expectations of the supervisory relationship.
2. Discuss how you will work towards establishing a positive and productive supervisory relationship. Also, discuss how you will address and resolve conflicts.
3. The supervisory experience will increase the supervisee's awareness of feelings, thoughts, behavior, and aspects of self which are stimulated by the client. Discuss the role of the supervisor in assisting with this process.
4. Share your thoughts with one another about the influence of race, ethnicity, gender, sexual orientation, religion, and class on the counseling and the supervision process.

Supervisee
1. Describe how you would like to increase your awareness of personal cultural assumptions, constructs, and ability to work with clients from diverse cultures.

Supervisor
1. If the supervisee needs to consult with you prior to the next supervision session, discuss how you would like to be contacted. Also, if you are unavailable during a period of time, inform the supervisee of an alternate supervisor who will be available in your absence.

Ethics and Issues in the Supervisory Relationship
1. Discuss the *Code of Ethics and Standards of Practice*. Review key issues not listed in this section.
2. A professional relationship is maintained between the supervisor and supervisee. The supervisor and supervisee do not engage in social interaction that interferes with objectivity and professional judgment of the supervisor.
3. After the initial supervisory meeting, the supervisee and supervisor can reestablish goals, expectations, and discuss roles of the supervisory process. The supervisor and supervisee provide one another with regular feedback.
4. During the initial counseling session, the supervisee will inform the client that she/he is in training and is being supervised. If the supervisee wishes to audiotape or videotape, the client needs to give written consent.
5. Discuss confidentiality and the importance of obtaining a written release from the client prior to consultation with other professionals who are serving the client.
6. The supervisor is ultimately responsible for the welfare of the supervisee's clients. During each supervisory session, the supervisee will review each client's progress and relate specific concerns to the supervisor in a timely manner.

Expectations of the Supervisory Process

Supervisor

1. Describe your theory of counseling and how it influences your counseling and supervision style.
2. Discuss your theory or model of supervision.

Supervisee

1. Discuss your learning style and your developmental needs.
2. Discuss your current ideas about your theoretical orientation.

Expectations of Supervisory Sessions

Supervisee

1. Discuss your expectations about the learning process and interest in reviewing audiotapes, videotapes, and case notes.

Supervisor

1. Describe the structure and content of the weekly supervisory sessions.
2. Discuss your expectations regarding supervisee preparedness for supervisory sessions (audiotapes, videotapes, case notes).

CACREP standards require students in their internship experience to receive a minimum one hour of individual supervision per week and 90 minutes of group supervision each week.

The weekly supervisory session will take place face-to-face in a professional environment that insures confidentiality. Decide the location, day, and time.

Location _____ Day _____ Time _____

Expectations Regarding Evaluation

Supervisee

1. Discuss your interest in receiving weekly feedback in areas such as: relationship building, counseling techniques, client conceptualization, and assessment.

Supervisor

1. Discuss your style of providing verbal feedback and evaluation.
2. Provide the supervisee with a copy of the formal evaluation you will use; discuss the evaluation tools and clarify specific items that need additional explanation.
3. Discuss the benefit of self-evaluation; provide a copy of self-evaluation forms, and clarify specific items that need additional explanation.

_____Supervisor's Signature   Date_____

_____Supervisee's Signature   Date_____

Maria A. Giordano, Michael K. Altekruse, & Carolyn W. Kern (2000). Unpublished manuscript. Reprinted by the permission of the authors.

DESCRIPTIVE CRITERIA FOR PROFESSIONAL
PERFORMANCE REVIEW POLICY STANDARDS (REVISED 5/05)

1. Openness to new ideas (1 = *closed* to 5 = *open*)

Was dogmatic about own perspective and ideas.	Was amenable to discussion of perspectives other than own.	Solicited others' opinions and perspectives about own work.
Ignored or was defensive about constructive feedback.	Accepted constructive feedback without defensiveness.	Invited constructive feedback and demonstrated interest in others' perspectives.
Showed little or no evidence of incorporating constructive feedback received to change own behavior.	Some evidence of effort to incorporate relevant feedback received to change own behavior.	Showed strong evidence of incorporation of feedback received to change own behavior.

2. Flexibility (1 = *inflexible* to 5 = *flexible*)

Showed little or no effort to recognize changing demands in the professional and interpersonal environment.	Effort to recognize changing demands in the professional and interpersonal environment was evident but sometimes inaccurate.	Showed accurate effort to recognize changing demands in the professional and interpersonal environment.
Showed little or no effort to flex own response to changing environmental demands.	Effort to flex own response to new environmental demands was evident but sometimes inaccurate.	Showed accurate effort to flex own response to changing environmental demands as needed.
Refused to flex own response to changing environmental demands despite knowledge of the need for change.	Flexed own response to changing environmental demands when directed to do so.	Independently monitored the environment for changing demands and flexed own response accordingly.
Was intolerant of unforeseeable or necessary changes in established schedule or protocol.	Accepted necessary changes in established schedule or protocol, but without effort to understand the reason for them.	Attempted to understand needs for change in established schedule or protocol to avoid resentment.
		Accepted necessary changes in established schedule and attempted to discover the reasons for them.

3. Cooperativeness with others (1 = *uncooperative* to 5 = *cooperative*)

Showed little or no engagement in collaborative activities.	Engaged in collaborative activities but with minimum allowable input.	Worked actively toward reaching consensus in collaborative activities.
Undermined goal achievement in collaborative activities.	Accepted but rarely initiated compromise in collaborative activities.	Was willing to initiate compromise in order to reach group consensus.
Was unwilling to compromise in collaborative activities.	Was concerned mainly with own part in collaborative activities.	Showed concern for group as well as individual goals in collaborative activities.

4. Willingness to accept and use feedback (1 = *unwilling* to 5 = *willing*)

Discouraged feedback from others through defensiveness and anger.	Was generally receptive to supervisory feedback.	Invited feedback by direct request and gave positive acknowledgement when received.
Showed little or no evidence of incorporation of supervisory feedback received.	Showed some evidence of incorporating supervisory feedback into own views and behaviors.	Showed evidence of active incorporation of supervisory feedback received into own views and behaviors.
Took feedback contrary to own position as a personal affront.	Showed some defensiveness to critique through "over-explanation of own actions"—but without anger.	Demonstrated a balanced willingness to give and receive supervisory feedback.
Demonstrated greater willingness to give feedback than receive it.	Demonstrated greater willingness to receive feedback than to give it.	

5. Awareness of own impact on others (1 = *unaware* to 5 = *aware*)

Words and actions reflected little or no concern for how others were impacted by them.	Effort to determine how own words and actions impacted others was evident but sometimes inaccurate.	Effort toward recognition of how own words and actions impacted others.
Ignored supervisory feedback about how words and actions were negatively impacting others.	Responded as necessary to feedback regarding negative impact of own words and actions on others, but at times, with resentment.	Initiated feedback from others regarding impact of own words and behaviors.

Regularly incorporated feedback regarding impact of own words and behaviors to effect positive change.

6. Ability to deal with conflict (1 = *unable* to 5 = *able*)

Was unable or unwilling to consider others' points of view.	Attempted but sometimes had difficulty grasping conflicting points of view.	Always willing and able to consider others' points of view.
Showed no willingness to examine own role in a conflict.	Would examine own role in a conflict when directed to do so.	Almost always willing to examine own role in a conflict.
Ignored supervisory advisement if not in agreement with own position.	Was responsive to supervision in a conflict if it was offered.	Was consistently open to supervisory critique about own role in a conflict.
Showed no effort at problem solving.	Participated in problem solving when directed.	Initiated problem-solving efforts in conflicts.
Displayed hostility when conflicts were addressed.		Actively participated in problem-solving efforts.

7. Ability to accept personal responsibility (1 = *unable* to 5 = *able*)

Refused to admit mistakes or examine own contribution to problems.	Was willing to examine own role in problems when informed of the need to do so.	Monitored own level of responsibility in professional performance.
Lied, minimized, or embellished the truth to extricate self from problems.	Was accurate and honest in describing own and others' roles in problems.	Invited constructive critique from others and applied it toward professional growth.
Consistently blamed others for problems without self-examination.	Might blame initially, but was open to self-examination about own role in problems.	Accepted own mistakes and responded to them as opportunity for self-improvement.
		Avoided blame in favor of self-examination.

8. Ability to express feelings effectively and appropriately
(1 = *unable* to 5 = *able*)

Showed no evidence of willingness and ability to articulate own feelings.	Showed some evidence of willingness and ability to articulate own feelings, but with limited range.	Was consistently willing and able to articulate the full range of own feelings.
Showed no evidence of willingness and ability to recognize and acknowledge the feelings of others.	Showed some evidence of willingness and ability to acknowledge others' feelings—sometimes inaccurate.	Showed evidence of willingness and accurate ability to acknowledge others' feelings.
Acted out negative feelings (through negative behaviors) rather than articulating them.	Expressions of feeling usually appropriate to the setting—responsive to supervision when not.	Expressions of own feelings was consistently appropriate to the setting.
Expressions of feeling were inappropriate to the setting.	Willing to discuss own feelings in supervision when directed.	Initiated discussion of own feelings in supervision.
Was resistant to discussion of feelings in supervision.		

9. Attention to ethical and legal considerations
(1 = *inattentive* to 5 = *attentive*)

Engaged in dual relationships with clients.	Was responsive to supervision for occasional personal-professional boundary confusion in verbal interactions with clients.	Maintained clear personal-professional boundaries with clients.
Acted with prejudice toward those of different race, culture, gender, or sexual orientation than self.	Was responsive to supervision for occasional insensitivity to diversity in professional interactions.	Demonstrated consistent sensitivity to diversity.
Endangered the safety and the well-being of clients.	Used judgment that could have put client safety and well-being at risk.	Satisfactorily ensured client safety and well-being.
Breached established rules for protecting client confidentiality.	Used judgment that could have put client confidentiality at risk.	Appropriately safeguarded the confidentiality of clients.

10. Initiative and motivation (1 = *poor initiative and motivation* to 5 = *good initiative and motivation*)

Often missed deadlines and classes.	Missed the maximum allowable classes and deadlines.	Met all attendance requirements and deadlines.
Rarely participated in class activities.	Usually participated in class activities.	Regularly participated in class activities.
Often failed to meet minimal expectations in assignments.	Met only the minimal expectations in assigned work.	Met or exceeded expectations in assigned work.
Displayed little or no initiative and creativity in assignments.	Showed some initiative and creativity in assignments.	Consistently displayed initiative and creativity in assigned work.

Note. Column 1 = unacceptable professional performance; Column 2 = acceptable professional performance; Column 3 = excellent professional performance.

From McAdams, C. R., III, Foster, V. A., & Ward, T. J. (2007). Remediation and dismissal policies in counselor education: Lessons learned from a challenge in federal court. *Counselor Education and Supervision, 46,* 212–229. Reprinted with permission.

THE PRACTICUM COMPETENCIES OUTLINE

Report on Practicum Competencies

A. Baseline Competencies:
1. Personality characteristics, intellectual, and personal skills students bring to the graduate training experience:
   a. interpersonal skills: encompass both verbal and nonverbal forms of communication, the ability to listen and be empathic and respectful of others, and the ability to be open to feedback.
   b. cognitive skills: includes an attitude of intellectual curiosity and flexibility, and abilities in problem-solving, critical thinking, and organized reasoning.
   c. affective skills: the ability to tolerate affect, to tolerate and understand interpersonal conflict, and to tolerate ambiguity and uncertainty.
   d. personality/attitudes: the desire to help others, openness to new ideas, honesty and integrity and the valuing of ethical behavior, and personal courage.
   e. expressive skills: the ability to communicate accurately one's ideas, feelings, and information in verbal, nonverbal, and written forms.
   f. reflective skills: the ability to examine and consider one's own motives, attitudes, and behaviors and one's effect on others.
   g. personal skills: personal organization, hygiene, and appropriate dress.
2. Knowledge from graduate classroom experience prior to or concurrent with practicum:
   a. assessment and clinical interviewing   c. ethical and legal standards
   b. intervention   d. individual and cultural differences

B. Skills Developed During Practicum
1. Relationship/interpersonal skills
2. Application of research
3. Psychological assessment
4. Intervention
5. Consultation/interprofessional collaboration
6. Diversity: Individual and cultural differences
7. Ethics
8. Leadership
9. Supervisory skills
10. Professional development: Building a foundation for life-long learning
    a. practical skills to maintain effective clinical practice
    b. professional development competencies
11. Metaknowledge/metacompetencies

The following table illustrates how each of the 11 above skills is then elaborated into subskills, with the expected level of attained competence for each. Elaborations of the remaining 10 skills can be found online at http://www.adptc.org/public_files/Practicum%20Competencies%20Final%20(Oct%20'06%Version).pdf

B. Description of Skills Leading to Competencies That Are Developed During the Practicum Experience	Completed Practicum

Competence Level expected by the completion of practicum is indicated in the column on the right. N = *Novice;* I = *Intermediate;* A = *Advanced.* These competencies are built upon fundamental personality characteristics, intellectual and personal skills (see below for definitions).

1. Relationship/Interpersonal Skills

The ability to form and maintain productive relationships with others is a cornerstone of professional psychology.

Productive relationships are respectful, supportive, professional, and ethical. Professional psychologists should possess these basic competencies when they first begin their clinical training. Although the ability to form such relationships is grounded in basic skills that most students will have developed over the course of their lives to date, helping the student hone and refine these abilities into professional competencies in the clinical setting is a key aim of the practicum.

In particular, the practicum seeks to enhance students' skills in forming relationships:

a) With patients/clients/families:	
i) Ability to take a respectful, helpful professional approach to patients/clients/families.	A
ii) Ability to form a working alliance.	I
iii) Ability to deal with conflict, negotiate differences.	I
iv) Ability to understand and maintain appropriate professional boundaries.	I
b) With colleagues:	
i) Ability to work collegially with fellow professionals.	A
ii) Ability to support others and their work and to gain support for one's own work.	I
iii) Ability to provide helpful feedback to peers and receive such feedback nondefensively from peers.	I
c) With supervisors, the ability to make effective use of supervision, including:	
i) Ability to work collaboratively with the supervisor.	A

Collaboration means understanding, sharing, and working by a set of common goals for supervision. Many of these goals will change as the student gains professional competence, although a core goal, of working cooperatively to enhance the student's skills as a clinician, will remain constant. It is this aspect of collaboration that is expected to be at the "A" level by the end of practicum training. Competencies ii and iii below may be considered aspects of collaboration with the supervisor

ii) Ability to prepare for supervision.	A
iii) Ability/willingness to accept supervisory input, including direction; ability to follow through on recommendations; ability to negotiate needs for autonomy from and dependency on supervisors.	A
iv) Ability to self-reflect and self-evaluate regarding clinical skills and use of supervision, including using good judgment as to when supervisory input is necessary.	I

d) With support staff :

i) Ability to be respectful of support staff roles and persons.	A

e) With teams at clinic:

i) Ability to participate fully in team's work.	A
ii) Ability to understand and observe team's operating procedures.	I

f) With community professionals:

i) Ability to communicate professionally and work collaboratively with community professionals.	I

g) For the practicum site itself:

i) Ability to understand and observe agency's operating procedures.	A
ii) Ability to participate in furthering the work and mission of the practicum site.	A
iii) Ability to contribute in ways that will enrich the site as a practicum experience for future students.	A

1. **Novice (N):** Novices have limited knowledge and understanding of (a) how to analyze problems and (b) intervention skills and the processes and techniques of implementing them. Novices do not yet recognize patterns and do not differentiate well between important and unimportant details; they do not have filled-in cognitive maps of how, for example, a given client may move from where he or she is to a place of better functioning.

2. **Intermediate (I):** Psychology students at the intermediate level of competence have gained enough experience through practice, supervision, and instruction to be able recognize some important recurring domain features and to select appropriate strategies to address the issue at hand. Surface-level analyses of the Novice stage are less prominent, but generalization of diagnostic and intervention skills to new situations and clients is limited, and support is needed to guide performance.

3. **Advanced (A):** At this level, the student has gained deeper, more integrated knowledge of the competency domain in question, including appropriate knowledge of the scholarly/research literature as needed. The student is considerably more fluent in his or her ability to recognize important recurring domain features and to select appropriate strategies to address the issue at hand. In relation to clinical work, recognition of overall patterns, of a set of possible diagnoses, and/or treatment processes and outcomes for a given case are taking shape. Overall plans, based on the more integrated knowledge base and identification of domain features are clearer and more influential in guiding action. At this level, the student is less flexible in these areas than the proficient psychologist [the next level of competence] but does have a feeling of mastery and the ability to cope with and manage many contingencies of clinical work.

From Hatcher, R. L., & Lassiter, K. D. (2007). Initial training in professional psychology: The practicum competencies outline. *Training and Education in Professional Psychology, 1,* 49–63. Copyright © 2007 by the American Psychological Association. Reprinted with permission.

SUPERVISORY SATISFACTION QUESTIONNAIRE

1. How would you rate the quality of the supervision you have received?

1	2	3	4
Excellent	*Good*	*Fair*	*Poor*

2. Did you get the kind of supervision you wanted?

1	2	3	4
No, definitely not	*No, not really*	*Yes, generally*	*Yes, definitely*

3. To what extent has this supervision fit your needs?

4	3	2	1
Almost all my needs have been met	*Most of my needs have been met*	*Only a few of my needs have been met*	*None of my needs have been met*

4. If a friend were in need of supervision, would you recommend this supervisor to him or her?

1	2	3	4
No, definitely not	*No, I don't think so*	*Yes, I think so*	*Yes, definitely*

5. How satisfied are you with the amount of supervision you have received?

1	2	3	4
Quite satisfied	*Indifferent or mildly dissatisfied*	*Mostly satisfied*	*Very satisfied*

6. Has the supervision you received helped you to deal more effectively in your role as a counselor or therapist?

4	3	2	1
Yes, definitely	*Yes, generally*	*No, not really*	*No, definitely not*

7. In an overall, general sense, how satisfied are you with the supervision you have received?

4	3	2	1
Very satisfied	*Mostly satisfied*	*Indifferent or mildly dissatisfied*	*Quite dissatisfied*

8. If you were to seek supervision again, would you come back to this supervisor?

1	2	3	4
No, definitely not	*No, I don't think so*	*Yes, I think so*	*Yes, definitely*

The score is the sum of the items.

Note: Developed by Ladany, N., Hill, C. E., & Nutt, E. A. (1996). Unpublished instrument. Reprinted with permission of the authors.

GROUP SUPERVISION SCALE

For each of the following items, please circle the number that best describes your experience with your group supervisor. Please use a five-point scale where 1 = *strongly disagree* and 5 = *strongly agree*.

1. The supervisor provides useful feedback regarding my skills and interventions.　1　2　3　4　5

2. The supervisor provides helpful suggestions and information related to client treatment.　1　2　3　4　5

3. The supervisor facilitates constructive exploration of ideas and techniques for working with clients.　1　2　3　4　5

4. The supervisor provides helpful information regarding case conceptualization and diagnosis.　1　2　3　4　5

5. The supervisor helps me comprehend and formulate clients' central issues.　1　2　3　4　5

6. The supervisor helps me understand the thoughts, feelings, and behaviors of my clients.　1　2　3　4　5

7. The supervisor encourages supervisee self-exploration appropriately.　1　2　3　4　5

8. The supervisor enables me to express opinions, questions, and concerns about my counseling.　1　2　3　4　5

9. The supervisor creates a safe environment for group supervision.　1　2　3　4　5

10. The supervisor is attentive to group dynamics.　1　2　3　4　5

11. The supervisor effectively sets limits, and establishes norms and boundaries for the group.　1　2　3　4　5

12. The supervisor provides helpful leadership for the group.　1　2　3　4　5

13. The supervisor encourages supervisees to provide each other feedback.　1　2　3　4　5

14. The supervisor redirects the discussion when appropriate.　1　2　3　4　5

15. The supervisor manages time well between all the group members.　1　2　3　4　5

16. The supervisor provides enough structure in the group supervision.　1　2　3　4　5

Scoring:　*Group Safety Scale:*　Sum items 7, 8, 9, 10, and 13; divide by 5

Skill Development and Case Conceptualization Scale: Sum items 1, 2, 3, 4, 5, and 6; divide by 6.

Group Management Scale:　Sum items 11, 12, 15, and 16

From Arcinue, F. (2002). The development and validation of the Group Supervision Scale. Unpublished doctoral dissertation, University of Southern California. Reprinted with permission of the author.

SUPERVISEE LEVELS QUESTIONNAIRE–REVISED

Please answer the items that follow in terms of your own *current* behavior. In responding to those items, use the following scale:

Never	Rarely	Sometimes	Half the Time	Often	Most of the Time	Always
1	2	3	4	5	6	7

1. I feel genuinely relaxed and comfortable in my counseling/therapy sessions.
     1   2   3   4   5   6   7

2. I am able to critique counseling tapes and gain insights with minimum help from my supervisor.
     1   2   3   4   5   6   7

3. I am able to be spontaneous in counseling/therapy, yet my behavior is relevant.
     1   2   3   4   5   6   7

4. I lack self-confidence in establishing counseling relationships with diverse client types.
     1   2   3   4   5   6   7

5. I am able to apply a consistent personalized rationale of human behavior in working with my clients.
     1   2   3   4   5   6   7

6. I tend to get confused when things don't go according to plan and lack confidence in ability to handle the unexpected.
     1   2   3   4   5   6   7

7. The overall quality of my work fluctuates; on some days I do well, on other days, I do poorly.
     1   2   3   4   5   6   7

8. I depend upon my supervision considerably in figuring out how to deal with my clients.
     1   2   3   4   5   6   7

9. I feel comfortable confronting my clients.
     1   2   3   4   5   6   7

10. Much of the time in counseling/therapy I find myself thinking about my next response instead of fitting my intervention into the overall picture.
      1   2   3   4   5   6   7

11. My motivation fluctuates from day to day.
      1   2   3   4   5   6   7

12. At times, I wish my supervisor could be in the counseling/therapy session to lend a hand.
      1   2   3   4   5   6   7

13. During counseling/therapy sessions, I find it difficult to concentrate because of my concern about my own performance.
      1   2   3   4   5   6   7

14. Although at times I really want advice/feedback from my supervisor, at *other* times I really want to do things my own way.

    1   2   3   4   5   6   7

15. Sometimes the client's situation seems so hopeless. I just don't know what to do.

    1   2   3   4   5   6   7

16. It is important that my supervisor allow me to make my own mistakes.

    1   2   3   4   5   6   7

17. Given my current state of professional development, I believe I know when I need consultation from my supervisor and when I don't.

    1   2   3   4   5   6   7

18. Sometimes I question how suited I am to be a counselor/therapist.

    1   2   3   4   5   6   7

19. Regarding counseling/therapy, I view my supervisor as a teacher/mentor.

    1   2   3   4   5   6   7

20. Sometimes I feel that counseling/therapy is so complex, I never will be able to learn it all.

    1   2   3   4   5   6   7

21. I believe I know my strengths and weaknesses as a counselor sufficiently well to understand my professional potential and limitations.

    1   2   3   4   5   6   7

22. Regarding my counseling/therapy, I view my supervisor as a peer/colleague.

    1   2   3   4   5   6   7

23. I think I know myself well and am able to integrate that into my therapeutic style.

    1   2   3   4   5   6   7

24. I find I am able to understand my clients' view of the world, yet help them objectively evaluate alternatives.

    1   2   3   4   5   6   7

25. At my current level of professional development, my confidence in my abilities is such that my desire to do counseling/therapy doesn't change much from day to day.

    1   2   3   4   5   6   7

26. I find I am able to empathize with my clients' feeling states, but still help them focus on problem resolution.

    1   2   3   4   5   6   7

27. I am able to adequately assess my interpersonal impact on clients and use that knowledge therapeutically.

    1   2   3   4   5   6   7

28. I am adequately able to assess the client's interpersonal impact on me and use that therapeutically.

    1   2   3   4   5   6   7

29. I believe I exhibit a consistent professional objectivity and ability to work within my role as a counselor without *undue overinvolvement* with my clients.

    1   2   3   4   5   6   7

30. I believe I exhibit a consistent professional objectivity and ability to work within my role as a counselor without *excessive distance* from my clients.

    1   2   3   4   5   6   7

Scoring key: *Self and Other Awareness items:*   1, 3, 5, 9, 10*, 13*, 24, 26, 27, 28, 29, 30

   Motivation items: 7, 11*, 15*, 18*, 20*, 21, 23, 25

   Dependency-Autonomy items: 2, 4*, 6*, 8, 12*, 14, 16, 17, 19*, 22

*indicates reverse scoring. To score: sum the items in the scale, then divide by the number of items.

Developed by Stoltenberg, C. D. Unpublished version of Supervisee Levels Questionnaire—Revised. Reprinted by permission of the author.

ANTICIPATORY SUPERVISEE ANXIETY SCALE (ASAS)

Directions: Complete before your supervision session.

Below are a number of statements that describe possible feelings or experiences you may have about your upcoming supervision session. Recall, if you have more than one supervisor or supervision session per week, please choose the supervision session you were asked to rate.

Please indicate your *current* thoughts and/or feelings about your *upcoming* supervision session by responding to the sentence stem: "in anticipation of my upcoming supervision session, I ...." Rate each item on a scale of 1 to 9; 1 meaning "not at all true of me," 5 meaning "moderately true of me," and 9 meaning "completely true of me." It is very important to answer all questions; otherwise your data will not be fully useable.

1	2	3	4	5	6	7	8	9
Not at all true		Mildly true		Moderately true		Very true		Completely true

"In anticipation of my upcoming supervision session, I ...."

_____	1	have difficulty focusing on what I will say to my supervisor
_____	2	feel my heart pounding
_____	3	feel anxious about how my supervisor might evaluate me
_____	4	feel self-conscious
_____	5	worry about how my peers will see me
_____	6	think less of myself because of my shortcomings as a therapist
_____	7	feel fearful that I might receive a negative evaluation from my supervisor
_____	8	notice I am having a hard time relaxing
_____	9	feel nervous
_____	10	feel annoyed with my limitations
_____	11	am concerned about my skills compared to other therapists
_____	12	can't help but compare myself to my peers
_____	13	feel overwhelmed
_____	14	begin to find fault with my therapy session
_____	15	feel apprehensive
_____	16*	feel calm
_____	17	feel antsy
_____	18	feel stressed out
_____	19	feel afraid I might lose face in front of my supervisor
_____	20	question my abilities as a therapist
_____	21	think that I won't perform at my best in the supervision session
_____	22	feel myself getting tense
_____	23*	feel relaxed
_____	24	worry that I might not make sense (be coherent in presenting the issues)
_____	25	wonder what my supervisor might be thinking of me
_____	26	become concerned about what my supervisor might think of me

_____ 27   worry that I might appear stupid
_____ 28   am uneasy about receiving criticism from my supervisor

*reverse scored item

To score the ASAS, reverse score items first, then sum items; higher scores indicate greater anticipatory supervisee anxiety.

From Ellis, M. V., Singh, N. N., Dennin, M. K., & Tosado, M. *The Anticipatory Supervisee Anxiety Scale.* Unpublished measure. University at Albany, SUNY, Albany, NY. Reprinted with permission. Additional supporting data can be found in Ellis et al. (1993), Singh and Ellis (2000), and Tosado (2004).

ROLE CONFLICT AND ROLE AMBIGUITY INVENTORY

Instructions: The following statements describe some problems that therapists-in-training may experience during the course of clinical supervision. Please read each statement and then rate the extent to which you have experienced difficulty in supervision in your most recent clinical training.

For each of the following, circle the most appropriate number, where 1 = *not at all,* and 5 = *very much so.*

I HAVE EXPERIENCED DIFFICULTY IN MY CURRENT OR MOST RECENT SUPERVISION BECAUSE:

1. I was not certain about what material to present to my supervisor.   1 2 3 4 5

2. I have felt that my supervisor was incompetent or less competent than I. I often felt as though I was supervising him/her.   1 2 3 4 5

3. I have wanted to challenge the appropriateness of my supervisor's recommendations for using a technique with one of my clients, but I have thought it better to keep my opinions to myself.   1 2 3 4 5

4. I wasn't sure how best to use supervision as I became more experienced, although I was aware that I was undecided about whether to confront her/him.   1 2 3 4 5

5. I have believed that my supervisor's behavior in one or more situations was unethical or illegal and I was undecided about whether to confront him/her.   1 2 3 4 5

6. My orientation to therapy was different from that of my supervisor. She or he wanted me to work with clients using her or his framework, and I felt that I should be allowed to use my own approach.   1 2 3 4 5

7. I have wanted to intervene with one of my clients in a particular way and my supervisor has wanted me to approach the client in a very different way. I am expected both to judge what is appropriate for myself and also to do what I am told.   1 2 3 4 5

8. My supervisor expected to me to come prepared for supervision, but I had no idea what or how to prepare.   1 2 3 4 5

9. I wasn't sure how autonomous I should be in my work with clients.   1 2 3 4 5

10. My supervisor told me to do something I perceived to be illegal or unethical and I was expected to comply.   1 2 3 4 5

11. My supervisor's criteria for evaluating my work were not specific.   1 2 3 4 5

12. I was not sure that I had done what the supervisor expected me to do in a session with a client.   1 2 3 4 5

13. The criteria for evaluating my performance in supervision were not clear.   1 2 3 4 5

14. I got mixed signals from my supervisor and I was unsure of which signals to attend to.   1 2 3 4 5

15. When using a new technique, I was unclear about the specific steps involved. As a result, I wasn't sure how my supervisor would evaluate my work.   1 2 3 4 5

16. I disagreed with my supervisor about how to introduce a specific issue to a client, but I also wanted to do what the supervisor recommended.   1 2 3 4 5

17. Part of me wanted to rely on my own instincts with clients, but I always knew that my supervisor would have the last word.   1 2 3 4 5

18. The feedback I got from my supervisor did not help me to know what was expected of me in my day to day work with clients.   1 2 3 4 5

19. I was not comfortable using a technique recommended by my supervisor; however, I felt that I should do what my supervisor recommended.   1 2 3 4 5

20. Everything was new and I wasn't sure what would be expected of me.   1 2 3 4 5

21. I was not sure if I should discuss my professional weaknesses in supervision because I was not sure how I would be evaluated.   1 2 3 4 5

22. I disagreed with my supervisor about implementing a specific technique, but I also waned to do what the supervisor thought best.   1 2 3 4 5

23. My supervisor gave me no feedback and I felt lost.   1 2 3 4 5

24. My supervisor told me what to do with a client, but did not give me very specific ideas about how to do it.   1 2 3 4 5

25. My supervisor wanted me to use an assessment technique that I considered inappropriate for a particular client.   1 2 3 4 5

26. There were no clear guidelines for my behavior in supervision.   1 2 3 4 5

27. The supervisor gave no constructive or negative feedback and as a result, I did not know how to address my weaknesses.   1 2 3 4 5

28. I did not know how I was doing as a therapist and, as a result, I did not know how my supervisor would evaluate me.   1 2 3 4 5

29. I was unsure of what to expect from my supervisor.   1 2 3 4 5

Scoring key: *Role Ambiguity items:*   1, 4, 8, 9, 11, 12, 13, 18, 20, 21, 23, 24, 26, 27, 28, 29

Role Conflict items: 2, 3, 5, 6, 7, 10, 14, 15, 16, 17, 19, 22, 25

From Olk, M., & Friedlander, M. L. (1992). Trainees' experiences of role conflict and role ambiguity in supervisory relationships. *Journal of Counseling Psychology, 39,* 389–397. Copyright © 1992 by the American Psychological Association. Reprinted with permission of the authors.

EVALUATION PROCESS WITHIN SUPERVISION INVENTORY

Please indicate the extent to which you agree or disagree with each of the following statements. For each, circle the appropriate number on a seven-point scale where 1 = *strongly disagree* and 7 = *strongly agree.*

1. The goals my supervisor and I generated for my training seem important.   1 2 3 4 5 6 7

2. My supervisor and I created goals that were easy for me to understand.   1 2 3 4 5 6 7

3. The objectives my supervisor and I created were specific.   1 2 3 4 5 6 7

4. My supervisor and I created goals that were realistic.   1 2 3 4 5 6 7

5. I think my supervisor would have been against my reshaping/changing my learning objectives over the course of our work together.   1 2 3 4 5 6 7

6. My supervisor and I created goals that seemed too easy for me.   1 2 3 4 5 6 7

8. I felt uncertain as to what my most important goals were for this training experience.   1 2 3 4 5 6 7

9. My training objectives were established early in our relationship.   1 2 3 4 5 6 7

10. My supervisor and I never had a discussion about my objectives for my training experience.   1 2 3 4 5 6 7

11. My supervisor told me what he/she wanted me to learn from the experience without inquiring about what I hoped to learn.   1 2 3 4 5 6 7

12. Some of the goals my supervisor and I established were not practical in light of the resources available at my site (e.g., requiring videotaping and not providing equipment).   1 2 3 4 5 6 7

13. My supervisor and I set objectives which seemed practical given the opportunities available at my site, (e.g., if career counseling skills was a goal, I was able to work with people with career concerns).   1 2 3 4 5 6 7

14. My supervisor welcomed comments about his or her style as a supervisor.   1 2 3 4 5 6 7

15. The appraisal I received from my supervisor seemed impartial.   1 2 3 4 5 6 7

16. My supervisor's comments about my work were understandable.   1 2 3 4 5 6 7

17. I did not receive information about how I was doing as a counselor until late in the semester.   1 2 3 4 5 6 7

19. My supervisor balanced his or her feedback between positive and negative statements.   1 2 3 4 5 6 7

20. The feedback I received from my supervisor was based upon his or her direct observation of my work.   1 2 3 4 5 6 7

21. The feedback I received was directly related to the goals we established.   1 2 3 4 5 6 7

Scoring: *First, reverse score the following items:*   5, 6, 8, 10, 11, 12, and 17.

Goal Setting: Sum of items 1–13.

Feedback: Sum of items 14–21.

SUPERVISORY WORKING ALLIANCE (SWA)–SUPERVISOR FORM

Instructions: Please indicate the frequency with which the behavior described in each of the following items seems characteristic of your work with your supervisee. After each item, check (*X*) the space over the number corresponding to the appropriate point of the following seven-point scale:

	1	2	3	4	5	6	7
	Almost Never						*Almost Always*

1. I help my supervisee work within a specific treatment plan with his/her client.
      1 2 3 4 5 6 7

2. I help my supervisee stay on track during our meetings.
      1 2 3 4 5 6 7

3. My style is to carefully and systematically consider the material that my supervisee brings to supervision.
      1 2 3 4 5 6 7

4. My supervisee works with me on specific goals in the supervisory session.
      1 2 3 4 5 6 7

5. In supervision, I expect my supervisee to think about or reflect on my comments to him or her.
      1 2 3 4 5 6 7

6. I teach my supervisee through direct suggestion.
      1 2 3 4 5 6 7

7. In supervision, I place a high priority on our understanding of the client's perspective.
      1 2 3 4 5 6 7

8. I encourage my supervisee to take time to understand what the client is saying and doing.
      1 2 3 4 5 6 7

9. When correcting my supervisee's errors with a client, I offer alternative ways of intervening.
      1 2 3 4 5 6 7

10. I encourage my supervisee to formulate his/her own interventions with his/her clients.
       1 2 3 4 5 6 7

11. I encourage my supervisee to talk about the work in ways that are comfortable for him/her.
       1 2 3 4 5 6 7

12. I welcome my supervisee's explanations about his/her client's behavior.
       1 2 3 4 5 6 7

13. During supervision, my supervisee talks more than I do.
       1 2 3 4 5 6 7

14. I make an effort to understand my supervisee.
       1 2 3 4 5 6 7

15. I am tactful when commenting about my supervisee's performance.
       1 2 3 4 5 6 7

16. I facilitate my supervisee's talking in our sessions.

   1 2 3 4 5 6 7

17. In supervision, my supervisee is more curious than anxious when discussing his/her difficulties with me.

   1 2 3 4 5 6 7

18. My supervisee appears to be comfortable working with me.

   1 2 3 4 5 6 7

19. My supervisee understands client behavior and treatment techniques similar to the way I do.

   1 2 3 4 5 6 7

20. During supervision, my supervisee seems able to stand back and reflect on what I am saying to him/her.

   1 2 3 4 5 6 7

21. I stay in tune with my supervisee during supervision.

   1 2 3 4 5 6 7

22. My supervisee identifies with me in the way he/she thinks and talks about his/her clients.

   1 2 3 4 5 6 7

23. My supervisee consistently implements suggestions made in supervision.

   1 2 3 4 5 6 7

The Supervisor form of the SWA has three scales, scored as follows:

Rapport: Sum items 10–16, then divide by 7.

Client Focus: Sum items 1–9, then divide by 9.

Identification: Sum items 17–23, then divide by 7.

SUPERVISORY WORKING ALLIANCE (SWA)–SUPERVISEE FORM

Instructions: Please indicate the frequency with which the behavior described in each of the following items seems characteristic of your work with your supervisor. After each item, check (X) the space over the number corresponding to the appropriate point of the following seven-point scale:

	1	2	3	4	5	6	7
	Almost Never						*Almost Always*

1. I feel comfortable working with my therapist.

                      1   2   3   4   5   6   7

2. My supervisor welcomes my explanations about the client's behavior.

                      1   2   3   4   5   6   7

3. My supervisor makes the effort to understand me.

                      1   2   3   4   5   6   7

4. My supervisor encourages me to talk about my work with clients in ways that are comfortable for me.

                      1   2   3   4   5   6   7

5. My supervisor is tactful when commenting about my performance.

                      1   2   3   4   5   6   7

6. My supervisor encourages me to formulate my own interventions with the client.

                      1   2   3   4   5   6   7

7. My supervisor helps me talk freely in our sessions.

                      1   2   3   4   5   6   7

8. My supervisor stays in tune with me during supervision.

                      1   2   3   4   5   6   7

9. I understand client behavior and treatment technique similar to the way my supervisor does.

                      1   2   3   4   5   6   7

10. I feel free to mention to my supervisor any troublesome feelings I might have about him/her.

                      1   2   3   4   5   6   7

11. My supervisor treats me like a colleague in our supervisory sessions.

                      1   2   3   4   5   6   7

12. In supervision, I am more curious than anxious when discussing my difficulties with clients.

                      1   2   3   4   5   6   7

13. In supervision, my supervisor places a high priority on our understanding the client's perspective.

                      1   2   3   4   5   6   7

14. My supervisor encourages me to take time to understand what the client is saying and doing.

                      1   2   3   4   5   6   7

15. My supervisor's style is to carefully and systematically consider the material I bring to supervision.

                      1   2   3   4   5   6   7

16. When correcting my errors with a client, my supervisor offers alternative ways of intervening with that client.

   1 2 3 4 5 6 7

17. My supervisor helps me work within a specific treatment plan with my clients.

   1 2 3 4 5 6 7

18. My supervisor helps me stay on track during our meetings.

   1 2 3 4 5 6 7

19. I work with my supervisor on specific goals in the supervisory session.

   1 2 3 4 5 6 7

The supervisee form of the SWA has two scales, scored as follows:

Rapport: Sum items 1–12, then divide by 12.

Client Focus: Sum items 13–19, then divide by 6.

SUPERVISORY STYLES INVENTORY

For supervisees' form: Please indicate your perception of the style of your current or most recent supervisor of psychotherapy/counseling on each of the following descriptors. Circle the number on the scale, from 1 to 7, which best reflects your view of him or her.

For supervisors' form: Please indicate your perceptions of your style as a supervisor of psychotherapy/counseling on each of the following descriptors. Circle the number on the scale, from 1 to 7, which best reflects your view of yourself.

	1	2	3	4	5	6	7
	Not very						*Very*
1. goal-oriented	1	2	3	4	5	6	7
2. perceptive	1	2	3	4	5	6	7
3. concrete	1	2	3	4	5	6	7
4. explicit	1	2	3	4	5	6	7
5. committed	1	2	3	4	5	6	7
6. affirming	1	2	3	4	5	6	7
7. practical	1	2	3	4	5	6	7
8. sensitive	1	2	3	4	5	6	7
9. collaborative	1	2	3	4	5	6	7
10. intuitive	1	2	3	4	5	6	7
11. reflective	1	2	3	4	5	6	7
12. responsive	1	2	3	4	5	6	7
13. structured	1	2	3	4	5	6	7
14. evaluative	1	2	3	4	5	6	7
15. friendly	1	2	3	4	5	6	7
16. flexible	1	2	3	4	5	6	7
17. prescriptive	1	2	3	4	5	6	7
18. didactic	1	2	3	4	5	6	7
19. thorough	1	2	3	4	5	6	7
20. focused	1	2	3	4	5	6	7
21. creative	1	2	3	4	5	6	7
22. supportive	1	2	3	4	5	6	7
23. open	1	2	3	4	5	6	7
24. realistic	1	2	3	4	5	6	7
25. resourceful	1	2	3	4	5	6	7
26. invested	1	2	3	4	5	6	7
27. facilitative	1	2	3	4	5	6	7
28. therapeutic	1	2	3	4	5	6	7
29. positive	1	2	3	4	5	6	7
30. trusting	1	2	3	4	5	6	7
31. informative	1	2	3	4	5	6	7
32. humorous	1	2	3	4	5	6	7
33. warm	1	2	3	4	5	6	7

Scoring key: *Attractive:*   Sum items 15, 16, 22, 23, 29, 30, 33; divide by 7.

Interpersonally sensitive: Sum items 2, 5, 10, 11, 21, 25, 26, 28; divide by 8.

Task oriented: Sum items 1, 3, 4, 7, 13, 14, 17, 18, 19, 20; divide by 10.

Filler items: 6, 8, 9, 12, 24, 27, 31, 32.

From Friedlander, M. L., & Ward, L. G. (1984). Development and validation of the Supervisory Styles Inventory. *Journal of Counseling Psychology, 31,* 542–558. Reprinted with permission of the authors.

THE FEMINIST SUPERVISION SCALE (FSS)

Instructions: For each of the following statements, decide to what degree it describes **your approach to clinical supervision.** Then write the number in the space to the left of each statement that best describes your approach to working with supervisees. There are no right or wrong answers; however, for the data to be meaningful, you must answer each statement given below as honestly as possible.

Almost	never true		Sometimes true		Almost always true	
1	2	3	4	5	6	7

_____ 1. I am actively involved in social change to improve women's lives.

_____ 2. I clarify supervisory boundaries, roles, and relationships with my supervisees.

_____ 3. I provide assistance in designing and developing specialized women's groups and workshops.

_____ 4. I facilitate open, flexible, and egalitarian interactions with my supervisees.

_____ 5. I utilize strategies that minimize power differences between my supervisees and myself.

_____ 6. I am actively involved in social change aimed at eliminating oppression.

_____ 7. I establish supervisor–supervisee relationships that are hierarchical.

_____ 8. I advocate for feminist/women's issues in my daily life and/or work.

_____ 9. I encourage my supervisees to examine how they may have benefited from privileges associated with their gender, race, class, sexual orientation, and/or ability level.

_____ 10. I am sensitive to power differences that exist between my supervisees and myself.

_____ 11. I recognize cultural diversity and oppression as it impacts my supervisees.

_____ 12. I analyze power differentials and dynamics in the supervisory relationship.

_____ 13. I help my supervisees understand how sociocultural variables and oppressive environments have precipitated and maintained clients' problematic behaviors.

_____ 14. I model accountability in the use of power.

_____ 15. I am actively involved in professional or political organizations that address the needs of women.

_____ 16. I facilitate my supervisees' awareness of and attention to the social, contextual nature of the therapeutic process.

_____ 17. I encourage my supervisees to work actively for social change to improve the status of women.

_____ 18. I facilitate my supervisees' understanding of the ways culture influences client development, behavior, and client symptom presentation.

_____ 19. I attend to power relations in the supervisory context.

_____ 20. I explore with my supervisees how social constructs, such as gender, ethnicity, and class, influence one's clinical understanding of the client.

_____ 21. I believe that supervisees and supervisors should be equal partners in the supervisory process.

_____ 22. I help my supervisees develop an awareness of stereotyping and biases underlying theoretical assumptions.

_____ 23. I address power differences that exist between my supervisees and myself.

_____ 24. I actively monitor the various responsibilities associated with multiple role relationships, including the overlap between professional and personal roles.

_____ 25. I teach my supervisees feminist therapy content and process.

_____ 26. I apply the basic tenets of feminist therapy to my supervision practices.

_____ 27. I offer conceptual frameworks that take into account cultural issues relevant to me.

_____ 28. I establish my position as the expert/teacher and the supervisee as inexpert/learner.

_____ 29. I help my supervisees integrate cultural and contextual information into therapeutic conceptualizations.

_____ 30. I provide my supervisees with readings and books about feminist theory and/or therapy.

_____ 31. I educate my supervisees about feminist issues.

_____ 32. I address with my supervisees issues of gender, race, ethnicity, sexual orientation, disability, and socioeconomic status as they impact the therapeutic relationship.

FSS Scoring Grid

In scoring the FSS, you first need to reverse score some of the items; that is, if a participant responds with a 7 it would be scored as a 1, if a participant responds with a 2 it would be scored as a 6, and so on. Reverse Score Items: 7 and 28

After reverse scoring items 7 and 28, mean total and subscale scores are used with higher scores indicating more feminist supervision practices.

Total score = Mean of all items

Subscale scores = Mean of items for each subscale

Items comprising the four FSS subscales:

1. *Collaborative Relationship (CR) Subscale* = Items 4, 5, 7, 21, 28
2. *Power Analysis (PA) Subscale* = Items 2, 10, 12, 14, 19, 23, 24

3. *Diversity and Social Context (DSC) Subscale:* Items 9, 11, 13, 16, 18, 20, 22, 27, 29, 32

4. *Feminist Advocacy and Activism (FAA) Subscale:* Items 1, 3, 6, 8, 15, 17, 25, 26, 30, 31

From Szymanski, D. M. (2003). The Feminist Supervision Scale (FSS): A rational/theoretical approach. *Psychology of Women Quarterly, 27,* 221–232. Reprinted with permission of Blackwell Publishing.

COUNSELOR SUPERVISOR SELF-EFFICACY SCALE

Directions: Each of the items listed below is related to a task performed in counselor supervision. Please rate your level of confidence for completing each task *right now*. Circle the number that reflects your confidence level. Please answer every question, regardless of whether you have actually performed the corresponding activity.

1	2	3	4	5	6	7	8	9	10
Not confident at all				*Somewhat confident*					*Completely confident*

1. Select supervision interventions congruent with the model/theory being used

| 1 | 2 | 3 | 4 | 5 | 6 | 7 | 8 | 9 | 10 |

2. Articulate to a supervisee the ethical standards regarding client welfare

| 1 | 2 | 3 | 4 | 5 | 6 | 7 | 8 | 9 | 10 |

3. Present procedures for assessing and reporting an occurrence of child abuse

| 1 | 2 | 3 | 4 | 5 | 6 | 7 | 8 | 9 | 10 |

4. Describe the strengths and limitations of the various supervision modalities (e.g., self-report, live observation, audiotape review)

| 1 | 2 | 3 | 4 | 5 | 6 | 7 | 8 | 9 | 10 |

5. Assist a supervisee to deal with termination issues

| 1 | 2 | 3 | 4 | 5 | 6 | 7 | 8 | 9 | 10 |

6. Assist a supervisee to include relevant cultural variables in case conceptualization

| 1 | 2 | 3 | 4 | 5 | 6 | 7 | 8 | 9 | 10 |

7. Model effective decision making when faced with ethical and legal dilemmas

| 1 | 2 | 3 | 4 | 5 | 6 | 7 | 8 | 9 | 10 |

8. Demonstrate knowledge of various counseling theories, systems, and their related methods

| 1 | 2 | 3 | 4 | 5 | 6 | 7 | 8 | 9 | 10 |

9. Structure supervision around a supervisee's learning goals

| 1 | 2 | 3 | 4 | 5 | 6 | 7 | 8 | 9 | 10 |

10. Assist a supervisee to develop working hypotheses about her/his clients

| 1 | 2 | 3 | 4 | 5 | 6 | 7 | 8 | 9 | 10 |

11. Solicit critical feedback on my work as a supervisor from either my peers or an evaluator

| 1 | 2 | 3 | 4 | 5 | 6 | 7 | 8 | 9 | 10 |

12. Understand key research on counselor development and developmental models as they pertain to supervision

| 1 | 2 | 3 | 4 | 5 | 6 | 7 | 8 | 9 | 10 |

13. Assist a supervisee to develop a strategy to address client resistance

| 1 | 2 | 3 | 4 | 5 | 6 | 7 | 8 | 9 | 10 |

14. Encourage a supervisee to share his/her negative feelings about supervision without becoming defensive

| 1 | 2 | 3 | 4 | 5 | 6 | 7 | 8 | 9 | 10 |

15. Listen carefully to concerns presented by a supervisee
    1   2   3   4   5   6   7   8   9   10

16. Identify key ethical and legal issues surrounding client confidentiality
    1   2   3   4   5   6   7   8   9   10

17. Address a supervisee's racial or ethnic identity as a counseling process variable
    1   2   3   4   5   6   7   8   9   10

18. Understand appropriate supervisor functions of teacher, counselor, and consultant
    1   2   3   4   5   6   7   8   9   10

19. Employ interventions appropriate to a supervisee's learning needs
    1   2   3   4   5   6   7   8   9   10

20. Describe the legal liabilities involved in counseling minors
    1   2   3   4   5   6   7   8   9   10

21. Establish a plan to safeguard a supervisee's due process within supervision
    1   2   3   4   5   6   7   8   9   10

22. Help a supervisee assess the compatibility between his/her in-session behaviors
    and espoused theoretical orientation
    1   2   3   4   5   6   7   8   9   10

23. Model strategies that may enhance a supervisee's case conceptualization skills
    1   2   3   4   5   6   7   8   9   10

24. Conduct supervision in strict accordance to the ethical standards governing
    my profession
    1   2   3   4   5   6   7   8   9   10

25. Facilitate a supervisee's cultural awareness
    1   2   3   4   5   6   7   8   9   10

26. Appear competent in interactions with a supervisee
    1   2   3   4   5   6   7   8   9   10

27. Receive critical feedback from a supervisee on my performance as a supervisor
    without becoming defensive or angry
    1   2   3   4   5   6   7   8   9   10

28. State a rationale for choosing a supervision intervention based on theory,
    client/counselor dynamics, and/or setting
    1   2   3   4   5   6   7   8   9   10

29. Recognize possible multiple relationship issues that may arise within supervision
    1   2   3   4   5   6   7   8   9   10

30. Demonstrate respect for a supervisee who has a different worldview from myself
    1   2   3   4   5   6   7   8   9   10

31. Assess a supervisee's multicultural competencies
    1   2   3   4   5   6   7   8   9   10

32. Address parallel processes as they arise within the supervisory relationship
    1   2   3   4   5   6   7   8   9   10

33. Communicate due process procedures to a supervisee if he/she is unhappy with the supervision I have provided

    1   2   3   4   5   6   7   8   9   10

34. Demonstrate respect for various learning styles and personal characteristics within supervision

    1   2   3   4   5   6   7   8   9   10

35. Facilitate case discussion during group supervision

    1   2   3   4   5   6   7   8   9   10

36. Balance the needs of the group with the individual needs of each supervisee during group supervision

    1   2   3   4   5   6   7   8   9   10

37. Model appropriate responses to affect presented in group supervision

    1   2   3   4   5   6   7   8   9   10

38. Offer adequate support to all members of a group during group supervision

    1   2   3   4   5   6   7   8   9   10

39. Integrate an understanding of supervisees' learning styles into the group supervision process

    1   2   3   4   5   6   7   8   9   10

Scoring key: *Theories and Techniques:*   1, 4, 8, 9, 10, 12, 13, 18, 19, 21, 22, 23, 28, 32

              Group Supervision: 35, 36, 37, 38, 39

              Supervisory Ethics: 2, 5, 7, 15, 24, 26, 29, 33

              Self in Supervision: 11, 14, 27, 30, 34

              Multicultural Competence: 6, 17, 25, 31

              Knowledge of Legal Issues: 3, 16, 20

From Barnes, K. L. (2002). Development and initial validation of a measure of counselor supervisor self-efficacy. Unpublished dissertation, Syracuse University. Reprinted with permission of the author.

MULTICULTURAL SUPERVISION COMPETENCIES QUESTIONNAIRE

This questionnaire is intended to evaluate the quality of multicultural supervision. If you have had a supervisor who is culturally or racially different from you, I would like you to complete this questionnaire with respect to this particular supervisor.

Your ethnic/racial identity _____

Your supervisor's ethnic/racial background _____

Your gender _____ Your supervisor's gender _____

How long ago? _____ How long did you have him/her as supervisor? _____

What was the level of your clinical training during this supervision?

_____

What was the nature of the clinical site where this supervision took place?

_____

Based on your experiences and observation, please rate the following statements according to the following scale:

1	2	3	4	5
Strongly Disagree	*Disagree*	*Undecided*	*Agree*	*Strongly Agree*

Circle the response code (e.g., 4 for Agree, or 2 for Disagree) at the end of each statement that most clearly reflects your opinion about this supervisor. Try to use 3 sparingly.

1. Understands my culture and value systems.   1 2 3 4 5

2. Shows openness and respect for culturally different supervisees.   1 2 3 4 5

3. Actively avoids cultural biases and discriminatory practices in working with minority students.   1 2 3 4 5

4. Understands the worldviews of supervisees and clients from other cultures.   1 2 3 4 5

5. Understands the tendency and the problem of racial stereotyping.   1 2 3 4 5

6. Makes an effort to understand and accommodate culturally different supervisees.   1 2 3 4 5

7. Is able to avoid racial stereotypes by taking into account both the uniqueness of individuals as well as the known characteristics of the culture.   1 2 3 4 5

8. Makes use of every opportunity to increase supervisees' multicultural competence in counseling.   1 2 3 4 5

9. Is able to clarify presenting problems and arrives at culturally relevant case conceptualization with clients from different cultural backgrounds.   1 2 3 4 5

10. Shows an understanding of how culture, ethnicity, and race influence supervision and counseling.   1 2 3 4 5

11. Is able to overcome cultural and language barriers in relating to minority students and clients.   1 2 3 4 5

12. Has never mentioned that race is an important consideration in supervision and counseling.   1 2 3 4 5

13. Demonstrates skills to balance between the generic characteristics of counseling and the unique values of different cultural groups.   1 2 3 4 5

14. Shows sensitivity and skills in supervising culturally different supervisees.   1 2 3 4 5

15. Shows unconditional acceptance of all supervisees, regardless of their race, ethnicity, and culture.   1 2 3 4 5

16. Recognizes the limitations of models and approaches based on Western assumptions in working with culturally different individuals.   1 2 3 4 5

17. Knows how to encourage discussion of cultural and racial issues in counseling and supervision.   1 2 3 4 5

18. Shows interest in learning new skills and enhancing own multicultural competence in supervision and counseling.   1 2 3 4 5

19. Recognizes that what is inappropriate from the standpoint of the majority culture may be appropriate for some minority cultures.   1 2 3 4 5

20. Takes into account cultural biases in assessing supervisees and forming clinical judgments.   1 2 3 4 5

21. Exhibits respect for other cultures without overly identifying self with minority culture or becoming paternalistic.   1 2 3 4 5

22. Is willing to advocate for minorities who experience institutional discrimination.   1 2 3 4 5

23. Understands the cultural reasons why minority students and clients tend to defer to authority figures.   1 2 3 4 5

24. Communicates effectively with culturally different supervisees at both the verbal and nonverbal levels.   1 2 3 4 5

25. Understands cultural differences in help-giving and help-seeking.   1 2 3 4 5

26. Believes that Western models and approaches of counseling are equally generalizable to ethnic minorities.   1 2 3 4 5

27. Gives emotional support and encouragement to minority students.   1 2 3 4 5

28. Is very rigid and dogmatic regarding what constitutes the proper approach of counseling.   1 2 3 4 5

29. Shows an interest in helping minority students overcome systemic and institutional barriers.   1 2 3 4 5

30. Welcomes my input even when I express different views and values.   1 2 3 4 5

31. Knows how to consult or refer to resources available in ethnocultural communities.   1 2 3 4 5

32. Takes into account racial biases and sociopolitical implications in counseling and supervision.   1 2 3 4 5

33. Considers supervisees' cultural and linguistic backgrounds in giving them feedback and evaluation.   1 2 3 4 5

34. Shows a genuine interest in learning about other cultures.   1 2 3 4 5

35. Recognizes individual differences in ethnic/racial identity.   1 2 3 4 5

36. Demonstrates a familiarity with the value systems of diverse cultural groups.   1 2 3 4 5

37. Knows that biases and assumptions of Western counseling models can have a negative effect on culturally different supervisees and clients.   1 2 3 4 5

38. Knows how to adapt knowledge of cultural differences to supervision and counseling.   1 2 3 4 5

39. Does not seem to be aware of own limitations in working with culturally different supervisees or clients.   1 2 3 4 5

40. Does not pay any attention to the demographics of supervisees.   1 2 3 4 5

41. Is able to develop culturally appropriate treatment plans for clients from different cultural backgrounds.   1 2 3 4 5

42. Makes an effort to establish a relationship of trust and acceptance with culturally different supervisees.   1 2 3 4 5

43. Is flexible in adjusting his/her supervisory style to culturally different supervisees.   1 2 3 4 5

44. Assists supervisees in formulating culturally appropriate assessment and treatment plans.   1 2 3 4 5

45. Makes use of the support network of minorities.   1 2 3 4 5

46. Does not seem to be aware of own implicit cultural biases in counseling and supervision.   1 2 3 4 5

47. Acknowledges that his or her own life experiences, values, and biases may influence the supervision process.   1 2 3 4 5

48. Actively interacts with minority students outside of counseling and classroom settings.   1 2 3 4 5

49. Knows something about how gender, socioeconomic status, and religious issues are related to minority status.   1 2 3 4 5

50. Shows some knowledge about the cultural traditions of various ethnic groups.   1 2 3 4 5

51. Is able to integrate own beliefs, knowledge, and skills in forming relationships with culturally different supervisees.   1 2 3 4 5

52. Is able to reduce my defensiveness, suspicions, and anxiety about having a supervisor from a different culture.   1 2 3 4 5

53. Shows no interest in understanding my cultural background and ethnic/racial heritage.   1 2 3 4 5

54. Negatively evaluates supervisees who do not conform to   1 2 3 4 5
    supervisor's own theoretical orientation and approach of
    counseling.

55. Has a tendency to abuse supervisory power (e.g., imposes view   1 2 3 4 5
    on supervisees).

56. Respects the worldview, religious beliefs, and values of   1 2 3 4 5
    culturally different supervisees.

57. Demonstrates competence in a wide variety of methods of   1 2 3 4 5
    assessment and interventions, including nontraditional ones.

58. Provides guidance to international students and new   1 2 3 4 5
    immigrants to facilitate their acculturation.

59. Makes minority supervisees feel safe to share their difficulties   1 2 3 4 5
    and concerns.

60. Is able to relate to culturally different supervisees, while   1 2 3 4 5
    maintaining own cultural values.

Scoring: Before scoring, reverse the scoring of the following items: 12, 26, 28, 39, 40, 46, 53, 54, 55

Attitude and beliefs (how the supervisor feels about multicultural issues and culturally different supervisees): 2, 12, 16, 19, 21, 26, 34, 39, 40, 46, 47, 56

Knowledge and understanding (what the supervisor knows about multicultural supervision): 1, 4, 5, 10, 23, 25, 36, 37, 49, 50

Skills and practices (how the supervisor demonstrates multicultural competencies in actual practices of supervision): 7, 8, 9, 13, 14, 17, 18, 20, 24, 28, 31, 32, 33, 35, 38, 41, 43, 44, 45, 52, 54, 57

Relationship (how the supervisor relates to culturally different supervisees): 3, 6, 11, 15, 22, 27, 29, 30, 42, 48, 51, 53, 55, 58, 59, 60

THE APPROVED CLINICAL SUPERVISOR CODE OF ETHICS, NATIONAL BOARD FOR CERTIFIED COUNSELORS

In addition to following your profession's Code of Ethics, clinical supervisors shall:

1. Ensure that supervisees inform clients of their professional status (e.g., intern) and of all conditions of supervision. Supervisors need to ensure that supervisees inform their clients of any status other than being fully qualified for independent practice or licensed. For example, supervisees need to inform their clients if they are a student, intern, supervisee or, if licensed with restrictions, the nature of those restrictions (e.g., associate or conditional). In addition, clients must be informed of the requirements of supervision (e.g., the audiotaping of all counseling sessions for purposes of supervision).

2. Ensure that clients have been informed of their rights to confidentiality and privileged communication when applicable. Clients also should be informed of the limits of confidentiality and privileged communication. The general limits of confidentiality are when harm to self or others is threatened; when the abuse of children, elders, or disabled persons is suspected; and in cases when the court compels the counselor to testify and break confidentiality. These are generally accepted limits to confidentiality and privileged communication, but they may be modified by state or federal statute.

3. Inform supervisees about the process of supervision, including supervision goals, case management procedures, and the supervisor's preferred supervision model(s).

4. Keep and secure supervision records and consider all information gained in supervision as confidential.

5. Avoid all multiple relationships with supervisees that may interfere with the supervisor's professional judgment or exploit the supervisee.

    Although all multiple relationships are not in of themselves inappropriate, any sexual relationship is considered to be a violation. Sexual relationship means sexual contact, sexual harassment, or sexual bias toward a supervisee by a supervisor.

6. Establish procedures with their supervisees for handling crisis situations.

7. Provide supervisees with adequate and timely feedback as part of an established evaluation plan.

8. Render assistance to any supervisee who is unable to provide competent counseling services to clients.

9. Intervene in any situation where the supervisee is impaired and the client is at risk.

10. Refrain from endorsing an impaired supervisee when such impairment deems it unlikely that the supervisee can provide adequate counseling services.

11. Refrain from offering supervision outside of their area(s) of competence.

12. Ensure that supervisees are aware of the current ethical standards related to their professional practice, as well as legal standards that regulate the practice of counseling. Current ethical standards would mean standards published by the National Board for Certified Counselors (NBCC) and other appropriate entities such as the American Counseling Association (ACA). In addition, it is the supervisor's responsibility to ensure that the supervisee is aware that state and federal laws might regulate the practice of counseling and to inform the supervisee of key laws that affect counseling in the supervisee's jurisdiction.

13. Engage supervisees in an examination of cultural issues that might affect supervision and/or counseling.
14. Ensure that both supervisees and clients are aware of their rights and of due process procedures.

ETHICAL GUIDELINES FOR COUNSELING SUPERVISORS, ASSOCIATION FOR COUNSELOR EDUCATION AND SUPERVISION

Adopted by ACES Executive Counsel and Delegate Assembly March, 1993

Preamble

The Association for Counselor Education and Supervision (ACES) is composed of people engaged in the professional preparation of counselors and people responsible for the ongoing supervision of counselors. ACES is a founding division of the American Counseling Association (ACA) and as such adheres to ACA's current ethical standards and to general codes of competence adopted throughout the mental health community. ACES believes that counselor educators and counseling supervisors in universities and in applied counseling settings, including the range of education and mental health delivery systems, carry responsibilities unique to their job roles. Such responsibilities may include administrative supervision, clinical supervision, or both. Administrative supervision refers to those supervisory activities which increase the efficiency of the delivery of counseling services; whereas, clinical supervision includes the supportive and educative activities of the supervisor designed to improve the application of counseling theory and technique directly to clients. Counselor educators and counseling supervisors encounter situations which challenge the help given by general ethical standards of the profession at large. These situations require more specific guidelines that provide appropriate guidance in everyday practice. The Ethical Guidelines for Counseling Supervisors are intended to assist professionals by helping them: 1. Observe ethical and legal protection of clients' and supervisees' rights; 2. Meet the training and professional development needs of supervisees in ways consistent with clients' welfare and programmatic requirements; and 3. Establish policies, procedures, and standards for implementing programs.

The specification of ethical guidelines enables ACES members to focus on and to clarify the ethical nature of responsibilities held in common. Such guidelines should be reviewed formally every five years, or more often if needed, to meet the needs of ACES members for guidance. The Ethical Guidelines for Counselor Educators and Counseling Supervisors are meant to help ACES members in conducting supervision. ACES is not currently in a position to hear complaints about alleged non-compliance with these guidelines. Any complaints about the ethical behavior of any ACA member should be measured against the ACA Ethical Standards and a complaint lodged with ACA in accordance with its *procedures* for doing so. One overriding assumption underlying this document is that supervision should be ongoing throughout a counselor's career and not stop when a particular level of education, certification, or membership in a professional organization is attained.

Definitions of Terms

Applied Counseling Settings—Public or private organizations of counselors such as community mental health centers, hospitals, schools, and group or individual private practice settings.

Supervisees—Counselors-in-training in university programs at any level who working with clients in applied settings as part of their university training program, and counselors who have completed their formal education and are employed in an applied counseling setting.

Supervisors—Counselors who have been designated within their university or agency to directly oversee the professional clinical work of counselors. Supervisors also may be persons who offer supervision to counselors seeking state licensure and so provide supervision outside of the administrative aegis of an applied counseling setting.

1. Client Welfare and Rights

1.01   The Primary obligation of supervisors is to train counselors so that they respect the integrity and promote the welfare of their clients. Supervisors should have supervisees inform clients that they are being supervised and that observation and/or recordings of the session may be reviewed by the supervisor.

1.02   Supervisors who are licensed counselors and are conducting supervision to aid a supervisee to become licensed should instruct the supervisee not to communicate or in any way convey to the supervisee's clients or to other parties that the supervisee is himself/herself licensed.

1.03   Supervisors should make supervisees aware of clients' rights, including protecting clients' right to privacy and confidentiality in the counseling relationship and the information resulting from it. Clients also should be informed that their right to privacy and confidentiality will not be violated by the supervisory relationship.

1.04   Records of the counseling relationship, including interview notes, test data, correspondence, the electronic storage of these documents, and audio and videotape recordings, are considered to be confidential professional information. Supervisors should see that these materials are used in counseling, research, and training and supervision of counselors with the full knowledge of the clients and that permission to use these materials is granted by the applied counseling setting offering service to the client. This professional information is to be used for full protection of the client. Written consent from the client (or legal guardian, if a minor) should be secured prior to the use of such information for instructional, supervisory, and/or research purposes. Policies of the applied counseling setting regarding client records also should be followed.

1.05   Supervisors shall adhere to current professional and legal guidelines when conducting research with human participants such as Section D-1 of the ACA Ethical Standards.

1.06   Counseling supervisors are responsible for making every effort to monitor both the professional actions, and failures to take action, of their supervisees.

2. Supervisory Role

Inherent and integral to the role of supervisor are responsibilities for:

  a. Monitoring client welfare;
  b. Encouraging compliance with relevant legal, ethical, and professional standards for clinical practice;
  c. Monitoring clinical performance and professional development of supervisees; and
  d. Evaluating and certifying current performance and potential of supervisees for academic, screening, selection, placement, employment, and credentialing purposes.

2.01   Supervisors should have had training in supervision prior to initiating their role as supervisors.

2.02   Supervisors should pursue professional and personal continuing education activities such as advanced courses, seminars, and professional conferences on a regular and ongoing basis. These activities should include both counseling and supervision topics and skills.

2.03   Supervisors should make their supervisees aware of professional and ethical standards and legal responsibilities of the counseling profession.

2.04   Supervisors of post-degree counselors who are seeking state licensure should encourage these counselors to adhere to the standards for practice established by the state licensure board of the state in which they practice.

2.05   Procedures for contacting the supervisor, or an alternative supervisor, to assist in handling crisis situations should be established and communicated to supervisees.

2.06   Actual work samples via audio and/or videotape or live observation in addition to case notes should be reviewed by the supervisor as a regular part of the ongoing supervisory process.

2.07   Supervisors of counselors should meet regularly in face-to-face sessions with their supervisees.

2.08   Supervisors should provide supervisees with ongoing feedback on their performance. This feedback should take a variety of forms, both formal and informal, and should include verbal and written evaluations. It should be formative during the supervisory experience and summative at the conclusion of the experience.

2.09   Supervisors who have multiple roles (e.g., teacher, clinical supervisor, administrative supervisor, etc.) with supervisees should minimize potential conflicts. Where possible, the roles should be divided among several supervisors. Where this is not possible, careful explanation should be conveyed to the supervisee as to the expectations and responsibilities associated with each supervisory role.

2.10   Supervisors should not participate in any form of sexual contact with supervisees. Supervisors should not engage in any form of social contact or interaction which would compromise the supervisor–supervisee relationship. Dual relationships with supervisees that might impair the supervisor's objectivity and professional judgment should be avoided and/or the supervisory relationship terminated.

2.11   Supervisors should not establish a psychotherapeutic relationship as a substitute for supervision. Personal issues should be addressed in supervision only in terms of the impact of these issues on clients and on professional functioning.

2.12   Supervisors, through ongoing supervisee assessment and evaluation, should be aware of any personal or professional limitations of supervisees which are likely to impede future professional performance. Supervisors have the responsibility of recommending remedial assistance to the supervisee and of screening from the training program, applied counseling setting, or state licensure those supervisees who are unable to provide competent professional services. These recommendations should be clearly and professionally explained in writing to the supervisees who are so evaluated.

2.13   Supervisors should not endorse a supervisee for certification, licensure, completion of an academic training program, or continued employment if the supervisor believes the supervisee is impaired in any way that would interfere with the performance of counseling duties. The presence of any such impairment should begin a process of feedback and remediation wherever possible so that the supervisee understands the nature of the impairment and has the opportunity to remedy the problem and continue with his/her professional development.

2.14   Supervisors should incorporate the principles of informed consent and participation; clarity of requirements, expectations, roles and rules; and due process and appeal into the establishment of policies and procedures of their institutions, program, courses, and individual supervisory relationships. Mechanisms for due process appeal of individual supervisory actions should be established and made available to all supervisees.

3. Program Administration Role

3.01   Supervisors should ensure that the programs conducted and experiences provided are in keeping with current guidelines and standards of ACA and its divisions.

3.02   Supervisors should teach courses and/or supervise clinical work only in areas where they are fully competent and experienced.

3.03   To achieve the highest quality of training and supervision, supervisors should be active participants in peer review and peer supervision procedures.

3.04   Supervisors should provide experiences that integrate theoretical knowledge and practical application. Supervisors also should provide opportunities in which supervisees are able to apply the knowledge they have learned and understand the rationale for the skills they have acquired. The knowledge and skills conveyed should reflect current practice, research findings, and available resources.

3.05   Professional competencies, specific courses, and/or required experiences expected of supervisees should be communicated to them in writing prior to admission to the training program or placement/employment by the applied counseling setting, and, in case of continued employment, in a timely manner.

3.06   Supervisors should accept only those persons as supervisees who meet identified entry-level requirements for admission to a program of counselor training or for placement in an applied counseling setting. In the case of private supervision in search of state licensure, supervisees should have completed all necessary prerequisites as determined by the state licensure board.

3.07   Supervisors should inform supervisees of the goals, policies, theoretical orientations toward counseling, training, and supervision model or approach on which the supervision is based.

3.08   Supervisees should be encouraged and assisted to define their own theoretical orientation toward counseling, to establish supervision goals for themselves, and to monitor and evaluate their progress toward meeting these goals.

3.09   Supervisors should assess supervisees' skills and experience in order to establish standards for competent professional behavior. Supervisors should restrict supervisees' activities to those that are commensurate with their current level of skills and experiences.

3.10   Supervisors should obtain practicum and fieldwork sites that meet minimum standards for preparing students to become effective counselors. No practicum or fieldwork setting should be approved unless it truly replicates a counseling work setting.

3.11   Practicum and fieldwork classes would be limited in size according to established professional standards to ensure that each student has ample opportunity for individual supervision and feedback. Supervisors in applied counseling settings should have a limited number of supervisees.

3.12   Supervisors in university settings should establish and communicate specific policies and procedures regarding field placement of students. The respective roles of the student counselor, the university supervisor, and the field supervisor should be clearly differentiated in areas such as evaluation, requirements, and confidentiality.

3.13   Supervisors in training programs should communicate regularly with supervisors in agencies used as practicum and/or fieldwork sites regarding current professional practices, expectations of students, and preferred models and modalities of supervision.

3.14   Supervisors at the university should establish clear lines of communication among themselves, the field supervisors, and the students/supervisees.

3.15   Supervisors should establish and communicate to supervisees and to field supervisors specific procedures regarding consultation, performance review, and evaluation of supervisees.

3.16   Evaluations of supervisee performance in universities and in applied counseling settings should be available to supervisees in ways consistent with the Family Rights and Privacy Act and the Buckley Amendment.

3.17   Forms of training that focus primarily on self-understanding and problem resolution (e.g., personal growth groups or individual counseling) should be voluntary. Those who conduct these forms of training should not serve simultaneously as supervisors of the supervisees involved in the training.

3.18   A supervisor may recommend participation in activities such as personal growth groups or personal counseling when it has been determined that a supervisee has deficits in the areas of self-understanding and problem resolution which impede his/her professional functioning. The supervisors should not be the direct provider of these activities for the supervisee.

3.19   When a training program conducts a personal growth or counseling experience involving relatively intimate self-disclosure, care should be taken to eliminate or minimize potential role conflicts for faculty and/or agency supervisors who may conduct these experiences and who also serve as teachers, group leaders, and clinical directors.

3.20   Supervisors should use the following prioritized sequence in resolving conflicts among the needs of the client, the needs of the supervisee, and the needs of the program or agency. Insofar as the client must be protected, it should be understood that client welfare is usually subsumed in federal and state laws such that these statutes should be the first point of reference. Where laws and ethical standards are not present or are unclear, the good judgment of the supervisor should be guided by the following list.

   a. Relevant legal and ethical standards (e.g., duty to warn, state child abuse laws, etc.);

b. Client welfare;
c. Supervisee welfare;
d. Supervisor welfare; and
e. Program and/or agency service and administrative needs.

REFERENCES

Abadie, P. D. (1985). *A study of interpersonal communication processes in the supervision of counseling.* Unpublished doctoral dissertation, Kansas State University.

Abbott, A. A., & Lyter, S. C. (1998). The use of constructive criticism in field supervision. *Clinical Supervisor, 17*(2), 43–57.

Abreu, J. M. (1999). Conscious and nonconscious African American stereotypes: Impact on first impression and diagnostic ratings by therapists. *Journal of Consulting and Clinical Psychology, 67,* 387–393.

Abroms, G. M. (1977). Supervision as metatherapy. In F. W. Kaslow (Ed.), *Supervision, consultation, and staff training in the helping professions* (pp. 81–99). San Francisco: Jossey-Bass.

Acker, M. (1992, July). *The relationship in clinical supervision.* Paper presented at the B.A.S.P.R. International Conference on Supervision, London.

Acuff, C., Bennett, B. E., Bricklin, P. M., Canter, M. B., Knapp, S. J., Moldawsky, S., & Phelps, R. (1999). Considerations for ethical practice in managed care. *Professional Psychology: Research and Practice, 30,* 563–575.

Adamek, M. S. (1994). Audio-cueing and immediate feedback to improve group leadership skills: A live supervision model. *Journal of Music Therapy, 31,* 135–164.

Adams, J. (1995). Perspectives on live supervision: Working live. *The Supervision Bulletin, 8*(2), 4.

Ahia, C. E., & Martin, D. (1993). The danger-to-self-or-others exception to confidentiality. In T. P. Remley (Series Ed.), *The ACA legal series* (Vol. 8). Alexandria, VA: American Counseling Association.

Aiello, J. R., & Douthitt, E. A. (2001). Social facilitation from Triplett to electronic performance monitoring. *Group Dynamics: Theory, Research, and Practice, 5,* 163–180.

Albee, G. W. (1970). The uncertain future of clinical psychology. *American Psychologist, 25,* 1071–1080.

Alderfer, C. (1983). *The supervision of the therapeutic system in family therapy.* Unpublished manuscript.

Allen, D. W. (Ed.). (1967). *Microteaching: A description.* Stanford, CA: Stanford Teacher Education Program.

Allen, J. (1976). Peer group supervision in family therapy. *Child Welfare, 55,* 183–189.

Allphin, C. (1987). Perplexing or distressing episodes in supervision: How they can help in the teaching and learning of psychotherapy. *Clinical Social Work Journal, 15,* 236–245.

Alonso, A. (1983). A developmental theory of psychodynamic supervision. *The Clinical Supervisor, 1*(3), 23–26.

Alonso, A., & Rutan, J. S. (1988). Shame and guilt in supervision. *Psychotherapy, 25,* 576–581.

Alpher, V. S. (1991). Interdependence and parallel processes: A case study of structural analysis of social behavior in supervision and short-term dynamic psychotherapy. *Psychotherapy, 28,* 218–231.

American Association for Marriage and Family Therapy (AAFMT). (2001). *Code of ethics* (Rev. ed.). Washington, DC: Author.

American Association for Marriage and Family Therapy (AAMFT). (2006). Standards of Accreditation, Version 11. Alexandria, VA: Author.

American Counseling Association (ACA). (2005). *Code of ethics* (Rev. ed.). Alexandria, VA: Author.

American Psychological Association (APA). (2002). *Ethical principles of psychologists and code of conduct.* Washington, DC: Author. Retrieved January 2, 2008, from http://www.apa.org/ethics/code2002.html

American Psychological Association (APA). (2008). *Guidelines and principles for accreditation of programs in professional psychology.* Washington, DC: Author.

Anderson, J. R. (1996). ACT: A simple theory of complex cognition. *American Psychologist, 51,* 355–365.

Anderson, S. A., Rigazio-DiGilio, S. A., & Kunkler, K. P. (1995). Training and supervision in family therapy: Current issues and future directions. *Family Relations, 44,* 489–500.

Anderson, S. A., Schlossberg, M., & Rigazio-DiGilio, S. (2000). Family therapy trainees' evaluations of their best and worst supervision experiences. *Journal of Marital & Family Therapy, 26*(1), 79–91.

Anderson, T. (1987). The reflecting team: Dialogue and meta-dialogue in clinical work. *Family Process, 26,* 415–428.

361

Andrews, J. D. W. (1989). Integrating visions of reality: Interpersonal diagnosis and the existential vision. *American Psychologist, 44,* 803–817.

Anonymous. (1991). Sexual harassment: A female counseling student's experience. *Journal of Counseling and Development, 69,* 502–506.

Anonymous. (1995). Perspectives on live supervision: A client's voice. *The Supervision Bulletin, VIII*(2), 5.

Ansbacher, H., & Ansbacher, R. (1956). *The individual psychology of Alfred Adler.* New York: Basic Books.

Aponte, H. J. (1994). How personal can training get? *Journal of Marital and Family Therapy, 20,* 3–15.

Approved Clinical Supervisor. (2000). Center for Credentialing and Education (an affiliate of the National Board for Certified Counselors, Inc.).

Arcinue, F. (2002). *The development and validation of the Group Supervision Scale.* Unpublished doctoral dissertation, University of Southern California.

Arkowitz, S. W. (2001). Perfectionism in the supervisee. In S. Gill (Ed.), *The supervisory alliance: Facilitating the psychotherapist's learning experience* (pp. 33–66). Northvale, NJ: Jason Aronson, Inc.

Aronson, M. L. (1990). A group therapist's perspectives on the use of supervisory groups in the training of psychotherapists. *Psychoanalysis and Psychotherapy, 8,* 88–94.

Arthur, A. R. (2000). The personality and cognitive-epistemological traits of cognitive behavioural and psychoanalytic psychotherapists. *British Journal of Medical Psychology, 73,* 243–257.

Arthur, G. L., & Gfoerer, K. P. (2002). Training and supervision through the written word: A description and intern feedback. *The Family Journal: Counseling and Therapy for Couples and Families, 10,* 213–219.

Association for Counselor Education and Supervision. (1990). Standards for counseling supervisors. *Journal of Counseling and Development, 69,* 30–32.

Aten, J. D., & Hernandez, B. C. (2004). Addressing religion in clinical supervision: A model. *Psychotherapy: Theory, Research, Practice, Training, 41,* 152–160.

Atwood, J. D. (1986). Self-awareness in supervision. *The Clinical Supervisor, 4*(3), 79–96.

Ault-Riche, M. (1988). Teaching an integrated model of family therapy: Women as students, women as supervisors. *Journal of Psychotherapy and the Family, 3,* 175–192.

Aveline, M. (1992). The use of audio and videotape recordings of therapy sessions in the supervision and practice of dynamic psychotherapy. *British Journal of Psychotherapy, 8,* 347–358.

Averitt, J. (1989). Individual versus group supervision of counselor trainees. Doctoral dissertation, University of Tennessee, 1988. *Dissertation Abstracts International, 50,* 624.

Avis, J. M., & Sprenkle, D. H. (1990). Outcome research on family therapy training: A substantive and methodological review. *Journal of Marital and Family Therapy, 16,* 241–264.

Bahrick, A. S. (1990). Role induction for counselor trainees: Effects on the supervisory working alliance. *Dissertation Abstracts International, 51*(3-B), 1484 (Abstract # 1991-51645).

Bahrick, A. S., Russell, R. K., & Salmi, S. W. (1991). The effects of role induction on trainees' perceptions of supervision. *Journal of Counseling and Development, 69,* 434–438.

Baker, D. E. (1990). The relationship of the supervisory working alliance to supervisor and supervisee narcissism, gender, and theoretical orientation. *Dissertation Abstracts International, 51*(7-B), 3602–3603 (Abstract # 1991-54991).

Baker, S. B., Daniels, T. G., & Greeley, A. T. (1990). Systematic training of graduate-level counselors: Narrative and meta-analytic reviews of three major programs. *Counseling Psychologist, 18,* 355–421.

Baker, S. B., Exum, H. A., & Tyler, R. E. (2002). The developmental process of clinical supervisors in training: An investigation of the supervisor complexity model. *Counselor Education and Supervision, 42,* 15–30.

Balint, E. (1985). The history of training and research in Balint groups. *Psychoanalytic Psychotherapy, 1,* 1–9.

Balint, M. (1948). On the psychoanalytic training system. *International Journal of Psychoanalysis, 29,* 163–173.

Bambling, M., King, R., Raue, P., Schweitzer, R., & Lambert, W. (2006). *Psychotherapy Research 16,* 317–331.

Bandura, A. (1994). Self-efficacy. In V. S. Ramachaudran (Ed.), *Encyclopedia of human behavior* (Vol. 4, pp. 71–81). Retrieved December 30, 2007, from http://www.des.emory.edu/mfp/BanEncy.html

Bargh, J. A., & Chartrand, T. L. (1999). The unbearable automaticity of being. *American Psychologist, 54,* 462–479.

Barlow, D. H. (Ed.). (2001). *Clinical handbook of psychological disorders: A step-by-step treatment manual* (3rd ed.). New York: Guilford Press.

Barnes, K. L. (2002). *Development and initial validation of a measure of counselor supervisor self-efficacy.* Unpublished dissertation, Syracuse University.

Barnes, K. L. (2004). Applying self-efficacy theory to counselor training and supervision: A comparison of two approaches. *Counselor Education and Supervision, 44,* 56–69.

Barnes, K. L., & Bernard, J. M. (2003). Women in counseling and psychotherapy supervision. In M. Kopala & M. Keitel (Eds.), *The handbook of counseling women* (pp. 535–545). Thousand Oaks, California: Sage Publications.

Barnett, J. E., Cornish, J. A. E., Goodyear, R. K., & Lichtenberg, J. W. (2007). Commentaries on the ethical and effective practice of clinical supervision. *Professional Psychology: Research and Practice, 38,* 268–275.

Baron, R. M., & Kenny, D. A. (1986). The moderator-mediator variable distinction in social psychological research: Conceptual, strategic, and statistical considerations. *Journal of Personality and Social Psychology, 51*(60), 1173–1182.

Barrett, M. S., & Barber, J. P. (2005). A developmental approach to supervision of therapists in training. *Journal of Contemporary Psychotherapy, 35,* 169–183.

Bartell, P. A., & Rubin, L. J. (1990). Dangerous liaisons: Sexual intimacies in supervision. *Professional Psychology: Research & Practice, 21,* 442–450.

Bartlett, F. C. (1932). *Remembering: An experimental and social study.* Cambridge: Cambridge University Press.

Bartlett, F. C. (1958). *Thinking.* New York: Basic Books.

Bateson, G. (1958). *Naven.* London: Cambridge University Press. (Original work published 1936)

Bateson, G. (1972). *Steps to an ecology of mind.* New York: Ballantine Books.

Bauman, W. F. (1972). Games counselor trainees play: Dealing with trainee resistance. *Counselor Education and Supervision, 11,* 251–256.

Baumeister, R. F., & Leary, M. R. (1995). The need to belong: Desire for interpersonal attachments as a fundamental human motivation. *Psychological Bulletin, 117,* 497–529.

Bava, S., Burchard, C., Ichihashi, K., Irani, A., & Zunker, C. (2002). Conversing and constructing spirituality in a postmodern training context. *Journal of Family Psychotherapy, 13,* 237–258.

Bear, T. M., & Kivlighan, D. M., Jr. (1994). Single-subject examination of the process of supervision of beginning and advanced supervisees. *Professional Psychology: Research and Practice, 25,* 450–457.

Beavers, W. R. (1986). Family therapy supervision: An introduction and consumer's guide. *Family Therapy Education and Supervision, 1*(4), 15–24.

Beck, A. T., Rush, A. J., Shaw, B. F., & Emery, G. (1979). *Cognitive therapy of depression.* New York: Guilford.

Beck, T. D., Yager, G. G., Williams, G. T., Williams, B. R., & Morris, J. R. (1989, March). *Training field supervisors for adult counseling situations.* Paper presented at the annual meeting of the American Association for Counseling and Development, Boston.

Behan, C. P. (2003). Some ground to stand on: Narrative supervision. *Journal of Systemic Therapies, 22,* 29–42.

Behling, J., Curtis, C., & Foster, S. A. (1988). Impact of sex-role combinations on student performance in field instruction. *The Clinical Supervisor, 6*(3), 161–168.

Beis, E. (1984). *Mental health and the law.* Rockville, MD: Aspen.

Belar, C. D., Bieliauskas, L. A., Klepac, R. K., Larsen, K. G., Stigall, T. T., & Zimet, C. N. (1993). National conference on postdoctoral training in professional psychology. *American Psychologist, 48,* 1284–1289.

Benedek, T. (1954). Countertransference in the training analyst. *Bulletin of the Menninger Clinic, 18,* 12–16.

Benjamin, L. S. (1974). Structural analysis of social behavior. *Psychological Review, 81,* 392–425.

Bennett, L., & Coe, S. (1998). Social work field instructor satisfaction with faculty field liaisons. *Journal of Social Work Education, 34,* 345–352.

Berger, M., & Dammann, C. (1982). Live supervision as context, treatment, and training. *Family Process, 21,* 337–344.

Berkel, L. A., Constantine, M. G., & Olson, E. A. (2007). Supervisor multicultural competence: Addressing religious and spiritual issues with counseling students in supervision. *The Clinical Supervisor, 26*(1/2), 3–15.

Bernard, J. L., & Jara, C. S. (1986). The failure of clinical psychology graduate students to apply understood ethical principles. *Professional Psychology: Research and Practice, 17,* 313–315.

Bernard, J. M., & Goodyear, R. K. (1992). Fundamentals of clinical supervision. Boston: Allyn & Bacon.

Bernard, J. M. (1979). Supervisor training: A discrimination model. *Counselor Education and Supervision, 19,* 60–68.

Bernard, J. M. (1981). Inservice training for clinical supervisors. *Professional Psychology, 12,* 740–748.

Bernard, J. M. (1982). *Laboratory training for clinical supervisors: An update.* Paper presented at the annual meeting of the American Psychological Association, Washington, DC.

Bernard, J. M. (1992). The challenge of psychotherapy-based supervision: Making the pieces fit. *Counselor Education and Supervision, 31,* 232–237.

Bernard, J. M. (1994a). Multicultural supervision: A reaction to Leong and Wagner, Cook, Priest, and Fukuyama. *Counselor Education and Supervision, 34,* 159–171.

Bernard, J. M. (1994b). Reaction: On-campus training of doctoral-level supervisors. In J. E. Myers (Ed.), *Developing and directing counselor education laboratories.* Alexandria, VA: American Counseling Association, 141–144.

Bernard, J. M. (1997). The Discrimination Model. In C. E. Watkins, *Handbook of psychotherapy supervision* (pp. 310–327). New York: Wiley.

Bernard, J. M. (2005). Tracing the development of clinical supervision. *The Clinical Supervisor, 24,* 3–21.

Berne, E. (1964). *Games people play.* New York: Grove Press.

Berne, E. (1972). *What do you say after you say hello? The psychology of human destiny.* New York: Grove Press.

Bernstein, B. L. (1993). Promoting gender equity in counselor supervision: Challenges and opportunities. *Counselor Education and Supervision, 32,* 198–202.

Bernstein, B. L., & Lecomte, C. (1979). Self-critique technique training in a competency-based practicum. *Counselor Education and Supervision, 19,* 69–76.

Bernstein, R. M., Brown, E. M., & Ferrier, M. J. (1984). A model for collaborative team processing in brief systemic family therapy. *Journal of Marital and Family Therapy, 10,* 151–156.

Betan, E. J., & Stanton, A. L. (1999). Fostering ethical willingness integrating emotional and contextual awareness with rational analysis. *Professional Psychology: Research and Practice, 30,* 295–301.

Betcher, R. W., & Zinberg, N. E. (1988). Supervision and privacy in psychotherapy training. *American Journal of Psychiatry, 145,* 796–803.

Beutler, L. E., Moleiro, C., & Talebi, H. (2002a). Resistance in psychotherapy: What conclusions are supported by research. *Journal of Clinical Psychology/In Session: Psychotherapy in Practice, 58,* 207–217.

Beutler, L. E., Moleiro, C., & Talebi, H. (2002b). Resistance. In J. C. Norcross (Ed.), *Psychotherapy relationships that work: Therapist contributions and responsiveness to patients* (pp. 129–144). New York: Oxford University Press.

Bhat, C. S., & Davis, T. E. (2007). Counseling supervisors' assessment of race, racial identity, and working alliance in supervisory dyads. *Journal of Multicultural Counseling and Development, 35,* 80–91.

Birk, J. M., & Mahalik, J. R. (1996). The influence of trainee conceptual level, trainee anxiety, and supervision evaluation on counselor developmental level. *The Clinical Supervisor, 14*(1), 123–137.

Bishop, D. R., Avila-Juarbe, E., & Thumme, B. (2003). Recognizing spirituality as an important factor in counselor supervision. *Counseling and Values, 48,* 34–46.

Blackwell, T. L., Strohmer, D. C., Belcas, E. M., & Burton, K. A. (2002). Ethics in rehabilitation counselor supervision. *Rehabilitation Counseling Bulletin, 45,* 240–247.

Blake, R. R., & Mouton, J. S. (1976). *Consultation.* London: Addison-Wesley.

Blocher, D. (1983). Toward a cognitive developmental approach to counseling supervision. *The Counseling Psychologist, 11,* 27–34.

Blocher, D. H. (1987). On the uses and misuses of the term theory. *Journal of Counseling and Development, 66,* 67–68.

Blodgett, E. G., Schmidt, J. F., & Scudder, R. R. (1987). Clinical session evaluation: The effect of familiarity with the supervisee. *The Clinical Supervisor, 5,* 33–43.

Bloom, B. S., Engelhart, M. D., Furst, F. J., Hill, W. H., & Krathwohl, D. R. (1956). *Taxonomy of educational objectives: Cognitive domain.* New York: McKay.

Bob, S. (1999). Narrative approaches to supervision and case formulation. *Psychotherapy: Theory/Research/Practice/Training, 36,* 146–153.

Boëthius, B. S., Ögren, M. L., Sjøvold, E., & Sundin, E. (2005). Experiences of group culture and patterns of interaction in psychotherapy supervision groups. *The Clinical Supervisor, 23,* 101–121.

Bogo, M. (2005). Field instruction in social work: A review of the research literature. *The Clinical Supervisor, 24*(1/2), 163–193.

Bogo, M., Regehr, C., Power, R., & Regehr, G. (2007). When values collide: Field instructors' experiences of providing feedback and evaluating competence. *The Clinical Supervisor, 26*(1/2), 99–117.

Bonney, W. (1994). Teaching supervision: Some practical issues for beginning supervisors. *The Psychotherapy Bulletin, 29,* 31–36.

Borders, L. D. (1989a). A pragmatic agenda for developmental supervision research. *Counselor Education and Supervision, 29,* 16–24.

Borders, L. D. (1989b). Developmental cognitions of first practicum supervisees. *Journal of Counseling Psychology, 36,* 163–169.

Borders, L. D. (1990). Developmental changes during supervisees' first practicum. *The Clinical Supervisor, 8*(2), 157–167.

Borders, L. D. (1991). A systemic approach to peer group supervision. *Journal of Counseling & Development, 69,* 248–252.

Borders, L. D. (1992). Learning to think like a supervisor. *The Clinical Supervision, 10*(2), 135–148.

Borders, L. D. (2001a). Counseling supervision: A deliberate educational process. In D. Locke, J. Myers, & E. Herr (Eds.), *Handbook of counseling* (pp. 417–432). Thousand Oaks, CA: Sage.

Borders, L. D. (2005). Snapshot of clinical supervision in counseling and counselor education: A five-year review. *The Clinical Supervisor, 24*(1/2), 69–113.

Borders, L. D. (2006, June). *Subtleties in clinical supervision.* Paper presented at the Annual International Interdisciplinary Supervision Conference, Buffalo, NY.

Borders, L. D., Bernard, J. M., Dye, H. A., Fong, M. L., Henderson, P., & Nance, D. W. (1991). Curriculum guide for training counseling supervisors: Rationale, development, and implementation. *Counselor Education and Supervision, 31,* 58–82.

Borders, L. D., & Brown, L. L. (2005). *The new handbook of counseling supervision.* Mahway, NJ: Lahaska Press.

Borders, L. D., & Cashwell, C. S. (1992). Supervision regulations in counselor licensure legislation. *Counselor Education and Supervision, 31,* 209–218.

Borders, L. D., Cashwell, C. S., & Rotter, J. C. (1995). Supervision of counselor licensure applicants: A comparative study. *Counselor Education and Supervision, 35,* 54–69.

Borders, L. D., & Fong, M. L. (1991). Evaluations of supervisees: Brief commentary and research report. *The Clinical Supervisor, 9*(2), 43–51.

Borders, L. D., Fong, M. L., & Neimeyer, C. J. (1986). Counseling students' level of ego development and perceptions of clients. *Counselor Education and Supervision, 26,* 36–49.

Borders, L. D. & Leddick, G. R. (1987). *Handbook of counseling supervision.* Alexandria, VA: Association for Counselor Education and Supervision.

Borders, L. D., & Leddick, G. R. (1988). A nationwide survey of supervision training. *Counselor Education and Supervision, 27*(3), 271–283.

Borders, L. D., & Usher, C. H. (1992). Postdegree supervision: Existing and preferred practices. *Journal of Counseling and Development, 70,* 594–599.

Bordin, E. S. (1979). The generalizability of the psychodynamic concept of the working alliance. *Psychotherapy: Theory, Research, and Practice, 16,* 252–260.

Bordin, E. S. (1983). A working alliance model of supervision. *The Counseling Psychologist, 11,* 35–42.

Borg, M. B., Jr. (2005). "Superblind": Supervising a blind therapist with a blind analysand in a community mental health setting. *Psychoanalytic Psychology, 22,* 32–48.

Bowen, M. (1978). *Family therapy in clinical practice.* New York: Aronson.

Bowlby, J. (1977). The making and breaking of affectional bonds. I. Aetiology and psychopathology in the light of attachment theory. *British Journal of Psychiatry, 130,* 201–210.

Bowlby, J. (1978). Attachment theory and its therapeutic implications. In S. C. Feinstein & P. L. Giovacchini (Ed.), *Adolescent psychiatry* (Vol. VI: Development and clinical studies, pp. 5–33). Chicago: University of Chicago Press.

Boxley, R., Drew, C., & Rangel, D. (1986). Clinical trainee impairment in APA approved internship programs. *The Clinical Psychologist, 39,* 49–52.

Boyd, J. (1978). *Counselor supervision: Approaches, preparation, practices.* Muncie, IN: Accelerated Development, Inc.

Bradey, J., & Post, P. (1991). Impaired students: Do we eliminate them from counselor education programs? *Counselor Education and Supervision, 31,* 100–108.

Bradley, C., & Fiorini, J. (1999). Evaluation of counseling practicum: National study of programs accredited by CACREP. *Counselor Education & Supervision, 30*(2), 110–119.

Bradley, L. J., & Gould, L. J. (1994). *Supervisee resistance.* Greensboro, NC: ERIC Clearinghouse on Counseling and Student Services. (ERIC Document Reproduction Service No. ED372344)

Bradshaw, W. H., Jr. (1982). Supervision in black and white: Race as a factor in supervision. In M. Blumenfield (Ed.), *Applied supervision in psychotherapy* (pp. 199–220). New York: Grune & Stratton.

Brandell, J. R. (1992). Focal conflict analysis: A method of supervision in psychoanalytic psychotherapy. *The Clinical Supervisor, 10*(1), 51–69.

Brantley, A. P. (2000). A clinical supervision documentation form. In L. VandeCreek & T. L. Jackson (Eds.), *Innovations in clinical practice: A sourcebook* (Vol. 18, pp. 301–307). Sarasota: Professional Resource Press.

Brashears, F. (1995). Supervision as social work practice: A reconceptualization. *Social Work, 40,* 692–699.

Brawer, P. A., Handal, P. J., Fabricatore, A. N., Roberts, R., & Wajda-Johnston, V. A. (2002). Training and education in religion/spirituality within APA-accredited clinical psychology programs. *Professional Psychology: Research and Practice, 33,* 203–206.

Brehm, J. (1966). *A theory of psychological reactance.* New York: Academic Press.

Brehm, S. S., & Brehm, J. W. (1981). *Psychological reactance: A theory of freedom and control.* New York: Wiley.

Breunlin, D., Karrer, B., McGuire, D., & Cimmarusti, R. (1988). Cybernetics of videotape supervision. In H. Liddle, D. Breunlin, & R. Schwartz, (Eds.), *Handbook of family therapy training and supervision* (pp. 194–206). New York: Guilford.

Bridges, N. A. (1999). The role of supervision in managing intense affect and constructing boundaries in therapeutic relationships. *Journal of Sex Education and Therapy, 24*(4), 218–225.

Bridges, N. A., & Wohlberg, J. W. (1999). Sexual excitement in therapeutic relationships: Clinical and supervisory management. *The Clinical Supervisor, 18*(2), 123–141.

Briggs, J. R., & Miller, G. (2005). Success enhancing supervision. *Journal of Family Psychotherapy, 16,* 199–222.

Brill, R., Wolkin, J., & McKeel, N. (1987). Strategies for selecting and securing the predoctoral clinical internship of choice. In R. H. Dana & W. T. May (Eds.), *Internship training in professions psychology* (pp. 220–226). New York: Hemisphere.

British Association for Counselling and Psychotherapy (BACP). (2007). Ethical framework for good practice in counselling & psychotherapy. Leicestershire, U.K.: Author. Retrieved December 28, 2007, from http://www.bacp.co.uk/ethical_framework

Broder, E., & Sloman, L. (1982). A contextual comparison of three training programmes. In R. Whiffen & F. Byng-Hall (Eds.), *Family therapy supervision: Recent developments in practice* (pp. 229–242). London: Academic Press, Inc.

Brown, L. M., & Gilligan, C. (1990, August). *Listening for self and relational voices: A responsive/resisting reader's guide.* Paper presented at the annual meeting of the American Psychological Association, Boston.

Brown, R. W., & Otto, M. L. (1986). Field supervision: A collaborative model. *Michigan Journal of Counseling and Development, 17*(2), 48–51.

Bruss, K. V., Brack, C. J., Brack, G., Glickauf-Hughes, C., & O'Leary, M. (1997). A developmental model for supervising therapists treating gay, lesbian, and bisexual clients. *The Clinical Supervisor, 15*(1), 61–73.

Bryant-Jefferies, R. (2005). *Person-centred counselling supervision; personal and professional.* Abingdon, UK: Radcliffe Publishing.

Bubenzer, D. L., Mahrle, C., & West, J. D. (1987). *Live counselor supervision: Trainee acculturation and supervisor interventions.* Paper presented at the American Association for Counseling and Development Annual Convention, New Orleans.

Bubenzer, D. L., West, J. D., & Gold, J. M. (1991). Use of live supervision in counselor preparation. *Counselor Education and Supervision, 30,* 301–308.

Buhrke, R. A. (1989). Incorporating lesbian and gay issues into counselor training: A resource guide. *Journal of Counseling and Development, 68,* 77–80.

Buhrke, R. A., & Douce, L. A. (1991). Training issues for counseling psychologists in working with lesbian women and gay men. *The Counseling Psychologist, 19,* 216–234.

Burgess, S. L. (1994). *The impaired clinical and counseling psychology doctoral student.* Unpublished doctoral dissertation, The California School of Professional Psychology, Alameda, CA.

Burian, B. K., & Slimp, A. O. (2000). Social dual-role relationships during internship: A decision-making model [Special issue]. *Professional Psychology: Research & Practice, 31*(3), 332–338.

Burkard, A. W., Johnson, A. J., Madson, M. B., Pruitt, N. T., Contreras-Tadych, D. A., Kozlowski, J. M., Hess, S. A., & Knox, S. (2006). Supervisor cultural responsiveness and unresponsiveness in cross-cultural supervision. *Journal of Counseling Psychology, 53,* 288–301.

Burke, W., Goodyear, R. K., & Guzzardo, C. (1998). A multiple-case study of weakenings and repairs in supervisory alliances. *American Journal of Psychotherapy, 52,* 450–462.

Burns, C. I., & Holloway, E. L. (1990). Therapy in supervision: An unresolved issue. *The Clinical Supervisor, 7*(4), 47–60.

Byng-Hall, J. (1982). The use of the earphone in supervision. In R. Whiffen & J. Byng-Hall (Eds.), *Family therapy supervision: Recent developments in practice* (pp. 47–56). London: Academic Press.

Cade, B. W., Speed, B., & Seligman, P. (1986). Working in teams: The pros and cons. *The Clinical Supervisor, 4,* 105–117.

Caligor, L. (1984). Parallel and reciprocal processes in psychoanalytic supervision. In L. Caligor, P. M. Bromberg, & J. D. Meltzer (Eds.), *Clinical perspectives on the supervision of psychoanalysis and psychotherapy* (pp.1–28). New York: Plenum.

Campbell, T. W. (1994). Psychotherapy and malpractice exposure. *American Journal of Forensic Psychology, 12,* 5–41.

Caplan, G. (1970). *The theory and practice of mental health consultation.* New York: Basic Books.

Caplan, G., & Caplan, R. (2000). Principles of community psychiatry. *Community Mental Health Journal, 36,* 7–24.

Caplow, T. (1968). *Two against one: Coalitions in triads.* Englewood Cliffs, NJ: Prentice-Hall.

Capraro, R. M., & Capraro, M. M. (2002). Myers-Briggs Type Indicator score reliability across studies: A meta-analytic reliability generalization study. *Educational and Psychological Measurement, 62,* 590–602.

Carey, J. C., & Williams, K. S. (1986). Cognitive style in counselor education: A comparison of practicum supervisors and counselors in training. *Counselor Education and Supervision, 26,* 128–136.

Carkhuff, R. R. (1969). *Helping and human relations* (Vol. 2). New York: Holt, Rinehart, and Winston.

Carkhuff, R. R., & Truax, C. B. (1965). Training in counseling and psychotherapy: An evaluation of an integrated didactic and experiential approach. *Journal of Consulting Psychology, 29,* 333–336.

Carlozzi, A. F., Romans, J. S. C., Boswell, D. L., Ferguson, D. B., & Whisenhunt, B. J. (1997). Training and supervision practices in counseling and marriage and family therapy programs. *Clinical Supervisor, 15*(1), 51–60.

Carroll, M. (1996). *Counseling supervision: Theory, skills, and practice.* London: Cassell.

Carroll, M. (2001). The spirituality of supervision. In M. Carroll & M. Tholstrup (Eds.), *Integrative approaches to supervision* (pp. 76–89). London: Jessica Kingsley Publishers.

Carroll, M. & Gilbert, M. C. (2005). *On being a supervisee: Creating learning partnerships.* London: Vukani Publishing.

Carson, R. C. (1969). *Interaction concepts of personality.* Chicago: Aldine.

Carter, J. W., Enyedy, K. C., Goodyear, R. K., Arcinue, F., Puri, N. N., & Getzelman, M. A. (in press). Concept mapping of the events supervisees find helpful in group supervision. *Training & Education in Professional Psychology.*

Carter, R. T., & Qureshi, A. (1995). A typology of philosophical assumptions in multicultural counseling and training. In P. Ponterotto, J. M. Casas, L. A. Suzuki, & C. M. Alexander (Eds.), *Handbook of multicultural counseling* (pp. 239–262). Thousand Oaks, CA: Sage.

Cashwell, C. S., Looby, E. J., & Housley, W. F. (1997). Appreciating cultural diversity through clinical supervision. *The Clinical Supervisor, 15*(1), 75–85.

Celenza, A. (1998). Precursors to therapist sexual misconduct: Preliminary findings. *Psychoanalytic Psychology, 15,* 378–395.

Center for Credentialing and Education. (2001). *Approved clinical supervisor.* Greensboro, NC: Author.

Chaiklin, H., & Munson, C. E. (1983). Peer consultation in social work. *The Clinical Supervisor, 1,* 21–34.

Chaimowitz, G. A., Glancy, G. D., & Blackburn, J. (2000). The duty to warn and protect: Impact on practice. *Canadian Journal of Psychiatry, 45,* 899–904.

Chambless, D. L., & Ollendick, T. H. (2001). Empirically supported psychological interventions: Controversies and evidence. *Annual Review of Psychology, 52,* 685–716.

Chang, C. Y., Hays, D. G., & Shoffner, M. F. (2003). Cross-racial supervision: A developmental approach for white supervisor working with supervisees of color. *The Clinical Supervisor, 22*(2), 121–138.

Chapin, J., & Ellis, M. V. (2002). *Effects of role induction workshops on supervisee anxiety.* Paper presented at the annual meeting of the American Psychological Association, Chicago.

Chen, E. C., & Bernstein, B. L. (2000). Relations of complementarity and supervisory issues to supervisory working alliance: A comparative analysis of two cases. *Journal of Counseling Psychology, 47,* 485–497.

Chickering, A. W. (1969). *Education and identity.* San Francisco: Jossey-Bass.

Chung, Y. B., Marshall, J. A., & Gordon, L. L. (2001). Racial and gender biases in supervisory evaluation and feedback [Special issue]. *Clinical Supervisor, 20*(1), 99–111.

Chur-Hansen, A., & McLean, S. (2006). On being a supervisor: The importance of feedback and how to give it. *Australasian Psychiatry, 14,* 67–71.

Cikanek, K., McCarthy Veach, P., & Braun, C. (2004). Advanced doctoral students' knowledge and understanding of clinical supervisor ethical responsibilities: A brief report. *The Clinical Supervisor, 23*(1), 191–196.

Claiborn, C. D., Etringer, B. D., & Hillerbrand, E. T. (1995). Influence processes in supervision. *Counselor Education and Supervision, 35,* 43–53.

Claiborn, C. D., Goodyear, R. K., & Horner, P. A. (2002). In J. C. Norcross (Ed.), *Psychotherapy relationships that work: Therapist contributions and responsiveness to patients* (pp. 217–234). New York: Oxford University Press.

Clarkson, P. (1994). In recognition of dual relationships. *Transactional Analysis Journal, 24,* 32–38.

Clifton, D., Doan, R., & Mitchell, D. (1990). The reauthoring of therapist's stories: Taking doses of our own medicine. *Journal of Strategic & Systemic Therapies, 9*(4), 61–66.

Clingerman, T. L., & Bernard, J. M. (2004). An investigation of the use of e-mail as a supplemental modality for clinical supervision. *Counselor Education and Supervision, 44,* 82–95.

Cobia, D. C., & Boes, S. R. (2000). Professional disclosure statements and formal plans for supervision: Two strategies for minimizing the risk of ethical conflicts in post-master's supervision. *Journal of Counseling & Development, 78*(3), 293–296.

Cobia, D. C., & Pipes, R. B. (2002). Mandated supervision: An intervention for disciplined professionals. *Journal of Counseling and Development, 80,* 140–144.

Coffey, D. (2002). Receiving corrective feedback: A special set of skills. Presentation at the Association for Counselor Education and Supervision Convention. Park City, UT.

Cohen, B. Z. (1987). The ethics of social work supervision revisited. *Social Work, 32,* 194–196.

Cohen, J. (1992). A power primer. *Psychological Bulletin, 112,* 155–159.

Cohen, R. J. (1979). *Malpractice: A guide for mental health professionals.* New York: Free Press.

Coll, K. M. (1995). Clinical supervision of community college counselors: Current and preferred practices. *Counselor Education and Supervision, 35,* 111–117.

Collins, D., & Bogo, M. (1986). Competency-based field instruction: Bridging the gap between laboratory and field learning. *The Clinical Supervisor, 4*(3), 39–52.

Committee on Professional Practice and Standards. (2003). Legal issues in the professional practice of psychology. *Professional Psychology: Research and Practice, 34,* 595–600.

Congress, E. P. (1992). Ethical decision making of social work supervisors. *The Clinical Supervisor, 10*(1), 157–169.

Constantine, J. A., Piercy, F. P., & Sprenkle, D. H. (1984). Live supervision-of-supervision in family therapy. *Journal of Marital & Family Therapy, 10,* 95–97.

Constantine, M. G. (1997). Facilitating multicultural competency in counseling supervision: Operationalizing a practical framework. In D. B. Pope-Davis & H. L. K. Coleman (Eds.), *Multicultural counseling competencies: Assessment, education and training, and supervision* (pp. 310–324). Thousand Oaks, CA: Sage Publications.

Constantine, M. G. (2001). Multiculturally-focused counseling supervision: Its relationship to trainees' multicultural self-efficacy. *The Clinical Supervisor, 20*(1), 87–98.

Constantine, M. G., & Sue, D. W. (2007). Perceptions of racial microaggressions among black supervisees in cross-racial dyads. *Journal of Counseling Psychology, 54,* 142–153.

Constantine, M. G., Warren, A. K., & Miville, M. L. (2005). White racial identity dyadic interactions in supervision: Implications for supervisees' multicultural counseling competence. *Journal of Counseling Psychology, 52,* 490–496.

Cook, D. A. (1994). Racial identity in supervision. *Counselor Education and Supervision, 34,* 132–141.

Cook, D. A., & Helms, J. E. (1988). Visible racial/ethnic group supervisees' satisfaction with cross-cultural supervision as predicted by relationship characteristics. *Journal of Counseling Psychology, 35,* 268–274.

Copeland, S. (1998). Counselling supervision in organizational contexts: New challenges and perspectives [Special issue]. *British Journal of Guidance & Counselling, 26*(3), 377–386.

Corey, G., Corey, M. S., & Callanan, P. (1993). *Issues and ethics in the helping professions* (4th ed.). Pacific Grove, CA: Brooks/Cole.

Cormier, L. S., & Bernard, J. M. (1982). Ethical and legal responsibilities of clinical supervisors. *The Personnel and Guidance Journal, 60,* 486–491.

Cornell, W. F. (1994). Dual relationships in transactional analysis: Training, supervision, and therapy. *Transactional Analysis Journal, 24,* 21–30.

Corrigan, J. D., & Schmidt, L. D. (1983). Development and validation of revisions in the Counselor Rating Form. *Journal of Counseling Psychology, 30,* 64–75.

Corrigan, J. D., Dell, D. M., Lewis, K. N., & Schmidt, L. D. (1980). Counseling as a social influence process: A review [Monograph]. *Journal of Counseling Psychology, 27,* 395–441.

Costa, L. (1994). Reducing anxiety in live supervision. *Counselor Education and Supervision, 34,* 30–40.

Couchon, W. D., & Bernard, J. M. (1984). Effects of timing of supervision on supervisor and counselor performance. *The Clinical Supervisor, 2*(3), 3–20.

Council for Accreditation of Counseling and Related Educational Programs. (CACREP). (2001). *The 2001 standards.* Alexandria, VA: Author. http://www.counseling.org/cacrep/2001standards700.htm

Counselman, E. F., & Gumpert, P. (1993). Psychotherapy supervision in small leader-led groups. *Group, 17,* 25–32.

Counselman, E. F., & Weber, R. L. (2004). Organizing and maintaining peer supervision groups. *International Journal of Group Psychotherapy, 54,* 125–143.

Counselor Education & Supervision, 29, 16–24.

Court, J. H., & Winwood, P. (2005). Seeing the light in cyberspace: A cautionary tale of developing a practical model for cybercounseling and cyber supervision within the University of South Australia. *Journal of Technology in Counseling, 4*(1), 1–17.

Covey, S. R., Merrill, A. R., & Merrill, R. R. (1994). *First things first.* New York: Simon & Schuster.

Covner, B. J. (1942a). Studies in phonographic recordings of verbal material: I. The use of phonographic recordings in counseling practice and research. *Journal of Consulting Psychology, 6,* 105–113.

Covner, B. J. (1942b). Studies in phonographic recordings of verbal material: II. A device for transcribing phonographic recordings of verbal material. *Journal of Consulting Psychology, 6,* 149–151.

Craig, C. H., & Sleight, C. C. (1990). Personality relationships between supervisors and students in communication disorders as determined by the Myers-Briggs Type Indicator. *The Clinical Supervisor, 8*(1), 41–51.

Cummings, A. L., Hallberg, E. T., Martin, J., Slemon, A., & Hiebert, B. (1990). Implications of counselor conceptualizations for counselor education. *Counselor Education and Supervision, 30,* 120–134.

D'Andrea, M., & Daniels, J. (1997). Multicultural counseling supervision: Central issues, theoretical considerations, and practical strategies. In D. Pope-Davis & H. Coleman (Eds.), *Multicultural counseling competencies: Assessment, education and training, and supervision. Multicultural aspect of counseling series* (Vol. 7, pp. 290–309). Thousand Oaks, CA: Sage.

Daniels, J., D'Andrea, M., & Kim, B. S. K. (1999). Assessing the barriers and changes of cross-cultural supervision: A case study. *Counselor Education & Supervision, 38*(3), 191–204.

Daniels, J. A., & Larson, L. M. (2001). The impact of performance feedback on counseling self-efficacy and counselor anxiety. *Counselor Education & Supervision, 41*(2), 120–130.

Dawes, R. M. (1994). *House of cards: Psychology and psychotherapy built on myth.* New York: The Free Press.

Day, S. X., & Schneider, P. L. (2002). Psychotherapy using distance technology: A comparison of face-to-face, video, and audio treatment. *Journal of Counseling Psychology, 49,* 499–503.

Deacon, S. A. (2000). Using divergent thinking exercises within supervision to enhance therapist creativity. *Journal of Family Psychotherapy, 11*(2), 67–73.

Deal, K. H. (2003). The relationship between critical thinking and interpersonal skills: Guidelines for clinical supervision. *The Clinical Supervisor, 22*(2), 3–19.

Dean, J. E. (2001). Sandtray consultation: A method of supervision applied to couple's therapy. *The Arts in Psychotherapy, 28,* 175–180.

Delaney, D. J. (1972). A behavioral model for the practicum supervision of counselor candidates. *Counselor Education and Supervision, 12,* 46–50.

deMayo, R. A. (2000). Patients' sexual behavior and sexual harassment: A survey of clinical supervisors.

Professional Psychology: Research & Practice, 31(6), 706–709.

Dennin, M. K., & Ellis, M. V. (2003). Effects of a method of self-supervision for counselor trainees. *Journal of Counseling Psychology, 50,* 69–83.

Dewey, J. (1933). *How we think.* New York: D. C. Heath.

Dickey, K. D., Housley, W. F. & Guest, C. (1993). Ethics in supervision of rehabilitation counselor trainees: A survey. *Rehabilitation Education, 7,* 195–201.

Disney, M. J., & Stephens, A. M. (1994). *Legal issues in clinical supervision.* Alexandria, VA: ACA Press.

Dixon, D. N., & Claiborn, C. D. (1987). A social influence approach to counselor supervision. In J. E. Maddux, C. D. Stoltenberg, & R. Rosenwein (Eds.), *Social processes in clinical and counseling psychology* (pp. 83–93). New York: Springer-Verlag.

Dodds, J. B. (1986). Supervision of psychology trainees in field placements. *Professional Psychology: Research and Practice, 17,* 296–300.

Dodenhoff, J. T. (1981). Interpersonal attraction and direct-indirect supervisor influence as predictors of counselor trainee effectiveness. *Journal of Counseling Psychology, 28,* 47–52.

Doehrman, M. (1976). Parallel processes in supervision and psychotherapy. *Bulletin of the Menninger Clinic, 40,* 3–104.

Dombeck, M. T., & Brody, S. L. (1995). Clinical supervision: A three-way mirror. *Archives of psychiatric nursing, 9,* 3–10.

Douce, L. (1989, August). *Classroom and experiential training in supervision.* Paper presented at the annual meeting of the American Psychological Association, New Orleans.

Dowd, E. T. (1989). Stasis and change in cognitive psychotherapy: Client resistance and reactance as mediating variables. In W. Dryden & P. Trower (Eds.), *Cognitive psychotherapy: Stasis and change* (pp. 139–158). New York: Springer.

Dowling, S. (1984). Clinical evaluation: A comparison of self, self with videotape, peers, and supervisors. *The Clinical Supervisor, 2*(3), 71–78.

Dressel, J. L., Consoli, A. J., Kim, B. S. K., & Atkinson, D. R. (2007). Successful and unsuccessful multicultural supervisory behaviors: A Delphi poll. *Journal of Multicultural Counseling and Development, 35,* 51–64.

Driscoll, J. (2000). *Practising clinical supervision: A reflective approach.* London: Bailliere Tindall.

Duan, C., & Roehlke, H. (2001). A descriptive "snapshot" of cross-racial supervision in university counseling center internships [Special issue]. *Journal of Multicultural Counseling and Development, 29*(2), 131–146.

Dudding, C. C., & Justice, L. M. (2004). An E-supervision model: Videoconferencing as a clinical training tool. *Communication Disorders Quarterly, 25,* 145–151.

Dunning, D., Johnson, K., Ehrlinger, J., & Kruger, J. (2003). Why people fail to recognize their own incompetence. *Current Directions in Psychological Science, 12,* 83–87.

Duys, D. K., & Hedstrom, S. M. (2000). Basic counselor skills training and counselor cognitive complexity. *Counselor Education and Supervision, 40,* 8–18.

Dye, A. (1994). Training doctoral student supervisors at Purdue University. In J. E. Myers (Ed.), *Developing and directing counselor education laboratories* (pp. 121–130). Alexandria, VA: ACA Press.

Edwards, D., Cooper, L., Burnard, P., Hanningan, B., Adams, J., Fothergill, A., & Coyle, D. (2005). Factors influencing the effectiveness of clinical supervision. *Journal of Psychiatric and Mental Health Nursing, 12,* 405–414.

Edwards, J. K., and Chen, M. W. (1999). Strength-based supervision: Frameworks, current practice, and future directions: A Wu Wei method. *The Family Journal, 7,* 349–357.

Efstation, J. F., Patton, M. J., & Kardash, C. M. (1990). Measuring the working alliance in counselor supervision. *Journal of Counseling Psychology, 37,* 322–329.

Einstein, A. (1933). *On the method of theoretical physics: The Herbert Spencer lecture,* delivered at Oxford 10 June 1933. Oxford: Oxford University Press.

Eisenberg, S. (1956). *Supervision in the changing field of social work.* Philadelphia: The Jewish Family Service of Philadelphia.

Ekstein, R. (1964). Supervision of psychotherapy: Is it teaching? Is it administration? Or is it therapy? *Psychotherapy, Research, and Practice, 1,* 137–138.

Ekstein, R., & Wallerstein, R. S. (1972). *The teaching and learning of psychotherapy* (2nd ed.). New York: International Universities Press, Inc.

Elizur, J. (1990). "Stuckness" in live supervision: Expanding the therapist's style. *Journal of Family Therapy, 12,* 267–280.

Ellis, A. (1974). *The techniques of Disputing Irrational Beliefs (DIBS).* New York: Institute for Rational Living.

Ellis, A. (1989). Thoughts on supervising counselors and therapists. *Psychology: A Journal of Human Behavior, 26,* 3–5.

Ellis, M. V. (1991a). Critical incidents in clinical supervision and in supervisor supervision: Assessing supervisory issues. *Journal of Counseling Psychology, 38,* 342–349.

Ellis, M. V. (1991b). Research in clinical supervision: Revitalizing a scientific agenda. *Counselor Education & Supervision, 30,* 238–251.

Ellis, M. V. (2001). Harmful supervision, a cause for alarm: Commentary on Nelson & Friedlander (2001) and Gray et al. (2001). *Journal of Counseling Psychology, 48,* 401–406.

Ellis, M. V., Anderson-Hanley, C. M., Dennin, M. K., Anderson, J. J., Chapin, J. L., & Polstri, S. M. (1994, August). *Congruence of expectation in clinical supervision: Scale development and validity data.* Paper presented at the annual meeting of the American Psychological Association, Los Angeles.

Ellis, M. V., Chapin, J. L., Dennin, M. K., & Anderson-Hanley, C. (August, 1996). *Role induction for clinical supervision: Impact on neophyte supervisees.* Paper presented at the annual meeting of the American Psychological Association, Toronto.

Ellis, M. V., & Dell, D. M. (1986). Dimensionality of supervisor roles: Supervisors' perceptions of supervision. *Journal of Counseling Psychology, 33,* 282–291.

Ellis, M. V., Dell, D. M., & Good, G. E. (1988). Counselor trainees' perceptions of supervisor roles: Two studies testing the dimensionality of supervision. *Journal of Counseling Psychology, 35,* 315–322.

Ellis, M. V. Dennin, M., DelGenio, J., Anderson-Hanley, C., Chapin, J., & Swagler, M. (1993, August). *Perfomance Anxiety in Clinical Supervision: Scale Construction and Validity Data.* Paper presented at the 101st Annnual Convention of the American Psychological Association, Toronto, Canada.

Ellis, M. V., & Douce, L. A. (1994). Group supervision of novice clinical supervisors: Eight recurring issues. *Journal of Counseling & Development, 72,* 520–525.

Ellis, M. V., Krengel, M., & Beck, M. (2002). Testing self-focused attention theory in clinical supervision: Effects of supervisee anxiety and performance. *Journal of Counseling Psychology, 49,* 101–116.

Ellis, M. V., & Ladany, N. (1997). Inferences concerning supervisees and clients in clinical supervision: An integrative review. In C. E. Watkins, Jr. (Ed.), *Handbook of psychotherapy supervision* (pp. 467–507). New York: Wiley.

Ellis, M. V., Ladany, N., Krengel, M., & Schult, D. (1996). Clinical supervision research from 1981 to 1993: A methodological critique. *Journal of Counseling Psychology, 43,* 35–50.

Ellis, M. V., & Robbins, E. S. (1993). Voices of care and justice in clinical supervision: Issues and interventions. *Counselor Education & Supervision, 32,* 203–212.

Elman, N. S., & Forrest, L. (2004). Psychotherapy in the remediation of psychology trainees: Exploratory interviews with training directors. *Professional Psychology: Research & Practice, 49,* 123–130.

Elman, N., Forrest, L., Vacha-Haase, T., & Gizara, S. (1999). A systems perspective on trainee impairment: Continuing the dialogue. *The Counseling Psychologist, 27,* 712–721.

Enyedy, K. C., Arcinue, F., Puri, N. N., Carter, J. W., Goodyear, R. K., & Getzelman, M. A. (2003). Hindering phenomena in group supervision: Implications for practice. *Professional Psychology: Research & Practice, 34,* 312–317.

Epstein, L. (2001). Collusive selection inattention to the negative impact of the supervisory interaction. In S. Grill (Ed.), *The supervisory alliance: Facilitating the psychotherapist's learning experience* (pp. 139–163). Northvale, NJ: Jason Aronson, Inc.

Erera, I. P., & Lazar, A. (1994). The administrative and educational functions in supervision: Indications of incompatibility. *The Clinical Supervisor, 12*(2), 39–55.

Ericcson, K. A., & Lehmann, A. C. (1996). Expert and exceptional performance: Evidence of maximal adaptation to task constraints. *Annual Review of Psychology, 47,* 273–305.

Erwin, W. J. (2000). Supervisor moral sensitivity. *Counseling Education and Supervision, 40,* 115–127.

Eshach, H., & Bitterman, H. (2003). From case-based reasoning to problem-based learning. *Academic Medicine, 5,* 491–496.

Estrada, D., Frame, M. W., & Williams, C. B. (2004). Cross-cultural supervision: Guiding the conversation toward race and ethnicity. *Journal of Multicultural Counseling and Development, 32,* 307–319.

Falender, C. A., Collins, C., & Shafranske, E. P. (2005, June). *Impairment in psychology training.*

International Interdisciplinary Conference on Clinical Supervision, Buffalo, NY.

Falender, C. A., Cornish, J. A. E., Goodyear, R. K., Hatcher, R., Kaslow, N. J., Leventhal, G., Shafranske, E., Sigmon, S., Stoltenberg, C., & Grus, C. (2004). Defining competencies in psychology supervision: A consensus statement. *Journal of Clinical Psychology, 60,* 771–785.

Falender, C. A., & Shafranske, E. P. (2007). Competence in competency-based supervision practice: Construct and application. *Professional Psychology: Research and Practice, 38,* 232–240.

Fall, M., & Sutton, J. M., Jr. (2004). *Clinical supervision: A handbook for practitioners.* Boston: Allyn & Bacon.

Falvey, J. E. (1987). *Handbook of administrative supervision.* Alexandria, VA: Association for Counselor Education and Supervision.

Falvey, J. E. (2002). *Managing clinical supervision: Ethical practice and legal risk management.* Pacific Grove, CA: Brooks/Cole.

Falvey, J. E., Caldwell, C. F., & Cohen, C. R. (2002). *Documentation in supervision: The focused risk management supervision system.* Pacific Grove, CA: Brooks/Cole.

Falvey, J. E., & Cohen, C. R. (2003). The buck stops here: Documenting clinical supervision. *The Clinical Supervisor, 22*(2), 63–80.

Feiner, A. H. (1994). Comments on contradictions in the supervisory process. *Contemporary Psychoanalysis, 30,* 57–75.

Fennell, D. L., Hovestadt, A. J., & Harvey, S. J. (1986). A comparison of delayed feedback and live supervision models of marriage and family therapist clinical training. *Journal of Marital and Family Therapy, 12,* 181–186.

Fine, M. (2003). Reflections on the intersection of power and competition in reflecting teams as applied to academic settings. *Journal of Marital and Family Therapy, 29,* 339–351.

Fiscalini, J. (1997). On supervisory parataxis and dialogue. *Contemporary Psychoanalysis, 21,* 591–608.

Fisher, B. (1989). Differences between supervision of beginning and advanced therapists: Hogan's hypothesis empirically revisited. *The Clinical Supervisor, 7*(1), 57–74.

Fitzgerald, L. E, & Osipow, S. H. (1986). An occupational analysis of counseling psychology: How special is the specialty? *American Psychologist, 41,* 535–544.

Fleming, J. (1953). The role of supervision in psychiatric training. *Bulletin of the Menninger Clinic, 17,* 157–159.

Fleming, J., & Benedek, T. (1966). *Psychoanalytic supervision.* New York: Grune & Stratton.

Fly, B. J., van Bark, W. P., Weinman, L., Kitchener, K. S., & Lang, P. R. (1997). Ethical transgressions of psychology graduate students: Critical incidents with implications for training. *Professional Psychology: Research and Practice, 28,* 492–495.

Follette, W. C., & Callaghan, G. M. (1995). Do as I do, not as I say: A behavior-analytic approach to supervision. *Professional Psychology: Research and Practice, 26,* 413–421.

Fong, M. L., Borders, L. D., Ethington, C. A., & Pitts, J. H. (1997). Becoming a counselor: A longitudinal study of student cognitive development. *Counselor Education & Supervision, 37*(2), 100–114.

Fong, M. L., Borders, L. D., & Neimeyer, G. J. (1986). Sex role orientation and self-disclosure flexibility in counselor training. *Counselor Education and Supervision, 25*(3), 210–221.

Fong, M. L., & Lease, S. H. (1997). Cross-cultural supervision: Issues for the white supervisor. In D. B. Pope-Davis & H. L. K. Coleman (Eds.), *Multicultural counseling competencies: Assessment, education and training, and supervision* (pp. 387–405). Thousand Oaks, CA: Sage Publications.

Ford, S. J. W., & Britton, P. J. (2002). *Multicultural supervision: What's really going on?* Presentation at the American Counselor Education and Supervision conference. Park City, UT.

Forrest, L., Elman, N., Gizara, S., & Vacha-Haase, T. (1999). Trainee impairment: A review of identification, remediation, dismissal, and legal issues. *Counseling Psychologist, 27*(5), 627–686.

Foster, J. T. (2002). *Attachment behavior and psychotherapy supervision.* Unpublished dissertation, Department of Psychological Research in Education, University of Kansas, Lawrence, KS.

Foster, J. T., Heinen, A. D., Lichtenberg, J. W., & Gomez, A. D. (2006). Supervisor attachment as a predictor of developmental ratings of supervisees. *American Journal of Psychological Research, 2,* 28–39. Retrieved December 30, 2007, from http://www.mcneese.edu/ajpr//vol2/AJPR%2006-08%20Foster%20et%20al.pdf

Foster, J. T., Lichtenberg, J. W., & Peyton, V. (2007). The supervisory attachment relationship as a predictor of the professional development of the supervisee. *Psychotherapy Research, 17,* 343–350.

Fox, R. (1983). Contracting in supervision: A goal oriented process. *The Clinical Supervisor, 1*(1), 37–49.

Fraenkel, P., & Pinsof, W. M. (2001). Teaching family therapy-centered integration: Assimilation and beyond. *Journal of Psychotherapy Integration, 11,* 59–85.

Frame, M. W. (2001). The spiritual genogram in training and supervision. *Family Journal—Counseling and Therapy for Couples and Families, 9*(2), 109–115.

Frame, M. W., & Stevens-Smith, P. (1995). Out of harm's way: Enhancing monitoring and dismissal processes in counselor education programs. *Counselor Education and Supervision, 35,* 118–129.

Frank, A. D. (1961). *Persuasion and healing.* Baltimore: Johns Hopkins University Press.

Frankel, B. R. (1990). Process of family therapy live supervision: A brief report. *The Commission on Supervision Bulletin, III*(1), 5–6.

Frankel, B. R., & Piercy, F. P. (1990). The relationship among selected supervisor, therapist, and client behaviors. *Journal of Marital and Family Therapy, 16,* 407–421.

Frawley-O'Dea, M. G., & Sarnat, J. E. (2001). *The supervisory relationship: A contemporary psychodynamic approach.* New York: Guilford Press.

Frayn, D. H. (1991). Supervising the supervisors: The evolution of a psychotherapy supervisors' group. *American Journal of Psychotherapy, 45,* 31–42.

Frazier, P. A., Tix, A. P., & Barron, K. E. (2004). Testing moderator and mediator effects in counseling psychology research. *Journal of Counseling Psychology, 51,* 115–134.

Freeman, S. C. (1993). Reiterations on client-centered supervision. *Counselor Education and Supervision, 32,* 213–215.

Freitas, G. J. (2002). The impact of psychotherapy supervision on client outcome: A critical examination of 2 decades of research. *Psychotherapy: Theory, Research, Practice, Training, 39,* 354–367.

French, J. R. P., Jr., & Raven, B. (1959). The bases of social power. In D. Cartwright (Ed.), *Studies in social power* (pp. 150–167). Ann Arbor, MI: Institute for Social Research.

Freud, S. (1973). Analysis of a phobia in a five-year-old boy. In J. Strachey (Ed.), *Standard edition of the complete psychological works* (Vol. X). London: Hogarth. (Original work published 1909)

Freud, S. (1986). On the history of the psychoanalytic movement. In *Historical and expository works on psychoanalysis.* Harmondsworth, U.K.: Penguin. (Original work published 1914)

Frick, D. E., McCartney, C. I., & Lazarus, J. A. (1995). Supervision of sexually exploitative psychiatrists: APA district branch experience. *Psychiatric Annuals, 25,* 113–117.

Fried, L. (1991). Becoming a psychotherapist. *Journal of College Student Psychotherapy, 5,* 71–79.

Fried, Y., Tiegs, R. B. & Bellany, A. R. (1992). Personal and interpersonal predictors of supervisors' avoidance of evaluating subordinates. *Journal of Applied Psychology, 77,* 462–468.

Friedberg, R. D., & Taylor, L. A. (1994). Perspectives on supervision in cognitive therapy. *Journal of Rational-Emotive & Cognitive Behavior Therapy, 12*(3), 147–161.

Friedlander, M. L., Keller, K. E., Peca-Baker, T. A., & Olk, M. E. (1986). Effects of role conflict on counselor trainees' self-statements, anxiety level, and performance. *Journal of Counseling Psychology, 33,* 73–77.

Friedlander, M. L., & Schwartz, G. S. (1985). Toward a theory of strategic self-presentation in counseling and psychotherapy. *Journal of Counseling Psychology, 32,* 483–501.

Friedlander, M. L., Siegel, S. M., & Brenock, K. (1989). Parallel process in counseling and supervision: A case study. *Journal of Counseling Psychology, 36,* 149–157.

Friedlander, M. L., & Snyder, J. (1983). Trainees' expectations for the supervisory process: Testing a developmental model. *Counselor Education and Supervision, 22,* 342–348.

Friedlander, M. L., & Ward, L. G. (1984). Development and validation of the Supervisory Styles Inventory. *Journal of Counseling Psychology, 31,* 542–558.

Friedman, D., & Kaslow, N. J. (1986). The development of professional identity in psychotherapists: Six stages in the supervision process. *The Clinical Supervisor, 4*(1–2), 29–49.

Friedman, R. (1983). Aspects of the parallel process and counter-transference issues in student supervision. *School Social Work Journal, 8*(1), 3–15.

Frohman, A. L. (1998). Building a culture for innovation. *Research Technology Management, 41,* 9–12.

Fruzzetti, A. E., Waltz, J. A., & Linehan, M. M. (1997). Supervision in dialectical behavior therapy. In C. E.

Watkins, Jr. (Ed.), *Handbook of psychotherapy supervision* (pp. 84–100). New York: John Wiley & Sons, Inc.

Fukuyama, M. A. (1994). Critical incidents in multicultural counseling supervision: A phenomenological approach to supervision. *Counselor Education and Supervision, 34,* 142–151.

Fulero, S. M. (1988). Tarasoff: 10 years later. *Professional Psychology: Research and Practice, 19,* 184–190.

Fuller, F. F., & Manning, B. A. (1973). Self-confrontation reviewed: A conceptualization for video playback in teacher education. *Review of Educational Research, 43,* 469–528.

Galassi, J. P., & Brooks, L. (1992). Integrating scientist and practitioner training in counseling psychology: Practicum is the key. *Counselling Psychology Quarterly, 5,* 57–65.

Gallant, J. P., & Thyer, B. A. (1989). The "bug-in-the-ear" in clinical supervision: A review. *The Clinical Supervisor, 7*(2), 43–58.

Gallant, J. P., Thyer, B. A., & Bailey, J. S. (1991). Using bug-in-the-ear feedback in clinical supervision: *Research on Social Work Practice, 1,* 175–187.

Garfield, S. L. (1983). Effectiveness of psychotherapy: The perennial controversy. *Professional Psychology: Theory, Research, and Practice, 14,* 35–43.

Garfield, S. L. (1986). Research on client variables in psychotherapy. In S. L. Garfield & A. E. Bergin (Eds.), *Handbook of psychotherapy and behavior change* (3rd ed., pp. 190–228). New York: John Wiley & Sons.

Gatmon, D., Jackson, D., Koshkarian, L., Koshkarian, L., Martos-Perry, N., Molina, A., Patel, N., & Rodolfa, E. (2001). Exploring ethnic, gender, and sexual orientation variables in supervision: Do they really matter? *Journal of Multicultural Counseling and Development, 29*(2), 102–113.

Gaubatz, M. D., & Vera, E. M. (2006). Trainee competence in master's-level counseling programs: A comparison of counselor educators' and students' views. *Counselor Education and Supervision, 26,* 32–43.

Gautney, K. (1994). What if they ask me if I am married? *The Supervisor Bulletin, VII*(1), 3, 7.

Gelso, C. A., & Carter, A. (1985). The relationship in counseling and psychotherapy. *The Counseling Psychologist, 13,* 155–243.

Gelso, C. J. (1979). Research in counseling: Methodological and professional issues. *The Counseling Psychologist, 8*(3), 7–36.

Gershenson, J., & Cohen, M. (1978). Through the looking glass: The experiences of two family therapy trainees with live supervision. *Family Process, 17,* 225–230.

Giddings, M. M., Vodde, R., & Cleveland, P. (2003). Examining student-field instructor problems in practicum: Beyond student satisfaction measures. *The Clinical Supervisor, 22*(2), 191–214.

Gilbert, P. (1998). What is shame: Some core issues and controversies. In P. Gilbert & B. Andrews (Eds.), *Shame: Interpersonal behavior, psychopathology, and culture* (pp. 3–38). New York: Oxford University Press.

Gill, S. (Ed.). (2001). *The supervisory alliance: Facilitating the psychotherapist's learning experience.* Northvale, NJ: Jason Aronson Inc.

Gilligan, C. (1982). *In a different voice.* Cambridge, MA: Harvard University Press.

Giordano, M. A., Altekruse, M. K., & Kern, C. W. (2000). *Supervisee's bill of rights.* Unpublished manuscript.

Gist, R. (2007, March 13). Message posted to the listserv of the Society for a Science of Clinical Psychology.

Gizara, S. S., & Forrest, L. (2004). Supervisors' experiences of trainee impairment and incompetence at APA-accredited internship sites. *Professional Psychology: Research and Practice, 35,* 131–140.

Glaser, R. D., & Thorpe, J. S. (1986). Unethical intimacy. *American Psychologist, 41,* 43–51.

Glidden, C. E., & Tracey, T. J. (1992). The structure of perceived differences in supervision across developmental levels. *Professional Psychology, 23,* 151–157.

Gloria, A. M., & Robinson, S. E. (1994). The internship application process: A survey of program training directors and intern candidates. *Counseling Psychologist, 22,* 474–488.

Globerman, J., & Bogo, M. (2003). Changing times: Understanding social workers' motivation to be field instructors. *Social Work, 48,* 65–73.

Goldberg, D. A. (1985). Process notes, audio, and videotape: Modes of presentation in psychotherapy training. *The Clinical Supervisor, 3,* 3–13.

Goldstein, A. P., Heller, K., & Sechrest, L. B. (1966). *Psychotherapy and the psychology of behavior change.* New York: John Wiley & Sons.

Gonccalves, O. F. (1994). Cognitive narrative psychotherapy: The hermeneutic construction of alternative meanings. *Journal of Cognitive Psychotherapy, 8,* 105–125.

Gonsalvez, C. & Freestone, J. (2007). Field supervisors' assessments of trainee performance: Are they reliable and valid? *Australian Psychologist, 42,* 23–32.

Gonzalez, R. C. (1997). Postmodern supervision: A multicultural perspective. In D. B. Pope-Davis & H. L. K. Coleman (Eds.), *Multicultural counseling competencies: Assessment, education and training, and supervision* (pp. 350–386). Thousand Oaks, CA: Sage Publications.

Goodyear, R. K. (1982). *Psychotherapy supervision by major theorists* [Videotape series]. Mahattan, KS: Kansas State University Instructional Media Center.

Goodyear, R. K. (1990). Gender configurations in supervisory dyads: Their relation to supervisee influence strategies and to skill evaluations of the supervisee. *The Clinical Supervisor, 8*(2), 67–79.

Goodyear, R. K. (2006, June). Supervision to foster reflective practice. Presentation at the 2nd International Interdisciplinary Conference on Clinical Supervision, Buffalo, NY.

Goodyear, R. K., Abadie, P. D., & Efros, F. (1984). Supervisory theory into practice: Differential perceptions of supervision by Ekstein, Ellis, Polster, and Rogers. *Journal of Counseling Psychology, 31,* 228–237.

Goodyear, R. K., Bunch, K., & Claiborn, C. D. (2005). Current supervision scholarship in psychology: A five year review. *The Clinical Supervisor, 24,* 137–147.

Goodyear, R. K., Cortese, J., Guzzardo, C. R., Allison, R. D., Claiborn, C. D., & Packard, R. (2000). Factors, trends and topics in the evolution of counseling psychology training. *Counseling Psychologist, 28,* 603–621.

Goodyear, R. K., & Guzzardo, C. R. (2000). Psychotherapy supervision and training. In S. D. Brown & R. W. Lent (Eds.), *Handbook of counseling psychology* (3rd ed., pp. 83–108). New York: John Wiley & Sons.

Goodyear, R. K., Murdock, N., Lichtenberg, J. W., McPherson, R., Petren, S., & O'Byrne, K. K. (2008). Stability and change in counseling psychologists' identities, roles, functions, and career satisfaction across fifteen years. *The Counseling Psychologist, 36,* 220–249.

Goodyear, R. K., & Nelson, M. L. (1997). The major supervision formats. In C. E. Watkins, *Handbook of psychotherapy supervision* (pp. 328–344). New York: Wiley.

Goodyear, R. K., & Robyak, J. E. (1982). Supervisors theory and experience in supervisory focus. *Psychological Reports, 51,* 978.

Goodyear, R. K., & Sinnett, E. D. (1984). Current and emerging ethical issues for counseling psychologists. *Counseling Psychologist, 12*(3), 87–98.

Goodyear, R. K., Wertheimer, A., Cypers, S., & Rosemond, M. (2003). Refining the map of the counselor development journey: Response to Rønnestad and Skovholt. *Journal of Career Development, 30,* 73–80.

Gordon, S. P. (1990). Developmental supervision: An exploratory study of a promising model. *Journal of Curriculum and Supervision, 5,* 293–307.

Gottlieb, M. C., Robinson, K., & Younggren, J. N. (2007). Multiple relations in supervision: Guidance for administrators, supervisors, and students. *Professional Psychology: Research and Practice, 38,* 241–247.

Graf, N. M., & Stebnicki, M. A. (2002). Using E-mail for clinical supervision in practicum: A qualitative analysis. *Journal of Rehabilitation, 68*(3), 41–49.

Granello, D. H. (1996). Gender and power in the supervisory dyad. *The Clinical Supervisor, 14*(2), 53–67.

Granello, D. H. (2000). Encouraging the cognitive development of supervisees: Using Bloom's taxonomy in supervision. *Counselor Education and Supervision, 40*(1), 31–46.

Granello, D. H. (2002). Assessing the cognitive development of counseling students: Changes in epistemological assumptions. *Counselor Education and Supervision, 41,* 279–293.

Granello, D. H. (2003). Influence strategies in the supervisory dyad: An investigation into the effects of gender and age. *Counselor Education and Supervision, 42,* 189–202.

Granello, D. H., Beamish, P. M., & Davis, T. E. (1997). Supervisee empowerment: Does gender make a difference? *Counselor Education and Supervision, 36,* 305–317.

Green, D., & Dye, L. (2002). How should we best train clinical psychology supervisors? A Delphi survey. *Psychology Learning and Teaching, 2,* 108–115.

Green, S. L., & Hansen, J. C. (1986). Ethical dilemmas in family therapy. *Journal of Marital and Family Therapy, 12,* 225–230.

Greenberg, L. S. (1984). Task analysis: The general approach. In L. N. Rice & L. S. Greenberg (Eds.), *Patterns of change: Intensive analysis of psychotherapy process* (pp. 124–148). New York: Guilford.

Grencavage, L. M., & Norcross, J. C. (1990). Where are the commonalities among the therapeutic common factors? *Professional Psychology Research and Practice, 21,* 372–378.

Grey, A. L., & Fiscalini, J. (1987). Parallel process as transference-countertransference interaction. *Psychoanalytic Psychology, 4,* 131–144.

Griffith, B. A., & Frieden, G. (2000). Facilitating reflective thinking in counselor education. *Counselor Education and Supervision, 40,* 82–93.

Gross, S. M. (2005). Student perspectives on clinical and counseling psychology practica. *Professional Psychology: Research and Practice, 36,* 299–306.

Gubi, P. M. (2007). Exploring the supervision experience of some mainstream counsellors who integrate prayer in counseling. *Counselling and Psychotherapy Research, 7,* 114–121.

Guest, C. L., Jr., & Dooley, K. (1999). Supervisor malpractice: Liability to the supervisee in clinical supervision. *Counselor Education and Supervision, 38*(4), 269–279.

Guest, P. D., & Beutler, L. E. (1988). Impact of psychotherapy supervision on therapist orientation and values. *Journal of Consulting & Clinical Psychology, 56,* 653–658.

Guiffrida, D. A. (2005). The emergence model: An alternative pedagogy for facilitating self-reflection and theoretical fit in counseling students. *Counselor Education and Supervision, 44,* 201–213.

Guiffrida, D. A., Jordan, R., Saiz, S., & Barnes, K. L. (2007). The use of metaphor in clinical supervision. *Journal of Counseling & Development, 85,* 393–400.

Gurk, M. D., & Wicas, E. A. (1979). Generic models of counselor supervision: Counseling/instruction dichotomy and consultation metamodel. *Personnel and Guidance Journal, 57,* 402–407.

Guth, L. J., & Dandeneau, C. J. (2007, June). *Nonlinear supervision process model (NSPM): Augmenting existing supervision theories.* Paper presented at the Annual International Interdisciplinary Supervision Conference, Buffalo, NY.

Gutheil, T. G., & Gabbard, G. O. (1993). The concept of boundaries in clinical practice: Theoretical and risk-management dimensions. *American Journal of Psychiatry, 150,* 188–196.

Gutheil, T. G., & Simon, R. I. (2002). Non-sexual boundary crossing and boundary violations: The ethical dimension. *Psychiatric Clinics of North America, 25,* 585–592.

Haas, L. J. (1991). Hide-and-seek or show-and-tell? Emerging issues of informed consent. *Ethics and Behavior, 1,* 175–189.

Haas, L. J., & Cummings, N. A. (1991). Managed outpatient mental health plans: Clinical, ethical and practical guidelines for participation. *Professional Psychology: Research and Practice, 22,* 45–51.

Haas, L. J., Malouf, J. L., & Mayerson, N. H. (1986). Ethical dilemmas in psychological practice: Results of a national survey. *Professional Psychology: Research and Practice, 17,* 316–321.

Hackney, H. L., & Goodyear, R. K. (1984). Carl Rogers' client-centered supervision. In R. F. Levant & J. M. Schlien (Eds.), *Client-centered therapy and the person-centered approach* (pp. 278–296). New York: Praeger.

Hadjistavropoulos, T., & Malloy, D. C. (2000). Making ethical choices: A comprehensive decision-making model for Canadian psychologists. *Canadian Psychology, 41,* 104–115.

Hahn, W. K. (2002). The experience of shame in psychotherapy supervision. *Psychotherapy, 38,* 272–284.

Hahn, W. K., & Molnar, S. (1991). Intern evaluation in university counseling centers: Process, problems, and recommendations. *The Counseling Psychologist, 19,* 414–430.

Haj-Yahia, M. M., & Roer-Strier, D. (1999). On the encounter between Jewish supervisors and Arab supervisees in Israel. *Clinical Supervisor, 18*(2), 17–37.

Haley, J. (1976). *Problem solving therapy.* San Francisco: Jossey-Bass.

Haley, J. (1987). *Problem solving therapy* (2nd ed.). San Francisco: Jossey-Bass.

Haley, J. (1996). *Learning and teaching therapy.* New York: Guilford Press.

Hall, J. E. (1988a). Protection in supervision. *Register Report, 14*(4), 3–4.

Hall, J. E. (1988b). Dual relationships in supervision. *Register Report, 15*(1), 5–6.

Hall, R. C. W., Macvaugh, III, G. S., Merideth, P., & Montgomery, J. (2007). Commentary: Delving further into liability for psychotherapy supervision. *The Journal of the American Academy of Psychiatry and the Law, 35,* 196–199.

Halpert, S. C., & Pfaller, J. (2001). Sexual orientation and supervision: Theory and practice. *Journal of Gay and Lesbian Social Services: Issues in Practice, Policy & Research, 13*(3), 23–40.

Hamilton, J. C., & Spruill, J. (1999). Identifying and reducing risk factors related to trainee-client sexual misconduct. *Professional Psychology: Research and Practice, 30,* 318–327.

Hamlin, E. R., II, & Timberlake, E. M. (1982). Peer group supervision for supervisors. *Social Casework, 67,* 82–87.

Handelsman, M. M., & Gottlieb, M. C., & Knapp, S. (2005). Training ethical psychologists: An acculturation model. *Professional Psychology: Research and Practice, 36,* 59–65.

Handley, P. (1982). Relationship between supervisors' and trainees' cognitive styles and the supervision process. *Journal of Counseling Psychology, 25,* 508–515.

Hanna, M. A., & Smith, J. (1998). Using rubrics for documentation of clinical work supervision. *Counselor Education and Supervision, 37,* 269–278.

Hansen, N. D., & Goldberg, S. G. (1999). Navigating the nuances: A matrix of considerations for ethical-legal dilemmas. *Professional Psychology: Research and Practice, 30,* 495–503.

Hardcastle, D. A. (1991). Toward a model for supervision: A peer supervision pilot project. *The Clinical Supervisor, 9*(2), 63–76.

Hardy, K. V. (1989). The theoretical myth of sameness: A critical issue in family therapy training and treatment. *Journal of Psychotherapy and the Family, 6*(1–2), 17–33.

Hardy, K. V. (1993). Live supervision in the postmodern era of family therapy: Issues, reflections, and questions. *Contemporary Family Therapy: An International Journal, 15,* 9–20.

Harkness, D., & Poertner, A. (1989). Research and social work supervision: A conceptual review. *Social Work, 34,* 115–119.

Harrar, W. R., VandeCreek, L., & Knapp, S. (1990). Ethical and legal aspects of clinical supervision. *Professional Psychology: Research and Practice, 21,* 37–41.

Harris, M. B. C. (1994). Supervisory evaluation and feedback. In L. D. Borders (Ed.), *Supervision: Exploring the effective components.* Greensboro, NC: ERIC/CASS.

Hart, G. (1982). *The process of clinical supervision.* Baltimore: University Park Press.

Hart, G. M., & Nance, D. (2003). Styles of counselor supervision as perceived by supervisors and supervisees. *Counselor Education and Supervision, 43,* 146–158.

Harvey, C., & Katz, C. (1985). *If I'm so successful, why do I feel like a fake? The impostor phenomenon.* New York: St. Martin's Press.

Harvey, O. J., Hunt, D. E., & Schroeder, H. M. (1961). *Conceptual systems and personality organization.* New York: Holt, Rinehart, and Winston.

Hatcher, R. L., & Lassiter, K. D. (2007). Initial training in professional psychology: The practicum competencies outline. *Training and Education in Professional Psychology, 1,* 49–63.

Hawkins, P., & Shohet, R. (1989). *Supervision in the helping professions.* Milton Keynes, UK: Open University Press.

Hawkins, P., & Shohet, R. (2000). *Supervision in the helping professions: An individual, group and organizational approach* (2nd ed.). Philadelphia: Open University Press.

Hayes, J. R. (1981). *The complete problem solver.* Philadelphia: Franklin Institute Press.

Hayes, R. L. (1989). Group supervision. In L. J. Bradley & J. D. Boyd (Eds.), *Counselor supervision* (2nd ed., pp. 399–421). Muncie, IN: Accelerated Development Inc.

Hayes, S. C. (2004). Acceptance and commitment therapy and the new behavior therapies: Mindfulness, acceptance and relationship. In S. C. Hayes, V. M. Follette, & M. Linehan (Eds.), *Mindfulness and acceptance: Expanding the cognitive-behavioral tradition* (pp. 1–29). New York: Guilford Press.

Hays, D. G., & Chang, C. Y. (2003). White privilege, oppression, and racial identity development: Implications for supervision. *Counselor Education and Supervision, 43,* 134–145.

Heath, A. (1982). Team family therapy training: Conceptual and pragmatic considerations. *Family Process, 21,* 187–194.

Heckman-Stone, C. (2003). Trainee preferences for feedback and evaluation in clinical supervision. *The Clinical Supervisor, 22*(1), 21–33.

Helms, J. E. (1990). *Black and white racial identity: Theory, research and practice.* New York: England Greenwood Press.

Helms, J. E., & Cook, D. A. (1999). *Using race and culture in counseling and psychotherapy: Theory and process.* Boston: Allyn & Bacon.

Helms, J. E., & Piper R. E. (1994). Implications of racial identity theory for vocational psychology. *Journal of Vocational Behavior, 44,* 124–138.

Hemlick, L. M. (1998). The role of shame in clinical supervision: Development of the Shame in Supervision Instrument. *Dissertation Abstracts International: Section B: The Sciences & Engineering Vol 58(7-B)*, Jan 1998, 3924.

Henderson, P. (1994). Administrative skills in counseling supervision. In L. D. Borders (Ed.), *Supervision: Exploring the effective components*. Greensboro, NC: ERIC/CASS. (ERIC Document Reproduction Services No. EDOCG9425)

Heppner, P. P., & Claiborn, C. D. (1989). Social influence research in counseling: A review and critique [Monograph]. *Journal of Counseling Psychology, 36*, 365–387.

Heppner, P. P., & Dixon, D. N. (1981). A review of the interpersonal influence process in counseling. *Personnel and Guidance Journal, 59*, 542–550.

Heppner, P. P., & Handley, P. G. (1982). A study of the interpersonal influence process in supervision. *Journal of Counseling Psychologist, 28*, 437–444.

Heppner, P. P., Kivlighan, D. M., Burnett, J. W., Berry, T. R., Goedinhaus, M., Doxsee, D. J., Hendricks, F. M., Krull, L. A., Wright, G. E., Bellatin, A. M., Durham, R. J., Tharp, A., Kim, H., Brossart, D. F., Wang, L., Witty, T. E., Kinder, M. H., Hertel, J. B., & Wallace, D. L. (1994). Dimensions that characterize supervisor interventions delivered in the context of live supervision of practicum counselors. *Journal of Counseling Psychology, 41*, 227–235.

Heppner, P. P., & Roehlke, H. J. (1984). Differences among supervisees at different levels of training: Implications for a developmental model of supervision. *Journal of Counseling Psychology, 31*, 76–90.

Herman, K. C. (1993). Reassessing predictors of therapist competence. *Journal of Counseling and Development, 72*, 29–32.

Heron, J. (1989). *Six-category intervention analysis* (3rd ed.). Surrey, U.K.: Human Potential Resource Group, University of Surrey.

Heru, A. M., Strong, D. R., Price, M., & Recupero, P. R. (2004). Boundaries in psychotherapy supervision. *American Journal of Psychotherapy, 58*, 76–89.

Heru, A. M., Strong, D. R., Price, M., & Recupero, P. R. (2006). Self-disclosure in psychotherapy supervisors: Gender differences. *American Journal of Psychotherapy, 60*, 323–334.

Hess, A. K. (1980). Training models and the nature of psychotherapy supervision. In A. K. Hess (Ed.), *Psychotherapy supervision: Theory, research, and practice* (pp. 15–28). New York: John Wiley & Sons.

Hess, A. K. (1986). Growth in supervision: Stages of supervisee and supervisor development. *The Clinical Supervisor, 4*(1–2), 51–67.

Hess, A. K. (1987). Psychotherapy supervision: Stages, Buber, and a theory of relationship. *Professional Psychology: Research and Practice, 18*, 251–259.

Hess, A. K., & Hess, K. A. (1983). Psychotherapy supervision: A survey of internship training practices. *Professional Psychology, 14*, 504–513.

Hewson, J. (1999). Training supervisors to contract in supervision. In E. Holloway & M. Carroll (Eds.), *Training counselling supervisors* (pp. 67–91). London: Sage Publications.

Hill, C. E., Carter, J. A., & O'Farrell, M. K. (1981). A case-study of the process and outcome of time-limited counseling. *Journal of Counseling Psychology, 30*, 428–436.

Hill, C. E., Charles, D., & Reed, K. G. (1981). A longitudinal analysis of changes in counseling skills during doctoral training in counseling psychology. *Journal of Counseling Psychology, 28*, 428–436.

Hill, C. E., & Knox, S. (2002). Self-disclosure. In J. C. Norcross (Ed.), *Psychotherapy relationships that work: Therapist contributions and responsiveness to patients* (pp. 255–266). New York: Oxford University Press.

Hill, C. E., O'Grady, K. E., Balenger, V., Busse, W., Falk, D. R., Hill, M., Rios, P., & Taffe, R. (1994). Methodological examination of videotape-assisted reviews in brief therapy: Helpfulness ratings, therapist intentions, client reactions, mood, and session evaluation. *Journal of Counseling Psychology, 41*, 236–247.

Hillerbrand, E. T. (1989). Cognitive differences between experts and novices: Implications for group supervision. *Journal of Counseling and Development, 67*, 293–296.

Hillerbrand, E. T., & Claiborn, C. D. (1990). Examining reasoning skill differences between expert and novice counselors. *Journal of Counseling and Development, 68*, 684–691.

Hilton, D. B., Russell, R. K., & Salmi, S. W. (1995). The effects of supervisor's race and level of support on perceptions of supervision. *Journal of Counseling and Development, 73*, 559–563.

Himsel, D. (2003). *Leadership Soprano's style: How to become a more effective boss.* Chicago: Dearborn Trade, A Kaplan Professional Company.

Hinett, K. (2002). *Developing reflective practice in legal education.* Warwick, U.K.: UK Centre for Legal Education, University of Warwick.

Hird, J. S., Cavalieri, C. E., Dulko, J. P., Felice, A. A., & Ho, T. A. (2001). Visions and realities: Supervisee perspective of multicultural supervision. *Journal of Multicultural Counseling and Development, 29,* 114–130.

Hird, J. S., Tao, K. W., & Gloria, A. M. (2004). Examining supervisors' multicultural competence in racially similar and different supervision dyads. *The Clinical Supervisor, 23*(2), 107–120.

Hoffman, L. W. (1990). *Old scapes, new maps: A training program for psychotherapy supervisors.* Cambridge, MA: Milusik Press.

Hoffman, L. W. (1994). The training of psychotherapy supervisors: A barren scape. *Psychotherapy in Private Practice, 13,* 23–42.

Hoffman, M. A., Hill, C. E., Holmes, S. E., & Freitas, G. F. (2005). Supervisor perspective on the process and outcome of giving easy, difficult, or no feedback to supervisees. *Journal of Counseling Psychology, 52,* 3–13.

Hogan, R. (1964). Issues and approaches in supervision. *Psychotherapy: Theory, Research, and Practice, 1,* 139–141.

Holloway, E., & Carroll, M. (Eds.). (1999). *Training counselling supervisors: Strategies, methods, and techniques.* London: Sage Publications.

Holloway, E. L. (1984). Outcome evaluation in supervision research. *The Counseling Psychologist, 12,* 167–174.

Holloway, E. L. (1987). Developmental models of supervision: Is it supervision? *Professional Psychology: Research and Practice, 18,* 209–216.

Holloway, E. L. (1988). Instruction beyond the facilitative conditions: A response to Biggs. *Counselor Education and Supervision, 27,* 252–258.

Holloway, E. L. (1992). Supervision: A way of teaching and learning. In S. D. Brown & R. W. Lent (Eds.), *Handbook of counseling psychology* (pp. 177–214). New York: John Wiley.

Holloway, E. L. (1995). *Clinical supervision: A systems approach.* Thousand Oaks, CA: Sage Publications, Inc.

Holloway, E. L. (1997). Structures for the analysis and teaching of psychotherapy. In C. E. Watkins, Jr.

(Ed.), *Handbook of psychotherapy supervision* (pp. 249–276). New York: Wiley.

Holloway, E. L., & Carroll, M. (1996). Reaction to the special section on supervision research: Comment on Ellis et al. (1996), Ladany et al. (1996), Neufeldt et al. (1996), and Worthen and McNeill (1996). *Journal of Counseling Psychology, 43,* 51–55.

Holloway, E. L., Freund, R. D., Gardner, S. L., Nelson, M. L., & Walker, B. R. (1989). Relation of power and involvement to theoretical orientation in supervision: An analysis of discourse. *Journal of Counseling Psychology, 36,* 88–102.

Holloway, E. L., & Hosford, R. E. (1983). Toward developing a prescriptive technology of counselor supervision. *The Counseling Psychologist, 11,* 73–77.

Holloway, E. L., & Johnston, R. (1985). Group supervision: Widely practiced but poorly understood. *Counselor Education and Supervision, 24,* 332–340.

Holloway, E. L., & Neufeldt, S. A. (1995). Supervision: Its contributions to treatment efficacy. *Journal of Consulting and Clinical Psychology, 63,* 207–213.

Holloway, E. L., & Roehlke, H. J. (1987). Internship: The applied training of a counseling psychologist. *The Counseling Psychologist, 15,* 205–260.

Holloway, E. L., & Wampold, B. E. (1983). Patterns of verbal behavior and judgments of satisfaction in the supervision interview. *Journal of Counseling Psychology, 30,* 227–234.

Holloway, E. L., & Wampold, B. E. (1986). Relationship between conceptual level and counseling-related tasks: A meta-analysis. *Journal of Counseling Psychology, 33,* 310–319.

Holmbeck, G. N. (1997). Toward terminological, conceptual, and statistical clarity in the study of mediators and moderators: Examples from the child-clinical and pediatric psychology literatures. *Journal of Consulting and Clinical Psychology, 65,* 599–610.

Holtzman, R. F., & Raskin, M. S. (1988). Why field placements fail: Study results. *The Clinical Supervisor, 6*(3), 123–136.

Horvath, A. O., & Greenburg, L. S. (1989). Development and validation of the working alliance inventory. *Journal of Counseling Psychology, 36,* 223–233.

Horvath, A. O., & Luborsky, L. (1993). The role of the therapeutic alliance in psychotherapy. *Journal of Consulting and Clinical Psychology, 61,* 561–573.

Horvath, A. O., & Symonds, B. D. (1991). Relation between working alliance and outcome in psychotherapy: A meta-analysis. *Journal of Counseling Psychology, 38,* 139–149.

Hotelling, K., & Forrest, L. (1985). Gilligan's theory of sex-role development: A perspective for counseling. *Journal of Counseling and Development, 64,* 183–186.

Howard, E. E., Inman, A. G., & Altman, A. N. (2006). Critical incidents among novice counselor trainees. *Counselor Education and Supervision, 46,* 88–102.

Hoyle, R. H. (Ed.). (1995). *Structural equation modeling: Concepts, issues, and applications.* Thousand Oaks, CA: SAGE Publications.

Hoyt, M. F., & Goulding, R. (1989). Resolution of a transference-countertransference impasse: Using Gestalt techniques in supervision. *Transactional Analysis Journal, 19,* 201–211.

Hutto, B. (2001). Some lessons best learned from psychotherapy supervision. *Psychiatric Times, 18*(7). Retrieved January 3, 2008, from http://www.psychiatrictimes.com/p010753.html

Hyrkäs, K. (2005). Clinical supervision, burnout, and job satisfaction among mental health and psychiatric nurses in Finland. *Issues in Mental Health Nursing, 26,* 531–556.

Igartua, K. J. (2000). The impact of impaired supervisors on residents. *Academic Psychiatry, 24*(4), 188–194.

Inman, A. G. (2006). Supervisor multicultural competence and its relation to supervisory process and outcome. *Journal of Marital and Family Therapy, 32,* 73–85.

Itzhaky, H., & Sztern, L. (1999). The take over of parent-child dynamics in a supervisory relationship: Identifying the role transformation. *Clinical Social Work Journal, 27,* 247–258.

Ivey, A. (1986). *Developmental therapy: Theory into practice.* San Francisco: Jossey-Bass.

Jackson, H., & Nuttall, R. L. (2001). A relationship between childhood sexual abuse and professional sexual misconduct. *Professional Psychology: Research and Practice, 32,* 200–204.

Jacobs, D., David, P., & Meyer, D. J. (1995). *The supervisory encounter: A guide for teachers of psychodynamic psychotherapy and analysis.* New Haven, CT: Yale University Press.

Jacobsen, C. H. (2007). A qualitative single case study of parallel process. *Counselling and Psychotherapy Research, 7,* 26–33.

Jakubowski-Spector, P., Dustin, R., & George, R. L. (1971). Toward developing a behavioral counselor education model. *Counselor Education and Supervision, 11,* 242–250.

James, W. (1981). *The Principles of psychology.* Cambridge, MA: Harvard University Press. (Original work published 1890)

Jerome, L. W., DeLeon, P. H., James, L. C., Folen, R., Earles, J., & Gedney, J. J. (2000). The coming age of telecommunications in psychological research and practice. *American Psychologist, 55,* 407–421.

Johnson, E., & Moses, N. C. (1988, August). *The dynamic developmental model of supervision.* Paper presented at the annual convention of the American Psychological Association, Atlanta.

Johnson, E. A., & Stewart, D. W. (2000). Clinical supervision in Canadian academic and service settings: The importance of education, training, and workplace support for supervisor development. *Canadian Psychology, 41,* 124–130.

Johnson, S. W., & Combs, D. C. (1997). The use of interactive television in live supervision. *TCA Journal, 25*(1), 10–18.

Johnson, W. B., & Campbell, C. D. (2002). Character and fitness requirements for professional psychologists: Are there any? *Professional Psychology: Research and Practice, 33,* 46–53.

Jordan, K. (1999). Live supervision for beginning therapists in practicum: Crucial for quality counseling and avoiding litigation. *Family Therapy, 26*(2), 81–86.

Jordan, K. (2006). Beginning supervisees' identity: The importance of relationship variables and experience versus gender matches in the supervisee/supervisor interplay. *The Clinical Supervisor, 25*(1/2), 43–51.

Juhnke, G. A. (1996). Solution-focused supervision: Promoting supervisee skills and confidence through successful solutions. *Counselor Education and Supervision, 36,* 48–57.

Kadushin, A. (1968). Games people play in supervision. *Social Work, 13,* 23–32.

Kadushin, A. (1976). *Supervision in social work.* New York: Columbia University Press.

Kadushin, A. (1992a). *Supervision in social work* (3rd ed.). New York: Columbia University Press.

Kadushin, A. (1992b). What's wrong, what's right with social work supervision. *The Clinical Supervisor, 10*(1), 3–19.

Kadushin, A. (1992c). Social work supervision: An updated survey. *The Clinical Supervisor, 10*(2), 9–27.

Kadushin, A. (2002). *Supervision in social work* (4th ed.). New York: Columbia University Press.

Kadushin, A., & Harkness, D. (2002). *Supervision in social work* (4th ed.). New York: Columbia University Press.

Kagan, H. K., & Kagan, N. I. (1997). Interpersonal process recall: Influencing human interaction. In C. E. Watkins, Jr. (Ed.), *Handbook of psychotherapy supervision* (pp. 296–309). New York: Wiley.

Kagan, N. (1976). *Influencing human interaction.* Mason, MI: Mason Media, Inc. or Washington, DC: American Association for Counseling and Development.

Kagan, N. (1980). Influencing human interaction— eighteen years with IPR. In A. K. Hess (Ed.), *Psychotherapy supervision: Theory, research and practice* (pp. 262–286). New York: Wiley.

Kagan, N., & Krathwohl, D. R. (1967). *Studies in human interaction: Interpersonal process recall stimulated by videotape.* East Lansing, MI: Michigan State University.

Kagan, N., Krathwohl, D. R., & Farquahar, W. W. (1965). *IPR—Interpersonal process recall by videotape: Stimulated recall by videotape.* East Lansing, MI: Michigan State University.

Kagan, N., Krathwohl, D. R., & Miller, R. (1963). Stimulated recall in therapy using videotape—a case study. *Journal of Counseling Psychology, 10,* 237–243.

Kahn, B. (1999). Priorities and practices in field supervision of school counseling students. *Professional School Counseling, 3*(2), 128–136.

Kanz, J. E. (2001). Clinical-supervision.com: Issues in the provision of online supervision. *Professional Psychology: Research & Practice, 32*(4), 415–420.

Kaplan, D. M., Rothrock, D., & Culkin, M. (1999). The infusion of counseling observations into a graduate counseling program. *Counselor Education and Supervision, 39*(1), 66–75.

Kaplan, M. (1983). A woman's view of DSM-III. *American Psychologist, 38,* 786–792.

Kaplan, R. (1987). The current use of live supervision within marriage and family therapy training programs. *The Clinical Supervisor, 5*(3), 43–52.

Kaslow, N. J., Celano, M. P., & Stanton, M. (2005). Training in family psychology: A competencies-based approach. *Family Process, 44,* 337–353.

Kaslow, N. J., & Rice, D. G. (1985). Developmental stresses of psychology internship training: What training staff can do to help. *Professional Psychology: Research and Practice, 16,* 253–261.

Katz, J. H. (1985). The sociopolitical nature of counseling. *The Counseling Psychologist, 13,* 615–624.

Kaul, T. J., & Bednar, R. L. (1986). Research on group and related therapies. In S. L. Garfield & A. E. Bergin (Eds.), *Handbook of psychotherapy and behavior change* (3rd ed., pp. 671–714). New York: John Wiley & Sons.

Kavanagh, D. J., Spence, S. H., Strong, J., Wilson, J., Sturk, H., & Crow, N. (2003). Supervision practices in allied mental health: Relationships of supervision characteristics to perceived impact and job satisfaction. *Mental Health Services Research, 5,* 187–195.

Keith, D. V., Connell, G., & Whitaker, C. A. (1992). Group supervision in symbolic experiential family therapy. *Journal of Family Psychotherapy, 3*(1), 93–109.

Kell, B. L., & Burow, J. M. (1970). *Developmental counseling and therapy.* Boston: Houghton Mifflin.

Kell, B. L., & Mueller, W. J. (1966). *Impact and change: A study of counseling relationships.* New York: Appleton-Century-Crofts.

Kelly, G. A. (1955). *The psychology of personal constructs* (2 vols). New York: Norton.

Kennard, B. D., Stewart, S. M., & Gluck, M. R. (1987). The supervision relationship: Variables contributing to positive versus negative experiences. *Professional Psychology: Research and Practice, 18,* 172–175.

Kerl, S. B., Garcia, J. L., McCullough, C. S., & Maxwell, M. E. (2002). Systematic evaluation of professional performance: Legally supported procedure and process. *Counselor Education and Supervision, 41,* 321–334.

Kerr, B. A., Claiborn, C. D., & Dixon, D. N. (1982). Training counselors in persuasion. *Counselor Education and Supervision, 22,* 138–148.

Kiesler, D. J. (1983). The 1982 Interpersonal Circle: A taxonomy for complementarity in human transactions. *Psychological Review, 90,* 185–214.

Killian, K. D. (2001). Differences making a difference: Cross-cultural interactions in supervisory relationships. *Journal of Feminist Family Therapy, 12*(2–3), 61–103.

King, D., & Wheeler, S. (1999). The responsibilities of counsellor supervisors: A qualitative study. *British Journal of Guidance and Counselling, 27*(2), 215–229.

Kinsella, J. A. (2000). Direct supervision: A computer feedback method used in the live supervision of first practicum marriage and family therapy students. *Dissertation Abstracts International: Section B: The Sciences & Engineering, 60*(9-B), 4870.

Kirschner, P. A., Sweller, J., & Clark, R. (2006). Why minimal guidance during instruction does not work: An analysis of the failure of constructivist, discovery, problem-based, experiential and inquiry-based teaching. *Educational Psychologist, 41*, 75–86.

Kitchener, K. S. (1984). Intuition, critical evaluation and ethical principles: The foundation for ethical decisions in counseling psychology. *The Counseling Psychologist, 12*, 43–55.

Kitchener, K. S. (1988). Dual role relationships: What makes them so problematic? *Journal of Counseling and Development, 67*, 217–221.

Kitzrow, M. A. (2001). Application of psychological type in clinical supervision. *The Clinical Supervisor, 20*(2), 133–146.

Kivlighan, D. M., Angelone, E. O., & Swafford, K. G. (1991). Live supervision in individual psychotherapy: Effects on therapist's intention use and client's evaluation of session effect and working alliance. *Journal of Counseling Psychology, 22*, 489–495.

Kleintjes, S., & Swartz, L. (1996). Black clinical psychology trainees at a "white" South African University: Issues for clinical supervision. *The Clinical Supervisor, 14*(1), 87–109.

Klitzke, M. J., & Lombardo, T. W. (1991). A "bug-in-the-eye" can be better than a "bug-in-the-ear": A teleprompter technique for on-line therapy skills training. *Behavior Modification, 15*, 113–117.

Knapp, S., & VandeCreek, L. (1997). Ethical and legal aspects of clinical supervision. In C. E. Watkins, Jr. (Ed.), *Handbook of Psychotherapy Supervision* (pp. 589–602). New York: Wiley.

Knapp, S. J., & VandeCreek, L. D. (2006). *Practical ethics for psychologists: A positive approach.* Washington, DC: American Psychological Association.

Knoff, H. M., & Prout, H. T. (1985). Terminating students from professional psychology programs: Criteria, procedures and legal issues. *Professional Psychology: Research and Practice, 16*, 789–797.

Knowles, Z., Gilbourne, D. Tomlinson, V., & Anderson, A. G. (2007). Reflections on the application of reflective practice for supervision in applied sport psychology. *The Sport Psychologist, 21*, 109–122.

Koch, L. C., Arhar, J. M., & Wells, L. M. (2000). Educating rehabilitation counseling students in reflective practice. *Rehabilitation Education, 14*, 255–268.

Koenig, T. L., & Spano, R. N. (2003). Sex, supervision, and boundary violations: Pressing challenges and possible solutions. *The Clinical Supervisor, 22*(1), 3–19.

Koerin, B., & Miller, J. (1995). Gate-keeping policies: Terminating students for nonacademic reasons. *Journal of Social Work Education, 31*, 247–260.

Kolbert, J. B., Morgan, B., & Brendel, J. M. (2002). Faculty and student perceptions of dual relationships within counselor education: A qualitative analysis. *Counselor Education and Supervision, 41*, 193–206.

Kollock, P., Blumstein, P., & Schwartz, P. (1985). Sex and power in interaction: Conversational privileges and duties. *American Sociological Review, 50*, 34–46.

Koob, J. J. (2002). The effects of solution-focused supervision on the perceived self-efficacy of therapists in training. *The Clinical Supervisor, 21*, 161–183.

Kopp, R. R., & Robles, L. (1989). A single-session, therapist-focused model of supervision of resistance based on Adlerian Psychology. *Individual Psychology, 45*, 212–219.

Kozlowska, K., Nunn, K., & Cousins, P. (1997). Adverse experiences in psychiatric training. Part 2. *Australian and New Zealand Journal of Psychiatry, 31*, 641–652.

Krause, A. A., & Allen, G. J. (1988). Perceptions of counselor supervision: An examination of Stoltenberg's model from the perspectives of supervisor and supervisee. *Journal of Counseling Psychology, 35*, 77–80.

Kruse, T. D., & Leddick, G. R. (2005, October). *A comparison of reflecting team techniques and live supervision.* Paper presented at the Association for Counselor Education and Supervision Conference, Pittsburgh, PA.

Kugler, P. (1995). *Jungian perspectives on clinical supervision.* Einsiedeln, Switzerland: Daimon.

Ladany, N., Brittan-Powell, C. S., & Pannu, R. K. (1997). The influence of supervisory racial identity interaction and racial matching on the supervisory working alliance and supervisee multicultural competence. *Counselor Education and Supervision, 36*, 284–304.

Ladany, N., Constantine, M. G., Miller, K., Erickson, C. D., & Muse-Burke, J. L. (2000). Supervisor countertransference: A qualitative investigation into its identification and description. *Journal of Counseling Psychology, 47*, 102–115.

Ladany, N., Ellis, M. V., & Friedlander, M. L. (1999). The supervisory working alliance, trainee self-efficacy, and satisfaction. *Journal of Counseling & Development, 77*, 447–455.

Ladany, N., & Friedlander, M. L. (1995). The relationship between the supervisory working alliance and trainees' experience of role conflict and role ambiguity. *Counselor Education and Supervision, 34,* 220–231.

Ladany, N., Friedlander, M. L., & Nelson, M. L. (2005). *Critical events in psychotherapy supervision: An interpersonal approach.* Washington, DC: American Psychological Association.

Ladany, N., Hill, C. E., Corbett, M. M., & Nutt, E. A. (1996). Nature, extent, and importance of what psychotherapy trainees do not disclose to their supervisors. *Journal of Counseling Psychology, 43,* 10–24.

Ladany, N., & Inman, A. G. (2008). Developments in counseling skills training and supervision. In S. D. Brown & R. W. Lent (Eds.), Handbook of counseling psychology (4th ed.). Hoboken, NJ: John Wiley.

Ladany, N., Inman, A. G., Constantine, M. G., & Hofheinz, E. W. (1997). Supervisee multicultural case conceptualization ability and self-reported multicultural competence as functions of supervisee racial identity and supervisor focus. *Journal of Counseling Psychology, 44,* 284–293.

Ladany, N., & Lehrman-Waterman, D. E. (1999). The content and frequency of supervisor self-disclosures and their relationship to supervisor style and the supervisory working alliance. *Counselor Education and Supervision, 38,* 143–160.

Ladany, N., Lehrman-Waterman, D., Molinaro, M., & Wolgast, B. (1999). Psychotherapy supervisor ethical practices: Adherence to guidelines, the supervisory working alliance, and supervisee satisfaction. *The Counseling Psychologist, 27,* 443–475.

Ladany, N., Marotta, S., & Muse-Burke, J. L. (2001). Counselor experience related to complexity of case conceptualization and supervision preference [Special issue]. *Counselor Education & Supervision, 40*(3), 203–219.

Ladany, N., & Melincoff, D. S. (1999). The nature of counselor supervisor nondisclosure. *Counselor Education & Supervision, 38,* 161–176.

Ladany, N., Walker, J. A., & Melincoff, D. S. (2001). Supervisory style: Its relation to the supervisory working-alliance and supervisor self-disclosure. *Counselor Education and Supervision, 40,* 263–275.

Ladmila, A. (1997). Shame, knowledge, and modes of inquiry in supervision. In G. Shipton (Ed.), *Supervision of psychotherapy and counseling: Making a place to think* (pp. 35–46). Philadelphia: Open University Press.

Lamb, D. H., & Catanzaro, S. J. (1998). Sexual and non-sexual boundary violations involving psychologists, clients, supervisees, and students: Implications for professional practice. *Professional Psychology: Research and Practice, 29,* 498–503.

Lamb, D. H., Catanzaro, S. J., & Moorman, A. S. (2003). Psychologists reflect on their sexual relationships with clients, supervisees, and students: Occurrence, impact, rationales and collegial intervention. *Professional Psychology: Research and Practice, 34,* 102–107.

Lamb, D. H., Catanzaro, S. J., & Moorman, A. S. (2004). A preliminary look at how psychologists identify, evaluate, and proceed when faced with possible multiple relationship dilemmas. *Professional Psychology: Research and Practice, 35,* 248–254.

Lamb, D. H., Cochran, D. J., & Jackson, V. R. (1991). Training and organizational issues associated with identifying and responding to intern impairment. *Professional Psychology: Research and Practice, 22,* 291–296.

Lamb, D. H., Presser, N., Pfost, K., Baum, M., Jackson, R., & Jarvis, P. (1987). Confronting professional impairment during the internship: Identification, due process, and remediation. *Professional Psychology: Research and Practice, 18,* 597–603.

Lamb, D. H., & Swerdlik, M. E. (2003). Identifying and responding to problematic school psychology supervisees: The evaluation process and issues of impairment. *The Clinical Supervisor, 22*(1), 87–110.

Lambert, M. E., & Meier, S. T. (1992). Utility of computerized case simulations in therapist training and evaluation. *Journal of Behavioral Education, 2,* 73–84.

Lambert, M. J. (1974). Supervisory and counseling process: A comparative study. *Counselor Education and Supervision, 14,* 54–60.

Lambert, M. J. (1980). Research and the supervisory process. In A. K. Hess (Ed.), *Psychotherapy supervision: Theory, research, and practice* (pp. 423–450). New York: John Wiley & Sons.

Lambert, M. J., & Arnold, R. C. (1987). Research and the supervision process. *Professional Psychology: Research and Practice, 18,* 217–224.

Lambert, M. J., Hansen, N. B., Umpress, V., Lunnen, K., Okiishi, J., & Burlingame, G. M. (1998). *Administration and scoring manual for the OQ-45.2.* American Professional Credentialing Service (e-mail: apcs@erols.com).

Lambert, M. J., & Ogles, B. M. (1997). The effectiveness of psychotherapy supervision. In C. E. Watkins, Jr. (Ed.), *Handbook of psychotherapy supervision* (pp. 421–446). New York: Wiley.

Lambert, M. J., Whipple, J. L., Smart, D. W., Vermeersch, D. A., Nielson, S. L., & Hawkins, E. J. (2001). The effects of providing therapists with feedback on patient progress during psychotherapy: Are outcomes enhanced? *Psychotherapy Research, 11,* 49–68.

Lampropoulos, G. K. (2002). A common factors view of counseling supervision process. *The Clinical Supervisor, 21,* 77–94.

Landis, L. L., & Young, M. E. (1994). The reflecting team in counselor education. Special section: Marriage and family training methods. *Counselor Education & Supervision, 33,* 210–218.

Lane, R. C. (1986). The recalcitrant supervisee: The negative supervisory reaction. *Current Issues in Psychoanalytic Practice, 2,* 65–81.

Lanning, W. L. (1971). A study of the relation between group and individual counseling supervision and three relationship measures. *Journal of Counseling Psychology, 18,* 401–406.

Lanning, W. (1986). Development of the supervisor emphasis rating form. *Counselor Education and Supervision, 25,* 191–196.

Larson, L. M., & Daniels, J. A. (1998). Review of the counseling self-efficacy literature. *The Counseling Psychologist, 26,* 179–218.

Larson, L. M., Suzuki, L. A., Gillespie, K. N., Potenza, M. T., Bechtel, M. A., & Toulouse, A. (1992). Development and validation of the Counseling Self-Estimate Inventory. *Journal of Counseling Psychology, 39,* 105–120.

Lawson, D. M. (1993). Supervision methods for addressing triangulation issues with counselors-in-training. *The Family Journal, 1,* 260–268.

Lawson, G., Hein, S. F., & Stuart, C. L. (in press). A qualitative investigation of supervisees' experiences of triadic supervision. *Journal of Counseling & Development.*

Lazarus, J. A. (1995). Ethical issues in doctor-patient sexual relationships. Special issue: Clinical Sexuality. *Psychiatric Clinics of North America, 18,* 55–70.

Lazovsky, R., & Shimoni, A. (2007). The on-site mentor of counseling interns: Perceptions of ideal role and actual role performance. *Journal of Counseling and Development, 85,* 303–314.

Leary, M. R., & Kowalski, R. M. (1990). Impression management: A literature review and two-component model. *Psychological Bulletin, 107,* 34–47.

Leary, T. (1957). *Interpersonal diagnosis of personality: A theory and a methodology for personality evaluation.* New York: Ronald Press.

Leddick, G. R. (1994). Counselor education clinics as community resources. In J. E. Myers (Ed.), *Developing and directing counselor education laboratories* (pp. 147–152). Alexandria, VA: ACA Press.

Leddick, G. R., & Bernard, J. M. (1980). The history of supervision: A critical review. *Counselor Education and Supervision, 19*(3), 186–196.

Lee, R. E., & Everett, C. A. (2004). *The integrative family therapy supervisor: A primer.* New York: Brunner-Routledge.

Lee, R. E., Nichols, D. P., Nichols, W. C., & Odom, T. (2004). Trends in family therapy supervision: The past 25 years and into the future. *Journal of Marital and Family Therapy, 30,* 61–69.

Lee, R. W., & Cashwell, C. S. (2001). Ethical issues in counseling supervision: A comparison of university and site supervisors. *The Clinical Supervisor, 20*(2), 91–100.

Lee, R. W., & Gillam, S. L. (2000). Legal and ethical issues involving the duty to warn: Implications for supervisors. *The Clinical Supervisor, 19*(1), 123–136.

Lee, S. R. (1997). A process study of student supervisory phone interventions in live supervision of marital therapy. *Dissertation Abstracts International: Section B: The Sciences and Engineering, 57*(8-B), 5332.

Lehrman-Waterman, D., & Ladany, N. (2001). Development and validation of the evaluation process within supervision inventory [Special issue]. *Journal of Counseling Psychology, 48*(2), 168–177.

Leonardelli, C. A., & Gratz, R. R. (1985). Roles and responsibilities in fieldwork experience: A social systems approach. *The Clinical Supervisor, 3*(3), 15–24.

Leong, F. T. L., & Wagner, N. S. (1994). Cross-cultural counseling supervision: What do we know? What do we need to know? *Counselor Education and Supervision, 34,* 117–131.

Lesser, R. M. (1983). Supervision: Illusions, anxieties, and questions. *Contemporary Psychoanalysis, 19,* 120–129.

Levenson, E. A. (1984). Follow the fox. In L. Caligor, P. M. Bromberg, & J. D. Meltzer (Eds.), *Clinical perspectives on the supervision of psychoanalysis and psychotherapy* (pp. 153–167). New York: Plenum Press.

Levine, F. M., & Tilker, H. A. (1974). A behavior modification approach to supervision and psychotherapy. *Psychotherapy: Theory, Research and Practice, 11,* 182–188.

Levinson, D. J. (1978). *The seasons of a man's life.* New York: Alfred A. Knopf, Inc.

Levy, L. H. (1983). Evaluation of students in clinical psychology programs: A program evaluation perspective. *Professional Practice: Research and Practice, 14,* 497–503.

Lewin, K. (1951). Field theory in social science; selected theoretical papers. D. Cartwright (ed.). New York: Harper & Row.

Lewis, B. L., Hatcher, R. L., & Pate, W. E., II. (2005). The practicum experience: A survey of practicum site coordinators. *Professional Psychology: Research and Practice, 36,* 291–298.

Lewis, G. J., Greenburg, S. L., & Hatch, D. B. (1988). Peer consultation groups for psychologists in private practice: A national survey. *Professional Psychology: Research and Practice, 9,* 81–86.

Lewis, H. B. (1971). *Shame and guilt in neurosis.* New York: International University Press.

Lewis, M. (2000). Self-conscious emotions: Embarrassment, pride, shame, and guilt. In M. Lewis & J. M. Haviland-Jones (Eds.), *Handbook of emotions* (pp. 623–636). New York: The Guilford Press.

Lewis, W. (1988). A supervision model for public agencies. *The Clinical Supervisor, 6*(2), 85–91.

Lewis, W., & Rohrbaugh, M. (1989). Live supervision by family therapists: A Virginia survey. *Journal of Marital and Family Therapy, 15,* 323–326.

Lewis, W. C. (2001). Transference in analysis and in supervision. In S. Gill (Ed.), *The supervisory alliance: Facilitating the psychotherapist's learning experience* (pp. 75–80). Northvale, NJ: Jason Aronson, Inc.

Lichtenberg, J. W., & Goodyear, R. K. (2000). The structure of supervisor-supervisee interactions. *Clinical Supervisor, 19*(2), 1–24.

Lichtenberg, J. W., Goodyear, R. K., & McCormick, K. (2000). The structure of supervisor-supervisee interactions. *The Clinical Supervisor, 19,* 1–24.

Liddle, B. (1986). Resistance in supervision: A response to perceived threat. *Counselor Education and Supervision, 26,* 117–127.

Liddle, H. A. (1988). Systemic supervision: Conceptual overlays and pragmatic guidelines. In H. A. Liddle, D. C. Breunlin, & R. C. Schwartz (Eds.), *Handbook of family therapy training and supervision* (pp. 153–171). New York: Guilford.

Liddle, H. A., Becker, D., & Diamond, G. M. (1997). Family rherapy supervision. In C. E. Watkins, Jr. (Ed.), *Handbook of psychotherapy supervision* (pp. 400–418). New York: John Wiley.

Liddle, H. A., Breunlin, D. C., Schwartz, R. C., & Constantine, J. A. (1984). Training family therapy supervisors: Issues of content, form and context. *Journal of Marital and Family Therapy, 10,* 139–150.

Liddle, H. A., Davidson, G., & Barrett, J. (1988). Outcome in live supervision: Trainee perspectives. In H. Liddle, D. Breunlin, & R. Schwartz (Eds.), *Handbook of family therapy training and supervision* (pp. 183–193). New York: Guilford Press.

Liddle, H. A., & Saba, G. W. (1983). On context replication: The isomorphic relationship of family therapy and family therapy training. *Journal of Strategic and Systemic Therapies, 2*(2), 3–ll.

Liddle, H. A., & Schwartz, R. C. (1983). Live supervision/consultation: Conceptual and pragmatic guidelines for family therapy trainers. *Family Process, 22,* 477–490.

Liese, B. S., & Beck, J. S. (1997). Cognitive therapy supervision. In C. E. Watkins, Jr. (Ed.), *Handbook of psychotherapy supervision* (pp. 114–133). New York: Wiley.

Lilienfeld, S. O., & Norcross, J. C. (2003, October 23). Colloquy live: The safety and efficacy of psychotherapy. *Chronicle of Higher Education.* Retrieved December 28, 2007, from http://chronicle.com/colloquylive/2003/10/psychotherapy/

Linehan, M. M. (1980). Supervision of behavior therapy. In A. K. Hess (Ed.), *Psychotherapy supervision: Theory, research and practice.* New York: Wiley.

Linton, J., & Hedstrom, S. (2006). An exploratory qualitative investigation of group processes in group supervision: Perceptions of master's-level practicum students. *Journal for Specialists in Group Work, 31,* 51–72.

Littrell, J. M., Lee-Borden, N., & Lorenz, J. A. (1979). A developmental framework for counseling supervision. *Counselor Education and Supervision, 19,* 119–136.

Lloyd, A. P. (1992). Dual relationship problems in counselor education. In B. Herlihy & G. Corey (Eds.), *Dual relationships in counseling* (pp. 59–64). Alexandria, VA: AACD.

Lochner, B. T., & Melchert, T. P. (1997). Relationship of cognitive style and theoretical orientation to psychology interns' preferences for supervision. *Journal of Counseling Psychology, 44*(2), 256–260.

Locke, L. D., & McCollum, E. E. (2001). Clients' views of live supervision and satisfaction with therapy. *Journal of Marital and Family Therapy, 27*(1), 129–133.

Loganbill, C., Hardy, E., & Delworth, U. (1982). Supervision: A conceptual model. *The Counseling Psychologist, 10,* 3–42.

Lopez, S. R. (1997). Cultural competence in psychotherapy: A guide for clinicians and their supervisors. In C. E. Watkins, Jr. (Ed.). *Handbook of psychotherapy supervision* (pp. 570–588). New York: John Wiley & Sons.

Lovell, C. (1999). Supervisee cognitive complexity and the Integrated Developmental Model. *Clinical Supervisor, 18*(1), 191–201.

Lower, R. B. (1972). Countertransference resistances in the supervisory relationship. *American Journal of Psychiatry, 129,* 156–160.

Lowy, L. (1983). Social work supervision: From models to theory. *Journal of Education for Social Work, 19*(2), 55–62.

Luepker, E. T. (2003). *Record keeping in psychotherapy and counseling: Protecting confidentiality and the professional relationship.* East Sussex, UK: Brunner-Routledge.

Luke, M., & Bernard, J. M. (2006). The School Counseling Supervision Model: An extension of the Discrimination Model. *Counselor Education and Supervision, 45,* 282–295.

Lumadue, C. A., & Duffey, T. H. (1999). The role of graduate programs as gatekeepers: A model for evaluating student counselor competence. *Counselor Education and Supervision, 39*(2), 101–109.

Magnuson, S. (1995). *Supervision of prelicensed counselors: A study of educators, supervisors, and supervisees.* Unpublished doctoral dissertation. University of Alabama.

Magnuson, S., Norem, K., & Wilcoxon, A. (2000). Clinical supervision of prelicensed counselors: Recommendations for consideration and practice. *Journal of Mental Health Counseling, 22*(2), 176–188.

Magnuson, S., Wilcoxon, S. A., & Norem, K. (2000). A profile of lousy supervision: Experienced counselors' perspectives. *Counselor Education and Supervision, 39,* 189–202.

Maher, A. R. (2005). *Supervision of psychotherapists: The discovery-oriented approach.* London: Whurr Publishers.

Maheu, M. M., & Gordon, B. L. (2000). Counseling and therapy on the Internet. *Professional Psychology: Research and Practice, 31,* 484–489.

Mahoney, M. (1974). *Cognition and behavior modification.* Cambridge, MA: Ballinger.

Mahoney, M. J. (1977). Reflections on the cognitive-learning trend in psychotherapy. *American Psychologist, 32,* 5–13.

Mahoney, M. J. (1991). *Human change processes: The scientific foundations of psychotherapy.* New York: Basic Books.

Maki, D. R., & Bernard, J. M. (2007). The ethics of clinical supervision. In R. R. Cottone & V. M. Tarvydas (Eds.), *Ethical and professional issues in counseling* (3rd ed., 347–368). Columbus, OH: Pearson Merrill Prentice Hall.

Maki, D. R., & Delworth, U. (1995). Clinical supervision: A definition and model for the rehabilitation counseling profession. *Rehabilitation Counseling Bulletin, 38,* 282–292.

Mallinckrodt, B., & Nelson, M. L. (1991). Counselor training level and the formation of the psychotherapeutic working alliance. *Journal of Counseling Psychology, 38,* 133–138.

Malouf, J. L., Haas, L. J., & Farah, M. J. (1983). Issues in the preparation of interns: Views of trainers and trainees. *Professional Psychology: Research and Practice, 14,* 624–631.

Manosevitz, M. (2006). Supervision by telephone: An innovation in psychoanalytic training—A roundtable discussion. *Psychoanalytic Psychology, 23,* 579–582.

Manzanares, M. G., O'Halloran, T. M., McCartney, T. J., Filer, R. D., Varhely, S. C., & Calhoun, K. (2004). CD-ROM technology for education and support of site supervisors. *Counselor Education and Supervision, 43,* 220–231.

Marek, L. I., Sandifer, D. M., Beach, A., Coward, R. L., & Protinsky, H. O. (1994). Supervision without the problem: A model of solution-focused supervision. *Journal of Family Psychotherapy, 5,* 57–64.

Markowski, E. M., & Cain, H. I. (1983). Live marital and family therapy supervision. *The Clinical Supervisor, 1*(3), 37–46.

Marks, J. L., & Hixon, D. F. (1986). Training agency staff through peer group supervision. *Social Casework, 67,* 418–423.

Martin, J. M. (1988). A proposal for researching possible relationships between scientific theories and the personal theories of counselors and clients. *Journal of Counseling and Development, 66,* 261–265.

Martin, J. M., Slemon, A. G., Hiebert, B., Hallberg, E. T., & Cummings, A. L. (1989). Conceptualizations of novice and experienced counselors. *Journal of Counseling Psychology, 36,* 395–400.

Martin, J. S., Goodyear, R. K., & Newton, F. B. (1987). Clinical supervision: An intensive case study.

Professional Psychology: Research and Practice, 18, 225–235.

Martino, C. (2001, August). Secrets of successful supervision: Graduate students' preferences and experiences with effective and ineffective supervision. In J. E. Barnett (Chair), *Secrets of successful supervision—Clinical and ethical issues.* Symposium conducted at the 109th Annual Convention of the American Psychological Association, San Francisco.

Matarazzo, R. G., & Patterson, D. R. (1986). Methods of teaching therapeutic skill. In S. L. Garfield & A. E. Bergin (Eds.), *Handbook of psychotherapy and behavior change* (3rd ed., pp. 821–843). New York: John Wiley & Sons.

Mathews, G. (1986). Performance appraisal in the human services: A survey. *The Clinical Supervisor, 3*(4), 47–6l.

Matthews, G., Davies, D. R., & Lees, J. L. (1990). Arousal, extraversion, and individual differences in resource availability. *Journal of Personality and Social Psychology, 59,* 150–168.

Mauzey, E., & Erdman, P. (1997). Trainee perceptions of live supervision phone-ins: A phenomenological inquiry. *Clinical Supervisor, 15*(2), 115–128.

Mauzey, E., Harris, M. B. C., & Trusty, J. (2000). Comparing the effects of live supervision interventions on novice trainee anxiety and anger [Special issue]. *Clinical Supervisor, 19*(2), 109–122.

McAdams, C. R., III, Foster, V. A., & Ward, T. J. (2007). Remediation and dismissal policies in counselor education: Lessons learned from a challenge in federal court. *Counselor Education and Supervision, 46,* 212–229.

McCarthy, P., Kulakowski, D., & Kenfield, J. A. (1994). Clinical supervision practices of licensed psychologists. *Professional Psychology: Research and Practice, 25,* 177–181.

McCarthy, P., Sugden, S., Koker, M., Lamendola, F., Maurer, S., & Renninger, S. (1995). A practical guide to informed consent in clinical supervision. *Counselor Education and Supervision, 35,* 130–138.

McColley, S. H., & Baker, E. L. (1982). Training activities and styles of beginning supervisors: A survey. *Professional Psychology, 13,* 283–292.

McCollum, E. (1995). Perspectives on live supervision: The supervisor's view. *Supervision Bulletin, 8*(2), 4.

McDaniel, S., Weber, T., & McKeever, J. (1983). Multiple theoretical approaches to supervision: Choices in family therapy training. *Family Process, 22,* 491–500.

McKenzie, P. N., Atkinson, B. J., Quinn, W. H., & Heath, A. W. (1986). Training and supervision in marriage and family therapy: A national survey. *American Journal of Family Therapy, 14,* 293–303.

McMahon, M., & Simons, R. (2004). Supervision training for professional counselors: An exploratory study. *Counselor Education and Supervision, 43,* 301–309.

McNamee, C. M., & McWey, L. M. (2004). Using bilateral art to facilitate clinical supervision. *The Arts in Psychotherapy, 31,* 229–243.

McNeill, B. W., Stoltenberg, C. D., & Pierce, R. A. (1985). Supervisee's perceptions of their development: A test of the counselor complexity model. *Journal of Counseling Psychology, 32,* 630–633.

McNeill, B. W., Stoltenberg, C. D., & Romans, J. S. (1992). The Integrated Developmental Model of supervision: Scale development and validation procedures. *Professional Psychology: Research & Practice, 23,* 504–508.

McNeill, B. W., & Worthen, V. (1989). The parallel process in psychotherapy supervision. *Professional Psychology: Research & Practice, 20,* 329–333.

McWilliams, N. (1994). *Psychoanalytic diagnosis: Understanding personality structure in the clinical process.* New York: The Guilford Press.

McWilliams, N. (2004). Some observations about supervision/consultation groups. *New Jersey Psychologist, Winter,* 16–18.

Mead, D. E. (1990). *Effective supervision: A task-oriented model for the mental health professions.* New York: Brunner/Mazel.

Mead, G. H. (1913). The social self. *Journal of Philosophy, Psychology, and Scientific Methods, 10,* 374–380.

Meichenbaum, D. (1977). *Cognitive-behavior modification.* New York: Plenum Press.

Menefee, D. S. (2007). *Perceptions of trainee attachment in the supervisory relationship.* Unpublished doctoral dissertation, University of Houston.

Messinger, L. (2004). Out in the field: Gay and lesbian social work students' experiences in field placement. *Journal of Social Work Education, 40,* 187–204.

Messinger, L. (2007). Supervision of lesbian, gay, and bisexual social work students by heterosexual field instructors: A qualitative dyad analysis. *The Clinical Supervisor, 26*(1.2), 195–222.

Meyer, R. G. (1980). Legal and procedural issues in the evaluation of clinical graduate students. *The Clinical Psychologist, 33,* 15–17.

Meyer, R. G., Landis, E. R., & Hays, J. R. (1988). *Law for the psychotherapist*. New York: W. W. Norton & Co.

Miars, R. D., Tracey, T. J., Ray, P. B., Cornfield, L., O'Farrell, M., & Gelso, C. J. (1983). Variation in supervision process across trainee experience levels. *Journal of Counseling Psychology, 30,* 403–412.

Michaelson, S. D., Estrada-Hernández, & Wadsworth, J. S. (2003). A competency-based evaluation model for supervising novice counselors-in-training. *Rehabilitation Education, 17,* 215–223.

Middleman, R. R., & Rhodes, G. B. (1985). *Competent supervision: Making imaginative judgments*. Englewood Cliffs, NJ: Prentice-Hall.

Miller, G. M., & Larrabee, M. J. (1995). Sexual intimacy in counselor education and supervision: A national survey. *Counselor Education and Supervision, 34,* 332–343.

Miller, K. L., Miller, S. M., & Evans, W. J. (2002). Computer-assisted live supervision in college counseling centers. *Journal of College Counseling, 5,* 187–192.

Miller, M. M., & Ivey, D. C. (2006). Spirituality, gender, and supervisory style in supervision. *Contemporary Family Therapy, 28,* 323–337.

Miller, S. B. (1996). *Shame in context*. Hillsdale, NJ: The Analytic Press.

Milne, D. (2006). Developing clinical supervision research through reasoned analogies with therapy. *Clinical Psychology and Psychotherapy, 13,* 215–222.

Milne, D. (2007). An empirical definition of clinical supervision. *British Journal of Clinical Psychology, 46,* 437–447.

Milne, D., & Aylott, H. (2006). An integrative model of clinical supervision, derived from a systematic review. Unpublished paper.

Milne, D., & James, I. (2000). A systematic review of effective cognitive-behavioral supervision. *British Journal of Clinical Psychology, 39,* 111–127.

Milne, D., & Westerman, C. (2001). Evidence-based clinical supervision: Rationale and illustration. *Clinical Psychology and Psychotherapy, 8,* 444–457.

Milne, D. L., & James, I. A. (2002). The observed impact of training on competence in clinical supervision. *British Journal of Clinical Psychology, 41*(1), 55–72.

Milne, D. L., & James, I. A. (1999). Evidence-based clinical supervision: Review and guidelines. *Clinical Psychology Forum, 133,* 32–36.

Milne, D. L., & James, I. A. (2005). Clinical supervision: Ten tests of the tandem model. *Clinical Psychology Forum, 151,* 6–9. Retrieved December 28, 2007, from http://www.bps.org.uk/downloadfile.cfm?file_uuid=2C9894A5-1143-DFD0-7E56-6AEC25CF5AB3&ext=pdf

Minuchin, S., & Fishman, C. (1981). *Family therapy techniques*. Cambridge, MA: Harvard Press.

Mitchell, R. W. (1991). *Documentation in counseling records*. Alexandria, VA: American Counseling Association Press.

Miyake, A., & Priti, S. (Eds.). (1999). *Working memory: Mechanisms of executive maintenance and active control*. Cambridge, U.K.: Cambridge University Press.

Mohl, P. C., Sadler, J. Z., & Miller, D. A. (1994). What components should be evaluated in a psychiatric residency. *Academic Psychiatry, 18,* 22–29.

Molnar, A., & de Shazer, S. (1987). Solution-focused therapy: Toward the identification of therapeutic tasks. *Journal of Marital and Family Therapy, 13,* 349–358.

Monks, G. M. (1996). A meta-analysis of role induction studies. *Dissertation Abstracts International: Section B: The Sciences & Engineering, 56*(12-B), Jun 1996, 7051.

Montalvo, B. (1973). Aspects of live supervision. *Family Process, 12,* 343–359.

Montgomery, L. M., Cupit, B. E., & Wimberley, T. K. (1999). Complaints, malpractice, and risk management: Professional issues and personal experiences. *Professional Psychology: Research and Practice, 30,* 402–410.

Montgomery, M. L., Hendricks, C. B., & Bradley, L. J. (2001). Using systems perspectives in supervision. *The Family Journal: Counseling and Therapy for Couples and Families, 9,* 305–313.

Moore, L. S., Dietz, T. J., & Dettlaff, A. J. (2004). Using the Myers-Briggs Type Indicator in field education supervision. *Journal of Social Work Education, 40,* 337–349.

Moorhouse, A., & Carr, A. (1999). The correlates of phone-in frequency, duration and the number of suggestions made in live supervision. *Journal of Family Therapy, 21*(4), 407–418.

Moorhouse, A., & Carr, A. (2001). A study of live supervisory phone-ins in collaborative family therapy: Correlates of client cooperation [Special issue]. *Journal of Marital and Family Therapy, 27*(2), 241–249.

Moorhouse, A., & Carr, A. (2002). Gender and conversational behavior in family therapy and life supervision. *Journal of Family Therapy, 24,* 46–56.

Morgan, M. M., & Sprenkle, D. H. (2007). Toward a common-factors approach to supervision. *Journal of Marital and Family Therapy, 33,* 1–17.

Mothersole, G. (1999). Parallel process: A review. *The Clinical Supervisor, 18,* 107–122.

Mueller, W. J. (1982). Issues in the application of "Supervision: A conceptual model" to dynamically oriented supervision: A reaction paper. *The Counseling Psychologist, 10,* 43–46.

Mueller, W. J., & Kell, B. L. (1972). *Coping with conflict: Supervising counselors and therapists.* New York: Appleton-Century-Crofts.

Mullen, J. A., Luke, M., & Drewes, A. (2007). Supervision can be playful too: Play therapy techniques that enhance supervision. *International Journal of Play Therapy, 16,* 69–85.

Munson, C. E. (1983). *An introduction to clinical social work supervision.* New York: Haworth Press.

Munson, C. E. (2002). *Handbook of clinical social work supervision* (3rd ed.). Binghamton, NY: Haworth Press, Inc.

Muratori, M. C. (2001). Examining supervisor impairment from the counselor trainee's perspective. *Counselor Education and Supervision, 41,* 41–56.

Murphy, J. A., Rawlings, E. I., & Howe, S. R. (2002). A survey of clinical psychologists on treating lesbian, gay, and bisexual clients. *Professional Psychology: Research and Practice, 33,* 183–189.

Murphy, J. W., & Pardeck, J. T. (1986). The "burnout syndrome" and management style. *Clinical Supervisor, 4,* 35–44.

Murphy, M. J., & Wright, D. W. (2005). Supervisees' perspectives of power use in supervision. *Journal of Marital and Family Therapy, 31,* 283–295.

Murray, G. C., Portman, T., & Maki, D. R. (2003). Clinical supervision: Developmental differences during pre-service training. *Rehabilitation Education, 17,* 19–32.

Muslin, H. L., Thurnblad, R. J., & Meschel, G. (1981). The fate of the clinical interview: An observational study. *American Journal of Psychiatry, 138,* 822–825.

Mutual Recognition Agreement of the Regulatory Bodies for Professional Psychologists in Canada. (2001, June). Retrieved December 28, 2007, From http://www.cpa.ca/cpasite/userfiles/documents/mra.pdf

Myers, I. B. (1962). *The Myers-Briggs Type Indicator.* Palo Alto, CA: Consulting Psychologists Press, Inc.

Myers, I. B., & McCaulley, M. H. (1985). *Manual: A guide to the development and use of the Myers-Briggs Type Indicator.* Palo Alto, CA: Consulting Psychologists Press.

Myers, J. E. (Ed.). (1994). *Developing and directing counselor education laboratories.* Alexandria, VA: ACA Press.

Myers, J. E., & Hutchinson, G. H. (1994). Dual role or conflict of interest? Clinics as mental health providers. In J. E. Myers (Ed.), *Developing and directing counselor education laboratories* (pp. 161–167). Alexandria, VA: ACA Press.

Nathanson, D. L. (1992). *Shame and pride: Affect, sex, and the birth of the self.* New York: W.W. Norton.

National Association of Social Workers. (1999). *Code of ethics* (rev. ed.). Washington, DC: Author.

National Board for Certified Counselors. (1993). *A work behavior analysis of professional counselors.* Greensboro, NC: Author.

Navin, S., Beamish, P., & Johanson, G. (1995). Ethical practices of field-based mental health counselor supervisors. *Journal of Mental Health Counseling, 17,* 243–253.

Neimeyer, R. A. (1995). An invitation to constructivist psychotherapies. In R. A. Neimeyer & M. J. Mahoney (Eds.), *Constructivism in psychotherapy* (pp. 1–8). Washington, DC: American Psychological Association.

Neiss, R. (1988). Reconceptualizing arousal: Psychobiological states in motor performance. *Psychological Bulletin, 103,* 345–366.

Nelson, M. L. (2002, October). *How to be a lousy supervisor: Lessons from the research.* Paper presented at the annual meeting of the Association for Counselor Education and Supervision, Park City, UT.

Nelson, M. L., & Friedlander, M. L. (2001). A close look at conflictual supervisory relationships: The trainee's perspective. *Journal of Counseling Psychology, 48,* 384–395.

Nelson, M. L., Gizara, S., Hope, A. C., Phelps, R., Steward, R., & Weitzman, L. (2006). A feminist multicultural perspective on supervision. *Journal of Multicultural Counseling and Development, 34,* 105–116.

Nelson, M. L., Gray, L. A., Friedlander, M. L., Ladany, N., & Walker, J. A. (2001). Toward relationship-centered supervision: Reply to Veach (2001) and

Ellis (2001). *Journal of Counseling Psychology, 48,* 407–409.

Nelson, M. L., & Holloway, E. L. (1990). Relation of gender to power and involvement in supervision. *Journal of Counseling Psychology, 37,* 473–481.

Nelson, M. L., & Neufeldt, S. A. (1998). The pedagogy of counseling: A critical examination. *Counselor Education and Supervision, 38,* 70–88.

Nelson, T. S. (1991). Gender in family therapy supervision. *Contemporary Family Therapy: An International Journal, 13,* 357–369.

Neufeldt, S. A. (1997). A social constructivist approach to counseling supervision. In T. E. Sexton & B. Griffin (Eds.), *Constructivist thinking in counseling research, practice, and supervision* (pp. 191–210). New York: Teachers' College Press.

Neufeldt, S. A. (1999). Training in reflective processes in supervision. In M. Carroll & E. L. Holloway (Eds.), *Education of clinical supervisors* (pp. 92–105). London: Sage.

Neufeldt, S. A., Iverson, J. N., & Juntunen, C. L. (1995). *Supervision strategies for the first practicum.* Alexandria, VA: American Counseling Assocation.

Neufeldt, S. A., Karno, M. P., & Nelson, M. L. (1996). A qualitative analysis of experts' conceptualization of supervisee reflectivity. *Journal of Counseling Psychology, 43,* 3–9.

Neufeldt, S. A., & Nelson, M. L. (1999). When is counseling an appropriate and ethical supervision function? *The Clinical Supervisor, 18,* 125–135.

Neukrug, E., Milliken, T., & Walden, S. (2001). Ethical complaints made against credentialed counselors: An updated survey of state licensing boards. *Counselor Education and Supervision, 41,* 57–70.

Neukrug, E. S. (1991). Computer-assisted live supervision in counselor skills training. *Counselor Education & Supervision, 31,* 132–138.

Nicholas, M. W. (1989). A systemic perspective of group therapy supervision: Use of energy in the supervisor-therapist-group system. *Journal of Independent Social Work, 3*(4), 27–39.

Nichols, M. (1984). *Family therapy: Concepts and methods.* New York: Gardner Press.

Nichols, W. C., Nichols, D. P., & Hardy, K. V. (1990). Supervision in family therapy: A decade restudy. *Journal of Marital and Family Therapy, 16,* 275–285.

Nigam, T., Cameron, P. M., & Leverette, J. S. (1997). Impasses in the supervisory process: A resident's perspective. *American Journal of Psychotherapy, 51,* 252–272.

Nilsson, J. E. (2007). International students in supervision: Course self-efficacy, stress, and cultural discussions in supervision. *The Clinical Supervisor, 16*(1/2), 35–47.

Nilsson, J. E., & Anderson, M. Z. (2004). Supervising international students: The role of acculturation, role ambiguity, and multicultural discussions. *Professional Psychology: Research and Practice, 35,* 306–312.

Nilsson, J. E., & Dodds, A. K. (2006). A pilot phase in the development of the international student supervision scale. *Journal of Multicultural Counseling and Development, 34,* 50–62.

Noelle, M. (2002). Self-report in supervision: Positive and negative slants. *Clinical Supervisor, 21,* 125–134.

Norcross, J. C., & Halgin, R. P. (1997). Integrative approaches to psychotherapy supervision. In J. C. E. Watkins (Ed.), *Handbook of psychotherapy supervision.* New York: Wiley.

Norcross, J. C., Hedges, M., & Castle, P. H. (2002). Psychologists conducting psychotherapy in 2001: A study of the division 29 membership. *Psychotherapy: Theory, research, practice, training, 39,* 97–102.

Norcross, J. C., & Napolitano, G. (1986). Defining our journal and ourselves. *International Journal of Eclectic Psychotherapy, 5,* 249–255.

O'Connor, T. S. J., Davis, A., Meakes, E., Pickering, R., & Schuman, M. (2004). Narrative therapy using a reflecting team: An ethnographic study of therapists' experiences. *Contemporary Family Therapy: An International Journal, 26,* 23–39.

O'Neil, J. M. (1981). Male sex-role conflicts, sexism, and masculinity: Implications for men, women, and the counseling psychologist. *The Counseling Psychologist, 9,* 61–80.

O'Neil, J. M., Good, G. E., & Holmes, S. (1995). Fifteen years of theory and research on men's gender role conflict. In R. F. Levant & W. S. Pollack (Eds.), *The new psychology of men* (pp. 164–206). New York: Basic Books.

O'Neil, J. M., Helms, B., Gable, R., David, L., & Wrightsman, L. (1986). Gender Role Conflict Scale: College men's fear of femininity. *Sex Roles, 14,* 335–350.

Ogloff, J. R. P., & Olley, M. C. (1998). The interaction between ethics and the law. The ongoing refinement of ethical standards for psychologists in Canada. *Professional Psychology: Research and Practice, 39,* 221–230.

Ögren, M. L., Jonsson, C. O., & Sundin, E. (2005). Group supervision in psychotherapy. The relationship between focus, group climate and perceived attained skill. *Journal of Clinical Psychology, 61*(4), 373–389.

Oliver, M. N. I., Bernstein, J. H., Anderson, K. G., Blashfield, R. K., & Roberts, M. C. (2004). An exploratory examination of student attitudes toward "impaired" peers in clinical psychology training programs. *Professional Psychology: Research and Practice, 35,* 141–147.

Olk, M., & Friedlander, M. L. (1992). Trainees' experiences of role conflict and role ambiguity in supervisory relationships. *Journal of Counseling Psychology, 39,* 389–397.

Olsen, D. C., & Stern, S. B. (1990). Issues in the development of a family therapy supervision model. *The Clinical Supervisor, 8*(2), 49–65.

Olsen, D. C., & Stern, S. B. (1990). Issues in the development of a family therapy supervision model. *Clinical Supervisor, 8*(2), 49–65.

Olson, M. M., Russell, C. S., & White, M. B. (2001). Technological implications for clinical supervision and practice. *The Clinical Supervisor, 20*(2), 201–215.

Orlinsky, D. E., Botermans, J. F., & Rønnestad, M. H. (2001). Towards an empirically grounded model of psychotherapy training: Four thousand therapists rate influences on their development. *Australian Psychologist, 36,* 139–148.

Orlinsky, D. E., Grawe, K., & Parks, B. K. (1994). Process and outcome in psychotherapy: Noch einmal. In A. E. Bergin & S. L. Garfield (Eds.), *Handbook of psychotherapy and behavior change* (3rd ed., pp. 270–376). New York: Wiley.

Osborn, C. J. (2004). Seven salutary suggestions for counselor stamina. *Journal of Counseling and Development, 82,* 319–328.

Osborn, C. J., & Davis, T. E. (1996). The supervision contract: Making it perfectly clear. *The Clinical Supervisor, 14*(2), 121–134.

Osborn, C. J., Paez, S. B., & Carrabine, C. L. (2007). Reflections on shared practices in a supervisory lineage. *The Clinical Supervisor, 26*(1/2), 119–139.

Osterberg, M. J. (1996). Gender in supervision: Exaggerating the differences between men and women. *The Clinical Supervisor, 14*(2), 69–83.

Overholser, J. C., & Fine, M. A. (1990). Defining the boundaries of professional competence: Managing subtle cases of clinical incompetence. *Professional Psychology: Research and Practice, 21,* 462–469.

Pack-Brown, S. P., & William, C. B. (2003). *Ethics in a multicultural context.* Thousand Oaks, CA: Sage Publications.

Page, S., & Wosket, V. (1994). *Supervising the counsellor: A cyclical model.* London: Routledge.

Page, S., & Woskett, V. (2001). *Supervising the counselor: A cyclical model.* London: Brunner-Routledge.

Panos, P. T. (2005). A model for using videoconferencing technology to support international social work field practicum students. *International Social Work, 48,* 834–841.

Panos, P. T., Roby, J. L., Panos, A., Matheson, K. W., & Cox, S. E. (2002). Ethical issues concerning the use of videoconferencing to supervise international social work field practicum students. *Journal of Social Work Education, 38,* 421–437.

Parry, A. (1991). A universe of stories. *Family Process, 30,* 37–50.

Parry, A., & Doan, R. E. (1994). *Story re-visions: Narrative therapy in the postmodern world.* New York: Guilford.

Patrick, K. D. (1989). Unique ethical dilemmas in counselor training. *Counselor Education and Supervision, 28,* 337–341.

Patterson, C. H. (1964). Supervising students in the counseling practicum. *Journal of Counseling Psychology, 11,* 47–53.

Patterson, C. H. (1983). Supervision in counseling: II. Contemporary models of supervision: A client-centered approach to supervision. *The Counseling Psychologist, 11*(1), 21–25.

Patton, M. J., & Kivlighan, Jr., D. M. (1997). Relevance of the supervisory alliance to the counseling alliance and to treatment adherence in counselor training. *Journal of Counseling Psychology, 44,* 108–115.

Patton, M. J., Kivlighan, Jr., D. M., & Multon, K. D. (1997). The Missouri psychoanalytic counseling research project: Relation of changes in counseling process to client outcomes. *Journal of Counseling Psychology, 44,* 189–208.

Peace, S. D., & Sprinthall, N. A. (1998). Training school counselors to supervise beginning counselors: Theory, research, and practice. *Professional School Counseling, 1*(5), 2–8.

Pearson, B., & Piazza, N. (1997). Classification of dual relationships in the helping professions. *Counselor Education and Supervision, 37*(2), 89–99.

Pearson, Q. M. (2000). Opportunities and challenges in the supervisory relationship: Implications for counselor supervision. *Journal of Mental Health Counseling, 22,* 283–294.

Pedersen, P. B. (1991). Multiculturalism as a generic approach to counseling. *Journal of Counseling and Development, 70,* 6–12.

Peleg-Oren, N. & Even-Zahav, R. (2004). Why do field supervisors drop out of student supervision? *The Clinical Supervisor, 23*(2), 15–30.

Penman, R. (1980). *Communication processes and relationships.* London: Academic Press.

Perlesz, A. J., Stolk, Y., & Firestone, A. F. (1990). Patterns of learning in family therapy training. *Family Process, 29,* 29–44.

Perris, C. (1994). Supervising cognitive psychotherapy and training supervisors. *Journal of Cognitive Psychotherapy, 8,* 83–103.

Perry, W. G., Jr. (1970). *Forms of intellectual and ethical development in the college years.* New York: Holt, Rinehart, and Winston.

Perry, W. G., Jr. (1981). Cognitive and ethical growth: The making of meaning. In A. W. Chickering (Ed.), *The modern American college* (pp. 76–116). New York: Jossey-Bass.

Peterson, M. (1993). Covert agendas in supervision. *The Supervision Bulletin, VI* (1), 1, 7–8.

Peterson, R. (2002, November 7). Discussant. Panel discussion: Landscapes. (M. Willmuth, Chair.) APPIC Competencies Conference, Scottsdale, AZ.

Petty, R. E., & Cacioppo, J. T. (1986). *Communication and persuasion: Central and peripheral routes to attitude change.* New York: Springer-Verlag.

Pfohl, A. H. (2004). The intersection of personal and professional identity: The heterosexual supervisor's role in fostering the development of sexual minority supervisees. *The Clinical Supervisor, 23*(1), 139–164.

Philp, K. M., Guy, G. E., & Lowe, R. D. (2007). Social constructionist supervision or supervision as social construction? Some dilemmas. *Journal of Systemic Therapies, 26,* 51–62.

Pierce, R. M., & Schauble, P. G. (1970). Graduate training of facilitative counselors: The effects of individual supervision. *Journal of Counseling Psychology, 17,* 210–215.

Pierce, R. M., & Schauble, P. G. (1971). Toward the development of facilitative counselors: The effects of practicum instruction and individual supervision. *Journal of Counseling Psychology, 17,* 210–215.

Piercy, F. P., Sprenkle, D. H., & Constantine, J. A. (1986). Family members' perceptions of live, observation/supervision: An exploratory study. *Contemporary Family Therapy, 8,* 171–187.

Pilkington, N. W., & Cantor, J. M. (1996). Perceptions of heterosexual bias in professional psychology programs. *Professional Psychology: Research and Practice, 27,* 604–612.

Pinsof, W. M., & Wynne, L. C. (1995). The efficacy of marital and family therapy: An empirical overview, conclusions, and recommendations. *Journal of Marital and Family Therapy, 21,* 585–613.

Pistole, M. C., & Watkins, C. E. (1995). Attachment theory, counseling process, and supervision. *The Counseling Psychologist, 23,* 457–478.

Poertner, J. (1986). The use of client feedback to improve practice: Defining the supervisor's role. *The Clinical Supervisor, 4*(4), 57–67.

Polanski, P. J. (2003). Spirituality in supervision. *Counseling and Values, 47,* 131–141.

Polkinghorne, D. (1988). *Narrative knowing and the human sciences.* Albany, NY: State University of New York Press.

Ponterotto, J. G. (1987). Client hospitalization: Issues and considerations for the counselor. *Journal of Counseling and Development, 65,* 542–546.

Pope, K. S., & Bajt, T. R. (1988). When laws and values conflict: A dilemma for psychologists. *American Psychologist, 45,* 1066–1070.

Pope, K. S., Levenson, H., & Schover, L. R. (1979). Sexual intimacy in psychology training: Results and implications of a national survey. *American Psychologist, 34,* 682–689.

Pope, K. S., Spiegel, K. P., & Tabachnik, B. G. (1986). Sexual attraction to clients: The human therapist and the sometimes inhuman training system. *American Psychologist, 41,* 147–158.

Pope, K. S., Tabachnik, B. G., & Spiegel, P. K. (1987). Ethics of practice: The beliefs and behaviors of psychologists and therapists. *American Psychologist, 42,* 993–1006.

Pope, K. S., & Vasquez, M. J. T. (1991). *Ethics in psychotherapy and counseling: A practical guide for psychologists.* San Francisco: Jossey-Bass.

Pope, K. S., & Vasquez, M. J. T. (2007). *Ethics in psychotherapy and counseling: A practical guide* (3rd ed.). San Francisco, CA: Jossey-Bass.

Pope, K. S., & Vetter, V. A. (1992). Ethical dilemmas encountered by members of the American

Psychological Association. *American Psychologist, 47*, 397–411.

Popper, K. (1959). *The logic of scientific discovery*. London: Hutchinson. (Original work published 1935)

Popper, K. (1968). Predicting overt behavior versus predicting hidden states. *Behavioral & Brain Sciences, 9*, 254.

Porter, N. (1994). Empowering supervisees to empower others: A culturally responsive supervision model. *Hispanic Journal of Behavioral Sciences, 16*, 43–56.

Porter, N., & Vasquez, M. (1997). Covision: Feminist supervision, process, and collaboration. In J. Worell & N. G. Johnson (Eds.), *Shaping the future of feminist psychology: Education, research, and practice*. Washington, DC: American Psychological Association.

Presbury, J., Echterling, L. G., & McKee, J. E. (1999). Supervision for inner-vision: Solution-focused strategies. *Counselor Education and Supervision, 39*, 146–155.

Prest, L. A., Darden, E. C., & Keller, J. F. (1990). "The fly on the wall" reflecting team supervision. *Journal of Marital and Family Therapy, 16*, 265–273.

Prest, L. A., Russel, R., & D'Souza, H. (1999). Spirituality and religion in training, practice, and personal development. *Journal of Family Therapy, 21*, 60–78.

Price, D. (1963). *Little science, big science*. New York: Columbia University Press.

Priest, R. (1994). Minority supervisor and majority supervisee: Another perspective of reality. *Counselor Education and Supervision, 34*, 152–158.

Prieto, L. R. (1996). Group supervision: Still widely practiced but poorly understood. *Counselor Education and Supervision, 35*, 295–307.

Prieto, L. R. (1998). Practicum class supervision in CACREP-accredited counselor training programs: A national survey. *Counselor Education and Supervision, 38*, 113–123.

Proctor, B. (1986). Supervision: A co-operative exercise in accountability. In A. Marken & M. Payne (Eds.), *Enabling and ensuring: Supervision in practice*. Leicester National Youth Bureau/Council for Education and Training in Youth and Community Work.

Proctor, B. (1991). On being a trainer. In W. Dryden & B. Thorne (Eds.), *Training and supervision for counselling in action* (pp. 49–73). London: Sage Publications.

Proctor, B. (2000). *Group supervision: A guide to creative practice*. London: Sage Publications.

Proctor, B., & Inskipp, F. (1988). *Skills for supervising and being supervised*. Sussex, U.K.: Alexia Publications.

Proctor, B., & Inskipp, F. (2001). Group supervision. In J. Scaife (Ed.), *Supervision in the mental health professions: A practitioner's guide* (pp. 99–121). London: Routledge.

Protinsky, H., & Preli, R. (1987). Interventions in strategic supervision. *Journal of Strategic and Systemic Therapies, 6*(3), 18–23.

Prouty, A. (2001). Experiencing feminist family therapy supervision. *Journal of Feminist Family Therapy, 12*, 171–203.

Prouty, A. M., Thomas, V., Johnson, S., & Long, J. K. (2001). Methods of feminist family therapy supervision. *Journal of Marital and Family Therapy, 27*, 85–97.

Putney, M. W., Worthington, E. L., & McCulloughy, M. E. (1992). Effects of supervisor and supervisee theoretical orientation and supervisor-supervisee matching on interns' perceptions of supervision. *Journal of Counseling Psychology, 39*, 258–265.

Quarto, C. J. (2002). Supervisors' and supervisees' perceptions of control and conflict in counseling supervision. *The Clinical Supervisor, 21*, 21–37.

Quinn, W. H., Atkinson, B. J., & Hood, C. J. (1985). The stuck-case clinic as a group supervision model. *Journal of Marital and Family Therapy, 11*, 67–73.

Rabinowitz, F. E., Heppner, P. P., & Roehlke, H. J. (1986). Descriptive study of process and outcome variables of supervision over time. *Journal of Counseling Psychology*, 292–300.

Raiger, J. (2005). Applying a cultural lens to the concept of burnout. *Journal of Transcultural Nursing, 16*, 71–76.

Raimy, V. C. (Ed.). (1950). *Training in clinical psychology*. New York: Prentice-Hall.

Ramos-Sanchez, L., Esnil, E., Goodwin, A., Riggs, S., Touster, L. O., Wright, L. K., Ratanasiripong, P., & Rodolfa, E. (2002). Negative supervisory events: Effects on supervision and supervisory alliance. *Professional Psychology: Research and Practice, 33*, 197–202.

Ratliff, D. A., Wampler, K. S., & Morris, G. H. B. (2000). Lack of consensus in supervision. *Journal of Marital & Family Therapy, 26*(3), 373–384.

Ray, D., & Altekruse, M. (2000). Effectiveness of group supervision versus combined group and individual supervision. *Counselor Education & Supervision, 40*(1), 19–30.

Recupero, P. R., & Rainey, S. E. (2007). Liability and risk management in outpatient psychotherapy supervision. *The Journal of the American Academy of Psychiatry and the Law, 35,* 188–195.

Reid, E., McDaniel, S., Donaldson, C., & Tollers, M. (1987). Taking it personally: Issues of personal authority and competence for the female in family therapy training. *Journal of Marital and Family Therapy, 13,* 157–165.

Reising, G. N., & Daniels, M. H. (1983). A study of Hogan's model of counselor development and supervision. *Journal of Counseling Psychology, 30,* 235–244.

Remley, T. R., Jr., & Herlihy, B. (2001). *Ethical, legal, and professional issues in counseling.* Upper Saddle River, NJ: Prentice-Hall.

Renfro-Michel, E. L. (2006). *The relationship between counseling supervisee attachment orientation and supervision working alliance.* Unpublished doctoral dissertation, Mississippi State University. Retrieved December 28, 2007, from http://sun.library.msstate.edu/ETD-db/theses/available/etd-04102006–111609/

Resnick, R. F., & Estrup, L. (2000). Supervision: A collaborative endeavor. *Gestalt Review, 4,* 121–137.

Retzinger, S. M. (1998). Shame in the therapeutic relationship. In P. Gilbert & B. Andrews (Eds.), *Shame: Interpersonal behavior, psychopathology, and culture* (pp. 206–222). New York: Oxford University Press.

Rice, L. N. (1980). A client-centered approach to the supervision of psychotherapy. In A. K. Hess (Ed.), *Psychotherapy supervision: Theory, research and practice* (pp. 136–147). New York: Wiley.

Richardson, B. K., & Bradley, L. J. (1984). Microsupervision: A skill development model for training clinical supervisors. *The Clinical Supervisor, 2*(3), 43–54.

Richman, J. M., Aitken, D., & Prather, D. L. (1990). In-therapy consultation: A supervisory and therapeutic experience from practice. *The Clinical Supervisor, 8*(2), 81–89.

Rickert, V. L., & Turner, J. E. (1978). Through the looking glass: Supervision in family therapy. *Social Casework, 59,* 131–137.

Rigazio-DiGilio, S. A. (1995). The four SCDS cognitive-developmental orientations. Unpublished document.

Rigazio-DiGilio, S. A. (1997). Integrative supervision: Pathways to tailoring the supervisory process. In T. C. Todd & C. L. Storm (Eds.), *The complete systemic supervisor: Context, philosophy, and pragmatics* (pp. 195–216). Needham Heights, MA: Allyn & Bacon.

Rigazio-DiGilio, S. A. (1998). Toward a reconstructed view of counselor supervision. *Counselor Education and Supervision, 38,* 43–51.

Rigazio-DiGilio, S. A., & Anderson, S. A. (1994). A cognitive-developmental model for marital and family therapy supervision. *The Clinical Supervisor, 12*(2), 93–118.

Rigazio-DiGilio, S. A., Daniels, T. G., & Ivey, A. E. (1997). Systemic Cognitive-Developmental Supervision: A developmental-integrative approach to psychotherapy supervision. In C. E. Watkins, Jr. (Ed.), *Handbook of psychotherapy supervision* (pp. 223–249). New York: John Wiley & Sons, Inc.

Rinas, J., & Clyne-Jackson, S. (1988). *Professional conduct and legal concerns in mental health practice.* Norwalk, CT: Appleton & Lange.

Rioch, M. J., Coulter, W. R., & Weinberger, D. M. (1976). *Dialogues for therapists: Dynamics of learning and supervision.* San Francisco: Jossey-Bass.

Rita, E. S. (1998). Solution-focused supervision. *Clinical Supervisor, 17*(2), 127–139.

Riva, M. T., & Cornish, J. A. E. (1995). Group supervision practices at psychology predoctoral internship programs: A national survey. *Professional Psychology: Research and Practice, 26,* 523–525.

Riva, M. T., & Cornish, J. A. E. (2008). Group supervision practices at psychology predoctoral internship programs: 15 years later. *Training and Education in Professional Psychology, 2,* 18–25.

Roberts, J. (1997). Reflecting processes and "supervision": Looking at ourselves as we work with others. In T. C. Todd & C. L. Storm (Eds.), *The complete systemic supervisor: Context, philosophy, and pragmatics* (pp. 334–348). Boston: Allyn & Bacon.

Roberts, W. B., Morotti, A. A., Herrick, C., & Tilbury, R. (2001). Site supervisors of professional school counseling interns: Suggested guidelines. *Professional School Counseling, 4,* 208–215.

Robiner, W. N., Fuhrman, M., & Ristvedt, S. (1993). Evaluation difficulties in supervising psychology interns. *The Clinical Psychologist, 46,* 3–13.

Robiner, W. N., Fuhrman, M., Ristvedt, S. L., Bobbit, B., & Schirvar, J. (1994). The Minnesota Supervisory Inventory (MSI): Development, psychometric characteristics, and supervisory evaluation issues. *Clinical Psychologist, 47,* 4–17.

Robiner, W. N., Saltzman, S. R., Hoberman, H. M., Semrud-Clikeman, M., & Schirvar, J. A. (1997). Psychology supervisors' bias in evaluations and letters of recommendation. *Clinical Supervisor, 16*(2), 49–72.

Robinson, W. L., & Reid, P. T. (1985). Sexual intimacies in psychology revisited. *Professional Psychology: Research and Practice, 16,* 512–520.

Robyak, J. E., Goodyear, R. K., & Prange, M. (1987). Effects of supervisors' sex, focus, and experience on preferences for interpersonal power bases. *Counselor Education and Supervision, 26,* 299–309.

Rock, M. L. (1997). Effective supervision. In M. R. Rock (Ed.), *Psychodynamic supervision: Perspectives of the supervisor and supervisee* (pp. 107–132). Northvale, NJ: Jason Aronson, Inc.

Rodenhauser, P. (1994). Toward a multidimensional model for psychotherapy supervision based on developmental stages. *Journal of Psychotherapy Practice and Research, 3,* 1–15.

Rodenhauser, P. (1997). Psychotherapy supervision: Prerequisites and problems in the process. In C. E. Watkins (Ed.), *Handbook of psychotherapy supervision* (pp. 527–548). New York: John Wiley.

Rodolfa, E., Bent, R., Eisman, E., Nelson, P., Rehm, L., & Ritchie, P. (2005). A cube model for competency development: Implications for psychology educators and regulators. *Professional Psychology: Research and Practice, 36,* 347–354.

Rodolfa, E., Rowen, H., Steier, D., Nicassio, T., & Gordon, J. (1994). Sexual dilemmas in internship training: What's a good training director to do? *APPIC Newsletter, 19*(2), 1, 22–24.

Rodway, M. R. (1991). Motivation and team building of supervisors in a multi-service setting. *The Clinical Supervisor, 9*(2), 161–169.

Rogers, C. R. (1942). The use of electrically recorded interviews in improving psychotherapeutic techniques. *American Journal of Orthopsychiatry, 12,* 429–434.

Rogers, C. R. (1951). *Client-centered therapy.* Boston: Houghton-Mifflin.

Rogers, C. R. (1957). Training individuals to engage in the therapeutic process. In C. R. Strother (Ed.), *Psychology and mental health* (pp. 76–92). Washington, DC: American Psychological Association.

Rogers, C. R., Gendlin, E. T., Kiesler, D. J., & Truax, C. B. (Eds.). (1967). *The therapeutic relationship and its impact: A study of psychotherapy with schizophrenics.* Madison: University of Wisconsin Press.

Rogers, G., & McDonald, P. L. (1995). Expedience over education: Teaching methods used by field instructors. *The Clinical Supervisor, 13*(2), 41–65.

Romans, J. S. C., Boswell, D. L., Carlozzi, A. F., & Ferguson, D. B. (1995). Training and supervision practices in clinical, counseling, and school psychology programs. *Professional Psychology: Research and Practice, 26,* 407–412.

Rønnestad, M. H., Orlinsky, D. E., Parks, B. K., & Davis, J. D. (1997). Supervisors of psychotherapy: Mapping experience level and supervisory confidence. *European Psychologist, 2,* 191–201.

Rønnestad, M. H., & Skovholt, T. M. (1993). Supervision of beginning and advanced graduate students of counseling and psychotherapy. *Journal of Counseling and Development, 71,* 396–405.

Rønnestad, M. H., & Skovholt, T. M. (2003). The journey of the counselor and therapist: Research findings and perspectives on professional development. *Journal of Career Development, 30,* 5–44.

Rosenbaum, M., & Ronen, T. (1998). Clinical supervision from the standpoint of cognitive-behavior therapy. *Psychotherapy: Theory, Research, Practice, Training, 35,* 220–230.

Rosenberg, J. I. (2006). Real-time training: Transfer of knowledge through computer-mediated, real-time feedback. *Professional Psychology: Research and Practice, 37,* 539–546.

Rosenberg, J. I., Getzelman, M. A., Arcinue, F., & Oren, C. Z. (2005). An exploratory look at students' experiences of problematic peers in academic professional psychology programs. *Professional Psychology: Research and Practice, 36,* 665–673.

Rosenblum, A. F., & Raphael, F. B. (1987). Students at risk in the field practicum and implications for field teaching. *The Clinical Supervisor, 5*(3), 53–63.

Rosenthal, L. (1999). Group supervision of groups: A modern analytic perspective. *International Journal of Group Psychotherapy, 49,* 197–213.

Rosenzweig, S. (1936). Some implicit common factors in diverse methods of psychotherapy. *American Journal of Orthopsychiatry, 6,* 412–415.

Ross, L. (1977). The intuitive psychologist and his shortcomings: Distortions in the attribution process. In L. Berkowitz (Ed.), *Advances in experimental social psychology* (Vol. 10). New York: Academic Press.

Rubel, D., & Okech, A. J (2006). The supervision of group work model: Adapting the Discrimination Model for supervision of group workers. *Journal for Specialists in Group Work, 31,* 113–134.

Rubinstein, M., & Hammond, D. (1982). The use of videotape in psychotherapy supervision. In M. Blumenfield (Ed.), *Applied supervision in psychotherapy* (pp. 143–164). New York: Grune & Stratton.

Rudolph, B., Craig, R., Leifer, M., & Rubin, N. (1998). Evaluating competency in the diagnostic interview among graduate psychology students: Development of generic scales. *Professional Psychology: Research and Practice, 29,* 488–491.

Russell, C. S., & Peterson, C. M. (2003). Student impairment and remediations in accredited marriage and family therapy programs. *Journal of Marital and Family Therapy, 29,* 329–337.

Russell, C. S., DuPree, W. J., Beggs, M. A., Peterson, C. M., & Anderson, M. P. (2007). Responding to remediation and gatekeeping challenges in supervision. *Journal of Marital and Family Therapy, 33,* 227–244.

Russell, G. M., & Greenhouse, E. M. (1997). Homophobia in the supervisory relationship: An invisible intruder. *Psychoanalytic Review, 84*(1), 27–42.

Russell, R. K., Crimmings, A. M., & Lent, R. W. (1984). Counselor training and supervision: Theory and research. In S. D. Brown & R. W. Lent (Ed.), *Handbook of counseling psychology* (pp. 625–681). New York: John Wiley & Sons.

Russell, R. K., & Petrie, T. (1994). Issues in training effective supervisors. *Applied and Preventive Psychology, 3,* 27–42.

Ryde, J. (2000). Supervising across difference. *International Journal of Psychotherapy, 5*(1), 37–48.

Ryder, R., & Hepworth, J. (1990). AAMFT ethical code: "Dual relationships." *Journal of Marital and Family Therapy, 16,* 127–132.

Saba, G. W. (1999). Live supervision: Lessons learned from behind the mirror. *Academic Medicine: Journal of the Association of American Medical Colleges, 74,* 856–858.

Safran, J. D., & Muran, J. C. (1996). The resolution of ruptures in the therapeutic alliance. *Journal of Consulting and Clinical Psychology, 64,* 447–458.

Safran, J. D., & Muran, J. C. (2000). Resolving therapeutic alliance ruptures: Diversity and integration. *Journal of Clinical Psychology: In Session: Psychotherapy in Practice, 56,* 233–243.

Safran, J. D., & Muran, J. C. (2001). A Relational approach to training and supervision in cognitive psychotherapy. *Journal of Cognitive Psychotherapy: An International Quarterly, 15,* 3–15.

Sagrestano, L. M. (1992). Power strategies in interpersonal relationships. *Psychology of Women Quarterly, 16,* 439–447.

Sakinofsky, I. (1979). Evaluating the competence of psychotherapists. *Canadian Journal of Psychiatry, 24,* 193–205.

Sampson, J. P., Kolodinsky, R. W., & Greeno, B. P. (1997). Counseling on the information highway: Future possibilities and potential problems. *Journal of Counseling and Development, 75,* 203–212.

Samuel, S. E., & Gorton, G. E. (1998). National survey of psychology internship directors regarding education for prevention of psychologist-patient sexual exploitation. *Professional Psychology: Research and Practice, 29,* 86–90.

Sansbury, D. L. (1982). Developmental supervision from a skill perspective. *The Counseling Psychologist, 10*(1), 53–57.

Sapyta, J., Riemer, M., & Bickman, L. (2005). Feedback to clinicians: Theory, research, and practice. *Journal of Clinical Psychology, 61,* 145–153.

Sarnat, J. E., & Frawley-O'Dea, M. G. (2001, April). *Supervisory relationship: Contemporary psychodynamic approach.* Discussion hour (S. A. Pizer, moderator) at the 21st Annual Spring meeting of the APA Division of Psychoanalysis, Sante Fe, NM.

Saxe, J. D. (1865). The blind men and the elephant. In *Clever stories of many nations.* Boston: Ticknor and Fields. Retrieved January 1, 2008, from http://www.noogenesis.com/pineapple/blind_men_elephant.html

Scanlon, C. R., & Gold, J. M. (1996). The balance between the missions of training and service at a university counseling center. *The Clinical Supervisor, 14*(1), 163–173.

Scarborough, J. L., Bernard, J. M., & Morse, R. E. (2006). Boundary considerations between doctoral students and master's students. *Counseling and Values, 51,* 53–65.

Schacht, A. J., Howe, H. E., & Berman, J. J. (1989). Supervisor facilitative conditions and effectiveness as perceived by thinking- and feeling-type supervisees. *Psychotherapy, 26,* 475–483.

Schein, E. (1973). *Professional education.* New York: McGraw-Hill.

Schermer, M. (2002). Introduction: Colorful Pebbles and Darwin's Dictum. In M. Schermer (Ed.), *The Skeptic Encyclopedia of Pseudoscience.* Santa Barbara, CA: ABC-Clio, Inc.

Schimel, J. L. (1984). In pursuit of truth: An essay on an epistemological approach to psychoanalytic supervision. In L. Caligor, P. M. Bromberg, & J. D. Meltzer (Eds.), *Clinical perspectives on the supervision of psychoanalysis and psychotherapy* (pp. 231–241). New York: Plenum Press.

Schlenker, B. R. (1980). *Impression management: The self-concept, social identity, and interpersonal relations.* Monterey, Calif.: Brooks/Cole Pub. Co.

Schlenker, B. R., & Leary, M. R. (1982). Social anxiety and self-presentation: A conceptualization and model. *Psychological Bulletin, 92,* 641–669.

Schmidt, J. P. (1979). Psychotherapy supervision: A cognitive-behavioral model. *Professional Psychology, l0,* 278–284.

Schneider, S. (1992). Transference, counter-transference, projective identification and role responsiveness in the supervisory process. *The Clinical Supervisor, 10*(2), 71–84.

Schön, D. (1983). *The reflective practitioner: How professionals think in action.* New York: Basic Books.

Schön, D. (1987). *Educating the reflective practitioner.* San Francisco: Jossey-Bass.

Schrag, K. (1994). Disclosing homosexuality. *The Supervisor Bulletin, VII*(1), 3, 7.

Schreiber, P., & Frank, E. (1983). The use of a peer supervision group by social work clinicians. *The Clinical Supervisor, 1*(1), 29–36.

Schroll, J. T., & Walton, R. N. (1991). The interaction of supervision needs with technique and context in the practice of live supervision. *The Clinical Supervisor, 9*(1), 1–14.

Schultz, J. C., & Finger, C. (2003). Distance-based clinical supervision: Suggestions for technology utilization. *Rehabilitation Education, 17,* 95–99.

Schultz, J. C., Ososkie, J. N., Fried, J. H., Nelson, R. E., & Bardos, A. N. (2002). Clinical supervision in public rehabilitation counseling settings. *Rehabilitation Counseling Bulletin, 45,* 213–222.

Schutz, B. M. (1982). *Legal liability in psychotherapy.* San Francisco, CA: Jossey-Bass.

Schwartz, R. C., Liddle, H. A., & Breunlin, D. C. (1988). Muddles in live supervision. In A. A. Liddle, D. C. Breunlin, & R. C. Schwartz (Eds.), *Handbook of family therapy training and supervision* (pp. 183–193). New York: The Guilford Press.

Scott, K. J., Ingram, K. M., Vitanza, S. A., & Smith, N. G. (2000). Training in supervision: A survey of current practices. *The Counseling Psychologist, 28,* 403–422.

Searles, H. (1955). The informational value of the supervisor's emotional experiences. *Psychiatry, 18,* 135–146.

Sechrest, L., Brewer, M. B., Garfield, S. L., Jackson, J. S., Kurz, R. B., Messick, S. J., Miller, N. E., Peterson, D. R., Spence, J. T., & Thompson, R. F. (1982). *Report of the task force on the evaluation of education, training, and service in psychology.* Washington, DC: American Psychological Association.

Segal, Z. V., Williams, J. M. G., & Teasdale, J. D. (2002). *Mindfulness-based cognitive therapy for depression: A new approach to preventing relapse.* New York: Guilford Press.

Sells, J. N., Goodyear, R. K., Lichtenberg, J. W., & Polkinghorne, D. E. (1997). Relationship of supervisor and trainee gender to in-session verbal behavior and ratings of trainee skills. *Journal of Counseling Psychology, 44,* 1–7.

Shapiro, C. H. (1988). Burnout in social work field instructors. *The Clinical Supervisor, 6*(4), 237–248.

Shaw, B. F., & Dobson, K. S. (1988). Competency judgements in the training and evaluation of psychotherapists. *Journal of Consulting and Clinical Psychology, 56,* 666–672.

Shechtman, Z., & Wirzberger, A. (1999). Need and preferred style of supervision among Israeli school counselors at different stages of professional development. *Journal of Counseling and Development, 77,* 456–464.

Sherry, P. (1991). Ethical issues in the conduct of supervision. *The Counseling Psychologist, 19,* 566–584.

Shilts, L., Rudes, J., & Madigan, S. (1993). The use of a solution-focused interview with a reflecting team format: Evolving thoughts from clinical practice. *Journal of Systemic Therapies, 12*(1), 1–10.

Shoben, E. J. (1962). The counselor's theory as personal trait. *Personnel and Guidance Journal, 40,* 617–621.

Shulman, L. (1982). *Skills of supervision and staff management.* Itasca, IL: F.E. Peacock Publishers.

Shulman, L. S. (2005, February 6–8). The signature pedagogies of the professions of law, medicine, engineering, and the clergy: potential lessons for the education of teachers. Presentation at the math science partnerships (msp) workshop: Teacher education for effective teaching and learning. Hosted by the national research council's center for education, Irvine, CA. Retrieved December 28, 2007, from http://hub.mspnet.org/media/data/shulman_signature_pedagogies.pdf?media_000000001297.pdf

Siegel, M. (1979). Privacy, ethics and confidentiality. *Professional Psychology, 10,* 249–258.

Simon, R. (1982). Beyond the one-way mirror. *Family Therapy Networker, 26*(5), 19, 28–29, 58–59.

Simonton, D. K. (1994). *Greatness: Who makes history and why.* New York: Guilford.

Singh, N., & Ellis, M V. (2000, August). *Supervisee Anxiety in Clinical Supervision: Constructing the Anticipatory Supervisee Anxiety Scales.* Paper presented at the 108th Annual Convention of the American Psychological Association, Washington, DC.

Skovholt, T. M., & Jennings, L. (2004). *Common factors training and supervision through the master therapist prism.* Paper presented at the 112th Annual Convention of the American Psychological Association, Honolulu, HI.

Skovholt, T. M., & Rønnestad, M. H. (1992a). *The evolving professional self: Stages and themes in therapist and counselor development.* Chichester, U.K.: Wiley.

Skovholt, T. M., & Rønnestad, M. H. (1992b). Themes in therapist and counselor development. *Journal of Counseling and Development, 70,* 505–515.

Skovholt, T. M., & Rønnestad, M. H. (1995). *The evolving professional self: Stages and themes in therapist and counselor development.* Chichester, U.K.: Wiley.

Skovholt, T. M., Rønnestad, M. H., & Jennings, L. (1997). Searching for expertise in counseling, psychotherapy, and professional psychology. *Educational Psychology Review, 9,* 361–369.

Slater, L. (2003, January 26). Full disclosure. *New York Times.* Retrieved Month XX, 200X, from http://www.nytimes.com/2003/01/26/magazine/26WWLN.html

Slavin, J. H. (1994). On making rules: Toward a reformulation of the dynamics of transference in psychoanalytic treatment. *Psychoanalytic Dialogues, 4,* 253–274.

Sloan, G., & Watson, H. (2001). John Heron's six-category intervention analysis: Towards understanding interpersonal relations and progressing the delivery of clinical supervision for mental health nursing in the United Kingdom. *Journal of Advanced Nursing, 36,* 206–314.

Smadi, A. A., & Landreth, G. G. (1988). Reality therapy supervision with a counselor from a different theoretical orientation. *Journal of Reality Therapy, 7*(2), 18–26.

Smith, J. L., Amrhein, P. C., Brooks, A. C., Carpenter, K. M., Levin, D., Schreiber, E. A., Travaglini, L. A., & Nunes, E. V. (2007). Providing live supervision via teleconferencing improves acquisition of motivational interviewing skills after workshop attendance. *American Journal of Drug and Alcohol Abuse, 22,* 163–168.

Smith, R. C., Mead, D. E., & Kinsella, J. A. (1998). Direct supervision: Adding computer-assisted feedback and data capture to live supervision. *Journal of Marital and Family Therapy, 24*(1), 113–125.

Smith, R. C., & Mead, D. E. (1996). *CRB Tracker.* Unpublished software program. St. Louis, MO and Provo, UT.

Smith, T. E., Yoshioka, M., & Winton, M. (1993). A qualitative understanding of reflecting teams: I. Client perspectives. *Journal of Systemic Therapies, 12,* 28–43.

Snider, P. D. (1985). The duty to warn: A potential issue of litigation for the counseling supervisor. *Counselor Education and Supervision, 25,* 66–73.

Snider, P. D. (1987). Client records: Inexpensive liability protection for mental health counselors. *Journal of Mental Health Counseling, 9,* 134–141.

Soisson, E. L., Vandecreek, L., & Knapp, S. (1987). Thorough record keeping: A good defense in a litigious era. *Professional Psychology: Research and Practice, 18,* 498–502.

Sommer, C. A., & Cox, J. A. (2003). Using Greek mythology as a metaphor to enhance supervision. *Counselor Education and Supervision, 42,* 326–335.

Sommer, C. A., & Cox, J. A. (2005). Elements of supervision in sexual violence counselors' narratives: A qualitative analysis. *Counselor Education and Supervision, 45,* 119–134.

Sommer, C. A., & Cox, J. A. (2006). Sexual violence counselors' reflections on supervision: Using stories to mitigate vicarious traumatization. *Journal of Poetry Therapy, 19*(1), 3–16.

Son, E. J., Ellis, M. V., & Yoo, S. K. (2007). The relations among supervisory working alliance, role difficulties, and supervision satisfaction: A cross-cultural comparison. *Korean Journal of Psychology, 26,* 161–162.

Sparks, D., & Loucks-Horsley, S. (1989). Five models of staff development for teachers. *Journal of Staff Development, 10*(4), 40–57.

Speed, B., Seligman, P. M., Kingston, P., & Cade, B. W. (1982). A team approach to therapy. *Journal of Family Therapy, 4,* 271–284.

Spelliscy, D., Chen, E. C., & Zusho, A. (2007, August). *Predicting supervisee role conflict and ambiguity: A path analytic model.* Paper presented at the annual meeting of the American Psychological Association, San Francisco.

Spence, S. H., Wilson, J., Kavanagh, D., Strong, J., & Worrall, L. (2001). Clinical supervision in four mental health professions: A review of the evidence. *Behaviour Change, 18,* 135–151.

Sperling, M. B., Pirrotta, S., Handen, B. L., Simons, L. A., Miller, D., Lysiak, G., Schumm, P., & Terry,

L. (1986). The collaborative team as a training and therapeutic tool. *Counselor Education and Supervision, 25,* 183–190.

Stein, D. M., & Lambert, M. J. (1995). Graduate training in psychotherapy: Are therapy outcomes enhanced? *Journal of Consulting and Clinical Psychology, 63,* 182–196.

Stenack, R. J., & Dye, H. A. (1982). Behavioral descriptions of counseling supervision roles. *Counselor Education and Supervision, 22,* 295–304.

Sterling, M. M., & Bugental, J. F. (1993). The meld experience in psychotherapy supervision. *Journal of Humanistic Psychology, 33,* 38–48.

Sternitzke, M. E., Dixon, D. N., & Ponterotto, J. G. (1988). An attributional approach to counselor supervision. *Counselor Education and Supervision, 28,* 5–14.

Stevens-Smith, P. (1995). Gender issues in counselor education: Current status and challenges. *Counselor Education and Supervision, 34*(4), 283–293.

Steward, R. J. (1998). Connecting counselor self-efficacy and supervisor self-efficacy: The continued search for counseling competence. *Counseling Psychologist, 26*(2), 285–294.

Steward, R. J., Breland, A., & Neil, D. M. (2001). Novice supervisees' self-evaluations and their perceptions of supervisor style. *Counselor Education & Supervision, 41*(2), 131–141.

Stewart, A. E., & Stewart, E. A. (1996). Personal and practical considerations in selecting a psychology internship. *Professional Psychology: Research and Practice, 27,* 295–303.

Stigall, T. T., Bourg, E. F., Bricklin, P. M., Kovacs, A. L., Larsen, K. G., Lorion, R. P., Nelson, P. D., Nurse, A. R., Pugh, R. W., & Wiens, A. N. (Eds.). (1990). *Report of the Joint Council on Professional Education in Psychology.* Baton Rouge, LA: Joint Council on Professional Education in Psychology.

Stiles, W. B., & Snow, J. S. (1984). Counseling session impact as viewed by novice counselors and their clients. *Journal of Counseling Psychology, 31,* 3–12.

Stiles, W. B., Shapiro, D. A., & Firth-Cozens, J. A. (1988). Do sessions of different treatments have different impacts? *Journal of Counseling Psychology, 35,* 391–396.

Stinchfield, T. A., Hill, N. R., & Kleist, D. M. (2007). The reflective model of triadic supervision: Defining an emerging modality. *Counselor Education and Supervision, 46,* 172–183.

Stoltenberg, C. (1981). Approaching supervision from a developmental perspective: The counselor-complexity model. *Journal of Counseling Psychologists, 28,* 59–65.

Stoltenberg, C., & Delworth, U. (1987). *Supervising counselors and therapists.* San Francisco: Jossey-Bass.

Stoltenberg, C. D. (2005). Enhancing professional competence through developmental approaches to supervision. *American Psychologist, 60,* 857–864.

Stoltenberg, C. D., McNeill, B. W., & Crethar, H. C. (1994). Changes in supervision as counselors and therapists gain experience: A review. *Professional Psychology: Research & Practice, 25,* 416–449.

Stoltenberg, C. D., McNeill, B. W., & Crethar, H. C. (1995). Persuasion and development in counselor supervision. *The Counseling Psychologist, 23,* 633–648.

Stoltenberg, C. D., McNeill, B. W., & Delworth, U. (1998). *IDM: An integrated developmental model for supervising counselors and therapists.* San Francisco: Jossey-Bass Publishers.

Stoltenberg, C. D., Pierce, R. A., & McNeill, B. W. (1987). Effects of experience on counselors needs. *The Clinical Supervisor, 5,* 23–32.

Stone, G. L. (1997). Multiculturalism as a context for supervision: Perspectives, limitations, and implications. In D. B. Pope-Davis & H. L. K. Coleman (Eds.), *Multicultural counseling competencies: Assessment, education, training, and supervision.* Thousand Oaks, CA: Sage Publications.

Stoppard, J. M., & Miller, A. (1985). Conceptual level matching in therapy: A review. *Current Psychological Research and Reviews, 4,* 47–68.

Storm, C., & Heath, A. W. (1982). Strategic supervision: The danger lies in discovery. *Journal of Strategic and Systemic Therapies, 1,* 71–72.

Storm, C. L. (1997). Back to the future: A review through time. In T. C. Todd & C. L. Storm (Eds.), *The complete systemic supervisor: Context, philosophy, and pragmatics* (pp. 283–287). Boston: Allyn & Bacon.

Storm, C. L., & Haug, I. E. (1997). Ethical issues: Where do you draw the line? In T. C. Todd & C. L. Storm (Eds.), *The complete systemic supervisor: Context, philosophy, and pragmatics* (pp. 26–40). Boston: Allyn & Bacon.

Storm, C. L., Todd, T. C., & Sprenkle, D. H. (2001). Gaps between MFT supervision assumptions and common practice: Suggested best practices. *Journal of Marital and Family Therapy, 27,* 227–239.

Storm, H. A. (1994). *Enhancing the acquisition of psychotherapy skills through live supervision.* Paper presented at the annual meeting of the American Psychological Association, Los Angeles.

Stout, C. E. (1987). The role of ethical standards in the supervision of psychotherapy. *The Clinical Supervisor, 5*(1), 89–97.

Stratton, J. S., & Smith, R. D. (2006). Supervision of couples cases. *Psychotherapy: Theory, Research, Practice, Training, 43,* 337–348.

Strean, H. S. (2000). Resolving therapeutic impasses by using the supervisor's countertransference. *Clinical Social Work Journal, 28,* 263–279.

Strein, W., & Hershenson, D. B. (1991). Confidentiality in nondyadic counseling situations. *Journal of Counseling and Development, 69,* 312–316.

Strong, S. R., & Hills, H. (1986). *Interpersonal Communication Rating Scale.* Richmond, VA: Virginia Commonwealth University.

Strong, S. R. (1968). Counseling: An interpersonal influence process. *Journal of Counseling Psychology, 15,* 215–224.

Strong, S. R., & Matross, R. P. (1973). Change process in counseling and psychotherapy. *Journal of Counseling Psychology, 20,* 25–37.

Strupp, H. H., & Binder, J. (1984). *Psychotherapy in a new key: A guide to time-limited dynamic psychotherapy.* New York: Basic Books.

Strupp, H. H., & Hadley, S. W. (1979). Specific versus nonspecific factors in psychotherapy. *Archives of General Psychiatry, 36,* 1125–1136.

Stryker, S., & Statham, A. (1985). Symbolic interactionism and role theory. In G. Lindzey & E. Aronson (Eds.), *The handbook of social psychology* (3rd ed., Vol. 1, pp. 311–378). New York: Random House.

Studer, J. R. (2005). Supervising school counselors-in-training: A guide for field supervisors. *Professional School Counseling, 8,* 353–359.

Sullivan, H. S. (1953). *The interpersonal theory of psychiatry.* New York: Norton.

Sumerel, M. B., & Borders, L. D. (1996). Addressing personal issues in supervision: Impact of counselor's experience level on various aspects of the supervisory relationship. *Counselor Education & Supervision, 35,* 268–286.

Supervision Interest Network, Association for Counselor Education and Supervision. (1990). Standards for counseling supervisors. *Journal of Counseling and Development, 69,* 30–32.

Supervision Interest Network, Association for Counselor Education and Supervision. (1993, Summer). ACES ethical guidelines for counseling supervisors. *ACES Spectrum, 53*(4), 5–8.

Sussman, T., Bogo, M., & Globerman, J. (2007). Field instructor perceptions in group supervision: Establishing trust through managing group dynamics. *The Clinical Supervisor, 26,* 61–80.

Sutter, E., McPherson, R. H., & Geeseman, R. (2002). Contracting for supervision. *Professional Psychology: Research and Practice, 33,* 495–498.

Sutton, J. M., Jr. (2000). Counselor licensure. In H. Hackney (Ed.), *Practice issues for the beginning counselor* (pp. 55–78). Boston: Allyn & Bacon.

Sutton, J. M., Jr., Nielson, R., & Essex, M. (1998). A descriptive study of the ethical standards related to supervisory behavior employed by counselor licensing boards. Paper presented at the annual conference of the American Association of State Counseling Boards, Tucson, AZ.

Swanson, J. L., & O'Saben, C. L. (1993). Differences in supervisory needs and expectations by trainee experience, cognitive style, and program membership. *Journal of Counseling and Development, 71,* 457–464.

Swenson, L. S. (1997). *Psychology and law for the helping professions* (2nd ed.). Pacific Grove, CA: Brooks/Cole.

Szymanski, D. M. (2003). The Feminist Supervision Scale (FSS): A rational/theoretical approach. *Psychology of Women Quarterly, 27,* 221–232.

Szymanski, D. M. (2005). Feminist identity and theories as correlates of feminist supervision practices. *The Counseling Psychologist, 33,* 729–747.

Talen, M. R., & Schindler, N. (1993). Goal-directed supervision plans: A model for trainee supervision and evaluation. *Clinical Supervisor, 11*(2), 77–88.

Tangney, J. P., Wagner, P., Fletcher, C., & Gramzow, R. (1992). Shamed into anger? The relation of shame and guilt to anger and self-reported aggression. *Journal of Personality & Social Psychology, 62,* 669–675.

Tarasoff, V. *Regents of the University of California.* 118 Cal. Rptr. 129, 529 P 2d 533 (1974).

Tarvydas, V. M. (1995). Ethics and the practice of rehabilitation counselor supervision. *Rehabilitation Counseling Bulletin, 38,* 294–306.

Taylor, B. A., Hernandez, P., Deri, A., Rankin, P. R., IV, & Siegel, A. (2006). Integrating diversity dimensions in supervision: Perspectives of ethnic minority AAMFT approved supervisors. *The Clinical Supervisor, 25*(1/2), 3–21.

Teitelbaum, S. H. (1990). Supertransference: The role of the supervisor's blind spots. *Psychoanalytic Psychology, 7,* 243–258.

Tennen, H. (1988). Supervision of integrative psychotherapy: A critique. *Journal of Integrative & Eclectic Psychotherapy, 7,* 167–175.

Thomas, F. N. (1996). Solution-focused supervision: The coaxing of expertise. In S. D. Miller, M. A. Hubble, & B. L. Duncan (Eds.), *Handbook of solution-focused therapy* (pp. 128–151). San Francisco: Jossey-Bass.

Thomas, J. T. (2007). Informed consent through contracting for supervision: Minimizing risks, enhancing benefits. *Professional Psychology: Research and Practice, 38,* 221–231.

Thoreson, R. W., Shaughnessy, P., Heppner, P. P., & Cook, S. W. (1993). Sexual contact during and after the professional relationship: Attitudes and practices of male counselors. *Journal of Counseling and Development, 71,* 429–434.

Thyer, B. A., Sowers-Hoag, K., & Love, J. P. (1988). The influence of field instructor-student gender combinations on student perceptions of field instruction quality. *The Clinical Supervisor, 6*(3), 169–179.

Tinsley, H. E. A., Bowman, S. L., & Ray, S. B. (1988). Manipulation of expectancies about counseling and psychotherapy: A review and analysis of expectancy manipulation strategies and results. *Journal of Counseling Psychology, 35,* 99–108.

Tinsley, H. E. A., Workman, K. R., & Kass, R. A. (1980). Factor analysis of the domain of client expectancies about counseling. *Journal of Counseling Psychology, 27,* 561–570.

Todd, T. C. (1997). Purposive systemic supervision models. In T. C. Todd & C. L. Storm (Eds.), *The complete systemic supervisor: Context, philosophy and pragmatics* (pp. 173–194). Boston: Allyn & Bacon.

Topolinski, S., & Hertel, G. (2007). The role of personality in psychotherapists' careers: Relationships between personality traits, therapeutic schools, and job satisfaction. *Psychotherapy Research, 17,* 365–375.

Toporek, R. L., Ortega-Villalobos, L., & Pope-Davis, D. B. (2004). Critical incidents in multicultural supervision: Exploring supervisees' and supervisors' experiences. *Journal of Multicultural Counseling and Development, 32,* 66–83.

Tosado, M. (2004). Supervision anxiety: Cross-validity data for the Anticipatory Supervisee Anxiety scale. Unpublished doctoral dissertation. University at Albanya, Albany, NY.

Tracey, J., & Sherry, P. (1993). Complementary interaction over time in successful and less successful supervision. *Professional Psychology: Research and Practice, 24,* 304–311.

Tracey, M., Froehle, T., Kelbley, T., Chilton, T., Sandhofer, R., Woodward, D., Blanchard, D., & Benkert, R. (1995, April). *Data centric counseling: The development of a computer-assisted observation system for use in process studies in counseling, supervision, and counselor training.* Paper presented at the annual meeting of the American Educational Reseach Association, San Francisco.

Tracey, T. J. (1993). An interpersonal stage model of the therapeutic process. *Journal of Counseling Psychology, 40,* 1–14.

Tracey, T. J., Ellickson, J. L., & Sherry, P. (1989). Reactance in relation to different supervisory environments and counselor development. *Journal of Counseling Psychology, 36,* 336–344.

Tracey, T. J., Hays, K. A., Malone, J., & Herman, B. (1988). Changes in counselor response as a function of experience. *Journal of Counseling Psychology, 35,* 119–126.

Tracey, T. J., Ryan, J. M., & Jaschik-Herman, B. (2001). Complementarity of interpersonal circumplex traits. *Personality and Social Psychology Bulletin, 27,* 786–797.

Tracey, T. J. G. (2002). Stages of counseling and therapy: An examination of complementarity and the working alliance. In G. S. Tryon (Ed.), *Counseling based on process research: Applying what we know* (pp. 265–297). Boston: Allyn & Bacon.

Tracey, T. J. G., Sherry, P., & Albright, J. M. (1999). The interpersonal process of cognitive-behavioral therapy: An examination of complementarity over the course of treatment. *Journal of Counseling Psychology, 46,* 80–91.

Triantafillou, N. (1997). A solution-focused approach to mental health supervision. *Journal of Systemic Therapies, 16,* 305–328.

Tromski-Klingshirn, D. (2006). Should the clinical supervisor be the administrative supervisor? The ethics versus the reality. *The Clinical Supervisor, 25*(1/2), 53–67.

Tromski-Klingshirn, D. M., & Davis, T. E. (2007). Supervisees' perceptions of their clinical supervision: A study of the dual role of clinical and administrative supervisor. *Counselor Education & Supervision, 46,* 294–304.

Tuckman, B. W. (1965). Developmental sequence in small groups. *Psychological Bulletin, 63,* 384–399.

Tuckman, B. W., & Jensen, M. A. C. (1977). Stages of small group development revisited. *Group and Organizational Studies, 2,* 419–427.

Tudor, K., & Worrall, M. (2004). *Freedom to practise: Person-centred approaches to supervision.* Ross-on-Wye, U.K.: PCCS Books.

Tudor, K., & Worrall, M. (2007). *Freedom to practise: Volume II: Developing person-centred approaches to supervision.* Ross-on-Wye, U.K.: PCCS Books.

Turban, D. B., & Jones, A. P. (1988). Supervisor-subordinate similarity: Types, effects, and mechanisms. *Journal of Applied Psychology, 73,* 228–234.

Turban, D. B., Jones, A. P., & Rozelle, R. M. (1990). Influences of supervisor liking of a subordinate and the reward context on the treatment and evaluation of that subordinate. *Motivation and Emotion, 14,* 215–233.

Turner, J. (1993). Males supervising females: The risk of gender-power blindness. *The Supervisor Bulletin, VI,* 4 & 6.

Twohey, D., & Volker, J. (1993). Listening for the voices of care and justice in counselor supervision. *Counselor Education & Supervision, 32,* 189–197.

Ungar, M., & Costanzo, L. (2007). Supervision challenges when supervisor are outside supervisees' agencies. *Journal of Strategic & Systemic Therapies, 26,* 68–83.

Upchurch, D. W. (1985). Ethical standards and the supervisory process. *Counselor Education & Supervision, 25,* 90–98.

Usher, C. H., & Borders, L. D. (1993). Practicing counselors' preferences for supervisory style and supervisory emphasis. *Counselor Education and Supervision, 33,* 66–79.

Utsey, S. O., Gernat, C. A., & Hammar, L. (2005). Examining white counselor trainees' reactions to racial issues in counseling and supervision dyads. *The Counseling Psychologist, 33,* 449–478.

Utsey, S. O., Hammar, L., & Gernat, C. A. (2005). Examining the reaction of white, black, and Latino/a counseling psychologists to a study of racial issues in counseling and supervision dyads. *The Counseling Psychologist, 33,* 565–573.

Vaccaro, N., & Lambie, G. W. (2007). Computer-based counseling-in-training supervision: Ethical and practical implications for counselor educators and supervisors. *Counselor Education & Supervision, 47,* 46–57.

Vacha-Haase, T., Davenport, D. S., & Kerewsky, S. D. (2004). Problematic students: Gatekeeping practices of academic professional psychology programs. *Professional Psychology: Research and Practice, 35,* 115–122.

Vander Kolk, C. (1974). The relationship of personality, values, and race to anticipation of the supervisory relationship. *Rehabilitation Counseling Bulletin, 18,* 41–46.

Vargas, L. A. (1989, August). *Training psychologists to be culturally responsive: Issues in supervision.* Paper presented at the Annual Convention of the American Psychological Association, New Orleans.

Vasquez, M. J. (1999). Trainee impairment: A response from a feminist/multiculturalist retired trainer. *Counseling Psychologist, 27,* 687–692.

Vasquez, M. J. T. (1992). Psychologist as clinical supervisor: Promoting ethical practice. *Professional Psychology: Research and Practice, 23,* 196–202.

Vaz, K. M. (2005). Reflecting team group therapy and its congruence with feminist principles: A focus on African American women. *Women & Therapy, 28*(2), 65–75.

Vogel, D. (1994). Narrative perspectives in theory and therapy. *Journal of Constructivist Psychology, 7,* 243–261.

Vygotsky, L. S. (1978). *Mind in society: The development of higher psychological processes* (M. Cole, V. John-Steiner, S. Scribner, & E. Souberman, Eds. and Trans.). Cambridge, MA: Harvard University Press.

Walker, J. A., & Gray, L. A. (2002, June). *Categorizing supervisor countertransference.* Paper presented at the annual meeting of the Society for Psychotherapy Research International Conference, Santa Barbara, CA.

Walker, R., & Clark, J. J. (1999). Heading off boundary problems: Clinical supervision as risk management. *Psychiatric Services, 50,* 1435–1439.

Walzer, R. S., & Miltimore, S. (1993). Mandated supervision: Monitoring, and therapy of disciplined health care professionals. *The Journal of Legal Medicine, 14,* 565–596.

Wampold, B. E. (2001). *The great psychotherapy debate: Models, methods, and findings.* Mahwah, NJ: Lawrence Erlbaum Associates, Publishers.

Wampold, B. E., & Holloway, E. L. (1997). Methodology, design, and evaluation in psychotherapy supervision research. In C. E. Watkins (Ed.), *Handbook of psychotherapy supervision* (pp. 11–27). New York: John Wiley.

Warburton, J. R., Newberry, A., & Alexander, J. (1989). Women as therapists, trainees, and supervisors. In M. McGoldrick, C. Anderson, & F. Walsh (Eds.), *Women in families: A framework for family therapy* (pp. 152–165). New York: Norton.

Ward, C. C., & House, R. M. (1998). Counseling supervision: A reflective model. *Counselor Education and Supervision, 38,* 23–33.

Ward, L. G., Friendlander, M. L., Schoen, L. G., & Klein, J. G. (1985). Strategic self-presentation in supervision. *Journal of Counseling Psychology, 32,* 111–118.

Ward, J., & Sommer, C. A., (2006). Using stories in supervision to facilitate counselor development. *Journal of Poetry Therapy, 19*(2), 1–7.

Wark, L. (1995). Defining the territory of live supervision in family therapy training: A qualitative study and theoretical discussion. *The Clinical Supervisor, 13*(1), 145–162.

Wark, L. (2000). Research: Trainees talk about effective live supervision. *Readings in family therapy supervision* (p. 119). Washington, DC: American Association for Marriage and Family Therapy.

Watkins, C. E., Jr. (1990a). Development of the psychotherapy supervisor. *Psychotherapy, 27,* 553–560.

Watkins, C. E., Jr. (1990b). The separation-individuation process in psychotherapy supervision. *Psychotherapy, 27,* 202–209.

Watkins, C. E., Jr. (1993). Development of the psychotherapy supervisor: Concepts, assumptions, and hypotheses of the supervisor complexity model. *American Journal of Psychotherapy, 47,* 58–74.

Watkins, C. E., Jr. (1994). The supervision of psychotherapy supervisor trainees. *American Journal of Psychotherapy, 48,* 417–431.

Watkins, C. E., Jr. (1995a). Considering psychotherapy supervisor development: A status report. *The Psychotherapy Bulletin, 29*(4), 32–34.

Watkins, C. E., Jr. (1995b). Psychotherapy supervisor and supervisee: Developmental models and research nine years later. *Clinical Psychology Review, 15,* 647–680.

Watkins, C. E., Jr. (1995c). Psychotherapy supervisor development: On musings, models, and metaphor. *Journal of Psychotherapy Practice & Research, 4,* 150–158.

Watkins, C. E., Jr. (1995d). Researching psychotherapy supervisor development: Four key considerations. *The Clinical Supervisor, 13*(2), 111–118.

Watkins, C. E., Jr. (1999). The beginning psychotherapy supervisor: How can we help? *The Clinical Supervisor, 18,* 63–72.

Watkins, C. E., Lopez, F. G., Campbell, V. L., & Himmell, C. D. (1986). Contemporary counseling psychology: Results of a national survey. *Journal of Counseling Psychology, 33,* 301–309.

Watkins, C. E., Schneider, L. J., Haynes, J., & Nieberding, R. (1995). Measuring psychotherapy supervisor development: An initial effort at scale development and validation. *The Clinical Supervisor, 13*(1), 77–90.

Watson, J. C. (2003). Computer-based supervision: Implementing computer technology into the delivery of counseling supervision. *Journal of Technology in Counseling, 3*(1).

Watson, M. F. (1993). Supervising the person of the therapist: Issues, challenges and dilemmas. Special Issue: Critical issues in marital and family therapy education. *Contemporary Family Therapy An International Journal, 15,* 21–31.

Watzlawick, P., & Beavin, J. (1976). Some formal aspects of communication. In P. Watzlawick & J. H. Weakland (Eds.), *The interactional view* (pp. 56–67). New York: Norton.

Watzlawick, P., Beavin, J. H., & Jackson, D. D. (1967). *Pragmatics of human communication: A study of interactional patterns, pathologies, and paradoxes.* New York: Norton.

Webb, A., & Wheeler, S. (1998). How honest do counsellors dare to be in the supervisory relationship? An exploratory study. *British Journal of Guidance & Counselling, 26,* 509–524.

Webster's New World Dictionary of the American Language. (1966). New York: World Publishing.

Wendorf, D. J. (1984). A model for training practicing professionals in family therapy. *Journal of Marital and Family Therapy, 10,* 31–41.

Wendorf, D. J., Wendorf, R. J., & Bond, O. (1985). Growth behind the mirror: The family therapy consortiums' group process. *Journal of Marriage & Family Therapy, 11,* 245–255.

Wessler, R. L., & Ellis, A. (1983). Supervision in counseling: Rational-Emotive Therapy. *The Counseling Psychologist, 11*(1), 43–49.

West, J. D., Bubenzer, D. L., & Delmonico, D. L. (1994). Preparation of doctoral-level supervisors. In J. E.

Myers (Ed.), *Developing and directing counselor education laboratories* (pp. 131–139). Alexandria, VA: ACA Press.

West, J. D., Bubenzer, D. L., Pinsoneault, T., & Holeman, V. (1993). Three supervision modalities for training marital and family counselors. Special Section: Marriage and family counselor training. *Counselor Education & Supervision, 33,* 127–138.

West, J. D., Bubenzer, D. L., & Zarski, J. J. (1989). Live supervision in family therapy: An interview with Barbara Oken and Fred Piercy. *Counselor Education and Supervision, 29,* 25–34.

West, W. (2003). The culture of psychotherapy supervision. *Counselling and Psychotherapy Research, 3,* 123–127.

Wester, S. R., & Vogel, D. L. (2002). Working with the masculine mystique: Male gender role conflict, counseling self-efficacy, and the training of male psychologists. *Professional Psychology: Research and Practice, 33,* 370–376.

Wester, S. R., Vogel, D. L., & Archer, J., Jr. (2004). Male restricted emotionality and counseling supervision. *Journal of Counseling & Development, 82,* 91–98.

Wetchler, J. L. (1989). Supervisors' and supervisees' perceptions of the effectiveness of family therapy supervisor interpersonal skills. *American Journal of Family Therapy, 17,* 244–256.

Wetchler, J. L., Piercy, F. P., & Sprenkle, D. H. (1989). Supervisors' and supervisees' perceptions of the effectiveness of family therapy supervisory techniques. *The American Journal of Family Therapy, 17,* 35–47.

Wetchler, J. L., & Vaughn, K. A. (1992). Perceptions of primary family therapy supervisory techniques: A critical incident analysis. *Contemporary Family Therapy: An International Journal, 14,* 127–136.

Wheeler, S., & King, D. (2000). Do counselling supervisors want or need to have their supervision supervised? An exploratory study. *British Journal of Guidance and Counselling, 28*(2), 279–290.

Wheeler, S., & Richards, K. (2007). The impact of clinical supervision on counselors and therapists, their practice and their clients. A systematic review of the literature. *Counselling and Psychotherapy Research, 7,* 54–65.

Whiston, S. C., & Emerson, S. (1989). Ethical implications for supervisors in counseling of trainees. *Counselor Education and Supervision, 28,* 318–325.

White, H. D., & Rudolph, B. A. (2000). A pilot investigation of the reliability and validity of the Group Supervisory Behavior Scale (GBS). *The Clinical Supervisor, 19,* 161–171.

White, L. J., Rosenthal, D. M., & Fleuridas, C. L. (1993). Accountable supervision through systematic data collection: Using single-case designs. *Counselor Education and Supervision, 33,* 32–46.

White, M. B., & Russell, C. S. (1997). Examining the multifaceted notion of isomorphism in marriage and family therapy supervision: A quest for conceptual clarity. *Journal of Marital and Family Therapy, 23,* 315–333.

White, R. W. (1959). Motivation reconsidered: The concept of competence. *Psychological Review, 66,* 297–323.

White, V. E., & Queener, J. (2003). Supervisor and supervisee attachments and social provisions related to the supervisory working alliance. *Counselor Education and Supervision, 42,* 203–218.

Whittaker, S. M. (2004). *A multi-vocal synthesis of supervisees' anxiety and self-efficacy during clinical supervision: Meta-analysis and interviews.* Unpublished dissertation, Virginia Polytechnic Institute and State University. Retrieved December 20, 2007, from http://scholar.lib.vt.edu/theses/available/etd-09152004-151749/

Wiggins, J. S. (1985). Interpersonal circumplex models: 1948–1983. *Journal of Personality Assessment, 49,* 626–631.

Wilbur, M. P., & Roberts-Wilbur, J. (1983). Schemata of the steps of the SGS model. Unpublished table.

Wilbur, M. P., Roberts-Wilbur, J., M., Hart, G., Morris, J. R., & Betz, R. L. (1994). Structured Group Supervision (SGS): A pilot study. *Counselor Education & Supervision, 33,* 262–279.

Wilbur, M. P., Roberts-Wilbur, J., Morris, J., Betz, R., & Hart, G. M. (1991). Structured group supervision: Theory into practice. *Journal for Specialists in Group Work, 16,* 91–100.

Wilcoxon, S. A. (1992). Videotape review of supervision-of-supervision in concurrent training: Allowing trainees to peer through the door. *Family Therapy, 19,* 143–153.

Wiley, M., & Ray, P. (1986). Counseling supervision by developmental level. *Journal of Counseling Psychology, 33,* 439–445.

Wiley, M. O. (1994, August). *Supervising oneself in independent practice: From student to solo practitioner.* Paper presented at the American Psychological Association, Los Angeles.

Williams, A. (1995). *Visual and active supervision: Roles, focus, technique.* New York: W.W. Norton.

Williams, A. B. (2000). Contribution of supervisors' covert communication to the parallel process. *Dissertation Abstracts International Section A: Humanities & Social Sciences Vol 61(3-A),* 1165.

Williams, E. N., Judge, A. B., Hill, C. E., & Hoffman, M. A. (1997). Experiences of novice therapists in prepracticum: Trainees', clients', and supervisors' perceptions of therapists' personal reactions and management strategies. *Journal of Counseling Psychology, 44*(4), 390–399.

Williams, L. (1994). A tool for training supervisors: Using the Supervision Feedback Form (SFF). *Journal of Marital & Family Therapy, 20,* 311–315.

Williams, M. H. (2000). Victimized by "victims": A taxonomy of antecedents of false complaints against psychotherapists. *Professional Psychology: Research and Practice, 31,* 75–81.

Winter, M., & Holloway, E. L. (1991). Relation of trainee experience, conceptual level, and supervisor approach to selection of audiotaped counseling passages. *Clinical Supervisor, 9*(2), 87–103.

Wise, P. S., Lowery, S., & Silverglade, L. (1989). Personal counseling for counselors in training: Guidelines for supervisors. *Counselor Education and Supervision, 28,* 326–336.

Wolpe, J., Knopp, W., & Garfield, Z. (1966). Postgraduate training in behavior therapy. *Exerta Medica International Congress Series, No. 150.* Proceedings of the IV World Congress of Psychiatry, Madrid, Spain.

Wong, P. T. P., & Wong, L. C. J. (1999). Assessing Multicultural Supervision Competencies. In W. J. Lonner, D. L. Dinnel, D. K. Forgays, & S. A. Hayes (Eds.), *Merging past, present and future in cross-cultural psychology* (pp. 510–519). Lisse, The Netherlands: Swets & Zeitlinger Publishers.

Wong, Y.-L. S. (1997). Live supervision in family therapy: Trainee perspectives. *The Clinical Supervisor, 15*(1), 145–157.

Wood, B., Klein, S., Cross, H., Lammers, C., & Elliot, J. (1985). Impaired practitioners: Psychologists' opinions about prevalence, and proposals for intervention. *Professional Psychology: Research and Practice, 16,* 843–850.

Woods, P. J., & Ellis, A. (1996). Supervision in rational emotive behavior therapy. *Journal of Rational-Emotive & Cognitive Behavior Therapy, 14,* 135–152.

Woodside, D. B. (1994). Reverse live supervision: Leveling the supervisory playing field. *The Supervision Bulletin, VII*(2), 6.

Woodworth, C. B. (2000). Legal issues in counseling practice. In H. Hackney (Ed.), *Practice issues for the beginning counselor* (pp. 119–136). Boston, MA: Allyn & Bacon.

Woody, R. H. and Associates. (1984). *The law and the practice of human services.* San Francisco: Jossey-Bass.

Woolley, G. (1991). Beware the well-intentioned therapist. *The Family Therapy Networker,* Jan/Feb, 15, 30.

Worthen, V., & McNeill, B. W. (1996). A phenomenological investigation of "good" supervision events. *Journal of Counseling Psychology, 43,* 25–34.

Worthington, E. L., Jr. (1987). Changes in supervision as counselors and supervisors gain experience: A review. *Professional Psychology: Research and Practice, 18,* 189–208.

Worthington, E. L., Jr., & Roehlke, H. J. (1979). Effective supervision as perceived by beginning counselors-in-training. *Journal of Counseling Psychology, 26,* 64–73.

Worthington, E. L., Jr., & Stern, A. (1985). Effects of supervisor and supervisee degree level and gender on the supervisory relationship. *Journal of Counseling Psychology, 32,* 252–262.

Worthington, R. L., Tan, J. A., & Poulin, K. (2002). Ethically questionable behaviors among supervisees: An exploratory investigation. *Ethics and Behavior, 12,* 323–351.

Woskett, V., & Page, S. (2001). *The cyclical model of supervision: A container for creativity and chaos.* In M. Carroll & M. Tholstrup, *Integrative approaches to supervision* (pp. 13–31). London: Jessica Kingsley Publishers.

Wright, L. M. (1986). An analysis of live supervision "phone-ins" in family therapy. *Journal of Marital and Family Therapy, 12,* 187–191.

Wulf, J., & Nelson, M. L. (2001). Experienced psychologists' recollections of internship supervision and its contributions to their development. *The Clinical Supervisor, 19,* 123–145.

Wynne, M. E., Susman, M., Ries, S., Birringer, J., & Katz, L. (1994). A method for assessing therapists' recall of in-session events. *Journal of Counseling Psychology, 41,* 53–57.

Yager, G. G., Wilson, F. R., Brewer, D., & Kinnetz, P. (1989). *The development and validation of an instrument to measure counseling supervisor focus and style.* Paper presented at the American Educational Research Association, San Francisco.

Yalom, I. D. (1985). *The theory and practice of group psychotherapy* (3rd ed.). New York: Basic Books.

Yalom, I. D. (1995). *The theory and practice of group psychotherapy* (4th ed.). New York: Basic Books.

Yerkes, R. M., & Dodson, J. D. (1908). The relation of strength of stimulus to rapidity of habit formation. *Journal of Comparative Neurology and Psychology, 18,* 459–482.

Yerushalmi, H. (1999). The roles of group supervision of supervision. *Psychoanalytic Psychology, 16,* 426–447.

Young, J., Perlesz, A., Paterson, R., O'Hanlon, B., Newbold, A., Chaplin, R., & Bridge, S. (1989). The reflecting team process in training. *Australia and New Zealand Journal of Family Therapy, 10,* 69–74.

Yourman, D. B. (2003). Trainee disclosure in psychotherapy supervision: The impact of shame. *Journal of Clinical Psychology, 59,* 601–609.

Zajonc, R. B. (1965). Social facilitation. *Science, 149,* 269–274.

Zarski, J. J., Sand-Pringle, C., Pannell, L., & Lindon, C. (1995). Critical issues in supervision: Marital and family violence. *The Family Journal: Counseling and Therapy for Couples and Families, 3*(1), 18–26.

Name Index

Binder, J., 164
Birk, J. M., 117
Bishop, D. R., 146
Bitterman, H., 8
Blackwell, T. L., 59
Blake, R. R., 91
Blocher, D. H., 89, 125, 181, 187, 248
Blodgett, E. G., 45
Bloom, B. S., 118
Bob, S., 87
Boes, S. R., 12, 59
Boëthius, B. S., 255
Bogo, M., 28, 36, 196, 197, 200, 201, 209, 210, 211, 216
Bonney, W., 285, 288, 289
Borders, L. D., 1, 14, 17, 25, 33, 34, 57, 66, 109, 117,
    120, 122, 123, 125, 181, 194, 219, 221, 222, 224,
    228, 232, 234, 237, 256, 257, 285, 286, 287, 288,
    289, 297, 300
Bordin, E. S., 82, 157, 158, 159, 182
Borg, M. B., Jr., 147
Bowen, M., 155, 156
Bowlby, J., 175
Boxley, R., 52
Boyd, J., 84
Bradey, J., 52
Bradley, C., 24
Bradley, L. J., 171, 288
Bradshaw, W. H., Jr., 129
Brandell, J. R., 225
Brantley, A. P., 212
Brashears, F., 5, 196
Brawer, P. A., 146
Brehm, J. W., 173
Brehm, S. S., 173
Breunlin, D., 227, 228
Bridges, N. A., 58, 63, 177
Briggs, J. R., 21, 25, 26, 28, 93
Brill, R., 203
Britton, P. J., 126, 137
Broder, E., 226
Brody, S. L., 178
Brooks, L., 31
Brown, L. L., 33, 34, 219, 224, 234, 237
Brown, L. M., 139
Brown, R. W., 209
Bruss, K. V., 144
Bryant-Jefferies, R., 84
Bubenzer, D. L., 263, 264, 271, 272, 273, 282
Bugental, J. F., 243
Buhrke, R. A., 144, 145

Burgess, S. L., 40
Burian, B. K., 63
Burke, W., 48, 120, 121, 168
Burns, C. I., 63
Burow, J. M., 18, 179
Byng-Hall, J., 264

Cacioppo, J. T., 187
Cade, B. W., 277, 278, 279, 280
Caligor, L., 81
Callaghan, G. M., 266
Campbell, C. D., 23
Campbell, T. W., 23, 67, 221
Cantor, J. M., 144
Caplan, G., 10
Caplan, R., 10
Caplow, T., 155
Capraro, M. M., 111
Capraro, R. M., 111
Carey, J. C., 111
Carkhuff, R. R., 84
Carlozzi, A. F., 226, 263, 281, 283
Carr, A., 142, 274, 282
Carroll, M., 5, 151, 152, 158, 219, 235, 243, 245, 246
Carson, R. C., 188
Carter, A., 84, 149, 157
Carter, R. T., 84, 129, 149, 157, 248, 249
Cashwell, C. S., 66, 209, 224
Catanzaro, S. J., 60
Celenza, A., 58
Chaiklin, H., 245, 252, 260
Chaimowitz, G. A., 72
Chambless, D. L., 85
Chang, C. Y., 128, 131
Chapin, J., 177, 179, 182
Chartrand, T. L., 179, 192
Chen, E. C., 139, 160, 164
Chen, M. W., 11
Chickering, A. W., 95, 240, 241
Chung, Y. B., 136, 141
Chur-Hansen, A., 33
Cikanek, K., 75
Claiborn, C. D., 1, 32, 120, 161, 177, 186, 187, 298,
    299, 300
Clark, J. J., 190
Clarkson, P., 62
Clifton, D., 87
Clingerman, T. L., 111, 124, 237, 238
Clyne-Jackson, S., 66
Cobia, D. C., 12, 59

SUBJECT INDEX

AAMFT, 3, 6, 222, 281
Academic components of training, 286–287
Academic dismissal, 42
Academy of Certified Social Workers (ACSW), 3
Accountability, 197–198, 199
Accrediting bodies, 3–4, 24
ACES. *See* Association for Counselor Education and Supervision (ACES)
Adherence to treatment protocols, working alliance and, 164
Adjourning group stage, 258–259
Administrative structure
  burnout and, 196
  evaluation and, 26
Administrative supervision, clinical supervision vs., 193–194
Advanced student phase, 97
Advising supervisees for clinical instruction, 203
Advocate, role as, 242
Agency, 198–199
Agency, service delivery
  field site supervisor as representative of, 210
  goals of, 201
  orientation, 205
  placement interview as metaphor for, 205
  Supervisee's Bill of Rights, 207, 311–313
  supervision contracts with, 205–207
Agreements of understanding (supervision contracts), 205–207
Alonso model of supervisor development, 293–294
Ambiguity role, 166
American Association for Marriage and Family Therapists (AAMFT), 3, 6, 222, 281
American Board of Professional Psychology, 3
American Psychological Association (APA), 1, 3, 6
  Division of Psychotherapy, 1
  ethical codes, 284
Americans with Disabilities Act, 40
Analysis competency in Bloom's Taxonomy, 119
Anchored evaluation rubrics, 29, 30
Androgenous supervisors, 143
Anticipatory Supervisee Anxiety Scale (ASAS), 331–332
Anxiety
  effects on supervisee, 178–181

sources of, 177
  of supervisee, 177–182
    games response to, 180–181
    impression management of, 180–181
    learning and, 178
    performance and, 178
    performance anxiety, 227
  of supervisor, 185
Anxious attachment, 175
APA Code of Ethics, 284
APPIC Competencies Conference, 89
Approved Clinical Supervisor (ACS) credential, 208
Arab supervisees, 137
Assessment. *See also* Evaluation
  quantified, 29
  of SITs, 285–286
Association for Counselor Education and Supervision (ACES), 6, 66, 67
  ethical guidelines, 355–360
Association of Psychology Postdoctoral and Internship Centers (APPIC), 6, 285, 287
Assumptive world, 79, 117
Attachment style
  supervisee, 162, 175
  supervisor, 161, 185
Attachment theory, 175
Attack on others, in reaction to shame, 177
Attack on self, in reaction to shame, 177
Attendance, group, 253
Attraction
  romantic, 178
  sexual, 178
    as positive transference, 184
    during supe-of-supe, 290–291
Audiotape, 182, 222–226
  client resistance to, 223
  in planning supervision, 223–225
  preselecting segments of, 224
  transcripts of, 225–226
  use of, 224
  written critique of, 225–226
Authoritative intervention, 92
Authoritative supervision, 248, 250
Authority, nature of supervisor's, 82
Autonomy, 125